Thomas Henry Dyer

Ancient Athens

Its History, Topography and Remains

I0592424

Thomas Henry Dyer

Ancient Athens
Its History, Topography and Remains

ISBN/EAN: 9783743316669

Manufactured in Europe, USA, Canada, Australia, Japa

Cover: Foto ©ninafisch / pixelio.de

Manufactured and distributed by brebook publishing software
(www.brebook.com)

ANCIENT ATHENS:

ITS HISTORY, TOPOGRAPHY, AND REMAINS.

πασῶν Ἀθῆναι τιμιωτάτη πόλις.

CHAPTER I.

Introductory—Nature of the Attic plain—The so-called Cranaan city on the western hills—Hypotheses respecting it—Early population of Attica—Poseidonia—Attic traditions and legends.

We shall relate so much of the early history of Athens as may serve to illustrate its progress as a city, and to explain the names and allusions which may occur in descriptions of its topography, its monuments, and its works of art. Whether this history be truth or fiction it is not our province to inquire. Such researches belong to the philosophical historian who undertakes to relate the political history of the people. For our more humble purpose it suffices to tell what the Athenians themselves believed, or generally admitted as authentic, respecting the origin and progress of their city, the introduction of their religious ceremonies, and the adventures of their most famous heroes, from which were taken the subjects of their poetry, their painting, and their sculpture. For the same reason we shall not stop to inquire whether their myths were of native growth, or—according to some modern views—imported from the East. Their primitive traditions as well as their early art point to an Eastern origin; but to pursue this subject would lead us too far from our design, and it has been already discussed by many able writers.

B

The immediately surrounding plain in which Athens lies is bounded on the north by Mount Parnes, which at its highest point attains an elevation of 4193 feet.[1] South-east of Parnes another smaller range, called Brilettus, Brilessus, or Pentelicum, of which the loftiest peak is 3884 feet high, encloses the plain on that side. Its southern declivities, consisting of marble, attract the eye of the spectator even from Athens by their whiteness where the quarries have been recently worked, whilst the ancient excavations have assumed a yellow tinge. A valley three or four miles in breadth separates the southern foot of Brilettus from Mount Hymettus, which, running in a southerly direction almost down to the sea, forms the eastern boundary of the plain. This chain, whose most elevated summit is about 3056 feet high, is divided almost in the middle by a deep ravine into two portions, of which the northern and larger is the proper Hymettus, whilst the other was called either the " Smaller " or the " Waterless " Hymettus.[2] On the south the plain is bounded by the waters of the Saronic Gulf, whilst Mount Ægaleos encloses its western side, running from a point on the coast nearly opposite to the capital of the Isle of Salamis in a northerly direction towards Parnes. This ridge, which is of no great elevation, separates the Athenian from the Eleusinian plain. The middle portion of it, through which ran the Sacred Way from Athens to Eleusis, was called Mount Pœcilum (τὸ Ποικίλον ὄρος), whilst its southern portion seems also to have borne the name of Corydallus; but authorities are not altogether agreed about the application of the names of the different portions of this ridge.

The plain thus enclosed, consisting for the most part of an arid limestone, is watered by two inconsiderable rivers—the Cephisus and the Ilissus. The former and larger of the two rises at the foot of Brilettus, at the place called after it, Cephisia, and with a volume increased by several small tributaries, flows by the western side of Athens at a distance of about three miles. When it contained sufficient water to reach the sea it discharged itself into the Bay of

[1] The measurements given are from the British survey.

[2] ὁ ἄνυδρος Ὑμηττός, Theophr. de Signis. Cf. Bursian, Geogr. von Griechenland, B. i. S. 254.

Phalerum; but now in the lower part of its course many rivulets were diverted from it for the purpose of watering the neighbouring gardens and plantations, its stream was often arrested in the summer time, and lost itself towards Piræeus in a stagnating marsh.' Its course is marked by a belt of vegetation, which forms a distinguishing feature in the landscape generally presented by the arid soil of Attica. In ancient times the Cephisus appears to have had only one bed, at present, among the olive woods below the village of Sepolia, it is divided into three. Of these the central one, though not now the largest, appears to represent the ancient stream, and terminates in the marsh of Halipedon. The eastern branch loses itself among the orchards ; the western, which is the strongest, falls into the basin of Piræeus, but in a very reduced and slender stream.² Hofrath Thiersch contested the account of Strabo that the Cephisus could ever have been dry. The inhabitants assured him that the water never failed after the longest drought ; and in confirmation of this with regard to ancient times he appeals to Sophocles' testimony of its sleepless springs (κρῆναι ἄυπνοι). Throughout the summer it waters two hundred gardens on its banks.² Chateaubriand remarked of the olive trees that they seemed old enough to be descended from that created by Athena.⁴ The Ilissus, which is little more than a brook, rises at the northern foot of Hymettus, and running close under the walls of Athens on its eastern side, also directs its course towards the Phaleric bay, but loses itself in the soil before reaching the sea. It is joined near Athens by another small stream, called Eridanus, which, however, is mostly dry ; and, except after heavy rains, there is but little water in the rocky and ravine-like bed of the Ilissus itself. It may possibly have been better supplied in ancient times, but it must have been always shallow, as we see from Phædrus proposing to Socrates to walk in its bed just for the pleasure of cooling their feet.⁵

---

[1] Strabo, ix. p. 400.

[2] F. Lenormant, Voie Sacrée, i. 235 sq.

[3] De l'état actuel de la Grèce, t. ii. p. 26.

[4] " Le Céphise coule dans cette forêt, qui par sa vieillesse semble descendre de l'olivier que Minerve fit sortir de la terre."— Itinéraire de Paris à Jérusalem. Œuvres. t. i. p. 120.

[5] ῥᾷστον οὖν ἡμῖν κατὰ τὸ ὑδάτιον βρέ-χουσι τοὺς πόδας ἰέναι καὶ οὐκ ἀηδές. ἄλλως;

In the plain just described, to the north east of Athens, and between
the Cephisus and the Ilissus, a chain of hills or small mountains, now
called Turco-vouni, of which the highest point is 1000 feet, runs
towards the city for a distance of about five miles, and terminates on the
north-east side of it in a remarkable isolated hill, having on its summit
a chapel dedicated to St. George. This hill is now, we believe, universally identified with the ancient Lycabettus, which must certainly
have lain in this quarter. The reasons for this opinion have been
collected by Leake in his 'Topography of Athens.'[1] The following
are the chief of them : Plato, in a fanciful description of the Acropolis
('Critias,' p. 112), says that it once extended to the Eridanus and
Ilissus, embracing on one side the Pnyx Hill, and having Lycabettus
for its boundary (ὅρον ἔχουσα) on the other. Now, the hill in question
adjoins those rivers and lies opposite to the Pnyx Hill, and the Acropolis is situated between the two. Again, Strabo says (p. 454) that the
town of Ithaca was as naturally connected with Mount Neritos as
Athens with Lycabettus. Now, the names of the other Attic mountains are satisfactorily ascertained, and the only unnamed one in the
immediate vicinity of Athens to which Strabo can be alluding is that
in question. Thirdly, Photius in his 'Lexicon' (voc. Πάρνης) quotes
from Aristophanes a line not now extant, which says that the clouds
vanished towards Parnes along Lycabettus ; and the Hill of St. George
lies in the direction between Athens and Mount Parnes. Lycabettus
is also mentioned by other ancient writers in a way which agrees with
the character and situation of this hill : as by Xenophon (Œcon.
xxix. 6); by Marinus, in his 'Life of Proclus,'[2] where he says that that
philosopher was buried near Lycabettus, in the more eastern suburbs
of the city, and Lycabettus lies north-east of it; also by Antigonus of
Carystus, by Theophrastus, 'De Signis,' and others.

τε καὶ τήνδε τὴν ὥραν τοῦ ἔτους τε καὶ τῆς
ἡμέρας.—Plat. Phædr. p. 229.

[1] Sect. iii. p. 204 sqq. See also Dr.
Wordsworth's 'Attica and Athens,' ch. viii.

[2] ἐτάφη ἐν τοῖς ἀνατολικωτέροις προ-
αστείοις τῆς πόλεως, πρὸς τῷ Λυκαβηττῷ.
—§ 36.

Pausanias, in his enumeration of the Attic mountains (i. 32), does not mention Lycabettus, but it is remarkable that he speaks of one called Anchesmus, a name which does not occur elsewhere.[1] The late Lord Broughton identified it with the hill we are speaking of on the north-east side of Athens;[2] and Leake himself says (p. 205), "We can hardly avoid the conclusion that this hill was Anchesmus.' If this be so, we might conclude that, in the time of Pausanias, Lycabettus had gotten a fresh name; for, as Leake observes in the same page, "there is still better reason to believe that it was the ancient Lycabettus." And indeed the passages just cited seem to prove that point incontestably. Leake offers another solution of the difficulty by observing (p. 211) that Anchesmus may never have been anything more than the specific name of the summit of St. George, while Lycabettus may have comprehended the whole chain. But more probably just the reverse was the case.[3] For, first, whether Plato included Lycabettus in his Acropolis, as some interpret, or whether it only formed the boundary of it, which we take to be the proper meaning of his words, it was evidently the hill terminating the chain; for he could hardly have been so extravagant as to fancy that the ancient Acropolis embraced a ridge several miles in length. Secondly, as Pausanias in the passage cited is enumerating the Attic mountains, he would doubtless mention *the whole range*, and not merely a particular summit, just as he mentions the whole range of Pentelicus, Parnes, and Hymettus. Nor does Leake's view derive any strength from the circumstance that Pausanias mentions on it a statue of Zeus, surnamed Anchesmius; for, allowing that the site of the chapel of St. George was anciently a hierum, from the Christian custom of erecting churches on such spots, still the Zeus erected there may have taken his name from the whole ridge rather than from the particular summit on which he actually stood.

Lying in the same direction as the ridge in question, and having the appearance of offsets from it, are other smaller hills, or rather

---

[1] καὶ Ἀγχεσμὸς ὄρος ἐστὶν οὐ μέγα, καὶ Διὸς ἄγαλμα Ἀγχεσμίου.

[2] Hobhouse, ' Journey,' &c., i. 292.

[3] This view is also adopted by Bursian, Geogr. v. Att. B. i. S. 255.

rocks, within the precincts of Athens itself. The nearest, distant from Lycabettus about a mile in a south-westerly direction, is the Acropolis, which rises to a height of about 500 feet above the sea, and has at its western foot another rock, smaller both in extent and height—the Areiopagus. Over against the southern side of the Acropolis, at a distance of about 500 yards, lies another isolated hill, called the Museium, of nearly equal height, but without so extensive a summit. This hill terminates precipitously on its south-eastern side, whilst to the north-west it sinks more gradually, and again rises into two less considerable heights—the Pnyx Hill, opposite to and south of the Areiopagus, and that called the Hill of the Nymphs, lying also at a little distance from the western foot of the Areiopagus. The rest of Athens to the east and north is almost level. Such is the nature of the plain which immediately surrounds Athens, and of the ground comprised within its walls.

According to ancient notions, the ground here described favoured in more ways than one the building of a city. The rocky soil served for excavating the foundations of those small primitive dwellings, of which numerous vestiges still remain ; whilst the isolated rocks which we have described, and especially that which in later times became the Acropolis of Athens, were admirably adapted to form defensive strongholds. According to tradition, the original city was in fact confined to the Acropolis, and obtained from its founder the name of Cecropia. But here a curious question arises. It is on the southern and western hills of Athens—that of the Museium, the Pnyx, the Nymphs' Hill, and Areiopagus—that are found those remains of houses to which we have just alluded ; and by some these are taken to have belonged to the original Athens, and to have formed what is called the Cranaan city. In order to decide this point, it is necessary to be acquainted with these remains, and we therefore insert a description of them, the substance of which is taken from the Report of a French gentleman residing at Athens, and addressed to the Minister of Public Instruction. For its general accuracy we can vouch from personal observation.[1] Although we do

---

[1] See the 'Archives des Missions scientifiques et littéraires,' t. v. p. 64, sq. The report is accompanied with a map of this part of Athens on a large scale, on which

not know the date of these constructions, they are undoubtedly centuries
older than the earliest Athenian building still extant, and therefore an
account of them may properly find a place at the very threshold of
this work.

Scattered over the southern and western hills, M. Burnouf counted
no fewer than 800 foundations of rooms excavated out of the living
rock; and there were probably a great many more, the traces of which
have been obliterated by soil and rubbish. The number of houses
which they represent was, however, of course less; for though some of
these excavations evidently constituted a single house, or rather cabin,
yet in other cases they appear to have been different chambers of one
and the same habitation. These chambers are all constructed on the
declivities of the hills. A certain space was marked out to form a
rectangular floor or area; the back wall, or at all events the lower
portion of it, was formed by the perpendicular excavation in the rock,
and the two side walls in the same manner; but as these descended
with the inclination of the hill, and so were of course higher at the
back than at the front, they would have required additional material to
complete them to the necessary height. How much of the back and
side walls could be completed out of the rock itself depended on the
greater or less steepness of the hill. The front, of course, must always
have been an artificial wall, and hence there are no remains of such
fronts, the stones composing them having probably been carried off in
modern times. Nevertheless, the doorway, which from the nature of the
construction must always have been in the front, may frequently be
recognized, sometimes with steps before it, and in two or three instances
with a *perron*, or flight of steps ascending from the basement to a
storey above. In the corner of a house on the furthest western hill
might even be discovered a piece of yellowish stucco.

Although, as we have said, some of these houses consisted of one

the remains are indicated. There is also
a map of the same region on a smaller
scale, but of clearer execution, in Curtius'
'Sieben Karten zur Topographie von
Athen' (No. 1), and some minor details
in Nos. 5 and 7.

small chamber, yet more frequently the rooms are grouped in such a
manner as to show that they were evidently connected and belonged to
the same house. Many of these groups are analogous to the plan of a
good Pompeian house, and must therefore have been the habitations of
wealthy persons. These were distinguished by peculiar conveniences,
as gutters for the rain, cisterns, large courts resembling the atria and
peristyles at Pompeii, and even places for the family sepulchres. This
last circumstance proves these houses to have been very ancient, for
such a mode of interment was not permitted in the more modern and
refined days of Athens.

The relative distribution of these houses appears to be as follows :—
On the north-western hill about 100; on the Pnyx hill, 200; on the
Observatory Hill (that of the Nymphs), 40; on the great western
hill, 150; on the Museium Hill, 250; and on the Areiopagus about 60.
They vary very much in their arrangement. On the Areiopagus the
chambers are scattered *pêle-mêle* and without order, whilst on the hills
behind the Pnyx they are disposed regularly in lines and streets. M.
Burnouf (p. 73) recognizes in this the natural march of civilization.
Accepting the Acropolis, which was always called πόλις, or ' the city '—
just as our old London within the walls is also distinguished by that
name—as the central point and the spot first inhabited, the earliest
additions would of course be in its immediate neighbourhood, and from
their period would be of a meaner character than the subsequent
extensions. Now, this is just what we find. The houses improve not
only in size, but also in regularity of disposition, as we advance from
the centre towards the circumference. Those on the Areiopagus and
the neighbouring portion of the Pnyx Hill show that primitive Athens
was a collection of little hovels, and this part of the town seems never
to have been improved. It is on the southern heights, which enjoyed
a prospect of the sea and received the refreshing breezes from it, that
the best houses, comparatively speaking, appear to have been built; but
even these would seem poor when contrasted with more modern habitations. Quite at the extremity of this southern suburb, and at the foot
of the hills, still larger foundations are seen, but, from their level site,

of course without side walls. As these lie near the great commercial route leading to the ports, M. Burnouf conjectures that they may have been warehouses.

Our limits will not allow us to enter into any detailed account of these houses, but we will select for description one or two of the best, which will give some idea of their nature. One of the most remarkable, to which M. Burnouf gives the name of the House of the Four Tombs, lies at the back of the Pnyx, near the ravine and road which divide it from the Museium Hill. The entrance was at the southern angle, where several steps led to the door and apparently a first enclosure or court, on the left of which are two tombs. Around the enclosure were chambers, resembling those which surround a Pompeian atrium. In a second enclosure on the right are four sepulchres. This also is surrounded by rooms, which probably formed part of the house. Another remarkable house, the last to the south-west on the same hill, is admirably placed. Being almost on a level with the top of the hill, it commanded on one side a view of the sea and harbours, whilst on the other it surveyed the Acropolis and its buildings and the distant mountains of Attica. In the interior of this house, also, is a small apartment or sacrarium, with a tomb.

Of these rock constructions, the largest and most complete is that commonly, but absurdly, known as the Prison of Socrates, lying on the north-east side of the Museum Hill, and facing the Acropolis. It is excavated out of the rock, which is here cut vertically to an average depth of about twenty-six feet, and a length of nearly fifty; thus forming a façade, in which are three doors, the middle one being the largest. It opens into a sort of lobby, having a large conical niche in the back wall, which probably is only the commencement of an excavation. There is a passage from this lobby to the room on the left, entrance to which is gained also by the third or most eastern door. This room is almost cubic, being about sixteen feet long, broad, and high. The floor is fashioned in the manner of an impluvium; a small gutter runs through the middle of it, and has its exit at the door. The apartment at the other extremity, to which the right hand or

westernmost door gives admittance, is somewhat smaller than that just described. It has a slanting roof, and at its right hand corner is a doorway leading into a circular apartment of singular construction. It is a rotunda, or tholus, about fifteen feet in diameter, with an elliptical vault, forming a sort of chimney with an opening on the upper surface of the rock, where its round and narrow shaft is half closed by a projecting ledge. At the western end of the façade of this singular dwelling, the rock projects at right angles to it about thirteen feet, and with the aid of carpentry, seems to have formed a sort of hall, or ante-room ; for on the side wall made by the rock, as well as on the façade, are numerous square holes, evidently intended to receive the joists of planking. The original destination of this place it is impossible to determine ; at present it serves as a stable for cattle.

The streets of this rock-town are of three kinds : main thoroughfares, or highways, smaller streets practicable for horses and cars, and lanes for foot passengers. The high roads led through a gate of the city, and there were only two of them in this quarter. One of these ran between the Pnyx and Museum hills, through a gate near the present little church of Agios Demetrius, which M. Burnouf, correctly we think, identifies with Pylæ Melitides (p. 79). We are not, however, so certain as to the road having been the Κοίλη 'Οδός ; but these are points which there will be occasion to discuss further on when we come to speak of the walls and regions of the city. In later times the road in question led to the port towns, and it is often used at this day by pedestrians. It probably served to convey merchandise from the ports, and it was a safe road for that purpose, as it ran between the Phaleric and the Long Wall. It is striated, or roughened with hammer and chisel, in order to secure the footing of beasts of burthen ; the ruts of wheels are still visible on it, and at its side runs a large kennel. The only other road having the appearance of a highway is one on the crest of the northwestern hill. It seems also to have led to the ports, but it was evidently not so much frequented as the other ; it has no kennel, and it is impossible to say through what gate it led.

The smaller striated streets, with marks of ruts, served for internal

communication, and are much more tortuous than the main roads. They have no traces of foot pavements, like those of Pompeii. Both these and the high roads were very narrow, which may account for a law passed in the time of Pericles,[1] when we may suppose that the traffic had a good deal increased, forbidding that the doors of houses should open outwards. The third class of streets, or rather lanes, were naturally more numerous; they were scarcely broad enough for two persons, and wound among the houses in a singular fashion. They were often provided with steps cut in the rock. Many such steps are seen on the east side of the Pnyx, but these were evidently intended for persons going to or from the ecclesia.

Nearly sixty cisterns (λάκκοι) may be observed on the hills, large pear-shaped excavations in the rock resembling a huge amphora. They vary in size, the average depth being thirteen or fourteen feet, while some have a depth of twenty. M. Burnouf is of opinion that they were intended only for water, as there are marks of ropes at their mouths, and their concave sides seem designed to avert collision with the pitcher. There is a depression round the mouth for a cover. Dr. Curtius thinks they may have also served as cellars, or for fruits, and Photius indeed says (voc. λάκκος) that the Athenians made broad or roomy excavations (ὀρύγματα εὐρυχωρῆ), both square and oval, which they plastered over, and kept wine and oil in them. This sort of λάκκος seems to have been a usual appendage to an Athenian house.[2] But those in question are rather deep than broad, and some of them were evidently intended for public use. We sometimes read of ὕδωρ λακκαῖον. It is also remarkable that there are none of these λάκκοι inside the circuit of the walls, and this circumstance, as well as the fashion of them, seems to show that they were reservoirs for water; for on those arid rocks outside the walls there could have been none but that supplied by the rain, whilst the inhabitants of the inner town would have had access to wells and fountains.

There are 111 tombs; but these also are all outside the wall, and there are none on the Areiopagus, the Observatory Hill or the northern

[1] According to M. Burnouf, p. 81.   [2] See Demosth. c. Aphob. p. 845, Reiske.

slope of the Pnyx Hill. They are oblong excavations in the rock, and have no uniform orientation, but are turned to all points of the compass. This seems at variance with the Attic laws and customs, by which apparently the head should be turned either to east or to the west, for the authorities seem to differ on this point.[1] The tombs are for the most part situated along the high roads; but some of them, as we have seen, were in the interior of or by the sides of houses. There are, besides these graves, sepulchral caverns of large size. Two are still remarkable : one on the south side of the western hill containing several tombs ; the other near the Pylæ Melitides, commonly called the Cimoncia, or sepulchre of the family of Cimon.

To this description of the remains of ancient Athens we need only add that on the west and on the north sides of the Observatory are two deep and rugged clefts in the rock, now used as abattoirs, or places for the slaughtering of cattle. As there are no similar clefts nearer than the Piræeus, or the chain of Anchesmus, it is probable that one of them was the barathron, or place of execution, described as being in the deme of the Keiriadæ.[2]

To what period did the rock city we have described most probably belong ? Curtius, in a *résumé* of the subject in the explanatory text to his maps of Athens,[3] recognizes, from Herodotus,[4] four epochs in the primeval history of Athens, viz.: 1. that of the Pelasgic Cranaoi ; 2. that of the Cecropidæ, from Cecrops ; 3. that of the Athenians from Erechtheus, whose story is connected with Athena ; and 4. that of the Ionians, from Ion. From their first ruler, Cranaos, Curtius continues—a ruler, however, whom Herodotus does not mention—the inhabitants were called Cranaoi, and their town Cranaë. The name of this king signifies ' rocky ' or ' stony,' hence the Cranaoi were the inhabitants of the rock city just described, and, indeed, its first inhabitants.

[1] They are collected by Petit, Leges Att. vi. 8, 18.

[2] Bekker, An. Græc. p. 219.

[3] Erläuternder Text, S. 17, ff.

[4] Ἀθηναῖοι δέ, ἐπὶ μὲν Πελασγῶν ἐχόντων τὴν νῦν Ἑλλάδα καλεομένην, ἦσαν Πελασγοί, οὐνομαζόμενοι Κραναοί. ἐπὶ δὲ Κέκροπος βασιλέος, ἐπεκλήθησαν Κεκροπίδαι· ἐκδεξαμένου δὲ Ἐρεχθέος τὴν ἀρχὴν Ἀθηναῖοι μετωνομάσθησαν· Ἴωνος δὲ τοῦ Ξούθου στρατάρχεω γενομένου Ἀθηναίοισι, ἐκλήθησαν ἀπὸ τούτου Ἴωνες.—viii. 44.

Now, without entering into any examination of this disputed passage, in which the name of Cranaos, contrary to Attic traditions, is placed before that of Cecrops, we may observe, first, that Curtius here assigns two etymologies for the name of the Cranai, namely, from their king and from the nature of the soil. But the best ancient authorities[1] derive the name of the Cranni only from their king, which indeed was the usual custom, and we cannot tell how he got his name, for the term Κραναὸς is applicable to other things besides the soil. Curtius, indeed, seeks to strengthen his argument by observing that Cranaos had to wife Pedias, i.e. *the plain*,[2] and that these were the oldest pair in Attica. But if any inference is to be drawn from this fanciful myth, it would appear to relate, not to the rock-city, or indeed to any part of Athens, but to the whole of Attica, which in the time of Cranaos emerged from Deucalion's flood, according to Apollodorus in the passage quoted.[3] The whole country seems to have been called Κραναή,[4] which appellation Cranaos changed to Atthis, on the death of his daughter of that name. Therefore, Κραναοὶ is equivalent to Ἀττικοί, the inhabitants of the district called Cranaö and afterwards Attica; and the Κραναὰ πόλις is the chief city of Cranaö,[5] as Athens might be called, κατ' ἐξοχήν, the Attic city. Secondly, even if we allow that Cranaos and his subjects derived their appellation from the rocks of Athens only, still there is nothing to show that it was from the western hills, for it might just as well have been from the rock of the Acropolis. And, indeed, Aristophanes gives the Acropolis that name.[6] And that this was the part of

---

[1] Strabo, p. 397; Hesych. voc. Κραναὴν πόλιν. And so Æschylus calls the Athenians παῖδες Κραναοῦ. Eumen. 1011.

[2] Attische Studien, i. S. 16; cf. Apollod. iii. 14, 5.

[3] Κέκροπος δὲ ἀποθανόντος, Κραναὸς αὐτόχθων ὤν, ἐφ' οὗ τὸν ἐπὶ Δευκαλίωνος λέγεται κατακλυσμὸν γενέσθαι, γήμας ἐκ Λακεδαίμονος Πεδιάδα τὴν Μήνητος, ἐγέννησε Κραναὴν καὶ Κραναίχμην καὶ Ἀτθίδα· ἧς ἀποθανούσης ἐπὶ παρθένου, τὴν χώραν Κραναὸς Ἀτθίδα προσηγόρευσε.

[4] Thus Stephanus Byz.: Κραναή· οὕτως ἐκαλεῖτο καὶ ἡ Ἀττική, ἀπὸ Κραναοῦ. Cf. Menander Rhetor. ap. Meurs. de Reg. Athen. cap. 13.

[5] Κραναὰ πόλις, Aristoph. Ach. 75; or in plur. Κρανααί, without πόλις.

ἔπειτα μείζω τῶν Κραναῶν ζητεῖς πόλιν;
—Av. 123.

[6] ὅ τι βουλόμεναί ποτε τὴν
Κραναὴν κατέλαβον,
ἐφ' ὅ τι τε μεγαλόπετρον, ἄβατον ἀκρόπολιν.—Lysistr. 480.

Athens first inhabited we think probable for many reasons. First, it was an almost inaccessible stronghold, a matter of the highest importance in founding an infant town. Secondly, as we have before observed, it always continued to bear the name of πόλις, or the city *par excellence*. Thirdly, appearances show that the rock city spread itself out from the Acropolis as from a centre. For the rock dwellings on the Areiopagus and immediately adjoining parts are, as we have already seen, much meaner and more irregularly placed than those further on, a circumstance which affords a strong presumption that they were the earliest offsets from the Acropolis. Lastly, this account of the growth of Athens is confirmed by the testimony of Thucydides, who names the Acropolis first as the proper city before the time of Theseus, and then the district under it looking rather to the south. And let us observe that the objects to which he appeals in confirmation of his statement did not lie in the direction of the southern and western hills but rather towards the southeast, as the Olympium, the Pythium, the temple of Gæa, the nearest one to the western hills being the temple of Dionysus in the Limnæ, under the south-east extremity of the Acropolis. The reason for the city spreading in this direction may have been the proximity of the Ilissus, for the soil is not so rocky and fit for foundations as the southwest hills, and there are consequently no traces here of any primitive dwellings. The mean houses on the Areiopagus and its vicinity may, however, have belonged to this early period. Let us observe that in this account Thucydides completely ignores the Pnyx Hill, where recent German topographers place from time immemorial a vast sanctuary of Zeus Hypsistos, on the area commonly supposed to have been the meeting place of the ecclesia. Truly, if there was such a place, a most singular and unaccountable omission![1] But on this subject we shall have to speak further on, and we will only add here that the constructions on the western hills bear not the slightest appearance of having been Pelasgic. Huge walls were the mode of building adopted by that people, of which there is not the slightest trace in the so-called rock

[1] τὸ δὲ πρὸ τούτου ἡ ἀκρόπολις ἡ νῦν οὖσα πόλις ἦν, καὶ τὸ ἐπ' αὐτὴν πρὸς νότον μάλιστα τετραμμένον.—ii. 15.

city. The wall at the Pnyx is not Pelasgic, but of a much later date.

For these reasons we are inclined to agree with M. Burnouf that the rock of the Acropolis was the first settlement of Athens, and the centre whence it spread itself, rather than with Dr. Curtius that the south-western hills were first inhabited, and the Acropolis afterwards forcibly seized by Cecrops; a view for which no traditions can be adduced, and which in itself seems highly improbable, as well for the reasons given as also from the consideration that settlers would hardly have chosen a place where they might so easily be overpowered and dominated from the neighbouring height. At the same time the rock city was no doubt of high antiquity. We do not infer this so much from the houses being hewn out of the rock, as the Athenians seem to have availed themselves of that mode of construction till a late period of their history, as appears from the Dionysiac theatre, not to mention the Pnyx, as its age and destination are contested points. But the custom of burying the dead in their own houses, as was evidently done in this quarter, was certainly very ancient, as appears from a passage in the dialogue entitled ' Minos,' sometimes ascribed to Plato.[1] The author alludes to a time when a victim was sacrificed before the body was carried out, and proceeds to say that in a still earlier age the dead were interred at home. Now the law prohibiting the sacrifice of victims in funerals was introduced by Solon,[2] and therefore burial in the house must have been long earlier than he. The fact, too, of this quarter having become almost deserted, as we see from several passages in the orators, shows that it must have been very ancient and old-fashioned. We cannot quit this subject without mentioning a tradition that the original inhabitants of Athens dwelt in caverns, of which indeed several may still be found there, and that the invention of brick houses was ascribed to Hyperbius and Agrolas (or Euryalus), who appear to have been Pelasgian, but of

---

[1] . . . οἶσθά που καὶ αὐτὸς ἀκούων, οἶοις νόμοις ἐχρώμεθα πρὸ τοῦ περὶ τοὺς ἀποθανόντας. ἱερεῖά τε προσφάττοντες πρὸ τῆς ἐκφορᾶς τοῦ νεκροῦ καὶ ἐγχυτριστρίας μεταπεμπόμενοι· οἱ δ' αὖ ἐκείνων ἔτι πρότεροι αὐτοὶ καὶ ἔθαπτον ἐν τῇ οἰκίᾳ τοὺς ἀποθανόντας.—p. 315 (p. i. t. ii. p. 254. Bekker).

[2] ἐναγίζειν δὲ βοῦν οὐκ εἴασεν.—Plut. Sol. 21.

their history we know nothing further. Were the first Athenian houses
really raised with brick on rock foundations? We seem to have a confirmation of the tradition in the lines of Æschylus :

> —— οὔτε πλινθυφεῖς
> δόμους προσείλους ἦσαν, οὐ ξυλουργίαν·
> κατώρυχες δ' ἔναιον, ὥστ' ἀήσυροι
> μύρμηκες, ἄντρων ἐν μυχοῖς ἀνηλίοις.[1]

> "—— they knew not then
> Of sunny homes with brick and timber made,
> But dwelt, like ants, in subterranean nooks
> Of darksome caverns."

Having thus described the environs of Athens, the site of the town
itself, and the earliest vestiges of its inhabitants, we will now proceed
to relate the chief primitive traditions of the Athenians. A favourite
one was that they were autochthones, or children of the soil, which they
were fond of proclaiming.[2] And in token of this origin, the more
ancient Athenians wore in their hair, over their foreheads, a golden
grasshopper, that insect being also reputed a product of the earth.[3] We
may observe, that this tradition is quite at variance with the statement
that the first inhabitants of Athens were of the wandering race of the
Pelasgi, though no doubt at some period there was a Pelasgic settlement in Attica. Strabo considers the Pelasgi as an immigrant race,
and even as having obtained their name from the Athenians, on account
of their wanderings after the manner of storks (πελαργοί).[4] The most
probable opinion seems to be that the Athenians were partly a mixture
of Ionians with the wandering and ubiquitous Pelasgi;[5] but that there

[1] Prom. 449 sqq. Cf. Pausan. i. 28, 3 ;
Plin. H. N. vii. 194.

[2] Thus Euripides:
ὦ σύγγον', ἐλθὼν λαὸν εἰς αὐτόχθονα
κλεινῶν Ἀθηνῶν, οἶσθα γὰρ θεᾶς πόλιν,
κ.τ.λ.—Ion, v. 29 sq. ; cf. οὐκ ἐπείσακ-
τον γένος, v. 590.
Cf. also Demosth. Orat. Fun.: μόνοι γὰρ
πάντων ἀνθρώπων, ἐξ ἧσπερ ἔφυσαν, ταύτην
ᾤκησαν, καὶ τοῖς ἐξ αὐτῶν παρέδωκαν.—p.
1390, Reiske ; and Plat. Menexen. p. 237
(p. ii. t. iii. p. 383, Bekk.), &c.

[3] Thucyd. i. 6 ; schol. ad Aristoph.
Nub. 980 ; Eustath. ad Il. x. p. 1388.
Cf. Aristoph. Eq. v. 1331 ; Ælian, V. H.
iv. 22 ; Athen. xii. 5.

[4] εἴρηται δὲ ὅτι κἀνταῦθα (i.e. in Attica)
φαίνεται τὸ τῶν Πελασγῶν ἔθνος ἐπιδη-
μῆσαν· καὶ ὅτι ὑπὸ τῶν Ἀττικῶν Πελαργοὶ
προσηγορεύθησαν διὰ τὴν πλάνην.—p. 397.
Cf. p. 221.

[5] See Herodot. i. 56, sq. ; ii. 51 ; vii. 94;
viii. 44. Cf. Clinton, Fast. Hell. vol. i. p. 56.

was what may be called an indigenous race settled in Attica before the advent of either of those peoples, and perhaps, even that not an unmixed one. . . All that we can affirm with any certainty in this obscure matter, which has occupied the researches of the learned without any positive results, is, that the Ionian race, though according to Attic traditions not the original one, ultimately became predominant. The autochthonal tradition is of course valuable only as showing that there was none running contrary to it, none of a first settlement of the population, which might consequently have been there from time immemorial. This tradition, however, will only apply to the city of Athens, and at most the plain already described as immediately surrounding it. But Attica in later ages consisted of two other plains besides the central one; the Thriasian plain on the west and that containing Mesogæa and Paralia on the east; not to mention Diacria in the northeast, a highland region, and the small plain of the Marathonian Tetrapolis. German critics have pointed out, by probable inferences from the religious systems of these districts, that they were originally inhabited by different races. Zeus, Athena, and Gæa were the primeval deities of Athens and its immediate district. In the western plain the worship of Demeter prevailed, Eleusis being the chief seat of it ; whilst in the eastern region the principal deity was the Brauronian Artemis.[1] Circumstances in the worship of Zeus and Athena, to which we shall have occasion to advert further on, show that they were the patrons of agriculture, which function was also among the principal characteristics of Demeter, whilst Artemis, on the other hand, was the goddess of the chace. Hence A. Mommsen has inferred that the inhabitants of the two first-named divisions were agriculturists, whilst those of the eastern districts were hunters;[2] for which last pursuit, however, that small extent of country was but ill adapted.

But traces of distinct worships, and consequently, of distinct settlements, have been shown to have existed in the immediate neighbourhood of Athens itself, nay, even in spots ultimately included within its walls.

---

[1] Worshipped not only at Brauron, her chief seat, but also at Myrrhinus, Athmonum, Munychia, and Rhamnus.   [2] Heortologie, S. i. il.

Mommsen has pointed out[1] that there was on the heights of Agræ, just on the other side of the Ilissus, and partly even on its western bank, a group of deities quite different from those on the Acropolis ; namely, the Heliconian Poseidon, Artemis Agrotera, and Aphrodite in the Gardens (ἐν κήποις), or the Celestial Aphrodite ; and hence he was led to think that this district might, in ancient times, have been a sort of foreigners' quarter, inhabited by Ionians from Helice in Ægialeia, who brought with them their Poseidon Heliconius, and also established there the other two deities. Wachsmuth has carried this idea still further.[2] He is of opinion that the colony at Agræ was quite an independent one, founding his view on the circumstance that the heights there offered an equally eligible place for a settlement as the Acropolis. He includes in its boundaries not only the Aphrodisium and the Lyceum, but also the Delphinium and Pythium. But this is an evident encroachment on the Athenian precincts ; for the two last adjoined the Olympium ; and the Pythium is expressly named by Thucydides (ii. 15) as one of the early Athenian sanctuaries. There is, however, some probability of the height itself, with the sanctuary of the Heliconian Poseidon, having been originally a distinct Ionian colony ; its close proximity to Athens is no valid objection to this view ; in the early days of colonization, the city itself, with the smallest possible strip of territory, was the state ; as we see in the case of Rome and other foundations in Italy. In the Athenian mythology, Athena and Poseidon are at first represented at variance ; but they are reconciled, and Poseidon, identified as Erechtheus—a myth to which we shall allude further on—shares the temple of the goddess. Welcker has observed,[3] that the Athenians took the worship of Poseidon from the Ionians, and that the identification of Poseidon with Erechtheus denoted the political union of the peoples. This view is supported by the circumstance that Attica bore also ·the name of Poseidonia.[4] From the Ionian union followed also the introduction of Apollo into Attic worship. There may be some general pro-

---

[1] Heortologie, p. 19, note.

[2] See 'Rheinisches Museum.' 1868, p. 170, sqq.

[3] Götterlehre, i. 636.

[4] Strab. p. 397.

bability in this view, which we mention here because it is connected
with the site and localities of Athens, but we must confess that we
cannot follow Wachsmuth with regard to the manner in which the
union was effected. But there will be occasion to return to this subject, on which he subsequently modified his opinion, and thought that
the settlement at Agræ was a Thracian one, the Helicomian Poseidon
being, he says, a Thracian god before he became an Ionian one. Wachsmuth quotes a fragment of Euripides, in proof of the Thracian genealogy
of Poseidon; but it is also shown by a passage in Isocrates who says
that Eumolpus, the son of Poseidon, with his Thracians, invaded Attica,
and contested with Erechtheus the possession of Athens, affirming that
Poseidon had occupied it before Athena.[1] This story is preferable
on chronological grounds; for which, however, it would be absurd to
look in myths like this, and indeed to discuss the subject is little better
than beating the air. For it may be observed that though the Heliconian Poseidon was undoubtedly an Ionian as well as a Thracian
god, yet if he took his name from Helice, the city founded by Ion,
that event, according to tradition, was subsequent to the reign of
Cecrops and the contest of Athena and Poseidon. There appears,
however, to have been a more ancient Helice in Thessaly; and Agræ
itself, according to Cleidemus, bore originally the name of Helicon.[2]
The only thing that we can settle with any probability is, that
there had once been an Ionian colony at Agræ, but the time and manner
of its foundation are utterly unknown. It is not improbable that feuds
between the settlers on the Acropolis and those at Agræ, may have
given rise to the story of the contest of Athena and Poseidon, which
may have been finally reconciled when Ion became king, or at all events,
leader of the Athenians.

Curtius has also conjectured with considerable probability, the existence of a Phœnician settlement almost in the heart of Athens. Salamis,

---

[1] Θρᾶκες μὲν γὰρ μετ' Εὐμόλπου τοῦ
Ποσειδῶνος εἰσέβαλον εἰς τὴν χώραν ἡμῶν,
ὃς ἠμφισβήτησεν Ἐρεχθεῖ τῆς πόλεως,
φάσκων Ποσειδῶ πρότερον Ἀθηνᾶς κατα-
λαβεῖν αὐτήν. Orat. Panath. p. 273.

[2] Ap. Bekker, Anec. Græc. p. 326: cf.
Strabo, p. 384, sq.; Paus. vii. 1, 2, and
24, 4.

he supposes, from the etymology of the name,[1] was a Phœnician colony, whence offshoots were planted on the adjoining continent. One of these was Melite, which continued till the latest period to be one of the city-demes of Athens. It was unmistakably connected with Salamis, for in it dwelt families who had emigrated from that island and from Ægina. Melitë, who gave name to the quarter, was a sea-nymph, whom ancient legends connect with the Æacidæ dwelling in those islands. She was also the mistress of Heracles, the Tyrian god (Melkarth), and the temple of Heracles in Melitë was the finest Heracleium at Athens.[2] Yet, though adopted among the Athenian deities, he was always regarded as a stranger, and thus he had been refused initiation in the mysteries, though he was initiated in the lesser ones in Melitë. Further, the name, Melitë, betokens a Phœnician settlement, as in Malta, in one of the Liburnian islands, and in Samothrace.[3]

We will now proceed to the historical and mythological traditions of the Athenians. We have no satisfactory history of Athens till about the time of Pisistratus. The many centuries which elapsed between its origin and the reign of that tyrant, are destitute of events that can properly be called historical. The details of history can be preserved only by contemporary record, of which there were no traces in the early times of Athens, as at Rome. There are, however, other means by which a general notion of leading events and prominent men may be conveyed to posterity. Such are the foundations of temples and other public buildings, with their inscriptions; the institution of sacred festivals recurring at appointed intervals, the origin and purpose of which would be preserved by the priests who officiated in them; and the verses of poets in honour of heroes. The ἀοιδοί, or bards, were the historiographers of ancient Greece; of whom Homer, though the most famous, was by no means the first. For he describes them himself as an institution of the heroic age, when he tells of Demodocus, the bard of King

---

[1] Salama, *peace*, or *place of peace*. Hence the worship of the Salaminian Zeus, Baal-Salam. Movers, Colon. 239. See Curtius, Erläuternder Text der sieben Karten, p. 9, sqq.

[2] Schol. ad Aristoph. Ran. 501.

[3] Movers, Colon. 347.

Alcinous, of Phemius in Ithaca, and the unnamed poet of the court of Agamemnon.[1] These bards were held in the highest honour; nay, even the heroic leaders of the Greeks disdained not to cultivate their pleasing art. Thus Odysseus and Ajax and Achilles playing on the lyre, and accompanying the instrument with his voice. His theme was the glorious deeds of distinguished men —δεῖος δὲ ἄμα κλέα ἀνδρῶν.[1] It would be idle to think that they were the deeds of fictitious personages. Such fictions would have excited no sympathy in the breasts of those rude and unsophisticated warriors; they are the product of a much later and more civilized state of society. The songs of Achilles celebrated, probably, only some isolated deeds. But besides Homer, Greece had also its cyclic poets, whose productions embraced a considerable period, or a biography. Thus, what is more to our purpose, we are told by Aristotle of a poem called Theseis, which recounted all the actions of Theseus;[3] and Pausanias mentions an Atthis (Ἀτθς.), or poetical account of Attica, by Hegesinoüs, which, however, had vanished before Pausanias was born.[4] But these, of course, were poor substitutes for regular history.

The pre-historic period of Athens may be divided into two portions: first, from its origin to the Trojan war, and second, from that event to the time of Pisistratus. The first of these may be called the legendary period, or heroic age. To the student of Attic antiquities and art, this period is by far the most important, as being that from which the Athenians drew the subjects of their poems, their sculpture, and their paintings. The second epoch is indeed almost a blank; for while the legends have vanished, there is little or nothing in the shape of genuine history to supply their place. The legendary or heroic period represents the struggles of advancing civilization with the evils, both physical and moral, of barbarism. The wild and unsubdued powers of nature have to be controlled; the lawless savages, who were continually infesting the progress of peaceful industry, to be tamed or exterminated. The exploits undertaken for these objects had naturally

[1] Odyss. viii. 537; i. 154; iii. 267.

[2] Iliad, ix. 189.

[3] Poet. c. 17. Cf. Plut. Thes. 28.

[4] Paus. ix. 29, 1.

a striking and poetical, sometimes almost a supernatural character; and it is no wonder that those who distinguished themselves most in such labours—a Heracles or a Theseus—should be exalted into heroes and demigods.   Sometimes these labours are undertaken to free the land from wild beasts and monsters; as the adventures of Heracles with the Nemean lion, or the Erymanthian boar, and of Theseus with the Crommyonian boar and Marathonian bull; or they represent the struggle with savage races, as in the stories of the Centaurs and Lapithæ. The war against the powers of nature is shown in the story of Heracles vanquishing the Lernæan hydra; an emblem, no doubt, of uncurbed and overflowing waters, which rendered the country unhealthy and unfit for cultivation.[1]   The fables of the introduction of the olive into Attica in the reign of Cecrops; of the vine and its produce in that of Amphictyon, depict the advance of agriculture. The progress of commerce is represented by the Argonautic expedition, and that of Heracles to the Hesperides.   The chastisement of evil doers, who preyed on the helpless and industrious, is the subject of several of the exploits of Theseus; as in the defeat and punishment of Periphetes, Sinis, the robber Sciron, and others.   In fact, these primitive heroes were a sort of knights-errant on a grand scale.

The human mind, especially in uncivilized ages, has a natural tendency to fix upon and glorify some particular individual as the hero of achievements, which must, for the most part, have been effected by combination, and to symbolize, in one grand and striking adventure, results which must have been slow and gradual.   This we take to be the natural and simple explanation of the heroic age and, its prodigies. Civilization once established, all such wonders cease; there is, in fact, no longer any scope for them.   And here, perhaps, we have the explanation why the heroic age may be said to terminate with the siege of Troy.   Such an event necessarily implies an advanced stage of civilization.   Considerable independent states must have been formed, possessing lagre navies; facts which imply laws and government, civil policy, agriculture, and commerce.   The wonders had ceased which had ushered

[1] Servius ad Virg. Æn. vi. 287.

in this state of things, and more commonplace conditions had succeeded them. Homer's heroes resemble not the more sublime types of a Heracles or a Theseus. They are men indeed of a superior and almost superhuman mould, and under the immediate protection of the gods, from whom some of them are descended, but they achieve nothing miraculous. And this strengthens the probability that the siege was really an historical event.

Concerning the antiquity of the heroic legends, and the manner of their formation, different opinions may be entertained. Preller is of opinion [1] that they can hardly be older than the age of Solon and Pisistratus. But this view is at variance with the fact that some of them are alluded to by Homer; as that of Erechtheus, and that of Theseus and Ariadne.[2] And, from the examples already cited from the same poet, of the antique custom of celebrating heroic deeds in song, it seems probable that such legends may have been even earlier than his days. The age of Theseus, the chief Athenian hero, preceded only by one generation the era of the Trojan war; but the legendary history of Attica mounts several centuries higher. To recount all its traditions forms no part of our plan. We shall content ourselves with selecting the more prominent ones, and those more especially which are connected with Athenian topography and art.

[1] Griechische Mythologie, B. ii. S. 135.   [2] Iliad, ii. 546, sqq.; Od. xi. 321, sqq

CHAPTER II.

CECROPS is commonly reputed to have been the first King of Athens.
There were, however, traditions of earlier sovereigns, as Ogyges, or
Ogygus; but he seems properly to have been a Theban king. His name is
synonymous with ' ancient' or ' primitive,' [1] and he was doubtless a fictitious personage. He is connected with Attica, as having been reputed
by some to have been the father of the hero Eleusis, the founder of the
town or that name.[2] In his reign occurred the great flood which,
according to tradition, covered Attica, as well as Bœotia, and left it
desolate near two centuries. We hear also of Draco, Actæus, or
Actæon. Porphyrion, and others, as earlier kings than Cecrops. But
the Athenian antiquary Philochoros declared all these names to be
fictitious.[3] To the same purpose is the testimony of Apollodorus, who
says that Cecrops ruled first in Attica; but he also mentions that he
married Agraulos, a daughter of Actæus.[4]

That there was a sovereign named Cecrops, may with probability be
inferred from the Acropolis, the original city, having been once called

---

[1] ὠγυγίου, παλαιοῦ, ἀρχαίου.—Hesych.
[2] Pausan. i. 38, 7.
[3] Ap. African. Chron. lib. iii. See Meursius De Reg. Ath. i. 6.
[4] Lib. iii. 14, 1, sq.

Cecropia, and its inhabitants Cecropidae.[1] Further, Cecropia was not only the name of one of the four original Attic tribes, but also of one of the later ten.[2] Cecrops was said to be an autochthon, or sprung from the soil (γηγενης), that is, he belonged to the primitive Attic race; to symbolize which he was depicted as half man half snake.[3] Hence he was called διφυης, or of a double nature, and by Ovid *geminus*.[4] Many rationalistic explanations have been given of this epithet, as that he had the understanding of a man and the strength of a dragon; that it was he who first instituted marriage, that from a good sovereign he became a tyrant, &c.[5] But ancient mythology was full of these double natures, as the centaur, the satyr, the mermaid, &c. Images representing the monstrous combination of the man-serpent still exist at Athens.

Cecrops was reputed to have been the founder not only of Athens, but also of the Attic state, and to have distributed the population into twelve cities or boroughs, namely, Cecropia, which he made his residence, Tetrapolis, Epacria, Decelea, Eleusis, Aphydna, Thoricus, Brauron, Cytherus, Sphettus, Cephisia, Phalerus.[6] But Strabo, in the same passage, remarks on the variations and uncertainty of Attic history, and it is quite improbable that the whole of Attica should have been subject to the founder of Athens. Thus we shall have to recount further on a war between Athens and Eleusis; and it may be doubted, as we have seen, whether even the plain immediately surrounding Athens formed part of her territory from the beginning. We must content ourselves with assuming only that the division into twelve demi had been effected before the time of Theseus.

As the founder of the state, Cecrops was also partly the founder of its religion. He is said to have erected the first altar to Zeus Hypatos (ὕπατος)—dwelling on high, worshipped on mountain tops—and to have forbidden living sacrifices to be offered to him; for which

[1] Herod. viii. 44; Eurip. Suppl. 658; Plin. H. N. vii. 194.

[2] Harpocr. in voc. Pollux, viii. c. 9, s. 109, sq.

[3] ὦ Κέκροψ ἥρως ἄναξ, τὰ πρὸς ποδῶν δρακοντίδη.—Aristoph. Vesp. 438.

Cf. Eurip. Ion. 1163.

[4] Metam. ii. 555.

[5] Demosth. Orat. Fun. p. 1398, Reiske: Athen. xiii. 1,&c. All the explanations are given by Tzetzes, Chil. v. 18, l. 637 sqq.

[6] Strab. p. 397.

he substituted cakes (πέλανοι).[1] These cakes, it appears, were still offered in the time of Pausanias on the altar of Zeus Policus—the same as Hypatos—before the Erechtheium. We cannot, however, quite reconcile this account with another passage in the same author, where he describes the sacrifice of an ox at this altar in the reign of Erechtheus.[2] This was the first occasion, he says, on which the priest called Bouphonos (Βουφόνος) slew an ox at the altar of Zeus Policus; but leaving the hatchet there, he fled from the place, and the hatchet was arraigned in the court of the Prytaneium. This was therefore evidently an innovation on the institution of Cecrops, and considered as a guilty one. But then, what of the πέλανοι, or cakes, which Pausanias says, continued to be offered? According to another account, they were the cause of the crime. The story is thus told by Porphyrius.[3] Sopatros, an Attic farmer, was assisting at a sacrifice at Athens, when an ox returning from labour ate some of the cakes on the sacrificial table, threw others on the ground, and trod upon them. Hereupon, Sopatros, in a rage, seized a hatchet and killed the ox. Stung with remorse, he buried the hatchet, and fled to Crete. A drought ensued, and the Pythian oracle being consulted by the Athenians, answered, that a Cretan fugitive must free them from it; the slayer must be punished, the slain ox recalled to life, though all were to partake of it. Sopatros was recalled, and invented the rites of the festival called Diipoleia; in which, after the ox had been slaughtered and divided, his skin was stuffed, and he was put in a plough, to betoken his revival! Childish as is this ceremony, it is but too typical of the slight varnish with which superstition, in all ages, has sought to cover and atone for sin.

Such was the institution of the Buphonia, called also Diipoleia. But, like all Attic legends, there are many versions of it. According to Androtion, cited by the scholiast on the 'Clouds' of Aristophanes (v. 981), the man who originally struck the ox was named Thaulon. His descendants formed an hereditary priesthood called Bouphoni and

---

[1] Paus. i. 26, 6; viii. 2, 1.
[2] i. 28, 11.
[3] De Abstinentia, ii. 29, sq. Lobeck,

Aglaophamus, p. 1083, is of opinion that all these bloodless sacrifices were of a late date, as Homer does not mention such.

Boutypi (Βουφόνοι, Βουτίπποι), whilst those who drove the ox were called Centriadæ (Κεντριάδαι), and those who cut it up, Daitri (Δαιτροι).' With the license of the Attic theatre, Aristophanes sneers at the festival as very archaic.'

Let us observe here, that the scene of these original ceremonies of the Zeus worship is on the Acropolis, and there is not a word about the vast and ancient sanctuary of Zeus, which a recent school of Athenian topographers pretends to have discovered upon the Pnyx Hill, on the site of the Eccleon.

Whether Zeus ever obtained among the Athenians the surname of Patrous (πατρῷος) is a disputed point. According to a scholiast on Aristophanes,' he got this name not as the progenitor of the Athenians, as Apollo was sometimes considered, but because they first welcomed the god, and were the only Hellenes who sacrificed to him according to their phratriæ, demi, and races, or families (συγγενειας). Plato, in a passage of the 'Euthydemus,' also recognizes him in these capacities, but denies that he was called πατρῷος, but only ἕρκειος and φράτριος.' Hence Porson and Lobeck have abjudicated this surname from the Athenian Zeus; the former confining its use to the tragic poets, and the latter still further restricting it to those who were actually descended from the deity. We must of course bow to the decision of these great critics; but at the same time we must confess that their explanations of the use of the epithet by Attic writers in other passages seems hardly satisfactory. Plato himself uses it in a passage in his 'Laws,' which Porson sets aside because they are feigned laws delivered to a fictitious republic. But the book was written for the

---

1 Schol. Arist. Pac. 418; Bekker, An. Graec. p. 288; Porphyr. loc. cit.

2 ἀρχαῖά γε, καὶ Διπολιώδη καὶ τεττίγων ἀνάμεστα
καὶ Κηκείδου καὶ βουφονίων.—Nub. 984. Cf. ibi schol.

3 Nubes, 1470.

4 οὐκ ἔστιν, ἦν δ᾽ ἐγώ, αὕτη ἡ ἐπωνυμία Ἰώνων οὐδενί, οὔθ᾽ ὅσοι ἐκ τῆσδε πόλεως ἀπῳκισμένοι εἰσὶν οὔθ᾽ ἡμῖν, ἀλλὰ Ἀπόλλων πατρῷος διὰ τὴν τοῦ Ἴωνος γένεσιν· Ζεὺς δ᾽ ἡμῖν πατρῷος μὲν οὐ καλεῖται, ἕρκειος δὲ καὶ φράτριος, καὶ Ἀθηνᾶ φρατρία.—p. 302 (ii. i. 153, Bekk.).

5 Porson, ad Eurip. Med. 1314; Lobeck, Aglaophamus, p. 770, sq.

6 ὁ δὲ μὴ ἀμύνων ἀρᾷ ἐνεχέσθω Διὸς ὁμογνίου καὶ πατρῴου κατὰ νόμον.—Leg. ix. p. 881 (iii. iii. 174, Bekk.). Cf. καταιδεσθῆτι πατρῴου Δία.—Arist. ph. Nub. 1468.

Athenians, and to put the laws prescribed for them under the protection of a deity whom they did not acknowledge seems hardly an eligible way of recommending them. In the 'Euthydemus,' may not Socrates be only fencing with the question of Dionysodorus, who was a foreigner, and trying to mystify him, by giving to the doubtful epithet πατρῷος only the sense of an actual progenitor, as in the case of Apollo, without regarding that signifying a fatherly care?

Macrobius says,[1] after Philochorus, that Cecrops first erected altars to Saturn and Ops—that is, to Cronos and Rhea. In the time of Pausanias, as we shall see in the sequel, there was a common sanctuary of these deities in the Olympium. The festival of Cronos (Κρόνια) was celebrated on the 12th of Hecatombæon, which month was at an earlier period called the Cronian month (μὴν Κρόνιος); and it seems to have resembled in its merriment and feasting the Roman Saturnalia.[2]

But what chiefly distinguished the reign of Cecrops was the contest of Athena and Poseidon for the possession of Attica. In like manner Hera and Poseidon are said to have contended for Argos.[3] Whether such contests denote the strife of hostile races, having different religions, or not, it may be remarked that the presence of a patron deity was indispensable to an ancient city, with whom its safety was inseparably connected. Hence, a prime object with the Greeks at Troy was to get possession of the Palladium; and the Romans, when besieging Veii, implored the aid of its patron goddess Juno, nor dared to carry off her image after it was captured, except with her own consent.[4] In the legend, the rival deities contend for the honour of presiding over the city. Poseidon coming first, strikes the rock of the Acropolis with his trident, and forthwith the salt water gushes out. Then comes Athena, and produces the olive. These symbols of their strife were long shown in after-ages; the olive tree in the Pandroseium; the sea water (Ἐρεχθηὶς θάλασσα) in the Erechtheium, where, indeed, the marks of the trident are still exhibited! In the version of Callimachus, which

---

[1] Saturn. i. 10.

[2] Demosth. c. Timocr. p. 708, Reiske; Plut. Thes. 12; Athen. xiv. 15.

[3] Pausan. ii. 15, 5.

[4] Livy, v. 21, sq. See also the form of evocation of the guardian deity of Carthage in Macrobius, Saturn. iii. 9.

seems to be the older one, the contending gods chose Cecrops for their
arbiter, who gave the victory to Athena.[1] Another account makes
Cecrops only the witness of the strife, which, by the appointment of
Zeus, is determined by the twelve gods.[2] St. Augustine gives a Euhemeristic version of the myth, taken from Varro.[3] An olive suddenly
sprung up on the Acropolis, and near it appeared some sea water.
Cecrops having consulted the Delphic oracle on these portents, was
told that the olive signified Athena, the sea water Poseidon; and it
was for the citizens to decide after which deity their city should be
named. At that time the women took part in public affairs, and
having a majority of one, declared in favour of the goddess. Poseidon,
in his anger, flooded all Attica, which caused the women to be deprived
of the suffrage; and it was further ordained that women should not
bear their mothers' name, and that no woman should be called Athenaia.
A fable to be pondered by the advocates of the political rights of
women !

The sacred olive being of wild and fortuitous growth, was stunted
and crooked, and thence called πάγκυφος.[4] Yet an ever-blooming
vigour was attributed to it :

στέφανον ἐλαίας ἀμφέθηκά σοι τότε,
ἣν πρῶτ᾽ Ἀθήνα σκόπελον εἰσηνέγκατο,
ὅς, εἴπερ ἔστιν, οὔποτ᾽ ἐκλείπει χλόην,
θάλλει δ᾽ ἐλαίας ἐξ ἀκηράτου γεγώς.[5]

"A garland then I placed around thy head
From the first olive on Athena's rock :
Which, while it lasts, will never cease to bloom,
But flourish ever like its parent stem."

And thus, after it had been burnt by the Persians when they captured
Athens, it is related that the priests only two days afterwards found
that it had thrown out a shoot a cubit long![6] From the victory
of Athena a chaplet of olive became the meed and ornament of
conquerors.

[1] Apud schol. Hom. Iliad. xvii. 54.   [4] Hesych. in voc. and in ἀστή.
[2] Apollod. iii. 14, 1.   [5] Eurip. Ion. 1433, sqq.
[3] Civ. Dei. xviii. 9.   [6] Herod. viii. 55.

From this moment the Erechtheium, where the monuments of the contest were preserved, appears to have become, as it afterwards continued to be, a temple of Athena. Thus Homer:

Οἳ δ' ἄρ' Ἀθήνας εἶχον, ἐϋκτίμενον πτολίεθρον,
δῆμον Ἐρεχθῆος μεγαλήτορος, ὅν ποτ' Ἀθήνη
θρέψε, Διὸς θυγάτηρ, τέκε δὲ ζείδωρος ἄρουρα,
κὰδ δ' ἐν Ἀθήνῃσ' εἷσεν, ἑῷ ἐνὶ πίονι νηῷ.
ἔνθάδε μιν ταύροισι καὶ ἀρνειοῖς ἱλάονται
κοῦροι Ἀθηναίων, περιτελλομένων ἐνιαυτῶν.[1] κ. τ. λ.

" Then those who held the well-built town of Athens,
Town of Erechtheus with the noble heart,
Earth-born, but fostered by Athena's care,
Jove's child, and in her own rich temple set.
Him, as the years revolve, the youth of Athens
With blood of bulls and rams propitiate."

These lines have by some critics been regarded as an interpolation of the age of Solon and Pisistratus; because, it is said, the word δῆμος could not have been applied to the Athenians in Homer's time, and because that poet never uses the word νηός.[2] But the charge cannot be supported, at all events by these proofs. Homer does not mention the *Athenians*, as forming a republican state, but *Athens*, as a town or district. Such a use of δῆμος is not uncommon in Homer. Thus, Βοιωτοὶ μάλα πίονα δῆμον ἔχοντες, Il. v. 710; and Λυκίης ἐνὶ πίονι δημῷ, Ib. xvi. 437; where it is evident that he is speaking, not of the people, but the soil. It is true, indeed, that the word has been interpreted by "Plutarch of the people";[3] but even if we should allow that Homer uses it in the sense of a republican state, still there is very good classical authority for it. That Athens was a democracy before the time of Pisistratus, and that it was established by Theseus, is affirmed by several classical authorities; as Aristotle, cited by Plutarch in this passage; by Isocrates, who says that Lycurgus modelled the Spartan democracy on that of Athens; by Demosthenes, who attributes to Theseus the foundation of a democratic state; and by Strabo, who

---

[1] Iliad, ii. 546 sqq.   [2] See Müller, Dorians, ii. 73, sq.   [3] Vit. Thes. 25.

describes Peisistratus and his sons as overthrowing it.' It is true that this earlier Athenian democracy had in it a strong aristocratic leaven, and differed very much from the later one produced by Ephialtes and Pericles breaking the power of the Areopagus and giving wages to the judges, as well as by the efforts of other demagogues, and by the power and consideration which the Athenian people obtained through their Persian victories,' but this is no valid objection against applying the word δῆμος to the original state. The objection drawn from the employment of the word νηός is quite unfounded. It would be extraordinary indeed if Homer, who so frequently speaks of priests and sacrifices, should have been ignorant of temples. But it is not true. He mentions, and by the name of νηός, a temple of Apollo at Cilla, and another of the same deity, with a large adytum, at Troy.' There is again an allusion in the 'Odyssey' to the temple of Erechtheus, not indeed under the name of νηός, but δόμος : —

ἵκετο δ᾽ ἐς Μαραθῶνα καὶ εὐρυάγυιαν Ἀθήνην,
δῦνε δ᾽ Ἐρεχθῆος πυκινὸν δόμον.

vii. 80.

" First she sought Marathon,
Then Athens, with its spacious streets, and reached
The splendid palace where Erechtheus dwelt."

Which is a confirmation of the allusion in the 'Iliad,' and a further proof that those lines were not forged ; for to assert that both passages are forged would be somewhat too hardy. And a comparison of them shows that the house of Erechtheus and the temple of Athena, into which it was afterwards converted, were identical.

The genesis of Erechtheus is given in the passage cited from the Iliad. He is there represented as the offspring of the cultivated, or corn-bearing, land (ἄρουρα, from ἀρόω, 'to till'), reared by the care of Athena ; a myth, having an analogous reference to agriculture with that of Demeter and Triptolemus. Erechtheus appears to have been

---

[1] See Isocr. Panath. p 264 E sq.: Demosth. c. Near. p. 1370, Reiske ; Strabo, ix. p. 397.

[2] Aristot. Polit. ii. 10 (p. 57).

[3] Iliad. i. 39 ; v. 446.

the earliest form of the name of the foster-son of Athena, and the only
one known to Homer and Herodotus. But in later authors we find the
name Erichthonius used in a way that identifies it with that of Erechtheus. Thus, Isocrates makes Erichthonius the successor of Cecrops;[1]
and the same view is adopted by Euripides, Pausanias, and others.[2]
The name thus written has been thought to have reference to his earth-
born origin (ἔρι χθόνιος, 'very earthy,' as ἐριβῶλαξ, ἐριθηλής, &c.).
According to some, ἔρι refers to that version of the myth which made
Erichthonius spring from the seed of Hephæstus, saturating the wool
which Athena flung to the earth. The etymology is hardly possible;
but from this form of the myth, Erichthonius is sometimes called the son
of Hephæstus and Gæa; which is also merely an allegory of the earth
being rendered fruitful by warmth. Hence the worship of Hephæstus
is often found combined with that of Athena, and, as we shall see
further on, he had an altar in the Erechtheium. Plato represents
Athena and Hephæstus as dwelling together, apparently in the Erechtheium, and exercising the arts in common, and Prometheus as
stealing from their temple the creative fire.[3]

The sequel of this myth is of the highest importance in the mythology of the Athenians. When Erechtheus, or Erichthonios, was born,
Athena placed him in a chest, which she delivered to Agraulos, Herse,
and Pandrosos, the daughters of Cecrops, with strict injunctions not to
pry into it. In the chest was a snake, under which form Erechtheus
was sometimes represented and worshipped, and which became one of
the symbols of Athena.[4] Pandrosos alone obeyed the commands of
the goddess; her sisters opened the box, and seeing Erechtheus and the
serpents, were seized with madness, and flung themselves from the
most precipitous part of the Acropolis. According to the version of
Apollodorus, they were killed by the snake. As a reward for her
fidelity, Pandrosos became the first priestess of Athena, and was lodged

[1] Orat. Panath. p. 258 D.

[2] γηγενοῦς Ἐριχθονίου. — Eur. Ion, 20.
Cf. v. 268 sqq.; Pausan. i. 2, 5; 18, 2;
Apollod. iii. 14, 6.

[3] Protagoras, p. 321 (i. i. p. 173, Bekk.).

[4] Apollod. loc. cit. According to Euripides, two snakes, δισσὼ δράκοντε.—Ion,
23.

in a compartment of her temple, in which also was the olive which Athena had produced. But Aglauros also obtained divine honours, and her name became an epithet of Athena. Her temple, however, was not on the Acropolis, but on its northern declivity, above the Anaceium or temple of the Dioscuri, at which spot she had fallen; but it communicated with the Erechtheium by means of a subterranean staircase. That Aglauros was no obscure deity is shown by the fact that she was one of the seven called to witness ($i\sigma\tau o\rho\epsilon\varsigma\ \theta\epsilon o i$) the oath taken by the Attic Ephebi, which indeed was sworn in her temple.[1] The other witnesses were Enalios (Poseidon), Ares, Zeus, Thallo, Auxo, Hegemonë. Thallo was one of the Horæ, and worshipped by the Athenians in conjunction with Pandrosos. Auxo and Hegemone were Charites, or Graces.[2]

Such were the main outlines of the myth; like every Attic one, it had minor variations, which we forbear to notice. It is plainly an agricultural allegory, like that of the contest of Athena and Poseidon, which Plutarch says was invented by the Attic kings to divert the population from a seafaring life to the pursuits of agriculture.[3] Cecrops' daughters are personifications of the properties of the atmosphere. Hersë and Pandrosos both signify the dew ($\epsilon\rho\sigma\eta$, $\delta\rho\acute{o}\sigma o\varsigma$), while Aglauros (= $\dot{\alpha}\gamma\lambda\alpha\acute{o}\varsigma$) denotes the splendour, or brightness, of day.[4] Thus Athena, when made the guardian deity of the city, with the name of Polias (= $\pi o\lambda\iota o\tilde{\upsilon}\chi o\varsigma$), was the patroness of agriculture. This attribute was lost, or at all events eclipsed, after the introduction of the worship of Demeter, and in after times she became more especially the president of art, science, and war.

The earliest pantheon of the greater gods among the Athenians seems to have consisted only of Zeus, Poseidon, Athena, Hephæstus, and Hermes, perhaps also Hera, as the spouse of Zeus, but she is a goddess who plays no great part in Athenian mythology. It is possible that

---

[1] Pollux, lib. viii. s. 106. Cf. Demosth. De falsa leg. p. 438. Reiske.

[2] Pausan. ix. 35, 1.

[3] Vit. Themist. 10. Dionysius Hal. (Ant. Rom. ii. 20) considers some of the Greek myths as allegories of natural phenomena.

[4] Another, and perhaps older, form of the name was $\ddot{\alpha}\gamma\rho\alpha\upsilon\lambda o\varsigma$, 'dwelling in the fields.' Hence, apparently, the demos Agraulë ('$A\gamma\rho\alpha\upsilon\lambda\acute{\eta}$, or '$A\gamma\rho\upsilon\lambda\acute{\eta}$) of the tribe Erechtheïs. See Leake, Demi. p. 183.

Ares also may have been included; at all events we have no notice of his subsequent introduction. The remaining gods, as Apollo, Artemis, Demeter, Aphrodite, &c., appear to have been of later adoption. Poseidon is generally allowed to have had possession of Attica before Athena; and it is remarkable that she, as well as Hephæstus and Hermes, are reputed to have been of Egyptian origin. Athena is said to have been the Egyptian *Neith*, Hephæstus *Phtha*, and Hermes *Thoth*. An Egyptian origin is also ascribed to Erechtheus, the offspring of Hephæstus and foster-child of Athena, who, when there was a dearth at Athens, is said to have brought corn from Egypt.[1] There was at all events a close connection between the Athenians and the Egyptian Saïtæ in the Delta. Plato says that the Saïtæ were very friendly to the Athenians and claimed a connection with them, but in what manner he does not explain.[2] According to Callisthenes and Phanidemus, quoted by Proclus in his commentary on this place, the Saïtæ were a colony from Athens, whilst Theopompus is also cited for a connection just the reverse.[3] Plato in this passage identifies Athena and the Egyptian Neith, and that there was a similarity of worship in the two places seems certain; but in which city it originated cannot be said. Herodotus records a tradition that Athena was the daughter of Poseidon and the Libyan lake Tritonis.[4] However this may be, it will be seen, when we come to describe the Erechtheium, that the deities worshipped in it were Athena, Poseidon, or rather Poseidon-Erechtheus, Zeus, Hermes, of the greater deities, and Pandrosos. Originally, perhaps, it was the house or palace of Cecrops, for we sometimes find it called simply δόμος or οἴκημα; and according to an ancient Athenian custom to which we have before adverted, Cecrops appears to have been buried in it, in a part called the Cecropeium. Subsequently it became the temple of Athena, surnamed Polias (= πολιοῦχος), as the guardian deity of the city. Here was the most ancient and revered image of her, a mere ξόανον, rudely carved out

[1] Diodor. Sic. i. 29.
[2] μάλα φιλαθήναιοι, καί τινα τρόπον οἰκεῖοι τῶνδε (τῶν Ἀθηναίων).—Tim. p. 21 (iii. ii. 12. Bekk.).
[3] See Meurs. De Fort. Athenar. i. 1. Cf. Herod. ii. 28, 59, 170.
[4] Herod. iv. 180.

of a piece of olive wood, yet much more sacred than the gold and ivory statue in the Parthenon, the work of Pheidias; for it was for the primitive statue that the peplus was worked. Before it a lamp continually burned.[1] For a long time it appears to have been the only, or at all events, the principal, temple on the Acropolis. Thus Herodotus, in his account of the capture of the Acropolis by the Persians, mentions only this one temple as having been burnt, and constantly alludes to it under the name of *the* temple (τὸ ἱρόν, ἐν τῷ ἱρῷ, &c.).[1] Nor can it be shown, we believe, from any ancient author, that there was any other temple on the Acropolis in use before the Persians were than this one dedicated to Athena Polias. Professor Ludwig Ross has indeed asserted the contrary, and maintained that Herodotus alludes to an earlier Hecatompedon, or Parthenon, which had become the seat of the worship of Athena before the Persian invasion.[3] But all the passages which he cites are capable of being referred to the one temple of Athena Polias. At the same time we do not deny that when the Acropolis was taken there was a large Hecatompedon in progress of erection on the site subsequently occupied by the Parthenon. Recent excavations have proved this fact too plainly to admit of any question. All we affirm is that it

[1] Strab. p. 396; Pausan. i. 26, 7.

[2] Lib. viii. c. 51, 53.

[3] Archäolog. Aufsätze, i. 129 sqq. The only passages that might raise any doubt are viii. 51 and 55. In the first the Persians are said to have found the *treasurers in the temple* (ταμίας τοῦ ἱροῦ); on which Ross denies that the public treasury could have been in the small and uniform Erechtheium. The public treasure, however, in the ante-Persian times, before it was augmented by the contributions of the allies, was doubtless small. As to the second, Ross remarks that in c. 55 Herodotus speaks of the Erechtheium as a temple not before mentioned, and therefore a separate one (ἔστι ἐν τῇ ἀκροπόλι ταύτῃ Ἐρεχθῆος τοῦ γηγενέος λεγομένου εἶναι νηός). But he has quoted only a small part of the passage. For Herodotus goes on to say that it was the *temple* (νηός) in which were the olive and the sea water (ἐν τῷ ἐλαίη τε καὶ θάλασσα ἔνι), and that the olive was burnt with the rest of the *hieram*, or sanctuary (ταύτην ὧν τὴν ἐλαίην ἅμα τῷ ἄλλῳ ἱρῷ κατέλαβε ἐμπρησθῆναι), thus showing that by νηός he means not the whole Erechtheium, but only a compartment of it. And a few lines further, "when they went up to the hieram or temple" (ὡς ἀνέβησαν ἐς τὸ ἱρόν), showing that there was only one hieram, and that it contained the temple with the burnt olive. The whole complex of buildings forming what we now call the Erechtheium does not appear to have obtained that name till a much later period.

D 2

was burnt when in an incomplete state, and before it had been dedicated
for public worship; and the unfinished columns which have been discovered show that this was the case. But we shall return to this subject when describing the city.

We will say a few words of the other gods who inhabited the temple in
conjunction with Athena. The principal one was Poseidon, who appears
to have been reconciled with Athena; but when and in what manner we
are unable to explain. Typical of the reconciliation there stood in the
temple a statue of Lethë, or Oblivion.[1] It would appear to have been
effected through Erechtheus, with whom Poseidon became identified,
under the name of Poseidon-Erechtheus, while the sea water which he
had called forth obtained the name of Erechthean ($\theta\acute{a}\lambda a\sigma\sigma a$ 'Ερεχθηΐς).
A double name of this sort was not unparalleled, for Athena was called
Athena-Aglauros and Athena-Nikë. Hence we find mentioned a priesthood of Poseidon-Erechtheus.[2] Butes, brother of the second Erechtheus,
was invested with this priesthood; and the office, afterwards combined
with a priesthood of Athena, was transmitted to his descendants, called
Eteobutadæ.[3] Butes himself obtained divine honours, and had an altar
in the Erechtheium by the side of that of Poseidon-Erechtheus.[4] Erechtheus appears also to have had a separate worship under the form of a
snake, and a live one was kept in the temple, called οἰκουρὸς ὄφις, or the
guardian serpent. Some of Poseidon's attributes show him associated
with Athena as the patroness of agriculture, for he is not only the god
of the sea, but also of rivers, springs, and moisture in general, and so
assists the productive powers of the earth. Under this aspect he
obtained the epithet of φυτάλμιος, 'nourishing' or 'producing,' and is
placed by Plutarch along with Zeus ὄμβριος (pluvius, 'descending in
showers') and Demeter προηροσία ('presiding over tillage'), among the
gods who patronized agriculture.[5] In this character he had a priesthood

[1] Plut. Sympos. ix. p. 740.

[2] Ps.-Plut. x. Orat. Vit. t. ix. p. 353,
Reiske; and in an inscription on one of
the thrones in the Dionysiac theatre:
Ποσειδῶνος γαιηόχου καὶ 'Ερεχθέως.

[3] Apollod. iii. 15, 1; Harpocrat. voc.
Βούτης.   [4] Pausan. i. 26, 6.

[5] Septem Sap. Conv. p. 158 (t. vi. p. 603,
Reiske). Cf. Cornutus, 22; Preller, Griech.
Mythol. i. 457.

at Athens, as is also shown by an inscription on one of the thrones of
the priests recently discovered in the theatre (Ποσειδῶνος Φυταλμίου.
A further proof of his connection with agriculture and Athens is, that
on the Holy Way leading from Athens to Eleusis, was a temple of
Demeter and Coré, with an altar of Zephyrus; and that Athena and
Poseidon were here associated with their worship.[1] Zephyr is the
husband of Chloris,[2] or Verdure, a name analogous to that of Chloe,
the epithet of Demeter, and the result of their union is Carpus, or
' fruit.'

Poseidon and Athena are connected by other attributes besides those
pertaining to agriculture. Poseidon was the creator of the horse:

> "   —   tuque O cui prima frementem
> Fudit equum magno tellus percussa tridenti,
> Neptune."
>
> Virg. Georg. i. 12.

The scene of the creation is variously laid in Thessaly and in Bœotia.[3]
According to the latter version, Areion, the first horse, belonged to
Adrastus, and was the offspring of Poseidon and one of the Furies, or
of Demeter in the shape of an Erinnys.[4] When Adrastus fled from
Thebes he reined in his horses at the Attic Colonus, and saluted both
Poseidon and Athena with the surname of Hippios.[5] But the boast of
Attica was the taming of the horse, which Athena shared with Poseidon.
Hence in the Œdipus Coloneus of Sophocles, the chorus sing their con-
joint praises at Colonus (v. 710 sqq.). For that Athena also claimed to

[1] Pausan. i. 37, 1.

[2] The Latin Flora, which, according to Ovid, Fast. v. 195, is only a corruption of the Greek word. Cf. Serv. ad Virg. Ecl. v. 48.

[3] Schol. ad Pind. Pyth. iv. 246: Philostr. Imag. ii. 14, where however the creation is differently related. Iliad, xxiii. 346, et ibi schol.

[4] Pausan. viii. 25, 5. Cf. Serv. ad Virg. Georg. i. 12; schol. Pind. Pyth. iv. 246, &c. But there are various versions of the story. It may be right, though perhaps hardly necessary, to apprise the reader, that in this and other cases we give only the more general and obvious outlines of Attic myths and legends: which however may suffice for the student of Athenian literature. Those who seek a more recondite interpretation of them are referred to the works of Creuzer, O. Müller, Preller, and the two Lenormants.

[5] Bekker, An. Græc. 350, 28: Etym. M. voc. ἱππία.

le the tamer of horses is shown by her epithets of ἱππία, 'the equestrian,' and χαλινῖτις, 'the bridler.' Pindar represents Athena as instructing Bellerophon how to bridle Pegasus, and afterwards commanding him to sacrifice a bull to Poseidon and to erect an altar to Athena Ἱππία.[1] The epithet ἵππιος is also connected with ships, the horses as it were of the sea, and so called by Homer ;[2] and under this epithet Poseidon is saluted in a chorus of the 'Knights' of Aristophanes as presiding over both ships and horses (v. 550 sqq.). Even in what might be regarded as his peculiar element he finds a rival in Athena, who prepares the Argo for Jason, and the fifty-oared vessel which aided the flight of Danaüs.[3] We find them associated in a common worship at the promontory of Sunium, where Athena had a temple, and Poseidon perhaps only an altar in it; unless, indeed, as Dr. Wordsworth suggests, the vestiges of a large building close by may have belonged to a temple of Poseidon.[4]

With regard to the horse, Erechtheus is further connected with Poseidon and Athena as being the first charioteer :

> "Primus Erichthonius currus et quatuor ausus
> Jungere equos, rapidisque rotis insistere victor."[5]

In this capacity he appeared on the western pediment of the Parthenon, in the group representing the contest of Athena and Poseidon, as driving a chariot behind the goddess.[6]

Zeus plays no great part in the pantheon of the original city. As

[1] Olymp. xiii. 90 sqq. ; 115. Cf. Paus. ii. 41. On the approach of the Persians, Cimon dedicates his bridle to Athena. Plut. Cim. 5.

[2] ἁλὸς ἵπποι, Od. iv. 708.

[3] Apollod. i. 9, 16 ; ii. 1, 4.

[4] Athens and Attica, ch. 27. See Aristoph. Eq. 556 sqq. and schol.

[5] Virg. Georg. iii. 113.

[6] ἐν τῇ ἀκροπόλει ὀπίσω τῆς θεοῦ ὁ Ἐρεχθεὺς γέγραπται ἅρμα ἐλαύνων.—Aristid. Panath. schol. p. 62, Dindorf. There can hardly be a doubt that the reference is to the pediment of the Parthenon. It might be objected that the word γέγραπται refers to a painting ; but it is a well-known fact that friezes and pediments were painted. In the drawing of Carrey of the western pediment, a figure is seen just behind Athena, driving a two-horse chariot. The quadriga appears to have been an addition of Virgil's ; for the Greek tradition mentions only a simple chariot: λέγεται γὰρ Ἐριχθόνιον μὲν τὸν τῆς θεοῦ τρόφιμον πρῶτον ἀνθρώπων ἅρμα ζεῦξαι ἵππων.—Aristid. Min. Orat. t. i. p. 12, Jebb.

THE AREIOPAGOS FROM THE SOUTH-EAST.

Hypatos: his altar is outside the temple; though as Zeus Herceius (ἑρκεῖος), the household god, the guardian of the fence, he had an altar within. Here also, like Athena, he was guardian of the city (πολιεύς). The introduction of the Olympian Zeus, and the building of a magnificent temple to him, belonged to a much later period. It was in honour of the Zeus of the Acropolis that one of the three sacred ἄροτοι, or ' ploughings,' was performed by the priest called Buzyges (βουζύγης), which became an hereditary office, like many others at Athens. Buzyges, who first yoked oxen to the plough, is sometimes identified with Epimenides.[1] Before the Eleusinium at Athens, and near the statue of Triptolemos, was a brazen ox being led along, and near it a statue of Epimenides in a sitting posture.[2]

Hermes is connected with the history of the Cecropids; for by Pandrosos[3] he had Ceryx, forefather of the Eleusinian Cerykes, or heralds; and by her sister Hersë he had Cephalos. Aglauros also is related to have had by Ares a daughter named Alcippë, whose story is of some importance for Athenian topography. She is related to have been ravished by Halirrhotius (' the raging sea wave '), son of Poseidon and the nymph Euryte, for which outrage he was slain by Ares. The scene of the murder was at a fountain on the south side of the Acropolis, where afterwards stood the temple of Asclepios. For this act Ares was arraigned before the gods on the hill, or rock, which lies before the western side of the Acropolis—a trial from which it obtained its name of Areiopagus ('Mars' Hill').[4] Æschylus, however, assigns the derivation of the name to the hill having been occupied by the Amazons when they made war upon Theseus, and from their offering sacrifice upon it to Ares.[5]

Mr. Clinton has observed[6] that the history of Attica before the Trojan æra is more obscure and more unsatisfactory than that of

[1] " Epimenides, qui postea Buzyges dictus est, secundum Aristotelem."—Serv. ad Virg. Georg. i. 19.

[2] Pausan. i. 14, 3.

[3] Pollux. viii. 103. But Pausanias says, by Aglauros. i. 38, 3.

[4] Eurip. Elketra. 1258 sqq.; cf. schol. ad Orest. 1665.

[5] Eumen. v. 685 sqq.

[6] See Fasti Hellenici, vol. i. p. 59; where the reader will find collected all the authorities upon the subject.

many other parts of Greece. It forms no part of our plan to attempt
to clear up this obscurity; we shall accept the commonly received
accounts. Scanty as it is, the chronicle of the Attic kings seems to be
eked out by duplicate sovereigns, and some of them are evidently mere
abstractions. According to Pausanias (i. 2, 5) Cecrops was not the first
king, but the successor of an earlier one called Actæus, or Actæon,
whose daughter he had married; while Apollodorus, though he says
that Cecrops first reigned over Attica, yet admits that he married a
daughter of Actæus, and that the country had previously been called
Acté, for which he substituted the name of Cecropia.[1] We shall here
content ourselves with giving the most commonly-received list of the
Attic kings down to the Trojan war. 1. Cecrops; 2. Cranaus; 3. Amphictyon; 4. Erechtheus or Erichthonius; 5. Pandion I., son of
Erichthonius; 6. Erechtheus II., son of Pandion; 7. Cecrops II.,
brother of Erechtheus; 8. Pandion II., son of Erechtheus; 9. Ægeus,
son of Pandion; 10. Theseus, son of Ægeus; 11. Menestheus, son of
Peteus, who led the Athenians to Troy. The reigns of these kings are
supposed to have occupied 376 years.

So vague are the accounts of this period, that it is not even certain
under which sovereign the city obtained the name of Athenæ. We
may here remark that this appellation was not peculiar to the capital of
Attica. Stephanus Byzantinus (in voc.) enumerates eight other cities
of the same name, amongst which the most famous was that in Bœotia,
near the lake Copaïs.[2] Hence, by way of distinction, we sometimes
find the capital of Attica called Athenæ Atticæ, even by late writers,
as Plautus:

"Immo Athenis gnatus, altus, educatusque Atticis."[3]

Rud. iii. 4.

The account of Plutarch, that the capital of Attica did not obtain
the name of Athens till the time of Theseus, when it embraced, besides

---

[1] See Apollodorus, iii. 14, 2 sqq. The
form *Actæon* is found in Strabo, p. 397;
Harpocr. voc. ἀκτή: and in Etym. M.

[2] Pausan. ix. 24, 2.

[3] Cf. Apul. Met. lib. i. p. 74; Macrob.
Sat. vii. 1; Ammian. xxvii. 9, 6, &c.

the Acropolis, the asty, or town, which had grown up around it, seems to be the most probable one;[1] though some authors place the assumption of the name in the reign of Amphictyon, and even of Cecrops; while Herodotus assigns it to the reign of Erechtheus.[2] Even the founding of Athens was sometimes ascribed to Athena, whence Sophocles characterises it as θεόδμητοι, divinely built;[3] and Æschylus calls it the city of Pallas.[4]

Of Cranaos we have already spoken. There was still a monument to him in the time of Pausanias in the demus Lampra, or Lamptra.[5] His son-in-law and successor, Amphictyon, was, according to some, an autochthon, according to others, a son of Deucalion; and the institution of the Amphictyonic council is sometimes attributed to him.[6] The reign of Amphictyon is chiefly remarkable in Attic mythology as that in which Dionysus first visited Attica; but it is not quite clear whether his worship was then established in the country. Amphictyon is said to have taught the Athenians to mix their wine with water, so that they could walk without reeling, and hence to have erected an altar of the upright Dionysus (Ὀρθοῦ Διονύσου). But he permitted a little pure wine to be brought in after dinner, just to show the power of the god.[7] The subject of Amphictyon feasting Dionysus and other gods was represented in terra cotta statues in the temenos of Dionysus near the Peiraic Gate, as we shall see in the description of the city.[8]

Dionysus, though not one of the Twelve Gods, plays a most important part in the Athenian pantheon, as his festivals were the occasion of the Attic drama, and the seasons of theatrical representations. As the Attic wine god he is the son of Zeus and Semele, preserved from the fire which blasted his mother only by the ivy which suddenly sprang up in the apartment.[9] As a god of the upper air, and of the vintage, he appears to be entirely Hellenic; whilst as a θεὸς χθόνιος, or subter-

[1] Thes. 24.
[2] viii. 44.
[3] Sophocles, Electr. v. 707.
[4] θεοὶ πόλιν σώζουσι Παλλάδος θεᾶς.
        Persæ, 347.
[5] i. 13, 2. Cf. Hesych. in voc.

[6] Pausan. i. 2, 6; x. 8, 1; Apollod. iii. 14, 5.
[7] Philochorus, ap. Athen. ii. 7. Cf. v. 8.
[8] Pausan. i. 2, 4.
[9] Eurip. Phœn. 651, et ibi schol.

rancan deity, the mystic Iacchus, or Bacchus, celebrated in the Trie-
terica, he was probably of Phrygian or Thracian origin. Two places
in Attica—Icaria and Eleutheræ—claimed to have introduced Dionysus
into Attica. Icaria lay in the eastern parts of the country, a few miles
south of Marathon, near Mount Icarius, celebrated for its vines. Eleutheræ was situated some twenty or thirty miles north of Eleusis, near
the southern foot of Mount Cithæron. In the first version the myth
ran as follows. Dionysus coming into Attica along with Demeter was
received by Icarius, the eponymous hero of the place, whom he taught
to cultivate the vine and make wine of its produce. Some peasants,
intoxicated with the draught Icarius had given them, and thinking
that he had poisoned them, slew him and buried him under a tree.
His daughter Erigonë, directed to his grave by his dog Mæra, hanged
herself on the tree.[1] Enraged at the death of his friend, Dionysus
afflicts all the maidens connected with his murderers with madness, so
that they hang themselves after the example of Erigonë. An oracle
promises relief when the corpses are found and expiation made; but as
the search was unavailing, the festival called αἰώρα, or ἐώρα, was instituted in memory of Erigonë, called also εὔδειπνος, in which little
figures or masks (oscilla) were hung on the trees.[2]

The other version of the myth was the more prevalent and the
more important one. According to this, it was Pegasus of Eleutheræ
who first introduced Dionysus into Attica. In ancient times Eleutheræ
was a town on the borders of Bœotia, and voluntarily annexed itself to
Attica. Even in the time of Strabo[3] it was by some ascribed to Bœotia.
Hence it was a natural channel through which the Theban wine god should
find his way into Attica. Near Eleutheræ he had a temple, whence the
ξόανον, or antique image, was carried in very early times to Athens, and
was preserved in the most ancient temple of Dionysus near the theatre.[4]
Besides the surname of Eleuthereus ('Ελευθερεύς), derived from the
place, the god, both here and at Athens, had also the surname of

[1] Apollod. iii. 14, 7.

[2] Hesych. and Etym. M. in voc.: Pollux,
iv. 55; Athen. xiv. 10.

[3] Page 412.

[4] Pausan. i. 20, 2: 38, 8.

Ἐλεύθερος or Ἐλευθεύς, the "free" or "liberal" (in Latin, *Liber*), which he had in common with Zeus.[1] Pausanias relates that Pegasus was noted in introducing him by a Delphic oracle, which had pronounced that the god would come among them in the time of Icarius.[2] The advent, therefore, was contemporary at Icaria and Athens; and it is strange to find Preller, after Osann and Bergk, regarding the Icarian and Eleutheran Dionysus as two distinct deities, and the former as the older and proper Attic god.[3] From the account of Pausanias, it appears that Icarius and Pegasus must have been contemporary, and the apparently divergent stories may perhaps be reconciled by assuming that Icarius harboured the god and first planted the vine in Attica, but that it was Pegasus who introduced his worship. And it is plain that Pegasus was more considered by the Athenians than Icarius, for it is he who is placed at the festal board with Dionysus and the other gods; and it is the Eleutheran Dionysus, as we have just said, whose antique image was first adored. There were, indeed, two temples of Dionysus in the Limnæ, one of which contained the antique Eleutheran image, and the other a more modern one, the work of Alcamenes;[4] but there is nothing to connect the latter with an Icarian Dionysus, and there is no more reason to suppose that the two statues represented different divinities than there is to assume that the Athena of the Erechtheium and the Athena of the Parthenon were different.

Amphictyon was succeeded by Erechtheus, or Erichthonios; but Isocrates says—identifying him with the Erechtheus of whom we have spoken—that he followed Cecrops, who had no male heir, and that henceforth the kingdom was transmitted to father and son, down to the time of Theseus;[5] whence we see the inextricable confusion of these legends.

Pandion I., the next on the list, is alluded to by Thucydides as an historical king, who allied himself with Tereus of Daulia in Phocis,

[1] Hesych. in voc.
[2] "Liberque non ob licentiam linguæ dictus est inventor vini, sed quia liberat servitio curarum animum."—Senec. De Tranq. c. 15 sub fin.
[3] i. 2. 4.
[4] Griech. Mythol. i. 525 and 527, note 2.
[5] Pausan. i. 20, 2.
[6] Panath. p. 258.

and gave him his daughter Procne in marriage.[1] The fable of Procne and her daughter Philomela is well known, but has no local Attic interest. According to some authors, the advent of Demeter into Attica took place in this reign, whilst others place it in that of his son and successor.

This was Erechtheus, the second of that name. The worship of Demeter and the mysteries connected with it became one of the most famous and revered of the Attic religious rites. Herodotus seems tacitly to connect the Thesmophoria of Demeter and Corë with certain mysteries performed at the Lake of Saïs, and describes them as having been brought into the Peloponnesus by the daughters of Danaüs, who taught them to the Pelasgic women. He goes on to say that, when the Peloponnesus was subdued by the Dorians, these rites perished except among the Arcadians — a pre-eminently agricultural people.[2] Thus we find that the inhabitants of Pheneus, in Arcadia, celebrated the mysteries much in the same way as they were performed at Eleusis. They had a story that Demeter had arrived among them during her wanderings; but the surname of Eleusinia, which they gave her, raises a presumption that they did not derive her worship in a direct line from the daughters of Danaüs, but rather from Eleusis; and indeed they acknowledged that Naos, who established it among them, was the great-grandson of Eumolpus, the original priest of the Eleusinia.[3] Still we find among the Pheneates traces of an Eastern origin of the ceremonies, for they gave to Demeter the surname of Kidaria, from κίδαρις, signifying a Persian tiara.[4] In their greater mysteries the priest personated this goddess by putting on a mask, and struck with rods the nether deities.[5]

It seems probable that the worship of Demeter may have been introduced into Attica long before the invasion of the Peloponnesus by the Dorians, and it may have come thither through Megara; for the Megarians asserted that they had erected temples to Demeter in the time of Car, son of Phoroneus,[6] who is supposed to have reigned six or

[1] Lib. ii. c. 29.
[2] Lib. ii. c. 171.
[3] Pausan. viii. 14, 8; 15, 1.
[4] Pollux, vii. s. 58.
[5] Pausan. loc. cit.
[6] Pausan. i. 39, 4.

seven centuries before the fall of Troy, and long before the advent of
Danaus into Greece.[1] Megara, indeed, seems to have taken its name
from certain underground caves, where Demeter and Persephone were
worshipped,[2] and similar ones appear to have been established at Eleusis.
But though the origin of the worship is wrapped in obscurity, everything connected with it seems to point to an Eastern origin.

But there is another, and perhaps the most probable way in which
the introduction of Demeter into Attica may be accounted for. One of
her surnames was Gephyræa (Γεφυραία).[3] Now the Gephyræans were
a tribe said to have been of Phœnician origin, to have come with Cadmus
into Bœotia, and to have settled at Tanagra, also called Gephyra. Being
afterwards driven out, they emigrated into Attica, where they were
allowed to settle on certain conditions, and where they established the
worship and orgies of Demeter.[4] The compiler of the 'Etymologicum
Magnum' is wrong in calling them a demos; they were merely a race,
which eventually became dispersed about in various parts of Attica; and
thus Harmodius and Aristogeiton, who were of Gephyræan origin, were
natives of Aphidna.[5] Besides the name of Gephyræa, Demeter with
them had also the name of Achæa ('Αχαία, Ion. 'Αχαίη).[6] Now, this
title may be accounted for in various ways. First, it may be derived
from Achaia in the Peloponnesus, where Demeter was peculiarly
honoured, and where, under the title of Παναχαία, she became the protectress of the Achæan League;[7] but as this title could have nothing
to do with the Gephyræans, it may here be left out of consideration.
Another derivation is from ἄχος—the grief, namely, of Demeter for the
loss of her daughter, as expressed in the Homeric hymn to the goddess:
'Οξὺ δέ μιν κραδίην ἄχος ἔλλαβεν (v. 40); and it appears that in Bœotia,
the ancient seat of the Gephyræans, there was a festival to Achæa

---

[1] See Clinton, Fast. Hell. i. p. 7 sq.

[2] Μέγαρα, κατάγεια οἰκήματά φησι ταῖν
θεαῖν, ἥγουν Δήμητρος καὶ Περσεφόνης.—
Phavorinus.

[3] Etym. M. voc. Γέφυρεῖς. So Stephanus Byz.: Γέφυρα, πόλις Βοιωτιάς· τοῖς
αὐτοῖς δέ φασι καὶ Ταναγραίους, ὡς Στρά-
βων καὶ 'Εκαταῖος· ἀφ' οὗ καὶ Γεφυραῖα

ἡδύν. Where Meursius corrects with certainty the last meaningless word by reading ἡ Δηώ. For Deo was the Eleusinian
Demeter (Att. Lect. v. 31).

[4] Herod. v. 57, 61; Strabo, p. 404.

[5] Herod. ib. 55; Plut. Sympos. i. 10.

[6] Herod. ib. 61.

[7] Pausan. vii. 24, 2.

called ἐπαχθής—'melancholy' or 'unpleasant.'[1] But let us observe that, in the character of the sorrowing mother, she has the epithet of ἀχθεία (from ἄχθος),[2] though it must be admitted that the same lexicographer gives also (under 'Αχαία) the derivation from ἄχος. But a scholiast on the 'Theriacs' of Nicander (v. 485), after alluding to the same derivation, gives also another from the sound of the cymbals[3] with which she sought her daughter; and this we are inclined to think the more probable one. In the celebration of the mysteries the hierophant appears to have sounded a kettle-drum (ἠχεῖον).[4] We are fortified in this opinion by Buttmann, who shows that, in the Homeric hymn to Demeter, ἀχέειν is not to be translated 'lament,' but 'sound,' the initial short ᾰ, for η, being an Ionicism ('Lexilogus,' 'Αχέειν). Hence Demeter had the epithet of χαλκόκροτος—'brass rattling';[5] and it is related that, when the Gephyræans emigrated from Tanagra, Demeter commanded them in a dream to follow the sound of the cymbals, and where it ceased, to build a city; and they also erected a temple of Demeter Achræa.[6] Hence Echo ('sound') is intimately connected with Demeter. Echo was the mother, by Pan, of Baubo, or Iambë—of whom we shall speak presently—and she had an altar on the road from Athens to Eleusis. Even the name of Iacchus seems to be connected with the noise of the Eleusinian festival, and signified the boisterous song sung on that occasion.[7]

Demeter is literally 'the earth-mother,' for the Doric Δα = Γα or Γη. But the goddess Γᾶ, Γῆ, or Γαῖα (Gæa) is different from Demeter. Gæa is 'the earth' in its widest and most general acceptation, whilst

---

[1] Plut. De Isid. et Os. t. vii. p. 489, Reiske. How M. Lenormant (Voie Sacrée, i. p. 250) makes out from this passage that the goddess herself had the surname of Ἐπαχθῆ or Ἐπαχῆ, we are at a loss to discover.

[2] Ἀχθεία, ἡ Δημήτηρ, μυστικῶς.—Hesych.

[3] ἢ διὰ τὸν τῶν κυμάτων (l. κυμβάλων) ἦχον. Ap. Albert. not ad Hesych.; schol. ad Aristoph. Ach. 708.

[4] Schol. ad Theocr. Id. ii. v. 36. Cf. Vell. Paterc. i. 4.

[5] Pindar, Isth. vii. 3, and schol.

[6] Ἀχαιὰ . . . ἢ ὅτι μετὰ κυμβάλων ἠχοῦσα τὴν Κόρην ἐζήτει· ἢ ὅτι τοῖς Ταναγραίοις μεταστᾶσιν ἐκ Τανάγρας, ἡ Δημήτηρ κατ' ὄναρ φανεῖσα, ἐκέλευσεν αὐτοὺς ἀκολουθῆσαι τῷ γενομένῳ ἤχῳ· καὶ ὅπου ἂν παύσηται, ἐκεῖ πόλιν κτίσαι· καὶ ἱδρύσαντο ἱερὸν Ἀχαιᾶς Δημήτερος.—Etym. M.

[7] παρὰ τὴν ἰαχὴν τὴν ἐν ταῖς χορείαις γιγνομένην, τουτέστι τὴν βοήν, γίνεται Ἴακος, καὶ πλεονασμῷ τοῦ κ Ἴακχος.—Ibid. in voc. Cf. Herod. viii. 65, τὴν φωνὴν . . . ἰακχάζοισι.

the added appellation of μητηρ denotes its fructifying power. Demeter is not only the patroness of agriculture, but also of the manner of civilized life which result from it. Hence her epithet of θεσμοφορος, or 'law-bringing,' shared also by her daughter Persephone; for they are an inseparable pair.' Thus we find them jointly invoked as τὰ θεσμοφόρω in the proclamation of the herald in the 'Thesmophoriazusæ' of Aristophanes,' which is probably a close imitation of that made at the festival of the Thesmophoria. But this festival was only a subsidiary one to that of the mysteries; for agriculture is a primary condition, without which civilization cannot exist, and therefore, as the cause of it, demands a more solemn recognition. The Thesmophoria were celebrated by the women alone, and lasted only three or four days; whilst the mysteries took up nine, and were open to the whole population.

Isocrates, whilst acknowledging that the mysteries originated in a myth—which was, doubtless, also the persuasion of every educated Athenian—has pointed out the twofold benefits which they typified; namely, in this life, agriculture and the civilization which results from it; in the life to come, the hope, through initiation, of a happy eternity.' So also Sophocles, in a fragment preserved by Plutarch,' asserts the influence of initiation as to the happiness or misery of a future state·

$$\text{——— ὡς τρισόλβιοι}$$
κεῖνοι βροτῶν, οἱ ταῦτα δερχθέντες τέλη
μόλωσ᾿ ἐς Ἅιδου· τοῖσδε γὰρ μόνοις ἐκεῖ
ζῆν ἐστι, τοῖς δ᾿ ἄλλοισι πάντ᾿ ἐκεῖ κακά.

"——— They are thrice blest
Who, having seen these sacred mysteries,
Descend into the grave. For they alone
Once more enjoy a life, where all the rest
Find nought but woe."

---

1 The most usual name for Persephonë is simply Corë (Κόρη), 'the maiden' or 'daughter.' Other forms are: Phersephonë, Persephassa, Phersephassa, Phersephatta.

2 Ver. 295. The other gods invoked there, besides Demeter and Corë, are Plutus, Calligeneia, Gaia κουροτρόφος ('boy-nourishing'), Hermes, and the Graces.

3 Panegyr. p. 46.

4 De aud. poetis, p. 21 (t. vi. p. 76. Reiske).

Some philosophers might despise the ceremony; yet to the latest period of paganism, initiation was eagerly sought by the highest and most distinguished persons; and Cicero, in a general condemnation of all nocturnal rites, excepted only this.[1]

The mysteries shadowed forth the analogy between the sowing of the seed and the committal of the dead body to the earth, from which both were to rise again with renewed vigour. Cicero, in another passage, adverts to a custom—which he says was as old as the time of Cecrops—of immediately burying the dead in the earth, and sowing seeds over their graves, so that they might repose, as it were, in the bosom of a mother.[2] Corë, the offspring of Demeter, passes, like the seed, a portion of her existence underground, or in Hades, and in the spring of the year rises again to the light of day. The myth ran as follows :

Demeter, when her daughter had been ravished by Aïdoneus, wandered over the earth, seeking her with lighted torches. The scene of the rape has been variously selected; but Attic traditions—with which alone we are here concerned—placed it either at Erineos, on the western or Eleusinian Cephisus, or at the chasm at Colonus, supposed to have been the threshold of Hades.[3] At length, having arrived at Eleusis—from which circumstance the place, according to some, derived its name (ἔλευσις, 'advent')—she sat down on the ἀγέλαστος πέτρα, or stone of grief, near the well called Callichoros, on which also Theseus was related to have sat before his descent into Hades.[4] Being introduced into the palace of Celeus, King of the Eleusinians, an old woman named Baubo,[5] Babo, or Iambë, made the goddess laugh by her obscene

---

[1] " Nam mihi quum multa eximia divinaque videntur Athenæ tuæ peperisse atque in vitam hominum attulisse, tum nihil melius illis mysteriis, quibus ex agresti immaniquevita exculti ad humanitatem et mitigati sumus. Initiaque ut appellantur, ita re vera principia vitæ cognovimus : neque solum cum lætitia vivendi rationem accepimus, set etiam cum spe meliore moriendi."—De Leg. ii. 14,36.

[2] Ibid. 25, 63.

[3] ὁ καταρράκτης ὁδός.—Soph. Œd. Col. 1590.

[4] Schol. Aristoph. Eq. 782.

[5] The name, slightly altered to Βαββώ, appears to be still used in these parts as a term of reproach towards a disreputable old woman. F. Lenormant, Voie Sacrée, i. p. 244. As Iambë, she is the eponymous inventor of the iambic verse, also employed for abuse. Cf. Apollod. i. 5, 1 ; Clemens Alex. Protrept. p. 17 ; Hor. Od. i. 16, 24.

jokes or gestures—a story doubtless invented to account for the jests uttered by the women in the festival of the Thesmophoria, and the 'gephyrismi,' or ribald language at the bridge, during the Eleusinian procession. According to another version of the story it was Phytalus, not Celeus, who received the goddess. She rewarded him by creating the fig-tree,[1] whence a suburb of Athens was called Ἱερὰ Συκῆ, or The Holy Fig Tree; for as the olive was sacred to Athena, so was the fig to Demeter. At this place there was a plantation of figs under the care of the Phytalidæ, the reputed descendants of Phytalus.

According to some accounts, it was Demeter herself who instituted the mysteries, and the first initiated in them were Triptolemus, Diocles, Eumolpus, and Celeus.[2] Triptolemus was the son of Celeus and Metaneira, or according to Pherecydes, of Oceanus and Gæa.[3] Demeter provided him with seed-corn and gave him a car yoked with dragons, in which being carried through the air, he sowed the whole earth. Eumolpus was the first hierophant, or chief priest of the mysteries, whose descendants, under the name of Eumolpids (Εὐμολπίδαι), continued to hold the same office. Sophocles represents them as having the golden key of the mysteries, with which they touched the tongues of the initiated, in token of the silence enjoined.[4] But who Eumolpus was is a subject of dispute. The most generally received opinion is that he was a Thracian, the son of Poseidon, who aided the Eleusinians in a war against Erechtheus, king of Athens.[5] According to some traditions, the first hierophant was a son of Deiope, the daughter of Triptolemus; according to others, he was the fifth in descent from the Thracian.[6] It is probable that the name of the Eumolpids was invented to explain one of their chief qualifications, namely, a good voice for singing (εὖ μέλπειν). Philostratus, in his life of Apollonius, the Attic Sophist, who became hierophant in his old age, observes that he

---

[1] Pausan. i. 37, 2.

[2] Isocrat. Panegyr. p. 46; Hom. Hymn. in Cer.

[3] Apollod. i. 5, 2.

[4] Œd. Col. 1051.

[5] Thucyd. ii. 15; Plat. Menex. 239 (ii. iii. 386, Bekk.); Iscer. Panegyr. p. 54.

[6] Schol. ad Soph. Œd. Col. 1051.

had not so fine a voice as his predecessors Heracleides, Logimus and Glaucus, though he excelled them in gravity, dignity, and grace.[1] Philostratus had said just before that he was intrusted with the voices, or sounds (φωνάς), which proceeded from the ἀνάκτορα, or shrines; whence, perhaps, we may conclude that the revelations made to the mystæ were delivered in a kind of song, or chant.[2] The stress here laid on a fine voice seems to show that singing was one of the chief functions of the hierophant, as the name of the functionaries would imply. Yet Donaldson has observed, after Müller, that " the Eumolpids were not singers of hymns, but dancers in the chorus of Demeter and Dionysus."[3] It is true that μολπή may mean a dance as well as a song, and indeed any kind of sport; yet singing is the most usual interpretation; and that the chorus at Eleusis was accompanied with singing we see from the account of Pausanias.[4] And in fact, the choruses did not begin till after the autopsy (αὐτοψία) in the adytum, where the voices were heard and revelations made. So also a fine sonorous voice was requisite for the herald of the mysteries.[5]

The celebration of the mysteries was no doubt at first rude and simple in comparison with what it afterwards became. At a later period it was necessary to have been first initiated in the Lesser Mysteries before admission to the Greater. The lesser mysteries seem to have been proper to Persephonë,[6] and were considered as a purification preparatory to the greater. They were called μυστικά, and the person admitted to them μύστης; while the greater were called ἐποπτικά, and when the mysta obtained this complete initiation he became an ἐπόπτης or epopt (from ἐποπτεύειν, ' to overlook ').[7] The ceremony,

---

[1] Vit. Soph. ii. c. 20, s. i. p. 600 sq.

[2] ἐπετράπη καὶ τὰς ἐξ ἀνακτόρων φωνάς. Meursius, Eleusinia, c. 13, has made nonsense of the passage, by translating ἐπετράπη, commutavit.

[3] Theatre of the Greeks, p. 14; Müller, Hist. of Greek Literat. vol. i. p. 25.

[4] ᾖσαν ἐς τὴν θεόν.—i. 38, 6.

[5] Κλεόκριτος δὲ ὁ τῶν μυστῶν κήρυξ, μάλ' ἔμφωνος (or εὔφωνος) ὤν, κ.τ.λ.—Xenoph. Hell. ii. 4, s. 20.

[6] Schol. Aristoph. Plut. v. 846.

[7] Harpocr. voc. ἀνεπόπτευτος; Suid. voc. ἐπόπται. The mystæ, however, though not epoptæ, were μεμυημένοι, 'initiated.'—Aristoph. Ran. 318, 336.

when completed, was called τελετη, from its being supposed to render
the partakers in it perfect. But according to some writers there were
three degrees of initiation. The lesser mysteries were instituted in
favour of Hercules, and therefore not till the time of Theseus, with
whom, in the Attic mythology, he was supposed to be contemporary.
Hercules, as a foreigner, could not be gratified with initiation into the
greater Eleusinia; but to compensate for his disappointment the lesser
were instituted.   A scholiast on Aristophanes[1] says that he was
initiated in the demos of Melite, in which, as we have before remarked
(supra, p. 20), he had in after times a celebrated temple. But Agræ
on the further side of the Ilissus, of which we have already spoken
(supra, p. 18), afterwards became the place of their celebration, and was
sacred to Demeter as well as to Artemis.[2]

The hierarchy presiding over the mysteries, consisted, first, of the
hierophant (ἱεροφάντης), who was the highest in rank of all the Athenian
priests.   He was also called the mystagogue (μυσταγωγός), because he
introduced the mystæ into the temple at Eleusis, on which occasion he
was assisted by the priest called Daiduchos (δᾳδοῦχος), or ' the torch-
bearer.'[3]   Besides these priests, there were the Hieroceryx (ἱεροκῆρυξ)
or ' holy herald,' and the ὁ ἐπὶ βωμῷ, or ' minister at the altar.' Marble
thrones inscribed with the names of all these priests except the last,
may still be seen in the Dionysiac theatre. The hierophant represented
the creator, the daiduchus the sun, the ὁ ἐπὶ βωμῷ the moon, and the
hieroceryx Hermes ;[4] the last no doubt as the conductor of the souls of
the dead, agreeably to that part of the allegory which related to a
future state. Not only the priests of the mysteries, but all the initiated
also were crowned with myrtle ; a plant specially dedicated to the
χθόνιοι θεοί, or subterranean gods--as were Demeter and Persephonē—
by Dionysus, when he descended into Hades in search of his mother
Semele.[5] So too, the image of Iacchus, the mystical Dionysus of the

---

[1] Ran. 504.

[2] Hesych. in voc. ; Polyæn. v. 17, 1.

[3] ἡμᾶς μὲν γὰρ ἱεροφάντης ἅμα καὶ δᾳδοῦχος εἴσω τῶν ἀνακτόρων εἰσέβαλε.—Sopater.

Divis. Quæst. ap. Meurs. Eleusinia. c. 13.

[4] Euseb. Præpar. Evang. lib. iii.

[5] Istros, ap. schol. ad Soph. Œd. Col.
651. Cf. schol. ad Aristoph. Ran. 333.

Eleusinia, was also crowned with myrtle, though in his more cheerful character of the wine-god, his diadem was composed of the ivy and the grape. Iacchus seems to be Dionysus yet in his infancy, and thus we find him called Dionysus at the breast.[1] May not therefore Iacchus represent the grape, still unsevered from the stem, and consequently still sucking its mother earth, whilst in mature age, as Dionysus, he presides over the produce of the grape, or wine? And this distinction between the two states of the god seems to have been recognised by some of the ancient interpreters of his allegorical existence; for Diodorus Siculus, explaining why he was thought to have had two mothers, says that one of his births was from the earth, the other from the vine.[2] Iacchus and Dionysus are also identified by other writers, as Sophocles and Strabo.[3] Iacchus is sometimes represented as the son of Zeus by Demeter, sometimes by Corë, and thus also like them a χθόνιος θεός, or terrene deity. And thus he seems to be identical with Ζαγρεύς, the chief god of the Orphic mysteries, which were also Bacchic.[4] Zagreus, like Iacchus, is the child of the first birth, from Zeus and Persephone, whilst Dionysus is of the second birth, from Zeus and Semele. Thus Nonnus: Ἀρχεγόνῳ Ζαγρῆϊ καὶ ὀψιγόνῳ Διονύσῳ. Zagreus is torn to pieces by the Titans, and Hera presents his heart to Zeus, who devours it; or, according to another version, presents it to Semele, from whom the Theban Dionysus, the wine-god, is born. Here doubtless we have an allegory of the vintage, and the tearing to pieces of Zagreus symbolizes the crushing of the grape. Zagreus is sometimes said to be Pluto's son, while sometimes he is identified with Pluto himself, the mighty hunter who captures all; his name being derived from ἀγρεύω and the intensive particle ζα.[5]

---

[1] Ἴακχος· Διόνυσος ἐπὶ τῶ μαστῶ. Photius and Suidas in voc.

[2] ὥστε τὴν μὲν ἐκ γῆς, τὴν δ' ἐκ τοῦ ἀμπέλου γένεσιν τοῦ θεοῦ, νομίζεσθαι.— iii. 62.

[3] See Sophocl. Ant. v. 1115 sqq. Ἴακχόν τε καὶ τὸν Διόνυσον καλοῦσι, καὶ τὸν ἀρχηγέτην τῶν μυστηρίων, τῆς Δήμητρος δαίμονα.—Strabo, 10, p. 468.

[4]   Ὀρφέα τ' ἄνακτ' ἔχων
        βάκχευε.—Eur. Hipp. 953.
Cf. Herod. ii. 81.

[5] Ζαγρεύς· ὁ Διόνυσος . . . δοκεῖ γὰρ ὁ Ζεὺς μιγῆναι τῇ Περσεφόνῃ· ἐξ ἧς χθόνιος ὁ Διόνυσος . . . παρὰ τὸ ζα, ἵν' ᾖ ὁ πάνυ ἀγρεύων. τινὲς τὸν αὐτὸν φασὶν εἶναι τῷ Πλούτωνι.—Etym. M. Cf. Phot. and Hesych. in voc.

That there was some esoteric dogma in the mysteries we may
perhaps infer from the account given by Pausanias of their celebration
at Pheneus in Arcadia, which no doubt bore a resemblance to those of
Eleusis and may even, as we have seen, have been the prototype of them.
The priest took from a sort of stone chest (πετρωμα) some writings,
which he read to the initiated, and again deposited them in the same
place.[1] But Pausanias always approaches the subject of the mysteries
with awe, and says as little about them as possible ; and since the revelation of them was forbidden under the most dreadful penalties, we know
little or nothing of their real nature. The initiatory ceremonies on
entering the adytum were calculated to inspire a holy terror.[2] In an
alternation of darkness and light, the ears of the mystae were saluted
with a variety of sounds, their eyes feasted with a variety of spectacles. Thunder rolled, lightnings flashed, blows were inflicted in the
darkness by the unknown hands of those previously initiated, and the
temple was filled with mystic lamentations. But suddenly, the scene
changed. A divine light dispelled the darkness, the mysta became an
epopt, cheerful meadows appeared, divine hymns were heard, dances
were seen and holy phantasms ; and, the initiation being complete,
the initiated were dismissed with the words Konx, Ompax (Κογξ,
Ὀμπαξ), to roam about at pleasure and join the dances, indispensable to
every mystery ; whence they who revealed them were said ἐξορχεῖσθαι
τὰ μυστήρια. The person to be initiated was required to fast, to drink
a mixture called cyceon (κυκεών) ; he took some object from a chest,
placed it in the calathus, or basket, and then returned it again from the
calathus into the chest. Might not this have been the ear of corn
(τεθερισμένος στάχυς), the last and most perfect mystery exhibited to
the epopt ? Among the things revealed appears to have been the
genesis of the god, typified apparently in a manner sufficiently gross.[3]
The final revelation seems to have been that Brimo (either Deo or

[1] Pausan. viii. 15, 1.

[2] οἱ μεμυημένοι ταῖς μελλούσας μυεῖσθαι
δεδίττονται.— Schol. ad Aristoph. Vesp.
1362.

[3] καὶ γὰρ αἱ τελεταὶ καὶ τὰ ὄργια τὰ

τοίτων εἶχεν αἰνίγματα· τῶν κτεῖς μὲν ἡ
Ἐλευσίς, ἡ φαλλαγωγία δὲ τὸν φαλλόν.—
Theodoret. Therap. vii. But according to
Tertullian, the φαλλός seems also to have
been exhibited at Eleusis : Simulacrum...

Persephone) had brought forth a holy son, Brimos;[1] which may perhaps mean that the seed-corn had produced other corn.

We learn not what doctrines or moral precepts, if any, were inculcated in the mysteries, but it was probably the revelation of these that was punished, like other impiety, with death; for many of the ceremonies practised seem to have been openly talked of, and even parodied on the stage, as we see in the 'Frogs' of Aristophanes. Eustratius, or whoever was the commentator on the first book of Aristotle's 'Nicomachean Ethics,' says, that it was for revealing, as it was thought, some of the more *mysterious parts* of initiation in his tragedies that Æschylus was compelled to take refuge at the altar of Dionysus; and being tried for the offence in the court of Areiopagus, obtained an acquittal by showing that he had never been initiated.[2] Now, we can only suppose that these were some doctrines which had occurred spontaneously to the poet's mind. And that they might easily have done so, being in fact not very recondite, may be inferred from the story of the Melian Diagoras, who having, it appears, been really initiated, dissuaded others from doing the same by representing the mysteries as trivial—an offence for which a reward of two talents was offered to whomsoever should bring him alive, and one for killing him.[3] But the whole subject of the mysteries is so obscure, that we will not venture any positive opinion upon this part of them.[4]

---

membri virilis revelatur.—Adv. Valent. c. i. But Meursius (Eleusis, c 11) thinks he is mistaken, and that the only object revealed was that shown by Baubo to Demeter.

[1] ἱερὸν ἔτεκε πότνια κοῦρον, Βριμὼ Βριμόν.—Philosophumena, ascribed to Origen, v. 8. See Lenormant, Voie Sacrée, t. i. p. 318; Clemens Alex. Protrept. ii. p. 15 (Potter); Arnob. adv. Gent. v. 20. Respecting the ceremonies of initiation, see the passages collected from Clemens, Arnobius, Porphyrius, Dio Chrysostom, Proclus, &c., by Meursius, in his 'Eleusinia,' c. 10, 11.

[2] τῶν μυστικοτέρων περιεργύτερον ἅπτεσθαι ἔοικε, in Ethic. Nicom. iii. 1; ap. Petit, Leg. Att. i. i. 15; Clemens Alex. Strom. ii. p. 461.

[3] Schol. Aristoph. Av. 1073; Nub. 828; Ran. 323.

[4] Those who would see how much or how little is known about the Eleusinian mysteries, should consult the first volume of Lobeck's 'Aglaophamus'; who, however, perhaps depreciates them too much. A comparison of Lobeck with Warburton's 'Divine Legation of Moses,' bk. ii. s. 4, will show how variously the same subject may be viewed by different minds.

Erechtheus is said to have been aided by Ion in his war against the Eleusinians and their allies, the Thracians, under Eumolpus. According to the most commonly received account, Ion was the grandson of Erechtheus, being the son of his daughter, Creusa, married to Xuthus. On chronological grounds, therefore, the story is hardly consistent; but in these Attic legends this is a point on which we must not be too particular. The favourite tradition was, that Ion was not the son of Xuthus, but of Apollo, who did violence to Creusa in a cave on the north-western side of the Acropolis. The cave, or a closely adjoining one, was at a much later period dedicated to Pan, and is till a conspicuous object. The story is told by Euripides

> KP.   — *αἰσθα Κεκροπιας πετρας*
> *πρόσβόρρον ἄντρον, ἃς Μακρας κεκλήσκομεν.*
> ΠΑΙ. *οἶδ', ἔνθα Πανὸς ἄδυτα καὶ βωμοὶ πέλας.*
> ΚΡ. *ἐνταῦθ' ἀγῶνα δεινὸν ἠγωνίσμεθα.*
> Π.Μ. *τίν'; ὡς ἀπαντᾷ δάκρυά μοι τοῖς σοῖς λόγοις.*
> ΚΡ. *Φοίβῳ ξυνῆψ' ἄκουσα δύστηνον γάμον.*[1]

> Cr.   "———— Thou know'st that northern cave
>   At the Cecropian rocks we call the High?
> Pan. Yes—where Pan's altars are and cavern-shrine.
> Cr. A fearful contest once I pass'd through there.
> Pan. Say what—thy words call tears into my eyes.
> Cr. Phœbus there made me his unwilling wife."

Ion, the fruit of this violence, was reputed the progenitor of the Ionians; and hence also Apollo derived his name of πατρῷος, or 'the ancestral.'[2] We may perhaps infer from the story that the worship of Apollo was introduced into Attica about this time by the Ionians. The genealogy seems to have been universally accepted;[3] but the Ionians, under the name of Iaones, had existed even in Attica before the period ascribed to Ion.[4] However this may be, it is related that Erechtheus with the aid of Ion—that is, of the Ionians—defeated Eumolpus and

---

[1] Ion, v. 936 sqq. Cf. v. 10 sqq.; Pausan. i. 28, 4, &c. From which passages we learn that the rocks at this point were called Μάκραι Πέτραι.

[2] Schol. Aristoph. Nub. 1470; Av. 1526.

[3] Harper. in Ἀπόλλων πατρῷος: Aristot. Met. iv. 28; &c.

[4] See Clinton, Fast. Hell. i. p. 55. note *.

the Thracians, when the Eleusinians surrendered, on condition of retaining their peculiar ceremonies.[1] According to the authority just quoted, Erechtheus fell in this war, and also Immaradus, the son of Eumolpus; but there was another tradition, that Eumolpus himself was killed by Erechtheus, for which he in turn was put to death by Poseidon, the father of Eumolpus[2]—a version, however, which Pausanias rejected.[3] Ion was now intrusted with the government of the Athenians, and is said to have been the first who divided them into four tribes.[4] According to some authorities, the festival of the Boëdromia was instituted in commemoration. of the aid rendered to the Athenians by Ion;[5] but there are other accounts of its origin.

Besides Creüsa, there are legends connected with the other five daughters of Erechtheus. In order to insure success in his war with the Eleusinians, he had been commanded by an oracle to sacrifice one of them. Protogeneia, the eldest, was selected as the victim; but two other of the maidens, Pandora and Chthonia, also put themselves to death. Hence they were called *par excellence* Παρθένοι, or 'the Virgins,' and are several times alluded to by Cicero under that name.[6] Some say that they were deified under the name of Hyades;[7] but, like all other Attic myths, not only is there a great diversity on this point, but also on the whole story; for Demosthenes says that Erechtheus sacrificed all his daughters, and that they obtained the name of Hyacinthides.[8] Of the other daughters, Procris was married to Cephalos, whose well-known tale has no local interest; whilst Oreithyia was carried off by Boreas.

The rape of Oreithyia is a celebrated Attic myth, and was made the subject of a tragedy both by Æschylus and Sophocles. The maiden was sporting on the banks of the Ilissus, when she was carried off by

---

[1] ἰδίᾳ τελεῖν τὴν τελετήν.—Pausan. i. 38, 3.

[2] Apollod. iii. 15, 4 sq.

[3] i. 27, 5.

[4] Strabo, viii. p. 383.

[5] Harpocr. in voc. βοηδρομεῖν γὰρ τὸ βοηθεῖν ὠνομάζετο, τουτέστιν ἐπὶ μάχην δραμεῖν.

[6] Pro Sestio, xxi. 48 (ubi vid. schol. Lob.); Tusc. Q. i. 48, 116; De N. Deor. iii. 19, 49.

[7] Schol. ad Arat. ap. Meurs.

[8] Orat. Funebr. p. 1397, Reiske. Cf. Phot. Lex. voc. Παρθένοι.

the blustering god.[1] They who have experienced with what violence
the north wind sometimes blows at Athens will easily realize the origin
of the fable. The scene of the occurrence, marked by an altar to
Boreas, was still pointed out in the later days of Athens. Plato looks
at the tale in a Euhemeristic light; and Socrates, in the 'Phaedrus,'
explains that Oreithyia was blown by the north wind from a rock at
this spot and killed, adding, that another version placed the scene at
the Areiopagus.[2]

It was about the same time that Leos is related to have sacrificed
his daughters in order to avert a pestilence. Their names were Praxi-
thea, or Phrasithea, Theope, and Euboule.[3] The Athenians erected a
monument to them called Leocorion, which in later times came to be
included in the agora or market-place.

The reigns of the two next sovereigns - Cecrops II. and Pandion II.
- offer nothing worthy of note. The reign of Ægeus, the adopted son
and successor of Pandion II., is more important, and chiefly as the
father of Theseus, the Attic national hero.

The childless Ægeus had consulted the Pythian oracle respecting
a remedy for that misfortune; and on his return to Athens was in-
veigled at Troezen into a connection with Æthra, daughter of Pittheus,
who ruled there. Ægeus leaves her pregnant, instructing her, if she
should bear a son, to conceal from him the name of his father, but to
bid him, when strong enough, to lift a rock, under which Ægeus had
concealed his sword and sandals, and to bring them to Athens. Ægeus is
sometimes identified with Poseidon; at least, in accordance with a custom
prevalent in ancient times, of glossing over slips like Æthra's by giving
out that the fruit of them was the offspring of a god. Theseus was said
to be the son of Poseidon.[4] Poseidon, therefore, was only his putative

[1] Apollod. iii. 15. 2 ; Pausan. i. 19. 6.

[2] Phaedr. p. 229 (i. i. 7, Bekk.).

[3] Ælian. V. H. xii. 28 ; Suid. voc. Λεω-
κόριον. All the authorities for the story
will be found collected in Meursius, Ceram.
Gem. c. 17.

[4] Plut. Thes. 6 ; Diod. Sic. iv. 59. M.
Lenormant, Voie Sacree. i. 255, would

identify Ægeus with Poseidon, from Strabo,
p. 405, and Virgil, Æn. iii. 74. But the
forms Ægeus and Ægeus are radically
different. In the next page, M. Lenormant repeats the erroneous story of the
Ægean Sea being named from Ægeus
precipitating himself into it. See below,
p. 61, note 2.

father.   After his return to Athens, Ægeus celebrated the Panathenaic
festival, in which Androgeus, son of Minos, king of Crete, was the victor
in every contest.   Ægeus became alarmed at his success, especially
as he had contracted a friendship with the Pallantidæ, who were his
rivals, and he therefore caused Androgeus to be murdered at Œnoë, in
Attica, as he was on his way to a sacred festival at Thebes.[1]   To avenge
this deed, Minos makes war on the Athenians, subdues them, and compels them to pay, either annually or at certain stated periods, a tribute
of seven youths and seven maidens, to be devoured by the Cretan
Minotaur.

The payment goes on some years; Theseus, arrived at the threshold
of manhood, dedicates his forelocks to Apollo at Delphi in the mode of
tonsure called Theseïs;[2] then lifts the rock, previously called Διὸς
Σθενίου βωμός, but thenceforwards πέτρα Θησέως;[3] and takes from
under it the sword and sandals.   With these trophies he set off for
Athens, and emulating Heracles, chose to go by land, because the road
was beset with dangers.   His exploits were six.   1. On the mountain
between Trœzen and Epidaurus he overcame Periphetes, son of Hephæstus, surnamed Korynētes, from the iron club (κορύνη) with which
he slew those who approached his haunt.   2. On the Corinthian Isthmus he put his relative, Sinis, to death after his own fashion, by com-
pelling him to bend a pine tree, which, by its revulsion, threw him into
the air.   As this was the boundary between Ionia and the Peloponnesus,
Theseus afterwards erected at the spot a column with inscriptions denoting their respective limits, and instituted here the Isthmian games.[4]
3. He despatched the Crommyonian boar.   4. He slew the robber Sciron
on the cliffs named after him, where he compelled the passers-by to wash
his feet, and then kicked them into the sea, as Theseus did him.
5. Near Eleusis he wrestled with and overthrew Cercyon, and then put

---

[1] Diod. Sic. iv. 60; Apollod. iii. 15, 7.
There are other accounts; as that Ægeus
sent him against the Marathonian bull,
&c.   Here, as elsewhere, we give only
the main and most generally accepted
outline.

[2] Plut. Thes. 5.

[3] Pausan. ii. 32, 7.

[4] Plut. Thes. 25; Strabo, p. 392.

him to death. 6. On the banks of the Eleusinian Cephissus he subdued Polypemon or Damastes, better known as Procrustes. Having achieved these labours, he crossed the Cephissus, and at the altar of Zeus Meilichios was purged by the Phytalidæ of the homicides he had committed.[1]

The contrast between manly strength and female delicacy, and the picture of the hero sunk for a while into effeminacy, were favourite topics with the ancients, and gave rise to the stories of Heracles in the service of Omphale, and of Achilles among the daughters of Lycomedes. After performing these exploits, Theseus, like Heracles, puts on the dress of a maiden and proceeds to Athens. His appearance provokes the ridicule of some labourers employed in building the temple of the Delphinian Apollo, which, according to the description of Pausanias,[2] must have been near the Olympium and the Ilissus. Enraged at their jeers, Theseus unyokes some oxen from a cart, and throws it over their heads upon the roof of the temple. Hence we see that the worship of Apollo had been introduced before this time, and that the city had extended itself beyond the original Cecropia.

In the interval, Ægeus had espoused Medea, a fugitive from Corinth, and Athens was distracted by factions. Medea recognised Theseus, who had not yet discovered himself to his father, and fearing his influence, persuaded Ægeus to poison him at dinner; but during the banquet Theseus happened to draw his father's sword, and Ægeus, recognising his son, dashed the poisoned cup from his lips. The spot where the poison was said to have fallen was still marked, in Plutarch's time, by an inclosure in the Delphinium, which therefore must have originally formed part of the royal palace.[3]

Aided by the herald Leos, Theseus now kills his uncle, Pallas, and overthrows his cousins, the Pallantidæ, who were aiming at the throne; for which act he was arraigned before the Delphinian tribunal and acquitted. His next exploit was the capture of the Marathonian bull, which annoyed the inhabitants of the Tetrapolis. Theseus brought it

[1] Pausan. i. 37, 2 sq. [2] i. 19, 1.
[3] Plut. Thes. 12.

to Athens and sacrificed it to the Delphinian Apollo, or, according to Pausanias,[1] to Athena.

The crowning exploit of Theseus was the destruction of the Cretan Minotaur.[2] Having performed his devotions in the temple of the Delphinian Apollo, he set sail from Phalerum, then the only port of Athens. Arrived at Crete, Minos taunted him by denying that he was the son of Poseidon, and challenged him to prove his parentage by bringing up a ring which he threw into the sea; whereupon Theseus plunged into his paternal waters, and re-appeared, not only with the ring, but also with a golden diadem presented to him by Amphitrite. The valour and youthful beauty of Theseus attracted the love of Ariadne, the daughter of Minos. Furnished by her with a sword and a clue, Theseus despatched the Minotaur, otherwise called Asterion, and extricated himself from the labyrinth. An elopement with Ariadne followed, whom, however—seduced by the charms of Ægle—he ungratefully abandoned at Naxos, whence she was carried off by Dionysus. Theseus made a long voyage before returning to Athens. Among other places he visited Delos, where he consecrated an image of Aphrodite, which, like all the primitive ξόανα, terminated in a quadrangular base instead of feet.[3] According to Suidas,[4] Dædalus first supplied such images with feet, whence he was said to have made them walk. But according to Pausanias, this image of Aphrodite was the work of Dædalus, and was carried off by Ariadne when she left Crete. In such instances, however, the name of Dædalus must only be taken to signify workmanship of a very archaic kind, which the ancients, in their love for identification, ascribed to Dædalus as the most celebrated of primitive artists. The same story is told of Isis, who is said to have separated the legs of Jupiter Ammon, which previously grew together—a fable taken, as Warburton observes, from the form of the Egyptian statues of the gods, which were made with the legs undivided.[5] At Delos

---

[1] i. 27, 10.

[2] The chief authorities are Plutarch, in his life of Theseus, and the Helenæ Encomium of Isocrates.

[3] Pausan. ix. 40, 2.

[4] In Δαιδάλου ποιήματα.

[5] Divine Legation, b. ii. s. 4, vol. ii. p. 3.

Theseus instituted the chorus called γέρανος, or 'the crane, which was danced round the altar of Apollo in commemoration of the labyrinth, the escape from which it imitated, being danced by many persons following one another in a line.[1]

Theseus had promised that on his return from Crete he would, if he had succeeded in his enterprise, hoist a white sail in place of the black one with which he had departed. But this promise he forgot, and the anxious Ægeus, as he watched from the Acropolis—at the spot afterwards occupied by the temple of Athena Nike—the arrival of the vessel, and fancied all his hopes defeated, precipitated himself from the rock and was dashed to pieces. Some authors, including Meursius, make him fall into the Ægean sea, which hence derived its name from him; but this is not only physically, but also etymologically impossible, for the sea is five miles off, and Αἰγαῖος, as we have already observed, cannot come from Αἰγεύς.[2] Theseus now became king of Attica, and, according to some, of Crete also. In commemoration of his success, he is said to have instituted two festivals - the Pyanepsia (πυανεψια) and Oschophoria (ὀσχοφόρια). The former was a harvest feast, celebrated in the month Pyanepsion, in honour of Apollo; the latter was established to commemorate the Cretan expedition. Two youths in female attire—for such had accompanied Theseus to Crete—carried a vine-branch with bunches of grapes and flowers on it (ὄσχος, ὄσχη, or ὤσχη) from the temple of Dionysus in Athens, accompanied by a chorus, to the temple of Athena Sciras, at Phalerum. This makes it more probable that the festival was in honour of Athena and Dionysus, as Photius says,[3] than of Dionysus and Ariadne, according to the version of Plutarch. The other and more striking institution was that of the Theoria, or annual legation to the Delian Apollo, which postponed for a time the death of Socrates; for the priest of Apollo had garlanded the prow of the Theoric vessel on the day before judgment

[1] Pollux, iv. 101; Plut Thes. 21; Lucian, De Salt. 34.

[2] See above, p. 57, note [4]. Meursius indeed (De Regibus Athen. iii. 4) quotes Suidas and the Etym. M. for his view; but both those late lexicographers are very untrusty guides; and a little further on Meursius quotes the true derivative form Αἰγεῖος (on a different occasion) from a better authority, Harpocration.

[3] Bibl'oth. 239 (p. 822 A. Bekker).

was pronounced against him, and from that time till its return the city was in a state of purification, and no public executions could take place. Theseus had vowed the legation when he sailed for Crete, and the vessel which had carried him thither was appropriated to the service, and called *Theoris* (θεωρίς).[1] Plutarch asserts that, by constant repairs, it was kept in existence till the time of Demetrius Phalereus,[2] and thus gave occasion for the exercise of sophistical ingenuity in discussing the question whether it were the same vessel or another.

Of the political acts of Theseus the most important for our present purpose is the making Athens the capital of Attica. According to some authors, it would appear as if he had actually transferred the inhabitants to Athens;[3] but the word συνοικεῖν, used by Thucydides and Plutarch to describe the event, means only a transference of the government to the capital; and, as Meursius observes, Strabo uses the word συνοικίζειν to designate the uniting of twelve different cities under one government.[4] It is, however, a fair inference from this fact that the ancient Cecropia was already by far the most considerable of the Attic towns, and also that the population must have increased very much after it became the exclusive seat of government. It was probably after this event, as we have already said, that the whole city, the Polis and the Asty, received the name of Athens; and in commemoration of it Theseus is said to have instituted the festivals called Panathenæa and Synoikia.[5] The former we certainly cannot well place at an earlier date, and probably it was much later. On the same occasion Theseus also introduced the worship of Aphroditē Pandemos ('Αφροδίτη πάνδημος); where we are not to take the word πάνδημος—as it was used in a later and more corrupt state of society—to characterize her as presiding over

---

[1] Plat. Phædo, init.: Xenoph. Mem. iv. 8.

[2] Thes. 23.

[3] τὴν πόλιν σποράδην καὶ κατὰ κώμας οἰκοῦσαν εἰς ταὐτὸ συναγαγών.—Isocr. Hel. Encom. p. 214 fin.: τοὺς δήμους . . . μεταγαγεῖν εἰς τὰς Ἀθήνας.—Diod. Sic. iv. 61. Still more plainly Cicero: "Theseus eos demigrare ex agris, et in astu, quod appel-latur, omnes se conferre jussit."—De Leg. ii. 2, 5.

[4] Κέκροπα πρῶτον εἰς δυοκαίδεκα πόλεις συνοικίσαι τὸ πλῆθος.—p. 397. τὸ ξυνώκισεν οὐκ ἔστιν ἐπὶ τοῦ ὁμοῦ ξυνοικισθῆναι ἐποίησεν, ἀλλ' ἐπὶ τοῦ μίαν πόλιν, τουτέστι μητρόπολιν, ἔχειν αὐτὴν [τὴν χώραν, sc.].—Schol. ad Thucyd. ii. 15. Cf. Plut. Thes. 24.

[5] Plut. and Thucyd. locc. citt.

prostitution, but rather as uniting the population together, and thus answering to the Roman goddess Concordia. Hence he united with her worship that of Peitho, or Persuasion.' The neglecting to observe this distinction has occasioned some serious mistakes in Athenian topography, as we shall see further on; for Solon afterwards erected near the agora a temple to the Aphrodite Pandemos of the grosser type.'

The history of Theseus, even after his accession to the throne of Attica, continues to be almost entirely mythical; but as his adventures, however fabulous, are connected with the antiquities and topography of Athens, we must give a brief sketch of them. Either alone or in conjunction with Heracles, he undertook an expedition to the Euxine against the Amazons, and carried off Antiope. This brought on an invasion of Attica by the Amazons; and Plutarch, after Cleidemus, has pretended to relate a battle which ensued at Athens itself. The left wing of the Amazons is said to have been posted at a place called, in Plutarch's time, the Amazoneium, whilst the right wing extended to the Golden Victory at the Pnyx.[3] Then, as Æschylus places their camp and main body on the Areiopagus,[4] it is evident that they must have faced towards the east and the Acropolis. This agrees with the scheme of the best topographers. We are unable to say where the Golden Victory was; but the Pnyx is a well-known, and, until within the last few years, undisputed place, suiting precisely with the description of Plutarch. About the Areiopagus, also, there can be no question; and from these two objects it may be inferred that the Amazoneium, or post of the left wing, lay as much to the north of the Areiopagus as the Pnyx did to the south. The Athenians attack the Amazonian right from the Museium, the hill next adjoining the Pnyx on the east; and the fight appears to have been in the road which led to the gate near the Heroum of Chalcodon, called, in the time of Plutarch, the Peiraic Gate; consequently, in the valley between the Pnyx and the Areiopagus, where, in the time of Cleidemus, were shown the

[1] Pausan. i. 22, 3.

[2] Athen. xiii. 25; Harpocr. v. πανδη-
μος.

[3] For a description of the battle s.
Plutarch, Theseus. 27.

[4] Eumenid. 688 sqq.

tombs of the Athenians who had fallen in the battle. The Athenians were repulsed and driven back to the spot where was afterwards the temple of the Eumenides, at the north-eastern extremity of the Areiopagus. But the reserve of the Athenians, which had been posted on the Ilissus and the high ground beyond it—namely, at the Palladium, the Lyceium, and on Ardettus—now came up and drove the right wing of the Amazons back to their camp with great slaughter. This seems to have put an end to the battle, and indeed to the war; and in the fourth month—that is, probably, of the war—a peace was made through the intervention of Hippolyta. For it was she, according to Cleidemus, and not Antiope, whom Theseus had carried off and married. Some related that Hippolyta was killed in the battle by Molpadia, and that her tomb, or stelë, was that near the temple of Gæa Olympia; while others held that it was Antiope who was killed and buried there.[1] However this may be, there was a place called Horcomosium, near the Theseium, where the treaty was sworn to. An ancient sacrifice was made to the Amazons before the Theseia, or festival of Theseus.

The author of the poem called 'Theseïs' made Antiope and the Amazons attack Theseus because he had married Phædra, and said that they were defeated by Heracles; but this account was regarded as less authentic. This marriage took place after the death of Antiope, by whom Theseus had had a son named Hippolytus, though Pindar calls him Demophon. We need not here relate the incestuous love of Phædra for Hippolytus, which forms the subject of a tragedy of

---

[1] Pausan. i. 2, 1; Plut. Thes. 27. Leake has made some strange mistakes about these passages. He says (p. 446, note): "There appears from Plutarch to have been a difference of opinion as to the name of the Amazon who was slain by Theseus. Some said Antiope, others Hippolyte, and according to Pausanias it was Molpadia." Nobody says that either Antiope or Hippolyte was slain by Theseus. Plutarch's words: ἔνιοι δέ φασιν μετὰ τοῦ Θησέως μαχομένην ['ΙπποͰύτην] πεσεῖν τὴν ἄνθρωπον: do not mean that she was fighting with him, but *on his side, along with him*. The only difference of opinion was, whether it was Antiope or Hippolyte who was killed by Molpadia, which last only Theseus is said to have slain. We might infer from Plutarch's words that it was doubtful whether the monument near the Olympium was that of Antiope or Hippolyte. Molpadia also had a monument, but it does not appear to have been at this spot. See Pausanias, l. c., who says it was Antiope who was slain by Molpadia.

Euripides. With regard to the further exploits of Theseus, authorities differed. Herodorus maintained that he took part only in the battle of the Centaurs and Lapithæ, whilst others held that he accompanied Jason to Colchis and aided Meleager in slaying the boar.[1] But it is evident from the many subjects of art taken from the war of the Amazons, and that of the Centaurs and Lapithæ, that these were regarded by the Athenians as the chief exploits in which Theseus had a share. The story of the enmity between the Centaurs and Lapithæ, and the fight which took place between them at the marriage of Peirithoüs and Deïdameia, to which Theseus was invited, is well known. He was said to have played a great part in subduing the Centaurs, but some accounts represent Heracles as the chief hero of the affair. Thessaly was famous for its horses, and the form of the Centaur, half horse, half man, was no doubt suggested by the rider and his horse. The form of the Centaur, noble though monstrous, became a favourite subject for the chisel of the Athenian sculptor, but did not attain its full perfection till the palmy days of art. The primitive form represented the whole figure of a man with the body and hind legs of a miserable little horse attached to him. It is in this way that Centaurs were represented on the chest of Cypselus.[2] Ross has given a drawing of a bronze Centaur of this kind,[3] on a very small scale, found in the excavations on the Acropolis, the whole character of which, especially the hair and beard, is quite in the archaic style. This, however, was by no means the first instance of the kind, for in the Florentine edition of Meursius' works such a Centaur wrestling with Heracles had been figured from an ancient gem in the Museum Victorianum.[4]

The amorous adventures of Theseus, who was a kind of ancient Don Giovanni, we need not enter into, as they present nothing of interest for Athenian art and antiquities. The strangest one was his carrying off Helen before she was of a marriageable age, when he himself was turned

[1] Plut. Thes. 29.

[2] Κένταυρος δὲ μετὰ τούτους τοὺς ὄπισθεν ἵππου πόδας, τοὺς δὲ ἔμπροσθεν αὐτῶν ἔχων ἀνδρός ἐστιν.—Paus. v. 19, 2 (Siebel).

[3] Archäol. Aufsätze, i. p. 104.

[4] Meursii Op. t. i. p. 915. Some others that have been discovered are mentioned by Ross. Ib. p. 105, note 1.

F

of fifty; in which adventure he was assisted by his friend Peirithoüs.[1] Theseus retained her at Aphidnæ under the care of his mother, and in requital of the services of Peirithoüs aided him in an attempt to abduct Persephonë, or Corë, from Hades—a tale which later writers rationalized by representing Aïdoneus as a king of the Molossi, who had a wife named Persephonë and a daughter named Corë. But this adventure proved the destruction of both. Peirithoüs was killed by the dog Cerberus, and Theseus was cast into prison, where he is said to have sat four years on a rock, or, according to Virgil, eternally—

> " sedet æternumque sedebit
> Infelix Theseus." [2]

From which long session, according to a malicious tale of the Athenians, his sitting-part grew as it were to the rock, from which he could not rise without leaving it behind. Hence the Athenians got the nickname of ἀπόγλουτοι (depyges), a characteristic, however, which they are said to have obtained by their assiduity in rowing.[3] Meanwhile Menestheus, great-grandson of Erechtheus, in the absence of Theseus stirred up the Athenians against him, and was assisted in his designs upon the throne by the Dioscuri, who came into Attica in search of their sister Helen. Echedemus, or Academus, the hero from whom the Academy took its name, flourished at this time, and indicated to the Tyndaridæ where their sister was confined. The Lacedæmonians invaded Attica; Aphidnæ was captured and Helen released; the Dioscuri were admitted into Athens at the persuasion of Menestheus, were initiated in the mysteries, and obtained divine honours under the name of Anaces. After a time Theseus was released by Heracles from the custody of Aïdoneus and returned to Athens, when he assigned all the shrines which had been dedicated to himself, except four, to Heracles. Thus they became Heracleia instead of Thesia.[4] In this story we have also no doubt the indication of a revolution, which is related as follows: The machinations

[1] The story is alluded to by Herod. ix. 73.

[2] Æneid, vi. 617.

[3] οἱ γὰρ Ἀθηναῖοι πάντες λεπτοὶ ἐτύγχανον τὰ ὀπίσθια ἀπὸ Θησέως.—Schol. ad

Aristoph. Eq. 1365. Cf. Lucilius Tharræus, Coll. Proverb. in Meursius, Theseus, c. 27.

[4] Philochorus ap. Plut. Thes. 35.

of Menestheus had done their work, Theseus became unpopular and found himself obliged to abdicate. At Gargettus, a place on the south-west side of Mount Pentelicus, he uttered a curse against the Athenians, at the spot which continued to be called Araterion or Araterion (from ἀρά or ἀρή, 'an imprecation'). Then he retired to the isle of Scyros, ruled at that time by Lycomedes, who treacherously put him to death.

From the preceding sketch of the life of Theseus it appears that the Athenians regarded him in two characters: as a mythological hero, and as a statesman who founded their political institutions. The question then arises whether he is a wholly fabulous personage, or a real person about whom an heroic halo has been thrown. There are some circumstances in his story which might lead us to incline to the latter opinion. He is very different from Heracles. The exploits of that demigod extend over the greater part of the known world; he founds no state, though the planting of colonies is ascribed to him; and there seems reason to suppose that the idea of him was suggested by the maritime enterprises of the Phœnicians. [The exploits of Theseus, on the contrary, are chiefly confined to Attica and its neighbourhood; and his ultimate expulsion from his kingdom, and death in a foreign land, have a certain historical air, since the legend of the founder-hero of a state, if wholly fictitious, would hardly end in misfortune and disgrace. He and his predecessor Ion seem to represent revolutions which temporarily raised an Ionian to power, of which, however, they were deprived by the legitimate line of the Erechtheidæ. Theseus is thrice mentioned by Homer; once in the Iliad and twice in the Odyssey.[1] It is said indeed that the line in the Iliad—

Θησέα τ' Αἰγείδην, ἐπιείκελον ἀθανάτοισιν—

must be spurious, because it also occurs in Hesiod.[2] But would it not be more reasonable to say that Hesiod took it from Homer? One of the reasons for abjudicating it from Homer is that it is not commented on by Eustathius and the scholiasts.[3] But if that is a test of

[1] Il. i. 265; Od. xi. 321, 630.
[2] Scut. Herc. 182.
[3] See Clinton, Fast. Hell. t. i. p. 64, note v.

spuriousness, then many other lines must be blotted out; and even if it be spurious, it must surely have got into the text long before the time of Eustathius. The probable time for such an interpolation would have been when Homer's text was revised by the Pisistratidæ. Thucydides treats Theseus as an historical personage and the founder of Attic unity,[1] and his memory may have been handed down not only by the verses of poets but also by the festivals instituted by him or in his honour, and by the traditions connected with them, which would have been preserved by the priesthood. But even so, all we can say of him is "stat nominis umbra." A person so called probably once ruled Attica, and made some important changes in its constitution; but the nature of them cannot be established with anything like historical accuracy.

In the reign of Theseus we find symptoms of the Athenians becoming a maritime people. Poseidon was a peculiarly Ionian god, and Theseus was his reputed son. Thus, in his time we find a harbour established at Phalerum, from which he sails for Crete; not to mention the share in the Argonautic expedition attributed to him by some authorities. In the next reign, the Athenians are related to have sailed for Troy with a considerable fleet.

What may have been the appearance of the city of Athens in the time of Theseus we have but scanty materials for judging. The Acropolis must of course have been always much the same; but with regard to the surrounding asty we have little to guide us. If we draw an inference from the inscription on the Arch of Hadrian, which professes to mark the boundary of the ancient Thesean city, we might, perhaps, conclude that the Acropolis was surrounded by a wall at about the same distance from it on every side as that object is from its south-eastern foot. That such a wall must have been erected at all events before the time of the Pisistratidæ is plain from the account which Thucydides gives of the attack upon Hipparchus by Harmodius and Aristogeiton; who being in the Cerameicus, not, be it observed, then called the *outer* Cerameicus, rush through the gate and slay him in the city.[2] It is probable, however, that this wall may have been built long after the time of Theseus,

---

[1] lib. ii. 15. [2] Thucyd. vi. 57.

and that Athens was then little more than a straggling village, which on the south-east may have extended nearly down to the Ilissus, in which direction the palace of Ægeus seems to have been. The Pelasgic fortifications about the Acropolis do not seem to have been constructed till after the 'Trojan war.' But to these subjects we shall have to return in another part of this work.

---

¹ Clinton places the probable date of the immigration into Attica of the Pelasgi, who built these walls, at sixty years after the fall of Troy.—Fast. Hell. vol. i. p. 96, note ³.

CHAPTER III.

THESEUS was succeeded by Menestheus, son of Peteos, of the line of the Erechtheidæ. He led the Athenians to Troy, and is twice men- tioned in the Iliad, where he is praised as being an able tactician:

τῶν αὖθ' ἡγεμόνευ' υἱὸς Πετεῶο Μενεσθεύς.
τῷδ' οὔπω τις ὁμοῖος ἐπιχθόνιος γένετ' ἀνὴρ
κοσμῆσαι ἵππους τε καὶ ἀνέρας ἀσπιδιώτας.[1]

Under Menestheus fifty ships did pass
Who for the ord'ring of a battle well
Of horse or foot the best of all men was.

HOBBES.

The same military ability is ascribed to him by Xenophon and Ælian.[2] According to an Attic tradition, he was one of the Greeks enclosed in the wooden horse Durius;[3] but there is little to connect his name with Athens. He died in the isle of Melos, on his return from Troy.[4] Menestheus was succeeded by Demophon, the son of Theseus. He was said by some to have brought the Palladium from Troy, by others to have seized it from Diomedes, who, when carrying it off, was driven by stress of weather on the Attic coast; and an involuntary homicide com- mitted on this occasion is said to have led to the establishment of the

[1] Iliad. ii. 552; cf. xii. 331.
[2] Xenoph. De Ven.; Ælian. Tact. c. 1.
[3] Pausan. i. 23, 10.
[4] Eusebii Chron.

court called ἐπὶ Παλλαδίῳ.[1] It would be useless to pursue any further
the history of the Athenian kings, whose reigns have neither the authen-
ticity of history nor the splendour of heroic fable, and therefore add
nothing towards the illustration of Athenian topography or art. With
Codrus the fifth king from Demophon, who generously offered up his
life for the safety of his country, the Attic monarchy ends.[1] Of the
administration of the archons who succeeded, the first being Medon, son
of Codrus, the same may be said as of the reigns of the kings, and we
will therefore pass on to the time of Solon and Peisistratus, when Attic
history begins to assume some consistency.

The first event which affords any notices of a topographical character is the attempt of Cylon to make himself tyrant of Athens. Cylon
had gained the Olympic victory in the 35th Olympiad (B.C. 640), and
elated apparently by this triumph, as well as by his marriage with
the daughter of Theagenes, tyrant of Megara, he with his brother and
adherents seized the Acropolis during another Olympic festival, interpreting in that way the response of the Delphic oracle that he should
undertake the enterprise during the greatest festival of Zeus; especially as he imagined that the one at Olympus was particularly connected
with himself (Olymp. 40, B.C. 620).[3] But the attempt proved a failure.
Cylon and his fellow conspirators were surrounded by the Athenians,
aided by the population of the rural districts; and finding their position
untenable, they were induced by a promise of security to quit the altar
of Athena, at which they had taken refuge, and to proceed to the Areiopagus for trial. But on their way thither, and just after they had
passed the Enneapylon, or Nine Gates, they were attacked and slain;
or as some authorities say, at the very altar of the Eumenides, to which
they had hastened for safety.[4]

[1] Harper. in voc.; Paus. i. 28, 9;
Pollux, viii. 10.

[2] For this event see Lycurg. Orat. in
Leocr. p. 194. Reiske; Cic. Tusc. Disp. i.
48, 116; Vell. Pat. i. 2, 3, &c.

[3] In the dates we have followed Clinton.

[4] Herod. v. 71; Thucyd. i. 126; Pausan.

i. 28, 1; schol. ad Aristoph. Eq. v. 443.
Thucydides says that Cylon and his brother
contrived to escape, but Herodotus relates
that Cylon was slain; and later writers
adopt sometimes one account, sometimes
the other.

The topographical particulars supplied by this event are that the
Acropolis must now have been fortified by the Pelasgi and become the
citadel of Athens; that the Court of Areiopagus held its sittings on the
hill which bore its name; and that on its eastern side, at no great distance from the entrance to the Acropolis, a shrine or temple of the
Eumenides, or Σεμναὶ Θεαί, had been established.

The murder of Cylon had been recommended to the Athenians by
the archon Megacles, and hence not only himself but his posterity also,
the Alcmæonidæ, became accursed in the sight of Athena (ἐναγεῖς τῆς
θεοῦ), whose sanctuary they had violated. Feuds arose between the
families of Cylon and Megacles; the city was visited by a pestilence
attributed to the anger of the offended deity; and at the suggestion of
Solon, the impious race was tried and condemned to banishment. In
order to a complete purgation, Epimenides, who by some was reckoned
among the Seven Wise Men, in place of Peisander, was summoned from
Crete.[1] To some of the expiatory ceremonies which he recommended,
we shall advert in the sequel. Epimenides is reputed to have been the
adviser of the legislation which Solon established in his archonship.[2]
(B.C. 594.) Two or three years afterwards, Anacharsis, the Scythian,
visited Athens in the archonship of Eucrates.

Solon was a descendant of Codrus, and also connected on the
maternal side with Peisistratus.[3] Our subject is no further concerned
with his legislation than the changes which it might have occasioned in
the aspect of the city. As he is the reputed author of the Ecclesia,
as well as of the Senate of Four Hundred, it is a probable supposition
that the Pnyx may have been constructed at this time, as well as the
senate-house on the north-west side of the Acropolis. That the
Athenians still availed themselves of the rocky nature of their soil in
the construction of their buildings, is evident from the Dionysiac
theatre, built a little later; for a great part of which the natural rock
of the Acropolis was used, while the rest was constructed of large and

---

[1] Plut. Sol. 12; Pausan. i. 28, 1; vii.   [2] Plut. loc. cit.; Diog. Laërt. Vit. Epim.
25, 1.   lib. i. s. 112 sq.
               [3] Plut. Sol. 1; Diog. Laërt. i. s. 48.

solid masonry. Precisely the same process was adopted at the Pnyx, and the huge circular wall which forms its northern boundary is evidently of a much later period than the Cyclopean or Pelasgic, to which some writers have attributed it. But of this we shall speak in another place. To remedy the want of water under which Athens suffered, Solon ordained that there should be a public well at a distance of every four stadia, about half a mile.[1] The laws of Solon were written on quadrangular wooden machines turning on an axis, and therefore called ἄξονες, and on triangular stones (κύρβεις). The axones seem to have been of considerable height, reaching from the floor to the ceiling of an apartment, and contained the laws relating to civil matters, while the cyrbeis contained those respecting religion. Both were at first preserved in the Acropolis; but as that was a sacred and enclosed place, and, especially after the Persian wars, not very accessible, Ephialtes subsequently caused them to be brought down into the agora, so that they might be more open to public inspection; when the cyrbeis were placed in the Stoa Basileios, and the axones in the Prytaneium.[2] It is probable that neither of these buildings was in existence in the time of Solon. He is said to have legalized prostitution, and to have consecrated out of its wages a temple to Aphrodite Pandemos;[3] which must not be confounded with that said to have been erected by Theseus. According to Apollodorus (ap. Harpocr. l.c.) one of them was in the ancient agora; whence some writers have inferred that there was anciently an agora on the southern side of the Acropolis, as the temple erected by Theseus appears to have been on that side.

After passing his laws, Solon travelled into Egypt and other places, and on his return found Athens torn by factions. At length, in spite of his opposition, which Solon was prepared to maintain even by force of arms, Peisistratus, who was at the head of the Diacrii or Hyperacrii, the mountaineers of northern Attica, succeeded in making himself tyrant (Ol. 55, B.C. 560). He is said to have effected this by a stratagem

---

[1] Plut. Sol. c. 23.

[2] Ibid. c. 25; Harpocr. voce. ἄξονες and κύρβεις; Pollux, viii. 10; Etym. M. voc. ἄξονες, &c.

[3] Athen. lib. xiii. 25; Harpocr. voc. Πάνδημος Ἀφροδίτη.

which could have been successful only in rude and ignorant times. He wounded himself and his mules, and in that state drove into the agora or market-place, where he accused the Pediæi, an opposite faction consisting of the rich proprietors of the Attic plains, of having attempted his life. The Athenians, moved by his state, and by the recollection of what he had done for them in war, granted his request for a guard, which at first consisted of only fifty citizens armed with clubs. But their number he soon increased, and then seized the Acropolis. In order to render himself still more secure, he disarmed the people by the following stratagem. He convoked an armed assembly at the Anaceium, or temple of the Dioscuri, where he addressed them in so low a tone of voice, that they requested him to proceed to the Propylæum, in order that all might hear. When the assembly were all attentive, the guards of Peisistratus seized their arms and carried them down to the temple of Aglauros, which was situated above the Anaceium, half way up the cliff of the Acropolis.[1]

Peisistratus held the tyranny thirty-three years, but with two intervals, for he was twice driven out; so that the actual duration of his enjoyment of supreme power was only about seventeen years.[2] Once he contrived to return by conciliating the Alcmæonidæ and Megacles, whose daughter he married. On this occasion also he is related to have practised a stratagem which could have been attempted only with a rude and ignorant people. He dressed up a tall and handsome woman, named Phya, a seller of garlands, to resemble Athena, and carried her in his chariot to Athens, when she told the Athenians that she was bringing Peisistratus to her own Acropolis, and commanded them to receive him. The second time Peisistratus returned by force of arms and with the aid of foreigners, after which he succeeded in retaining the tyranny till his death in a good old age[3] (Ol. 63.2, B.C. 527).

Peisistratus was a genial tyrant, and on the whole ruled with

---

[1] Polyæn. Strat. i. 21, 2. From the arms being carried *down* (κατήνεγκαν) we might perhaps infer that, by 'Propylæum,' Poly-æus means the entrance to the Acropolis.

[2] Herod. i. 59 sqq.; Aristot. Pol. v. 12.

[3] Herod. ib. c. 60; Polyæn. ib. s. 1.

clemency and justice. He retained Solon's laws; but in order, apparently, to render his hold of power more secure, he adopted the policy of dispersing the Athenians into the country and making them wear a labourer's dress.[1] This must have tended to check the growth of the city, though he is nevertheless related to have done much towards its adornment. Thus, he is said to have built the Pythium, to have laid the foundations of the magnificent temple of Zeus Olympius, to have founded the gymnasium at the Lyceum, and to have constructed the fountain called Enneacrunos.[2] The Academy must have been in existence at this time, as Charmus, who lived in the reign of Peisistratus, is said to have dedicated there a statue of Eros; and Hipparchus is related to have enclosed the place with a wall.[3] Peisistratus is also reputed to have founded the earliest public library, and to have first arranged in a connected series the works of Homer, which had been previously sung in detached rhapsodies. Let us observe, however, that the fame of having introduced Homer's poems at Athens is sometimes ascribed to his son, Hipparchus;[4] whilst, on the other hand, Solon is related, before this time, to have made the rhapsodists sing portions of the poems one after the other.[5] All that we can conclude then, is, that it must have been about the time of Peisistratus and his sons that the recitation of the Homeric rhapsodies became a public entertainment at Athens during the great Panathenæa, which, as we have before observed, were probably now instituted.[6] And hence we may also, perhaps, infer that the oldest Odeium was now erected, for the purpose of these recitations and other entertainments of a similar kind. For the literary progress of the Athenians at this period

---

[1] Dio Chrysos. Orat. vii. (t. i. p. 132, Teubner); Orat. xxv. (p. 311 ib.). The dress may be inferred from Aristophanes, Lysistr. 1155 (κἀντὶ τῆς κατωνάκης, κ.τ.λ.).

[2] See Hesych. ἐν Πυθίῳ χέσαι: Vitruv. vii. Præf.; Harpocr. voc. Λύκειον.

[3] Suidas. τὸ Ἱππάρχου τεῖχος.

[4] A. Gell. N. A. vii. (vi.) 17: Cic. De Orat. iii. 34. 137; Ælian, V. H. xiii. 14:

cf. viii. 2: Plat. Hipparch. p. 228 (i. ii. 237, Bekk.).

[5] τά τε Ὁμήρου ἐξ ὑποβολῆς γέγραφε ῥαψωδεῖσθαι, οἷον ὅπου ὁ πρῶτος ἔληξεν ἐκεῖθεν ἄρχεσθαι τὸν ἐχόμενον. — Diog. Laërt. Vit. Sol. lib. i. s. 57.

[6] According to Eusebius, Chron. the Panathenaic agon was instituted anno 1451. Ol. 53.4 (B.C. 566). See Clinton under that year.

is also testified by another circumstance, that Thespis had begun to lay the foundations of the drama. Solon, just before he went into exile, is said to have addressed much the same reproach to Thespis as Cardinal Ippolito d'Est did to Ariosto when he asked him, on the subject of his 'Orlando Furioso,' where he had picked up such a parcel of idle stuff?[1] But from such rude beginnings were soon to spring some of the sublimest productions of human genius.

It is curiously illustrative of the carelessness of the Athenians for their history, that their best authors should be divided in opinion as to which was the eldest of Peisistratus' three sons, and whether he was succeeded by Hippias or Hipparchus. In the time of Thucydides, who lived only about a century later, the commonly received opinion was that Hipparchus was his successor; but in support of his view to the contrary, he can appeal to no written records; whilst among the Romans—a much ruder people, yet careful of their history and traditions—it had been customary, long before the time of Peisistratus, to record in writing the most memorable public events. All that Thucydides can appeal to in support of his view is hearsay, probability, and an inscription on a pillar. The arguments from probability are certainly rather weak, as Meursius has shown.[2] That Hippias alone of the three brothers should have had children does not prove him the eldest, especially considering the peculiar tastes of Hipparchus; nor is there much force in the argument drawn from the difficulty which Hippias would have experienced in seizing the reins of government on the assassination of his brother, had he been previously in a private station; for this, as Meursius observes, might have been effected by the address and coolness with which he proceeded to disarm the people before the death of Hipparchus was generally known. On the other hand, we think there is great weight in the circumstance that the name of Hippias immediately succeeded that of his father on the pillar erected on the Acropolis in memory of the unjust usurpation of the Peisistratids. Meursius explains this by saying that the name of Hippias was put first because he was the most harsh and cruel of

<hr>

[1] Plut. Sol. c. 29.   [2] Peisistratus, c. 11.   For the whole story see Thucyd. vi. 54–59.

them. But if harshness regulated the collocation, this would be a good reason for putting Hippias even before his father. The Athenians were evidently not governed by that circumstance. They regarded the whole family as tyrants and usurpers;' and if they were guided in their views of them by cruelty, why should the celebrated songs in praise of Harmodius and Aristogeiton, the tyrannicides, have been made, who slew Hipparchus, the mildest of them, yet so far from getting rid of the tyranny, only for a while augmented its severity? In spite, however, of the remarks of Thucydides, the opinion which he contested was not extirpated; and Plato, or whoever was the author of the dialogue entitled ' Hipparchus,' continued to adopt it,* believing Hipparchus to have been the eldest son. Later writers have only followed one or the other of these authorities, and it were useless therefore to cite them.

But whether the eldest or not, Hipparchus was doubtless, as Plato says, the best and wisest of the brothers; all good actions are ascribed to him, all evil ones to Hippias. He was a patron of poetry, which is equivalent to saying that he was a patron of literature, for prose composition was an art yet unknown. He entertained Anacreon and Simonides; also Onomacritus, till he was detected in interpolating the oracles ascribed to Musæus.[3] In order to instruct the people he placed Hermæ in the streets, having moral apophthegms inscribed on their sides, whence they obtained the name of *Hipparchic* ('Iππάρχειοι).[4] In short, so mild and benignant was the rule of the Peisistratids, before the murder of Hipparchus, that it was compared to the reign of Cronus or Saturn.[5] Hipparchus drew in a measure his fate upon himself. Slighted by Harmodius, he revenged himself by grievously insulting his sister. She was summoned to attend some procession as a Canephoros, or basket-bearer, an honour coveted by the foremost families in the land; but when she appeared, Hipparchus rejected her as unworthy of it. Stung

---

[1] κοινῶς δὲ πάντες οἱ Πεισιστρατίδαι τύραννοι ἐλέγοντο.—Schol. ad Aristoph. Vesp. v. 500.

[2] Ἱππάρχῳ, ὃς τῶν Πεισιστράτου παίδων ἦν πρεσβύτατος καὶ σοφώτατος.—p. 228 (i. ii. 237, Bekk.).—οἱ (Ἱππάρχου sc.)

καὶ ἀποθανόντος τρία ἔτη ἐτυραννεύθησαν Ἀθηναῖοι ὑπὸ τοῦ ἀδελφοῦ αὐτοῦ Ἱππίου.—Ib. p. 229.

[3] Herod. vii. 6; Plat. Hipp. l. c.

[4] Harpocr. voc. Ἑρμαῖ.

[5] Plat. l. c.

by this insult, Harmodius and his lover Aristogeiton plotted the overthrow and death of the tyrants. The festival of the great Panathenæa
was chosen for carrying their plan into execution, because on that
occasion the citizens were allowed to appear in arms. Hippias was
occupied in arranging the procession in the Ceramcicus, outside the
walls; Harmodius and Aristogeiton, who were to take part in it, were
also there, and observing one of their friends talking familiarly with
Hippias they fancied that they were betrayed. Under this impression,
and with a determination to effect something, they rushed through
the gate into the city, and meeting with Hipparchus near the Leocorion,
or monument of Leos, they slew him. But Harmodius was instantly
killed by the guards, whilst Aristogeiton was soon afterwards seized
and put to the torture.[1] A memorable incident in Athenian history!
and recorded by inscriptions, statues, and frequent allusions to it by
poets and orators, but more especially by some famous scolia, or songs,
in the mouth of every citizen. The following is one of them :

$$\text{ἐν μύρτου κλαδὶ τὸ ξίφος φορήσω,}$$
$$\text{ὥσπερ Ἁρμόδιος κ' Ἀριστογείτων,}$$
$$\text{ὅτε τὸν τύραννον κτανέτην,}$$
$$\text{ἰσονόμους τ' Ἀθήνας ἐποιησάτην.[2]}$$

My sword I'll bear in myrtle hid,
  As once Harmodius and his lover,
Who slew Hipparchus and thus did
  Their country's equal laws recover.

Freedom and equality were not, however, as the song had it, the
immediate result of the act of the tyrannicides; which in spite of
its celebrity, was, as we have seen, prompted rather by private pique
than by patriotic motives. On the contrary, Hippias ruled three or
four years longer with increased severity.[3] We will mention some of his
acts that are connected with the monuments and topography of Athens.
There was a courtesan named Leæna, beloved by Aristogeiton. Hippias

---

[1] Thucyd. loc. cit.; Herod. v. 55.

[2] Athen. xv. 50, where there are four
different forms of it. Some able critics,
however, as Lowth, Prunck, Schneidewin,

&c., consider these to be four stanzas of
one and the same poem. Cf. Aristoph.
Lysis. 633, et ibi schol.; Acharn. v. 68.

[3] Herod. ib. 62; Thucyd. l. c.

put her to the torture, to extort from her a confession of Aristogeiton's accomplices, but rather than do so she bit off her tongue.[1] In commemoration of the act, and by a play upon her name, a statue of a lioness without a tongue was erected on the Acropolis. From one of his regulations it would appear that the upper storeys of some of the Athenian houses overhung the streets, that they had steps, or *περροι*, before them, as we have already remarked concerning the so-called Cranaan city, with railings, and that the doors opened outwards. For, according to the treatise on domestic economy ascribed to Aristotle, Hippias ordered all such things to be sold, and the owners were compelled to buy them in.[2] He is also said to have instituted a tribute payable to the priestess of Athena on the occasion of deaths and marriages; a measure of wheat, another of barley, and an obol.[3]

Hippias was ejected by the Alcmaeonids, a powerful Athenian family, which had been banished for a previous attempt to upset the Pisistratids. As we have already said, Megacles, one of their members, had played a conspicuous part in the affair of Cylon. Cleisthenes was now at their head. He is said to have bribed the priestess at Delphi by building a temple with a marble façade, while he had only contracted to erect one of tufa (πώρινος λίθος);[4] and the oracle persuaded the Lacedæmonians to liberate Athens from the tyrant. The first attempt, under Anchimolius, failed. The Lacedæmonians landed at Phalerum, but Hippias had obtained 1000 cavalry from Thessaly, and having cleared all the country about Phalerum to facilitate their evolutions, the invaders were completely defeated. On the next invasion, which was undertaken by land, Cleomenes and the Spartans were successful, captured Athens, and shut up Hippias in the Pelasgicum, where he would have been able to defy them. But his children and nephews, who had been sent out of the country, were seized, and in order to recover them he agreed to evacuate Athens in five days.[5] This event took place in Ol. 67.3 (B.C. 510).

---

[1] Polyæn. viii. 45. Cf. Lactant. De Falsa Rel. i. 20; who, however, tells the story differently.

[2] De cura rei fam. ii. 2. 4.

[3] Ibid. It was probably a registration fee.

[4] Herod. v. 62. Plutarch, however, ascribes this story to the malignity of Herodotus (t. ix. p. 415. Reiske).

[5] Herod. v. 65. Cf. Aristoph. Lysistr. 1150 sqq.

No sooner was the tyrant expelled than dissensions arose between Cleisthenes and Isagoras, the chiefs of the Alcmæonids, till Cleisthenes, by courting the democracy, obtained the expulsion of his opponent. By some he is celebrated as having perfected Solon's constitution; and it is certain, at all events, that he broke up the power of the aristocracy by admitting foreigners, metics, and slaves to citizenship, and especially by increasing the number of the tribes from four to ten, and thus demolishing the influence of the Eupatrids arising from local connections. The names of the ten tribes were Erechtheïs, Ægeïs, Pandionis, Leontis, Acamantis, Œneïs, Cecropis, Hippothoöntis, Aiantis, and Antiochis. Cleisthenes also increased the number of the Senators to five hundred, fifty being elected for each tribe; and these bodies of fifty, under the name of Prytanes, presided by turns over public affairs.[1] But it will suffice to have adverted to so many of these political changes as will serve to explain subsequent allusions.

We will now mention a few things that lie more within our immediate scope. We have adverted above to Thespis and the beginnings of the drama. It seems probable that Peisistratus introduced at Athens the cyclic chorus and dithyramb,[2] the Doric dialect of which shows that it was not of native growth. Peisistratus was a native of Philaidæ, near Brauron, where the festival of Dionysus was celebrated in a very boisterous manner.[3] Thespis was also a Diacrian, born at Icaria, where, as we have seen, the culture of the vine and the worship of Dionysus were very early introduced. And as the Diacrians formed the extreme democratic party, this may account for Solon's dislike of the innovations of Thespis. The view that Peisistratus introduced the cyclic chorus is rather confirmed by the circumstance that the tripods, the prize of the victors in it, were placed in the Pythium, or temple of Apollo, which Peisistratus had built,[4] as well as by the tradition that a mask of Dionysus preserved at Athens was said to be a portrait of that tyrant.[5] However this may be, the dithyrambic chorus, with Thespis'

---

[1] Aristot. Pol. iii. c. 1. Cf. Herod. vi. 131; Isocr. Areop. p. 143, &c.

[2] See Donaldson, Theatre of the Greeks, p. 45 sq.

[3] Aristoph. Pax, 874, and schol.

[4] Photius, voc. Πύθιον.

[5] Athen. xii. c. 44.

important addition of an actor, was welcomed by the lively genius of the Athenians and speedily developed into the regular drama. Choerilus is said to have been the first who exhibited a tragedy in Ol. 64.2 (B.C. 523), four years after the death of Peisistratus.[1] He was soon followed by Phrynichus, who gained the tragic prize in B.C. 511, the year before the expulsion of Hippias, and thus the drama may be said to have been completely established during the sovereignty of the Peisistratids.

Attic tragedy appears to have been originally performed in extempore wooden theatres (ἴκρια), and it was the fall of one of these, during the representation of a piece by Pratinas, which led to the building of the stone theatre.[2] As to the place in which these scaffoldings were erected opinions are very much divided. Some writers place them in the agora, on the north-west side of the Acropolis; others in the Lenæum on the south-east side; whilst others, again, think that sometimes one sometimes the other of these spots was selected; and perhaps this last opinion is the most correct. That these primitive exhibitions sometimes took place in the agora must be admitted, except we are to reject in a lump the testimony of scholiasts and lexicographers. Photius, Eustathius, and others say so expressly;[3] and it further appears, that above the spot where the stage was erected, and therefore probably near the ascent to the Acropolis on the north-west side, there stood a poplar tree, which those who could not get a place in the theatre were accustomed to mount, whence the proverb 'a view from the poplar' (ἀπ' αἰγείρου or παρ' αἴγειρον θέα), to denote a bad place.[4] And that the agora was on this side of the Acropolis in the time of the

[1] Suidas, voc. Χοιρίλος.

[2] Idem, voc. Πρατίνας.

[3] Ἴκρια· τὰ ἐν τῇ ἀγορᾷ ἀφ' ὧν ἐθεῶντο τοὺς Διονυσιακοὺς ἀγῶνας πρὶν ἢ κατασκευασθῆναι τὸ ἐν Διονύσου θέατρον.—Phot. Cf. Eustath. ad Hom. Od. iii. 350. Leake, who held that the primitive wooden theatre was only in the Lenæum, charges Photius with error in saying ἐν τῇ ἀγορᾷ (vol. i. p. 217), but adduces nothing in support of the charge.

[4] Ἀθήνησιν αἴγειρος ἦν, ἧς πλησίον τὰ ἴκρια ἐπήγνυτο εἰς τὴν θέαν πρὸ τοῦ θεάτρου γενέσθαι· οὕτω Κρατῖνος.—Bekk. An. Græc. p. 354. Ἀπ' αἰγείρου θέα καὶ παρ' αἴγειρον· ἡ ἀπὸ τῶν ἐσχάτων· αἴγειρος γὰρ ἐπάνω ἦν τοῦ θεάτρου, ἀφ' ἧς οἱ μὴ ἔχοντες τόπον ἐθεώρουν.—Ib. p. 419. Cf. Hesych. in Αἴγειροι θέα, and Ἀπ' αἰγείρων.

Peisistratids is evident from the circumstance that Peisistratus, the son of Hippias, erected in it the Altar of the Twelve Gods, which remained there in the time of Thucydides, as we shall see further on.

On the other hand there are some passages which show that dramatic contests also took place in the Lenæum or peribolos sacred to the Lenæan Dionysus, at the south-east foot of the Acropolis, before the theatre was built;[1] but these were probably in the festival called the Lenæa (τὰ Λήναια), celebrated in the month Gamelion, when these representations would very naturally take place in the proximity of the temple of the Lenæan Dionysus; while those during the great Dionysia, we may conclude, were originally held in the wooden theatre in the agora. The existence of a primitive orchestra here, near the spot where afterwards stood the statues of Harmodius and Aristogeiton, is strongly confirmative of this view.[2] This orchestra was probably first used for the performances of the cyclic chorus. We have only the evidence of Suidas, in the article Πρατίνας, before quoted, respecting the building of the stone theatre and its date, which he fixes in Olympiad 70.1, or B.C. 500. It was constructed in the Lenæum, or Dionysiac enclosure, which, as we have said, lay under the south-east

---

[1] Ληναῖον· περίβολος μέγας Ἀθήνῃσιν, ἐν ᾧ τοὺς ἀγῶνας ἦγον πρὸ τοῦ τὸ θέατρον οἰκοδομηθῆναι, ὀνομάζοντες ἐπὶ Ληναίῳ· ἔστιν δὲ ἐν αὐτῷ καὶ ἱερὸν Διονύσου Ληναίου. Phot. Lex.; Bekk. An. Graec. p. 278; Hesych. Ἐπὶ Ληναίῳ ἀγών. Let us observe here that the phrase ἐπὶ Ληναίῳ, as in Aristophanes, Acharn. 504—αὐτοὶ γάρ ἐσμεν οὑπὶ Ληναίῳ τ' ἀγών—though it may have originally meant a contest in or at the Lenæum, came in process of time to denote rather an agon in honour of the Lenæan Dionysus, or the Lenæan festival. In fact, as a designation of place, it would have ceased to have any meaning, as the plays at the Great Dionysia were also performed at the Lenæum. The words of the law quoted by Demosthenes (Mid. p. 517,

Reiske), ἡ ἐπὶ Ληναίῳ πομπή, do not admit such a meaning, for it would be absurd to imagine a solemn procession confining itself to a place like the Lenæum. ἐπὶ Ληναίῳ means the Lenæan festival in Plato, Protagoras, 327 D (i. i. 187, Bekk.): ἄγριοί τινες, οἷοί περ οὓς πέρυσι Φερεκράτης ὁ ποιητὴς ἐδίδαξεν ἐπὶ Ληναίῳ. Sometimes the form occurs: Διονύσια τὰ ἐπὶ Ληναίῳ.—Boeckh, C. Inser. Gr. i. No. 157; Rangabé, 'Ant. Helléniques,' t. ii. p. 601. Cf. Wieseler, 'Disputatio de loco,' &c., p. 13, note 40.

[2] Ὀρχήστρα . . . τόπος ἐπιφανὴς εἰς πανήγυριν, ἔνθα Ἁρμοδίου καὶ Ἀριστογείτονος εἰκόνες.—Tim. Lex. Plat. Ὀρχήστρα· πρῶτον ἐκλήθη ἐν τῇ ἀγορᾷ, εἶτα καὶ τοῦ θεάτρου τὸ κάτω ἡμίκυκλον.—Phot. Lex.

THEATRE OF POMPEII.

side of the Acropolis. The upper part of the κοῖλον, or place for the audience, was excavated out of the cliff, whilst the lower part, including the stage, was constructed of wood and masonry. At first, probably, it was but a rude construction in comparison with what Lycurgue the orator made it about a century and a half later. There is even reason to believe that the stone and marble seats for the spectators were not added till that time, except, perhaps, those higher ones actually cut out of the rock; for we find Cratinus and Aristophanes alluding to the ἴκρια, or wooden benches, long after the stone theatre was in existence.[1] A passage in the 'Thesmophoriazusae' of Aristophanes seems to confirm our notion that the lower benches were still constructed of wood. One of the women in the play, after alluding to Euripides' abuse of the female sex, and the bad impressions of them it had given the men, proceeds to say:

ὥστ' εὐθὺς εἰσιόντες ἀπὸ τῶν ἰκρίων
ὑποβλέπουσ' ἡμᾶς, σκοποῦνταί τ' εἰθέως. – v. 394.

"The men no sooner fill the wooden seats
Than they stare up and scrutinize us thence:"

a passage which seems to show not only that the women sat apart from the men, but also that they occupied the upper seats, which were of stone.[2] The excavations undertaken in 1862, the results of which will be described in the proper place, have now laid bare the whole of this magnificent theatre: one of the most important and interesting revelations of classical antiquity that has been made in our days.

An event was now at hand that was to change the whole face of Athens—its capture by the Persians. But before relating it, let us endeavour to realize the appearance of the primitive, or as it has been sometimes called, the Thesean city.

First, then, we must remark that it was surrounded with a wall. This is clear, from the account given above, from Thucydides, of the assassination of Hipparchus, where it is said that Harmodius and Aristogeiton rushed *through the gate* into the city (p. 78).

[1] ἰκρίων ψόφησις. Crat. Inc. Fab. Frag. no. li. Meineke.   [2] The scholiast on the passage observes: ὡς ἔτι ἰκρίων ὄντων ἐν τῷ θεάτρῳ.

All we can collect about this wall is, that it was of considerably less extent than the one afterwards built by Themistocles, who is said to have enlarged it on every side.[1] Supposing that the Gate of Hadrian, from the inscription on it, marked the boundary of the Thesean city on the south-east, then we may, perhaps, assume that the wall described a rude circle round the Acropolis with a radius about equal to the distance of that gate from it. That the configuration of it was circular we may infer from the oracle delivered to the Athenians before the Persian wars :

> Ὦ μέλεοι, τί κάθησθε ; λιπὼν φεῦγ᾽ ἔσχατα γαίης
> δώματα καὶ πόλιος τροχοειδέος ἄκρα κάρηνα.[2]

"Why linger ye? O wretches, fly to earth's remotest end,
Nor seek your wheel-shap'd town, your homes, and fortress to defend."

In this case it is probable that the remains of a wall still traceable on the crest of the Museum and Pnyx hills may, as Curtius suggests,[3] have belonged to the primitive enclosure. We have already seen that a wall must have existed in the time of the Peisistratids; but that it was built by them, as the author just mentioned thinks, is hardly probable. Their public works have been recorded, and it is not likely that one so important should have been omitted in the list. The fact of this enclosure being ascribed to Theseus, moreover, shows that it had originated time out of mind. If carried round with the radius mentioned it would have included the Areiopagus, and the modern bazaar; but the high ground on the north-west on which stands the so-called Theseium, and the Olympium and neighbouring temples on the south-east, would have been excluded. In the midst stood the Acropolis, strongly fortified with a wall all round, and especially at its western entrance, with a fortress called the Enneapylon. Above this, probably, was a propylæum. On the summit of the Acropolis, besides the Erechtheium, and perhaps a few

[1] Thucyd. i. 93.

[2] Herod. vii. 140.

[3] Erläuternder Text, S. 31. Curtius also mentions that vestiges of an ancient wall running in the direction of Hadrian's Gate, are still perceptible in the modern Street of Victory (ὁδὸς τῆς Νίκης). Att.

Stud. i. 59. The statement of Isocrates, that the Athenians abandoned the city on the approach of the Persians, because it was not fortified (Panath. p. 243), seems to be a random assertion, contrary to the testimony of the historians.

other monuments, a new and larger temple of Athena, called the Hecatompedon, appears to have been rising, but not yet completed. Round its sides were various temples, some of them mere caverns in the cliff, others lower down were built of masonry. These will be described in the sequel. At the south-east side was the new Dionysiac theatre, at the south-west side various public buildings and temples bordering the agora, the statues of the tyrannicides, the shrine of the Eumenides, &c. Such perhaps, was the general appearance of Thesean Athens, when besieged by the Persians.

That event happened in the archonship of Calliades, B.C. 480. The Pythian oracle had directed the Athenians to defend themselves with wooden walls. The sagacity, or complicity, of Themistocles, interpreted this to mean that they must take to their ships; and this view had been supported by the refusal of the sacred serpent in the Erechtheium to take its food. The counsels of Themistocles prevailed. Athens was almost deserted; a few only, unable or unwilling to fly, shut themselves up in the Acropolis; and in order to carry out what they supposed to be the commands of the oracle, erected some wooden outworks, or palisades, before the entrance. The Persians, on their arrival, found the gates and wall of the asty undefended, and encamped without opposition on the Areiopagus. Arming their arrows with burning tow, they soon set fire to and destroyed the wooden fence. But the garrison, even after the destruction of the defence on which they had superstitiously relied, still held out obstinately: Xerxes began to despair, when, probably on a hint from the Athenian exiles of the Peisistratid faction who accompanied him, he succeeded in introducing his men into the Acropolis through the temple of Aglauros below,[1] no

---

[1] Such is the account given by Herodotus, viii. 51 sqq. It is therefore surprising how Curtius can assume, without adducing the least authority, that the fortifications of the Acropolis were demolished after the departure of the Peisistratids, and that the only defence during the Persian siege was the palisade: " Die Burg, zur Tyrannenzeit noch Citadelle, war nach Abzug der Pisistratiden demolirt worden und am Aufgange nur nothdürftig mit Holzwerk verrammelt." — Erläuternder Text, p. 31. The palisade was evidently a mere superstitious compliance with the oracle, and the Persians still found the walls inassailable. The existence of the

doubt by means of the subterranean communication which modern researches have proved to exist. The garrison were now put to the sword; the temple was despoiled, and the whole Acropolis burnt. A day or two afterwards, Xerxes permitted the Athenian exiles to go up and sacrifice on the Acropolis; when they found that the sacred olive, although it had been burnt along with the temple, had thrown out a shoot a cubit long.[1] Ten months afterwards, the Persian general Mardonius again entered Athens unopposed, the citizens having fled to Salamis. On this occasion he completed the destruction of the city, overthrowing all the temples, walls, and houses, except a few in which the Persian leaders had lived.[2]

---

secret communication between the Ere-chtheium and the temple of Aglauros had been ingeniously conjectured by Dr. Words-worth before it was actually discovered.—

Athens and Attica, ch. xii.

[1] Herod. ib. c. 55.

[2] Idem, ix. c. 3, 13; Thucyd. i. 89.

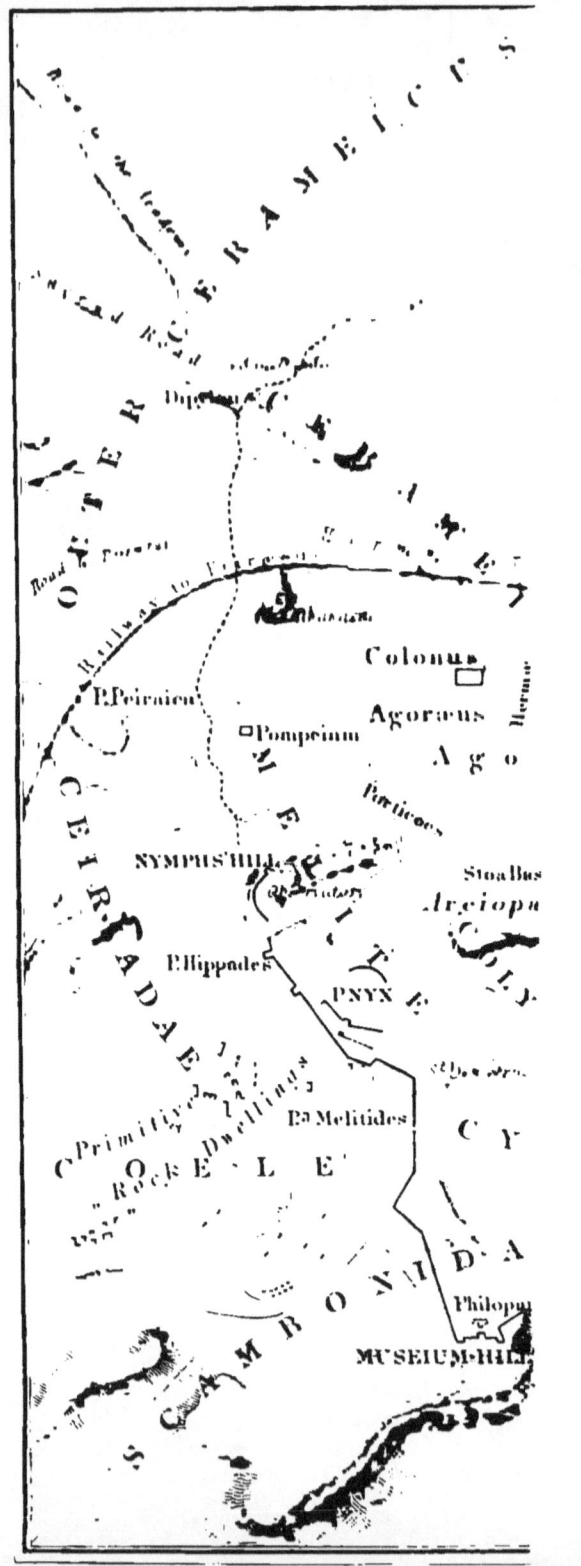

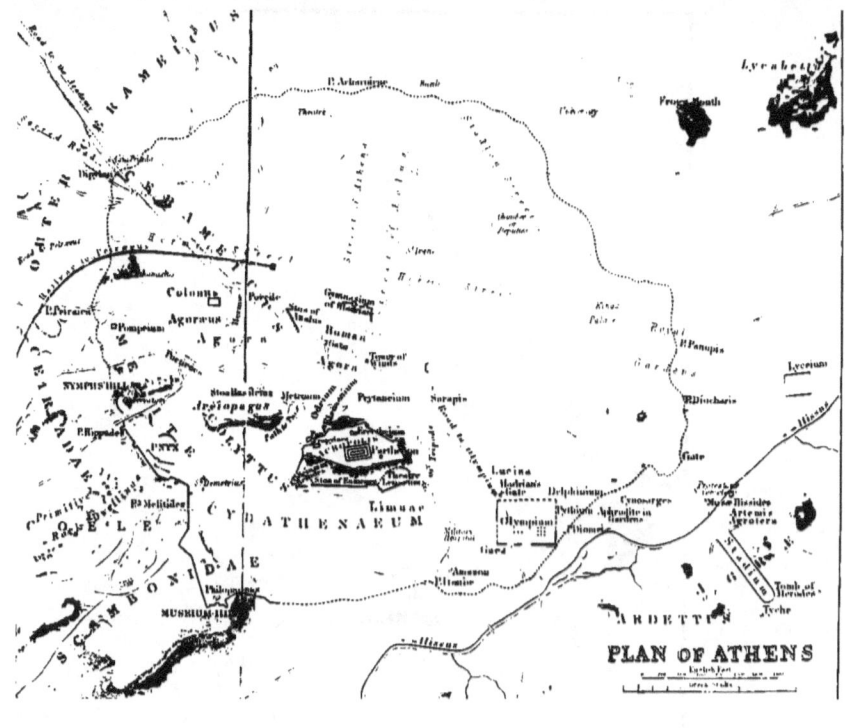

PLAN OF ATHENS

Athens in the time of Themistocles — City Wall — Dipylon — Ceramicus — Agora — Sacred Gate — Names of Dipylon — Peiraic Gate — Colonus Agoraeus — Melite — Ceriadæ — Psarathium — Gate Melitides — Cele — Gate Hippades — Objects in Melite — Collytus — Cydathenæum — Limnæ — Scambonidæ — Itonian Gate — Demos — Diocharean — Acharnenæan — Eretria — Demi and Gates — Circumference of Wall — Population — Peiræan Wall — Phalerum — Long Walls — Harbours — Peiræus, its divisions — Total circumference — Other works.

ALTHOUGH the narratives of the destruction of Athens may be somewhat exaggerated, there can be no doubt that when the inhabitants returned to it there was an immense deal to be done, both in repairing and reconstructing, before it could be again rendered properly habitable. But the views of Themistocles, who was now at the head of affairs, extended beyond this. In reconstructing the walls he was determined to give them a larger circuit; and especially, with a view to that naval superiority of the Athenians, which was always uppermost in his thoughts, he resolved to construct new harbours. These works, planned, though not entirely executed by him, mark him as the founder of the substantial greatness of Athens; its embellishment, which naturally came later, was left to be accomplished by Cimon and Pericles.

The course of the Themistoclean walls has long been a subject of controversy amongst topographers, and cannot be said even yet to be completely decided. Most writers, however, are agreed upon a general outline which does not offer any very important discrepancies.[1] The

---

[1] In order to avoid useless controversy, we shall not here discuss the hypothesis of Forchhammer, now, we believe, universally abandoned. The line of wall adopted by that topographer—whose general merits we are very far from wishing to depreciate—would almost seem to have been arrived at by placing one leg of his compasses on

line drawn by Curtius, one of the most recent, most authoritative, and perhaps most innovating of Athenian topographers, does not very materially differ, except on the southern side, from that laid down by Leake many years before; nor is it a matter of much consequence, except in a purely antiquarian view, whether the general line deviated a few yards to the right or left. The situation of the gates is more important, as they are frequently mentioned in the classic authors, and because the direction of the streets and the site of some of the monuments depend upon them. We shall therefore first endeavour to ascertain the situation of the principal gates, which if once determined, the line of wall between them may be laid down with tolerable accuracy. At the same time it will be convenient to describe, in connection with the gates, the different city regions; for Athens, as Themistocles made it, remained very much the same down to the latest times.

Unfortunately, however, there is only one gate, though the most important one—the Dipylon—on whose site we can pronounce with anything like certainty, and about which topographers are almost universally agreed.[1] We learn from Plutarch that the Dipylon was anciently called the Thriasian Gate (Θριασίαι Πύλαι);[2] and this is confirmed by Harpocration,[3] who repeats the same story as Plutarch, that Anthemocritus, the herald despatched by Pericles to the Megarensians, having been put to death by them, was buried near that gate. Now, as Thria was a *demos*, or borough, lying north-west of Athens, the Thriasian Gate would be on the corresponding side of the city. Again, it is universally allowed that the Academy lay north-west of Athens, and the route to it was through the Dipylon, from which it was about a mile distant.[4] From this gate issued also the Sacred Way leading to Eleusis,

---

the Acropolis and drawing a circle round it, answering to the measure given by Thucydides. In this way he brings the Ilissus within the city, contrary to all ancient testimony, and without pretending to support his views by any vestiges of ancient remains.

[1] Dr. Wordsworth stands, we believe, alone in placing it on the site commonly ascribed to the Peiraic Gate.

[2] Pericl. c. 30.

[3] Voc. Ἀνθεμόκριτος.

[4] Liv. xxxi. 25; Cic. De Fin. v. 1.

which was bordered with tombs, among which Pausanias saw that of
Anthemocritus, before mentioned.[1] These ancient notices are confirmed
by some recent discoveries of tombs near the church of Agia Triada,
a little northwards of the bottom of the modern Hermes Street, the
assumed site of the Dipylon; especially the tomb of Dexileos, a knight
who fell at Corinth, which we shall have occasion to describe in another
part of this work.

A further proof of the site of this gate may be derived from its
having stood in the quarter of the city called Cerameicus; whence it was
also called the Cerameican Gate.[2] And that the Cerameicus lay on the
north-west side of the city is evident from its having included the
Academy as well as the agora,[3] whence the Cerameicus was sometimes
called Academeia; whilst on the other hand the agora, from its being in
that region, came to be called by later writers the Cerameicus. Hence,
from its lying both within and without the walls, these respective parts
were designated the Inner and the Outer Cerameicus.[4] After the building of the wall of Themistocles, it was the Dipylon which formed the
boundary between the two. Whether there was an Inner Cerameicus, in
the Thesean city may be a question. Thucydides, in the passage which
we have quoted above (p. 76) respecting the assassination of Hipparchus,
merely says that Hippias was arranging the Panathenaic procession
in the Cerameicus, without adding the distinguishing epithet *outer* :
which might lead us to infer that part of that region was first included
within the walls by Themistocles. We may add here that the deme
Cerameicus belonged to the tribe Acamantis. Pausanias says that the
Cerameis derived their name from Ceramus (Κέραμος), a son of Bacchus
and Ariadne ; but Philochorus says that they were so called from their
exercising the trade of potters : though he also states that they sacrificed
to Ceramus, who seems to have been the eponymous hero of the potters.[5]

This will be a proper place, in connection with the Dipylon and

[1] i. 36. 3.

[2] Hesych. voc. Δημιάσι πύλαις.

[3] Hesych. voc. Ἀκαδημία.

[4] εἰσὶ δὲ δύο Κεραμεικοί, ὁ μὲν ἔξω τείχους, ὁ δὲ ἐντός.—Idem, voc. Κεραμεικός.

τὸν ἐντὸς τοῦ Διπύλου Κεραμεικόν.—Plut.
Sull. 14. παρὰ τῷ Πυθοδώρῳ, ἐκτὸς τείχους ἐν Κεραμεικῷ.—Plat. Parm. p. 127.

[5] Pausan. i. 3, 1 : Ἡ περσατ. in Κερα-
μεῖς and Κεραμεικός.

Cerameicus, to settle the situation of the agora. We have shown above (p. 81) that, at least as early as the time of the Peisistraids, the agora must have lain at the north-west foot of the Acropolis. There was ample room for it between that spot and the Areiopagus on one side, and the Thesean wall on the other; but in all probability it was enlarged when the new wall was built. The site for it is marked out by the nature of the ground. The narrow valleys on the southern and western sides of the Acropolis and Areiopagus, which must have been still deeper in ancient times, afford not sufficient space for a large market place, in which, besides the usual transactions of buying and selling, assemblies of the people were sometimes held, religious processions took place, and, on certain occasions, evolutions of cavalry were exhibited.[1] But on the northern side the ground is open and level to any extent in a northerly direction, whilst on the east and west two gentle eminences leave a space between them of four or five hundred yards, amply sufficient for the purposes required. Of these eminences the western one, on which stands the reputed temple of Theseus, and which, as we shall show further on, was Colonus Agoræus, is still sufficiently defined; while the eastern one, from its being covered with buildings, is not so immediately perceptible. It is that on which stands the gate of the new agora. M. Pervanoglu has pointed out[2] that this building stands on its ancient level, as is plain from the gateway and the road which passes through it; whilst the floor of the portico of Attalus, on the western side of it, is buried to a depth of about eight mètres (twenty-six feet), and that of the Tower of the Winds on the east, six mètres (nineteen and a half feet). Anciently, therefore, this gate must have stood on a ridge of ground between twenty and thirty feet higher than the level of the agora, which has been raised by rubbish and ruins in the same way as the Roman Forum. Hence the surrounding hills, the Acropolis, the Areiopagus, and Colonus Agoræus on the west, whose height has not been increased by the same cause, must have presented more marked and striking features in ancient times than they do now, and have formed a well-defined boundary for the agora.

[1] Xenoph. Hipparch. c. 3, s. 2.   [2] Philologus, t. xxiv. p. 457.

That the site here described was that of the agora is strongly corroborated by some inscriptions, belonging to the fourth century or,
found upon it about twenty years ago, under the northern side of the
Areiopagus. The subjects of them are here unmaterial, the only thing
important for our object being that two of them are ordered to be
placed before the Bouleuterion, or senate house, and a third near the
statue of Zeus Eleutherios.[1] All these inscriptions were found together,
under the foundations of a small house. They cannot, therefore, have
been in their original place; but it is not likely that they were brought
from any great distance, and it will be seen when we come to treat of
the agora as described by Pausanias, that the statue and portico of Zeus
Eleutherios and the Bouleuterion lay not very far from each other and
near the spot where the inscriptions were discovered.

Proceeding in a southerly direction from the Diplyon, which stood
at the north-westernmost angle of the walls, the next gate must have
been one between the little hill, or rock, on which stands the church of
St. Athanasius, and the northern foot of the Nymphs' Hill. It is altogether improbable that there should have been another gate in the
intervening space; for, first, the distance is too inconsiderable (less
than three hundred yards) to admit of one; and, secondly, the nature
of the ground, from the rock just mentioned and the more extended
height of Colonus Agoraeus in its rear, would have afforded no com-
modious approach to such a gate from within. Dr. Ernst Curtius,
indeed, affirms that there are vestiges of a gate in the hollow between
Agia Triada and Agios Athanasios, and thinks this may have been
the Peiraïc Gate.[2] Now this was a very natural place for a gate, for
the nature of the ground would make it a convenient outlet from the
city. But a gate here would most probably have been the original
Dipylon, the site of which, there is good reason to believe, must have

[1] See Rangabé. Ant. Hellén. t. ii. Nos.
381, 430, 478. Cf. Kumanudes, Pro-
gramme of Archaeol. Soc. in Athens, July,
1861, p. 16; Arch. Ephemeris, 4104, 57:
4108, 51; Curtius. Att. Stud. ii. 29.

[2] Erläuternder Text der sieben Karten,
S. 32. As the aspirate is dropped in
modern Greek, we have written Agios for
Ἅγιος.

been altered. For the whole hillock on which the church of Agia Triada stands is made ground, as appears from the ancient tombs discovered near it a few years ago, of which we shall speak in the sequel, buried at a depth of about thirty feet. These could not have been within the walls, because burial inside the city was not permitted. The nature of the soil, and the fact of the lower and more ancient tombs having later ones, of the Roman period, above them, show that the tumulus is artificial. There are two occasions on which it may probably have been made: the siege of Athens by Philip V. in B.C. 200, and that by Sulla in B.C. 86. It may perhaps be referred to the former. Sulla captured Athens by throwing down part of the wall near the Heptachalcum, probably between the Peiraïc Gate and Dipylon,[1] which he had learnt was not sufficiently guarded. The making of the mound not only for the purpose of attack, but also of destroying the celebrated tombs before the Dipylon and spoiling the finest approach to Athens is quite in accordance with what we hear of Philip's spiteful proceedings.[2] However this may be, a new Dipylon seems to have been erected, not very far from the original one. Curtius, in the map of Athens in his 'Attische Studien' (No. 1), and also in his 'Sieben Karten,' included Agia Triada and the tombs near it in his line of wall, but in his plan in the 'Erläuternder Text' to the latter (p. 38) has drawn a new and doubtless more correct line, two or three hundred yards to the east. It is not at all likely, as he suggests there, that the law forbidding burials in the city had been altered before the time of the Corinthian war (B.C. 394).

At the spot indicated near the foot of the Nymphs' Hill there are evident remains of a gate, as well as vestiges of a wall in the direction of the Dipylon. Now, what was the name of this gate? Forchhammer, who is followed by one or two writers, placed here what he calls the Sacred Gate; not indeed precisely at the spot where the vestiges of one exist, but in conformity with his arbitrary hypothesis for enlarging the circuit of the wall some two hundred yards before it, where there

---

[1] Plut. Sull. 14.

[2] "Diruta non tecta solum sed etiam sepulcra; nec divini humanive juris quid- quam præ impotenti ira est servatum."— Liv. xxxi. 25.

are traces neither of wall nor gate. But this 'Sacred Gate' is quite
an imaginary one. The only author who mentions it is Plutarch, in his
account of the siege of Athens by Sulla.[1] As the passage is an important one for Athenian topography, we will here state the substance of it.
Sulla appears to have been encamped in the Outer Cerameicus, before
the Dipylon; for it was here that some of his men overheard a conversation between two old Athenians, who were complaining that the portion of wall about the Heptachalcum had not been sufficiently guarded.
At this quarter, therefore, Sulla made his attack, by destroying the wall
between the Peiraic and the Sacred Gates. Over this breach he entered
the city in the middle of the night, amid the braying of horns and
trumpets and the ferocious shouts of the soldiery, bent on blood and
plunder. The slaughter in the agora alone, which, as we have seen, lay
in this quarter, was so great that the whole Inner Cerameicus was
drenched with blood, so that, according to some accounts, it even flowed
through the Dipylon. We may remark, by the way, that this passage
is strongly confirmatory of the agora having occupied the site we have
assigned to it. For though the story of the blood flowing through the
gate is no doubt an exaggeration, yet it would have been too gross a one
to attempt had the agora been on the south side of the Areiopagus,
as some topographers have assumed.

Now, if the gate at the north foot of the Nymphs' Hill was the
Sacred Gate, then we must look still further southwards for the Peiraic
Gate; and the first at all probable place we can find for it is between
the Nymphs' Hill and the Pnyx Hill. But the intervening space is the
most improbable one in the world for the attack. Not only is it at a
considerable distance from the Cerameicus, but also the ground outside
was and is covered with deep hollows and ravines which would have
rendered the marshalling of troops impracticable; whilst even allowing
this difficulty to have been overcome, they would have had to advance
into the city through a narrow gorge, where the besieged would have
had every advantage.

The Dipylon had many names. Besides being called, as we have seen,

[1] Sull. c. 14.

the Thriasian Gate and the Ceramcican Gate, it had also the appellation of Demiades Pylæ (Δημιάδες Πύλαι), because it was a favourite resort of prostitutes.[1] And as it derived a bad name from this circumstance, so it may have obtained the good one of the Sacred Gate from its being the outlet to the Sacred Way leading to Eleusis; which, however, in spite of its name, was a high road and common thoroughfare. When Plutarch, in his account of the siege of Athens by Sulla, speaks in the same chapter of the Dipylon and the Sacred Gate, it does not necessarily follow that they were two distinct gates, for these may have been only two different names for the same one. Had there been a gate expressly set apart for the Eleusinian procession, we should assuredly have heard of it from some ancient author; and the absurdity of the supposition is apparent, because, even according to the hypothesis, the road leading out of it very speedily joined the high road to Eleusis. Further, that the Sacred Way issued *immediately* from the Dipylon is shown by the passages before cited (supra, p. 88) respecting the tomb of Anthemocritus. Plutarch and Harpocration say that it was *close* to the Dipylon,[2] whilst Pausanias places it *on the Sacred Way*.[3]

---

[1] Hesych. Δημιάσι. Cf. Lucian, Dialog. Meretr. (t. iii. p. 287, Reitz).

[2] παρὰ τὰς Θριασίους πύλας, αἱ νῦν Δίπυλον ὀνομάζονται.— Plut. Pericl. 30; πρὸς ταῖς Θριασίαις πύλαις.—Harp. Ἄνθεμ.

[3] ἰοῦσι δ' ἐπ' Ἐλευσῖνα ἐξ Ἀθηνῶν, ἣν Ἀθηναῖοι καλοῦσιν ὁδὸν ἱεράν, Ἀνθεμοκρίτου πεποίηται μνῆμα.—i. 36, 3. It is possible that the gate which Plutarch calls 'Sacred' may have been that which some call Eriai, 'sepulchral' (Ἡρίαι from ἠρίον, a 'barrow,' or sepulchral tumulus). It would require but a slight alteration of his text (ἡρίας for ἱερᾶς), and Meursius has corrected in the same way a passage in Theophrastus: πόσους οἴει κατὰ τὰς ἱερὰς πύλας ἐξενηνέχθαι νεκρούς; (Charact. περὶ ἀναισθησίας :) where he reads ἡρίας for ἱεράς. See Athen. Att. iii. 12. This reading is also adopted by Dr. Sheppard,

in his edition of the 'Characters' of Theophrastus, p. 130. An ἠρίον was a barrow such as there appears to have been before the Dipylon; which, however, does not seem to have been *made* for that purpose, but to have been *converted* to it. There have actually been found here vast heaps of bones, which would justify and illustrate the question of Theophrastus. Plutarch, thus corrected, would not stand alone in his denomination of this gate, but be borne out by Theophrastus, and by the Etymol. M. (as emended by Meursius): Ἡρίαι· πύλαι Ἀθήνῃσι· διὰ τὸ τοὺς νεκροὺς ἐκφέρεσθαι ἐκεῖ ἐπὶ τὰ ἠρία, ὅ ἐστι τοὺς τάφους. It must be confessed, however, that there is no authority for an adj. ἠρίος, or ἠραῖος, the form suggested, but not adopted, by Sylburgius in his note on this passage (of which the original reading

Assuming therefore that the Dipylon and Plutarch's Sacred Gate were identical, we will now proceed to adduce some evidence that the Peiraic Gate occupied the spot we have indicated for it between the Nymphs' Hill and the church of St. Athanasius. We have already given an account from Plutarch of the battle between Theseus and the Amazons (supra, p. 634, and though the description is no doubt fanciful, yet it may be used by way of topographical evidence, since Plutarch or rather Cleidemus, whom he quotes, describes the position and movements of the hostile armies according to the localities as they existed in his time. We have seen that the Amazons faced the east, that their line extended from the Areiopagus to the Pnyx, and that they were attacked by the Athenians coming from the Museum Hill. The battle, therefore, must have taken place in the valley between the Pnyx and the Areiopagus, and it was here that their tombs were afterwards shown in the road between those hills leading to the Peiraic Gate. It is impossible to avoid this consequence. The only other possible roads would have been one between the Museum and Pnyx, and perhaps another between the Pnyx and the Nymphs' Hill. But these would not suit the line of battle, for they run to the south, and therefore the attack must have come from the north instead of the east, and the Amazonian line could not have stood as described by Plutarch and Æschylus.

Another argument in favour of the spot selected for the Peiraic Gate has been advanced by the late Professor Ross. Demosthenes relates that as he was coming up late from Peiræeus, Nicostratus struck him with his fist, and seizing him round the waist, was thrusting him towards the stone-quarries, when he was rescued by some passengers who heard his cries.[1] Now, there are no quarries, nor remains of any, on the road from Peiræeus to Athens, except those just under the Nymphs' Hill. Hence this passage would further show, that in the

---

is: Ἡραῖ αἱ πύλαι Ἀθηναῖοι), and that it rests only on a probable conjecture. We do not know why Leake (i. p. 447) writes this word with an aspirate (Heriæ). Har-

pocration, whom he cites, has ἡρία.
[1] Demosth. c. Nicostr. p. 1252, Reiske. C. Ross, 'Theseion,' Vorw. S. x.

time of Demosthenes this gate was the usual road to Peiræeus, and had consequently obtained the name of Peiraïc.

We will add another consideration. It will be seen when we come to the description which Pausanias gives of his route through Athens, that he must have entered at this gate, or at all events could not have entered at one further to the south, for in that case the road between it and the agora would have been too long for the objects which he describes, and would not have suited in other respects. Especially, if he had entered by a more southern gate, he must necessarily have passed the Pnyx, and could hardly have done so without noticing it. Yet he says not a word about it. And this strengthens the conclusion before arrived at, that the gate in question must have been that on the usual line of road between Athens and Peiræeus. We will assume, then, that the Peiraïc Gate must have stood in the valley beneath the Nymphs' Hill and the Church of St. Athanasius; and this is also the conclusion, we believe, of most recent topographers.

We have before observed that the height which lay between this gate and the Dipylon, and formed the western boundary of the agora, was Colonus Agoræus. Pherecrates, in his drama called 'Petalë,' distinguishes the Colonus within the walls from the Colonus Hippius without, in the following lines:

Οὗτος πόθεν ἦλθες;—Εἰς Κολωνὸν ᾠχόμην,
οὐ τὸν ἀγοραῖον, ἀλλὰ τὸν τῶν ἱππέων.[1]

"Holla, whence came you?—I have been to Colonus; not the Agoræan, but that of the horsemen."

Both these Coloni seem to have been demes or boroughs, and Colonus Hippius is thought to have belonged to the tribe Ægeïs, while the Agoræus was of the tribe Antiochis. This point, however, is far from being satisfactorily cleared up, for Colonus appears also in inscriptions under the tribes Leontis and Ptolemaïs.[2] The name, ἀγοραῖος, shows

[1] See the third argument to the Œdipus Col. and Meineke, Frag. Com. Græc. p. 114 (132).

[2] See Ross, Demen v. Attica, p. 11; Sauppe, De Demis, p. 19; Leake, Demi of Attica, p. 32, 189.

plainly enough that one of them must have been within the city, and, indeed, this is expressly said by Harpocration, who observes that it was near the agora, at the place where the Hephaesteum and Eurysaceium are.[1] And these two objects, as will be seen in the sequel, cannot be conveniently placed, except on this height. Pollux even says that Colonus was in the agora.[2] To the like effect is the testimony of a scholiast on Aristophanes, who remarks that it had become customary to call all the district behind the Great Stoa "Colonus", but that this was not correct, for all that part was Melite, as was recorded in the definitions of the boundaries.[3] And we shall see directly that Melite was conterminous with Colonus.

For, first, it was near the agora. In the 'Parmenides' of Plato, Cephalus meets Adeimantus and Glaucon in the agora, and they conduct him to Antiphon, who lived *near*, in Melite.[4] Again, Demosthenes, in his speech against Conon, says, that when walking in the agora he was met near the Leocorium by Ctesias, who passed on *up to* Melite:[5] whence we may infer that, besides being near the agora, Melite lay on high ground. And the Hill of the Nymphs must have formed part of it. For Plutarch observes that there was in Melite a temple of Artemis Aristobulē, founded by Themistocles near his own house; and here, in Plutarch's time, the corpses of the executed were thrown.[6] This is confirmed by other authorities. Plato, in his 'Republic,'[7] says that Leontius coming up to Athens from Peiræus, outside the northern Long

---

[1] τοὺς μισθωτοὺς Κολωναίτας ὠνόμαζον, ἐπειδὴ παρὰ τῷ Κολωνῷ εἱστήκεσαν, ὅς ἐστι πλησίον τῆς ἀγορᾶς, ἔνθα τὸ Ἡφαίστειον καὶ τὸ Εὐρυσάκειόν ἐστιν. ἐκαλεῖτο δὲ ὁ Κολωνὸς οὗτος ἀγοραῖος.—voc. Κολωναίτας.

[2] ὁ δὲ [Κολωνὸς] ἦν ἐν ἀγορᾷ.—lib. vii. s. 133.

[3] οὕτως μέρος τι νῦν σύνηθες γέγονε τὸ Κολωνὸν καλεῖν τὸ ὀπισθεν τῆς μακρᾶς στοᾶς, ἀλλ' οὐκ ἔστι. Μελίτη γὰρ ἅπαν ἐκεῖνο, ὡς ἐν τοῖς ὁρισμοῖς γέγραπται τῆς πόλεως.—Schol. in Av. v. 998. Hence it appears that the boundaries of the different Athenian regions were laid down in some public documents, or inscriptions. See the notes of Casaubon and Schweighäuser ad Athenæum, xii. 57. And indeed stones bearing the word ὅρος have been found in various parts of Athens.

[4] οἰκεῖ δὲ ἐγγὺς ἐν Μελίτῃ.—p. 126, fin.

[5] παρῆλθε πρὸς Μελίτην ἄνω.—p. 1258, Reiske.

[6] Vit. Them. c. 22.

[7] p. 439 sub fin. (iii. 1. 263, Bekk.): ἀνιὼν ἐκ Πειραιῶς ὑπὸ τὸ βόρειον τεῖχος ἐκτός, αἰσθανόμενος νεκροὺς παρὰ τῷ δημίῳ κειμένους.

Wall, perceived some corpses lying at the hangman's house. There must, therefore, have been a gate outside the northern wall, which could have been no other than the Peiraïc Gate just described, and near it the public executioner (ὁ δήμιος) lived, who was obliged to perform his office outside the walls.[1] Another confirmation has recently come to light. In a life of the philosopher Secundus, of which Tischendorf has published a portion from an Egyptian papyrus, we read : " I was going down to Peiræeus, for near the road to it is the place for executions."[2] Now there may still be seen at this spot a deep chasm or ravine, answering admirably to the βάραθρον into which the bodies of the executed were thrown. It was probably the same as the ὄρυγμα mentioned in the Λέξεις Ῥητορικαὶ as being in the deme of Ceiriadæ, and as the receptacle into which were thrown those condemned to death.[3] Whence we may infer that the Ceiriadæ were seated just outside the walls here, or partly without and partly within ; and Sauppe has inferred that they were a suburban *deme*, from an inscription in which are found named together Peiræeus, Ceiriadæ, Phalerum, Melitë.[4] This agrees well with the place we have assigned them, lying between Melitë within the city on one side and Peiræeus and Phalerum on the other. In the 'Plutus' of Aristophanes, Chremylus asks :

οὔκουν ὑπόλοιπόν σοι τὸ βάραθρον γίγνεται ;—(v. 431)

as much as to say, " Can't you go and hang yourself?" The scholiast on this passage describes the *barathrum* as a dark, well-like place, having hooks (ὄγκινοι) in its sides, into which malefactors were thrown. In the passage quoted from Bekker's 'Anecdota' it is said to have resembled a trap, so that those who trod on it fell in. The Athenians voted to throw Miltiades into it, and would have done so had not the

[1] Poll. lib. ix. s. 10.

[2] See Curtius, Att. Stud. No. i. p. 8. Sauppe (Philol. xvii. p. 152) reads the passage as follows : κατέβαινον εἰς Πειραιᾶ, ἦν γὰρ ὁ τύπος ἐκείνῃ ὁ τῶν κολαζομένων.

[3] Ἀθήνησι δὲ ἦν ὄρυγμά τι ἐν Κειριαδῶν δήμῳ τῆς Οἰνηΐδος φυλῆς, εἰς ὃ τοὺς ἐπὶ

θανάτῳ καταγνωσθέντας ἐνέβαλλον.—Bekk. An. Græc. p. 219 voc. βάραθρον. But other authorities make the Keiriadæ belong to the tribe Hippothoöntis. Harpocr. voc. βάραθρον. Cf. Hesych.

[4] De Demis urb. Athenarum, p. 16 sq.

Prytanes interfered. The δημιος, or executioner, was called ὁ ἐπι τω προς
τῷ ὀρύγματι;' or ὁ ἐπι του ὀρύγματος, 'the superintendent of the
chasm;' where Taylor, without necessity, would read τῷ ὀρύγματι.'
But to return to the regions.

Melite, besides the Nymphs' Hill, must also have comprehended the
Pnyx, as appears from a scholium on the 'Birds' of Aristophanes, to
which we have before referred. The scholiast there says. "Is not,
some say, the whole of that district in which the Pnyx is included the
Colonus called μισθιος?' so usual is it partly become to call all that
district behind the Long Stoa 'Colonus,' though it is not. For all that
part is Melite, and is so described in the boundary-records (ὁρισμοῖς)
of the city." [4]

If we were certain of the position of the Long Stoa, this passage
would settle with absolute precision the situation of Melite; but unfortunately it is the only place in which that portico is named. There
can, however, be little doubt that it was the portico which extended
from the Peiraic Gate to the agora, which Pausanias describes on entering the city, but to which he gives no name (i. 2, 6 sq.). For the street
from the Peiraic Gate to the agora must have been of considerable
length, and therefore have admitted a Long Stoa; while the Nymphs'
Hill, which we have shown to be a part of Melite, as well as the Pnyx,

[1] Deinarch. c. Demosth. iv. 46, Reiske;
Pollux, viii. c. 7.

[2] Lycurg. c. Leocr. iv. p. 221, Reiske.

[3] Another name for Colonus Agoraeus,
as a place for hiring labourers.

[4] μήποτε οὖν τὸ χωρίον, φασί τινες, ἐκεῖνο
πᾶν ᾧ περιλαμβάνεται καὶ ἡ πνίξ, Κολω-
νός ἐστιν ὁ ἕτερος ὁ μίσθιος λεγόμενος:
οὕτως μέρος τι νῦν σίνηθες γέγονε τὸ Κολωνὸν καλεῖν τὸ ὄπισθεν τῆς μακρᾶς στοᾶς,
ἀλλ' οὐκ ἔστι. Μελίτη γὰρ ἅπαν ἐκεῖνο, ὡς
ἐν τοῖς ὁρισμοῖς γέγραπται τῆς πόλεως.—
v. 998. Dobree has spoilt the sense by
reading οἱ ἕτερος for ὁ ἕτερος: which
would in fact make three Coloni: one in
which was the Pnyx, another the μίσθιος

or ἀγοραῖος, and a third the ἵππιος. What
the scholiast means is: "The Pnyx is
not in that other Colonus called μίσθιος;"
that is, ἄρρ. in contradistinction to
the Colonus ἵππιος. Forchhammer para-
phrases the passage as follows: "Es wäre
wohl die Gegend, sagen einige, jene eben-
in der auch die Pnyx begriffen ist, der
Kolonos sein, der eine von den beiden,
welcher der Lohnarbeiter heisst."— p. 72.
Leake has overlooked this scholium, and
has placed Melite and the Gate Melitides
on the northern side of the city, instead of
the southern: consequently displacing
also the adjoining deme Collytus.

would be accurately spoken of by the scholiast as lying *behind* it. At all events, the scholiast's words show that the Pnyx was in Melitë, and we may pretty confidently assume that this region must have extended within the walls from Colonus Agoræus on the north to the valley or ravine on the south, which separates the Pnyx Hill from the Museum; but we should not be inclined with Forchhammer (p. 64) to include also the latter hill within its boundaries; because we think that the scholiast, by mentioning the Pnyx, meant to designate its extreme boundary.

Having thus endeavoured to fix the limits of Melitë, our next task is to discover the situation of the gate called Melitides, mentioned by Pausanias and by Marcellinus, in his life of Thucydides. From its name, it must have lain somewhere in this region. Now, there are but two possible places for it; viz. on the road between the Nymphs' Hill and the Pnyx Hill, or on that between the Pnyx and the Museum. A further indication of its site is that Thucydides was buried near it, in the place called Cœlë (Κοίλη, or Κοίλη ὁδός—'the hollow way');[1] where also was buried Cimon, the father of Miltiades, outside the city, as Herodotus adds.[2] Now this Cimon was contemporary with Peisistratus, and we must therefore look for Cœlë outside the primitive or Thesean wall; the remains of which in this quarter of the city may, as we have before remarked, be those still visible along the crest of the Pnyx and Museum Hills. We should therefore be inclined to identify as κοίλη ὁδός, or the hollow way, the deep, ravine-like road which runs between these hills. It answers well enough to the name, and there are traces of graves at the spot. The Pylæ Melitides therefore would be near the church of St. Demetrius. The name of the other gate in Melitë, between the Nymphs' Hill and the Pnyx, may probably have been Hippades, or the Equestrian Gate, as assumed by Leake. What gives some little colour to the assumption is, that there were displays of horsemanship at Phalerum, and probably a hippodrome near Peiræeus, for which this gate would have been convenient.[3] Rangabé would derive its name

---

[1] Marcellinus, Vit. Thucyd. sub fin.; Pausan. i. 23, 11.

[2] vi. 103.

[3] Xenoph. Mag. Eq. iii. 1.

from its being accessible only to horsemen and not to chariots,' and this answers well enough to the description of the road by M. Burnouf (above, p. 10). We need only add here that Hyperides, the orator, was interred before the Pylæ Hippades.'

The deme of Melite belonged to the tribe Cecropis. We have already had occasion to observe that it was named after the nymph Melite, one of the mistresses of Heracles, who, according to Hesiod, was a daughter of Myrmex, according to Musæus, of Dius, son of Apollo.' The splendid temple of Heracles ἀλεξίκακος, or 'the averter of evil,' to which we have before adverted, was built in this quarter, according to the scholiast on Aristophanes, in the time of the great plague of Athens, and the statue of the demi-god within it was the work of Ageladas, the master of Pheidias.' But the scholiast must be mistaken, as Muller observes,' either in the time of the building of the temple or in the name of the artist who made the statue; for Ageladas, the master of Pheidias, could hardly have been living in the time of the great plague. He may have been led to his opinion by the epithet ἀλεξίκακος, which however was much older than this period, and probably brought from Delphi to Athens.' In Melite was the Melanippeion, or heroum of Melanippus, son of Theseus,' and the Eurysaceium, or heroum of Eurysaces, son of Ajax, who dwelt in Melite.' Here also in Plutarch's time the house of Phocion could still be seen, roofed with bronze tiles, but in other respects, modest and simple enough.' In the same quarter was a large house in which the tragic actors rehearsed.[10]

The district called Collytus,[11] which also appears to have been a deme or borough of the tribe Ægeis, must have been conterminous with

' Nuove Mem. dell' Inst. 1865, p. 347.

² X. Orat. Vit. (Plut. t. ix. p. 375, Reiske).

³ Harpocr. voc. Melite. But according to our present copies of Hesiod, she was a daughter of Nereus and Doris. Theog. 246.

⁴ Schol. ad Aristoph. Ran. 504; Harpocr. voc. ἐκ Μελίτης.

⁵ De Phidiæ Vita. p. 13 sq.

⁶ Muller, Dorer. i. p. 455.

⁷ Harpocration, voc. Μελανιππειον.

⁸ Plut. Solon, 10; Harper. in voc.

⁹ Plut. Phoc. 18.

¹⁰ Plut. Lex. voc. Μελιτέων οἶκος. Hesych.

¹¹ In inscriptions always written Κολλυτός, in codices generally Κόλιττος.— Sauppe, De Demis. p. 7.

Melitë; for Strabo says that their boundaries, though not marked with posts or walls, were yet known with accuracy enough to say, this is Collytus, this is Melitë.[1] In order more precisely to ascertain its position we may remark that Photius calls it a street ($\sigma\tau\epsilon\nu\omega\pi\acute{o}\varsigma$) in the very middle of the city, having an eponymous hero of the deme, and privileged with the use of the agora.[2] Now all these particulars point precisely enough to the valley lying between the Pnyx and the Areiopagus. For it would have been conterminous with Melitë, in the very heart of the city, and abutting on the agora at its northern extremity. We may infer from a passage in Plutarch, that it was a favourite place of residence,[3] and this also agrees very well with the central situation which we have assigned to it. Dr. Wordsworth indeed says that it was the least respectable quarter of Athens, adding: " Hence it seems that Demosthenes (De Cor. 288. 19, p. 288, Reiske) when he speaks of Æschines as acting with very limited success in a tragic character, intends to add to the bitterness of his sarcasm by specifying also that the representation was in Collytus."[4]   But he does not produce any

[1] As the passage has been differently interpreted we will here insert it : $\mu\grave{\eta}$ $\check{o}\nu\tau\omega\nu$ $\gamma\grave{a}\rho$ $\dot{a}\kappa\rho\iota\beta\tilde{\omega}\nu$ $\check{o}\rho\omega\nu$, $\kappa\alpha\theta\acute{a}\pi\epsilon\rho$ $Ko\lambda\upsilon\tau\tauo\tilde{\upsilon}$ $\kappa\alpha\grave{\iota}$ $M\epsilon\lambda\acute{\iota}\tau\eta\varsigma$ ($o\acute{\iota}o\nu$ $\sigma\tau\eta\lambda\tilde{\omega}\nu$ $\grave{\eta}$ $\pi\epsilon\rho\iota\beta\acute{o}\lambda\omega\nu$) $\tauo\tilde{\upsilon}\tauo$ $\mu\grave{\epsilon}\nu$ $\phi\acute{a}\nu\alpha\iota$ $\check{\epsilon}\chi\epsilon\iota\nu$ $\grave{\eta}\mu\tilde{a}\varsigma$, $\check{o}\tau\iota$ $\tauo\tilde{\upsilon}\tauo$ $\mu\acute{\epsilon}\nu$ $\grave{\epsilon}\sigma\tau\iota$ $Ko\lambda\upsilon\tau\tau\acute{o}\varsigma$, $\tauo\tilde{\upsilon}\tauo$ $\delta\grave{\epsilon}$ $M\epsilon\lambda\acute{\iota}\tau\eta$, $\tauo\grave{\upsilon}\varsigma$ $\check{o}\rhoo\upsilon\varsigma$ $\delta\grave{\epsilon}$ $\mu\grave{\eta}$ $\check{\epsilon}\chi\epsilon\iota\nu$ $\epsilon\grave{\iota}\pi\epsilon\tilde{\iota}\nu$.—lib. i. p. 65, Cas. Dr. Wordsworth (Athens and Attica, p. 151), Leake (Topography of Athens, p. 442, note 3), and Meursius (De pop. Attica, under Colyttus), take this to mean that the boundaries between Melitë and Collytus were actually marked by posts or walls. But then what is the meaning of the last words?—that you cannot tell the boundaries ($\tauo\grave{\upsilon}\varsigma$ $\check{o}\rhoo\upsilon\varsigma$ $\delta\grave{\epsilon}$ $\mu\grave{\eta}$ $\check{\epsilon}\chi\epsilon\iota\nu$ $\epsilon\grave{\iota}\pi\epsilon\tilde{\iota}\nu$). Strabo is talking of places that have no precise boundaries, and illustrates what he means by saying, "just as is the case with Colyttus and Melitë," that is, they are equally without precise boundaries, and you can only say, in a general way, this

is so and so. This is the interpretation of Forchhammer (Topographie, p. 79, note 129) and Sauppe (De Demis, p. 7), and it appears to us to be the more correct one.

[2] Myriob. cod. 243, p. 375 B, Bekk. $\sigma\tau\epsilon\nu\omega\pi\grave{o}\varsigma$ does not necessarily mean a narrow street. $\sigma\tau\epsilon\nu\omega\pi\acute{o}\varsigma$· $\grave{\eta}$ $\dot{a}\gamma\upsilon\iota\acute{a}$, $\kappa\alpha\grave{\iota}$ $\pi\lambda\alpha\tau\epsilon\tilde{\iota}\alpha$, $\kappa\alpha\grave{\iota}$ $\check{a}\mu\phi\omega\deltao\varsigma$. Hesych. and Diodorus Sic. (xii. 10, extr.) use it as equivalent to $\pi\lambda\alpha\tau\epsilon\tilde{\iota}\alpha$. But it may also mean a pass or ravine between two hills, as in the Œdipus T. of Sophocles, v. 1399, and this definition also suits very well the place in question.

[3] $\tau\grave{o}$ $\delta\acute{\epsilon}$ $\sigma\epsilon$ $\mu\grave{\eta}$ $\kappa\alpha\tauo\iota\kappa\epsilon\tilde{\iota}\nu$ $\Sigma\acute{a}\rho\delta\epsilon\iota\varsigma$, $o\grave{\iota}\theta\acute{\epsilon}\nu$ $\grave{\epsilon}\sigma\tau\iota$· $o\grave{\upsilon}\delta\grave{\epsilon}$ $\gamma\grave{a}\rho$ $'A\theta\eta\nu\alpha\tilde{\iota}o\iota$ $\pi\acute{a}\nu\tau\epsilon\varsigma$ $\kappa\alpha\tauo\iota\kappao\tilde{\upsilon}\sigma\iota$ $Ko\lambda\upsilon\tau\tau\acute{o}\nu$.—De Exil. p. 601 (t. viii. p. 372, Reiske).

[4] Athens and Attica, p. 151. We may observe here that Dr. Wordsworth and Leake place Collytus at quite the opposite or northern side of the town.

evidence for this view except that Lucian probably assigned Collytus to Timon, the man-hater, as an appropriate place for his extraction. But a misanthrope might perhaps be sought more successfully in a fashionable than a disreputable neighbourhood; and Timon must have been a rich man to build himself a tower near the Academy. The character which Æschines was performing in Collytus was that of Œnomaus; but it does not seem at all probable that Demosthenes meant any sarcasm by adding the name of the place; for that is inserted also by Harpocration[1] in relating the same adventure, after Demochares, and by Apollonius, in his sketch of the life of Æschines;[2] and the intention of these writers could hardly have been sarcastic, but merely to identify the occurrence. Besides Æschines appears to have lived in Collytus, for he says in one of his letters, that he had dwelt there forty-five years.[3] Nay, it seems not improbable that the mishap may actually have occurred in the house in Melite, where, as we have said, the tragic actors rehearsed; for, as we have seen, the boundaries of Melitë and Collytus were not very accurately defined, and one might often have been mentioned for the other. Dr. Wordsworth's charge might, perhaps, derive some colour from a passage in Plutarch's life of Demosthenes, where the orator retorting upon Demades, who had compared himself to Athena, exclaimed: "This Athena was caught in adultery not long ago in Collytus."[4] But everybody knows that such things might happen in the most fashionable quarters. Collytus was the deme of Plato, the most eloquent of Attic writers,[5] though according to some accounts he was actually born in Ægina, whither his father had been sent to divide lands; so that it appears a man retained his paternal deme wherever he might happen to be born. We have already said that Timon the misanthrope was also a Collytean.[6]

---

[1] voc. Ἰσχανδρος.

[2] ap. Reiske, Orat. t. iii. p. 13.

[3] Ibid. p. 674. The genuineness of these letters has indeed been much questioned, but some of them seem to be authentic. We have touched on this subject in another place. At all events the writer, in so precise a statement, would probably have followed some authority or tradition.

[4] cap. 11.

[5] Diog. Laert. Vit. Plat. lib. iii. s. 3.

[6] Lucian. Tim. 7; Pausan. i. 30, 4.

From what has been said, we hope it will appear with as much certainty as can be reasonably expected in such a matter, that the more important half of the city, from the Acropolis westwards, was occupied by the four regions or demes mentioned, namely, the Inner Cerameicus, including the agora, Colonus Agoræus, Melitë, and Collytus. The Acropolis itself appears to have been uninhabited, at all events after the Persian wars, and the same must have been the case with the eastern portion of the Areiopagus, appropriated to the court of the same name; its western and southern slopes may perhaps have formed part of Melitë or Collytus. In the eastern quarters of Athens it is not easy to arrange with anything like precision the situation of the different regions. It seems, however, highly probable, as Leake has assumed, that the region called Cydathenæum, whose name suggests a reference to some ancient and distinguished part of Athens, may have lain under the southern and eastern side of the Acropolis, as we know from Thucydides that this was the oldest part of the city, and contained some of the most primitive and venerable shrines. We learn from Hesychius that it was a deme within the city, belonging to the tribe Pandionis.[1] This region, therefore, would have contained the district called Limnæ, or 'the marsh,' for such, from its low situation, it might once very probably have been. It was no deme, as the scholiast on Callimachus improperly calls it,[2] who appears to have confounded it with a place of the same name on the borders of Messenia, but only a district (τόπος, χωρίον).[3] The Limnæ included the Lenæum, or enclosure sacred to the Lenæan Dionysus, containing two temples to him and the Dionysiac theatre, which will be described in the sequel.

It is not probable that the Cydathenæum embraced the Museium Hill, and the whole of the valley under its eastern side to the walls of Themistocles. We should be inclined to place here the Scambonidæ, though we have little or no evidence to adduce in support of the conjecture, except that there was a lane in that region called after Myrmex

---

[1] Κυδαθηναῖος δῆμος τῆς Πανδιονίδος φυλῆς ἐν ἄστει.--in voc.

[2] In Hymn. 3; cf. Strabo, viii. p. 362;

[3] Harpocr. in voc.; schol. ad Aristoph. Ran. 218.

Pausan. iii. 2, 6; iv. 31, 3.

(Μυρμηκος ἀτραπός), son of Melanippus, who, as we have seen, had a heroum in Melite, which must in part have adjoined the Museum.[1] Aristophanes seems facetiously to allude to it as the 'Ant's Path,' an interpretation which it would literally admit.[1] It seems at all events pretty certain that the Scambonidæ were a city deme of the tribe Leontis. It is mentioned by Aristophanes and Pausanias, and by Plutarch, as the deme of Alcibiades,[3] but there is nothing in these passages to show its situation.

There must doubtless have been a gate in the valley under the eastern side of the Museium, about two hundred and fifty yards south of the present Military Hospital, where there are evident traces of the ancient wall; and there is tolerably satisfactory proof that this must have been the Itonian Gate. The existence of a gate at this spot may be inferred not only from the nature of the ground but also from the account of Pausanias, who, when describing his arrival at Athens from Phalerum mentions having seen here the monument of Antiopē. Now, as Phalerum lay more to the east than Peiraeus, a gate leading to it may be conveniently sought in this quarter; and it appears from a passage before cited from Plutarch (supra, p. 64) that a monument either to Antiope or Hippolyta, he was uncertain which, lay here, near the temple of the Olympian Gæa.[4] The name of the gate may be inferred from a passage in the dialogue entitled 'Axiochus,' sometimes ascribed to Plato. Socrates is there described as having gone out at a gate leading to Cynosarges[5]—therefore to the north-east of the one we are considering— and to have got to the Ilissus, when he sees Cleinias and others running towards Callirrhoë, which must have been on his right hand. They all turn back in order to visit Cleinias' father, who lived near the gate

---

[1] Hesych. and Phot. in voc. This Myrmex, being the grandson of Theseus, must have been different from the father of Melite.

[2] Thesmoph. 100.

[3] Aristoph. Vesp. 81; Pausan. i. 38. 2; Plut. Alc. 22. Leake (vol. i. p. 634) and Sauppe (De Demis, p. 16) place Scambonidæ within the city.

[4] τὴν στήλην τὴν παρὰ τὸ τῆς Γῆς τῆς Ὀλυμπίας ἱερόν.—Thuc. 27. The site of this temple will be shown in the description of the city by Pausanias.

[5] ἐξιώντι μοι ἐς Κυνόσαργες καὶ γενομένῳ μοι κατὰ τὸν Ἰλισσόν, κ.τ.λ.—Axiochus. init.

called the Pylæ Itoniæ,[1] where was the monument of the Amazon, keeping along outside the wall. Recent discoveries have confirmed the existence of a gate at this spot.[2]

The gate at which Socrates had gone out when he met with Cleinias must have been near the south-eastern extremity of the peribolos of the Olympium, which is the only place where he could have seen Cleinias running towards Callirrhoë, and suits the description of his turning back with him and keeping along under the city wall till they arrived at the Itonian Gate. It suits also with the circumstance of Socrates being on his road to Cynosarges, which, from a gate near the Olympium, would have lain on his left hand a little higher up the stream. For Pausanias, when describing this quarter, and also proceeding up the river, or to his left, enumerates the objects after the Olympium in the following order: the temple of Apollo, Aphrodite in the Gardens, Cynosarges, the Lyceium, Artemis Agrotera, and then the Stadium. We have described more particularly the site of Cynosarges in another part of this work when accompanying the route of Pausanias, and therefore it may suffice to say here that it probably stood nearly opposite the Stadium, but a little to the west of it. Cynosarges lay in the district, or deme, called Diomeia, after its eponymous hero Diomus, a son of Collytus. Diomus was sacrificing here to Heracles when a white dog ran off with part of the victim, whence the name of the place.[3] Diomeia probably extended a good way beyond the river outside the walls, but lay not at all within it. The gate at which Socrates went out seems to have been the Diomeian Gate, which is mentioned by Hesychius.[4] But this proves nothing as to Diomeia being a city deme, as the gates were often named

---

[1] τὴν παρὰ τὸ τεῖχος ἥειμεν ταῖς Ἰτωνίαις, πλησίον γὰρ ᾤκει τῶν πυλῶν, πρὸς τῇ Ἀμαζονίδι στήλῃ.—p. 365 (iii. iii. 508, Bekk.). But the text seems to be wrongly punctuated, and perhaps we should read: τὴν παρὰ τὸ τεῖχος ᾖμεν, ταῖς Ἰτωνίαις πλησίον γὰρ ᾤκει τῶν πυλῶν—"we took the road along the wall, for he lived near the Itonian Gate:" literally, "near the Itonian of the gates." We find a similar

idiom in Thucydides: τοὺς ἄλλους μετὰ τοῦ Κλεαρίδα καθίστη ἐπὶ τὰς Θρᾳκίας καλουμένας τῶν πυλῶν.—v. 10.

[2] Philologus, xxv. p. 337.

[3] Hesych. Suid. Stephan. Byz. in Κυνόσαργες.

[4] μήποτε οὖν ἀντὶ τοῦ, Διομῆσι πύλαις, Δημιάσιν εἶπεν, διὰ τὴν ἐγγύτητα τῶν ὀνομάτων;—Hesych. in Δημιάσι πύλαις.

from distant places to which they led, as the Porta Acharnensis, Peiraïeus, and the ancient appellation of the Dipylon, Thriasis. Plutarch in his treatise on banishment, says, "Would Athenians who had removed from Melite to Diomeia consider themselves exiles and foreigners?"[1] Why he should have selected Diomeia for the comparison is not plain, unless from its being without the walls, though only just without; so that residence there might literally, but hardly virtually, be deemed exclusion from the city.

The next gate must be sought some seven hundred yards to the north-east of the Diomeian, at a point near the palace garden where the line of wall having reached its easternmost extension forms a rather acute angle and trends away to the north-west. This gate, as will be shown when describing the route of Pausanias, must have been the Diocharis, leading to the Lyceium. The only other gate in all the remaining line of wall which we can lay down with any probability and from inference, is the Acharnian.[2] The borough of Acharnæ, from which it took its name, must have lain about seven or eight miles due north of Athens. This may be shown as follows: Brasidas, having passed Eleusis and the Thriasian plain, defeats the Attic cavalry at Rheitoi, and advances through Cropeia, having Mount Ægaleos on his right - consequently in a northerly direction—till he arrives at Acharnæ.[3] Again, Thrasybulus, having taken post at Phylé, on Mount Parnes, descends, and attacks the Athenian camp at Acharnæ, and thence marches to Peiræeus.[4] He was therefore marching in a southerly direction, and Acharnæ might lie in about the middle of a line drawn from Phylé to Peiræeus. It is a reasonable inference, therefore, that the gate leading to it might lie in about the middle of the northern portion of the city wall; and it is here that Curtius places it, at the top of the modern Æolus Street, between the bank and the new theatre; a site which had been previously selected by Leake, and also, though beyond the true line, by Forchhammer.

[1] p. 601. t. viii. p. 372. Reiske.

[2] Ἀχαρικαὶ πύλαι Ἀθήνησιν.—Hesych. voc. Ἀχάρνη.

[3] Thucyd. ii. 19.

[4] Xenoph. Hell. ii. 4. 2; Diodor. Sic. iv. 32.

Besides the seven gates mentioned, namely, Dipylon, Peiraïcæ, Hippades, Melitides, Itoniæ, Diomeiæ, and Diocharis—there were doubtless several more, the names of which are not found in ancient writers. It cannot be doubted, also, that there were more city demes or regions than the seven we have described; and a glance at the map will show that a large space in the northern and eastern quarters of the town has been left unaccounted for. According to Strabo, the district on the northern side of the Acropolis, on which the Roman market-place was built, had been called in ancient times Eretria ;[1] but there is no trace, either in writers or inscriptions, of any Attic deme of that name. It may be observed that the seven demes which we have named as being within the walls—Cœlë was without—all belonged to different tribes, viz., the Ceramenses to the tribe Acamantis, the Colonenses to Antiochis, the Melitenses to Cecropis, the Collytenses to Ægeïs, the Ceiriadæ to Hippothoöntis, the Cydathenæenses to Pandionis, and the Scambonidæ to Leontis. It is, therefore, a plausible conjecture of Sauppe's,[2] that when Cleisthenes made a new division of the tribes he so arranged that a deme, or part of one, belonging to each should have a place within the walls. And if this view is correct, it furnishes an additional reason for excluding Diomeia from the city, as that deme belonged to the tribe Ægeïs, already represented by the Collytenses. According to this principle, there would remain three city demes to be accounted for, situated in the north-eastern part of Athens, but what were their names and positions we have no materials for deciding. It is not surprising that this quarter should not be so well known as the others. It seems to have been the last occupied, and to have had no temples or other public buildings to attract attention, and call forth allusions from the ancient writers ; and thus Pausanias does not appear to have visited more than that part of it which lay immediately under the Acropolis.

Whether the civic *demi* were the same as the *comæ* (κῶμαι), into which Solon and Cleisthenes are said to have divided the city,[3] is a

[1] lib. x. p. 447.

[2] De Demis, p. 19.

[3] διελόμενοι τὴν μὲν πόλιν κατὰ κώμας,

τὴν δὲ χώραν κατὰ δήμους.—Isocr. Areop. p. 149.

question that has caused a great difference of opinion among the learned. We find such comae mentioned by ancient writers, and their inhabitants under the name of cometae (κωμῆται)[1]. In the passage cited from Isocrates, the comae of the town are paralleled with the demi of the country; from which we might infer that, though different in name, they were the same in character; and, if this be not so, we are unable to say what the comae were.

Although we can indicate the sites of only seven gates, yet they are so placed that, with the aid of vestiges of the wall still discoverable between them, its line may be laid down with tolerable accuracy. It is well known that the itinerary stade, as computed from actual observation, and in comparison with the measurements given in ancient authors, differs from the Olympic stade in being one-sixth less, and consisting of five hundred feet instead of six hundred feet; and as the measurement of the Long Walls given by Thucydides agrees exactly with this smaller stade,[2] it may be assumed that he applied the same standard to the walls of the city. Now he says that the *guarded* part of the walls (τὸ φυλασσόμενον) was forty-three stadia in length, and that the part between the Phaleric and the Long Wall was unguarded, but gives no dimensions.[3] But the whole circuit of the wall as we have described it, taking, with Leake, the remains on the Pnyx Hill and the Museium to be part of it, and that the line passed through the gates we have laid down, only measures about forty-three smaller stadia, allowing for irregularities of surface, angles, and towers, and thus leaves nothing to spare for the unguarded part. Hence, we might almost be inclined to suspect that the words τὸ φυλασσόμενον are a gloss that has crept into

---

[1] Aristoph. Nub. 965: Lysistr. 5. οἱ δὲ τοὺς ἐν τῇ πόλει δήμους κώμας φασὶ προσαγορεύεσθαι· καὶ κωμήτας τοὺς δημότας ἐν πόλει.—Phot. Lex. voc. κώμην. Cf. Sauppe, De Demis, p. 11.

[2] Curtius, Erläuternder Text, S. 32.

[3] τοῦ τε γὰρ Φαληρικοῦ τείχους στάδιοι ἦσαν πέντε καὶ τριάκοντα πρὸς τὸν κύκλον τοῦ ἄστεος, καὶ αὐτοῦ τοῦ κύκλου τὸ φυλασσόμενον τρεῖς καὶ τεσσαράκοντα· ἔστι δὲ αὐτοῦ ὃ καὶ ἀφύλακτον ἦν, τὸ μεταξὺ τοῦ τε μακροῦ καὶ τοῦ Φαληρικοῦ· τὰ δὲ μακρὰ τείχη πρὸς τὸν Πειραιᾶ τεσσαράκοντα σταδίων, ὧν τὸ ἔξωθεν ἐτηρεῖτο· καὶ τοῦ Πειραιῶς ξὶν Μουνυχίᾳ ἑξήκοντα μὲν σταδίων ὁ ἅπας περίβολος, τὸ δ' ἐν φυλακῇ ὂν, ἥμισυ τούτου.—Thucyd. ii. 13.

the text of Thucydides, especially as they cannot be construed grammatically; for, as the sentence stands, the neuter singular τὸ φυλασσόμενον must be made to agree with the plural verb ἦσαν. It may be added that Thucydides has been very precise in giving the *whole* measure of the peribolus of the Peiraïc fortification, though only half of it was guarded, yet, as the text stands, he omits giving the whole circuit of the city walls. We dare not, however, venture to propose any emendation of a passage which has been passed over by so many great critics.[1] The dictum of the scholiast that the unguarded part was seventeen stadia is evidently intended to make up the round number of sixty for the whole peribolus. It is impossible to believe so absurd a statement, as it would leave nearly a third of the *enceinte* unguarded.

The only tolerably probable method of reconciling present appearances with the words of Thucydides is a hypothesis of Dr. Curtius,[2] that the remains of the wall traversing the Pnyx and Museium hills belong to the primitive or Thesean inclosure. This may likely enough have been the case; for the wall in question, as we have before observed (p. 84), probably surrounded the Acropolis at a radius about equal to the distance from the Acropolis to the Arch of Hadrian, which answers very well to the situation of the existing vestiges. The ancient wall must doubtless have traversed the summit of the hills, for it would have been of little use in the valley. And as Themistocles is said to have enlarged the circuit on every side, it is not unlikely, as Curtius thinks, that his wall embraced all that hilly region which from the Museium, the Pnyx Hill, and the Nymphs' Hill, slopes down to the Ilissus, ending near that river in an abrupt and narrow apex, and thus forming an irregular triangle. Curtius supports his view by the fact that there are vestiges, though scanty ones, of a line of wall in the circuit indicated. This would give the *enceinte* a circumference of about fifty smaller stades, consequently leaving seven stades for the unguarded part adverted to by Thucydides. It is difficult to verify this

<hr>

[1] Curtius, Att. Stud. i. 75, note, suspects the whole member ἔστι δὲ αὐτοῦ . . . τοῦ Φαληρικοῦ to be a gloss: but his only objection to it, the position of the καὶ before ἀφύλακτον, is quite unfounded.

[2] Attische Stud. No. 1, S. 58 sqq.

last assumption, because we do not know where the Phaleric Long
Wall joined the city wall   The junction, however, was probably
near the Itonian Gate, since Pausanias arrives there in walking
from Phalerum to Athens. If this gate, as we have endeavoured to
show (p. 105), lay somewhere in front of the Military Hospital, then
a distance of seven stades would about bring us to the point where
the southern Long Wall began.   But the question is beset with
almost insuperable difficulties, and we will here mention one of them.
It has been seen above (p. 100), that there were tombs before the
gate Melitides, which must therefore have been in the wall which
traverses the summit of the Pnyx Hill; and as Thucydides the historian was buried there, long after the time of Themistocles, how
can we reconcile this fact with his having enclosed all this quarter
in his wall?

Nothing can be decided about the population of Athens. In the
time of Xenophon there appear to have been 10,000 houses;[1] but it
is not stated whether this enumeration was confined to the city, or
included the population of the ports and suburbs. Mr. Clinton takes
it of the asty only, and assuming that each house contained 12
persons, consequently reckons that there were 120,000 inhabitants in
the city proper; to which he adds 40,000 more for Peiraeus, Munychia,
and Phalerum.[2] Boeckh assumes that the population of the same places
was 180,000.[3] Leake gives them at 192,000, taking the houses of the
asty and suburban demi at 12,000, and allowing 16 inhabitants for
each house.[4] Those who are curious in the matter are referred to the
authors cited, for any minute examination of it would demand more
space than we can afford; and after all, the data are so unsatisfactory
that nothing like an approach to accuracy can be made. Thus, for
instance, even 12 persons to each house (the lowest number assumed
in the foregoing calculations) appears very large for the miserable
hovels of which Athens principally consisted. But it must be always

[1] Mem. Socr. iii. 6. 14.   Eng. tr.
[2] Fast. Hell. vol. ii. p. 484 (395).   [4] Topogr. of Athens, vol. i. app. 21.
[3] Public Economy of Athens, p. 39.   p. 622, 2nd ed.

remembered that the slaves outnumbered the free citizens in the proportion probably of 4 or even 6 to 1.

Themistocles appears to have completed the city wall and the ring wall at Peiræus; but the Long Walls which connected the port towns with Athens, though seemingly designed by him,[1] were executed by his successors. The haste with which he carried out the walling of the city, the stratagem by which he gained time for it, by amusing the Lacedæmonians, and the signs which the wall showed of its hurried construction, are related by Thucydides.[2] The walls at Peiræus, on the contrary, were built in the strongest and most durable manner of solid masonry. They were of immense thickness, but carried up to only half the height that Themistocles had intended. Their actual height is stated by Appian[3] to have been forty $\pi\eta\chi\epsilon\iota\varsigma$, or more than sixty feet. Appian there says that they were built by Pericles in the Peloponnesian war, which is doubtless an error into which he has fallen through the circumstance that Pericles completed the Peiræan fortifications by the addition of the middle or southern wall. Remains of the Peiraïc wall still extant confirm Thucydides' account of the solidity of its construction.[4] It will be convenient here, in order to keep the subject together, to describe the port towns and the Long Walls, though these, as we have said, were not completed till some time afterwards.

Here a much debated question arises, which from its topographical importance must be examined. Till about thirty years ago Phalerum, the original port of Athens, was generally thought to have been situated at the western side of the bay of the same name, in that little natural cove or harbour now called Phanari. But Dr. Ulrichs, who was professor of Latin literature at the university of Athens at the

---

[1] τὴν πόλιν ὅλην ἁρμοττόμενος πρὸς τὴν θάλασσαν. . . . Θεμιστοκλῆς δ᾽ οὐχ ὡς ὁ κωμικὸς λέγει, τῇ πόλει τὸν Πειραιᾶ προσέμαξεν, ἀλλὰ τὴν πόλιν ἐξῆψε τοῦ Πειραιῶς.—Plut. Them. 19. The passage in Aristophanes is Eq. 815; where the scholiast remarks: αἰνίττεται διὰ τούτων τὰ μακρὰ τείχη παρὰ τοῖς Ἀθηναίοις καλού-

μενα. These passages seem to show that the Long Walls lay at least in the plan of Themistocles; but Leake doubts whether he ever contemplated them (vol. i. p. 417).

[2] lib. i. c. 90 sqq.

[3] Bell. Mithr. t. i. p. 324, ed. Toll.

[4] Leake, vol. i. p. 411.

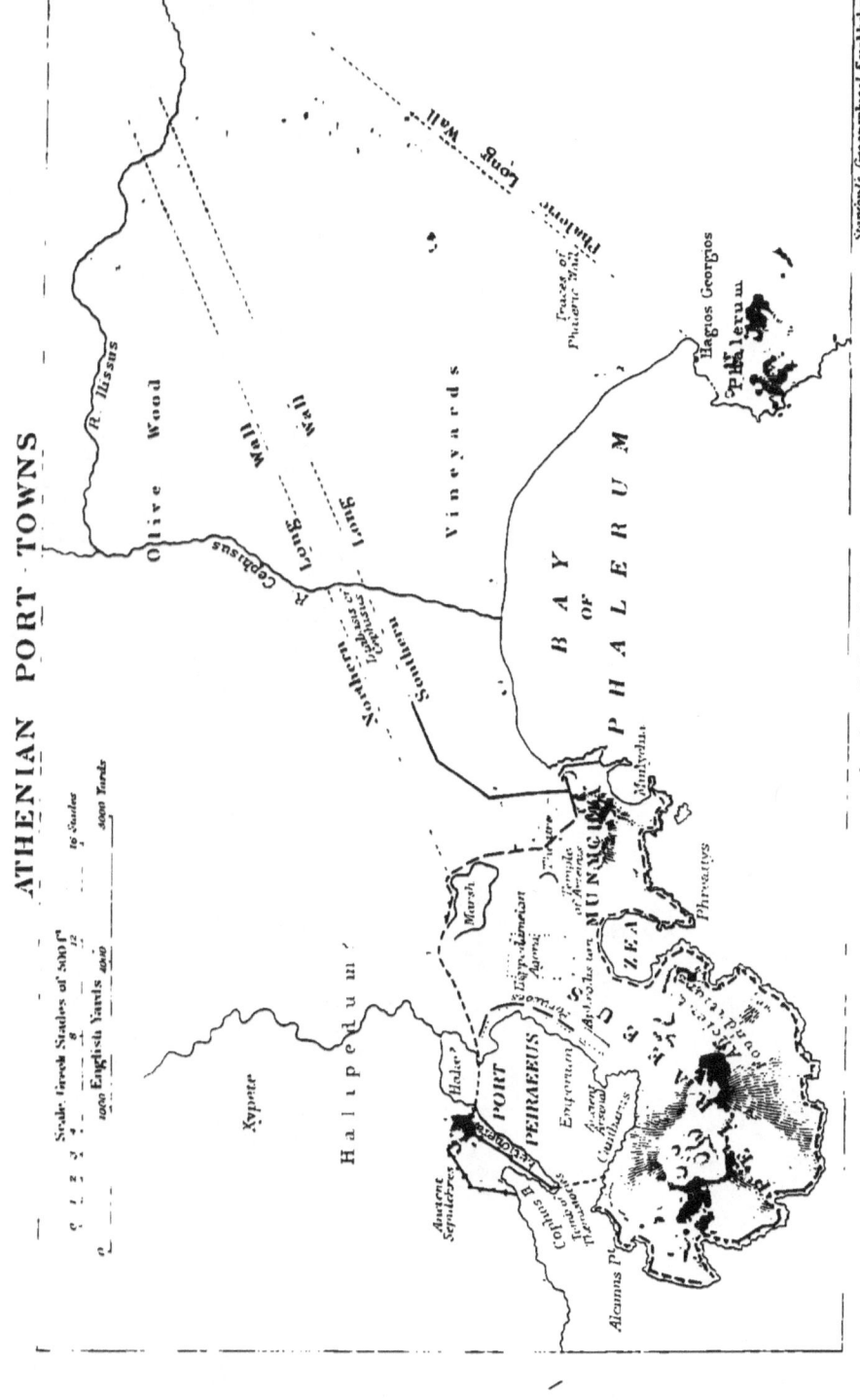

ATHENIAN PORT TOWNS

London: Bell & Daldy.

Stanford's Geographical Establishment.

time referred to, was induced to place it on the opposite side of the bay, near the church of St. George (Ἅγιος Γεώργιος), and it must be confessed that this view obviates some difficulties attendant upon the previous one. For instance, it can hardly be disputed that Athens was at one time connected with its ports by means of three long walls, the Phaleric, the Northern, and the Southern; yet if all the ports were in the Peiraïc peninsula, it is difficult to imagine what could have been the use of the third wall; while, if Phalerum lay on the east side of the bay, it is evident that the southern, or middle wall, would have been required as a protection against a hostile landing in the bay. And it has never, we believe, been pretended that any traces of a third Long Wall could be discovered in a line between Athens and Peiraeus.

It has indeed been sometimes asserted, that a third wall never existed, and some colourable grounds are not wanting for this opinion. Thus, when Athens was taken by the Lacedæmonians in B.C. 404, it was only proposed that ten stades of *each of the two*[1] Long Walls should be levelled, and no mention is made of a third. But it is evident that the partial destruction of both the Long Walls between Athens and Peiraeus would have admitted an enemy into the whole system of fortifications. He would then have been *within* the Phaleric Wall, and the port of Phalerum would have lain at his mercy.[2] Hence the Athenians seem to have discovered that the Phaleric Wall was of little or no use; especially as an attack from the south was hardly to be expected, that side of the town being covered by Mount Hymettus; and Athens, we believe, was never threatened in that quarter but once, namely, in the second year of the Peloponnesian war.[3] For these reasons, the Phaleric Wall seems to have been allowed to fall into decay; and an inscription relating to the repairs of the Long Walls,

---

[1] προεκαλεῖτο δέ, τῶν μακρῶν τειχῶν ἐπὶ δέκα σταδίους καθελεῖν ἑκάτερον.— Xenoph. Hell. ii. 2, 15. Cf. Lysias c. Agorat. p. 451 sqq. (Reiske).

[2] See Forchhammer, Topogr. p. 9. It may be observed, however, that the two Peiraïc Long Walls were sometimes regarded as forming *one* fortification, the interior of which was inhabited; and in this view the demolition by the Spartans may possibly have included the Phaleric Long Wall.

[3] Thucyd. ii. 55.

apparently about B.C. 335, mentions only two, the North Wall and the South.[1] Hence later writers allude only to the north and south walls, or those which connected Athens with Peiræeus; called by Greek authors σκέλη, and by Latin ones *brachia*.[2] These passages, indeed, might be urged in favour of the view that there were never more than two; but the evidence on the other side is too strong to be overcome. For we find three distinct names for the walls: the North Wall, the South Wall, and the Phaleric; and we find the South Wall sometimes called the *Middle* Wall (τὸ διὰ μέσου τεῖχος),[3] which clearly indicates three. And Harpocration, quoting Antiphon and Aristophanes, says categorically, that there were three walls, called respectively the North, the South, and the Phaleric.[4]

Again, it is said that one of the reasons of Themistocles for transferring the harbour from Phalerum to Peiræeus was, that the latter offered the convenience of three ports instead of one.[5] Now, it is difficult to say what these three ports could have been unless they were those of Peiræeus, Munychia, and Zea, at present called Port Drako,[6] Fanari, and Paschalimani or Stratiotiki. And even if the largest port, Drako, could be conveniently divided into three, so as to answer the requirements of Pausanias' description, we should then have one port too many, and unaccounted for, namely, that of Zea. These arguments are supported by the fact that at the part of the bay indicated, near Agios Georgios, there are undoubted remains of an ancient harbour, and

---

[1] See Leake, vol. i. p. 617.

[2] Æsch. De falsa Leg. p. 335 sqq. Reiske; Liv. xxxi. 26; Strabo, p. 395, &c.

[3] Plat. Gorg. 455 (ii. i. 22, Bekk.).

[4] Ἀντιφῶν πρὸς Νικοκλέα· τριῶν ὄντων τειχῶν ἐν τῇ Ἀττικῇ, ὡς καὶ Ἀριστοφάνης φησὶν ἐν Τριφάλητι, τοῦ τε βορείου, καὶ τοῦ νοτίου καὶ τοῦ Φαληρικοῦ, διὰ μέσου τούτων ἔλεγετο τὸ νότιον, οὗ μνημονεύει καὶ Πλάτων ἐν Γοργίᾳ.—voc. διὰ μεσ. τείχους.

[5] Pausan. i. 1, 2.

[6] Dhrako (δράκων) in modern Greek means not only a serpent, but also any monster, and in the present instance appears to have signified a colossal lion of white marble which stood at the head of the harbour; whence the Italians gave it the name of Porto Leone. Wheler saw it in this place. He describes it as ten feet high in a sitting posture, and from its having a hole answering to its mouth he took it to have been a fountain.—Journey, p. 418. It was carried to Venice after the capture of Athens by the Venetians in 1687.—Leake, Topography, &c. vol. i. p. 371.

of other objects which may have belonged to the town of Phalerum, described by Pausanias; as the tambour of a large Doric pillar, quarried stones, cisterns hewn in the rocks, fragments of tile and pottery.[1] The author may add the testimony of a gentleman[2] who accompanied Dr. Ulrichs in two or three of his visits to this spot, and discovered by diving the foundations of a mole of solid Hellenic masonry. The same gentleman also observed in company with the learned professor distinct vestiges of an ancient wall in the direction between Athens and Agios Georgios. And Curtius says that at its termination large square blocks of stone (Quaderreihen) project into the sea, for the purpose of protecting a landing-place.[3]

Ulrichs' hypothesis agrees well enough with the measurement given by Thucydides of the Phaleric Wall, which, he says, was thirty-five stades.[4] Measuring from the Itonian Gate, where it is probable that this wall may have begun, since Pausanias, as is evident from the objects which he mentions, arrived at that gate in walking from Phalerum, there are thirty-two of the smaller stades between it and Agios Georgios in an absolutely straight line, and something may surely be allowed for so trifling a deviation from it, especially near the terminus. That there must have been an interval between it and the Long Wall, and that consequently they started from different points, is plain from Thucydides' saying that this interval was unguarded. On the other hand, if the Phaleric Wall was carried to Phanari, on the western side of the bay, it would be impossible to bring it under forty stades, from whatever point of the city wall it may have started. Again, Pausanias says,[5] that Phalerum was anciently selected for the port of

[1] Dr. Ulrichs' pamphlet, p. 9, Eng. tr.

[2] Sir Patrick Colquhoun, then residing at Athens as Hanseatic consul. I am informed by Dr. Finlay the historian, a resident of Athens, that the Albanian peasantry called the spot Phalerea before Ulrichs' opinion was broached.

[3] Dr. Ulrichs does not speak very confidently. He says: "I think I recognized it many points in the vineyards, elevated some feet above the marshy hollow, on the right hand side of the road from Athens, indisputable remains of the old Phaleric Wall." Pamph. p. 9. Dr. Curtius says more positively that there are remains in two places, consisting of courses of stone resting on rubble. Erläuter. and Text, p. 84.

[4] lib. ii. 13.   lib. i. 1. 2.

Athens, because the sea there is at a less distance from it than at any other point; an assertion which suits St. George but not Fanari. It was also conveniently situated for the south-eastern quarter of the city, which, as we have seen, was the earliest inhabited.

Assuming then that Phalerum lay near St. George and the Three Towers (Τρεῖς Πύργοι) on the eastern side of the bay, we will now proceed to the Peiræeus; first remarking that in this view Cape Colias must be placed a few miles further south, at a promontory on which stands the church of Agios Cosmas.

The whole peninsula, probably once an island, which projects into the Saronic Gulf at a distance of about five miles south-west of Athens, appears to have been called Peiræeus, and formed one of the Attic demes of the tribe Hippothoöntis. The largest of its three harbours seems also to have borne the name par excellence of Peiræeus, and it is thus that we must interpret a passage in Harpocration, where he says that one of the headlands of Peiræeus was called Eetioneia.[1] The word which he uses (ἄκρα) more generally signifies a "height," and the peninsula is actually divided into two heights; a more extensive but less elevated one in its southern portion, and a higher and smaller one on the north-east where the peninsula joins the main land. But the former could not have been Eetioneia, which, as is plain from Thucydides, was the narrow tongue of land which projects itself into the sea on the western side of the large harbour. As the passage is of great topographical importance, we give it in a note.[2] The entrance to the

---

[1] 'Ητιωνία . . . οὕτως ἐκαλεῖτο ἡ ἑτέρα τοῦ Πειραιέως ἄκρα.

[2] ᾠκοδόμουν δὲ ἔτι προθυμότερον τὸ ἐν τῇ 'Ητιωνείᾳ τεῖχος· ἦν δὲ τοῦ τείχους ἡ γνώμη αὕτη . . . οὐχ ἵνα τοὺς ἐν Σάμῳ ἦν βίᾳ ἐπιπλέωσι, μὴ δέξωνται ἐς τὸν Πειραιᾶ, ἀλλ' ἵνα τοὺς πολεμίους μᾶλλον, ὅταν βού-λωνται, καὶ ναυσὶ καὶ πεζῷ δέξωνται· χηλὴ γάρ ἐστι τοῦ Πειραιῶς ἡ 'Ητιώνεια, καὶ παρ' αὐτὴν εὐθὺς ὁ ἔσπλους ἐστίν· ἐτει-χίζετο οὖν οὕτω ξὺν τῷ πρότερον πρὸς ἤπειρον ὑπάρχοντι τείχει, ὥστε καθεζομένων

ἐς αὐτὸ ἀνθρώπων ὀλίγων ἄρχειν τοῦ γε ἔσπλου· ἐπ' αὐτὸν γὰρ τὸν ἐπὶ τῷ στόματι τοῦ λιμένος στενοῦ ὄντος τὸν ἕτερον πύργον ἐτελεύτα τό τε παλαιὸν τὸ πρὸς ἤπειρον καὶ τὸ ἐντὸς τὸ καινὸν τεῖχος, τειχιζόμενον πρὸς θάλασσαν. διῳκοδόμησαν δὲ καὶ στοάν, ἥπερ ἦν μεγίστη καὶ ἐγγύτατα τούτου εὐθὺς ἐχομένη ἐν τῷ Πειραιεῖ, καὶ ἦρχον αὐτοὶ αὐτῆς, ἐς ἣν καὶ τὸν σῖτον ἠνάγκαζον πάντας τὸν ὑπάρχοντά τε καὶ τὸν ἐσπλέοντα ἐξαι-ρεῖσθαι καὶ ἐντεῦθεν προαιρουμένους πωλεῖν. —viii. 90. This passage suffices to show

harbour was formed by the extremity of this tongue, and by a headland called Alcimus, projecting towards it from the opposite shore.
These were prolonged by moles, called χηλαι, or "claws," from their
resemblance to a crab; and at the extremity of each was a tower. Such
was the usual construction of Greek harbours, formed, where possible,
of land-locked basins, and capable of being shut up by means of a chain
from mole to mole, which rendered them λιμένες κλειστοι, or enclosed
ports. There are vestiges of such a mole at Munychia. The inlet in the
west of Eetioneia was perhaps the Κωφός Λιμήν (the dumb or noise-
less harbour).[1] The Thieves Harbour (Φωρῶν Λιμήν) where skippers
might run in and out as they pleased, must, according to Strabo's
description, have been the next inlet on the west, opposite the little
island of Psyttaleia.[2] The north-eastern height of the peninsula, called
Munychia, was usually considered a part of Peiraeus.[3] Strabo describes
Munychia as a hill (λόφος) forming a sort of distinct peninsula, which
it may be said to do from having the harbour of Zea (Paschalimani)
on the west and the bay of Phalerum on the east. Strabo adds, that
under it lay three harbours, by which he can only mean Peiraeus, Zea,
and Munychia;[4] for as Ulrichs observes,[5] after the sentence referred to
he proceeds to describe Athens, and then two or three pages further on
returns to the sea-coast and mentions Phalerum.[6] Strabo's description
does not suit the southern part of the peninsula, where Leake places
Munychia; for, although there is a height there, it has not near the
elevation of that in the north-eastern quarter, nor can the three
harbours be said to lie under it. The description tallies only with the

---

the double meaning of Peiraeus, as a
port and as a district; the name being
used in the former sense in the first
two instances, and in the latter in the
third. So also Bekker, Anecdota Gr.:
Ἠετιώνεια, μέρος τι τοῦ Πειραιῶς.—p.
262, 25.

[1] Xenoph. Hell. ii. 4, 31.

[2] Strabo, p. 395; Demosth. πρὸς Λα-
κρίτου παραγραφήν. p. 932, Reiske.

[3] Μουνυχία τόπος τοῦ Πειραιῶς.—Plut.
Lex.

[4] εἶθ' ὁ Πειραιεὺς καὶ αὐτὸς ἐν τοῖς δήμοις
ταττόμενος, καὶ ἡ Μουνυχία· λόφος δ' ἐστὶν
ἡ Μουνυχία χερρονησίζων, καὶ κοῖλος . . .
ὑποπίπτουσι δ' αὐτῷ λιμένες τρεῖς.—p. 395.

[5] Topography of the Harbours, Mr.
Ewing Pye Colquhoun's translation. p. 9.

[6] μετὰ δὲ τὸν Πειραιᾶ, Φαληρεῖς δῆμος
ἐν τῇ ἐφεξῆς παραλίᾳ.—p. 398.

north-eastern height, and this is an additional proof that Phalerum could not have lain here. The three harbours of Peiræeus are mentioned by other writers, as Scylax,[1] Nepos,[2] and Pausanias;[3] and since, as Ulrichs further remarks,[4] each of these three harbours was an enclosed one (κλειστός), and capable of being defended by means of a boom or other contrivance,[5] we can understand these passages only of the three harbours in the Peiræean peninsula; the great harbour being one of them; for it cannot be pretended that it had within itself any second, or third, enclosure. It is true that Pausanias does not mention Zea, for the reason probably that it was quite a military port, and consequently travellers did not land there. Hesychius (in voc.) gives two derivations of its name; from ζεία, "barley" or "spelt," and from an Athenian name for Hecatë. The latter seems far the more probable one; for the corn-market was at the head of the great Peiræean harbour, while Hecatë was a Thracian deity, and, as we shall see further on, there was a Thracian colony in Peiræeus, which established there the worship of Bendis. Near Zea was situated the court called Phreattys, for the trial of involuntary homicides who had gone into exile for a certain time, and were obliged to plead their cause before they were suffered to land; which they did from a ship moored off the shore. The place seems to have been called indifferently Ἐν Ζέᾳ and Ἐν Φρεαττοῖ.[6]

But though the large Peiræean port consisted only of one basin with a single entrance, it was nevertheless appropriated to two different purposes, the northern and apparently the larger portion of it being set aside for commerce, whilst the southern part was used for the Athenian

---

[1] ὁ δὲ Πειραιεὺς λιμένας ἔχει τρεῖς.— Peripl. Atticæ.

[2] "Quum enim Phalereo portu neque magno neque bono Athenienses uterentur, hujus consilio triplex Piræi portus constitutus est, isque mœnibus circumdatus."—Vit. Them. c. 6.

[3] τοῖς τε γὰρ πλέουσιν ἐπιτηδειότερος ὁ Πειραιεὺς ἐφαίνετό οἱ προκεῖσθαι, καὶ λιμένας τρεῖς ἀνθ' ἑνὸς ἔχειν τοῦ Φαληροῖ.—i. 1, 2. Munychia is also mentioned as a

port by Isæus, De Philoct. hered. p. 137.

[4] Ibid. p. 14.

[5] ὁ Πειραιεὺς λιμένας ἔχει τρεῖς πάντας κλειστούς.—Schol. in Aristoph. Pac. 144. Ζέα, ἡ Ἑκάτη παρὰ Ἀθηναίοις καὶ εἰς τῶν ἐν Πειραιεῖ λιμένων· ἔχει δὲ ὁ Πειραιεὺς λιμένας τρεῖς κλειστούς.—Hesych. in Ζέα.

[6] Bekk. An. Græc. p. 311; Pollux, viii. s. 120; Photii Bibl. 1593 B, p. 535 A, Bekk.; Demosth. adv. Aristocr. p. 645 sq.

nary.   We have seen, from the passage of Thucydides quoted a little
before (p. 116, note 2), that next adjoining to the inner wall of
Eetioneia, which seems to have crossed the mouth of the shallow inlet
at the top of the harbour (which was probably Hala),[1] a long portico was
erected, stretching along the north-eastern shore, and that it was appropriated as a warehouse for the storing and sale of corn, whether imported or of home growth.   There were other porticoes along the
shore.   The scholiast on Aristophanes, in the scholium just quoted,
beginning from the south, describes the port as containing, first, the
harbour of Cantharus, in which were the neoria or dockyards ; then the
Aphrodisium, or temple and temenos of Aphrodite ; lastly, five porticoes,
of which that just described must have been the last, and furthest
to the north-west.   But we shall have to treat more at length of the
buildings here when we come to Pausanias' description of Peiraeus ;
at present we are only concerned for its main topographical features.
All this northern part appears to have been called the Emporium.
Cantharus, or the portion devoted to the ships of war, lay to the south
of a projecting headland, on which are now situated the quarantine
buildings.   In October, 1834, in digging the foundations of a magazine
at this spot, some marble blocks were found, containing inscriptions
relative to the Athenian dockyards.[2]   From the names of archons which
can be deciphered, these documents appear to have extended over a
period of fifty-five years from Olymp. 100.3 to Olymp. 114.2.   The
names of only three harbours are mentioned in them—Munychia, Zea,
and Cantharus.   The last is alluded to by Aristophanes :

ἐν Πειραιεῖ δήπου ᾽στὶ Κανθάρου λιμήν.

---

[1] " From the eastern end of the Eetonia,
a strong pier, for the most part perfect,
extends in a straight line through the water
to the other bank ; over this the walls of
the Eetonia must have extended and
joined the other ring walls of Piraeus.
The name Hala will consequently be the
most appropriate to the shallow basin
separated by the dam towards the north,
and which, according to the new plan of
Piraeus, has become gradually filled up."
Ulrichs' pamphlet, p. 22.

[2] Ludwig Ross forwarded copies of them
to Boeckh, who published them under the
title of ' Urkunden über das Seewesen des
Attischen Staates.' Berlin, 1840.

[3] Pax, v. 145 : " The harbour forsooth
of Cantharus is in Peiraeus."

The number of ship-sheds (νεώσοικοι) in the three harbours is given at 372; namely, in Munychia, 82; Zea, 196; Cantharus, 94. This pretty nearly agrees with the account of Strabo, who says that the Athenian ports had room for 400 ships.[1] The numbers, too, suit the size of the respective harbours; for the length of shore at Zea is about twice as much as that of either of the other two. Phalerum had probably ceased to be used as a station for ships of war after the destruction of the Phaleric Wall; but that it served at all events as a commercial port down to a very late period appears from the description of it given by Pausanias.

The circuit of the wall at Peiræeus, including Munychia, is given by Thucydides at 60 stades;[2] and such would be about the measure of a line, on the lesser scale, carried round the peninsula from a point a little to the westward of Eetioneia. Then the Long Walls measuring each 40 stades, and the ring wall of the city 43 (without the unguarded part), the whole circumference of the fortification, regarded as one, would, according to Thucydides, be $43+40+60+40 = 183$ stades. Dion Chrysostom sets it down at 200 in his sixth oration; but in his twenty-fifth he calls the Peiraic wall 90 stades,[3] thus exceeding by 30 stades the measure given by Thucydides. His former computation was perhaps founded on the account of that historian as supplemented by his scholiast, as we have shown, absurdly; in the latter he is evidently talking at random. Assuming that by 43 stades Thucydides meant only the guarded part of the wall, and allowing 7 stades for the unguarded portion, which is the largest probable number, then we arrive at a total circumference of 190 stades. And we may observe from the first

---

[1] p. 395. In the scholium on the Pax just cited, it is said that there were sixty νεώρια in Cantharus. Νεώριον seems to have had a more extended sense than νεώσοικος. Thus the Λέξεις 'Ρητορικαί. Νεώσοικοι· καταγώγια ἐπὶ τῆς θαλάττης ᾠκοδομήμενα εἰς ὑποδοχὴν τῶν νεῶν, ὅτε μὴ θαλαττεύοιεν· τὰ νεώρια δὲ ἡ τῶν ὅλων περιβολή.—Bekk. An. Græc. p. 282. But even thus we cannot reconcile the numbers.

[2] lib. ii. 13.

[3] καίτοι διακοσίων σταδίων εἶναι τὴν περίμετρον τῶν 'Αθηνῶν, τοῦ Πειραιῶς συντιθεμένου καὶ τῶν διὰ μέσου τειχῶν πρὸς τὸν περίβολον τοῦ ἄστεος· οἰκεῖσθαι γὰρ οὐ πάλαι καὶ ταῦτα σύμπαντα.—De Tyrannide, p. 199. Reiske (t. i. p. 96, Teubner). καὶ ὕστερον τὸν Πειραιᾶ τειχίσαι πλειόνων ἢ ἐνενήκοντα σταδίων.—De Genio, p. 521, Reiske (i. 312, Teubner).

passage quoted from Dion Chrysostom that the space between the Long Walls, while they existed, was, as we have said, an inhabited fortification. They were between 500 and 600 feet apart.

In addition to the walls of the asty and the Peiraeeus, it is probable that Themistocles also built the north wall of the Acropolis. There is, indeed, no direct evidence of the fact; but neither is there any of its having been done by anybody else; and as Cimon, who succeeded Themistocles as leader of the Athenians, is related to have constructed the south wall, it is a reasonable inference that he found the northern one completed. The mode in which it is constructed corroborates this view. A considerable portion of it consists of fragments of columns and other architectural members, just as the wall which he built round the asty was constructed;[1] and much of them is calcined, showing that they had belonged to the buildings on the Acropolis burnt by the Persians. Besides the fortifications, Themistocles seems only to have erected two temples—that of Artemis Aristobulë in Melitë, already mentioned, and one of Aphroditë Aparchos in Peiraeeus, from the circumstance of a dove having perched on his trireme during the battle of Salamis.[2]

After all his great services to his country, Themistocles turned traitor, and died in exile in the service of Persia. Yet the Athenians seem to have forgiven him, if the account of Diodorus be true, that they deposited his remains in a tomb just at the entrance of the great Peirnïc harbour.[3] No spot could have been selected for it more appropriate to the memory of the man whose master-mind had created that great stronghold of their naval supremacy. Plato, the comic writer, is supposed to allude to it in the following lines:

> Ὁ σὸς δὲ τύμβος ἐν καλῷ κεχωσμένος
> τοῖς ἐμπόροις πρόσρησις ἔσται πανταχοῖ.
> τούς τ' ἐκπλέοντας εἰσπλέοντάς τ' ὄψεται,
> χὡπόταν ἅμιλλ' ᾖ τῶν νεῶν θεάσεται.[4]

---

[1] Thucyd. i. 93.
[2] Schol. in Hermog. περὶ ἰδεῶν, cap. περὶ γλυκύτητος (Rhet. Graec. ii. p. 407, Ald. ap. Leake, i. 368, note 3).
[3] Plutarch, Them. 32; who, however, says that Diodorus spoke rather from conjecture than knowledge.
[4] Plut. ibid.

Which may be thus translated:

> Thy piled-up tomb well placed upon that strand
> The merchants will salute on every hand;
> Outward and homeward bound alike 'twill face,
> And view the ships contending in the race.

Where the allusion seems to be to the regattas during the Panathenaïc festival. If the lines of Plato really refer to Themistocles—and it would be difficult to name another to whom they would be more appropriate—then the tomb must have been erected within some twenty years after his death, for Plato was about that time his junior. At all events, the tradition that Themistocles was interred here prevailed at Athens down to the time of Pausanias, who mentions the tomb.

Peiræeus is still a fine harbour, and capable of receiving large vessels. Dodwell remarks [1] that there was sometimes not a single boat in it; while Lord Broughton, who visited Athens only a few years later (1810), saw in it only one Hydriote merchantman, chartered to carry off the spoils of Lord Elgin.[2] Its aspect is much changed since that time, and men-of-war, as well as many merchant vessels, may now be seen in it.

---

[1] Tour, vol. i. p. 421.   [2] Hobhouse's Journey, vol. i. p. 362.

CHAPTER V.

AFTER the ostracism of Themistocles, in B.C. 471, Cimon took the lead
in the affairs of Athens. Besides the public money at his disposal, he
had large private possessions, and his generous and munificent temper,
with the additional stimulus of a love of popularity, led him to employ
a large share of these resources in strengthening and adorning the
city. We have remarked that the Long Walls lay only perhaps in the
plan of Themistocles, and that he contributed nothing to their execution. According to Plutarch,[1] Cimon laid the foundations of the
Phaleric and the northern Long Wall after his victory at the Eurymedon
(B.C. 466)—a work of great labour and expense, as they had to be
carried through swampy ground, which it was necessary to render firm
by means of huge stones and rubble. These foundations were perhaps
hardly completed at the time of his temporary exile (B.C. 461); and at
his recall (B.C. 456), which appears to have been effected by a compact
with Pericles arranged through Cimon's sister Elpinicē,[2] he found the
walls finished; for, according to Thucydides,[3] the Athenians began to

[1] Cim. c. 13. [2] Plut. Pericl. 10. [3] lib. i. c. 107. 108.

erect them at the time of the battles in the Megarid (B.C. 457), and they
were completed after the battle of Tanagra in the following year. They
could hardly have been built in so short a time had not the foundations
been previously laid. Pericles appears to have had the chief conduct
of affairs during Cimon's exile, and it is not, therefore, surprising that
we sometimes find the Long Walls ascribed entirely to him. Cimon
seems also to have erected, before his banishment, the south wall of the
Acropolis, the masonry of which is of a more regular kind than that of
the north wall. Whether he also built the little temple of Athena Nikë,
which stands on the western abutment of the south wall, is a disputed
point. Ross, in his work on the Acropolis, so magnificently begun, but
of which, unfortunately, only the first number was completed, ascribes
it to Cimon, and fortifies his opinion by arguments drawn from the age
of Calamis, who imitated at Olympia the statue of Athena Nikë, and of
Alcamenes, who made the statue of the triple Hecatë which stood near
the temple;[1] also from the consideration that no such structure is
ascribed to Pericles, whose works are particularly enumerated, while
those of Cimon are not, and the improbability that such a building
should have been undertaken during the Peloponnesian war.[2] On the
other hand, Curtius, who generally either ignores or opposes the views
of Ross, abjudicates the temple from the age of Cimon, on account of
the style of the sculptures which adorned it.[3] But that some temple
must have stood at this spot before the Propylæa were built is, we think,
conclusively shown by Michaëlis, who remarks that the south wing of
the Propylæa does not advance so far westward as the north wing, evidently on account of the temple existing there.[4] We certainly cannot
imagine any other probable cause why so grand and important a structure as the Propylæa should have been curtailed of its fair proportions.
At the same time there is much truth in Curtius' remark about the
sculptures, which from their style were certainly not præ-Pheidian; but
these were very probably added at a later period.

[1] Pausan. ii. 30, 2.   [4] See Gerhard's Archäol. Anzeiger, June
[2] Die Akropolis von Athen, p. 9 sq.   1862.
[3] Erläuternder Text, p. 37.

Another work which may be attributed to Cimon is the Theseum most probably not the structure which now bears that name—as a receptacle for the remains of Theseus, which he brought from Scyros.[1] It is also probable that he may have erected some of the porticoes in the agora. In his time flourished an excellent school of painting, which included, besides Polygnotus, Micon and Panænus, even Phidias himself; for the great sculptor began life as a painter, and is said to have adorned the temple of Zeus Olympius with his pictures.[2] We may perhaps place in the time of Cimon the introduction of painted scenery at the theatre, for Vitruvius says that this was done by Agatharchus for one of the tragedies of Æschylus.[3] Polygnotus was an amateur who never painted for money. He was an admirer of Cimon's sister, Elpinicë, and therefore in some sort her brother's rival. He adorned with his art the portico called Peisianaction in the agora, which hence obtained the name of Pœcilë, and is said to have introduced into one of the pictures a portrait of Elpinicë in the character of Laodicë.[4] Polygnotus seems to have been generally assisted in his pictures by Micon, a professional and mercenary artist, who probably supplied those technical details in which Polygnotus may have been deficient. It is possible that Cimon may have erected the colossal statue of Athena Promachos in the Acropolis.[5] The artist, whoever he was, left it imperfect, for the engraving on the shield was done by Mys from the drawing of Parrhasius, who lived in the time of Socrates.[6] Cimon adorned the agora by planting it with plane trees, and improved the Academy by introducing into it streams of water and laying out shady walks.[7] His own gardens he threw open for the recreation of the public.

Cimon died in B.C. 449, and it was Pericles, his successor in the administration of affairs, to whom Athens owed those magnificent

[1] Plut. Cim. 8.

[2] Plin. H. N. xxxv. 54. If this be true the Olympium must have been in a sufficiently advanced state to admit of being used.

[3] lib. vii. Præf.

[4] Plut. Cim. c. 4.

[5] The scholiast on Demosthenes in Androt. p. 597. Reiske even places it before the battle of Salamis.

[6] Pausan. i. 28, 2.

[7] Plut. Cim. 13.

buildings which made it unrivalled in the world. Pericles also completed the fortifications of Athens, for it was by his advice that the southern or middle long wall was built. Socrates, when a youth, had heard him recommending the measure.[1] This third wall, executed by Callicrates, seems to have been built about B.C. 445, or perhaps a little later.

The chief glory of the administration of Pericles was the restoration of the Acropolis. Half a century had elapsed since its destruction by the Persians, yet its buildings still lay in calcined ruins. It is even uncertain whether the Erechtheium, the venerable temple of Athena Polias, had been restored. We know that the Athenians suffered several of their temples to lie in ashes in order to cherish among the people an immortal hatred of the Persians. We can hardly imagine, however, that the buildings on the Acropolis were left so long in ruins from this cause. The reason more probably was, the want of funds. To free Athens from the danger of another capture was the first care of her rulers, and the sums spent upon the fortifications must have been enormous. These having been completed, Pericles could turn his attention to the embellishment of Athens, and the funds supplied by the contributions of the allies furnished ample means for all his magnificent designs. That he should have erected so superb a structure as the Parthenon, and yet have suffered the original and more sacred temple of Athena to lie in ruins, seems hardly probable. Yet there is no account of his having restored it; and hence, perhaps, we may conclude that this had been done, though in a somewhat hasty and perfunctory manner, by Themistocles. For before the end of the century, as we shall see further on, it had either to be rebuilt, or thoroughly repaired.

The delay, however, was fortunate, not only for the Athenians, but for the world and for all time, since it placed at the disposal of Pericles the genius of such an artist as Pheidias, and such architects as Ictinus and Mnesicles, whose incomparable works became for after-ages models to be imitated, but never equalled. And Pheidias was only the head of

[1] Plato, Gorgias, p. 22, Bekk.

a school of first-rate artists. As M. Beulé has observed,[1] it is impossible to suppose that the sculptures of the Parthenon, executed in so short a time, were the work of one pair of hands. The pediments alone contained 40 or 50 figures, for the most part of colossal dimensions; to which must be added the 84 figures of the metopes, and 300 of the frieze. Besides, sculpture in marble does not appear to have been Pheidias' forte, and Pliny seems uncertain whether he had done anything in that material.[2] Chasing (τορευτική) was his more peculiar art, and his ivory statues his chief glory.[3] Beulé is of opinion that the statue in the Parthenon, with its accessories, would alone have occupied him several years; and when we consider that he had to direct all the works of Pericles, he could not have spared much time for statuary. Alcamenes and Agoracritus were his pupils, to whose works he sometimes put the finishing touches,[4] and to them, perhaps, is to be assigned much of the sculpture of the Parthenon; but, as Pheidias was the presiding genius, and doubtless the designer of the whole, his reputation has overshadowed that of his assistants.

The Odeium, on the eastern side of the Dionysiac theatre, seems to have been the first building completed by Pericles. The date of it may be proximately determined by the following lines:

ὁ σχινοκέφαλος Ζεὺς ὁδὶ προσέρχεται
ὁ Περικλέης τῳδεῖον ἐπὶ τοῦ κρανίου
ἔχων, ἐπειδὴ τοὔστρακον παροίχεται.[5]

" But here comes Pericles, squill-headed Zeus,
Bearing his own Odeium on his pate
Now that the ostracism is done and past."

The point of the joke—for ancient jokes must sometimes be explained—lay in the circumstance that the conical roof of the Odeium resembled the peaked cranium of Pericles. The allusion seems to be to the

---

[1] L'Acropole, t. ii. p. 97 sq. But perhaps the author carries the idea, though just enough in itself, too far when he says: " Phidias, comme Hercule, est le héros de travaux impossibles."

[2] "Et ipsum Phidiam tradunt sculpsisse marmora."—H. N. xxxvi. 15.

[3] Idem xxxiv. 49; Quint. xiv. 10; Diod. Sic. xxvi. 1.

[4] Plin. H. N. xxxvi. 16.

[5] Fragm. of 'Thraittæ' of Cratinus, ap. Plut. Pericl. 13.

ostracism of Thucydides, son of Melesias, the rival of Pericles, by which Pericles obtained the sole administration.[1] As this took place in B.C. 444, the Odeium must have been finished before that date. The Parthenon appears to have been the next work of Pericles; for, according to the testimony of Philochorus, the statue of Athena had been placed in it in the archonship of Theodorus (B.C. 438); while the Propylæa were begun in the following year, in the archonship of Euthymenes, and completed in five years.[2] After the erection of his chryselephantine statue of Athena, Pheidias was accused of embezzling some of the gold appropriated to it, and fled to Elis, where he died a few years after, in the archonship of Pythodorus.

It may be inquired why a new temple to Athena should have arisen close to her older and more sacred one? But such a question is not more reasonable than to ask why the Athenians should have substituted for the little ancient image of the goddess, made of olive wood, and between four and five feet high, a magnificent statue of gold and ivory. The increase of population, the progress of refinement and art, had demanded a larger temple and a more splendid worship. But superstition still invested the primitive sanctuary with a peculiar veneration, and the Athena of the Erechtheium continued to be regarded as the guardian deity of the Acropolis. The statue, though rude, was the more divine because its origin was lost in obscurity, and might therefore be regarded as celestial, and modern art concealed its defects in the folds of a magnificent peplus. That a more ancient temple of Athena had existed at the spot occupied by the new one, and also that there had previously been Propylæa, can hardly be doubted; but notices of them in ancient authors are vague and scanty. We have shown above (p. 27, note 1) that the passages in Herodotus sometimes adduced in order to show the existence of an ancient Parthenon *actually in use*, before the Persian wars, prove no such thing. It is noticeable that Pausanias calls the Erechtheium, not a temple, but an οἴκημα; and Professor Ross's opinion is not improbable, that it was originally the

---

[1] See Leake, vol. i. p. 461 sq.

[2] Schol. in Aristoph. Pac. 604; Harpocr. voc. Προπύλαια ταῦτα; Plut. Pericl. 13.

abode, or the reputed abode, of Erechtheus, and was converted into a temple when he became a god and was made equal to Poseidon. The only ancient authority who mentions a previous temple distinct from the Erechtheium—for nothing can be concluded from the account in Thucydides (i. 126) of the affair of Cylon—is Hesychius, whose testimony as to its existence is direct, since he says[1] that the new Hecatompedon was fifty feet larger than that burnt by the Persians; a remark which, as Leake observes (i. 556), is quite inapplicable to the small temple of the Erechtheium. Hence it appears that both the old Parthenon and the new were called Hecatompedon; and this, indeed, seems to have been the more usual name for it, at all events in later times; for the 'Etymologicum Magnum,' when speaking of it, adds, "*some* call it the Parthenon."[2] The authorities just quoted derive the name from its dimensions; and if these be taken from the *cella* of the more modern building, they are not far from the mark, for the whole temple is a great deal more; and it could only be with reference to its length that there was a difference of 50 feet between the old Parthenon and the new, for the whole breadth of the new, on the upper stylobate, is only 100 feet, and we can hardly suppose that it was twice as big as the old. Leake, however (p. 557), takes the name Hecatompedon to express the measure of the front on the upper stylobate of the new building, which is just 100 Greek feet; but this is open to the objection just stated. And, indeed, the name of Parthenon seems to have been properly confined to the *cella* of the goddess. In the inscriptions which contain lists of objects in the temple we find parts of it mentioned under the names of Pronaos, Parthenon, and Hecatompedon. The meaning of the first name is plain enough, but respecting the other two opinions may differ. Boeckh is of opinion that the whole building was called Hecatompedon, and that the Parthenon was that portion of it which contained the statue.[3] According to Hesychius (voc. Ἐκατόμπεδος νεώς) the temple was prepared for " the Virgins;" a name applied κατ' ἐξοχὴν to the daughters of Erechtheus

---

[1] voc. Ἐκατόμπεδος νεώς.   voc. Ἐκατόμπεδον.   The same in Bekker's
[2] καλοῦσι γὰρ αὐτόν τινες Παρθενῶνα.—   An. Græc. p. 247.
[3] Corp. Inscrr. Gr. t. i. p. 177.

K

(Id. voc. Παρθένοι); whence we may infer that, according to his view, the temple derived its name from them, though he does not expressly say so. But here he seems to be confounding the Parthenon with the temple of Athena Polias, or Erechtheium, as the later scholiasts and lexicographers sometimes do. The account of the scholiast on the oration of Demosthenes against Androtion is more correct, that it was dedicated to Athena more especially as the virgin goddess (παρθένου Ἀθηνᾶς).[1] With regard to the name Hecatompedon, we may observe that the word ἑκατόν is often used with a very loose signification in compounds; and thus we find ἑκατόμβη in Homer of a sacrifice of only six oxen.[2] And Harpocration refers the name not to its measure, but to its beauty and harmony of proportions.[3]

If the ancient testimonies respecting a previous Hecatompedon are not very satisfactory, the remains of it discovered in the excavation of the Acropolis in 1835 and following year afforded very convincing proof of its existence. Its foundations were then laid bare, and were easily distinguished from those of the newer building, which indeed consist of the old ones enlarged. There are besides, on the Acropolis, many architectural remains, which could have belonged to nothing but this ancient temple. Thus in its north wall, reputed, as we have before remarked, to have been built by Themistocles, have been inserted twenty-six drums of columns, of Pentelic marble, from 5 ft. 6 in. to 6 ft. 2 in. in diameter. Built into the same wall, at the part called μακραὶ πέτραι, are also portions of a very ancient Doric entablature. The architrave, triglyphs, and guttæ are of *poros* stone;[4] the metopes, which have no sculptures, are of white marble. There are indications of these having been painted according to the

---

[1] Schol. August. ad Demosth. c. Androt. p. 597; t. ii. p. 134, Reiske.

[2] Il. vi. 93.

[3] ὁ Παρθενὼν ὑπό τινων Ἐκατόμπεδος ἐκαλεῖτο διὰ κάλλος καὶ εὐρυθμίαν, οὐ διὰ μέγεθος.—In voc. Where we see, on the other hand, Hecatompedon noted as the less usual name.

[4] Writers are not agreed about the nature of πῶρος, or πώρινος λίθος. Some consider it a kind of tufa. Theophrastus (De Lapid. c. ii.) describes it as resembling Parian marble in grain and colour, but less heavy. If it was used, as Pliny says (xxxvi. 53), to polish marble, it must have been friable. Cf. Siebel, ad Paus. v. 10, 2.

ancient system of polychromy; the triglyphs blue, the intervals red, and the guttæ black. The calcined metopes show that they must have belonged to some temple on the Acropolis burnt by the Persians. On the east and south-east side of the Acropolis were also discovered, buried in the ground, more than a dozen columns similar to those built into the wall, and bearing, like them, marks of fire. These columns seem not to have been completely finished, the fluting having been only begun at top and bottom; and hence it is conjectured that the temple was burnt before it was perfected.[1] At the base they were nearly of the same diameter as the columns of the present Parthenon, but tapered more towards the top, and were probably not so tall. From the measure of the ancient foundations and of these architectural remains, Professor Ross is inclined to think that Leake was right in his conjecture, that the old Hecatompedon had six columns in front and thirteen or fourteen at the sides. Strack, on the contrary, is of opinion that it was an octastyle, with eight columns in front and sixteen at the sides; and that it must have been a finer specimen of the old Doric than the Parthenon of Pericles.[2]

Besides these remains of the original Parthenon, many objects were discovered in the excavations on the Acropolis, which must have belonged to the times before the Persian wars, and to the temples which then existed upon it. Such were an image of Athena, of a centaur in the primitive style, fragments of architectural ornaments, pateræ, lamps, &c.[3]

The old Parthenon, with the other principal buildings of the Acropolis, must have lain in ruins, as we have before remarked, for about half a century, that is, from the Persian wars to the time of . Pericles. Callicrates and Ictinus were the architects of the new one,[4] about which Ictinus and Carpion published a book.[5] It was built entirely of Pentelic marble, on a stylobate of the same material 5 ft. 6 in. in height, with four steps resting on a rustic basement of lime-

---

[1] See Ross, Aufs. i. 129; ii. 285, &c.

[2] See his paper in Gerhard's Archäolog. Zeitg., April and May, 1862. Cf. Leake, vol. i. p. 556; Penrose, p. 74.

[3] Ross, Aufs. i. 104 sqq.

[4] Strabo, ix. p. 396; Plut. Pericl. 13; Pausan. viii. 41, 5.

[5] Vitruv. vii. Præf. s. 12.

stone. The length of the upper step was 227 ft. 7 in., its breadth 101 ft. 2 in. By this elevation, and the natural rise of the Acropolis, the floor of the peristyle was very nearly on a level with the top of the Propylæa; the pavement of that building, at its eastern entrance, being about 44 feet below the pavement of the Parthenon.

The Propylæa of Pericles appear in like manner to have been built over the remains of another structure of the same kind. Under their south wing, and impinging on the present great central hall, or megaron, a considerable piece of polygonal wall of unhewn stone was discovered in the excavations of 1840. Adjoining it were remains of a building of *poros* stone, with marble thresholds and antæ, and traces of a marble lining to the walls.[1] These remains do not lie precisely in the same direction as the present building, but are inclined more to the north-west. There are traces of the ancient megaron in the angle between the south wing and megaron of the present building. The slabs of marble which lined it show evident signs of fire, their surface being cracked and partly calcined. In the same slabs are holes for nails or hooks. Ross imagines,[2] rather fancifully, we think, that here were suspended the chains of the Chalcidians mentioned by Herodotus;[3] for these holes seem to have been in the interior of the building, whilst Herodotus says that the chains were hung up *before* it (ἀντίον). There can be little doubt, however, that by μέγαρον he meant the central hall of the old Propylæa, which lies in the direction he describes. His testimony as to the burning of the walls is both strongly corroborated by present appearances, and serves to identify the remains. Since the Acropolis still lay in ruins when he saw it, the Propylæa which he mentions in the same chapter must have been the ancient ones, and not the structure of Pericles; though some have imagined that he means the latter, and have consequently fixed the date of his visit to Athens in B.C. 431;[4] which is destitute of all pro-

---

[1] Ross, Archäol. Aufs. i. 78 sq.

[2] Ib. p. 80.

[3] ἅπερ [πέδαι] ἔτι καὶ ἐς ἐμὲ ἦσαν περιεοῦσαι, κεκράμεναι ἐκ τειχέων περιπεφλευσμένων πυρὶ ὑπὸ τοῦ Μήδου, ἀντίον δὲ τοῦ μεγάρου τοῦ πρὸς ἑσπέρην τετραμμένου. —Herod. v. 77. Where he most probably means the walls of the Acropolis.

[4] See the life of Herodotus in Smith's Dict. of Biography, vol. ii. p. 431 B.

bability. For he was then upwards of fifty years old, and a man of his culture, and so curious to see places of renown, would surely have seen Athens before that time of life. But though the Acropolis must have lain in ruins more than forty years, its walls had been built by Themistocles and Cimon, and perhaps one or two minor buildings erected or restored. A more particular description of the buildings upon it will be given when we come to narrate the tour of Pausanias.

Another great work of Pericles was the temple of Demeter at Eleusis. It was not finished at the breaking out of the Peloponnesian war, which arrested its progress. Plutarch records three architects having been employed upon it, Corœbus, Metagenes, and Xenocles; but Strabo and Vitruvius ascribe it to Ictinus.[1] It was not completed till the time of Demetrius Phalereus. Pericles, with the aid of the Ionian architect Hippodamus of Miletus, also greatly improved and adorned the Peiraïc peninsula. Architecture appears at this time to have been in a much more advanced state in the Asiatic Greek cities than in European Greece, at all events so far as regards the general laying out of the towns and the regularity of the streets. Hippodamus, who, according to Aristotle,[2] was a political philosopher, with some rather crotchety and self-conceited notions, as well as an architect, formed the plan of building cities of 10,000 inhabitants and dividing them into three classes; one consisting of mechanics, another of husbandmen, and the third of soldiers. These notions at all events betray a love of method and regularity, and we may infer analogically that the towns which he laid out—and he had a good deal of practice, for besides Peiræeus he built Thurii and Rhodes—were marked by order and convenience. At Piræeus he constructed the market place, which continued to be called after him the Hippodameian agora. Here Timotheus, against whom one of the orations of Demosthenes is directed, appears to have had a house.[3] It was Hippodamus, probably, who constructed the

---

[1] Plut. Pericl. 13; Strab. p. 395; Vitruv. vii. Præf.

[2] Polit. ii. 8. The expression of Aristotle, τὸν Πειραιᾶ κατέτεμε, may possibly mean

that he levelled great part of the ground in order to make his agora and the approaches.

[3] Adv. Timoth. p. 1190, Reiske.

theatre, of which there are still vestiges on the western declivity of the Munychian height. The temple of the Munychian Artemis and the Bendideium, or temple of Bendis, which lay further up the hill, seem to have been of much more ancient foundation. Xenophon's description of the struggle of Thrasybulus with the Thirty Tyrants affords some valuable indications for the topography of the Peiræeus. It would appear from this account that the Hippodameian agora must have lain to the east of the northern portion of the great harbour, and that a road led from it up the hill to the objects just mentioned. Thrasybulus, after marching from Phylë to Peiræeus, concentrated his small force on the Munychian height, as it was not sufficient to defend the whole place. The Thirty and their faction marching from Athens, took possession of the Hippodameian agora, and thence moved to attack Thrasybulus; who, however, gained an easy victory, as he was planted on high ground and his adversaries had to advance up a narrow thoroughfare.[1] Diodorus Siculus, in his account of the same action, describes Munychia as an uninhabited but fortified hill.[2]

Subsequently, when Pausanias and Lysander jointly besieged Thrasybulus in Peiræeus, Pausanias, who commanded the right wing, encamped at Halipedum. Therefore, as the Spartan line must have faced southwards, Halipedum must have been on the western side of Peiræeus. Next day, Pausanias went to Cophos Limen to observe how he could circumvallate Peiræeus. From this account we should be disposed to think that Cophos Limen was the narrow inlet or harbour

[1] Xenoph. Hell. ii. 4, s. 11 sqq.; Diodor. Sic. xiv. 33. Leake (vol. i. p. 386, note) objects to Diodorus' account "that the Thirty *besieged* Munychia (προσέβαλον τῇ Μουνυχίᾳ), since it is evident that the action was fought in Peiræeus, to the northward of the Munychian peninsula." But first, προσβάλλειν does not mean to *besiege*, but to *assault*; second, the action was no doubt fought in Peiræeus, or rather perhaps on the borders of Peiræeus and Munychia, though not to the northward, but westward of the latter. Leake's

criticism arises from his misplacing Munychia in the southern part of the Peiraïc peninsula, and Phalerum at its north-eastern harbour. Thus in the next note he goes on to say: "By the hill of Phalerum is meant that which extends from Port Phalerum to near the head of Port Aphrodisium [Peiræeus]." But the texts cited are only another proof that Phalerum is wrongly located there. What Leake calls the Hill of Phalerum is the Munychian height.

[2] λόφον ἔρημον καὶ καρτερόν.—loc. cit.

outside Eëtioneia, as it appears not to have been included in the fortifications, and would have been a proper place for Pausanias' survey.
Thrasybulus attacks him here, but is repulsed and driven back into the
theatre of Peiræeus. This must be the same theatre which Thucydides[1] calls the Dionysiac theatre near Munychia; and indeed it
appears to have been just on the borders of that district. Thrasybulus
renewed the attack from the theatre, and routed the Lacedæmonians,[2]
who retired to some rising ground four or five stades distant. But
having received reinforcements from hence they attacked the Athenians
in turn, killed 150 of them, and drove others into the marsh at Hale.

The military strength of Munychia had been observed by Epimenides
in the time of Solon, and a prediction of his is recorded, that if the
Athenians knew the annoyance the place would cause them, they would
eat it up with their own teeth.[3] The prophecy, however, was not verified till some centuries after his time, when, in B.C. 322, Munychia was
occupied by a Macedonian garrison.

Artemis, as the peculiar deity of the Peiræeus, was probably connected with the Brauronian Artemis.[4] Munychia, on which her temple
stood, is by some thought to have derived its name from a fanciful
epithet, designating her as the sole goddess of the night ($\mu o\nu o$-$\nu\nu\chi i a$);[5]
but according to Harpocration (in voc.) it was named after a king
Mounychos. From her situation on this height, Callimachus gives her
the epithet of $\lambda\iota\mu\epsilon\nu o\sigma\kappa\acute{o}\pi o\varsigma$, 'watcher of the harbour.'[6] Her festival
was celebrated on the 16th of the month Munychion, when large round
cakes having lights round them ($\dot{a}\mu\phi\iota\phi\tilde{\omega}\nu\tau\epsilon\varsigma$), to represent the full
moon, were offered.[7] At a later period another festival, in commemo-

---

[1] viii. 93.

[2] Xenoph. ibid. s. 30 sqq. Some Lacedæmonians killed in this action were
buried before the Dipylon.—s. 33.

[3] Plut. Sol. 12; Diog. Laërt. i. 114;
Tzetzes, Chil. v. 18.

[4] Welcker, Gr. G. i. 170 sqq.

[5] Preller, Gr. Mythol. i. 236. The form
of the name with an iota ($Mo\nu\nu\iota\chi i a$), found

in inscriptions, seems to be later. See A.
Mommsen, Heortol. p. 403.

[6] $\pi\acute{o}\tau\nu\iota a$ $Mo\nu\nu\nu\chi i\eta$ $\lambda\iota\mu\epsilon\nu o\sigma\kappa\acute{o}\pi\epsilon$. — In
Dian. 259. Hence is it not more probable
that she got her name of $Mo\nu\nu\nu\chi i a$ from
the place, like her epithet $B\rho a\nu\rho\omega\nu i a$?
This was a common practice.

[7] Pollux, vi. 75; Athen. xiv. 53; Phavor.
$\dot{a}\mu\phi\iota\phi\tilde{\omega}\nu\tau\epsilon\varsigma$.

ration of the victory at Salamis, appears to have been combined with it, because, says Plutarch, the full moon shone on the victors;[1] but this is a mistake, as the battle took place when the moon was fast waning.[2] The temple of the Munychian Artemis was doubtless much older than the age of Pericles; but it is possible that the Bendideium or temple of Bendis, the Thracian Artemis,[3] may have been erected in his time.[4] Bendis was regarded with much reverence by the Athenians. Aristophanes, in his 'Lemniæ,' called her the Great Goddess ($\mu\epsilon\gamma\acute{a}\lambda\eta$ Θεός) ;[5] and she appears in her own country to have had an image of solid gold.[6] There seems to have been a Thracian settlement in the Peiræcus. The Bendideium appears to have nearly adjoined the temple of Artemis. Leake (p. 393) places the latter temple on the low ground near the harbour of Stratiotiki (Zea), (which he calls Munychia), where he says the remains of a temple may be observed. But this spot was hardly in Munychia, and does not at all answer to the description of Strabo. The Bendideium he places some four hundred yards to the south-west of it, where there are some considerable remains; but then he is puzzled to explain Xenophon's account, given above, of the march of the Thirty towards the two temples, which, according to his hypothesis, must have lain in different directions. It seems probable that the ruins which Leake observed, may have belonged to a temple of Zea or Hecatë, from whom the harbour derived its name; but we cannot adduce any evidence for its existence. May not the other remains which Leake ascribes to the Bendideium have belonged to the temple of Zeus Soter and Athena? Such a position would answer well enough to the account

[1] De Glor. Athen. 7.

[2] See Mommsen, Heort. p. 403 sq. notes.

[3] Plat. Rep. init. and scholia.

[4] Mommsen (ib. p. 426) fixes the introduction of the Bendideia at Athens in the time of Socrates. But this does not at all appear from the opening lines of Plato's 'Republic,' which he quotes as his authority. It was the *demotes* of the Peiræcus who were celebrating the feast for the first time, and it does not say what feast. According to the scholiast it was the lesser Panathenæa, and he says that these followed the Bendideia.

[5] Hesych. and Phot. voc. Μεγάλη Θεός. In Photius we should read τὴν Βένδιν for Τελβαιναιν.

[6] Lucian, Jupit. Tragœdus, c. 8, and scholia.

of Strabo, who says, that in his time Peiræeus was reduced to a small village round the ports and the temple of Zeus Soter.[1] The theatre, which stood below the temples, must have been a place of some importance, as assemblies of the people were sometimes held there.[2] There were probably two theatres in the peninsula, as we hear sometimes of the Munychian theatre, and sometimes of the Peiraïc; and there are vestiges of a second on the western side of the port of Zea. There was also, probably, a sanctuary or temple of Dionysus in the Peiraeeus, for the Dionysiac festival was celebrated there, much as at Athens, with a procession and theatrical contests.[3] Socrates would go down to Piræeus whenever Euripides brought out a piece there, for he was a great admirer of that poet.[4]

Pericles is also said to have erected at Peiræeus a portico for the purpose of a meal or flour market (ἀλφιτόπωλις στοά, or simply Ἀλφιτόπωλις).[5] But though he effected so much for that peninsula, and also for Athens by adorning it with temples and other public buildings, yet the streets of the city were suffered to remain narrow, crooked, and inconvenient, insomuch that Dicæarchus, who lived about a century later, observes that a stranger unexpectedly carried thither might doubt whether he was in the far-famed Athens, till he beheld the Odeium, the theatre, and the Parthenon.[6]

Pericles had been enabled to achieve these great works by diverting from its proper destination the tribute collected from the allies for the purpose of securing Greece against the Persians. Aristeides had first assessed this tax, B.C. 477, at the yearly sum of 460 talents, which were

---

[1] p. 396. That Athena was worshipped there with Zeus see Pausan. i. 1, 3; Liv. 31, 30.

[2] Lysias adv. Agorat. p. 464,479, Reiske.

[3] ὅταν ἡ πομπὴ ᾖ τῷ Διονύσῳ ἐν Πειραιεῖ καὶ οἱ κωμῳδοὶ καὶ οἱ τραγῳδοί.—Law ap. Demosth. in Meid. p. 517, Reiske.

[4] Ælian, V. H. ii. 13. We know not why Leake (p. 391) calls the contest which Socrates beheld a *music* contest. An inscription brought to England by Chandler,

and now in the British Museum, records that Callidamas was to have a front seat (προεδρίαν) in the theatre whenever the Peiræenses celebrated the Dionysii. Boeckh, C. Inscr. Gr. No. 101.

[5] Aristoph. Eccl. 685; Acharn. 547, and schol.

[6] Vit. Græc. p. 8. But Demosthenes remarks an alteration in this respect. Adv. Aris'ocr. p. 689, Reiske.

deposited in the temple of Apollo at Delos.[1] When Pericles obtained the direction of affairs he raised the contribution to 600 talents, and carried the balance at Delos, 2000 talents, to Athens.[2] How much his buildings cost it is impossible to say with any certainty. The only datum we have for the calculation is, that the Propylæa cost about 2000 talents (about £460,000).[3] Leake thinks this very much exaggerated, as money in those times went two or three times further than at present. He remarks that the Parthenon would have required double the sum of the Propylæa, and all the buildings together 8000 or 9000 talents. But a collection of 600 talents a year during the fifteen years of the administration of Pericles would amount to 9000, without including the balance from Delos. He may also be supposed to have raised the domestic taxes, and there was no occasion during his time to make preparations against the Persians. But the whole subject is obscure, and those who wish for further information are referred to Leake's third appendix.

The breaking out of the Peloponnesian war and the death of Pericles two or three years afterwards (b.c. 429) arrested any further improvements, and from this period down to the taking of Athens by Lysander there is but little to record. It was, however, during this interval that the Erechtheium was either restored or rebuilt. We may infer from several circumstances that the Erechtheium, though partially burnt by the Persians, was not so much injured as to have been rendered altogether unserviceable. For only two days after, as we have already said, some Athenian exiles, by order of Xerxes, went up to it to sacrifice; and Herodotus, in the chapter in which he records this, speaks of the temple in a manner which shows that it was in existence in his

[1] Demosth. c. Aristocr. p. 689 sq. ; Plut. Aristid. 24 sq.

[2] The amount of the balance appears as follows : the confederate treasure is said to have been 10,000 talents (Isocrat. de Pace, p. 173, Steph.), and Pericles is said to have carried to the Acropolis 8000 talents, without reckoning the sacred money from Delos

(χωρὶς τῶν ἱερῶν).—Ibid. p. 184.

[3] Harpocr. Προπυλαία ταῦτα says 2012 ; Diodor. Sic. (xii. 40) says that the Propylæa and the siege of Potidæa cost 4000 talents ; and as the siege of Potidæa cost 2000 talents (Thucyd. ii. 70) this account agrees pretty nearly with that of Harpocration.

time,[1] when it is quite impossible, from his age, that he can have meant the temple rebuilt in the archonship of Callias, B.C. 406. Müller, who places the visit of Herodotus to Athens about the third year of the Peloponnesian war, thinks that the temple was in a serviceable state, in which we agree with him; but for his opinion that it had been rebuilt of wood, or with a wooden roof, he produces no authority, and it is therefore a mere conjecture. He is, too, evidently in error about the date of Herodotus' visit, which must have been much earlier, since, as we have seen (supra, p. 132), he beheld the old Propylæa in their burnt state, whereas in the third year of the Peloponnesian war, he would have found those of Pericles just newly erected.[2] We have already ventured an opinion (supra, p. 126) that it had been partially restored by Themistocles, for it is contrary to all probability, as well as to the testimony of Herodotus just quoted, that it should have been suffered to lie in a useless state. Both these considerations, as well as the small size of the temple in comparison with most of the works of Pericles, yet at the same time its exceeding sanctity and venerableness, militate, we think, against Leake's conclusion, taken apparently from Stuart, that "Upon the whole it appears that this building, although designed by Pheidias and his colleagues, was not terminated until towards the end of the Peloponnesian war, or even after its conclusion, perhaps about the year B.C. 393."[3] The building then finished was, it appears to us much more likely, a wholly or nearly wholly new one, undertaken in the archonship of Diocles, B.C. 409, or a little before, because the ancient one, badly restored, had fallen into a state of complete decay. Nothing, we should imagine, but a case of the last necessity could have induced the Athenians to apply their funds to such a purpose in the very thick of the Peloponnesian war.

[1] ἔστι ἐν τῇ ἀκροπόλι ταύτῃ 'Ερεχθέος τοῦ γηγενέος λεγομένου εἶναι νηός, ἐν τῷ ἐλαίη τε καὶ θάλασσα ἔνι.—viii. 55.

[2] "Tamen sanctuarium totius civitatis inter Thesei, Parthenonis, Propylæorumque struendorum contentionem neglectum est atque florente reipublicæ statu sacra augustissima haud dubie in ædicula lignea vel ligno tecta fieri permissum." Then in a note, after quoting the above passage from Herodotus, he says of it: "Quæ scripta puto sub tertium fere annum belli Peloponnesiaci."—De Minervæ Poliadis templo, apud Rose, Inscr. Gr. p. 149.

[3] vol. i. p. 577.

The history of the rebuilding of the Erechtheium is attended with considerable difficulties. We have only two or three ancient authorities on the subject, and these are apparently discrepant. One of these is an inscription brought to England by Dr. Chandler, and now in the British Museum, containing an account of the state of certain works going on at the Erechtheium in the archonship of Diocles. The name of 'Erechtheium' is not, indeed, to be found in the inscription, but the temple is identified plainly enough by the words " in which is the primeval image " (ἐν ᾧ τὸ ἀρχαῖον ἄγαλμα), as well as by other unmistakable allusions.[1] This inscription has been since supplemented, as it is supposed, by another, or rather several fragments of one, discovered in the Pinacotheca in 1836, and published by Rangabé in his 'Antiquités Helléniques.'[2] A third authority is a passage in Xenophon's 'Hellenica,' stating that the *old* temple of Athena was set on fire in the archonship of Callias, which was three years later than that of Diocles, or in B.C. 406.[3] If, then, Chandler's inscription refers to the *rebuilding* of the Erechtheium, how could Xenophon call it the *old* temple, when it had been hardly three years in existence?

Leake attempts to get rid of this difficulty by asserting that " the *old* temple " (παλαιός) was the usual name for the Erechtheium; and he adduces from Strabo a passage in which it is called the *archaic* temple (ἀρχαῖος).[4] But these words are far from being synonymous; and the proof of it is, that they are not unfrequently used together in the same sentence by Greek writers.[5] Παλαιός refers to duration of time, *old in years;* whilst ἀρχαῖος relates to origin, *primitive, primeval*,

[1] The inscription will be found in Leake, vol. i. App. xvii. p. 586 sqq.; Rose, Inscr. Grac. p. 145 sqq.; and Boeckh, C. Inscr. Gr. No. 160. There is an elaborate explanation of it in both the last-named works. The name of the archon is somewhat defaced on the stone, but is perfect enough to show that the reading is Διοκλεος, as the author has satisfied himself by personal inspection.

[2] vol. i. Nos. 56–60.

[3] τῷ δ' ἐπιόντι ἔτει, ᾧ ἥ τε σελήνη ἐξέλιπεν ἑσπέρας, καὶ ὁ παλαιὸς τῆς Ἀθηνᾶς νεὼς ἐνεπρήσθη, Πίτιος μὲν ἐφορεύοντος, ἄρχοντος δὲ Καλλίου Ἀθήνῃσιν.—i. 6, 1.

[4] ὅ τε ἀρχαῖος νεὼς ὁ τῆς Πολιάδος, ἐν ᾧ ὁ ἄσβεστος λύχνος.—p. 396.

[5] As by Lysias c. Andoc.: κατὰ τὸ νόμιμον τὸ παλαιὸν καὶ ἀρχαῖον (p. 253,

and has, therefore, only incidentally a meaning of antiquity. A thing may be old, and yet not the original; whilst the original, though commonly, but not necessarily, very old, must at all events be the first of its kind. Wherefore, when Strabo speaks of the Erechtheium as ἀρχαῖος, he means the original foundation consecrated to Athena, without regard to the actual building, and as contrasted with the newer one of the Parthenon. But where Xenophon applies the term παλαιὸς to it he can mean nothing but the building itself; the old temple, which had been succeeded in his time by a new one.

The difficulty would in a great degree vanish, if it could be shown that the archonship of Diocles was later than that of Callias, for which the scholiast on the 'Plutus' of Aristophanes affords some colour, by affirming that Diocles was archon fourteen years after Chabrias;[1] since, as the latter was archon in B.C. 415, the year of Diocles would then fall in B.C. 401; which would suit very well with the rebuilding of a temple burnt in B.C. 406. But the archonship of Diocles is too well established to be shaken by this passage of the scholiast. Thus the anonymous defendant in Lysias' oration entitled Ἀπολογία δωροδοκίας,[2] enumerates his liturgies under successive archons in the following chronological order: Theopompus (B.C. 411), Glaucippus (B.C. 410), Diocles (B.C. 409), Alexias (B.C. 405), and Eucleides (B.C. 403). Again: Euripides exhibited his 'Orestes' either in the archonship of Diocles, or in that of Theopompus, two years earlier;[3] and as he died in the archonship of Callias (B.C. 406), Diocles cannot be placed later than that archon. Besides, the inscription is written in characters that were in official use before the date of Eucleides; who, as we have seen, was six years later than Diocles, and two years before the date assigned by the scholiast.

We cannot agree with Leake that the injury which the temple

Reiske); where Taylor would have substituted τὸ πάτριον for τὸ παλαιόν, but where Reiske shows the difference between the two words. Cf. Demosth. adv. Androt. p. 597, Reiske: ἀλλ' ἐκεῖνα μὲν ἀρχαῖα καὶ παλαιά. We must confess, however, that

Boeckh also takes ἀρχαῖος and παλαιὸς to be equivalent. C. Ins. Gr. i. p. 264.

[1] ἵνα δὴ ἐπὶ Χαβρίου τις ταῦτα γενέσθαι δῷ . . . ἔστι δὲ ἕως Διοκλέους ἔτη ιδ΄.—v. 179.

[2] p. 698 sqq. Reiske.

[3] Schol. ad Eur. Orest. v. 365.

sustained under Callias, "seems not to have been great."[1] In that case, Xenophon would hardly have mentioned it in his history as an event so remarkable that it might serve to fix the chronology of the year, together with the phenomenon of the moon rising eclipsed.[2] Nor can we follow Leake when he says that " the word employed by Xenophon (ἐνεπρήσθη) implies only a conflagration ;" meaning, we presume, a partial one, though *conflagration* usually denotes a very extensive fire. The word ἐμπίπρημι has indeed special reference to the *act* of setting fire to anything ; a *purposed* act, and therefore, in cases of a criminal complexion, a wilful one. And thus it is used, both by Strabo and Plutarch, of the act of Herostratus in burning the temple of Artemis at Ephesus.[3] In this sense it answers to our word *to fire*, and has reference more to the act itself than to the effects of it. Yet it by no means excludes the idea of total destruction. When Achilles in Homer says :

> μὴ δὴ πυρὸς αἰθομένοιο
> νῆας ἐνιπρήσωσι, φίλον δ' ἀπὸ νόστον ἕλωνται
>
> (*Il.* xvi. 81)

> " For fear the ships should all be set on fire ;
> Then lost the Greeks are without remedy,
> And to their country never shall retire "
>
> (HOBBES)

he means, lest they set fire to the ships *and destroy* them, otherwise how should the return of the Greeks be cut off? And when Thucydides says : τό τε πεδίον ἀναβάντες ἐδῄουν, καὶ τὸν σῖτον ἐνεπίμπρασαν (vi. 94), he means that the Athenians set fire to the corn and *consumed it.* Hence, from this word alone, we should be inclined to suspect that the burning of the Erechtheium was a wilful act, and therefore the

---

[1] vol. i. p. 577. We may observe here that the words in Xenophon, ᾧ ἦ τε σελήνη ἐξέλιπεν το ἄρχοντος δὲ Καλλίου Ἀθήνησιν, are regarded by Müller as a gloss ; but this view is satisfactorily disposed of by Boeckh, loc. cit.

[2] The fact of the moon rising eclipsed in Olym. 93.3, the archonship of Callias, has been shown by Petavius (ap. Boeckh, Corp. Inser. Græc. vol. i. p. 264).

[3] ὡς δὲ τοῦτον (τὸν νεὼν) Ἡρόστρατός τις ἐνέπρησεν.—Strabo, xiv. p. 640 ; καθ' ἣν ἡμέραν ὁ τῆς Ἐφεσίας Ἀρτέμιδος ἐνεπρήσθη νεώς.—Plut. Alex. M. c. 3.

more memorable and the fitter to mark a date. We can indeed produce no authority for this view, but neither can any be adduced for the burning of the temple at all except Xenophon's; and as he is the only historian who relates the events of that period in any detail, this circumstance is no serious objection to our hypothesis.

We will now examine whether the inscription published by Rangabé helps to throw any light upon the subject.

Chandler's inscription is a report of the state of the works at the Erechtheium; Rangabé's, discovered in 1836, is a statement of disbursements on account of some works there. That it relates to the Erechtheium is evident, although no building is named; for it mentions the altar of the θυηχόος, or 'sacrificer,' which is also found in Chandler's inscription; and alludes also, like that, to the Cecropium.[1] It is not plain to what date it belongs; but it is evidently of a different one from Chandler's, since the architect mentioned in it is not the same; that specified in Chandler's being Philocles of Acharnæ, whilst Rangabé's inscription has Archilochus of Agrylæ. This renders somewhat improbable, but does not altogether exclude, Rangabé's supposition,[2] that his inscription relates to the finishing of the temple two years later than that of Chandler, or in B.C. 407. A stronger objection to this view is that some of the works mentioned in it were evidently completed at a later date than those noted as finished in the archonship of Diocles. Thus, for instance, Chandler's inscription adverts to the figures in the frieze of Eleusiniac stone as having been completed and fixed under the inspection of the Epistatæ it records;[3] whilst Rangabé's, supposed to be two years later, specifies payments for making these figures[4]— a long while for artists to be kept out of their money. What is

---

[1] τῷ βωμῷ τῷ τοῦ θυηχοῦ λίθοι πεντέλεικοι μῆκος τετράποδες, κ.τ.λ.—Chandler, l. 188 sq.; παρ(ὰ) τῷ (θυ)ηχο βωμῷ.—Rangabé, No. 57 A, l. 62; ἐν τῇ προστάσει τῇ πρὸς τῷ Κεκροπίῳ.—Chand. l. 58 sq.; (Κ)εκροπιο, Rang. No. 56 B. l. 24. The form θυηχόος, with a χ, is not recognised by Liddell and Scott, but it is found in the

inscriptions and in the codex of Photius' Lexicon. See Porson's Addenda, p. 689.

[2] vol. i. p. 61.

[3] πρὸς ᾧ τὰ ζῷα καὶ ἐτέθη ἐπὶ τῶν ἐπιστατῶν τούτων.—line 42 sq.

[4] See the beginning of the fragment No. 57 A, lines 1 to 22.

perhaps still more conclusive is a payment for lead for fixing the figures.[1] This might lead to the supposition that Rangabé's inscription referred to a state of things a little before, instead of two years after that of Chandler. But, as Rangabé himself observes, it relates to a more advanced state of the works, or even to their completion; as it alludes to the taking down of the scaffolding, which could only be done when the building was complete. And many of the payments are for things which would be done last, such as painting the interior of the portico, gilding the eyes of the volutes, &c.

We are thus led to the conclusion that these inscriptions relate to two wholly different operations; that Chandler's refers to some works, perhaps only very extensive repairs, going on in the time of Diocles, which had then become necessary, from the temple's antiquity, as well as from the partial damage it had sustained from the Persian fire. These repairs were probably accompanied with some architectural alterations, as perhaps the substitution of the coræ for pillars, the addition of the frieze with the little figures, &c.; while, at the same time, the foundations, general plan, and portions of the superstructure were preserved; so that Xenophon might be justified in calling it the *old* temple, when describing its destruction by fire. This view derives some confirmation from the opinion of Boeckh, that Chandler's inscription refers to a building in a tolerably complete state, which would be the case with one only under repair.[2] Soon after the fire it must have been rebuilt on a very similar plan, and with the same decorations of the frieze and of the southern portico, or Cecropium, and it is probably to this re-erection that the inscription published by Rangabé refers. This view is corroborated by the circumstance, that though some particulars of the present building appear to agree with Chandler's inscription, yet the measures assigned to them do not. Thus Stuart observes: "In the 44th line, it [the inscription] mentions columns on the walls next the Pandrosium, and in the 62nd, pilasters next to the Cecropium; some other particulars occur in it which seem to belong to the present

---

[1] μόλυβδος ἐωνήθη δύο ταλάντω εἰς πρόσθεσιν τῶν ζῳδίων.—No. 57 B, line 38 sq.

[2] Corp. Inscr. Gr. t. i. p. 271.

building, but the measures assigned to them prove the contrary. This circumstance is a confirmation of a passage in Xenophon, where this temple is said to have been burnt, about three years after this survey was taken, though the names of the archon and ephorus are generally believed to be interpolated." [1]

The original building was probably of the Ionic order, which was preserved in the subsequent reconstructions, perhaps as a sacred characteristic. For this order may be considered more proper to the Athenians, as Ionians, than the Doric, though at a more advanced period they adopted the latter in preference, and most of the extant specimens of their architecture are of that order—as the Parthenon, the Propylæa, and the so-called temple of Theseus.

The most splendid period of Athenian history was now drawing to a close. The loss of the army in Sicily and the battle of Ægospotami brought the Athenians under subjection to Sparta (B.C. 404). By the treaty which they made, under the influence of famine, they consented to the destruction of the Long Walls and the Peiraïc fortification, and to deliver up all their ships but twelve.[2] The demolition of the walls and the burning of the fleet were conducted—or rather, perhaps, inaugurated—to the sound of flutes; the allies of the Lacedæmonians looking on crowned with chaplets, regarding that day as the commencement of Grecian freedom.[3] Thus was established the tyranny of the Thirty, overthrown by Thrasybulus in the following year. We have before adverted to the military operations by which that revolution was effected (supra, p. 134). It is evident, from the account of the actions in the Peiræcus, that a very considerable portion of the fortifications must have been demolished by the Lacedæmonians.[4] For we have seen

---

[1] Antiquities of Athens, vol. ii. ch. ii. p. 18. Mr. Wilkins also observed a discrepancy between the actual measurements and those of the inscription. See Rose, Inscr. Gr. p. 178. On the other hand, however, M. Rangabé affirms that the particulars agree. Ant. Hellén. t. i. p. 60.

[2] Xenoph. Hell. ii. 2, 20.

[3] Xenoph. ibid. s. 23; Plut. Lysand. 15.

[4] Leake observes, vol. i. p. 391, note 2: "That *some* demolition of the Peiraïc walls was executed is evident from Xenophon, but he also shows that it was *very speedily* and therefore not effectually done. Οἱ δὲ τριάκοντα ᾑρέθησαν μέν, ἐπεὶ τάχιστα τὰ μακρὰ τείχη καὶ τὰ περὶ τὸν Πειραιᾶ

that Pausanias went to Cophos Limen to survey how Peiræcus might be most easily blockaded by erecting a fortress,[1] from which we can only infer that the northern portion, at least, of the Peiraic wall was down, or what would have been the use of a new fortification? Again, Pausanias, when repulsed by the Thrasybulians, retires to some rising ground about half a mile off. He must have retreated northwards, for had he retired southwards he would have been liable to be cut off from his allies by the Thrasybulians; whereas, from the spot where he rallied his men, he sent a message to his associates to come to his aid. There is a slight eminence just outside Peiræcus on approaching it from Athens.[2] Having been reinforced, Pausanias attacks the Thrasybulians with a heavy phalanx, kills many of them, and drives others into the mud at Halæ.[3] Now Halæ, if not the extreme northern inlet of the Peiræan harbour, must at all events have been outside the walls somewhere in this direction; and there is, according to Curtius' map, some low swampy ground half a mile to the east of that inlet, which would answer admirably to Xenophon's description, though this, indeed, is within the enclosure. But the whole account of these engagements is unintelligible on the supposition that the northern wall of the Peiræcus was still standing. Both Lacedæmonians and Athenians are evidently manœuvering on open ground, for no mention is made of wall or gate,

---

καθηρέθη. Hellen. ii. 3, 11." It is hardly necessary to say that the sense is : "The Thirty were elected *as soon as* the walls were demolished." Theramenes had brought home worse terms of peace than had at first been contemplated ; that the whole of the Long Walls should be demolished, instead of a length of ten stadia ; also that the fleet should be given up, and the Peiraïc wall pulled down. Lysias c. Agorat. p. 453, Reiske. Probably this demolition was not carried out literally ; but, that the destruction must have been great, appears from what Lysias says a little further on : ἔτι δὲ (μέμνησθε) τὰ τείχη ὡς κατεσκάφη, καὶ αἱ νῆες τοῖς

πολεμίοις παρεδόθησαν, καὶ τὰ νεώρια καθηρέθη, καὶ Λακεδαιμόνιοι τὴν ἀκρόπολιν ὑμῶν εἶχον, καὶ ἡ δύναμις ἅπασα τῆς πόλεως παρελύθη.—p. 471.

[1] Such seems to be the meaning of πῇ εὐαποτειχιστότατος εἴη ὁ Πειραιεύς.—Xen. Hell. ii. 4, 31.

[2] "Advancing further towards the sea the ground is more stony, and the plain in parts uncultivated, and the road ascending a low rocky hill brings you at once upon the Piræus."—Hobhouse's Journey, vol. i. p. 361. It is laid down in Curtius' plan of the Peiræcus, where the height is given at fifty feet.

[3] Xen. Hell. ii. 4, 34.

and the last engagement must, partly at least, have been outside the line of walls.

In ten years, however, by the victory of Conon at Cnidus (B.C. 394) the Athenians regained their naval superiority. One of the first cares of Conon after his success was to restore the Long Walls and the Peiraïc fortification, and the means which he adopted for that purpose show that there was a great deal to be done. For Conon not only employed in the work the crews of his own fleet, consisting of eighty triremes, but also hired builders and masons, sparing no expense that was necessary; whilst the Athenians themselves, the Bœotians, and other cities, voluntarily took upon themselves part of the labour.[1] Conon also erected, or rather, perhaps, enlarged and improved the Aphrodisium on the shore of the Peiræan harbour, in commemoration of his victory at Cnidus, where Aphroditë was the reigning goddess.[2]

For more than half a century from this time the history of the city is a blank. In his third Olynthiac oration Demosthenes refers indignantly to the trumpery public works then undertaken in comparison with those of the preceding age, though the luxury of private houses had much increased, and some of them had become more splendid than the public buildings.[3] But in B.C. 337, Lycurgus the orator, son of Lycophron, obtained the administration of the Athenian finances, and by his taste and munificence restored in no inconsiderable degree the splendour of the Periclean age. Lycurgus was of an old and wealthy family, and the confidence reposed in him by his fellow-citizens may be estimated from the circumstance that they had deposited in his hands, apparently as a sort of banker, 650 talents[4] (near £260,000)—a trifling

[1] Xenoph. Hell. iv. 8, 10; Diodor. Sic. xiv. 85. According to the latter author the Thebans alone sent 500 workmen.

[2] Pausan. i. 1, 4.

[3] p. 36 sq. Reiske.

[4] Psephisma at end of Vit. X. Orat. (Plut. Oper. t. ix. p. 385, Reiske). The Life says 250. The following account of Lycurgus is taken from that work, and from Pausanias, lib. i. 29, 16. Two fragments of the psephisma of Stratocles in honour of Lycurgus have been discovered at Athens, one in 1859 at Panagia Pyrgotissa, near the Stoa of Attalus, and the other in 1862 in the Dionysiac theatre. The first, published by Kumanudis in the Ἐπιγραφαὶ

sum, indeed, in these days of millionnaires, but large for a small state
like Athens. He held the administration for about the same time as
Pericles, but the revenue during that period exceeded that brought in
by Pericles by 6500 talents. The demagogues, after the time of that
minister, had raised the tribute of the allies by degrees to 1300 talents.[1]
Much of this fund was expended by Lycurgus in augmenting the military and naval strength of Athens. He brought into the Acropolis a
great quantity of arms, including 50,000 javelins, which were no doubt
deposited in the arsenal to the east of the Parthenon, of which, it is
thought, the foundations have been discovered in building the new
Museum.[2] Partly by building, and partly by repairing, he fitted out a
fleet of 400 triremes, and completed the ship sheds and arsenal, which
he found in an imperfect state. He instituted, at the Peiræeus, an
agon in honour of Poseidon, with not less than three cyclic choruses.
It was probably also under his direction that the walls were repaired.
From an inscription found in 1829, it appears that this work was executed when his son Habron was treasurer, most probably in the lifetime of his father, and by his instructions.[3] Much, also, was devoted
to the adornment of the city and the gratification of the tastes of the
Athenians. He provided for the Panathenaïc processions Victories of
solid gold (ὁλοχρύσους), gold and silver vases, and gold ornaments for a
hundred canephoroi. Being a man of cultivated mind, and a patron of
the drama, he restored the credit of the comic stage by bringing in a law
to revive an agon that had grown obsolete; namely, that the comedians
should contend in the theatre in the festival of the Chytri, or pot feast,

---

'Ελληνικαί, was very mutilated and illegible;
the second, which will be found in the
number of the 'Αρχαιολογικὴ 'Εφημερὶς
published in June, 1863 (No. 241), contains about twenty lines of the psephisma
more or less perfect. A great part agrees
verbatim with the copy in the pseudo-
Plutarch; the differences were no doubt
owing to the scribe who copied it. The
fragments have also been published by

Dr. Carl Curtius in the 'Philologus' for
1866 (t. xxiv. p. 83 sqq.).
[1] Plut. Arist. 24. According to the
author of the 'Lives of the Orators,' it
was Lycurgus who raised it to 1200.—
p. 351.
[2] Carl Curtius in Philol. xxiv. 269.
[3] See the Inscr. in Rangabé, t. ii. p.
381 sqq. Cf. Müller, De Munimentis
Athen.

and that the victor should be inserted in the *Didascaliæ* of the asty.[1] Comedy had begun to decline in the archonship of Callias (B.C. 406), when the choruses had been reduced; and not many years afterwards, Cinesias dealt it an almost mortal blow by procuring a law for abolishing the comic choregia altogether.[2] Lycurgus also procured a decree that bronze statues should be erected to Æschylus, Sophocles, and Euripides, doubtless those seen by Pausanias in the theatre;[3] and that copies of their tragedies should be preserved in the public record office and read by the town clerk when the actors were performing them, who were not to act them except in this manner.[4] A regulation adopted, apparently, to prevent the text of those great geniuses being corrupted by the caprice or negligence of the actors. The same dramatic tastes led Lycurgus to complete the Dionysiac theatre when director of it.[5] We have seen that even in the palmy days of the Attic drama the lower seats were of wood (supra, p. 83); and it seems probable that

---

[1] Such seems to be the meaning of the following obscure sentence : εἰσήνεγκε δὲ καὶ νόμους, τὸν μὲν περὶ τῶν κωμῳδῶν ἀγῶνα τοῖς χύτροις ἐπιτελεῖν ἐφάμιλλον ἐν τῷ θεάτρῳ, καὶ τὸν νικήσαντα εἰς ἄστυ καταλέγεσθαι, πρότερον οὐκ ἐξόν, ἀναλαμβάνων τὸν ἀγῶνα ἐκλελοιπότα.—Vit. X. Or. p. 347, Reiske. Petit (Legg. Att. p. 145) renders : "victorem civitate donato." But most of the dramatic poets must have been already Attic citizens. Wyttenbach translates : "victorque in asty reciperetur," which is unintelligible.

[2] Schol. ad Aristoph. Ran. 406; cf. Boeckh, Public Econ. of Athens, p. 461, Engl. trans.

[3] lib. i. c. 21.

[4] This we take to be the meaning of the following sentence : καὶ τὰς τραγῳδίας αὐτῶν ἐν κοινῷ γραψαμένους φυλάττειν, καὶ τὸν τῆς πόλεως γραμματέα παραναγινώσκειν τοῖς ὑποκρινομένοις οὐκ ἐξεῖναι γὰρ αὐτὰς ὑποκρίνεσθαι.—Vit. X. Or. p. 348. The passage is evidently corrupt. Some have emended it by reading αὐτοὺς for αὐτάς,

which, however, scarcely makes better sense ; and some by inserting ἄλλως after αὐτάς. The fault seems to be in οὐκ, which in a prohibitive sense ought to be μή, as we find just after μηδενὶ ἐξεῖναι, κ.τ.λ. Therefore we would read : οὕτως ἐξεῖναι γάρ, κ.τ.λ. Dr. Donaldson, Theatre of the Greeks, p. 167 (6th edit.), interprets the law to mean that "the actors were obliged to compare the acting copies of the plays of the three great tragedians with the authentic copies of their works preserved in the state archives ; and it was the duty of the public secretary to see that the texts were accurately collated." But first, this would have been no check on the actor when performing ; secondly, παραναγινώσκειν τοῖς ὑποκρινομένοις cannot mean to collate the texts, but to read them while they were acting, to see that they were correctly delivered.

[5] καὶ τὸ θέατρον τὸ Διονυσιακὸν ἐξειργάσατο.—Pseph. in Vit. X. Orat. p. 385. ἐπετέλεσε μὲν τὸ θέατρον.—Pausan i. 29, 16.

Lycurgus's improvements consisted of substituting stone ones for them, and perhaps also adding the marble thrones for those entitled to the προεδρία, or first row, which recent excavations have brought to light. He may also have adorned the theatre generally, since, as we have seen, he placed in it the statues of the great tragic triumvirate.

In addition to these works he also perfected the Panathenaïc stadium by levelling the ravine in which it is, and putting a stone kerb round the course. He made a gymnasium at the Lyceum, planted that place, and built a palæstra there. These were his most memorable works; but he also adorned the city with many other objects, which are not particularly specified. For his services, Stratocles procured a decree that he should have a bronze statue in the agora, and that his eldest representative for ever should be entitled to dine in the Prytaneium. He died in B.C. 323.

But these were about the last public works of any importance executed by the Athenians from their own resources and as an independent state. Athens, however, no doubt received many minor embellishments during this and the following period, especially in the erection of small temples and tripods in commemoration of choragic victories. The monument of Lysicrates, in the Street of the Tripods, belongs to the year B.C. 335; and probably other monuments of the same kind were erected there about the same time. In 320 Thrasyllus constructed the little temple over the theatre with the statue of Dionysus above it, which some years after (271) received the tripods consecrated by his son.

Lycurgus was one of the nine orators demanded by Alexander. The power of Macedon was now gaining the supremacy; and after the defeat of the confederate Greeks at Crannon by Antipater, the Athenians were compelled to receive a Macedonian garrison in Munychia (B.C. 322). One of the measures of Antipater was the disfranchisement of the poorer Athenian citizens, to whom new homes were offered in Thrace. It is said that 12,000 were removed thither,[1] so that considerably more than half of the Athenians who enjoyed the franchise must

---

[1] Plut. Phoc. 28; Diod. Sic. xviii. 18. The number of 22,000 (πλείους δισμυρίων καὶ δισχιλίων) is evidently a mistake, as the whole number of citizens was only 21,000.

have been in a state of pauperism, as the new qualification was only 2000 drachmas. The orators were now silenced; Demosthenes had poisoned himself, others had been put to death by Antipater, and Phocion, supported by Menyllus, the commander of the Macedonian garrison, governed almost at his discretion the 9000 citizens who remained at Athens. It seems not improbable that the Pnyx was destroyed at this period to gratify Antipater's hatred of the popular assembly and its orators; but we can adduce no authority for such a conjecture. The bema still bears the signs of having been fractured with great violence, and it is not an object which would have attracted the iconoclastic fury of the Christians. After the death of Phocion, Cassander, the Macedonian commander, by treaty with the Athenians, appointed Demetrius the Phalerean governor of Athens, under the title of superintendent or guardian (ἐπιμελητής) of the city (B.C. 318). During ten years Demetrius ruled Athens in uninterrupted peace. He was a man of taste, a lover of learning, and himself a voluminous author, by which qualities he had probably recommended himself to the attention of Cassander. Birth or dignity, at all events, gave him no title to the post which he held, for he appears to have been a slave in the family of Conon, though of a superior order.[1] He had, however, received a good education, had been a hearer of Theophrastus, and had had some experience in public affairs, as he appears to have had a share in the administration when Harpalus fled from Alexander to Athens[2] (B.C. 324). Being of a philosophic and literary turn of mind, he at first used well the power with which Cassander had invested him, and, in imitation of Peisistratus and Pericles, he endeavoured to improve Athens by laws, and other regulations. He is said to have first brought into the theatre a class of men called Homeristæ, who appear to have differed from the ancient rhapsodists by chanting the verses with a sort of modulation or recitative.[3] He is related to have improved the city with buildings,[4] but we can indicate none in Athens itself; the only

[1] Diodor. Sic. xviii. 74.

[2] Diog. Laërt. in Vit. v. 76; Ælian, V. H. xii. 43; Diog. L. ibid. 75.

[3] Athen. xiv. 12.

[4] If that is the meaning of κατασκευαῖς, Diog. L. loc. cit.

works of his that we know of being the completion of the Eleusinian temple by the addition of a portico, and the building of a magnificent arsenal or armoury at Peiræus, which, if we may trust Pliny,[1] was capable of supplying 1000 ships. Both these works were executed by the celebrated architect Philo, who wrote a treatise upon the latter, and another upon the symmetry of temples.[2]

Demetrius, in a census which he took of the Athenians, is said to have found 21,000 freemen, 10,000 metics, or resident aliens, and 400,000 slaves;[3] which probably means in all Attica. It is very difficult to reconcile these numbers with the account before given of the removal of 9000 citizens to Thrace by Antipater. The number of resident aliens, and also of the slaves, in proportion to the citizens, seem both enormous. From the same place of Athenæus, it appears that private individuals sometimes had 1000 slaves; but, if true, these could only have been proprietors of mines or very large manufacturers.

Demetrius had at first lived plainly and frugally, as became a philosopher, and he even passed sumptuary laws to restrain the luxury of the Athenians. But the possession of almost unlimited wealth and power corrupted his mind, and the latter part of his administration became as notorious for its dissoluteness and profligacy, as the beginning had been commendable for the opposite qualities.[4] The conquered Athenians had lost their self-respect, and had already sunk down to be that herd of slaves and flatterers which they remained ever after. They encouraged and applauded the vices and the vanity of their ruler. In the year of his archonship (B.C. 309), when he celebrated the Dionysiac pomp, the poet who composed the choral hymn alluded to his noble birth, and compared him in beauty and splendour to the sun; and at the instance of some parasite as many bronze statues are said to have been erected to him as there were days in the year.[5] The Athenians, of course, felt no real affection or respect for the man whom they so basely flattered; and when his namesake Demetrius, called Poliorcetes, from his

[1] H. N. vii. 125; Strab. p. 395.
[2] Vitruv. vii. Præf. 12.
[3] Ctesicles ap. Athen. vi. c. 103.
[4] Duris and Carystius, ap. Athen. xii. 60.
[5] Plin. H. N. xxxiv. 27; Strabo, p. 398.

engineering talent, the son of Antigonus, another of the Macedonian
diadochi, or successors of Alexander, and the rival of Cassander, unexpectedly arrived at Peiraeus, with his fleet, and found the entrance
of the port unguarded, the Athenians at once submitted, and even
welcomed his arrival (B.C. 308).

Demetrius at first displayed the greatest moderation. He dismissed the Phalerean in safety to Thebes, and though longing to see
the glories of Athens, declined to enter the city till he had reduced the
garrison in Munychia.[1] Thus after a lapse of about fifteen years, the
Athenian republic was nominally restored. But the Athenians were no
longer fit to exercise the rights of freemen. They hastened to put
their necks under the yoke with all the signs of the most abject sub-
mission. They gave to Antigonus and Demetrius the title of their
saviour gods (σωτῆρες) and abolishing the office of the eponymous
archon, chose annually in his place a priest of the saviours. The names
of Antigonus and Demetrius were embroidered on the peplus along
with those of Zeus and Athena; a profanation, however, at which the
offended deities expressed their displeasure by rending it in a storm, as
the Panathenaïc ship passed along the agora. The place where Poliorcetes had first alighted from his chariot was dedicated to Demetrius
Catæbates (καταιβάτης), the epithet of Jove when he descends in the
thunderbolt. Two new Attic tribes were instituted, called Antigonis
and Demetrias, and the senate conformably augmented to the number
of 600. Stratocles procured a decree that the ambassadors sent to the
saviours should be called Theori, like those sent to perform the national
sacrifices at Delphi and Olympia; and it was ordained that Demetrius
should be consulted as if he were an oracle. The month Munychion
was renamed Demetrion, and the festival of the Dionysia called
Demetria. But in the midst of all this abject adulation, the comic poet
Philippides gave token that the ancient Attic wit and spirit was not
entirely extinct, by attacking in his verses the decrees of Stratocles.

---

[1] The principal authorities for these
events are Plutarch, Vit. Demetr. and
Diodorus Sic. xx. sqq. There is a brief
sketch of the period in Pausanias, lib. i.
c. 25 sq.

Nothing was now left to the Athenians but the choice of a master. In B.C. 304, Cassander attempted to regain possession of Athens, but his enterprise was defeated by Demetrius. Hence a fresh occasion for exalting him. He was now lodged in the Parthenon, in the house, as he called it, of his elder sister. He contaminated the abode of the virgin goddess by his boundless lust, to which were sacrificed the wives and children of the citizens; so that whilst he dwelt there the temple was considered most pure when he only indulged himself with his courtesans Chrysis, Lamia, Demo, and Anticyra. In a subsequent temporary visit to Athens, he expressed a desire to be initiated without delay, and to pass at once from the Lesser Mysteries to the state of an epopt. The extravagance of this request may be estimated when it is remembered that the Lesser Mysteries were celebrated in the month Anthesterion, the Greater in Boëdromion, and that it was not allowed to become an epopt till at least a year after the latter. The daiduchus Pythodorus alone ventured to remonstrate, but in vain. It was decreed that the month Munychion (or Demetrion) should be called Anthesterion, and Demetrius was initiated in the Lesser Mysteries at Agræ. Then the name of the month was again changed to Boëdromion, when the greater ceremonies were performed, and Demetrius at once admitted to be an epopt: Stratocles, as Philippides said, having thus reduced the year to one month. Such servility had its natural effect, and excited the contempt instead of the gratitude of Demetrius.

When put to the test, the feelings of the Athenians proved just as sincere as in the case of the Phalerean. After the overthrow and death of Antigonus at Ipsus, and the flight of Demetrius (B.C. 301), they passed a decree that no kings should be admitted into the city, and relegated his wife Deidamia to Megara. After the victory of Demetrius over Ptolemy at Cyprus, both he and his father Antigonus had assumed the regal title (B.C. 306), and the rest of the diadochi soon followed the example. During the eclipse of Demetrius, Cassander had endeavoured to regain possession of Athens, and invaded Attica; but this enterprise he was forced to relinquish by the Athenian general Olympiodorus, who opposed him with some forces which he had brought from Ætolia; and

Cassander had then conciliated a faction at Athens through Lachares, the leading demagogue of the day, whom he excited with the hope of becoming tyrant of Athens. In this state of things, Demetrius, whose power had revived, beheld a prospect of recovering Athens. His first attempts were unsuccessful, and raised against him a Macedonian party, headed by Demochares, besides the faction of Lachares. But in B.C. 296 he laid siege to Athens, devastated Attica from one side to the other, and reduced the Athenians to the extremity of famine. Lachares used the conjuncture to make himself absolute master of Athens, when he drove Demochares into exile, and exercised his power with extreme cruelty, impiety, and rapaciousness.[1] But in spite of this tyranny, and their state of almost absolute starvation, the Athenians. probably at the instigation of Lachares, passed a decree that to propose a capitulation should be deemed a capital offence. At last, the tyrant, having rendered himself insupportable to the Athenians, and seeing that the city must fall into the hands of Demetrius, fled to Thebes, carrying off the golden shields from the Acropolis, and all the movable ornaments from the chryselephantine statue of Athena.

Lachares had no sooner departed than the gates of Athens were thrown open to Demetrius. The conqueror bade the citizens assemble in the theatre. With fear and trembling they took their seats in that favourite place of amusement, apprehending that they themselves were to become the subject of no mimic tragedy. They found the scene occupied by soldiers, and the logeum, or stage, surrounded with the bodyguard of Demetrius. Soon the conqueror made his appearance at the principal entrance, like some tragic actor, whilst every heart throbbed with anxiety and expectation. But his first words when he had descended to the logeum soothed all their apprehensions. With a mild voice and friendly words he gently reproved them, promised them a donation of one hundred thousand bushels of corn, and restored those magistrates whom he knew to be most popular. The theatre rung with acclamations and applause at so unexpected a change of things, and

___

[1] τυράννων ὧν ἴσμεν τά τε ἐς ἀνθρώπους μάλιστα ἀνήμερον καὶ ἐς τὸ θεῖον ἀφειδέστατον.—Pausan. i. 25, 5.

amidst the general excitement the rhetor Democleides proposed and carried a decree that Peiræeus and Munychia should be delivered up to Demetrius. This, of course, was a work of supererogation. Demetrius would no doubt have occupied those fortresses without asking the permission of the Athenians; and soon afterwards, to keep them more securely in subjection, and to prevent their insurrections from diverting him from his other projects, he also seized and fortified the Museium Hill, which lies over against the Acropolis.[1] (B.C. 295.)

In the obscurity of the Macedonian period there is little to be discovered of the history of the city. We shall content ourselves with noting the principal events. When the arms of Pyrrhus began to prevail over those of Demetrius, the Athenians seized the opportunity of revolt. Under the conduct of Olympiodorus, they expelled the garrisons which Demetrius had placed on the Museium, and recovered Peiræeus and Munychia. Encouraged by these successes, they abolished the priesthood of the saviours, and restored the annual archonship[2] (B.C. 288). Demetrius made an attempt to recover Athens, which was frustrated by Pyrrhus, whose aid the Athenians had invoked. Pyrrhus entered Athens, but after sacrificing on the Acropolis retired, advising them to admit no more kings. In B.C. 268 Antigonus Gonatas laid siege to Athens, which, though said to have continued five or six years with intermissions, was without success. Antigonus, enraged at their obstinacy, laid waste Attica and burnt the temple and sacred grove of Poseidon at Colonus.[3] At length his efforts were successful; Athens was compelled to capitulate and to admit Macedonian garrisons into the Museium, Peiræeus, Munychia, Salamis, and Sunium. It was during the period of their subjection to Antigonus that Zeno, the Stoic philosopher, was intrusted with the keys of the city, and on his death Antigonus, who loved and admired him, persuaded the Athenians to bury him in the Cerameicus.[4] One of the most dreadful of the Mace-

[1] Plut. Demetr. 34. Let us observe here that no mention is made of Phalerum; which shows that it had ceased to be a military port, and is another proof that it lay not at the Peiraïc peninsula.

[2] Pausan. i. 26; Plut. Demetr. 46.
[3] Pausan. i. 30, 4: iii. 6.
[4] Diog. Laërt. vii. 6, 11.

donian inflictions was the siege of Athens by Philip V. in B.C. 200.
He repulsed a sally of the Athenians from the Dipylon, but was unable
to take the city by assault; and as the Athenians were now aided by
the Romans, who had begun to play a part in the affairs of Greece,
Philip was obliged to retreat, and pitched his camp at Cynosarges.
Hence he wreaked his vengeance on the surrounding suburbs, destroying
not only Cynosarges with its temple of Hercules, its gymnasium, and
sacred groves, but the Lyceium also, and every pleasant or holy place
around the city, sparing neither the buildings nor even the tombs.
But after an unsuccessful attempt on Eleusis he retreated to Megara,
and thence to Corinth.[1]

During the struggle with the Macedonians, the Athenians were
probably assisted with money by some of the Eastern princes. We
know, at all events, of several who aided in embellishing their city,
and on whom they lavished the tokens of their adulation. One of the
Ptolemies, most probably Philadelphus, built near the Theseium, about
B.C. 260, the gymnasium which bore his name; and in return for his
benefactions the Athenians changed the name of the tribe Antigonis to
that of Ptolemaïs.[2] Attalus I., king of Pergamus, who formed an
alliance with the Athenians against Philip, visited Athens in B.C. 200.
He was received with the most striking demonstrations of popular goodwill and reverence. As he approached the city from Peiræeus not
only the magistrates and knights, but also all the citizens with their
wives and children went forth to meet him. When he entered the
Dipylon, which gate was probably selected as being the noblest entrance
of Athens, all the priests and priestesses ranged themselves on each
hand, every temple was open, and at all the altars stood victims ready
for the sacrifices which he was entreated to perform. He showed himself a still more liberal benefactor than Ptolemy. He adorned Athens
with a stoa, long known only from the mention of it by Athenæus
(v. 50), situated on the north-east side of the agora, as the discovery of
the architrave and inscription within the last few years has proved.
Its remains had previously been assigned to the gymnasium of Ptolemy.

---

[1] Liv. xxxi. 24 sq.; 30.   [2] Pausan. i, 17, 2; Cic. de Fin. v. 1.

Attalus also placed in the Acropolis at the eastern extremity of the southern or Cimonian wall a series of sculptures, representing the Gigantomachia, the battle with the Amazons, the battle of Marathon, and the overthrow of the Gauls in Mysia.[1] He also laid out a garden at the Academy. The Athenians rewarded him as they had done Ptolemy, by giving the name of Attalis to the tribe Demetrias.[2]

Eumenes II., the son and successor of Attalus (B.C. 197-159), inherited his father's love for the Athenians, and built for them a portico which appears to have lain on the west side of the theatre, as Vitruvius, after mentioning it, observes by way of distinction, that the Odeium of Pericles was on the left hand of those leaving the theatre, and consequently on the east.[3] It has been sometimes mistakenly identified with the arches near the Odeium of Regilla.

Antiochus IV., surnamed Epiphanes, king of Syria, was another of those princes who took a pride in adorning Athens. About the year B.C. 174 he formed the design of completing the Olympium, and appears to have employed for that purpose a Roman architect named Cossutius, but in what state he found it, or how far he advanced it, it is impossible to say. According to some authorities, he began it. The work was interrupted by his death, and it was some centuries yet before the temple was destined to be completed. Some writers say that he left it half finished, if we are to take the word ἡμιτελές literally.[4] Antiochus also appears to have placed above the theatre the gilded Gorgon's head.[5]

In B.C. 146 the Achæan League, the last bulwark of Grecian independence, was overthrown by the Romans, and subsequently all Greece, as far as the borders of Macedonia and Epirus, under the name of Achaia, became a Roman province.

---

[1] These have been recognized in some recently discovered sculptures. See Brunn, Bullet. dell' Instit. 1865, p. 116.

[2] Polyb. xvi. 25; Liv. xxxi. 12 sq.; Pausan. i. 5, 5; 8, 1.

[3] lib. v. c. 9.

[4] See Vitruv. vii. Præf. 15, 17; Athen. v. 21; Antiochus Epiphanes qui Athenis Olympeium inchoavit.—Vell. Pat. i. 10; cf. Liv. xli. 20. τὸ Ὀλύμπιον, ὅπερ ἡμιτελὲς κατέλιπε τελευτῶν ὁ ἀναθεὶς βασιλεύς.—Strab. 396.

[5] Pausan. v. 12, 2.

CHAPTER VI.

THE Athenians had lived more than half a century in peace and security under the Roman domination, and might have continued to do so had they not suffered themselves to be misled by a philosopher whose doings form one of the strangest episodes in their history. Aristion, or Athenion, for we find his name written both ways,[1] was of servile origin, but having inherited his master's property, he got himself illegally enrolled an Attic citizen. He now professed himself a Peripatetic, and having made a good deal of money by teaching in various places, returned to Athens, where he procured an embassy to Mithridates Eupator, king of Pontus, and succeeded by his address in completely insinuating himself into the monarch's favour. Mithridates was then at the height of his power, and Aristion, in his letters to the Athenians, painted it in such glowing colours that he inspired them with the hope of throwing off the Roman yoke, and regaining their ancient liberty by the aid of so powerful an ally. The extent to which he had dazzled them may be judged from

---

[1] Athenæus, who gives the most elaborate account of his history (lib. v. c. 47 sqq.), from Poseidonius, the Stoic philosopher and instructor of Cicero, alone calls him Athenion. All other writers call him Aristion: Strab. p. 398; Pausan. i. 20, 3; Plut. Syll. 12; Appian, B. M. p. 189 sqq., &c. He may possibly have changed his name, as Casaubon suggests (ad Athen. l. c.).

the circumstance that on his return, being driven to Carystus, in Euboea, by a storm, they despatched some ships of war to bring him home, with a silver-footed couch on which to enter the city. The whole population flocked out as he approached Athens, expecting some wonderful tidings from Mithridates; but the wiser part could not help admiring the freaks of fortune on contrasting the pomp of his entry, exceeding any the Romans had indulged in, with his former state of a poor schoolmaster in a ragged cloak. The actors and others connected with the Dionysiac theatre especially welcomed him, hailing him as the messenger of the new Dionysus, and invited him to the hearth of their guild to participate in their prayers and sacrifices. Instead of his former hired lodgings, he now dwelt in the house of one of the richest men in Athens, brilliant with embroidery, pictures, statues, and plate. When he went abroad in a splendid chlamys, and wearing a golden ring engraved with the head of Mithridates, he was preceded and followed by a crowd of slaves, and those thought themselves happy who could but get near enough to him to touch the hem of his garment.

The day after his arrival, a great crowd, both citizens and strangers, assembled spontaneously in the agora to hear what he had to tell them. Having ascended the rostra placed before the stoa of Attalus for the use of the Roman praetors, he began with a good deal of affectation and grimace to magnify and extol the power of Mithridates; then, after pausing a while to let his speech take full effect, he proceeded to exhort his auditors no longer to endure the state in which they were, a state of anarchy purposely prolonged by the Roman senate in settling what form of government they would have. "Let us," he exclaimed, "no longer submit to see our closed temples, and squalid gymnasia, our deserted theatre, our dumb tribunals, our Pnyx, consecrated by divine oracles, ravished from the people! Shall we endure the sacred voice of Iacchus to be silenced, the venerable temple of the Eleusinian goddesses to be shut up,[1] and the schools of the philosophers to be reduced to silence?"

[1] Such seems to be the meaning, as Casaubon observes, of the words τὸ σεμνὸν ἀνάκτορον τοῖν θεοῖν κεκλειμένον (Athen. v. 51). They would also apply to the

The utterances of such a person, with such an object, should of course be used with caution in drawing inferences regarding the earlier condition of Athens under the Roman dominion. At the same time what he brings forward are matters of fact which must have been notorious to all his audience, so that the most passionate advocate, the most unscrupulous impostor, could hardly have ventured to falsify them. And we must recollect that we have Poseidonius, a most respectable philosopher, and a contemporary, as a voucher for the speech. We are aware, indeed, that Strabo says[1] that the Romans left the Athenians their laws and liberty; by which, however, he perhaps only means that they became what the Romans called a ' Libera Civitas;' that is, they were allowed their own municipal government. For only at the end of the preceding page he had observed that the Athenians, after the expulsion of the Thirty Tyrants, preserved their democracy *down to the time of the Roman domination,* and that though they were sometimes unjustly treated by the Macedonian kings, in order to compel their obedience, yet they preserved under them their form of government untouched.[2] The fact seems to be, that, under the Romans, they retained their magistrates and their customary laws, only with the vital exception that their public assemblies were abolished. This agrees with the statement of Aristion about the people being deprived of the Pnyx. The ecclesia had lost its imperial functions, and with regard to state policy, the Athenians were no longer autonomous. The Mysteries, though afterwards revived, may at first have been temporarily suppressed by the Romans from their hatred of midnight and secret meetings; but we can adduce no evidence in support of the statement of Aristion. It was about the same time that the secret Bacchanalian societies were suppressed in Italy.

temple of the Dioscuri; but the preceding allusion to Iacchus indicates the true meaning, and the temple of the ἄνακες was hardly important enough to be introduced into an appeal such as this.

[1] p. 398.

[2] ἐφύλαξαν δὲ τὴν δημοκρατίαν μέχρι τῆς Ῥωμαίων ἐπικρατείας. καὶ γὰρ εἴ τι μικρὸν ὑπὸ τῶν Μακεδονικῶν βασιλέων παρελυπήθησαν, ὥσθ' ὑπακούειν αὐτῶν ἀναγκασθῆναι, τόν γε ὁλοσχερῆ τύπον τῆς πολιτείας τὸν αὐτὸν διετήρουν.—p. 397, fin.

M

The speech of Aristion made a great impression on the people, and especially the baser portion of them. With much clamour they hastened to the theatre, and elected Aristion their general.[1] Then he strutted into the orchestra, and, after thanking them, said: "Now you are your own masters, but I am your head; and if you support me, I shall be able to do as much alone as all of you together." So speaking, he dictated what colleagues he would have. Having thus made himself master of Athens, his first step was to get rid of the well-inclined citizens, and lest they should escape he set a guard at all the gates. In short, he appears to have been a sort of Greek Robespierre, and established a Reign of Terror. Many citizens let themselves down at night from the walls and fled; but Aristion sent horsemen after them, and some of them were killed, and the others brought back in chains. Having surrounded himself with a well-armed guard,[2] he began to play the tyrant. He laid snares to detect those who were inclined to the Roman cause; he filled not only the town, but the country also, with his satellites and spies; those who endeavoured to escape were brought back and put to death with torments; the rich were plundered to such an extent that he is said to have filled several wells with money, which, however, is probably an exaggeration; and he promulgated a sort of curfew law, that nobody should go out after sunset, even with a lanthorn. He was helped in his doings by Apellicon, a philosopher of the same kidney, whose literary and antiquarian taste had led him to purchase the library of Aristotle and a great many more. Having been detected in purloining from the Metroum some ancient autograph psephismata,[3] Apellicon had been obliged to fly for his life; but he

---

[1] στρατηγὸν ἐπὶ τῶν ὅπλων. In the time of Athenæus, the civil magistrates were called *strategi*. The fact of the people going to the theatre to elect Aristion, instead of to the Pnyx, seems to show that the latter was now quite out of use. Even the assemblies in the theatre had been suppressed, for Aristion notes the θέατρον ἀνεκκλησίαστον (Athen. v. 51).

[2] This seems to have consisted of 2000 soldiers, whom Mithridates had sent with him to Athens. Appian, Bell. Mithr. p. 189.

[3] This anecdote appears to show that the proposers of psephismata made a draft of them, and that, when carried, they were engraved on bronze tablets or stone.

contrived to return, and joined Aristion. By him he was despatched to plunder Delos; but through his blundering, the enterprise completely miscarried, and Apellicon himself nearly fell into the hands of the Romans.[1] In these events, as well as in their earlier history, we see how prone the Athenians were to be led away and deceived by any clever and specious intriguer.

These and other machinations of the king of Pontus against the Romans, brought on the Mithridatic war, the conduct of which was intrusted to Sulla. Landing in Greece, he marched through Bœotia. Thebes, which had also thrown off its allegiance, now submitted without striking a blow. Sulla then arrived in Attica, and telling off part of his army to invest Athens, he himself undertook the siege of Peiræeus; into which Mithridates' general, Archelaüs, had thrown himself with a considerable force. An attempt to escalade the walls having failed, Sulla found himself compelled to institute a regular siege, which lasted many months, and obliged him during the winter to construct a fortified camp at Eleusis. Archelaüs made a most vigorous defence, burning Sulla's machines as soon as they were erected before the walls; so that to construct new ones he cut down the timber in the sacred groves of the Academy and Lyceum. Provoked at this obstinacy, Sulla turned the siege into a blockade; and directing all his force against Athens, which was now suffering the extremities of famine, took it by assault (B.C. 86). The attack was made, as we have already had occasion to observe,[2] between the Dipylon and the Peiraïc Gate, near the monument called Heptachalcum. Then followed a dreadful massacre, which spared neither sex nor age, and inundated the streets and agora with blood.

During the siege Aristion with a few followers had taken refuge in the Acropolis, having first burnt the Odeium of Pericles, lest its materials might assist the Romans to scale and capture the citadel. Here his

---

[1] Such is the account of Athenæus, v. 53; but Appian relates that Archelaüs, having reduced Delos, which had revolted from the Athenians, sent the sacred treasure to Athens by Aristion, along with 2000 soldiers, and that he was thus enabled to seize the tyranny (Bell. Mithr. p. 189). And this perhaps is the more probable account.

[2] Above, p. 93.

conduct was of a piece with the rest of his character. He and his companions passed the day in feasting, drinking, dancing, and making merry, whilst the citizens were starving, and endeavouring to support life by boiling down old shoes, and gathering a herb called parthenion, which grew on the Acropolis. He even aggravated their misfortunes by insult. To the Hierophantis, who had begged a measure of corn, he sent some pepper; he suffered the holy lamp of Athena to be extinguished for want of oil; and when the senate and priests came to entreat him to propose terms to Sulla, he dispersed them with arrows. When the city was taken, the siege of the Acropolis was assigned to Curio, and after some time, the want of water, which was supplied only by the rain, compelled Aristion to submit. He, and those who had held office under him, were then put to death. Peiræeus was soon afterwards reduced, when the arsenal, docks, and principal buildings were burnt by Sulla. He re-established at Athens the laws previously imposed by the Romans, and deprived the citizens of the right of voting and electing their magistrates; with a promise, however, that these privileges should be ultimately restored to them.[1]

After this time the Long Walls and the walls of Peiræeus were never rebuilt; and indeed there was no longer any occasion for them, since Athens had ceased to be a naval power. Thus Strabo, as we have already remarked, describes the Peiræeus in his time as almost deserted. Sulla, however, appears to have committed no more devastation than was necessary for military purposes. His cutting down the timber at the Lyceum and Academy was not a wanton act, like those of Philip V., but done to procure the implements of war. Pausanias, however, who gives a more unfavourable account of his proceedings than the other authorities, charges him with decimating in the Cerameicus those who had shown themselves adverse to him when Taxiles, the general of Mithridates, advanced during the siege to the relief of Athens; and Sulla's cruelty and contempt for human life render the charge not improbable. Pausanias also accuses Sulla of many other ferocious acts, unworthy of a Roman, and especially with the impiety of dragging

[1] Appian, Bell. Mithr. p. 195 sq.; Plut. Sull. c. 12 sqq.

Aristion from the altar of Athena, to put him to death; to which Pausanias, with his usual devoutness, ascribes the horrible malady with which he was afterwards seized.[1] Sulla does not appear to have carried off any works of art from Athens, as Mummius did from Corinth; but he is said to have sent some of the columns of the Olympium to Rome, to be used in the temple of the Capitoline Jupiter, which he was rebuilding.[2] These must have been the columns provided by Antiochus Epiphanes. They could hardly have been of so gigantic a size as those used when the temple was completed by Hadrian; for these would have been out of all proportion to the much smaller temple on the Capitol; unless indeed the height of the ancient temple was very much increased, and not proportionably to its other dimensions. As there was apparently little hope in Sulla's time that the Olympium would ever be finished, this can hardly be regarded as a greater spoliation than the acquisitions of Lord Elgin. Sulla, who had some literary tastes, seized indeed the library of Apellicon; but this might justly be regarded among the spoils of war, like the forty pounds of gold and the six hundred pounds of silver which he took from the Acropolis, or the captured slaves whom he caused to be sold.[3] To Apellicon, perhaps, is partly due the corrupt state in which we have the text of Aristotle; but he appears to have been helped in depraving it by the grammarian Tyrannio, after the books had been carried to Rome.[4] Apellicon was rather a book collector than a philosopher; and as the manuscripts of Aristotle were in a very damaged state when they came into his possession, from having been kept in a cellar or well, he supplied the obliterated parts out of his own head, and, according to Strabo, published a very faulty edition.[5] But though Sulla committed no wanton destruction at Athens, he appears to have done nothing to repair the damage caused by the siege, for which, indeed, he had perhaps neither time nor means. The Odeium of Pericles was left to be restored shortly afterwards by Ariobarzanes III., surnamed Eusebes, king of Cappadocia, another of those princes who took a pride in associating their names with Athens.

---

[1] lib. i. c. 20.
[2] Plin. N. H. xxxvi. 45.
[3] Appian, B. M. p. 196; Plut. Sull. 26.
[4] Plut. ibid.
[5] Strab. p. 609.

It appears to have been restored on the original plan, since Pausanias, a century or two after, still notes its resemblance to the tent of Xerxes.[1] The Romans, indeed, did nothing for Athens till the time of Augustus, and their rule, during the republican period, tended rather to the damage than the benefit of the city, and indeed of Greece in general. The arch-plunderer Verres, when legatus of Dolabella, is charged by Cicero with carrying off many pictures and statues from Achaia, and with taking a great quantity of gold from the Parthenon.[2] The ruined and prostrate state of Ægina, Megara, Piræus, Corinth, is pictured in a letter of Servius Sulpicius to Cicero.[3] Corinth was rebuilt by a colony of freedmen sent thither by C. Cæsar, who enriched themselves and filled Rome with the most beautiful specimens of the ceramic art, by plundering the tombs.[4] The establishment of the empire benefited Greece by putting an end to the extortions of the irresponsible republican magistrates.

From the time of Sulla, the Athenians made no further attempts to free themselves from Roman domination; though when Rome herself was torn with civil faction, they inclined towards the republican, in that case, the conservative party, as was natural enough from their ancient sympathies and traditions. On the same side were many of the most gifted and best educated of the Romans themselves; men who had formed their minds, like Cicero, and subsequently Livy, Horace, and others, by the study of Greek literature, which many of them had imbibed at the fountain-head, in Athens itself. For after its reduction by Sulla, that city had become a sort of Roman university, and to have studied there came to be regarded as an almost indispensable part of a liberal education. Athens being filled with young men of this sort, its citizens would naturally have been swayed also by them in the part which they took in the great political question of the day; and therefore we can feel no surprise that they should have erected statues to Brutus and Cassius by the side of those of Harmodius and Aristogeiton.[5]

[1] lib. i. 20, 3.   [4] Strab. p. 381.

[2] Cic. in Verr. II. i. 17, 45.   [5] Dion Cass. xlvii. 20.

[3] Epp. ad Fam. lib. iv. 5.

The Athenians sided with Pompey against Cæsar ; yet, after they had surrendered to his legatus, Fufius Calenus, Cæsar appears to have borne them no grudge for the part which they took against him, and bequeathed them money wherewith to adorn their city ; at least Augustus, as we shall see, gave him credit for so doing. Brutus visited Athens a little before the fatal day of Philippi, and was received with acclamations and honorary decrees. His warlike projects were then concealed. He seemed only to be making an agreeable holiday, and his time was chiefly spent in hearing the philosophers Theomnestus and Cratippus. But he was secretly making preparations for the campaign ; and he employed himself in conciliating the young Romans then studying at Athens, among whom was Cicero's son, of whom he appears to have thought very highly.[1] The Athenians erected statutes to Brutus and Cassius. In the subsequent struggle between Antony and Octavianus they sided with Antony, whose agreeable vices were, perhaps, as welcome to them as the austerer character of Brutus. Antony entered warmly into all their pursuits. He heard their philosophers, beheld their games and contests, was initiated in their mysteries ; he loved to be called Philhellene, and still more Philathenæus, and made them many presents.[2] He was passing the winter at Athens when the news arrived of the victory of Ventidius over the Parthians, on which occasion he feasted the Greeks and accepted the post of gymnasiarch at Athens. When presiding at the games he left at home the ensigns of his dignity, adopted the Attic costume, and caressed the contending youths. And when he went forth to the war he plucked a fillet from the sacred olive, and, in obedience to an oracle, took with him a vessel filled with water from the Clepsydra.[3] His wife Octavia was an especial favourite with the Athenians, who showed her many marks of honour. When, on a subsequent visit to Athens, Antony brought Cleopatra with him, she desired to receive some testimonies of the same kind, and the Athenians sent to her house a decree they had made in her honour by ambassadors specially appointed for the purpose, among whom was Antony as an

---

[1] Plut. Brut. 24.
[2] Idem, Ant. 23.
[3] Ibid. 33 sq.

Athenian citizen.[1] When he departed for his last unfortunate campaign the gods seemed to declare against him. The statue of Dionysus, which formed one of the group in the Gigantomachia erected by Attalus on the Acropolis, was blown down by the wind and fell into the theatre; an omen which derived its significance from the fact that Antony affected to trace his descent from that god, and called himself the younger Dionysus. It was probably the beauty of the deity that occasioned this selection, as afterwards in the case of Antinoüs. But, indeed, the character of the deity was nearer to human nature, especially to Pagan human nature, than that of any other god. His voluptuous character, associated with merriment and revelry, and without anything awful or repulsive, was calculated to excite goodwill, whilst his Indian triumphs saved it from contempt. Hence, perhaps, it was that so many sovereigns and potentates affected a connection with him. The same storm overthrew the colossal statues which had been erected to Attalus and Eumenes, which, by an absurd practice that the Romans were not ashamed to adopt, had been re-inscribed to Antony.[2]

When Octavianus, by the overthrow of Antony at Actium, became master of the Roman world, he could very well afford to despise the political opinions of the Athenians; but to have wit and genius on his side was always part of his policy, and we need not, therefore, be surprised that he not only forgave them, but even became a remarkable benefactor. His sister Octavia, too, may have pleaded in their favour, who during her residence at Athens with her husband obtained, as we have said, the love of the Athenians. He mulcted them, indeed, in some of the territories which Antony had bestowed upon them, who had given them the islands of Ægina, Icus, Ceos, Sciathus, and Peparethus.[3] Of these Augustus took away Ægina, and also deprived them of Eretria in Eubœa.[4] By forbidding them to sell their citizenship he deprived them of a source of revenue, but at the same time must have increased their respectability. The foundation of Nicopolis and Patras must doubtless have proved detrimental to Athens and other Greek

[1] Plut. Ant. c. 57.   [3] Appian, B. C. v. p. 675.
[2] Ibid. 60.   [4] Dion Cass. liv. 7

cities. These acts Augustus probably deemed necessary in a political view; but he compensated the Athenians by improving their city. It is to this time that we must refer the Propylæum of the new agora, which still exists, consisting of four Doric columns, supporting an entablature and pediment, and forming its entrance on the west; while the Horologium, commonly called the Tower of the Winds, which faces it, though executed at the expense of a private individual, no doubt formed part of the general design, and marked the boundary of the market on the east. These buildings and their topographical relations are described in another place,[1] we are here only concerned about the origin of them. An inscription records that the Propylæum was built out of the gifts of C. Julius Cæsar and of Augustus; and as the former is called a god, whilst the latter is only styled son of a god, we may conclude that it was erected during the lifetime of Augustus. Besides, it was hardly probable that the Athenians should have allowed the gifts of Cæsar to have lain unemployed during the long reign of his successor. But it appears not to have been finished till after the death of Augustus. For, in another inscription, which stood under a statue, probably an equestrian one, of Lucius Cæsar, grandson and adopted son of Augustus, that emperor is styled θεός, or 'god,' and must therefore have been dead.[2] Lucius had died before his grandfather, A.D. 2.

But there may be reason to think, that though this gateway was not built till the reign of Augustus, the agora to which it formed an ornamental entrance had been laid out before that time. Leake is of opinion that the new agora was formed in the course of the last century before the Christian era, which is probable enough (p. 218). But we cannot agree with what he adds, that the religious motive, or ostensible reason, of the change was probably the defilement of the Ceramic agora by Sulla's massacre. There is no reason or authority for believing that the Athenians regarded it in that light; nor is it likely that the Romans would have taken a step equivalent to a condemnation of them-

[1] After the description of the agora by Pausanias in the next chapter, where the inscriptions will be found.

[2] Leake (p. 214, note [3]) is not quite accurate in saying that Augustus is styled a god "in these inscriptions." He is only styled "son of a god" in the principal one.

selves. Perhaps a more probable cause was, that the Romans, as we have seen, had forbidden the assemblies of the people in the Pnyx and the theatre, and had erected the rostra of the prætor before the stoa of Attalus in the ancient agora, before which the people were summoned to hear the decrees of their masters. The agora, as in the primitive times, had again become the place of assembly, but under very different circumstances, and hence it was found convenient to appropriate another place to the market-people and traders.

We have no means of ascertaining exactly when the Horologium of the Syrian, Andronicus of Cyrrhus, was erected. We know that it must have been built before the year B.C. 35, when Varro's treatise, ' De Re Rustica,' was published, as it is mentioned in that work,[1] but we know not how long before. Its situation was evidently selected with reference to the new agora, and hence an additional reason for thinking that the latter was founded before the Augustan period.

In the reign of Augustus the kings in alliance with Rome formed the resolution of completing the Olympian temple at Athens, and dedicating it to his Genius;[2] but it does not appear that any steps were taken in pursuance of it. The temple certainly remained in an unfinished state long after, for Lucian represents Zeus inquiring of Menippus, who probably lived in the first century of our era, when the Athenians meant to finish his temple?[3] The only monument which Augustus had at Athens was a little circular temple on the Acropolis, dedicated to Roma and Augustus, of which we shall speak in a subsequent chapter. To his son-in-law, Agrippa, an equestrian statue was erected before the Propylæa, of which the lofty basis is still extant. Agrippa appears to have built a theatre in the Cerameicus, called the Agrippeium, but of which we know only the name from Philostratus.[4] A gymnasium called Diogeneium, probably also connected with the new agora, and intended to supplant the Ptolemeium, may also have been constructed about the same period as the agora; but we know little more of it than the name.

The following emperors down to Hadrian seem to have done little

---

[1] lib. iii. c. 5, 17.

[2] Suet. Aug. 60.

[3] Icaro-Menippus, c. 24.

[4] Vit. Sophist. lib. ii. 5, 3, and 8, 2.

or nothing for Athens; but they did the next best thing, they left it unmolested. Even Caligula and Nero, though they robbed Greece of many works of art, seem to have spared Athens. Of the Greek statues enumerated by Pliny as brought to Rome by Nero, not one, Leake observes, is said to have been taken from Athens.[1] Pictures that were movable and not executed on walls, seem to have suffered more than statues. Pliny says, that there were supposed to be 3000 statues at Athens in his time.[2] Yet Nero had despoiled Delphi of no fewer than 500 bronze statues of gods and mortals.[3] It is plain, from the account of Pausanias, that Athens at a still later period preserved its most celebrated dedications. One reason for its escape may be that Nero had never visited it, and thus had not been tempted by the treasures which it contained. For though he had been as near to it as Corinth, the conscious matricide feared to go thither, because it was the abode of the avenging Furies.[4] In spite of his monstrous character, and the tyranny and cruelty which he exercised at Rome, Nero appears to have felt an affection for Greece, and he is said to have restored the whole province of Achaia to liberty, whatever that may mean;[5] a reward, apparently, for the adulation which the Greeks had displayed towards him.

The reigns of the next three emperors—Galba, Otho, Vitellius—were too short and stormy to allow of their paying any attention to the affairs of Athens. Vespasian was a lover of Greek art and literature, and was fond of quoting Greek verses. But war and politics were his predominant pursuits; and he again subjected Achaia, which Nero had liberated; that is, apparently, made it again tributary, and directly dependent on the Roman governor. For the Greeks had converted their newly-acquired liberty into license and sedition, and Vespasian observed that they had forgotten how to use it.[6] It does not appear that he or either of his sons, Titus and Domitian, did anything for Athens. The last named tyrant had no love for learning, and banished

[1] vol. i. p. 44; Plin. N. H. xxxiv. 8.
[2] Ibid. s. 36.
[3] Pausan. x. 7, 1.
[4] Dion Cass. lxiii. 14.

[5] Plin. N. H. iv. 22 (Sillig); Suet. Nero, 24.
[6] Philostr. V. Apollon. v. 41; Pausan. vii. 17, 2.

all philosophers from Rome.[1] Nerva and Trajan, also, appear to have neglected Athens, though the latter visited it once. But it was in his reign that the monument of the Syrian Philopappus was erected on the Museium Hill, as may be gathered from the Latin inscription on it; which, as it gives the title of Dacicus to Trajan, but not that of Parthicus, must have been erected, as Leake observes,[2] between A.D. 101 and 108.

With the accession of the Emperor Hadrian, A.D. 117, a new era of prosperity dawned upon Athens. Hadrian had early displayed a great inclination for the Greek language and literature, even to the neglect of the Latin, so that in his quæstorship he incurred some ridicule by his mispronunciation when reading a speech of Trajan's in the senate. Hence he obtained the name of Græculus.[3] In the fifth or sixth year of his reign he visited Athens, and was initiated in the Eleusinian mysteries. The laws of these rites, as we have already observed, seem to have been relaxed in favour of these great persons, who became at once mystæ and epopts.[4] Yet there was no need of this haste in the case of Hadrian, who seems to have spent about three years at Athens. During this visit he undertook the office of Agonotheta, and gave orders for those works which he dedicated on a subsequent occasion. His second or third visit seems to have been in about A.D. 129. On this occasion, according to Spartianus, he became archon eponymous; but, according to Phlegon of Tralles, he had held that office before, when he visited Athens previously to his accession, in the sixth consulship of Trajan (A.D. 112); and, if he is right, Hadrian must have been twice archon.[5] He is said to have exhibited in the Panathenaïc stadium a *venatio* of 1000 wild beasts, which is probably an exaggeration.

Hadrian did so much for Athens, that a large part of its eastern side, including the Olympium, was called after him Hadrianople. The entrance to this district was marked by an arch or gateway he erected,

[1] Suet. Dom. 10; A. Gell. N. A. xv. 11.
[2] vol. i. p. 496.
[3] Æl. Spart. in Vit. c. 1 and 3.
[4] Ibid. 13, with the note of Salmasius.
[5] Ibid. 19, and the note of Salmasius, c. 13, 6. Xiphilinus, in his abridgment of Dion Cassius (lxix. 16) agrees with Spartianus, that Hadrian was archon on this occasion, when he dedicated the Olympian temple. His first visit was made an era from which to date. Boeckh, C. Inscr. Gr. No. 288.

bearing inscriptions which showed it to be the boundary between the ancient city of Theseus and that which he had erected or improved. This part of the town was also called New Athens (Novæ Athenæ), as appears from the inscription on Hadrian's aqueduct. It extended beyond the Themistoclean wall, which indeed appears to have been pulled down for the purpose; for in the foundations of some of the ancient towers may still be seen mosaic floors belonging to Roman villas:[1] and thus, as we shall see further on, Pausanias, when describing objects that lay in this quarter, and certainly beyond the ancient enclosure, does not mention passing through any gate. Thus Hadrianople appears to have formed an open suburb, with country houses along the banks of the Ilissus.

As Curtius observes (loc. cit.), Hadrian, in restoring the Olympium, had in view rather his own glorification, as master of the world, than that of the ruler of Olympus; and indeed, it appears from some inscriptions found at this spot, that he usurped the title of the deity, and called himself Olympius.[2] Besides his colossal statue, the temple was surrounded with a whole forest of statues of him, the anathemata of Greek cities; and thus Athens was exalted to be the metropolis of the Hellenic world. Besides finishing this magnificent temple, Hadrian built for the Athenians a gymnasium with a hundred columns of Libyan marble, which is supposed to have stood at the little church of Gorgopiko, near the new cathedral, where Leake observed several marbles with inscriptions relating to gymnastic victories, and where there are some fragments of columns, &c.[3] We should, however, be rather inclined to ascribe these remains to the gymnasium called Diogeneion, which must have lain somewhere in this quarter. Hadrian founded a temple of Hera, and another of Zeus Panhellenius; also a Pantheon with a hundred and twenty columns of Phrygian marble, with porticoes of the same material, having apartments adorned with gilt roofs and alabaster, and containing sculptures, pictures, and a library.[4] At the bazaar is an extensive and well-preserved portion of a Corinthian colonnade, evidently part of

---

[1] Curtius, Erläuternder Text, S. 47.

[2] Leake, vol. i. p. 168.

[3] Ibid. p. 262, note; Breton, Athènes, p. 242.

[4] Such seems to be the meaning of the somewhat obscure passage of Pausanias, i. 18, 9. See Siebelis' note.

the façade or screen of a quadrangular enclosure, in which these buildings may have stood. The architectural details resemble those of Hadrian's arch at the Olympium,[1] and thus confirm the idea that it is a structure of that emperor. Its site also tends to the same conclusion, since its southern side occupies the breadth of the new or Roman agora, and lines drawn from its eastern and western sides would touch the Tower of the Winds on the one hand and the Propylæum of the agora on the other. Hence we may infer that it was accommodated to the area of the new market-place, and was designed as a finish to one of its sides. But into this question we shall enter more at length further on. Hadrian also undertook an aqueduct for bringing water from the Cephisus. Two Ionic columns, with part of the architrave, belonging to the frontispiece of a reservoir, were seen by Stuart about midway between the city walls and the Hill of St. George, or Lycabettus; and on digging he found vestiges of the other two columns. These have now disappeared; but the piers of some arches which must have belonged to the same aqueduct are still extant five or six miles to the north of Athens, near the village of Dervísh-Agú.[2] As the architrave was imperfect, only half the inscription was preserved; but Spon found at Spalatro a perfect copy of it in a MS. two centuries old. From this it appears that the aqueduct was completed and dedicated by Antoninus Pius[3] in the second year of his reign (A.D. 140).

Besides adorning Athens with these buildings, Hadrian also presented the Athenians with the island of Cephallenia, gave them large sums of money, and a donation of corn annually. He also instituted games, called Hadrianeia in honour of himself.[4] He was the greatest benefactor the Athenians ever had, and for this the inclination to be so sufficed, since his means were unlimited; and the Athenians could

---

[1] Wilkins, Atheniensia, p. 165.

[2] Leake, vol. i. p. 202; Stuart, Ant. of Athens, vol. iii. ch. 4; Wheler's Journey, p. 374.

[3] It runs as follows: IMP . CAESAR . T. AELIUS . HADRIANUS . ANTONINUS . AUG . PIUS . COS . III . TRIB . POT . II . P. P. AQUAEDUCTUM . IN . NOVIS . ATHENIS .

COEPTUM . A . DIVO . HADRIANO . PATRE . SUO . CONSUMMAVIT . DEDICAVITQ . See Wheler's Journey, p. 374; Leake, vol. i. p. 203.

[4] Dion Cass. (Xiphilinus), lxix. 16; cf. Salmasius ad Spart. V. Hadr. (Hist. Aug. t. i. p. 176).

hardly do less than repay him by creating a thirteenth tribe with the name of Hadrianis.[1] It also appears, from inscriptions lately discovered, that the name of one of the Attic months was changed to Hadrianon in his honour.[2]

The two Antonines, who succeeded Hadrian, were also favourably disposed towards the Athenians; but, with the exception of the completion of Hadrian's aqueduct by Pius, already mentioned, we know not of any buildings which they erected. We observed in the theatre a pedestal inscribed to M. Aurelius, son of Antoninus, as προστάτης Ἀθηναίων, equivalent perhaps to the Roman *patronus*. M. Aurelius visited Athens for the purpose of being initiated, and he established there masters in every branch of learning with annual salaries, whose lectures were to be public. He had himself studied under Greek teachers, and among the rest, Herodes Atticus,[3] whom he ever afterwards treated with the greatest respect. Philostratus has preserved a letter of Aurelius, in which he bids Herodes, if he have ever injured him, to demand retribution in the temple of Athena previously to the emperor's initiation.[4]

The sophists formed a remarkable feature in Athenian life under the empire, and we will here say a few words respecting them. The chief of the sophists at Athens was said to occupy the throne or cathedra (ὁ τῶν σοφιστῶν θρόνος). When the sophist Adrian filled that post, he appeared in a magnificent garment, and wearing the most precious gems; he drove to the school in a chariot with silver harness, and a crowd of Greeks escorted him home.[5] A still higher post, to which Adrian was ultimately promoted, was the sophistical chair at Rome, called the upper throne (ὁ ἄνω θρόνος). The lectures here were delivered in the Athenæum instituted by Hadrian.[6] To excel as a sophist was in those days a sure road to wealth and distinction. M. Aurelius, it is

---

[1] Pausan. i. 5, 5.

[2] Vischer, in Neues Schw. Museum, 1863, p. 56.

[3] Capitolin. V. Ant. Phil. c. 2; Dion Cass. lxxi. 31. M. Aurelius himself, however, who enumerates his teachers in the first book of his 'Meditations,' does not mention Herodes.

[4] Vit. Sophist. lib. ii. 1, 12; cf. ibid. x. 4.

[5] Philostr. ibid. c. 2.

[6] Aur. Victor, Hadr. 2.

said, overwhelmed Adrian and his family with wealth and honours,[1] though he was no admirer of the sophists. It was probably when he was young. On the other hand, Lucian, in his 'Nigrinus,'[2] says that these showy philosophers were not much esteemed at Athens.

That the character of the Athenians gradually became very much deteriorated after the loss of their independence cannot, we think, admit of a question. The disfranchisement and removal of so many citizens by Antipater, the oppression of the Romans, the cruelty of Sulla, and the custom of selling their franchise in order to increase their revenue, had indeed effected a great change in the population of Athens itself. In the reign of Tiberius, Piso described the Athenians as virtually extinct, and the present race as nothing but the offscourings of various nations.[3] In a speech intended to excite animosity against Germanicus for the favour he had shown them, something must no doubt be allowed for exaggeration; but that there was a considerable degree of truth in the assertion is confirmed by the fact, that in the time of the Antonines the Attic dialect in all its purity was no longer to be looked for at Athens itself, but in the midland districts of Attica, the population of which had not been mixed with barbarians and foreigners.[4] Nevertheless, as Dr. Finlay observes,[5] the Romans had perhaps formed too contemptible an opinion of the Greeks from the adventurers who flocked to Rome from the Grecian cities of the East.

The Romans had left the Greeks a considerable appearance of autonomy. The Amphictyonic Council still continued to meet in the time of the Antonines, and Augustus had added Nicopolis to its members.[6] The Olympic, Pythian, and Isthmian games were still celebrated.[7] With regard to the Athenians, they were allowed to send a guard, as in the old times, to the temple of Apollo at Delos.[8] The court of Areiopagus continued to exercise its functions, and indeed with independence and vigour, for in the reign of Tiberius it refused to

---

[1] Philostr. ibid. c. 4.

[2] cap. 13.

[3] "Colluviem nationum."—Tac. Ann. ii. 55.

[4] Philostrat. V. Sophist. ii. 1, 7.

[5] Greece under the Romans, p. 78.

[6] Pausan. x. 8, 2 sq.

[7] Id. v. 9, 2 sq.; x. 7, 2; ii. 2, 2.

[8] Id. viii. 33, 1.

spare, even at the intercession of Piso, a person whom it had condemned of fraud.[1] But intercourse with the Romans, aided by the
foundation of Roman colonies in Greece, as Nicopolis and Patrae, helped
to deteriorate the Greek character. The influence of the two nations
on each other was of an opposite kind. The literature of Rome was
developed, and the rough Roman mind received a polish which it could
never, like the Attic genius, have attained by its own efforts. "Graecia
capta ferum victorem cepit;" but in the process the victors inoculated
the Greeks with some of their own barbarousness.

This was particularly shown by the introduction of gladiatorial
combats into Greece. At what time this took place we have no means
of ascertaining, but such combats were certainly exhibited in the Dionysiac theatre at Athens in the first century of our era. For Dion
Chrysostom, who flourished at that period, animadverts upon the subject
with indignation, and observes that often a gladiator was killed on one
of those thrones where the hierophant and other priests sat; alluding
evidently to the marble arm-chairs which formed the first row in the
theatre, and which, as will be seen when we come to describe it, the
recent excavations have discovered *in situ.* The Athenians, as we learn
from the same passage of Dion, had borrowed the spectacle from the
Corinthians, who in the later times were, as we have seen, a Roman colony.
The Corinthians, however, displayed more decency in its use, for they
exhibited these combats outside their walls, in a sort of squalid hole, or
ravine, in which one would not even like, says Dion, to bury a gentleman.[2] It was, indeed, a sad profanation that the theatre which had
witnessed the performance of the masterpieces of Æschylus, Sophocles,
and Euripides, should be desecrated by so brutal a spectacle. From the
life of Apollonius by Philostratus, we learn that the Athenians gave

---

[1] Idem, i. 28, 5 ; Tac. Ann. ii. 55.

[2] οἷον εὐθὺς τὰ περὶ τοὺς μονομάχους
οὕτω σφόδρα ἐζηλώκασι Κορινθίους . . .
ὥστε οἱ Κορίνθιοι μὲν ἔξω τῆς πόλεως θεω
ροῦσιν, ἐν χαράδρᾳ τινί, πλῆθος μὲν δυναμένῳ
δέξασθαι τόπῳ, ῥυπαρῷ δὲ ἄλλως καὶ ὅπου
μηδεὶς ἂν μηδὲ θάψειε μηδένα τῶν ἐλευθέρων,

Ἀθηναῖοι δὲ ἐν τῷ θεάτρῳ θεῶνται τὴν καλὴν
ταύτην θέαν ὑπ' αὐτὴν τὴν ἀκρόπολιν, οὗ τὸν
Διόνυσον ἐπὶ τὴν ὀρχήστραν τιθέασιν, ὥστε
πολλάκις ἐν αὐτοῖς τινα σφάττεσθαι τοῖς
θρόνοις, οὗ τὸν ἱεροφάντην καὶ τοὺς ἄλλους
ἱερεῖς ἀνάγκη καθίζειν.—Orat. xxxi. t. i.
p. 385 sq. (Teubner).

a great deal of money for criminals, adulterers, fornicators, burglars, cut-purses, kidnappers, and others, and made them fight. When the Athenians invited Apollonius of Tyana to their assembly, then held in the theatre, that philosopher, who visited Greece in the reigns of Nero and Galba, wrote to them that he would not enter a place polluted with gore. "I wonder," he said, "that the goddess herself hath not forsaken the Acropolis since you shed so much blood before her eyes. If you go on in this fashion you will soon sacrifice hecatombs of men instead of oxen in your Panathenæa. And canst thou, Dionysus, endure to enter the theatre and receive the libations of the wise Athenians in the midst of such slaughter? Thou hadst better begone, for Cithæron is purer."[1] Lucian represents Demonax as exhorting the Athenians, when they were deliberating about the introduction of these combats in emulation of the Corinthians, first to destroy the altar of Pity.[2] But if Demonax was born, as is commonly supposed, about A.D. 90, the story is refuted by the authorities already quoted—for both Dion Chrysostom and Apollonius had animadverted on the custom.

Of the sophists to whom we have alluded, Herodes Atticus was one of the richest and most distinguished. He was of an ancient Marathonian family, and his father had become suddenly possessed of immense additional wealth by the discovery of a hidden treasure. A great part of this he had bequeathed to the Athenians, by directing that each citizen should receive a mina annually; but his son tricked them out of it by proposing an immediate payment of five minæ apiece, and when they came to receive the money he deducted all debts due to his father and grandfather, so that the greater part of them got little or nothing, while many remained still indebted. Hence, after he had completed the Stadium, it was pleasantly said that it was called Panathenaïc, because built with the money of all the Athenians. Herodes also derived much wealth from his mother, and further increased his fortune by marrying a rich lady named Regilla. When he presided at the Panathenaïc festival he promised the Athenians and other Greeks assembled in the Stadium to view the games that on the next occasion they

---

[1] Vit. Apollon. Tyan. lib. iv. c. 22.   [2] Vit. Demon. c. 57.

should find it covered with marble. And he was as good as his word, by completing within the four years a structure finer than any theatre in existence. On one side of the Stadium he erected a Temple of Tyché, or Fortune, with an ivory statue of the goddess who rules the world. She was indeed a divinity to which he was much indebted. In the same Panathenæa he improved the ship which bore the peplus, and made the latter more splendid. He altered the chlamys worn by the Athenian ephebi from black to white.[1] They had previously worn black on public occasions in memory of the herald Copreus, whom the Athenian youths had killed when he was in the act of dragging the Heracleidæ from the altar of Pity. Lastly, Herodes built the Odeium, the ruins of which may still be seen under the Acropolis, and dedicated it to the memory of his wife Regilla; whom, however, he had been accused, though falsely, of murdering, by causing her to be whipped in the eighth month of her pregnancy. Besides these magnificent buildings at Athens, Herodes erected many more in various Greek cities.[2]

Thus, in the reign of Marcus Aurelius, Athens attained, through the munificence of Herodes, the acme of its splendour. Its ancient monuments still remained in their original perfection, but from this time little or nothing appears to have been added to them, and soon after the process of decay must have commenced. It was therefore a fortunate circumstance that it should have been visited and described while in the maturity of its beauty by an inquisitive and intelligent traveller

[1] Philostr. V. Soph. ii. 1, 3, p. 550. There is a great difference of opinion among the learned on this point. Meursius (Panath. c. 22) is of opinion that black was worn even in the Panathenaïc procession. Petit, on the other hand, denies that this could have been the case, as there was a law forbidding the use of dyed garments on that occasion (Leg. Att. p. 95, ed. Wesseling, 1742). Palmer supports Meursius, and replies to Petit's objection that the black garments were not dyed but made of black wool. Olearius (ad Philostr. l. c.) sides with Petit, while Wesseling (ad Petit l. c.) cites a passage from Suidas (voc. ἀσκοφορεῖν) in which it is said that the metics in the pomp wore a purple chiton, and the citizens a dress of whatever colour they liked (οἱ δὲ ἀστοὶ ἐσθῆτα εἶχον, ἣν ἐβούλοντο). This however does not invalidate the words of Philostratus, which, as Wesseling observes, refer only to the ephebi as a distinct class.

[2] The life of Herodes has been written by Philostratus (Vit. Soph. lib. ii. 1). Aulus Gellius, who was his pupil, also gives some anecdotes of him (N. A. i. 2; ix. 2; xix. 12).

like Pausanias. A city so beautiful and so renowned as Athens had of course attracted the notice of writers long before his time. About the time of the Persian wars, Pherecydes and Hellanicus had composed works on the history and antiquities of Attica, and these were followed by other writers—as Clitodemus, or Clidemus, Marsyas of Pella, Ister, Phanodemus, and others.[1] These works, no doubt, contained many particulars concerning the early state of Athens as a city; but in a later age several books were published with the express purpose of describing it for the use of travellers. One of the earliest and most noted of these authors was Polemo, who lived about two centuries before the Christian era. From his employing himself in collecting inscriptions, Polemo obtained the name of Στηλοκόπας, or the Pillar-cutter. He wrote a work in four books on the anathemata in the Acropolis; another, in one book, on the paintings in the Propylæa; and a third on the Sacred Way leading to Eleusis.[2] Heliodorus, who lived at about the same time, also employed himself in describing Athens, and the elaborateness with which he performed this task may be inferred from the fact that he devoted fifteen books to the description of the Acropolis alone. He also wrote a book concerning the monuments of Athens, and another on the tripods consecrated there.[3] Other writers on the same subject were Diodorus, surnamed ὁ Περιηγητής (the Cicerone or Guide), Menacles, or Callistratus, and Ammonius of Lamptra, who wrote a book upon altars.[4] But of these writers only a few scattered fragments remain, and Pausanias is the only professed periegetes of Athens whose work has come down to us. His book, therefore, and the few meagre notices in Strabo, are the chief sources of our knowledge about ancient Athens, aided by what incidental allusions we can gather from the classical writers. But as the works of the periegetæ were extant in the time of Pausanias, he was probably led from that cause to treat of Attica and Athens less fully than

---

[1] See Heyne, ad Apollodor. iii. 14 (p. 809).

[2] Strab. p. 386; Athen. vi. 26, x. 48, 50, xi. 43, 72, xiii. 51; Harpocr. passim.

[3] Vit. X. Orat. p. 375, Reiske; Harpocr.

voce. Θετταλός, Ὀνήτωρ, Προπύλαια, Νίκη Ἀθηνᾶ.

[4] Plut. Thes. 36; Them. 32; Cimon, 16; Harpocr. voce. Ἑκατόμπεδον, Κεραμεικός, Ἑρμαῖ; schol. Aristoph. Av. 394, &c.

of other countries, and thus the omission of what an ancient reader
might have deemed superfluous becomes to us an irreparable loss. We
would gladly have sacrificed some of his historical narratives for a
more detailed account of the objects which he saw, or a sketch of those
which he has altogether omitted. He tells us himself that he had
selected only the things chiefly memorable.[1] Still we have reason to be
thankful for a book which conveys so good a general idea of ancient Athens.

The little that we know of Pausanias is gathered from his own
writings and from some passages in Stephanus of Byzantium.[2] From
a comparison of these it would appear that he was a native of the
Lydian Magnesia (Magnesia ad Sipylum), and that he flourished in
the reigns of Hadrian and the two Antonines. He speaks of Antinoüs
as his contemporary, though he had never seen him;[3] whence we may
conclude that he was at all events a youth at the time of Antinoüs'
death, which happened several years before A.D. 138, the date of the
death of Hadrian. In another passage[4] he alludes to the second Antoninus, or Marcus Aurelius, and his wars against the Germans and
Sauromatæ, which, however, lasted during the greater part of the
reign of that emperor. In the first book of his Eliacs[5] he says that
two hundred and seventeen years had elapsed since C. Julius Cæsar made
Corinth a colony; and as this happened about B.C. 46,[6] it follows that he

---

[1] ὃ δὴ ἐν τῇ συγγραφῇ μοι τῇ Ἀτθίδι
ἐπανόρθωμα ἐγένετο, μὴ τὰ πάντα με ἐφεξῆς,
ἀλλὰ τὰ μάλιστα ἄξια μνήμης ἐπιλεξάμενον
ἀπ' αὐτῶν εἰρηκέναι, δηλώσω δὴ πρὸ τοῦ
λόγου τοῦ ἐς Σπαρτιάτας.—lib. iii. 11, 1.
From the word ἐπανόρθωμα here, some
critics have been led to think that Pausanias was referring to a second edition
of his Attica. But from a passage in
that book it would appear that he had
adopted the principle of selection from the
very first : ἀπέκρινε δὲ ἀπὸ τῶν πολλῶν ἐξ
ἀρχῆς ὁ λόγος μοι τὰ ἐς συγγραφὴν ἀνήκοντα.
—i. 39, 3. Wherefore ἐπανόρθωμα seems
to mean ' an improved method :' i.e. on that
of former writers. He tells us in another

place that he passed over what others had
written about Hermolychus and Phormio
(i. 23, 12). His book therefore may perhaps
be regarded as partly an abridgment of
former ones.

[2] In Δῶρος, Ἀσκάλων, Σελευκόβηλος, &c.

[3] lib. viii. 9, 4.

[4] Ibid. 43, 4.

[5] v. 1, 1 ; cf. ii. 1, 2.

[6] Leake says, p. 21, note : " Corinth and
Carthage were taken and destroyed in the
same year, B.C. 146. 102 years afterwards,
or B.C. 44, they were both restored and
colonized by Julius Cæsar." But the term
of 102 years cannot be fixed from the
authorities he cites ; viz., Dion Cass. xliii.

must have been writing that book in A.D. 171. As he was not yet in the middle of his work, if he wrote his books in consecutive order, we may presume that he probably lived through the reign of Aurelius, who died in A.D. 178, and we shall therefore, perhaps, not be very far wrong in placing his life between the years 110 and 180.

Like Herodotus, whom he has sometimes been thought to imitate, Pausanias was a great traveller.[1] He appears to have visited Thebes in Egypt;[2] it may perhaps be affirmed from a passage in his Bœotica that he had seen the temple of the Libyan Ammon;[3] and he says in his Eliaca Priora[4] that he had a personal knowledge of the Dead Sea and the Lake of Tiberias. He appears also to have visited Rome and Italy, and many parts of the Mediterranean, and to have travelled over most or all of the countries in which the Greek language was spoken. The fruits of his travels were a work on Syria,[5] now lost, and another entitled Ἑλλάδος Περιήγησις, containing a description of the principal states of Greece proper, viz.: Attica, Corinth, Laconia, Messenë, Elis, Achaia, Arcadia, Bœotia, and Phocis. The primary object of Pausanias in visiting these countries appears to have been to describe the works of art which they contained, and thus to prepare a sort of guide-book for the travelling connoisseur of antiquity. His attention was chiefly directed to statues and pictures; he seldom or

---

50; Appian, De Rebus Pun. ad fin.; Pausan. v. 1, 2, cf. ii. 1, 2. Clinton also mentions the restoration of these colonies under the same year, which was that of Cæsar's assassination; but without fixing it in that year. The expression of Diodorus (Excerp. Wesseling, ii. 591) that it was almost exactly 100 years from their destruction to their restoration (διεληλυθότων σχεδὸν ἐτῶν ἑκατόν) seems to justify the assumption that the latter took place in B.C. 46. But Pausanias' expression 'to his time' (ἐς ἐμέ) is very vague.

[1] We do not see how Leake (p. 29) can

infer from iv. 35, 6, that Pausanias had "particularly examined Joppa." Where it is evident that he speaks only from hearsay; since he goes on to mention that he had seen *with his own eyes* (ἰδὼν οἶδα) some black water at Astura, warm baths of Atarneus, opposite Lesbos. Whence we conclude that he had not seen with his own eyes the water described at Joppa.

[2] i. 42, 2.

[3] ix. 16, 1.

[4] v. 7, 3.

[5] Stephanus Byzant. voc. Σελευκόβηλος. Tzetzes, Chil. vii. 167.

never describes the architecture of a building. But he mentions the temples and other structures which were worthy of notice either from their importance, their antiquity, their beauty, or the historical associations connected with them; and as he does this, at all events when treating of Athens, in the local order in which they stood, his book incidentally becomes a valuable topographical guide. But Pausanias was not only a lover of art. He was also a devout pagan, and a curious inquirer into history and antiquities; and hence his work rises sometimes almost to the dignity of history, from its containing many mythological and historical relations which are not to be found in any other author.

It is perhaps a fortunate thing for us, that Pausanias possessed no false and affected enthusiasm for art. He does not, like some of our modern æsthetical critics, treat us to long disquisitions intended rather to display the beauties of the writer's style than that of the objects on which it is employed. Hence he has not only more space for the enumeration of works of art, but we may also have a more confident reliance that those mentioned, were really masterpieces. He has, indeed, on this account, been accused of coldness and insensibility; and it has been said that his highest expression of admiration for anything is, that it is " worth seeing" (θέας ἄξιον). But, as he travelled over Greece in quest of works of art, he could hardly have been indifferent to their beauties; and in his days the appreciation of them must have differed from our own. The statues, at all events, must then have been a hundredfold more numerous, and even those of the second class made a nearer approach to excellence than our modern ones. Amidst such a galaxy of beauty, to say that an object was worth seeing would have conveyed a different idea to ancient ears than it does to us, who from the paucity of master-works are apt to fall into raptures over the few which come under our observation.

It is of much more importance to us that Pausanias should have been correct than that he should have been enthusiastic; and it is fortunate that in this respect he appears to have been all that we could desire. Some eminent critics have arrived at this conclusion merely

from a study of his text. Thus Bayle (in his ' Dissertation on Hippo-
manes') quotes him in preference to Pliny; and Mitford preferred him
as an authority to Diodorus Siculus and Plutarch.[1] But it is much
more satisfactory to find that the correctness of his descriptions has
been verified by eye-witnesses in modern times. Thus the late Lord
Broughton writes: "Pausanias alone will enable you to feel at home in
Greece; and it is true that the exact conformity of present appearances
with the minute descriptions of the Itinerary, is no less surprising
than satisfactory."[2] This judgment has been remarkably confirmed by
recent excavations at the Acropolis, as will be seen when we come to
treat of it.

Pausanias probably omits no place or building which contained
statues or pictures by the great masters; but the rule by which he
mentioned some objects, and passed over others, appears capricious.
That he should have left most of the Roman buildings unnoticed may
perhaps be attributed to national feeling; but it is difficult to discover
why he should not have named several interesting objects of Greek
antiquity, which must have lain in his route, as the Leocorion, the
altar of the Twelve Gods, &c. But the most striking omission in
the eyes of any modern visitor of Athens is the Pnyx. Perhaps the
most probable way of accounting for this is, that the quarter of the
Pnyx not containing any remarkable buildings or objects of art, and the
place of assembly itself being then in a state of ruin and dilapidation,
it did not form one of the regular places to which visitors were conducted. And this leads us to speak of the method in which Pausanias
wrote his book.

The renown of Athens, and the treasures of art which it contained,
made it the resort of strangers from all parts of the world; and we can
hardly doubt that there were professed ciceroni, who, like the valets-de
place of continental Europe, conducted them to the principal objects of
interest. It has been not improbably supposed that the work of Pausanias was intended as a supplement to the bald and parrot-like details

---

[1] Hist. of Greece, i. 78.   [2] Hobhouse, Journey through Albania, i. 214.

of such guides.[1] However this may be, it is certain that his periegesis
of Athens was conducted in the strictest and most methodical order.
This is a fact of the utmost importance for Athenian topography. If he
visited the different objects without any settled method, and put them
down at random in his book, it can be no guide to their situation;
while on the other hand, if he took them in the local order in which
they occurred, it is evident that his work affords a most valuable topographical clue. It becomes, therefore, important to show that such was
really his plan.

The best proof of Pausanias' strictly methodical way of proceeding
is his description of the Acropolis; because the objects there being still
pretty perfect, we are able to follow him step by step. Here everything is noted in the order in which it occurs; first, the temple of
Nikë Apteros, then the Propylæa and Pinacotheca, next several statues
and other objects, which, as we shall see further on, recent excavations
have discovered to be in the precise situation which he indicates. He
then proceeds round the south side of the Acropolis, and after describing
the Parthenon and adjacent objects, returns by the Erechtheium, and
the northern side. Hence a presumption that his description of the
whole city was done in the same methodical way. And that this was
the case is confirmed by another of his routes, viz., that from the
Prytaneium round the base of the Acropolis to its entrance, which also
contains well identified objects: some still existing, as the choragic
monument of Lysicrates and the theatre; and others so well ascertained from classical authorities as to leave no doubt about their site.
The same thing may also be inferred from the general method of his
book, which is divided into several convenient portions or walks, beginning with those nearest to the ports; a method which it would have
been quite unnecessary to follow if the description of the objects had
been his only aim, and if he had not also consulted the convenience of
the visitor, by taking him through the various parts of the city in a
regular order. We will therefore proceed to sketch out these various

[1] See Ulrichs, Reisen u. Forschungen in Griechenland, Th. ii. S. 148 ff.

routes, and then accompany him through each of them; which will be a method as convenient to us as it was to the ancients, for acquiring a knowledge of the city and its monuments.

Pausanias assumes that the traveller may have landed either at Phalerum or Peiræcus; and therefore conducts him to the city by each of the roads leading from those ports, in order that he may describe the objects found on them; but it is only on his second walk, namely, from Peiræcus, that he actually makes his entry. By what gate he entered is a contested point; and as the topography of the most important portion of his periegesis, embracing the agora and its neighbourhood, depends upon this question, we must endeavour to determine it.

If, as we have shown, the agora lay to the north of the Areiopagus, there are only two gates which will at all suit the account of Pausanias, viz., the Dipylon, at the north-west angle of the walls, and the Porta Peiraïca, between the so-called Hill of the Nymphs and the church of Agios Athanasios. Any entrance to the southward of these, as between the Hill of the Nymphs and the Pnyx Hill, or between the latter and the Muséium Hill, would leave too long a space between the gate and the agora to be filled up by the objects described by Pausanias; and accordingly topographers who have adopted such an entrance, as Forchhammer and Dr. Wordsworth, place their agora on the south side of the Areiopagus. Another objection is, that had Pausanias entered on this side, he must have passed near the Pnyx, and could hardly have avoided mentioning so important an object.

Dr. Curtius is the chief advocate for the Dipylon. One of his principal arguments is drawn from the Pompeium and the temple of Demeter which Pausanias mentions as just within the Gate, and which Curtius thinks were placed there through a kind of mystical connection with Eleusis, to which the Dipylon led.[1] This appears to us altogether fanciful. Besides, it is evident that the Pompeium was intended not only for the preparation of the Eleusinian processions, but also of the

---

[1] Attische Stud. i. 66, and ii. 17, note.

Panathenaïc. For Pausanias says that it was not only for yearly processions, but also for those which recurred at a longer interval;[1] by which he must mean the great Panathenæa. Let us also observe that the image of Iacchus, which Pausanias tells us was preserved in the temple of Demeter near the gate by which he entered, was carried through the agora in the Eleusinian procession;[2] which of course it would have been had the temple and the Pompeium been near the Peiraïc Gate; but not if the procession started from the Dipylon.

It has been inferred from some passages in ancient authors, that the Dipylon formed the ordinary entrance to the city from Peiræeus. Thus, after landing at Peiræeus, Attalus is described as entering the city by that gate;[3] and in the 'Navigium' of Lucian,[4] Lycinus, one of the party coming up from Peiræeus, says that he will make his vow in the last half stadium before arriving at the Dipylon. Now, on such an occasion as the entrance of Attalus, which was a state one and attended by crowds, the Dipylon might have been selected as the handsomest and most convenient entrance. Indeed, there was not so great an interval between the two gates as to make it a matter of very much importance by which one entered; and for some parts of the city the Dipylon might have been the more convenient. But the very name of the Peiraïc Gate proves that it was the usual entrance from the Peiræeus, and therefore that it must have offered the shortest route to the heart of the city; and a glance at the map shows that this was so.

It is probable that, for the greater part of the distance one and the same road would have served from the Peiræeus, both to the Dipylon and the Peiraïc Gate; and this was probably the ἀμαξιτός, or carriage-road mentioned by Xenophon[5] as leading to Peiræeus, and by Plato as running *under* and *outside* the northern Long Wall;[6] but on nearing the city it must have branched into two—one branch proceeding to the

---

[1] οἰκοδόμημα ἐς παρασκευήν ἐστι τῶν πομπῶν, ἃς πέμπουσι, τὰς μὲν ἀνὰ πᾶν ἔτος, τὰς δὲ καὶ χρόνον διαλείποντες.—i. 2, 4.

[2] Schol. ad Aristoph. Ran. 323.

[3] Polyb. lib. xvi. c. 25.

[4] c. 17.

[5] Hellen. ii. 4, 10.

[6] Republ. iv. p. 439 (iii., i. p. 203, Bekk.).

Porta Peiraïca, the other in a more northerly direction to the Dipylon. It must have been in the first-named portion of the road, and near the gate (οὐ πόρρω τῶν πυλῶν), that Pausanias saw the monument consisting of a warrior standing by his horse, which has not improbably been identified with the heroum of Chalchedon, father of one of the wives of Theseus, and which, according to Plutarch,[1] stood at the Peiraïc Gate. And this forms another probable argument that Pausanias entered by that gate. He must certainly have gone out at the Dipylon to visit the Academy (c. 29); and he mentions quite a different set of objects outside of it.

Another circumstance, which will appear when we come to describe the agora, is, that the buildings and other objects on it cannot be arranged with so much regularity and with such conformity to the text of Pausanias, if we suppose him to have entered by the Dipylon, as they can if he passed through the Peiraïc Gate.[2]

Assuming, then, that he entered by this last, we will proceed to sketch out his different routes in the interior of the city. His first day's work (c. 2—14) embraces the street leading from the gate to the Cerameicus or agora, and all the buildings and monuments which lay on the south side of the agora, as far as the Eleusinium and the temple of Eucleia, which must have marked its eastern boundary; after which he returns to that part of the agora at which he had entered it, viz., the Stoa Basileius, and proceeds to describe the remainder of it.

In this route, however, he is supposed to have committed an irregularity which does not occur in any other, and to have suddenly left the agora, to which it was devoted, in order to visit the fountain Enneacrunos and other objects assumed to have been in quite a distant part of the city, the description of which has no reasonable connection with

---

[1] Thes. 27. See Leake, p. 233 sq.; Bursian, Geogr. v. Griech. i. 278 f.

[2] The argument of Bursian and others that Pausanias must have entered by the Peiraïc Gate, because it is some time before he arrives at the Cerameicus, whereas had he passed through the Dipylon, he was already in it, would have been conclusive but for the fact that Pausanias speaks of the Cerameicus only as the *agora*, and not as the *district*.

the present route. All this part of the city forms the subject of a subsequent tour, in describing which he mentions objects which must have been close to those he has described before, if they were really there; yet he does not say that he has been there previously, or assign any reason for this arbitrary and inconvenient separation of things supposed to have been united. When we consider the regularity of his method in all the other parts of his work, there is a *prima facie* improbability that he should have done this; but as the inquiry is rather long, we have discussed it in an Appendix.[1]

All the remaining walks of Pausanias are accomplished in the most regular manner, and afford not the slightest ground for suspecting a deviation. In his fourteenth chapter (§ 5) he begins a new walk, having completed the description of the south side of the agora, which formed the subject of his first. Starting again from the same point, the Stoa Basileius, he now completes his description of the west and north sides of the agora or Ceramicus, and their neighbourhood, and then proceeds into the new, or Roman, agora, which lay to the east of it. The description of this and the adjacent objects, as the gymnasium of Ptolemy, the Theseium, and the sanctuaries, &c., under the north side of the Acropolis, beyond the eastern limit of the agora, as far as and including the Prytaneium, completes this route. His third walk begins from the Prytaneium (c. 18, 4), just beyond which building two roads branched off. One of these, leading to the Olympium and the objects on both banks of the Ilissus, is the subject of this third walk (c. 18, 4, to c. 20). For his fourth walk he returns again to the Prytaneium, and takes the other road through the street of Tripods, round the eastern and southern base of the Acropolis to its western entrance, and entering by the Propylæa, visits all the objects of interest on its summit. Having returned to the Propylæa, his fifth walk (c. 28, 4, to 29, 1) is employed on the objects around and below them, and the mention of the Areiopagus leads him to give an account of the other Attic courts of justice. This closes his description of the

---

[1] See Appendix No. 1.

city; and the remainder of his book is occupied in describing the Academy, the Sacred Way, Eleusis, and the towns, mountains, and islands of Attica.

Having thus given the reader a general notion of the plan and method of Pausanias, we will now accompany him in his walks, supplying, so far as we can, some additional particulars which he left unnoticed, and describing, where they exist, the present state of the monuments which he saw. This will convey a tolerably accurate idea of Athenian topography, so far as it can be determined, which a description of the Panathenaïc and Eleusinian processions will help to complete.

CHAPTER VII.

PAUSANIAS (c. i.) mentions three Athenian ports—MUNYCHIA, PHALERUM, and PEIRÆEUS. Of the first he only says that it contained a temple of the Munychian Artemis. It was, perhaps, more particularly a military port and seldom a landing-place for strangers.

PHALERUM was an Attic deme of the tribe Æantis, having for its eponymous hero Phalerus, a grandson of Erechtheus. From its greater antiquity it was natural that it should contain more objects of curiosity and veneration than the other ports, and Pausanias notices several here, the first of them being a temple of Demeter close to the port. In a passage of his Phocica (x. 35, 2) he again adverts to this temple, and says that it was in a half burnt state, as it was left by the Persians, the Greeks who opposed them having resolved that several of their temples should remain in that condition, as memorials of perpetual enmity. Near it was a temple of Athena Sciras, which, as we learn further on,[1] was founded by a soothsayer named Sciros, from Dodona, at the time when the Eleusinians were waging war with Erechtheus. A little beyond it was a temple of Zeus. There were also altars to the unknown gods, to certain heroes, to the children of Theseus, and to Phalerus, who, according to Athenian tradition, sailed with Jason to Colchis. There was also an altar, according to diligent antiquaries, of Androgeus, son of Minos, here worshipped as a hero. The objects enumerated by

[1] i. 36, 3; cf. Strab. ix. 393.

Pausanias may be supplemented with a tomb of Aristeides,[1] and a place called the Oschophorium.[2] Demetrius Phalereus, the last of the Attic orators, whose native place it was, and who is Plutarch's authority about Aristeides, said that he had also possessed a farm here. According to Diogenes Laërtius,[3] the sepulchral monument of Musæus, bearing an epitaph which he gives, was at Phalerum; but Pausanias, as we shall see further on, places it at the Museium Hill, a view to which the name of the hill gives some colour. The spring at the Acropolis called Clepsydra was said to have run underground into the harbour of Phalerum.[4] This place was famous for a little fish called aphyë (ἀφύη), which, when caught in other places, seems not to have been much relished.[5]

The mention of the anonymous altars suggests the idea that St. Paul may probably have landed at Phalerum, from that well-known passage in his speech to the Athenians,[6] where he says that, when coming through (διερχόμενος) he observed an altar inscribed To the Unknown God.[7] Such altars, called βωμοὶ ἀνώνυμοι, were not uncommon in the Attic demes. Diogenes Laërtius, in his life of Epimenides (i. 110), explains their origin as follows. The Athenians, when labouring under a great pest, sent for Epimenides from Crete, who expiated the city by collecting on the Areiopagus a number of black and white sheep, and suffering them to stray whither they would; when, wherever one of them might lie down, sacrifice was to be offered to the proper god. St. Chrysostom, on the other hand, says[8] that such altars were erected by the Athenians for fear of having overlooked some deity. There appears, however, to have been an altar of this kind in

[1] Plut. Arist. 1.

[2] Hesych. in voc.

[3] lib. i. 3.

[4] Schol. Aristoph. Lysistr. 912; Vesp. 853; Av. 1694.

[5] Athen. iv. 13; iii. 71; vii. 22.

[6] Acts xvii. 22. In this passage the word δεισιδαιμονεστέρους should, perhaps, be interpreted "somewhat religious" *rather than* "too superstitious" as in our ver-

sion; for it may have a good, as well as a bad, sense, and an orator like St. Paul would hardly have begun his address with a sort of insult.

[7] According to Œcumenius, cited by Meursius (Peiræeus, c. 10), the full inscription was Θεοῖς Ἀσίας, καὶ Εὐρώπης, καὶ Λιβύης, Θεῷ ἀγνώστῳ καὶ ξένῳ. Cf. Philostr. V. Apollon. vi. 11.

[8] Homilies on the Acts, xxxviii.

Athens itself; for in the dialogue entitled 'Philopatris,' attributed, most probably falsely, to Lucian, Critias is made to swear by the Unknown God in Athens.[1]

CAPE COLIAS, whither, after the destruction of the Persian fleet, the remnants of it were carried by the waves, is about twenty stades distant from Phalerum. It had an image of Aphroditë Colias, and of the deities called Genetyllides, which Pausanias took to be the same as those called by the Phocæans Gennaïdæ.

On the road from PHALERUM TO ATHENS was a temple of Hera, having neither roof nor doors. It was said to have been burnt by Mardonius, and appears to have been one of those left unrestored by the Athenians for the reason before given. The image of the goddess was by some ascribed to Alcamenes; but as it was damaged by the fire, it could not have been his work, since he lived after the Persian wars (c. 1, 4).[2] On arriving at the city there was a monument of the Amazon Antiopë (c. 2, 1). Pausanias, therefore, must have arrived at the Itonian Gate, where this monument was, as we have before shown.[3]

Such were the objects to be seen at Phalerum, and on the road between it and Athens. At PEIRÆEUS Pausanias adverts to the docks or SHIP-SHEDS (νεὼς οἶκοι), and the tomb erected to THEMISTOCLES, at the largest harbour, after his bones had been brought from Magnesia. Plutarch describes it as an immense κρηπίς, or base, with an altar-like elevation on it.[4] We have spoken of this monument before (supra, p. 121). But the most remarkable object was a temenos sacred to ZEUS AND ATHENA, with bronze images of both the deities. Zeus held in his hands a sceptre and a figure of Nikë or Victory, whilst Athena had a lance. There was also a picture by Arcesilaüs of Leosthenes, who defeated the Macedonians, and his sons (c. 1, 2).

Strabo appears to allude to this temple under the title of ZEUS SOTER, or the Saviour,[5] and he says that there were in it small porticoes,

[1] Νὴ τὸν "Αγνωστον ἐν 'Αθήναις.—c. 9.

[2] Such appears to be the meaning of Pausanias in this obscure passage. (The quotations from that author, where no book is cited, are of course from the 'Attica').

[3] Above, p. 61 and 105.

[4] Vit. Them. c. 32.

[5] τὸ ἱερὸν τοῦ Διὸς τοῦ Σωτῆρος.—ix. p. 396.

containing some admirable pictures by the most celebrated artists. These had probably vanished in the time of Pausanias, or else he mentions only that of Arcesilaüs on account of its superior excellence, or for its subject. Arcesilaüs was an encaustic painter, who flourished a little after Alexander the Great.[1] Pliny alludes to the statue of Athena as a very admirable one, the work of Cephisodotus.[2]

On the shore was A LONG PORTICO, which the coast people used as a market, and there was another market for those who lived further off. Among the porticoes was a place called DEIGMA, where samples were shown of goods on sale ($\delta\epsilon\hat{i}\gamma\mu\alpha$, 'a sample'), and where, also, there seems to have been counters of bankers or money-changers. It was from its nature a kind of exchange, or meeting-place for Athenians and foreigners, consequently a gossiping place, as it is characterized by Aristophanes.[3] Xenophon records a kidnapping of merchants and skippers from it,[4] and Polyænus a plundering of the bankers' counters by Alexander of Pheræ.[5] Behind the portico were statues of ZEUS AND DEMOS, executed by Leochares. Images of the people personified were sufficiently common at Athens. Parrhasius is said to have painted the Athenian Demos in a very ingenious manner, representing all its conflicting passions—its anger, clemency, pride, humility, &c.,[6] as they are so humorously sketched by Aristophanes in his 'Knights' (v. 719 sq., 1111 sq.). Such personifications were not altogether peculiar to the Athenians, for Pausanias mentions at Sparta a colossal statue of the Spartan people.[7] The conjunction, however, of Demos with Zeus at Peiræus shows that the people were not only personified but also deified. This fact was denied by Boeckh;[8] but it has been subsequently placed beyond doubt by the discovery of a throne in the Dionysiac theatre inscribed to the priest of Demos and the Graces. Several other inscriptions to the same purport have been discovered.

---

[1] Plin. H. N. xxxv. 122 (Sillig).
[2] Ibid. xxxiv. 74.
[3] Eq. 975, et ibi schol. Cf. Harpocr. in voc.; Demosth. adv. Polycl. p. 1214.
[4] Hellen. v. 1, 21.
[5] Stratag. vi. 2, 2.
[6] Plin. H. N. xxxv. 69.
[7] lib. iii. 11, 8.
[8] In the Monats-Bericht der Berl. Akad. Oct. 1853.

Conon erected near the sea a temple of Aphrodite (c. 1, 3), after defeating the Lacedæmonians off Cnidos,[1] where Aphroditë was particularly worshipped, and had three temples. But perhaps Conon's work was only an enlargement of the temple which, as we have already mentioned, Themistocles erected to Aphroditë Aparchos in the Peiræeus. This APHRODISIUM has been mistaken by Leake and others for the name of one of the ports, from a misunderstanding of the scholia to the 'Pax' of Aristophanes (v. 144). Of the harbours of the Peiræeus, the scholiast mentions only Cantharus, because that is the one which occurs in the text of his author. Callicrates, or Menecles, cited in that scholium, says that Cantharus is one of the three shut-up (κλειστοὺς) harbours of Peiræeus, and that it had sixty ship-sheds; then came (εἶτα) the Aphrodisium, and then five stoæ encircling the (Peiraïc) harbour. These no doubt formed the portico alluded to by Pausanias, as used by the seaboard people for a market, which was probably in five divisions, to allow of thoroughfares. The other two shut-up harbours were Munychia and Zea on the east side of the Peiraïc peninsula.

At the time of Pausanias' visit, Peiræeus must have been in a sad state of decay. Already in the time of Alexander the Great, Philiscus, the comic poet, had compared it, with allusion to its walls, to a great empty walnut-shell :

Πειραιεὺς κάρυον μέγ᾽ ἐστὶ καὶ κενόν.[2]

and, as we have before observed, Strabo found there only a few houses round the ports and the temple of Zeus Soter. Dodwell saw there at the beginning of the present century, the remains of a great quantity of wells, cisterns, and subterranean chambers cut in the rock,[3] which must have given it much the appearance of the rock-city on the southern hills of Athens.

On the road from Peiræeus to Athens, Pausanias observed remains of the Long Walls which Conon had restored after the battle of Cnidos

[1] Xenoph. Hell. iv. 3, 10 sq.
[2] Anthol. Jacobs, xiii. p. 708.
[3] Tour, i. p. 426. He calls it Mouny-

chia ; by which however he appears to mean the southern part of the Peninsula

(c. 2, 2). Those built by Themistocles after the evacuation of the city
by the Persians, had been pulled down, as already observed, by the
Lacedaemonians. The most remarkable tombs on the road were those of
MENANDER and of EURIPIDES. But the latter was only a cenotaph; for
Euripides was buried in Macedonia, where he had been a guest at the
court of King Archelaüs. At a little distance from the gate was another
tomb, having on it a warrior standing by his horse. Pausanias knew
not whom it represented, but only that it was the work of Praxiteles.
It belonged probably to the heroum of Chalcodon (above, p. 63).

The first object on entering the city was a building called the
POMPEIUM, in which were prepared the solemn religious processions,
whether they were annual, or whether they recurred after an interval
of years. Pausanias gives no further account of it; but we know from
other sources that it contained a bronze statue or bust (εἰκών) of Socrates,
executed by Lysippus,[1] and a painted portrait of Isocrates.[2] As the
depot of the sacred vessels of gold and silver (ἱερὰ σκευή, πομπεῖα) used
in the processions and games, it must have contained a considerable
treasure, which indeed Pericles enumerated among the resources of the
state.[3] Alcibiades was accused of using these vessels for domestic purposes.[4] They were under the custody of the Architheori. Harpocration
says,[5] from Philochorus, that the confiscated property of the Thirty
Tyrants was applied to the making of such utensils; but these, as we
have seen, could not have been the first. Lycurgus, the orator, among
his other benefactions to the Athenians, presented them with some gold
and silver *pompeia.*[6]

Near the Pompeium was a TEMPLE OF DEMETER, with statues of herself, of her daughter Corë, or Pherephatta, and of Iacchus, holding a
torch. It was written on the wall, in Attic letters, that they were the
work of Praxiteles. We have before adverted to this Iacchus as being
carried through the agora in the procession to Eleusis, accompanied

[1] Diog. Laërt. ii. 43. Tertullian, Apo-
log. says it was of gold.

[2] Vit. X. Orat. Plut. Reiske, ix. 338.

[3] Thucyd. ii. 13.

[4] Plut. Alc. 13; Andoc. in Alc. p. 126,
Reiske.

[5] voc. πομπείας.

[6] Vit. X. Orat. (Plut. Reiske, ix. p. 346).

with hymns. Forchhammer[1] has a very probable conjecture that it was
in this temple, which must have lain in Melitë, that Hercules was
related to have been initiated in the Lesser Mysteries. It was very
likely the PHEREPHATTEIUM mentioned by Demosthenes in his speech
against Conon;[2] and it seems to have been also called IACCHEIUM
(᾽Ιακχεῖον) from the image of Iacchus preserved here.[3] Near it was an
equestrian statue of Poseidon, hurling his trident at Polybotes;[4] but
the modern inscription ascribed the statue to some other person. We
have here, therefore, an instance of the misappropriation of ancient
statues; but the vainglory of the appropriator, most probably a Roman,
Pausanias frustrates by concealing his name. Pausanias calls it an
εἰκών, the term for a portrait-statue, which this now purported to be;
while ἄγαλμα is the proper word for the statue of a god.

Two PORTICOES extended from the gate to the Cerameicus, by which
term, as we shall show presently, Pausanias means the agora. But as
such a use of it might tend to confuse the modern reader, we shall con-
tinue to use the word agora. Measuring from the Peiraïc Gate to the
agora, these porticoes must have been between two and three stadia, or
upwards of a quarter of a mile, long. There is a portico at Bologna
about two miles long. We may perhaps assume from the scholium
quoted in p. 99, that the portico nearest the gate was called the Long
Stoa. It would appear from what Himerius says of them, that they
served as shops, or places of business.[5] They appear to have contained
various buildings, and they probably had openings for thoroughfares. We
have seen that the portico at Peiræus, which Pausanias speaks of in the
singular number, is called *five* porticoes by the scholiast on Aristophanes.
Before the porticoes were bronze statues of men and women of renown.
One of them contained sanctuaries of the gods, a GYMNASIUM named after
Hermes, and the HOUSE OF POLYTION; in which, says Pausanias, some

---

[1] Topographie, p. 32. Cf. schol. Aristoph. Ran. 501.

[2] p. 1259.

[3] "Iaccheum Athenis aliud non novimus
nisi in Ceramici urbani finibus ad portam
Piraeensem Cereris templum, ubi una

lacchus."—Boeckh, C. Ins. Gr. i. p. 471.

[4] The story of Polybotes is related by
Apollodorus, i. 6, 2; Strabo, x. p. 489;
Phavorinus, v. Πολυβώτης.

[5] στοαί, ἐφ᾽ ὧν ἀγοράζουσιν οἱ ᾽Αθηναῖοί
τε καὶ οἱ λοιποί.—Orat. iii. 12.

not of the meanest of the Athenians are said to have parodied the
Eleusinian mysteries.

There can be no doubt that the allusion is to the story of Alcibiades,
who with his drunken companions mutilated the Hermæ and mocked
the sacred mysteries; in which parody Theodorus sustained the part of
the ceryx or herald, Polytion that of the torch-bearer, and Alcibiades
that of the hierophant; whilst the other jovial companions represented
the mystæ, or initiated.[1]   In the εἰσαγγελία, or act of accusation, the
scene is said to have taken place in the house of Alcibiades (ἐν τῇ οἰκίᾳ
τῇ ἑαυτοῦ.—Plut. c. 22); but the other authorities give the house of
Polytion.   We will however take this occasion to observe that the house
of Alcibiades was most probably in this neighbourhood; for just here, as
we shall see further on, was the EURYSACEIUM, or monument of Eurysaces,
son of Ajax, from whom Alcibiades traced his descent; and it is therefore not unlikely that the monument was erected by his forefathers.
The vicinity too of the temple of Demeter may have suggested the
profane scene which he was charged with having enacted; whilst the
neighbouring Pompeium would have conveniently supplied the necessary utensils.   However this may be, the house of Polytion seems to
have been proverbial for its magnificence.   But after the profanity to
which we have alluded, it was probably confiscated, and the house and
grounds dedicated to Dionysus Melpomenos; at all events such was its
destination at the time when Pausanias saw it.   It contained images of
Athena Paionia (or Medica), of Zeus, of Mnemosynë, and of the Muses
and Apollo, executed and dedicated by Eubulides.   There was also a
mask of Acratus, a dæmon of the Dionysiac rout, built into the wall.

Pausanias does not mention the names of the stoæ which lined the
street leading from the Porta Peiraïca to the agora; but it is probable,
from its containing a GYMNASIUM OF HERMES, that the one nearest the
market-place was called the PORTICO OF THE HERMÆ (ἡ τῶν Ἑρμῶν στοά),
to which Æschines adverts in his speech against Ctesiphon.[2]   It seems

[1] Plut. Alc. 19; Thucyd. vi. 28; Isocr. De
Bigis, p. 348; Andoc. De Myster. p. 6 sq.
Reiske; who gives the names of other
participators.

[2] ἔδωκεν αὐτοῖς ὁ δῆμος τρεῖς λιθίνους
Ἑρμᾶς στῆσαι ἐν τῇ στοᾷ τῇ τῶν Ἑρμῶν.—
c. Ctesiph. p. 572, Reiske.

also to have been called the PORTICO OF THE THRACIANS (ἡ τῶν Θρᾳκῶν στοά), probably as a sort of by-name, because frequented by persons of that nation when staying at Athens; for it is not probable that the Athenians should have given one of their porticoes that name as a proper appellation. This seems to be the stoa alluded to by Aristophanes in the 'Ecclesiazusæ,' where Praxagora says that placing herself by the statue of Harmodius, she will distribute the different lots, marked with letters of the alphabet, showing the places where those who obtained them were to dine:

> καὶ κηρύξει τοὺς ἐκ τοῦ βῆτ' ἐπὶ τὴν στοιὰν ἀκολουθεῖν
> τὴν βασίλειον δειπνήσοντας · τὸ δὲ θῆτ' ἐς τὴν παρὰ ταύτην.
>
> v. 684.

"Those who get the letter be'a will be told to come and dine at the Stoa Basileios; and those who get theta at the one next to it."

As the beta here refers to the Stoa Basileios, we may conclude that the theta is also the initial letter of a stoa, and that it relates to the Stoa of the Thracians; which as the last in the street would adjoin the Stoa Basileios, as indicated in this passage. And we may probably infer hence that the tickets of the dicasts were distributed to them at the statue of Harmodius, as, in this parody, the tickets for dinner.

Next to the temenos of Dionysus, was a building having images of terra cotta. Among them was represented the Athenian king AMPHICTYON FEASTING DIONYSUS with other gods, and Pegasus of Eleutheræ, who introduced him among the Athenians (c. 2, 6);[1] in which, however, he was aided by the Delphic oracle, reminding him of the residence of the god in the time of Icarius.

Pausanias now arrives at the Cerameicus (c. 3, 1), by which, as we have said, he means the agora; for Cerameicus signified both the region and

---

[1] Such appears to be the meaning of the passage, which seems to be wrongly punctuated, though the editors do not notice it. Perhaps we should read: μετὰ δὲ τὸ τοῦ Διονύσου τέμενός ἐστιν οἴκημα ἀγάλματα ἔχον ἐκ πηλοῦ. βασιλεὺς 'Αθηναίων 'Αμφικτύων, ἄλλους τε θεοὺς ἑστιῶν καὶ Διόνυσον, ἐνταῦθά ἐστιν, καὶ Πήγασος 'Ελευθερεύς, κ.τ.λ.

the market-place. We do not believe, however, that it is found in the latter sense in any of the classical Greek authors; that is to say, in any authors down to the end of the orators. Nor, we believe, can the phrase ἀρχαία ἀγορά, or ancient market place, be found in them, but only in writers of a later age. Apollodorus appears to have used it,[1] who lived in the second century B.C.; but by that time a new market-place may have been constructed by the Romans, or rather, perhaps, he is speaking of a still more ancient and primitive agora, which may have existed in the early days of the city on the south side of the Acropolis. The new agora had been made at all events before the time of Strabo, who flourished in the Augustan period; for he mentions that the agora had been removed to a district once called Eretria.[2] Now it seems very probable that after the establishment of the new agora, the former one came to be called, by way of distinction, "Cerameicus," from the district in which it lay. In any event it is certain that *Cerameicus* came to be used as equivalent to *agora*, as we will show by a few examples.

In the 'Lives of the Ten Orators,' ascribed to Plutarch,[3] who lived in the last half of the first century of our era, it is said that a bronze statue was erected to Lycurgus *in the Cerameicus;*[4] whilst in the original psephisma at the end of the Lives, the statue is ordered to be erected *in the agora*.[5] And Pausanias also mentions the statue as being in the Cerameicus.[6] Whence we may conclude that in the time of these writers the name of Cerameicus was synonymous with that of agora.

Again, Pausanias in his description of the Cerameicus (loc. cit.),

---

[1] Apud Harpocr. voc. Πάνδημος Ἀφροδ.

[2] οἱ δ' ἀπὸ τῆς Ἀθήνῃσιν Ἐρετρίας, ἢ νῦν ἐστιν ἀγορά.—p. 447.

[3] The 'Lives of the Ten Orators' were certainly not by Plutarch. Anybody may convince himself of this who will compare the lives of Demosthenes in the 'Parallel Lives,' and in the 'Lives of the Orators.' The author of the latter appears to have been a more careful writer than Plutarch, as he quotes psephismata in support of his statements. At the same time it cannot be doubted that he was a late writer.

[4] ἐν Κεραμεικῷ.—Plut. Oper. t. ix. p. 353, Reiske.

[5] στῆσαι αὐτοῦ τὸν δῆμον χαλκῆν εἰκόνα ἐν ἀγορᾷ.—Ibid. p. 386.

[6] i. 8, 3.

mentions in it a statue of Demosthenes. But in the psephisma ap-
pended to the life of Demosthenes, it is directed that he should have
a statue in the agora.[1] And indeed, the author of the life here says
that it was in the agora;[2] and in another place he identifies the spot
more accurately, by saying that it was near the enclosed space and the
altar of the Twelve Gods;[3] which as we have seen (supra, p. 82), was
erected in the agora by Peisistratus the son of Hippias. Hence it
would seem that some of these later writers use the words indifferently,
and that there was no universal or exclusive custom in the matter. For
thus Lucian, a late writer, mentions the statues of Harmodius and Aristogeiton as being in the agora;[4] whilst Pausanias and Arrian, who
both lived in the time of the Antonines, speak of them as being in the
Cerameicus.[5] But Aristotle, a classical writer, says they were in the
agora.[6] The usage, therefore, of the later writers seems to have sometimes varied in this matter, though it appears to have inclined for
Cerameicus; and Pausanias doubtless adopted the latter appellation for
the sake of clearness in his topographical description, as he had to
speak of two market places—the regular Athenian agora, and the later
one established by the Romans.

In Grecian cities, the market place or agora was the centre both of
political and social life. It was here that the assemblies of the people
were originally held, and it was not till the riper years of Athenian
history that a separate place, the Pnyx, was set apart for them. It was
in and about the agora, as being the heart of the city, that the legisla-
tive chambers, the courts of law, and the other establishments for conducting the public business, were placed; and from this cause, as well
as from the large resort for purposes of traffic, the agora became the
seat not only of the finest public buildings, but also of the principal
monuments erected in honour of public men.[7] It was to these that the

[1] Plut. Op. ix. 380.
[2] Ibid. p. 369.   [3] Ibid. p. 367.
[4] De Parasit. c. 48 (t. ii. p. 873, Reitz).
[5] Paus. i. 8, 5; Arrian, Exp. Alex. iii.
16, 8.

[6] καὶ εἰς ὃν πρῶτον ἐγκώμιον ἐποιήθη,
οἷον εἰς Ἱππόλοχον, καὶ Ἁρμόδιον καὶ Ἀρισ-
τωγείτονα, τὸ ἐν ἀγορᾷ σταθῆναι.—Rhet.
i. 19, 6.

[7] ἁπάντων γὰρ ὑμῖν τῶν καλῶν ἔργων τὰ

attention of Pausanias was exclusively directed; but as we should scarcely obtain a complete knowledge of Athenian life without also surveying it as a market, and a place of resort for idlers and gossips, we shall say a few words about it under those aspects also.

The laws respecting the agora appear to have been very strict. Although we cannot affirm that Plato, in his 'Laws,'[1] speaks of the actual usage, yet we may infer that he wrote conformably to Athenian notions when he lays it down that all buying and selling must be done in the proper place in the agora, and for ready money; those who conducted their business in other places, and on credit, were to do so at their own risk, and were not to be allowed to claim the benefit of the laws. This could hardly have been the actual practice; still there was a habit of ready-money dealing among the Athenians which gave rise to the proverb "Attic faith" (Ἀττικὴ πίστις), and is probably alluded to by Plautus in the 'Asinaria'—"Græca mercari fide." There was an express law against speaking falsely in the market, that is, we suppose, making fraudulent misrepresentations, either on the part of buyer or seller.[2] The Agoranomi, of whom there were five at Athens and five at Piræus, were charged with seeing that this law was observed, as well as all other regulations concerning sales.[3] They appear to have had the power to punish citizens by fines, and metics and slaves by flogging. They were also the receivers of the market dues.[4] It was forbidden to taunt any citizen with being a dealer in the agora.[5]

Goods were sold in booths or stalls (σκηναί), but tradespeople were not allowed to set them up wherever they pleased. Each trade had its allotted place in the agora called a circle (κύκλος), apparently because the booths were pitched in a ring. Everything but meat appears to have been sold in these κύκλοι.[6] When the agora was wanted for

ὑπομνήματα ἐν τῇ ἀγορᾷ ἀνάκειται.—Æsch. c. Ctesiph. p. 575, Reiske.

[1] lib. xi. p. 915 (iii. 3, 235, Bekk.).

[2] Harpocrat. in κατὰ τὴν ἀγορὰν ἀψευδεῖν. Cf. Demosth. in Lept. p. 459, Reiske.

[3] Harpocr. in Ἀγοράνομοι.

[4] In later times the Agoranomi seem to have been identified with the Logistæ (schol. Aristoph. Acharn. 720); but originally these were distinct magistrates. Cf. ibid. v. 896.

[5] Demosth. in Eubul. p. 1308, Reiske.

[6] Schol. ad Aristoph. Eq. 137.

public occasions the booths were cleared away. The circles were named after the articles sold in them : as the fish market, the unguent market, the green-cheese market, &c. (τὸ ὄψον, τὰ μύρα, ὁ χλωρὸς τυρός).[1]

Eupolis names several κύκλοι in the following lines :

περιῆλθον εἰς τὰ σκόροδα καὶ τὰ κρόμμυα
καὶ τὸν λιβανωτόν, κεἰ θὺ τῶν ἀρωμάτων
καὶ περὶ τὰ γέλγη.[2]

" I went about to the garlic market, the onion shops, the frankincense shops, and towards the spice dealers, and the trippery market."

Particular spots in the market appear to have been frequented by certain townspeople as a rendezvous. Thus the Deceleians were to be found at the barber's shop near the Hermæ, and the meeting-place for the Platæans was at the green-cheese market,[3] and others, according to their wants or their trades, at the shoemaker's shop, the unguent market, &c.

We sometimes hear of ἀγορᾶς κύκλος in a different sense from that just mentioned, and signifying apparently not any particular division of the agora but the whole of it, or rather the persons assembled in it, as in the following passage of the 'Orestes' of Euripides :—

ὀλιγάκις ἄστυ κἀγορᾶς χραίνων κύκλον.—v. 909.

" Keeping aloof from the city and the market-place."

Whence Leake has been led to think[4] that the Athenian agora was actually of a circular form. And he is confirmed in this idea by another passage in the 'Hipparchics' of Xenophon, where it is said that

---

[1] Thus Lysias : ἐλθόντα εἰς τὸν χλωρὸν τυρόν.—cont. Pancl. p. 732, Reiske. Cf. Taylor, Lect. Lysiacæ, c. 12. And Aristophanes : τὰ μειράκια ταυτὶ λέγω, τὰν τῷ μύρῳ. — Eq. 1375, " in the unguent market." Where the scholiast observes that it was an Attic usage to name places after what was sold in them, and thus to say τὸ μύρον for τὸ μυροπώλιον. Again in the 'Ranæ': παρὰ τοὺς ἰχθῦς ἀνέκυψεν

(1068), "at the fish market."

[2] Fragm. ap. Meineke, p. 211. Asses' flesh seems to have been a common meat in antiquity. The place where it was sold was called μεσκόνια. Poll. ix. 5.

[3] Lysias c. Pancl. p. 731 sq. ; ἕκαστος γὰρ ὑμῶν εἴθισται προσφοιτᾶν ὁ μὲν πρὸς μυροπώλιον, ὁ δὲ πρὸς κουρεῖον, ὁ δὲ πρὸς σκυτοτομεῖον.—Idem, περὶ τοῦ Ἀδυνάτου, p. 754. [4] vol. i. p. 217 sq.

the cavalry are to ride *roun l* the agora.[1]   Hence he imagines the agora
to have described a sort of half-circle round the southern part of the
Areiopagus.   But with regard to the first passage we may observe that
the scene of the 'Orestes' is laid at Argos, and therefore can prove
nothing respecting the agora at Athens, even if κύκλος here had really
any reference to material form.   But ἀγορᾶς κύκλος means not the
market-place itself, but the public assembly of the Argives who had
met in it to try Orestes, of the proceedings of which the whole speech
of the ἄγγελος is a description.   The ill-favoured but manly man
alluded to in the passage in question as getting up and speaking in
favour of Orestes is described as rude and rustic, seldom coming into
the city or attending the public assembly, which is all the line means.
That this was Porson's view of it is plain enough from his note : "Sed
primo observandum est, nuncium, hoc est ipsum Euripidem, cum tacita
quadam indignatione loqui, quasi *homines urbani* rusticorum commercio
se pollui crederent."[2]   He does not illustrate the passage further,
because perhaps he thought that the use of κύκλος to denote *a circle of
people* was too common to need it.

In the passage from Xenophon, κύκλῳ περὶ τὴν ἀγορὰν περιελαύνειν
means only to make the circuit of it, and indeed κύκλος here would
refer rather to the horsemen than to the ground which they traversed.
By a similar mode of reasoning to Leake's we might infer from the
phrases "forum circumire," or "to drive round Grosvenor Square," that
the Roman forum and the London square were round.   The same rule
too would make the ἱερὰ circular as well as the agora in which they
were, which is absurd.

We are inclined, therefore, to think that the agora, the site of which
we have already indicated, formed a parallelogram of about three hundred
and fifty yards in length from east to west, and two hundred and fifty
in breadth from north to south.   This would have formed a noble and
spacious area, and that it must have been such is evident from Xeno-

---

[1] κύκλῳ περὶ τὴν ἀγορὰν καὶ τὰ ἱερὰ   "contaminating, forsooth, with his presence
περιελαύνειν.—iii. 2.   the fine city gentlemen."

[2] χραίνω has a quasi-ironical meaning :

phon s speaking about the cavalry galloping from the Hermae to the Eleusinium. The same inference may be drawn from its having sometimes served for assemblies of the people, and from the numerous large buildings which lined its sides.

On certain festivals the whole agora became a sort of τέμενος, or hallowed spot, and was marked out with vessels of holy water (περιρ-ραντήρια), beyond which certain persons were not allowed to go. Among such persons were those who had not performed military service, or had shown cowardice by deserting the ranks,[1] or had been guilty of lewd and abominable conduct.[2] When any one was to be condemned by ostracism the whole agora was boarded in, ten entrances being left, one apparently for each of the tribes.[3] That the Athenian agora, like the Roman Forum,[4] was the resort of idlers and loungers, and especially when the hours of business were over, needs no further illustration than the account given by Demosthenes in his speech against Conon, of his promenade in it, and the revellers whom, much to his annoyance, he encountered. In the earlier times the Scythian bowmen, called Τοξόται or Σκύθαι, one thousand in number, who were under the orders of the Prytanes, and discharged the office of policemen by keeping order in the assemblies, &c., were stationed under tents, or booths, in the middle of the agora, but were subsequently removed to the Areiopagus.[5] Two of these men went about with a rope dipped in a red dye when it was necessary to compel the people to go to the ecclesia, a practice graphically described by Aristophanes in his ' Acharnenses ':

οἱ δ' ἐν ἀγορᾷ λαλοῦσι, κἄνω καὶ κάτω
τὸ σχοινίον φεύγουσι τὸ μεμιλτωμένον.—v. 21.

"See in the market how they talk and chatter,
And send about to shun the red-dy'd rope."

---

[1] ὁ μὲν τοίνυν νομοθέτης τὸν ἀστράτευτον, καὶ τὸν δειλόν, καὶ τὸν λιπόντα τὴν τάξιν, ἔξω τῶν περιρραντηρίων τῆς ἀγορᾶς ἐξείργει.—Æsch. c. Ctesiph. p. 566, Reiske.

[2] Idem, c. Timarch. p. 47.

[3] Schol. ad Aristoph. Eq. 851. Cf. Plut. Arist. 7.

[4] "vespertinumque pererro
Sæpe forum."—Hor. Sat. i. 6, 113.

[5] Schol. ad Aristoph. Ach. 54.

Those who got marked with the rope were punished. For the same purpose all the avenues of the agora were closed with hurdles, except those which led to the ecclesia, and all buying and selling was suspended.[1] But to return from this digression.

On entering the agora, Pausanias says (c. 3, 1) that the first building on the right was the Στοὰ Βασίλειος, or REGAL PORTICO, so called apparently because the archon basileus took his seat in it during his year of office. Pausanias walking eastward from the Peiraïc Gate, must have entered the agora at its south-western side, or a little to the north of the western extremity of the Areiopagus. At this point, therefore, must have lain the Stoa Basileios; and in the time of Stuart traces of the foundations of an extensive building were visible here, running in a line eastward, as the stoa would have done.[2] If we may admit the epistles of the pseudo-Æschines as topographical evidence, it must have extended nearly up to the ascent of the Acropolis, and consequently to the eastern extremity of the Areiopagus; thus lining the greater part of the southern side of the agora. For in the fourth epistle it is said that the Athenians honoured Pindar with a bronze statue, which existed in the time of the writer (καὶ ἦν αὐτὴ καὶ εἰς ἡμᾶς ἔτι), and stood before the Stoa Basileios; while Pausanias mentions this statue as being near the temple of Ares, which, as we shall see further on, lay at the north-eastern end of the Areiopagus, and not far from those of Harmodius and Aristogeiton, on the ascent to the Acropolis. The very words of the epistle which we have cited prove it to be a forgery. For when a man says that an object *was* in existence down to his time, he implies that it had ceased to exist, which with regard to this statue is manifestly false of Æschines, since we know from Pausanias that it was in existence several centuries later. The real Æschines would have said, ' which *is* before the Stoa Basileius.' And that this stoa extended to so great a distance is contradicted by the fact that it was succeeded to the eastward by other buildings, which must have stood between it and the temple of

---

[1] Schol. ad Aristoph. Ach. 22.
[2] See the plan of Athens, in the third volume of the ' Antiquities.'

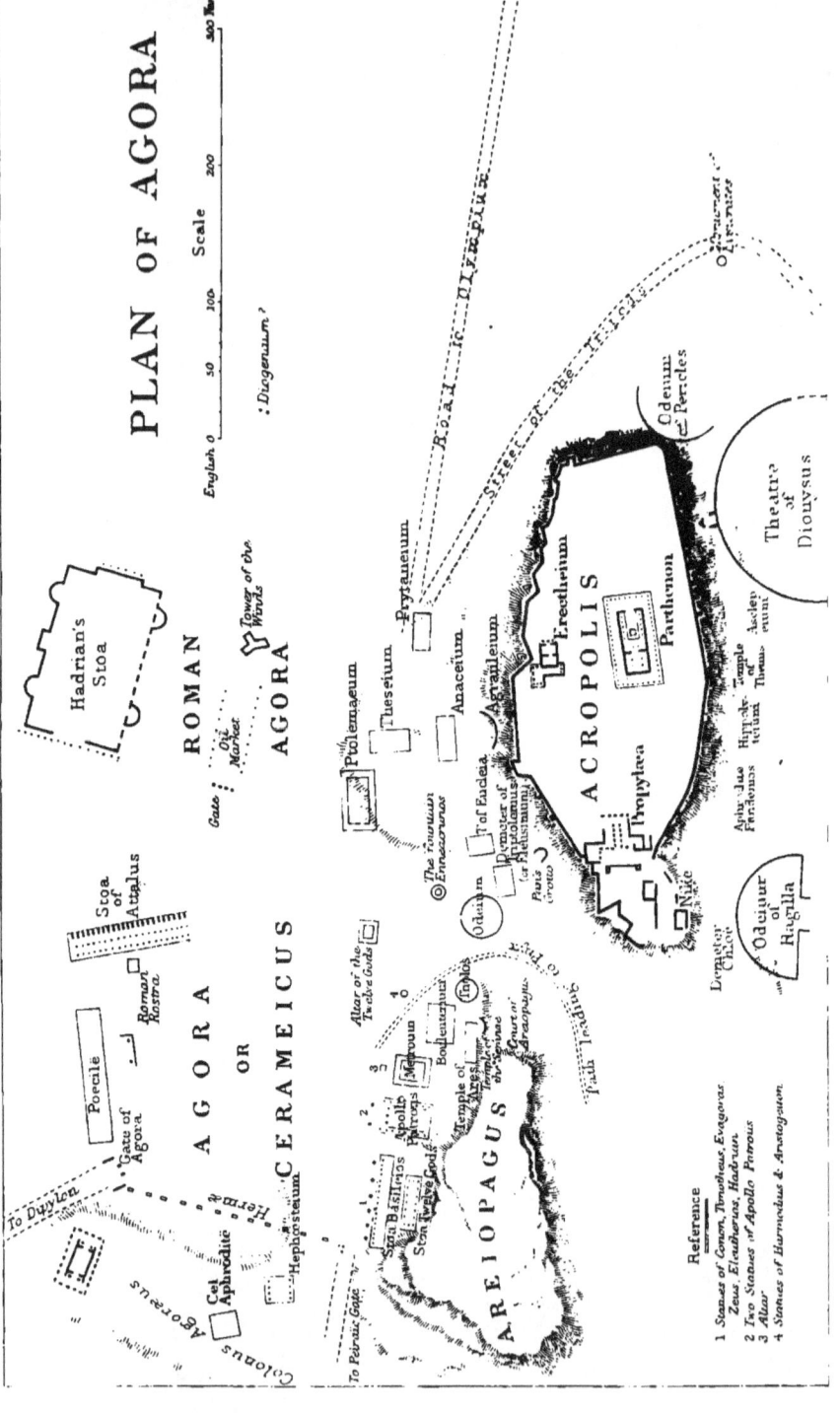

PLAN OF AGORA

Scale

English 0   50   100   200   300 Yards

Ares. We must therefore here reject the testimony of the pseudo-Æschines altogether as that of an ignorant forger.[1]

On the tiled roof of the Stoa Basileius were figures in terra cotta representing Theseus hurling Sciron into the sea, and Hemera, or Aurora, carrying off Cephalus. Near the portico were statues of Conon and his son Timotheus, and of Euagoras, the Cyprian king, who persuaded the King of Persia to make over his Phœnician triremes to Conon. We learn from Demosthenes that Conon's statue was of bronze, and doubtless the rest of the group were of the same material.[2]

The Council of the Areiopagus appears sometimes to have assembled in the Stoa Basileius, and on these occasions it was surrounded with a rope in order to keep off persons who had no business there.[3] The rope was drawn at a distance of fifty feet, and policemen stood by to prevent improper persons from approaching.[4] It was to the Stoa Basileius that Socrates was summoned to answer the charges brought against him by Melitus and others, as Plato tells at the end of his 'Theætetus.' Before it stood an altar at which the Thesmothetæ, after undergoing an examination by the Senate, took an oath to perform their office in a just and proper manner.[5] In this stoa were preserved the κύρβεις, or stone-pillars on which the laws relating to religion were engraved,[6] and which, as we have observed, were brought hither bý Ephialtes from the Acropolis.

Close to the Stoa Basileius was a statue of Zeus, surnamed Eleutherius, and another of the Emperor Hadrian, who was remarkable for his benevolence towards his subjects, and particularly towards the Athenians. Such is the eulogy of him by Pausanias, to which we may

---

[1] There are now twelve letters extant under the name of Æschines. Photius considered only nine to be genuine (Cod. 61 and 264). Taylor denounced them all as spurious, and the fourth by name (Reiske, Æsch. t. iii. p. 654). But M. Le Bas has asserted the genuineness of the tenth from an inscription found at Delos. 'Expédition de Morée,' t. iii. p. 25.

[2] c. Lept. p. 478, Reiske.   C. Nep.

Timoth.; Xenoph. Hell. iii. 4, 1; Isocr. Euag. p. 200, Steph.

[3] τὴν ἐξ Ἀρείου πάγου βουλὴν ὅταν ἐν τῇ βασιλείῳ στοᾷ καθεζομένη περισχοινίσηται, κ.τ.λ.—Demosth. in Aristog. 776.

[4] Jul. Poll. lib. viii. 124.

[5] Pollux, viii. 86.

[6] Aristot. ap. Harpocr. in voc.; Phot. Lex.

add that the Athenians in return held him in high honour, and put him on a level with Zeus himself, as we see among other things already mentioned, by his statue being erected here in company with that of the father of the gods. And there can be little doubt that the statue in question, like that of Zeus, was also inscribed with the title of Eleutherius; for, as we shall see further on, there is in the theatre a throne inscribed to the priest of Hadrian Eleutherius. Harpocration [1] quotes a passage from Hyperides to the effect that Zeus was so called because the neighbouring portico, of which we shall speak presently, was built by freedmen (ἐξελεύθεροι); and another from Didymus, in correction of this, affirming that Zeus obtained the name from his having delivered the Athenians from the Persians. This last was doubtless its true origin, as it is found on other objects besides this statue, and the view of Didymus is confirmed by Aristides.[2] Moreover, Isocrates, in a passage lately cited, calls the statue in question that of Zeus Soter, or the Saviour; which, as we have shown in another place, was equivalent to that of Eleutherius.[3]

Behind the statues just mentioned was a portico which Pausanias (3, 2) does not name, but we know from other sources that it was called the PORTICO OF ZEUS ELEUTHERIUS, and consequently derived its name from the statue of that deity. It is adverted to by Plato in the beginning of his 'Theages' under that title. Harpocration (voc. Βασίλειος Στοά) speaks of the two porticoes as being parallel to each other (παρ' ἀλλήλας), and Pausanias describes it as behind (ὄπισθεν) the Stoa Basileius. Its site near the Pompeium is further fixed by a passage in Diogenes Laërtius who, in his life of Diogenes says, that that philosopher used to point to those buildings as prepared for his abode by the Athenians.[4] The stoa had some celebrated pictures. Pausanias mentions one of the TWELVE GODS from which it seems to have sometimes taken its name. On the further wall was a picture representing Theseus, with personifications of Democracy and the Demos. This

[1] voc. Ἐλευθ. Ζεύς.
[2] Aristid. Panath. i. 125, Jebb.
[3] Euagor. 200 c.
[4] δεικνὺς τὴν τοῦ Διὸς στοὰν καὶ πομπεῖον αὐτῷ κατεσκευακέναι (τοὺς Ἀθηναίους) ἐνδιαιτᾶσθαι.—lib. vi. § 22.

juxtaposition shows at least the belief of the Athenians that Theseus was the founder of their democracy ; but Pausanias expresses his incredulity of it, and thinks that the opinion was derived from the choruses and tragedies of poets. Another picture, representing the battle of Mantineia, Pausanias adverts to when describing that city,[1] where there appears to have been a copy. It represented a cavalry engagement, in which the most conspicuous figures were, on the Athenian side, Gryllus, the son of Xenophon, and on that of the Thebans, Epaminondas. All these pictures appear to have been painted by Euphranor. Plutarch[2] mentions the picture of the battle and that of Theseus together as the work of that artist; and Eustathius[3] says, that when he was painting the Twelve Gods in the portico in question he took his idea of Zeus from accidentally hearing, when passing a school, those noble lines of Homer :—

> ἦ, καὶ κυανέῃσιν ἐπ' ὀφρύσι νεῦσε Κρονίων·
> ἀμβρόσιαι δ' ἄρα χαῖται ἐπερρώσαντο ἄνακτος
> κρατὸς ἀπ' ἀθανάτοιο, κ.τ.λ.

> " This said, with his black brows he to her nodded,
> Wherewith displayed were his locks divine ;
> Olympus shook at stirring of his godhead,
> And Thetis from it jump'd into the brine.
>   HOBBES.

But a similar story is told of Pheidias and his statue of Zeus at Elis. Pliny[4] also alludes to these pictures as being the work of Euphranor. We learn from the ' Phocica ' of Pausanias,[5] that in this portico of Zeus were once suspended the shields of celebrated warriors, till they were carried off by Sulla's soldiers after the capture of Athens.

Euphranor also executed the statue of APOLLO PATROUS, which stood in the neighbouring temple of that god, for he was a sculptor as well as a painter. Some writers have indeed thought that Pausanias means here a picture of Apollo ; but deities in the temples dedicated to them were, we believe, represented exclusively by statues, and Pausanias

---

[1] viii. 9, 4.
[2] De Glor. Athen. t. vii. p. 363, Reiske.
[3] Ad Il. i. 529.
[4] H. N. xxxv. 129.
[5] x. 21, 3.

comples the work in question with the Apollos of Leochares and Calamis, who were undoubtedly sculptors. Apollo Patrous, the reputed ancestor of the Athenians through Ion, was the same as the Pythian Apollo.[1] The statues of the god by Leochares and Calamis stood before the temple. That of Calamis represented him in his character of ἀλεξίκακος, or the 'Averter of Evil'—a name which he obtained from averting, by means of a Delphic oracle, the plague which infested Athens at the beginning of the Peloponnesian war. The archons, when elected, sacrificed to Apollo Patrous as their ancestral god.[2] An altar of Apollo in the agora most probably stood before this temple.[3]

Next followed the METROUM, or temple of the Mother of the Gods. Near it was the BOULEUTERIUM, or senate-house of the Five Hundred.

The worship of the Phrygian goddess Rhea at Athens, and a temple to her on the agora, are calculated to excite surprise; but, besides the authority of Pausanias, its existence is also testified by inscriptions.[4] Julian (Orat. v.) says that the Athenians were the first to receive this deity in Greece, and in what remote times, may be inferred from a passage in Pausanias,[5] from which we learn that an ancient image of the goddess in Peloponnesus was referred to the time of the Tantalidæ; that is, to time out of mind. Hence, as Curtius remarks,[6] there is no occasion to refer the introduction of the worship at Athens to the time of the Persian wars, with Gerhard, or, with Preller, to the time of the Peisistratidæ.[7] Curtius thinks that the Hellenes may have brought it from Asia Minor.

In the Metroum was a statue of the goddess by Pheidias. Æschines confirms the position of the Metroum next to the Bouleuterium.[8] It was a place of deposit not only for laws, psephismata, and other public

---

[1] καλῶ καὶ τὸν Ἀπόλλω τὸν Πύθιον, ὃς πατρῷός ἐστι τῇ πόλει.—Demosth. De Cor. p. 274, Reiske. ἑαυτῇ δὲ πατρῷον τὸν Ἀπόλλω τὸν Πύθιον.—Aristid. Panath. t. i. p. 112, Jebb.

[2] Schol. ad Aristoph. Nub. 1470. Cf. ad Av. 1527.

[3] X. Orat. Vit. Lycur. sub fin. (Plut.

Reiske, ix. 356).

[4] See Philologus, Suppl. ii. 588; Rhein. Mus. xix. 301.

[5] iii. 22, 4.

[6] Att. Stud. ii. 58 sq.

[7] Griech. Myth. i. 512.

[8] παρὰ τὸ βουλευτήριον.—c. Ctesiph. p. 576, Reiske.

records,[1] but also for wills, accounts, and other private documents.[2]
Hence this temple, as well as the temple of Apollo Patrous, the Bouleuterium, and the Tholos, being all places of public registration, were
called the "Archives" (τὰ ἀρχαῖα).[3] The Lyceium was also an ἀρχεῖον,
and contained the archives of the polemarch. We hear also of another
called the Parasitium, the position of which we cannot indicate; but it
appears to have been mentioned in an inscription in the Anaceium, and
in a regal law.[4] The name of the officer (Parasitos) who deposited the
first-fruits of the sacred corn in the Parasitium became a term of
reproach. Three inscriptions having reference to the Metroum have
been found at the church of Hypapante, opposite the north-west
angle of the Acropolis;[5] a circumstance which tends to confirm its
position.

The Metroum must have stood at the north-eastern foot of the
Areiopagus, as appears from the legend of a Metragyrtes,[6] who was
said to have first initiated the Athenian women in the worship of the
Mother of the Gods; wherefore the Athenians cast him headlong
into a chasm which once existed here, through which the Eumenides
were fabled to have descended.[7] But a pestilence having supervened,
they were directed by an oracle to expiate their act by building a
senate-house at the spot, making an enclosure round it, and dedicating
the whole to the Mother of the Gods. They also erected a statue of
the Metragyrtes, and filled up the chasm.[8] From this legend we may
infer that the Metroum was a sort of adjunct to the Bouleuterium,
and the story was probably invented to explain this connexion. The
Metroum appears to have stood at the corner of a street or turning.
We infer this from the speech of Æschines against Timarchus, which
shows that there was a street or road at it, by which the people went

[1] Æschin. l. c.; Lycurg. c. Leocr. p. 184, Reiske; Photius in Μητρῷον.

[2] Diog. Laërt. x. 16 et ibi Ménage.

[3] Thus the Tholus is described as τόπος τις ἐν τοῖς ἀρχείοις. Bekk. An. Græc. p. 264.

[4] J. Poll. vi. s. 35; Athen. vi. 27.

[5] Rangabé, Ant. Hell. ii. Nos. 1153–1155.

[6] *Metragyrtes* was another name for a *Gallus*, or priest of Cybelë.

[7] πάγον παρ' αὐτὸν χάσμα δύσονται χθονός.—Eurip. Electr. 1280.

[8] Photius and Suidas, voc. Μητραγύρτης.

from the agora to the Pnyx,[1] and which must consequently have run
between the Acropolis and the Areiopagus. Again, it was the same
road which led up to the Acropolis, since Arrian says that the statues
of Harmodius and Aristogeiton stood upon it, about opposite (καταντικρὺ μάλιστα) the Metroum.[2] This temple no doubt faced the north,
and before it was the altar at which, as described in the passage from
Æschines, Pittalacus, the public slave, took refuge. The statues of
Harmodius and Aristogeiton, therefore, would have been opposite its
eastern side. Inside the Metroum was a large earthenware cask, in
which Diogenes was said to have lived.[3]

From the south-western corner of the agora to the road just
mentioned, leading from the agora to the Acropolis, and onwards to
the Pnyx, we have, therefore, three buildings in consecutive order, all
facing to the north—the Stoa Basileius, the temple of Apollo Patrous,
and the Metroum, while the Stoa of Zeus Eleutherius lay behind the
Basileius. The buildings next mentioned, the Bouleuterium and Tholus,
are no longer in the line, but face to the east and to the road already
mentioned leading to the Acropolis and the Pnyx. This may be inferred
from Pausanias saying that the statues of the eponymous heroes which
came next to the Tholus were *higher up* the ascent (ἀνωτέρω, cap. 5, 1).
The north-eastern extremity of the Areiopagus forms a kind of bay,
leaving plenty of room for these structures; and it is here, indeed, that
Curtius places them, though he arrives there in a very different manner.

---

[1] ὁ Πιττάλακος ἔρχεται γυμνὸς εἰς τὴν
ἀγοράν καὶ καθίζει ἐπὶ τὸν βωμὸν τὸν τῆς
Μητρὸς τῶν θεῶν· ὄχλου δὲ συνδραμόντος,
οἷον εἴωθε γίγνεσθαι, φοβηθέντες ὅ τε 'Ηγησή-
σανδρος καὶ ὁ Τίμαρχος μὴ ἀνακηρυχθῇ αὐτῶν
ἡ βδελυρία εἰς πᾶσαν τὴν πόλιν—ἐπῄει δὲ
ἐκκλησία—θέουσι πρὸς τὸν βωμὸν καὶ αὐτοί,
κ.τ.λ.—p. 84, Reiske. We believe that
ἐπῄει here is usually rendered *instabat*, 'a
meeting of the ecclesia *was at hand*.' But
we take the meaning to be that given in
Reiske's Index Græc. Æsch.: "coibat, ad-
ventabat in forum concio." The members
were actually proceeding to the Pnyx, and
on passing the Metroum would observe
the suppliant Pittalacus. Hence the haste
of Hegesander and Timarchus to get him
from the altar, and out of the agora.
ἀνακηρυχθῇ means only 'should be
rumoured about' (περιβόητος γένηται,
schol. ad loc.).

[2] καὶ νῦν κεῖνται 'Αθήνησιν ἐν Κεραμεικῷ
αἱ εἰκόνες [of Harmodius and Aristogeiton]
ᾗ ἄνιμεν ἐς πόλιν, καταντικρὺ μάλιστα τοῦ
Μητρῴου, οὐ μακρὰν τῶν Εὐδανέμων τοῦ
βωμοῦ.—Arrian, Exped. Alex. iii. 16, 8.

[3] Diog. Laërt. vi. 23.

In the Bouleuterium, lying next to the Metroum at the commencement of the ascent, was an ancient wooden image (ξόανον) of Zeus Boulæus; an Apollo, the work of Peisias, and a statue of Demos, or the Athenian people personified, and probably deified, by Lyson. Also pictures of some Thesmothetæ, painted by Protogenes the Caunian. The portrait of Callippus, who led the Athenians to Thermopylæ to oppose the entrance of the Gauls into Greece, was done by Olbiades, an artist who seems not to be otherwise known. Pausanias then enters upon a long digression concerning the Gauls.

In the Senate House, Zeus Boulæus and Athena Boulæa had a common shrine (ἱερόν), at which the senators sacrificed on entering, an act that was called εἰσιτήρια θύειν, or εἰσιτήρια ὑπὲρ τῆς βουλῆς ἱεροποιεῖν.[1] Here was also an altar of Hestia (Vesta) Boulæa, by whom it was customary to swear. The altar served as a refuge.[2]

Near the Bouleuterium was the Tholus, where the Prytanes sacrificed (Paus. 5, 1). It was a round building, with a dome of stone, and not wood, as was more usual; and hence its name, from its likeness to a sort of conical hat called θολία.[3] All that Pausanias thought worth mentioning in it were some small silver statues (ἀγάλματα) of gods.

Still further up stood statues of the ten eponymous heroes of the Attic tribes. The Eponymi—for so they are called substantively— comprised Hippothoön, son of Poseidon and Alopë; Antiochus, son of Heracles and Mideia; Ajax, son of Telamon; and from among the Athenians themselves, Leos, who sacrificed his daughters for the public good; Erechtheus, who conquered the Eleusinians and killed their leader Immaradus, son of Eumolpus; Ægeus; Oineus, the bastard son of Pandion; and Acamas, one of the children of Theseus. Also Cecrops and Pandion; but Pausanias knew not how to rank these, or whether they were the first or second of the name; upon which subject

[1] Antiphon De Choreut. p. 789; Demosth. De falsa leg. p. 400; c. Meid. p. 552, Reiske; cf. Petit, Leg. Att. p. 275.

[2] καὶ τὴν Ἑστίαν ἐπώμοσε τὴν Βουλαίαν. —Æsch. De fal. Leg. p. 227, Reiske; Vit. X.

Orat. p. 328; Xenoph. Hell. ii. 3, 52; Harpocr. voc. Βουλαία.

[3] Tim. Lex. Plat. in voc.; Photius, ib.; Bekk. An. Græc. i. 264.

he makes a short digression. To these ten were afterwards added Attalus the Mysian, Ptolemy the Egyptian, and more recently, in the time of Pausanias himself, the emperor Hadrian.

From these thirteen Eponymi, therefore, we have the tribes Hippothoöntis, Antiochis, Æantis, Leontis, Erechtheïs, Ægeïs, Œneïs, Acamantis, Cecropis, Pandionis, Attalis, Ptolemaïs, Hadrianis. It does not appear from Pausanias whether there were statues here of the last three Eponymi.

By an ordinance of Solon, laws to be proposed in the assembly were written on tablets and exhibited before the statues of the Eponymi, for the inspection of the people.[1]   Here, also, were posted up the names of those drawn for military service abroad.[2]

Pausanias devotes his next two chapters to an account of Ptolemy and Attalus, and does not resume his description of the city till c. 8, s. 3. After the statues of the Eponymi came some images of gods; among them of Amphiaraüs, the mode of whose deification is related further on (c. 34, 2), viz. that he was swallowed up with his chariot by the earth as he was flying from Thebes;[3] a fable derived probably from the place called Harma.   He had a temple at Oropus, whose inhabitants were the first to deify him, with a white marble statue and an altar, which, as it was of a rather singular kind, we will here describe.   It was divided into five compartments, one of which was dedicated to Heracles, Zeus, and Apollo Pæan; another to heroes and their wives; a third to Hestia, Hermes, Amphiaraüs, and his son Amphilochus; a fourth to Aphroditë, Panaceia, Iaso[4] (a daughter of Amphiaraüs), Hygicia, and Athena Paionia; whilst the fifth and last was devoted to the Nymphs, to Pan, and the rivers Acheloüs and Cephissus.

Amphilochus, who here plays only a subordinate part, seems however to have cast his father into the shade, and to have ultimately usurped all the honours of the temple; for Livy, in describing the visit of

---

[1] Andoc. De Myst. p. 40; Demosth. c. Lept. p. 485; id. c. Timocr. p. 705; Phot. voc. ἐπώνυμοι; Suid. voc. ἄρχων.

[2] Schol. Aristoph. Pac. 1183.

[3] Cf. Apollod. iii. 6, 8.

[4] Panaceia and Iaso are also coupled together in the 'Plutus' of Aristophanes, v. 701 sq.

Æmilius Paullus to Oropus, mentions only him as the object of worship.[1] Bayle indeed (Amphilochus, note C.) charges Livy with being mistaken; but at all events, from Pausanias' own showing, Amphilochus was in more repute than his father; for he tells us that an altar had been erected to him at Athens, and that he had an oracle at Mallos in Cilicia, considered the most truthful of the age. Both Livy and Pausanias say that the temple had a fountain near it; but, according to the latter, it only served for convalescents to throw gold and silver coins into; which doubtless soon emerged from its depths.

Next to Amphiaraüs was a statue of Eirenë, or Peace, bearing in her arms her son Plutus. The reading of the MSS. here is Pluto (Πλούτωνα); but Pausanias in another passage (ix. 16, 1), reverts to this statue, and says that Cephisodotus, the brother of Phocion's wife,[2] who executed this statue, did as well in representing Eirenë *with Plutus*, as the maker of a statue at Thebes, who represented him nursed by Tychë, or Fortune. Plutus and Pluto, however, were nearly allied not only in their names but also in their attributes. Aristophanes confounds them in his ' Plutus;'[3] and Posidonius and Demetrius Phalereus, treating of the Attic and Spanish mines, speak of Pluto as equivalent to Plutus.[4] Near this image probably stood the altar which the Athenians erected to Eirenë after the peace procured by Cimon;[5] or, according to Nepos,[6] after the naval victory of Timotheus over the Lacedæmonians.

Here also was a bronze statue of Lycurgus, the orator; of Callias, who according to the prevalent opinion at Athens, made the peace with Artaxerxes; and of Demosthenes, the work of Polyeuctus.[7] That of Demosthenes stood near the περισχοίνισμα and the altar of the Twelve Gods;[8] and as Pausanias (c. 8, 5) also says that it stood near the temple of Ares, all these must have been neighbouring objects. The statue of Demosthenes appears to have stood with the palms of the hands reversed, or upwards, and the fingers rather closed, as appears from the

[1] lib. xlv. 27.

[2] Plut. Phoc. 19.

[3] v. 727, ubi v. scholia.

[4] Apud Strab. iii. p. 147.

[5] Plut. Cim. 13.

[6] Timoth. c. 2.

[7] Vit. X. Orat. p. 367, Reiske.

[8] Ibid.

anecdote of the soldier who hid his money in them, which was further concealed by the dropping of the leaves of the plane tree which stood over it.[1] We see from this that the agora was not bare of trees; indeed to plant planes in it was considered a meritorious work, and was enumerated among the benefactions of Cimon.[2]

Pausanias has omitted to speak of the ALTAR of the TWELVE GODS. It was dedicated by Peisistratus, son of Hippias; but the Athenians by subsequently enlarging the altar, obliterated the original inscription.[3] Like the umbilicus on the Roman forum, it appears to have been the standard point for measuring distances. Herodotus records the distance of Pisa from it;[4] and in an inscription is recorded the distance to Peiræeus.[5]

The TEMPLE OF ARES must doubtless have been upon the hill which bore his name; and the foundations of a small temple may still be observed on the side of it, beneath the spot where the Areiopagites took their seats. As their place of meeting was on the summit of the Areiopagus, in an unenclosed place in the open air, it seems probable that the rope-railing or περισχοίνισμα, before-mentioned, was intended to prevent the profanation by unhallowed feet of so revered a spot. Bursian[6] thinks it was the spot marked off for the purpose of ostracism.[7] But surely an act so seldom resorted to would scarcely have had a spot constantly appropriated to it; and the word used by Plutarch is not περισχοίνισμα but δρύφακτα, a 'railing' or 'lattice.' On this subject, however, we need say nothing more at present, as we shall come again, with Pausanias, to the Areiopagus, a description of which closes another tour.

Besides the statue of Ares, the work of Alcamenes, there were in the temple two statues of Aphroditë, an Athena executed by Locrus, a Parian, and an Enyo, or Bellona, by the sons of Praxiteles. Round

---

[1] Plut. Demosth. 31.
[2] Idem, Cim. 13; cf. Aristoph. Frag. No. 162.
[3] Thucyd. vi. 54.
[4] lib. ii. 7.

[5] Boeckh, C. I. No. 525; Leake, i. p. 435.
[6] Geogr. v. Griechenl. t. i. p. 281.
[7] Referring to Plut. Arist. 7; Vit. X. Orat. p. 847; Poll. viii. 20; Etym. M. 349.

about the temple were statues of Heracles, Theseus, and Apollo, binding his hair with a fillet.[1] Besides these divinities there were also some statues of men; as Calades, or Calliades, an Athenian legislator, and Pindar; who, for having lauded the Athenians in one of his odes, received from them this and other rewards. Of the Calades or Calliades here mentioned, but little seems to be known. Meursius[2] thinks he was a caricaturist mentioned by Pliny (xxxv. 113);[3] but it is not likely that the Athenians should have erected a statue to an artist of that kind in so conspicuous a place. In fact we are not aware that any artist whatsoever obtained the honour of a statue. We take the view of Palmerius to be the best, who reads Καλλιάδης, and thinks that he was the archon eponymus in the year in which Xerxes invaded Attica (B.C. 480). This would agree with his being described as a legislator. According to the pseudo-Æschines in the Epistle before cited (p. 206), the statue of Pindar was a bronze one, draped, and represented the bard in a sitting posture, with a lyre in his hands and on his knees an open book. It is not improbable that this description may have been taken from some better-informed author.

Pausanias has now finished his account of the objects on the right hand side of the road leading to the Acropolis and Pnyx, as far up as the temple of Ares; and he therefore crosses over to the statues of Harmodius and Aristogeiton, which, he says, were not very far off (οὐ πόρρω). That he may have passed over some objects which stood higher up than these is sufficiently probable. We have seen that Arrian, in a passage before cited (p. 212), mentions an ALTAR OF THE EUDANEMI, from which the statues in question were not far distant; but this altar is not mentioned by Pausanias. The Eudanemi appear to have been a kind of heralds connected with the ceryces of the Eleusinian Mysteries, for

---

[1] Leake translates (p. 116): "having his head bound with a fillet"; which would imply another figure binding it; unless, indeed, he merely means that there was a fillet round his head. But ἀναδούμενος, we take it, is the *middle* participle (ἀναδούμενος ταινίᾳ τὴν κόμην), and means that he was binding his own hair—a picturesque attitude! He is said to have done so after slaying the Python.

[2] Ceram. Gem. c. 9. He would read: ὃς λέγεται κώμους γράψας: "qui dicitur commessationes pinxisse."

[3] Where, however, we read 'Calates.'

Arrian in the passage alluded to, adds that whoever has been initiated at Eleusis knows the altar of Eudanemus on the floor there.[1] Eudanemus was the son of Poseidon and a nymph; and according to Hesychius (in voc.) the name was an Attic form equivalent to Ἄγγελος, 'a messenger.' Angelus also was the name of a son of Poseidon among the Samians,[2] and doubtless the same whom the Athenians called Eudanemus. The Eudanemi would seem to have been his descendants, and like many other Athenian families, to have held an hereditary hierarchical office.

The STATUES OF HARMODIUS AND ARISTOGEITON bring us back to the line which Pausanias had quitted in order to describe the objects lying upon the road to the right, leading to the Acropolis and Pnyx. Whether these objects could be strictly said to be on the agora may admit of question; but at all events they were so near and so intimately connected with it, as 'to be properly comprised in the same tour. The statues of the tyrannicides appear to have been regarded with a particular veneration. From an inscription in the collection of Dr. Finlay,[3] it appears that no other statue was allowed to be placed by their side, and we must therefore conceive them to have stood comparatively isolated. There would appear however to have been two pairs of them; for Pausanias says that the modern ones were the work of Critias, and that the more ancient were made by Antenor. The latter, which were first erected after the expulsion of the Pisistratidæ (B.C. 510), had been carried off by Xerxes, but were restored by order of Alexander the Great, when at Susa; the order, however, appears not to have been executed till after his death, by Seleucus,[4] or, according to Pausanias here, by Antiochus, son of Seleucus. It appears from the Marmor Oxoniense that the second pair was erected in B.C. 478,[5] and that Nesiotes had been concerned in their execution. The rule, however,

[1] ὅστις δὲ μεμύηται ταῖν θεαῖν ἐν Ἐλευσῖνι, οἶδε τὸν Εὐδανέμου βωμὸν ἐπὶ τοῦ δαπέδου ὄντα.—Alex. Anab. iii. 16, 8.

[2] Pausan. vii. 4, 6.

[3] Given by Dr. Wordsworth in his 'Athens,' p. 91.

[4] App. l. c. and vii. 19, 2.

[5] Apud Leake, vol. i. p. 117. Cf. Lucian, Philopseud. 18.

about placing no other statues close to those of the tyrannicides, seems on some extraordinary occasions to have been violated. Thus gilded statues of Antigonus and Demetrius, in chariots, were erected near (πλησίον) them;[1] whilst bronze ones of Brutus and Cassius were placed actually by their side (παρά, the very word of the inscription) as having emulated the noble action of the Athenian patriots.[2] These, however, had no doubt been removed on the accession of Augustus, and those of Antigonus and Demetrius had probably disappeared long before, as Pausanias mentions none of them.

Pausanias now arrives (c. 8, 6) at the ancient and original ODEIUM, which, as we have shown in an appendix (No. 1), lay at this spot, and not, as is commonly supposed, outside the walls, on the banks of the Ilissus. Before it were statues of several of the Ptolemies, who had been good benefactors to the Athenians. Next to these stood Philip, and his son Alexander, and Lysimachus, Alexander's spear-bearer (c. 9, 4 sq.). On the motion of Demades, the Athenians had voted divine honours to Philip, who appears to have been adored as a god at Cynosarges.[3] According to Ælian,[4] Demades even proposed that Alexander should be made the thirteenth god; an idea which exceeded the bounds even of Athenian servility, and for which the orator was fined 100, or as Athenæus more probably says,[5] ten talents. The Athenians, however, appear to have voted that he should be called Dionysus; who was not one of the Twelve Gods, and whose name was sometimes lightly bestowed; as for instance on Antinoüs. But Alexander was not content with that title, and further required to be called Sarapis.[6] A statue of Pyrrhus appears also to have stood near the Odeium (c. 11, 1). Within the entrance was a fine statue of Dionysus, besides other things worth seeing (c. 14, 1).

The Odeium was constructed before the theatre was in existence, and was intended for the recitations of rhapsodists and the performances

[1] Diod. Sic. xx. 46.

[2] Dio Cass. xlvii. 20.

[3] Demades ὑπὲρ τῆς δωδεκαετίας, t. iv. p. 268, Reiske, compared with Apsines De

Arte Rhet. cap. περὶ προοιμίου.

[4] V. H. v. 12.

[5] lib. vi. 58.

[6] Diog. Laërt. vi. 63.

of citharœdists.[1] It was therefore probably made in the time of Hipparchus, son of Peisistratus, who, according to Plato, first introduced at Athens the poems of Homer, and caused the rhapsodists to recite them during the Panathenæa, relieving one another by turns; a practice which still continued to exist in Plato's time.[2] Both Hesychius and the scholiast on the 'Wasps' of Aristophanes (v. 1104), call the Odeium a τόπος, or 'place'; and the latter adds, "resembling a theatre" (θεατροειδής); whence we may infer that it was not constructed with the regularity and perfection of the Dionysiac theatre. Forchhammer observes[3] that Suidas confounds this Odeium with that of Pericles; and it may be added that Meursius[4] confounds all three; that is, the later one of Herodes Atticus also. Forchhammer also justly remarks that an elaborate building like the Odeium of Pericles, could not justly be called *a place*. The ancient one must have been of very considerable size, as, in the time of the Thirty, the hoplites, numbering about 3000, and the cavalry, were ordered to assemble in it; whilst on another occasion the cavalry slept in it, with their horses.[5] In these later times, and after the building of the Odeium of Pericles, it seems to have been converted, at least occasionally, into a storehouse for corn, and an office for the σιτοφύλακες and μετρονόμοι.[6]

Near this spot and the statues of Harmodius and Aristogeiton was an ORCHESTRA used on festivals for choric dances and more especially, we may suppose, before the theatre was built.[7] This increases the probability that the Odeium also was at this spot; for it was natural that these places for public spectacles and recreation should have been placed near one another, and in the very heart of the city. We may conjecture also that it was round this orchestra that the WOODEN THEATRE was erected, which by its fall occasioned the building of the stone one at the Acropolis. That this structure was in the agora, we

[1] Hesych. in voc.

[2] See the Hipparchus, p. 228 (i. 2, 238, Bekk.).

[3] Topographie, p. 41.

[4] Ceram. Gem. c. xi.

[5] Xenoph. Hell. ii. 4, s. 9 and 21.

[6] Demosth. c. Phorm. p. 918; c. Neær. 1362 sq.; Poll. viii. 33.

[7] 'Ορχήστρα· τόπος ἐπιφανὴς εἰς πανήγυριν, ἔνθα 'Αρμοδίου καὶ 'Αριστογείτονος εἰκόνες.—Tim. Lex. Plat. 'Ορχήστρα· πρῶτον ἐκλήθη ἐν τῇ ἀγορᾷ.—Phot. Lex.

know from Photius.[1] Near it was a black poplar tree, from which a distant view of the stage could be obtained over the heads of the spectators seated on the scaffolding. This poplar is also identified as having been in the agora by Hesychius, who says that it was customary for those remote spectators to suspend little tablets on it.[2] Hence " a view from the poplar " (αἰγείρου θέα or θέα παρ' αἰγείρῳ) became proverbial for a bad and cheap position;[3] a passage moreover from which we may conclude, that seats on the scaffolding had to be paid for at a price which kept out the vulgar. We might conclude from the nature of the case that the poplar was on rising ground, even if we had not the express testimony of Suidas to that effect,[4] and it must therefore have been on the rising ground, if not on the cliff, at the north-west extremity of the Acropolis. We see from the practice of Pausanias, that it was customary to speak of these neighbouring spots as in the agora, though not precisely upon it. If we have rightly fixed the locality of these objects, the poplar must also have been near the Odeium; and we think that, with a slight emendation, we may claim for this view also, the authority of the lexicographers. Hesychius says that the poplar was near *the* hierum, or temple (πλησίον τοῦ ἱεροῦ).[5] This absurd and meaningless way of speaking can of course arise only from a corruption of the text, as the commentators are unanimously agreed. So far as we know, the only emendation proposed is that of Meursius,[6] who would read πλησίον τοῦ ἱκρίου—*prope tabulatum*. But he should have given us an example of ἵκριον in the singular; which we do not think is to be found. We would read: πλησίον τοῦ 'Ωδείου, 'near the Odeium.' It matters not that Suidas has the same reading as Hesychius; for the article of that late and blundering lexicographer is a mere verbatim

---

[1] Ἴκρια · τὰ ἐν τῇ ἀγορᾷ, ἀφ' ὧν ἐθεῶντο τοὺς Διονυσιακοὺς ἀγῶνας πρὶν ἢ κατασκευασθῆναι τὸ ἐν Διονύσου θέατρον.

[2] ἐκ τῆς ἐν τῇ ἀγορᾷ αἰγείρου τὰ πινάκια ἐξῆπτον οἱ ἔσχατοι. Sub 'Απ' αἰγείρων.

[3] θέα παρ' αἰγείρῳ, τύπος αἴγειρον ἔχων, ὅθεν ἐθεώρουν · εὐτελὴς δὲ ἐδόκει ἡ ἐντεῦθεν θεωρία · μακρόθεν γὰρ ἦν, καὶ εὐώνου (?) ὁ τόπος ἐπωλεῖτο.—Hesych.

[4] αἴγειρος γὰρ ἐπ ά νω ἦν τοῦ θεάτρου. Sub 'Απ' αἰγείρου θέα.

[5] Sub Αἰγείρου θέα.

[6] Att. Lect. iv. 33.

transcript from Hesychius. Pausanias does not mention this orchestra, and we may probably conclude, therefore, that it had disappeared before he visited Athens.

Near the Odeium was the ENNEACRUNUS (c. 14, 1), or fountain fitted up with nine pipes by Peisistratus, as we have before observed. Pausanias here remarks that this was the only spring ($\pi\eta\gamma\dot{\eta}$) in the city, though there were many wells; but he afterwards mentions another spring near the same place and the grotto of Pan (c. 28, 4), and a fountain ($\kappa\rho\dot{\eta}\nu\eta$) at the temple of Asclepius, on the south side of the Acropolis. As he couples the Enneacrunus with the $\phi\rho\dot{\epsilon}\alpha\tau\alpha$, or wells, the water of which was used for drinking, it has been supposed that the water of the other two which he mentions was not potable; and that he therefore excludes them from his computation. And indeed at present the springs at the Acropolis are of a brackish nature, with the exception of one just at this spot supposed to be the ancient Clepsydra; which, however, may not improbably have been connected with the Enneacrunus. We will say more on this subject when we come to treat of the Clepsydra.

Above the Enneacrunus was a temple of DEMETER and CORË, and another of TRIPTOLEMUS, with a statue of him. From the word 'above' ($\dot{\upsilon}\pi\dot{\epsilon}\rho$), we may infer that Pausanias is now under the north-western extremity of the Acropolis, and that the temples in question stood on the shelving ground at the foot of the cliffs, and therefore rather higher than the fountain, which lay more northwards. He begins to relate the legend of Triptolemus, but is deterred from finishing it by religious scruples occasioned by a dream, and refrains from saying more about the temple, which, though at Athens, was called, he says, the Eleusinium.

From the narrative of Pausanias, therefore, it appears that this temple of Triptolemus, called the ELEUSINIUM, lay *above* the Enneacrunus and *under* the Acropolis; and this last site for it is confirmed by Clemens and Arnobius.[1] Can anything be plainer? On the other

---

[1] Ἰμμάραδος δὲ ὁ Εὐμόλπου καὶ Δαείρας ὑπὸ τῇ ἀκροπόλει κεκήδευνται.—Clem. οὐχὶ ἐν τῷ περιβόλῳ τοῦ Ἐλευσινίου, τοῦ Protrept. p. 13. "Daciras et Immaradus

hand, how can those who hold that the Enneacrunus was at the Ilissus, and the Eleusinium near it, explain away these passages of three irreproachable authorities, which affirm that the Eleusinium was close under the Acropolis? Forchhammer, in part, prudently avoids the problem, by ignoring Clemens and Arnobius; whilst with regard to Pausanias, he simply denies that it appears from his words that any of the temples was identical with the Eleusinium.[1] But this fact is too plain to admit of dispute. Having mentioned the temple and image of Triptolemus at the end of the first section of this chapter (c. 14), Pausanias proceeds in the second section to give an account of him, but stops before he comes to the end of it; observing that he was hindered by a vision from saying more about this temple, which was called the Eleusinium. And he then commences the third section by saying : " Before this temple, which has the statue of Triptolemus," &c.,[2] thus clearly showing that he has been all along speaking of one and the same temple, and leaving no pretext for disputing that the Eleusinium, and the temple of Triptolemus, were identical. Leake, in his first edition, rightly perceived this, and consequently consistently, though wrongly, fixed the Eleusinium, together with the temple of Demeter, &c., at the Ilissus, in conformity with the theory which places the Enneacrunus there. Staggered, however, apparently, by the passages of Clemens and Arnobius, which so evidently fix the Eleusinium under the Acropolis, and disregarding the authority of Pausanias as to its identity with the temple of Triptolemus, he in his second edition[3] placed it, as a separate and substantive hierum, in the cavern in the east side of the Acropolis! A most unfortunate choice! For even admitting the possibility that it

---

fratres (conditi scribuntur) in Eleusinii concepto, quod civitati subjectum est."— Arnob. adv. Gentes, vi. p. 193, Maire. Also in an inscription discovered not very long ago : ἐν Ἐλευσεινίῳ τῷ ὑπὸ τῇ πόλει.— Philistor, ii. p. 239. In such cases ὑπὸ τῇ πόλει means *directly under*, or on the side of the hill.

[1] Topographie, p. 48.

[2] πρόσω δὲ ἰέναι με ὡρμημένον τοῦδε τοῦ λόγου, καὶ ὁπόσα ἐξήγησιν ἔχει τὸ Ἀθήνησιν ἱερόν, καλούμενον δὲ Ἐλευσίνιον, ἐπέσχεν ὄψις ὀνείρατος . . . . . s. 3. πρὸ τοῦ ναοῦ τοῦδε ἔνθα καὶ τοῦ Τριπτολέμου τὸ ἄγαλμα, κ.τ.λ.—cap. 14.

[3] vol. ii. p. 296.

can be thus separated from the temples of Triptolemus and of Demeter and Corë, it is highly improbable that a temple so important and so venerated, with statues in and before it, should have been thrust into this dark and gloomy hole ; and, secondly, that it was not, appears indisputably from the circumstance that in the Panathenaïc procession, the ship with the peplus went round it ; a feat which could not have been performed had this cavern been the temple. Yet in spite of these plain and palpable difficulties, Curtius, in his most recent topographical work,[1] also places the Eleusinium under the eastern side of the Acropolis, though not indeed, like Leake, *in* the grotto. Such are the errors and inconsistencies into which they who place the Enneacrunus with its adjoining objects at the Ilissus, must necessarily fall.

Before the Eleusinium was the image of a brazen ox being led to sacrifice. Here also was a seated statue of Epimenides of Gnossus, who is said to have slept forty years.

The Eleusinium appears to have been accounted one of the holiest places in Athens, and to have been ranked in this respect with the Acropolis and the Theseium. Plutarch[2] mentions these three places together as worthy of the highest reverence ; and it was the same three from which, on account of their superior sanctity, the country people were excluded when they flocked into Athens at the commencement of the Peloponnesian war.[3] It was forbidden, under the penalty of 1000 drachms, to carry the suppliant olive-branch (ἱκετηρία) into the Eleusinium and place it on the altar ; that it was death without trial appears to be a false assertion. The day after the Eleusinian mysteries had been celebrated at Eleusis the senate met in the Eleusinium for the trial of any crimes committed during their celebration, and the forbidding of a suppliant bough to be brought thither seems to imply that their judgment was inexorable.[4] It may, perhaps, be some confirmation of the site of the Eleusinium, that the little metropolitan church

---

[1] See his plan of the agora at p. 55 of the Erläuternder Text to his seven maps of Athens.

[2] De Exil. viii. p. 394, Reiske.

[3] Thucyd. ii. 17.

[4] See Andoc. De Myst. t. iv. p. 55 sqq. Reiske.

situated towards the extremity of the agora, contains some Eleusinian bas-reliefs.[1]

Simon, a great master of the equestrian art, had set up before the Eleusinium a bronze horse, or, according to Pliny, an equestrian statue of himself, on the base of which were inscribed the titles of his works.[2] On festival days Xenophon would have the cavalry proceed round the agora, beginning at the Hermæ and making the circuit of the various shrines, in honour of the gods. When they had completed the circuit and got back to the Hermæ, then he would have them start again in squadrons of tribes, and gallop as far as the Eleusinium.[3] This would seem to show that it must have stood in an open space and at the extremity of the agora, as we have placed it. The only object which Pausanias sets beyond it is the little temple of EUCLEIA, built from the Persian spoils, to which we have adverted elsewhere. Here, then, was the termination of the agora, even if the last two or three objects could properly be called on it; and a line drawn about due north from this spot will cut the gateway dedicated to Athena Archegetis, which formed the entrance to the new Roman market-place, lying to the east of the ancient one.

Here Pausanias terminates his first walk within the city, and his description of the objects on the southern side of the agora.

[1] Rangabé in Mem. dell' Inst. 1865, p. 360.

[2] Xenoph. De re eq. i. 1; xi. 6; Plin.

H. N. xxxiv. 76.

[3] De Off. Mag. Eq. iii. 2.

Q

CHAPTER VIII.

The Hephæsteium — Colonus Agoræus—Aphrodite Urania—Amazoneium — Pseudo-Theseium — Pœcile Stoa—Hermæ— Hermes Agoræus — Pœcile described — The Stoics—Altar of Mercy—Old and new Agora—Aphrodite Pandemus—Propylæum of Athena Archegetis—Leocoreium—Temenos of Æacus—Statues—Agrippeium—Stoa of Attalus—Rostra—Boundaries of Roman agora—Appearance of the ancient agora — Oil market—Hadrian's façade—Its destination—Tower of the Winds—Ptolemæum—Theseium—Diogeneium—Anaceium—Temple of Aglaurus—Prytaneium—Field of hunger.

To commence his second tour, Pausanias returns to the Stoa Basileios, and proceeds from that point to describe the objects on the west and north sides of the market-place. Some of these, like the temple of Ares, &c., on the south side, were not exactly in the agora, but they were so immediately adjacent to it as to appear to form part of it, and thus naturally belong to its description. Such was the case with the objects on the rising ground which flanks the western side of the agora, and on which stands the so-called temple of Theseus. The first object which Pausanias mentions here is the HEPHÆSTEIUM, or temple of Hephæstus, which, he says, lay *above* the agora and the Stoa Basileios.[1] And that it was really on a height appears also from a passage in the speech of Andocides concerning the Mysteries, where he says that Diocleides, seeing Euphemus sitting in the Chalceium, and leading him *up* (ἀναγαγών) to the Hephæsteium, began to tell his story.[2] We should always recollect, moreover, that in ancient times this height must have been much more marked than it is at present. The valley of the agora,

[1] ὑπὲρ δὲ τὸν Κεραμεικὸν καὶ στοὰν τὴν καλουμένην βασίλειον.—i. 14, 5. We have pointed out in Appendix No. 1, Pausanias' usual construction of ὑπέρ with an acc. to signify *above*.

[2] ἰδὼν δὲ Εὔφημον ἐν τῷ Χαλκείῳ καθήμενον, ἀναγαγὼν αὐτὸν εἰς τὸ Ἡφαιστεῖον, λέγειν, κ.τ.λ.—t. iv. p. 20, Reiske.

and perhaps also the other valleys in the heart of the city, has been filled up by débris to a height of some twenty feet, whilst the eminences have not undergone any corresponding elevation.

Before describing the objects on it, we will say a few words about this civic Colonus, for so this height was called. It was originally the place of resort for labourers seeking to be hired, and hence obtained the name of ὁ μίσθιος.[1] Subsequently, however, the place of hire appears to have been changed to the Anaceium, or temple of the Dioscuri,[2] which, as we shall see further on, lay under the Acropolis, beyond the eastern boundary of the agora. We have the authority of Solon for the tradition that Eurysaces, one of the sons of Ajax, dwelt in this neighbourhood after he and his brother Philæus had made over to Athens the island of Salamis, and become Athenian citizens; whilst Philæus took up his abode at Brauron in Attica, and became the eponymous hero of the demus of the Philaïdæ, to which Peisistratus belonged.[3] From Eurysaces, on the other hand, Alcibiades was descended;[4] and, as we have already observed, his ancestors probably erected the heroum called EURYSACEIUM. It lay on Colonus Agoræus, near the Hephæsteium, but is not mentioned by Pausanias.[5] The CHALCEIUM mentioned in the passage from Andocides is by some thought to have been a market for ironmongery lying under the Colonus Agoræus, and the vicinity of the temple of Hephæstus gives some colour to this opinion; but possibly it may mean only a blacksmith's shop.

By the statue of Hephæstus stood one of Athena, at which Pausanias was not surprised, being acquainted with the myth about Erichthonius; and as Athena was represented with grey eyes—another proof, by the way, that statues were painted—he concluded that the myth was of Libyan origin. For, according to the Libyans, she was the offspring of Poseidon and the Lake Tritonis, and had grey eyes like her

<hr />

[1] Above, p. 99.

[2] Ἀνακεῖον, Διοσκούρων ἱερόν, οὗ νῦν οἱ μισθοφοροῦντες δοῦλοι ἑστᾶσιν. — Bekk. Anecd. p. 212, 12.

[3] Plut. Solon, 10.

[4] Id. Alc. 1.

[5] Harpocr. voc. Κολωναίτας; but under Εὐρυσάκειον he says that it was in Melitë. That district and Colonus Agoræus were, however, conterminous. Poll. Onom. vii. s. 133.

father, whence her usual epithet of γλαυκῶπις. The legend is given by Herodotus (iv. 180). But Plato considers both Athena and Hephæstus to have been the offspring of the same father, and thus as having a congenial nature;[1] a view certainly more adapted to their association in the Athenian temples, for we shall find them again associated at the Erechtheium. There, however, Athena was the principal deity, and Hephæstus subordinate to her; an order which was reversed at the Hephæsteium. The statue of Hephæstus here was probably that praised by Cicero,[2] the work of Alcamenes, in which lameness was gracefully expressed. The Hephæsteium appears to have been used like a sort of police-office for the examination of suspected persons.[3]

Near it, and therefore apparently also in the Colonus Agorœus, was a temple of APHRODITË URANIA, or the heavenly Venus, who was first worshipped (according to Pausanias, c. 14, 6) by the Assyrians, then by the Paphians of Cyprus, and by the Phœnicians who dwelt at Ascalon in Palestine. It was Ægeus who first introduced the worship at Athens, being at that time childless himself, and his sisters in the same condition, through the anger, he thought, of Urania. The Athmoneans, however, an Attic demus, asserted that a temple of Aphroditë Urania was built in their borough by Porphyrion, who reigned before Actæus; but, observes Pausanias, the people of the demi have many other stories which differ from those of the citizens of Athens. The statue of the goddess was the work of Pheidias. Aphroditë Urania was the eldest of the Fates,[4] and appears also to have been called Nemesis;[5] but at Athens she seems also to have assumed a sensual character. She had another sanctuary near the Ilissus, which we shall have to speak of further on.

There still exists in good preservation in this quarter a temple which Pausanias apparently does not notice, the so-called temple of Theseus. That it could not possibly have been the Theseium we shall see further

---

[1] Critias, p. 109 (iii. ii. p. 150, Bekk.).

[2] De Nat. Deor. i. 30, 83; cf. Val. Max. viii. 2, 3.

[3] Isocr. Trapez. p. 361 (520, Oxon. 1822):

Andoc. de Myst. p. 20, Reiske.

[4] Pausan. i. 19, 2; C. I. No. 1444.

[5] Inscr. on a throne. See Philol. xix. p. 361; Mommsen, Heortol. p. 18.

on. We may also say, with tolerable confidence, that it could not have been the Hephaesteium with which Pervanoglu identifies it,[1] since the site of it does not well agree with the account of Pausanias, from which that building would appear to have stood pretty close to the Stoa Basileius, whilst the so-called Theseium is some distance to the north of it. Nor does the architectural character of this last edifice appear to be well adapted to a temple of Aphroditë Urania, the only one, besides that of Hephaestus, which Pausanias notices as lying at this spot. There was, indeed, another monument in this quarter, which Pausanias also omits to notice—the Amazoncium. That its site was hereabouts appears plainly from Plutarch's description of the attack on Athens by the Amazons, whose left wing is said to have extended to the Amazoncium (on the north), whilst their right wing reached to the Pnyx on the south, about an equal distance from their centre.[2] We have the testimony of Harpocration that the Amazoncium was a temple; and from the same passage we learn that it was reputed to have been built by the Amazons;[3] but it was no doubt erected to their memory by the Athenians. We learn from Ammonius, quoted by Harpocration, that they had been hallowed at Athens;[4] and from the same chapter of Plutarch, that sacrifice was offered to them previously to the festival of the Theseia. The importance attributed to the Amazons by the Athenians appears from several circumstances. In the time of Plutarch[5] there still existed near the Theseium a place called Horcomosium, where the treaty between them and Theseus was reputed to have been made. Besides the Amazoncium, we must remember that there was a separate monument to Antiopë at the place where she fell, near the Itonian Gate. And when we consider that Theseus, the great hero of the Athenians, had married one of the band, we need not be surprised if so handsome a temple, or rather, perhaps, heroum, should have been erected to them as that which still exists. Nor would the sculptures which ornamented it have been inappropriate as illustrating the military achievements of

---

[1] In the Philologus, t. xxvii. p. 660 sqq.

[2] Thes. c. 27.

[3] Ἀμαζόνιον—ἔστι δὲ ἱερὸν ὁ Ἀμαζόνες

ἱδρύσαντ.—οἳ ι voc.

[4] περὶ βωμῶν καὶ θυσιῶν.—Harp. loc. cit.

[5] loc. cit.

Theseus, of which the war with the Amazons was not the meanest, and might well have been regarded by the Athenians with more interest than the rest, as forming part of their domestic history. But it will be proper here to give some account of the temple in question in its present state, in order that the reader may be better able to judge for himself of its probable destination.

VIEW OF THE SO-CALLED THESEIUM.

The so-called THESEIUM is the first ancient monument that meets the view on approaching Athens from Peiræeus, and it is in so perfect a state of preservation that, at a little distance, it might almost be taken for a modern structure. Indeed, it now serves as a sort of museum in which are kept many valuable relics of ancient sculpture, and in particular the famous bas-relief of a Marathonian hero, as large as life, carefully preserved under a glass, and still bearing very visible traces of colour. The temple is of the Doric order, and is of the kind called hexastylos peripteros; that is, having six columns at each front, and thirteen at each side, counting over again the end columns of the fronts. The dimensions of the temple at the top of the stylobate are rather more

than 104 ft. in length, and 45 ft. in breadth. The dimensions of the cella are about 61 ft. 6 in. in length, with a pronaos at the eastern end of about 12 ft. 6 in.; and the breadth within the walls is between 20 ft. and 21 ft. It is wholly built of Pentelic marble, and was formerly used as a church dedicated to St. George.

The name of Theseium appears to have been first given to this building by the Jesuit Babin in a treatise on Athens composed in 1572, an edition of which, with notes, was published by Spon in 1674, a little before his journey to Athens. It is a mistake to suppose that the name rested on an ancient tradition, for it is mentioned by no topographer previous to Babin; and Cyriacus of Ancona, who visited Greece in 1437, and collected some inscriptions there, calls it the temple of Mars.[1] But the name given to it by Babin was adopted by Spon and Wheler, and prevailed to the present times unquestioned, till in 1838 Ludwig Ross disputed its correctness in a Greek pamphlet published at Athens, and since republished in German, in 1852. His view, so far as the negative portion of it is concerned, has been adopted by several of the leading German topographers; and there can be little doubt of its correctness. Two ancient authorities alone suffice to show that the Theseium could not have stood on the Colonos Agoraeus. Plutarch says that it was "in the middle of the city,"[2] and the temple in question is quite at its outskirts, not far from the Dipylon. Still stronger evidence may be drawn from the methodical tour of Pausanias, who does not mention the Theseium here, but further on, when speaking of the opposite, or eastern, side of the agora.

It is more difficult to determine the affirmative side of the question, and say to what divinity this temple was really dedicate. Ross contends at some length, that no certain inference can be drawn from the sculptures on the frieze and metopes of a temple, as to the god adored in it. A safer conclusion may be drawn from sculptures on the pediments; but those which once existed on the eastern front have now disappeared, and it seems doubtful whether the western front ever had any at all. It is natural, however, to think that the subjects even

---

[1] Ross, Thes. ium, p. 2 sq.   [2] καὶ κεῖται μὲν ἐν μέσῃ τῇ πόλει.—Thes. cap. ult.

of the friezes and metopes would at all events have some relation to
the deity who owned the temple. The frieze of the pronaos appears to
represent the battle of the Gods and Giants; that of the posticus, the
combat of the Centaurs and Lapithæ. The metopes of the eastern front
have evidently for their subjects the labours of Heracles; those of the
northern and southern sides, of which there are only four on each side
at the eastern end, show the exploits of Theseus. It is from these
sculptures that the temple has been commonly assigned to Theseus, but,
as we have seen, wrongly. They might afford a general presumption
that the temple belonged to some warlike deity or hero, and Ross
has assigned it to Ares. But the temple of that god lay, as we have
seen, on the Areiopagus. The sculptures have no appropriate reference
to Hephæstus; and this is another reason, besides the site, for rejecting
the hypothesis of Pervanoglu. They are, perhaps, more adapted on the
whole to Heracles than Theseus, and Curtius is inclined to consider
it an HERACLEIUM; founding his view on a scholium to the 'Frogs' of
Aristophanes, in which it is said that Heracles had a very conspicuous
temple in Melitë.[1] According to the same scholiast it was built in
commemoration of the great plague; and the statue of the hero was the
work of Ageladas, the master of Pheidias. These particulars accord well
enough with the building in question. But it is a fatal objection
to this view, that the temple is not in Melitë, but in Colonus Agoræus.
For, as we have shown above (p. 97), the latter was a city deme, and
if it lay not here, we know not where to place it. At all events,
we have here another omission of Pausanias, who does not mention
this building, whatever it may have been. The conjunction of Heracles
with Theseus in the sculptures, would not have been unsuitable to
an Amazoneium, since he aided the Attic hero in his war with the
Amazons, and the position of the building answers well enough to the
allusion in Plutarch's description of the Amazonian line of battle (see
above, p. 63). Hence it appears to us not at all improbable that
it may have been the Amazoneium; but there are not sufficient grounds
for giving any decided opinion on the subject. The building in ques-

---

[1] ἐν Μελίτῃ ἐστὶν ἐπιφανέστατον ἱερὸν Ἡρακλέους ἀλεξικάκου.—ad v. 504.

history of Athens, both in its mythical and later periods. In the description of the monuments Pausanias has been followed; his omissions being supplied, so far as was possible, by accounts taken from other authors. And as mere archæology is but a barren, and, for most persons, unattractive study, the author has endeavoured to impart some life and interest to the subject by connecting it, where practicable, with the literature and manners of the Athenians.

As Colonel Leake's 'Topography of Athens' is still in many respects one of the best works on the subject, the author had at first contemplated preparing a new edition of it, with additions, so as to bring it up to the present time. But the form of Leake's book is little favourable to such a process, as consisting rather of a series of detached essays than forming a homogeneous whole; so that to have supplemented it with further notes and dissertations would have seriously aggravated this defect in its method. And as the author has sometimes found himself compelled to differ from Leake's views, the discussion of such points would have still further tended to swell the notes and appendices. He will here, however, heartily acknowledge the aid which he has derived from the Colonel's book, as well as from the slighter, but scholarly, sketch of the subject in Dr. Wordsworth's 'Athens and Attica.' He must also confess his obligations to many foreign writers; as Forchhammer, Müller, Ross, Curtius, Rangabé, Breton, Le Normant, Beulé, and others, whose names he may be excused from inserting here, as he has been careful to cite them in his notes whenever they may have afforded any information. The Germans, as usual, have gone more deeply into the subject than any other people; but the author ventures to think that the profundity of their studies, to which he is much indebted, and perhaps the desire of saying something original, has occasionally led them into paradox. Those who are always for burrowing miss sometimes what lies near the surface.

The works of Meursius are, of course, the great storehouse for all

PREFACE.

THE following work was projected and begun during a visit to Athens in the year 1869. The important discoveries lately made at that place, and especially the excavation of the Dionysiac theatre in 1862, suggested the idea that there might be room for a new book on Athenian topography and antiquities. The theatre, with its glorious recollections of the dramatic poets, will always be one of the most interesting features of ancient Athens; yet, as revealed by the excavation, it remains, so far as the author is aware, undescribed in any substantive work on Athens, whether English or foreign, though scattered notices on the subject occur in German and other periodicals. No description of the theatre will be found in the second edition of Breton's 'Athènes,' dated in 1868. This part of the work, therefore, will probably be new to many readers. The comparatively very perfect state of some of the most important portions of the theatre, as the orchestra and first row of seats, serves to throw much light on its arrangements, and has led the author to inquire, in an Appendix, into the correctness of some of the prevailing hypotheses respecting the method of the dramatic performances.

The present work is intended neither for the accomplished antiquary nor the professional architect, but for the reader who may wish to gain a general knowledge of the origin and progress of the city, and a satisfactory idea of its buildings, monuments, and works of art. These could hardly be understood without some acquaintance with the

ANCIENT ATHENS:

ITS HISTORY, TOPOGRAPHY, AND REMAINS.

BY

THOMAS HENRY DYER, LL.D.

" I pray you let us satisfy our eyes
With the memorials and the things of fame
That do renown this city."—TWELFTH NIGHT, iii. 3.

LONDON:
BELL AND DALDY, YORK STREET, COVENT GARDEN.
1873.

Thomas Henry Dyer

Ancient Athens

LIST OF ILLUSTRATIONS.

CHAPTER XI.

CHAPTER XII.

CHAPTER XIII.

APPENDIX.

CHAPTER VIII.

CHAPTER IX.

CHAPTER X.

CHAPTER IV.

CHAPTER V.

CHAPTER VI.

CHAPTER VII.

TABLE OF CONTENTS.

the learning of the subject, and these the author has diligently consulted. It would, perhaps, be difficult to add, from the ancient writers, many more passages bearing on the matter to those which that learned Dutchman has collected. His works, however, are to be used with caution, for he had no local knowledge of Athens; and the progress of criticism has thrown a different light on some of the passages which he cites.

The author cannot conclude this preface without acknowledging his obligations to the friendship of Mr. George Long, who was kind enough to read the sheets as they were passing through the press. That gentleman's accurate and extensive scholarship has been of the greatest service to him; and it is hoped that no larger share of errors will be found in the work than is perhaps unavoidable, considering the long period and the vast variety of minute particulars which it embraces.

BRIGHTON, *February*, 1873.

tion appears to have been converted by the Byzantines into a church
dedicated to St. George.[1]

After describing the Hephæsteium and the temple of Aphroditē
Urania, Pausanias proceeds to the STOA called PŒCILĒ. The two
former buildings were, as we have said, probably on the skirts of
the agora; but the Pœcilē, as we know from several authorities, was
actually on it. Thus, Æschines alludes to it as forming one of the
glories of the agora.[2] The same inference may be drawn from Pausanias saying that close to the Stoa there was a bronze statue of
Hermes Agoræus; and from comparing this with Lucian, from whom
we learn that the Hermes Agoræus was by the Pœcilē;[3] and with the
scholiast on this passage, who says that the Hermes was styled
Agoræus because it was erected in the agora.[4] A further proof, if any
were needed, might be drawn from what we hear about the house
of Meton, the astronomer, which was near the Pœcilē, and to which he
set fire when he was feigning madness, in order to prevent either himself or his son being drafted on the Sicilian expedition.[5] Now we
know from Aristophanes and his scholiast that Meton's house was on
Colonus:

$$\text{ὅστις εἴμ' ἐγώ; Μέτων,}$$
$$\text{ὃν οἶδεν Ἑλλὰς χὠ Κολωνός.}^6$$

" Who I am ? why, Meton ;
Known at Colonus, and throughout all Greece."

And this will serve to fix the Pœcilē still more precisely at the north-
west corner of the agora. For the gate and the Hermes indicate a roadway into it, and there could have been none over the high ground
of Colonus. This, no doubt, formed the entrance into the agora from
the Dipylon.

We must here note a very remarkable feature of this part of the

---

[1] Mommsen, Athen. Christ. cap. xiii.
No. 116.

[2] προέλθετε οὖν τῇ διανοίᾳ καὶ εἰς τὴν
στοὰν τὴν ποικίλην· ἁπάντων γὰρ ὑμῖν τῶν
καλῶν ἔργων τὰ ὑπομνήματα ἐν τῇ ἀγορᾷ
ἀνάκειται.—c. Ctesiph. p. 575, Reiske.

[3] Ἑρμῆς ὁ Ἀγοραῖος ὁ παρὰ τὴν Ποικίλην.
—Jup. Trag. 33.

[4] ὡς ἐν τῇ ἀγορᾷ ἱδρυμένος.—Ibid.

[5] Ælian, V. H. xiii. 12.

[6] Aves, 997, et ibi schol.

agora which Pausanias altogether omits; namely, a line of HERMÆ, which stood between the Stoa Basileius and the Pœcile.[1] They would thus have formed a boundary to the agora, under the Colonus Agoræus. It was here that the phylarchi, or commanders of the horse, taught youths the rudiments of horsemanship, such as mounting and dismounting, as appears from the following fragment of the 'Hippotrophos' of Mnesimachus:

σteῖχ' eἰs ἀγορὰν
πρὸs τοὺs 'Ερμᾶs,
οὗ προσφοιτῶσ' οἱ φύλαρχοι,
τούs τε μαθητὰs τοὺs ὡραίουs,
οὓs ἀναβαίνειν ἐπὶ τοὺs ἵππουs
μελετᾷ Φείδων καὶ καταβαίνειν.[2]

"Go to the Hermæ
In the agora, where the Phylarchs
Also gather, and where Pheidon
Teaches his pupils when they're old enough,
To get on their horses, and get off again."

This also was the spot whence the cavalry started, on festivals, to make the tour of the agora,[3] and was therefore the best place for viewing the spectacle. Hence Demetrius, being commander of the horse in the Panathenæa, erected a scaffold above the heads of the Hermæ, from which his Corinthian mistress Aristagora might get a good view of the pageant.[4] It is here that the horsemen represented on the western side of the frieze of the Parthenon, may be supposed to be mounting their horses. It was an article of impeachment against Socrates, that he lounged about these Hermæ and the tables of the money-changers.[5] A barber's shop in the neighbourhood appears, as we have before observed, to have been the rendezvous of the Deceleians.[6] Some of the

[1] Μενεκλῆs, ἢ Καλλίστρατοs, ἐν τῷ περὶ Ἀθηναίων γράφει ταυτί· ἀπὸ γὰρ τῆs Ποικίληs καὶ τῆs τοῦ βασιλέωs στοᾶs εἰσιν οἱ Ἑρμαῖ καλούμενοι· διὰ γὰρ τὸ πολλοὺs κεῖσθαι καὶ ἱπὸ ἰδιωτῶν καὶ ἀρχόντων ταύτην τὴν προσηγορίαν εἰληφέναι συμβέβηκεν.—Harpocr. voc. Ἑρμαῖ.

[2] See Meineke, Fragm. p. 788; Athen. ix. c. 67.
[3] Xenoph. De Off. Mag. Eq. iii. 2.
[4] Athen. iv. 64 (ed. Schweigh.).
[5] Porphyrius, ap. Theodoret. Therap. xii.
[6] Lysias in Pancl. 731, Reiske: ἐπὶ τὸ κουρεῖον τὸ παρὰ τοὺs Ἑρμᾶs.

Hermæ in the agora appear to have been very ancient. On one of them was an inscription in antique characters relating to the treatment which Agamemnon had experienced at the hands of the Achivi.[1] To be allowed to erect a Hermes appears to have been considered a mark of honour, and those in the agora had been set up by private persons as well as by magistrates.[2]

Statues of Hermes were the most common, as well as the most ancient, form of sculpture; hence *Hermoglyph* (ἑρμογλύφος), or Hermes-carver, continued till a late period to be the name for a sculptor.[3] The Athenians were the first who made them square and without limbs (Ἑρμαῖ τετράγωνοι), which form was selected as the firmest.[4] Nevertheless sex was indicated, as we see still on the numerous portrait busts that have been preserved of gymnasiarchs, of which there are many in the Barbakeion at Athens, executed much in the same fashion as the Hermæ. Only these last were represented like Priapus; a circumstance which is said to have occasioned their mutilation by Alcibiades. Hence in the 'Lysistrata' of Aristophanes, represented soon after the Sicilian expedition, the chorus advise the Athenian in eager search for his wife to resume his clothes, lest the Hermocopidæ should see him.[5]

Before arriving at the Pœcilë, Pausanias comes to a GATE OF THE AGORA, which probably stood at its north-western angle, and formed the entrance to the market-place from the Dipylon. Hence we may perhaps conclude that the north side of the agora was also enclosed in some way. Forchhammer, indeed, translating very literally the scholiast on Aristophanes, thinks that the statue of Hermes Agoræus, and consequently the gate, stood in the middle of the market-place, forming a sort of triumphal arch, the model of those built afterwards by the Romans.[6] The gate had indeed a trophy on it commemorating the victory of the Athenians over Pleistarchus in a cavalry engagement.

[1] Harpocr. in Ἑρμαῖ.

[2] See the passage in Æsch. c. Ctesiph. quoted above, p. 233; and cf. Harp. l. c.

[3] Some, however, derive it from ἕρμα, a large stone. See Winkelmann, Storia delle Arti, t. i. p. 8, Ital. trans.

[4] Pausan. i. 24, 3; iv. 33, 4; viii. 32, 1; Galen, Protrep. c. 3.

[5] ver. 1093.

[6] ἐν μέσῃ γὰρ τῇ ἀγορᾷ ἵδρυται Ἑρμοῦ Ἀγοραίου ἄγαλμα.—Schol. ad Eq. 297: Forchhammer, Topogr. p. 56.

On the other hand, Demosthenes and Isaeus call it a πυλίς, or small gate, and Philochorus (ap. Harpocr.) a πύλων, or gatehouse;[1] neither of which terms answers very well to the idea of a triumphal arch; which, indeed, seems to have been a Roman invention.

The HERMES AGORÆUS must have been of quite a different character from the Hermæ which lined the side of the agora. These cubic ones seem to have been made of stone; but the Hermes Agoræus was a bronze statue, and apparently of great beauty, as artists often took casts of it.[2] It was an ancient statue, having been erected by the archons in pursuance of the commands of the senate and people, when the fortifications at Peiræeus were begun, as recorded in an elegiac distich inscribed on its base.[3] An altar stood before it, erected by Callistratus when master of the horse;[4] a fact which shows that it was regarded as an ἄγαλμα, or divine image.

The PŒCILÈ STOA was originally called Peisianacteios (πεισιανά-κτειος),[5] and obtained the name of ποικίλη, 'variegated,' after it had been adorned with paintings. It probably faced the south, and the Stoæ Basileius and Eleutherius on the opposite side of the agora.

May not the remains of a portico still traceable a little southward of the church of St. Philip, and about midway between the so-called Theseium and the Stoa of Attalus, have belonged to the Pœcilè? These remains consist only of two gigantic figures with legs terminating in snakes, and which appear to have performed the office of pillars in supporting a portico.[6] These figures project a considerable way into the area of the agora, but not more than about 120 feet from a line extended from the northern wall of the Stoa of Attalus, which would not give too great a depth for a large stoa like the Pœcilè, including the

<hr />

[1] περιτυχὼν αὐτῷ περὶ τὸν Ἑρμῆν τὸν πρὸς τῇ πυλίδι.—Demosth. c. Euerg. p. 1146, Reiske; τῆς συνοικίας τῆς παρὰ τὴν πυλίδα. —Isaeus, de Philoct. Herod. p. 134, Reiske; οἱ ἄρχοντες ἀνέθεσαν Ἑρμῆν παρὰ τὸν πυ-λῶνα τὸν Ἀττικόν.—Harpocr. voc. Ἑρμῆς πρὸς τῇ πυλίδι. Where we see that Har-pocration himself calls it πυλίς. Leake would read ἀστικὸν for ἀττικόν, p. 121.

[2] Lucian, Zeus Trag. 33, and schol.

[3] Harpocr. loc. cit.

[4] Vit. X. Orat. t. ix. p. 357 (Reiske).

[5] Plut. Cim. 4; cf. Diog. Laërt. vii. 5 (ed. Meibom, Amst. 1692), with Ménage's note. It probably took its name from Peisianax, Cimon's brother-in-law. Bur-sian, Geogr. p. 286.

[6] See Curtius, Att. Stud. ii. p. 49.

portico, or colonnade, in front of it. And if these figures formed the easternmost end of a portico stretching towards the west for about 400 feet, it would, with the addition of the gate of the agora, have pretty well occupied its northern side. The snake-like termination of the figures, so evidently referring to the myth of Erichthonius, seems at all events to bespeak for the building an ancient and genuine Attic origin.

The first picture in the Pœcilë represented the Athenians at Œnoë, drawn up in order of battle, and preparing to engage the Lacedæmonians. Pausanias then proceeds to speak of the *middle* wall; whence we may conclude with Siebelis (ad loc.) that the portico was closed on three sides, and that the middle wall, or that facing the entrance, was double the length of the side walls, as it appears to have contained two pictures, and the others only one. The first of the pictures on the centre wall represented Theseus and the Athenians combating the Amazons. The subject of the second picture was the Greeks and their kings debating about the outrage of Ajax on Cassandra after the capture of Troy. Here Ajax himself was represented, as well as Cassandra and other captive women.

The last of the paintings[1] had for its subject the battle of Marathon. In the foreground, the Athenians and Platæans—the only Greeks who aided them against the Persians—were seen engaged with the Persians in equal combat, the Platæans aided by Bœotian dogs.[2] Beyond these, in the middle ground, the barbarians were flying, and pushing one another into the marsh. This lake or marsh was that formed by the Charadras, under the hills of the isthmus of Rhamnus.[3] In the extreme distance were the Phœnician ships, and the Greeks slaying the barbarians who were attempting to get on board. In the picture were also represented the divinities and heroes who were thought to have aided

---

[1] τελευταῖοι (or τελευταῖον) δὲ τῆς γραφῆς εἰσὶν οἱ μαχεσάμενοι Μαραθῶνι. — Paus. c. 15, 4. Leake translates (i. p. 122) : "at one end of the picture are those who fought at Marathon." But that battle could hardly have been represented as part of the picture of the Greeks at Troy. The gen. sing. τῆς γραφῆς, as Siebelis observes, refers to *all* the paintings.

[2] Demosth. c. Neær. 1377, Reiske ; cf. Ælian, de Nat. Anim. vii. 38.

[3] Hobhouse's Journey, &c. i. p. 431.

the Athenians in the fight; as the hero Marathon, son of Apollo, after whom the district was named; Theseus ascending through the earth as if from Hades; Athena and Heracles, the latter of whom the Marathonians claimed to have been the first to worship. Among the combatants most conspicuously represented, were the Athenian polemarch Callimachus, Miltiades, one of the generals, and the hero Echetlus, or Echetlæus. This last, as Pausanias relates further on (c. 32, 4), was the man of rustic aspect who appeared in the battle, and after slaying many of the barbarians with a ploughshare, suddenly vanished. To the Athenians who inquired about him, the oracle only replied that they must honour the hero Echetlæus. There was also in the picture a head of Butes, but only as far as the eyes, the rest of the figure being hid behind a mountain, whence, from being so easily painted, the proverb θᾶττον ἢ Βούτης.[1]

The picture of the battle of Marathon was, no doubt, that which most attracted the attention of the Athenians, as we may conclude from the copious notices which they have left us of it. According to Pausanias (lib. v. 11, 2) it was painted by Panænus, who appears to have been a brother of Pheidias.[2] Ælian, on the other hand, attributes it either to Micon or Polygnotus;[3] but the disjunctive particle shows that he was not very certain about the matter. The truth seems to be that Polygnotus painted the Greeks in council; Micon, the battle with the Amazons, and Panænus, the battle of Marathon; but we have no notice of the artist who painted the first picture representing the Athenians and Lacedæmonians at Œnoë. These three artists, therefore, were contemporary, and flourished about the middle of the fifth century B.C. We have Plutarch's authority that Polygnotus painted the council before Troy; and that the head of Laodicë, one of the captive Trojan women, was a portrait of Cimon's sister, Elpinicë, of whom he was enamoured.[4] For Polygnotus was no vulgar artist painting only for gain, but did this picture *gratis;* while Micon was

---

[1] Hesych. voc. θᾶττον.
[2] Plin. H. N. xxxv. 54.
[3] De Nat. Animal. vii. 38.
[4] Plut. Cim. 4.

paid for his labour.[1] Micon painted the battle of the Amazons, as we learn from the 'Lysistrata' of Aristophanes :

τὰς δ' Ἀμαζόνας σκόπει,
ἃς Μίκων ἔγραψ' ἀφ' ἵππων μαχομένας τοῖς ἀνδράσιν.

v. 678.

"See the Amazons
Drawn by Micon, fighting, mounted,
With the male sex."

In the battle of Marathon, Panænus is said to have introduced five portraits, those of Miltiades, Callimachus, and Cynægirus, on the Athenian side, and those of Dates and Artaphernes on the side of the Persians. We may infer from Pliny, that these were among the first portraits done in colours, since he considers them to have been a great advance in art.[2] The Athenians appear to have allowed Miltiades the honour of this portrait, instead of an inscription, which had been refused.[3] The portrait of Cynægirus must have been quite in the background, for he had his hand cut off in endeavouring to prevent the Persians escaping in the ships.[4] Panænus may probably have taken the portraits of the Athenian commanders from busts. It may perhaps be inferred from Pausanias saying, in his account of the theatre (c. 21, 3), that the statue of Æschylus there was much posterior to his death, and to the picture in which his valour at Marathon was represented, that Panænus had also inserted a likeness of Æschylus. The Portico, with its pictures, appears to have been preserved down to the time of Synesius and the reign of Arcadius and Honorius, when a proconsul of Achaia, who affected indignation that the Pœcilë, as the seat of the Stoic philosophy, should have acquired more veneration than even the temples themselves, carried off the pictures ;[5] whence perhaps we may infer that they were painted on board, or at all events, not on the wall. Whether the four pictures mentioned by Pausanias were the only ones in the Portico does not seem

[1] Plin. N. H. xxxv. 59.
[2] Ibid. 57 ; cf. Nep. Milt. 6.
[3] Æsch. c. Ctesiph. p. 576.
[4] Herod. vi. 114.
[5] Synes. Epist. cxxxv.; and the note of Ménage, ad Diog. Laërt. vii. 5.

to be certain. An anonymous 'Life of Sophocles'[1] says, that he was
painted in the Pœcilë playing on the lyre, which he did in his 'Thamyris.'
A scholiast on Aristophanes[2] says that there was a picture by Apollodorus,
or Pamphilus, of the suppliant Heracleidæ at Athens, "in the Portico of
the Athenians;" by which he probably means the Pœcilë *par excellence*.
But the whole account is obscure; though the lines of Aristophanes
seem certainly to refer to a picture.

In the Portico were brazen shields of the Sionæi and their allies, as
the inscriptions showed.[3]   Other shields, smeared with pitch in order to
preserve them, were said to be those captured from the Lacedæmonians
in the island of Sphacteria.. There was also a bronze statue with only
one hand, of which Demonax ironically said that the Athenians had at
length honoured Cynægirus with a statue; though it does not appear
that it was really his.[4] Before the Portico stood a bronze statue of
Solon, and another of Seleucus, the companion of Alexander; and this
gives occasion to Pausanias to fill the remainder of the chapter (c. 16)
with an account of Seleucus. The statue of Solon seems to be that
alluded to by Demosthenes in his second speech against Aristogeiton.[5]

Diogenes Laërtius relates that, under the domination of the Thirty
Tyrants, 1400 citizens were massacred in the Pœcilë without a trial;[6]
and, according to Æschines, Diogenes assigns this massacre as the
reason which induced Zeno to select the Pœcilë for his discourses,
hoping thereby to render the place more retired and less liable to
such profanations. From its size and beauty it was the most celebrated portico at Athens, and hence was called "the Stoa" *par
excellence*,[7] and in Latin authors, "Porticus," or "the Porch." Its
celebrity was no doubt also greatly owing to Zeno having selected it for
his lectures, and founded here the Stoic sect, or philosophy of the

---

[1] Prefixed to his works.

[2] εἰς τὴν στοὰν τῶν Ἀθηναίων.—ad Plut.
v. 385.

[3] On their revolt from the Athenians,
see Thucyd. iv. 120 sqq.

[4] Lucian, Demon. 53.

[5] Σόλωνα ψηφίσασθαι χαλκοῦν ἐν τῇ

ἀγορᾷ στῆσαι.—p. 807, Reiske. Cf. Ælian,
V. H. viii. 16.

[6] Diog. Laërt. vii. 5; Æsch. de falsa leg.
p. 628, Reiske (who says 1500).

[7] ἐπελθε τὰς ἐν Λυκείῳ (σχολάς), τὰς ἐν
Ἀκαδημίᾳ, τὴν στοάν, τὸ Παλλάδιον, τὸ
ᾠδεῖον.—Plut. De Exil. viii. 386, Reiske.

Porch; whence στοά sometimes stands absolutely for that school of philosophy itself.[1] Hence Persius characterizes it by the epithet of "sapiens;" at the same time alluding to the pictures in it of the Medes in pantaloons:

> "Quæque docet sapiens braccatis illita Medis
> Porticus." *Sat.* iii. 53.

The only other object which Pausanias mentions on the agora—which, if he mean the same place, he now for the first time calls by that name (c. 17, 1)—is an ALTAR OF MERCY or Compassion (Ἔλεος). Arguing from the traditions connected with it, this appears to have been a very ancient altar. For Euripides represents the Heracleidæ, sitting upon it in suppliant guise, to have thus obtained the aid of the Athenians against Eurystheus; and in like manner, Adrastus having laid upon it the suppliant bough (ἱκετηρία) induced Theseus to make war upon Creon, and compel him to bury the bodies of the Thebans;[2] an act regarded as one of the most signal displays of the philanthropy for which the Athenians were famous, and celebrated accordingly. Statius has some fine lines on the subject, which, as they also help to show the nature of the altar and its surrounding objects, we here insert:

> " Urbe fuit mediâ nulli concessa potentum
> Ara deûm; mitis posuit Clementia sedem
> Et miseri fecere sacram; sine supplice nunquam
> Illa novo; nulla damnavit vota repulsa.
> Auditi quicunque rogant, noctesque diesque
> Ire datum et solis numen placare querelis.
> Parca superstitio: non turea flamma nec altus
> Accipitur sanguis, lacrimis altaria sudant,
> Mœstarumque super libamina serta comarum
> Pendent, et vestes mutata sorte relictæ.
> Mite nemus circa, cultuque insigne verendo
> Vittatæ laurus et supplicis arbor olivæ.
> Nulla autem effigies, nulli commissa metallo
> Forma deæ; mentes habitare et pectora gaudet."[3]

The deity had no image, no sacrifice; she resided only in the hearts and minds of men. The little grove of olives and laurels that grew

---

[1] Ζήνων ὁ Κιττιεὺς ὁ τῆς στοᾶς κτίστης.— Athen. viii. 35, "the founder of the Porch."

[2] Apollod. ii. 8, s. 1; iii. 7, s. 1.

[3] Thebaid. xii. 481 sqq.

R

around the altar, the locks of hair and the abandoned dresses suspended over it, were probably to be seen in the time of Statius; for, as
we shall show elsewhere, all the forms of ancient superstition were preserved till a very late period at Athens, and Libanius admonishes the
Emperor Julian that he had seen the altar in question.[1] Nay, it is even
alluded to by Claudian.[2] It was no doubt for the sake of compliment-
ing the Athenians, that Pausanias alluded to it, for it could have had
nothing to recommend it in the way of art; and he goes on to mention,
as further proofs of the philanthropy and piety of the Athenians, other
altars which they had erected to moral qualities personified; as
Modesty, Fame, and Alacrity; but without giving any indication of
their site. That of Fame is twice alluded to by Æschines.[3]

But was the altar of Mercy really on the old agora; that is, the
agora which Pausanias calls Cerameicus? None of the ancient authors
who allude to it say so, the nearest indication of its site being that it
was in the middle of the city. The fact of Pausanias changing his
way of speaking of the market, and now calling it the *agora* instead of
the *Cerameicus*, the name which he had used before, raises the presumption that he had now passed into a different market. The writers
of the classical period of Attic literature never call the agora *Cerameicus*.
We have already observed that that name for it came into use in later
times, and was doubtless adopted in order to prevent confusion between
the ancient and modern agora. The fact of a new, or Roman, market-
place may certainly be inferred from Strabo's words implying that one
had been established at the Athenian Eretria.[4] Bursian thinks that
Strabo is here alluding to the transference, probably by Peisistratus,
of a still more ancient and primitive agora from the south side of the
Areiopagus to the north side.[5] But the north side of the Areiopagus
we know to have been called Cerameicus, not Eretria, and therefore this
supposition falls to the ground. Forchhammer indeed observes, that in

[1] In Presbeut. ap. Meurs. Cer. Gem. c. 16.   [4] οἱ δ᾽ ἀπὸ τῆς Ἀθήνησιν Ἐρετρίας, ἣ νῦν
[2] De Bell. Gild. 404 sq.   ἐστιν ἀγορά.—p. 447.
[3] C. Timarch. p. 140; De fals. Leg.   [5] Geogr. v. Griechenland, i. p. 280.
p. 311.

spite of Strabo's *now* (νῦν), there is no reason why he may not have been alluding to the agora in the Cerameicus, which district might, in very early times, have been occupied by a demus called Eretria.[1] But if one demus had been supplanted by another, the Eretrians by the Cerameicans, Strabo would surely have said "where the Cerameicus now is," not "where the agora now is." And such a change must have been effected by a revolution, of which we have no indication. The existence of an ancient agora on the south side of the Areiopagus, or rather perhaps of the Acropolis, rests, we believe, entirely on a passage in Harpocration, where, in a quotation from Apollodorus, an ancient agora is mentioned (τὴν ἀρχαίαν ἀγοράν).[2] It is not improbable that there may have been a primitive agora there, which, however, must have been removed to the north side, certainly in, and probably long before, the time of Peisistratus. An argument is sometimes drawn from the temple of Aphroditē Pandemos mentioned in Harpocration. But there were two distinct temples of that name ; one erected to commemorate the union of the Attic boroughs into one metropolis under Theseus ; the latter, as shown in the passage quoted,[3] was built by Solon out of the wages of legalized prostitution ; and, consequently, the word πάνδημος has a very different signification as applied to the two temples, Apollodorus gives a third meaning, derived from the whole people being assembled in the agora for the ecclesia, which, however, has no very palpable reference to any kind of Aphroditē.

The assumption of a Roman agora is strengthened—we had almost said confirmed—by the still existing PROPYLÆUM of four columns, which has sometimes been taken for the portico of a temple, and sometimes,

---

[1] Topographie, p. 54.

[2] As the article is an important one, we give it entire : Πάνδημος Ἀφροδίτη · Ὑπερίδης ἐν τῷ κατὰ Πατροκλέους, εἰ γνήσιος. Ἀπολλόδωρος ἐν τῷ περὶ θεῶν πάνδημόν φησιν Ἀθήνησι κληθῆναι τὴν ἀφιδρυθεῖσαν περὶ τὴν ἀρχαίαν ἀγορὰν διὰ τὸ ἐνταῦθα πάντα τὸν δῆμον συνάγεσθαι τὸ παλαιὸν ἐν ταῖς ἐκκλησίαις, ἃς ἐκάλουν ἀγοράς. Νίκανδρος ἐν ς΄ Κολοφωνιακῶν Σόλωνά φησι σώματα ἀγοράσαντα εὐπρεπῆ ἐπὶ στέγης (?) στῆσαι διὰ τοὺς νέους, καὶ ἐκ τῶν περιγενομένων χρημάτων ἱδρύσασθαι Ἀφροδίτης Πανδήμου ἱερόν. ἔστι δὲ τὸ πάνδημον πάγκοινον.

[3] Nicandros is confirmed by Philemon (ap. Athen. lib. xiii. c. 25) with regard to Solon having instituted a public place of prostitution. We there read ἐπ' οἰκημάτων, for the unintelligible ἐπὶ στέγης.

R 2

with more justice, for the gateway to a market-place. This structure consists of four Doric columns, 4 ft. 4 in. in diameter at the base, and, including the capital, 26 ft. in height. The space between the middle columns is about 12 ft.; between the side ones under 5 ft. Over the middle of the pediment which they support is a large acroterium 9 or 10 ft. in length, with an inscription to Lucius Cæsar, the grandson of Augustus, of whom, apparently, it supported an equestrian statue.[1] Lucius died in the second year after the birth of Christ, aged nineteen, and the building, therefore, was completed about this time. But the space beyond the gateway may have been used as a market-place long before the propylæum itself was erected; for Cicero, in a passage where he is evidently speaking of the ancient agora,[2] calls it the Ceramcicus, and it is not probable that it obtained that name before the establishment of the new agora. Indeed, this market-place did not receive its final completion till the time of Hadrian, whose stoa, or Pantheon, added the finish to its northern side.

That the propylæum in question formed the portico of a temple was held by the older topographers, as Wheler, who considered it to be the portico of a temple of Augustus; but this we now know to have been upon the Acropolis.[3] Forchhammer[4] and Ross[5] are among the most eminent modern writers who hold it to have been the portico of a temple dedicated to Athena Archegetis, or protectress of the city, founding their opinion upon the inscription on the architrave, which purports that it was dedicated by the Athenian people to that goddess from the money bestowed by C. Julius and Augustus Cæsar.[6] For the

---

[1] ὁ δῆμος Λούκιον Καίσαρα αὐτοκράτορος θεοῦ υἱοῦ Σεβαστοῦ Καίσαρος υἱόν.

[2] De Fin. i. 11, 39, speaking of the statue of Chrysippus. See a little further on. The De Finibus was written about B.C. 50.

[3] See Journey, &c. p. 358.

[4] Topographie, p. 57.

[5] Theseion, p. 41.

[6] ὁ δῆμος ἀπὸ τῶν δοθεισῶν δωρεῶν ὑπὸ Γαίου Ἰουλίου Καίσαρος θεοῦ καὶ αὐτο-

κράτορος Καίσαρος θεοῦ υἱοῦ σεβαστοῦ Ἀθηνᾷ Ἀρχηγέτιδι, στρατηγοῦντος ἐπὶ τοὺς ὁπλίτας Εὐκλέους Μαραθωνίου, τοῦ καὶ διαδεξαμένου τὴν ἐπιμέλειαν ὑπὲρ τοῦ πατρὸς Ἡρώδου, τοῦ καὶ πρεσβεύσαντος. ἐπὶ ἄρχοντος Νικίου τοῦ Σαραπίωνος Ἀθμονέως. It was erected, therefore, in the reign of Augustus; for Julius was a god, i.e., dead, and Augustus emperor. Leake, vol. i. p. 213.

same reason the arches of the aqueduct which supplied the water-clock at the Tower of the Winds might be regarded as part of a temple dedicated to Athena Archegetis, for they have a similar inscription.[1] To dedicate a forum or market to some deity was a Roman custom; and thus the Forum Julium at Rome was consecrated to Venus Genetrix, that of Augustus to Mars Ultor, and that of Nerva, like this at Athens, to Minerva.

Meursius seems to have been the first[2] who, from the passage in Strabo before cited, inferred the existence of a new agora. But among more modern topographers, the honour belongs to Stuart of having held this colonnade to have formed the entrance to it; an opinion founded on its style of architecture and the inscriptions on and near it. The architectural objections to its being a temple are stated by Stuart as follows: "The wall in which the door is placed extended on each side beyond the lateral walls of the portico; whereas, the usual plan of temples is a rectangular parallelogram, and their lateral walls are continued without interruption from the antæ of the portico to the posticus or back front. Besides this, the diameters of these columns are in a smaller proportion to their height than the diameters of any that are found in the ancient temples of this order; which circumstance, considering the distinction which Vitruvius has made between the proportion of those columns which are employed in temples and of those which are placed in buildings of inferior dignity (lib. v. c. 9), adds a considerable weight to this opinion."[3] Bötticher has adduced another objection: that the crepidoma of this structure consists only of a single step,[4] an anomaly not hitherto found in any temple. And he further points out that the width of the intercolumniations, the middle one being two and a half times as wide as each of the side ones, shows that the former was intended for carriages and the latter for foot-passengers, and consequently that the whole must have formed

[1] Curtius, Erläuternder Text to his maps, p. 44.

[2] Ceramicus Geminus, c. 16; and Athen. Att. i. 6.

[3] Ant. of Athens, vol. i. p. 2. See also Leake, vol. i. p. 211 sqq. who adopts Stuart's view, and adds some particulars.

[4] Bericht, p. 225.

a gate. It is indeed surprising how Ross[1] should have supposed that it was a *tetrakionia*, or small temple, under which, in the Macedonian times, the patron goddesses of towns were placed, as such a structure must necessarily have been quadrangular, with the columns at the angles.

Still stronger reasons against its having been a temple may be drawn from the inscriptions upon and near it. Two of these we have already mentioned—namely, that on the architrave, containing the dedication to Athena, and that on the middle acroterium under the statue of Lucius Cæsar.[2] The style of the former one would, as Leake justly observes, have been unexampled on a temple. Still more inappropriate to such an edifice would have been the statue of a youth like Lucius Cæsar for its frontispiece. This circumstance alone is, we think, quite sufficient to dispose of its pretensions to be a temple. Two other inscriptions afford satisfactory proof that it formed the entrance to an agora. One of these is on the jamb of the doorcase, and contains an edict by the Emperor Hadrian respecting the sale of oil and the duties payable on it.[3] Truly a very appropriate inscription for the interior of a temple! Forchhammer, indeed, asserts that the stone bearing the inscription was brought hither from some other place. But recent researches by Bötticher[4] and others have confirmed the accuracy of Stuart's report, that it is in its original position; and Ross allowed this,[5] though he still adhered to the hypothesis of a temple. The fourth inscription was on the pedestal of a statue to Julia Augusta, with the title of Πρόνοια, or Providence, standing just within the Propylæum; and as the two agoranomi, or superintendents of the market, under whose magistracy the statue was erected, are named in the inscription, we have here a further proof that it stood in a forum.[6] Hence some of

[1] Theseion, p. 41.

[2] See p. 244.

[3] This is too long to be inserted here. It will be found in Boeckh, C. Ins. Gr. No. 355, and in Wheler's 'Journey,' p. 389.

[4] Bericht, p. 226.

[5] Theseion, p. 42, note 124.

[6] Ἰουλίαν θεὰν Σεβαστὴν Πρόνοιαν ἡ βουλὴ ἡ ἐξ Ἀρείου πάγου, καὶ ἡ βουλὴ τῶν ἑξακοσίων καὶ ὁ δῆμος, κ.τ.λ.—The base with the inscription is figured at the end of Stuart's first chapter. See also Boeckh, C. I. No. 313 and Leake, i. 214, note 3.

the leading modern topographers, as Bötticher and Curtius,[1] have adopted the view of Stuart and Leake, that the colonnade in question was the propylaeum of the new market. Curtius, indeed, is of opinion that it was no mere ordinary gate, but intended for state occasions, and that the Panathenaïc procession passed through it on its road to the Eleusinium. This, however, it could hardly have done, if, as we have shown before, the Eleusinium lay nearly parallel with it, under the north-west extremity of the Acropolis. Besides, the inscription about the oil was hardly fitted for a triumphal arch.

We are of opinion, then, that when Pausanias speaks of the agora, he has really passed out of the ancient market-place, or Cerameicus, into the new or Roman agora. The only thing he finds in it worthy of mention is the altar of Mercy, which was undoubtedly a very ancient Athenian monument; but there must have been other things in or near it worth a word or two, which however he does not mention, probably because they were recent or Roman. Before touching upon these, however, we must return awhile into the Cerameicus, where Pausanias has also passed over a good many objects, and some of them important from their antiquity.

Amongst these was the LEOCORIUM, or monument to the daughters of Leo, who, in pursuance of an oracle, were sacrificed to Athena by their father in order to avert a plague; for which act they were honoured by the Athenians with a little chapel or heroum. That it was a very ancient monument is plain from the circumstance of its commemorating a human sacrifice; and that it existed in the time of Hippias and Hipparchus, that is, B.C. 514, appears from Thucydides,[2] for it was at the Leocorium that, as we have already related, Harmodius and Aristogeiton slew Hipparchus. It must, therefore, have been within the walls of the ancient Thesean city, for Harmodius and Aristo-

---

[1] Bötticher, Bericht, p. 223 sqq.; Curtius, Erläuternder Text, p. 44. Bursian in his 'Geographie' still maintains the notion of a temple; but in Pauly's Real-Enc. (i. 1979) recognizes the Athena Archegetis as a foundation for a branch of market commerce: so that, as Curtius observes (ibid. note), the matter becomes a verbal dispute.

[2] i. 20, and vi. 57.

geiton being outside the walls in the Cerameicus, where Hippias also was, preparing the Panathenaïc procession, and seeing him conversing with one of their band, they were seized with the fear that their conspiracy had been betrayed, and rushing through the gate, fell in with Hipparchus at the spot in question (above, p. 78). Now, let us observe that Thucydides does not speak about the *inner* and the *outer* Cerameicus, but mentions only one; for the distinction between the outer and inner one did not arise till the circuit of the walls was extended by Themistocles, and part of the Cerameicus included within them, the boundary being at the Dipylon. At this period, therefore, the Cerameicus seems to have lain entirely outside the walls, and consequently the Leocorium could not have been in it. But it was certainly in the agora. For Demosthenes says, in his speech against Conon,[1] that as he was walking about one evening in the agora he fell in with Ctesias at the Leocorium. The lexicographers, on the other hand, say that it was in the middle of the Cerameicus (ἐν μέσῳ τῷ Κεραμεικῷ).[2] This, however, is only another proof that in later times Cerameicus usurped the name of agora, and also that it must have extended itself under that appellation towards the Acropolis and Areiopagus beyond its original limits, which were the Thesean wall. Nevertheless, the Leocorium may very well have stood about the middle of the agora, which eventually may have embraced a space outside the ancient wall as well as within it. We may also hence infer that the agora, as it existed in the time of the dramatists and orators, differed from that of the epoch of Pisistratus, since the Thesean wall would then have been in the way. Its final arrangement, at all events, must have been posterior to Themistocles. The Leocorium must have been a monument of some importance, as it is mentioned by Hegesias[3] with the Thescium and the few other monuments to which he adverts at Athens, which renders it the more singular that Pausanias should not have alluded to it. It is also mentioned by Cicero and several other

---

[1] p. 1258, Reiske. Demosthenes adds: ἐγγὺς τῶν Πυθ)βώρου, which we are unable to explain. There was an ancient Theban sculptor named Pythodorus. Pausan. ix.

24, 2.

[2] Harpocr., Hesych., Photius, Suidas, in voc.

[3] Ap. Strab. lib. ix. p. 396.

writers.[1] We learn from Ælian that it had a temenos attached to it,[2] so that it must have filled some space.

Of other larger objects of Athenian antiquity omitted by Pausanias in his description of the agora we may also mention a TEMENOS OF ÆACUS (Αἰακόντειον) which the Athenians had vowed in their war with the Æginetans, and which Herodotus had seen.[3] Also Solon's TEMPLE OF APHRODITE PANDEMOS, to which we have before adverted, and which was probably the same as that of Aphroditë Hetæra mentioned by Hesychius.[4] Ross conjectures that it may have been near the temple of Aphroditë Urania at the Colonus Agoræus, or even identical with it;[5] but the latter notion seems altogether improbable, and we have seen that the Urania was established long before the time of Solon.

That Pausanias should have omitted many of the statues on the agora, of which there was such a multitude, is not surprising. Among them was a Hermes with four heads, a fine work of art by Telesarchides.[6] A statue of Chrysippus, who being a small man, was nearly hidden by a horseman that stood near, whence Carneades pleasantly called him Crypsippus (Κρύψιππος).[7] And this may account for Pausanias having overlooked him. Statues of Diphilus, Berisades, Satyrus, and Gorgippus.[8] Chabrias kneeling with shield and spear thrust forwards, an attitude in which he had taught his troops to resist the enemy. This *pose* afterwards afforded an example to athletes to be taken in the posture in which they had been victorious.[9] And doubtless there were many other statues.

Pausanias was, perhaps, purposely silent about the buildings erected by foreigners on the agora, of which there must have been two or three of considerable size. Such was the AGRIPPEIUM, or theatre of Agrippa, mentioned only by Philostratus, but in two passages.[10] The same author speaks of a BOULEUTERIUM, or hall of the persons connected with the

---

[1] De Nat. Deor. iii. 19, 50.

[2] Var. Hist. xii. 28.

[3] lib. v. c. 89 ; cf. Hesych. in voc.

[4] voc. 'Εταίρας.

[5] Theseion, p. 39 sq.

[6] Anthol. Epigr. ap. Meurs. Ceram. Gem.

c. 15 : cf. Phot. Lex. 'Ερμῆς τετρακέφαλος.

[7] Diog. Laërt. vii. 183 ; cf. Cic. de Fin. i. 11, 39.

[8] Dinarch. c. Demosth. p. 33 sq., Reiske.

[9] C. Nep. Vit. Chabr. c. 1.

[10] Vit. Sophist. ii. 5, 3, and 8, 2.

stage (τεχνιτῶν βουλευτήριον), which he describes as situated near the
gates of the Cerameicus.[1] It is possible, however, that both these buildings may not have been exactly on the agora, but in that part of the
Inner Cerameicus which lay between it and the Dipylon. The boulen-
terium he further specifies as being near the horsemen (οὐ πόρρω τῶν
ἱππέων), by which he may possibly mean the tombs of the equites just
outside the Dipylon. The large STOA OF ATTALUS, which Pausanias also
omits to notice, was however undoubtedly in the agora, and stood at the
northern extremity of its eastern side. Athenæus is the only ancient
writer who mentions it, in his account of Aristion before given (supra,
p. 160). This stoa was built by Attalus I., of Pergamus, about two
centuries B.C. The remains of it were taken by Stuart and others for
the gymnasium of Ptolemy; but in 1862 the inscription of the architrave was discovered, showing that the building was erected by Attalus
and Apollonis. The excavation of the ruins discovered a building of
more than 120 yards in length from south-east to north-west, consisting of an open portico with a wall at the back, in which were twenty-
one doors leading into as many rooms about $5\frac{1}{2}$ yards deep. Before the
wall, at a distance of between 6 and 7 yards, stood a row of columns,
and before these again, at a rather larger interval, another row, of
which the columns were rather slenderer. This double colonnade was
attached by walls at each end to the back wall, so as to form one
building. In front, the portico was approached by three steps, before
which ran a gutter.[2] Curtius is of opinion that the agora was enlarged
northwards to make room for this stoa, but this does not seem probable.
The discovery of it may serve to give us some idea of the length of
such structures. If the Stoa Basileius was of equal dimensions, it
would have lined about half the side of the Areiopagus. The Pœcilë,
perhaps, may even have been larger, and thus would have served to
enclose the larger part of the north side of the agora, which, from the
nature of the ground, would not have been so long as the opposite one.

---

[1] Vit. Sophist. ii. 8, 2. Of the word
τεχνῖται used absolutely for οἱ περὶ τὸν
Διόνυσον τεχνῖται see Olearius ad Philostr.

V. Apollon. v. 7, note 20. Cf. A. Gell. N. A.
xx. 4; Ar. Rhet. iii. 2; Diod. Sic. xx. 108.

[2] Curtius, Att. St. ii. p. 30 sq.

Before quitting the ancient agora we will endeavour to realize the prospect which it would have offered to a person standing in the midst of it on a festival day, when the booths of the dealers had been removed. On the eastern side the prospect would have been confined not so much by public buildings, as by the ridge on which stood the propylæum of Athena Archegetis, though probably a view of that structure would have been obtained through the opening, or street, which led to it. The most notable building on this side would have been the stoa of Attalus at its northern extremity. On the north side would have been seen the magnificent Pœcilë, filling a great part of the line, with the statues before it, and near it the gate of the agora with its trophy, and the statue of Hermes Agoræus. The western side, bounded by the Coloneau Hill crowned with magnificent buildings, and lined at its foot with a fringe of Hermæ, would have offered a still finer *coup-d'œil*. But the most magnificent view must have been that on the south. The fine stoæ and temples which lined the side of the Areiopagus, with the statues standing like sentinels before them; beyond these, the deep bay or recess, which mounted steeply towards the Propylæa of the Acropolis, also lined with handsome public buildings rising one above the other, and almost literally filled with a crowd of the finest statues, among which those of Harmodius and Aristogeiton stood out in isolated dignity; the whole crowned with the Acropolis and its buildings as a back-ground, must have presented a scene which the imagination can hardly conceive. The dazzling whiteness of the marble buildings would have been relieved by the platanes and other trees which rose among them and afforded an agreeable shade; while the noble expanse of the agora was diversified by the sacred groves and shrines, such as the Leocorium and others, which were sprinkled upon it.

The gateway of Athena Archegetis, leading into the new or Roman agora, lay nearly parallel with the southern end of the stoa of Attalus, but about a hundred yards to the east of it. In this market-place Pausanias, as we have seen, mentions only the altar of Mercy; but there must have been other objects, though of late construction, upon it, some of which still remain. The principal of these is the Corinthian façade, commonly called the stoa of Hadrian, which probably enclosed the whole northern side of the market. The reasons for this opinion are, that the western side of this building is on a line with the gateway inscribed to Athena; while, if a straight line were drawn southwards from its eastern side, it would just enclose the Tower of the Winds, which fronts the gateway, and which from its nature, as Curtius observes, in all probability stood in an open space. The southern front of the façade is about 126 yards in length; and, supposing this to give the breadth of the new agora, and that in length it extended an equal distance on both sides of the Propylæum, we should thus have a parallelogram of about 180 yards long by 126 broad. This is a small area as compared with the ancient agora, but it would have been nearly twice as large as the Forum Julium or Forum Augusti at Rome, and even larger than the Forum Trajani.

The middle space of this area, between the Propylæum and the Horologium of Andronicus, seems to have been surrounded with a colonnade or portico, the remains of which were discovered some ten years ago.[1] The columns are of Hymettian marble, between 17 and 18 feet in height, with bases and capitals of Pentelic marble. They seem to have enclosed a quadrangular space about 100 yards long from west to east, and 66 or 67 broad from north to south; and it has been conjectured, with great probability, from the inscription already mentioned at the entrance of the Propylæum, that this space formed the oil-market. Such a market would have been very appropriately placed under the presidency of Athena.

Before we quit this agora we must give a short account of the building commonly called the stoa of Hadrian, and of the Tower of the Winds, which also stood upon it; both which Pausanias has omitted to notice here, though he alludes to the former building in another place.

The STOA OF HADRIAN occupied, as we have already remarked, the northern side of the new agora. It stood on the site of the present

[1] See Curtius, Erl. Text, p. 45. Pervanoglu, in the Philologus, xxvii. p. 670, conjectures that these columns may have belonged to the Ptolemæum. But their size is too small for so celebrated a gymnasium, and indicates rather the mere portico of a market.

bazaar, and enclosed a space of 376 ft. in length from east to west, and 252 ft. in breadth from north to south. Stuart, who has given a description of its remains,[1] took it to be the Pœcilë; not, indeed, the original building, which from the style of its architecture it could not have been, but a reconstruction. The northern side of the western façade is still pretty perfect. This façade consisted of a wall, before which stood detached, at a distance of less than two feet, a row of Corinthian columns, originally eighteen in number. The four middle ones, which are fluted, whilst the rest are plain, supported a pediment and formed a portal or entrance, with an ascent of six steps. The seven columns to the north of the portal are pretty perfect. Each stands on its own base, and is rather less than 29 ft. in height and 3 ft. in diameter. At the extremity the wall projects as far as the columns do, forming a pteroma faced with a Corinthian pilaster. The portal and the façade to the south of it are much defaced. The plan of the remainder of the building was partially traced by Stuart. The northern wall had three remarkable projections. The middle one, 34 ft. wide, was rectangular, and probably formed the entrance; those on each side were circular, 31 ft. in diameter, and formed recesses or bows on the inside of the building, meant seemingly for exhedræ, or places for retirement and conversation. The south wall, facing the new agora, was probably similar.

In the interior of the building were traces of a colonnade, or peristyle, which encompassed the whole quadrangle at a distance of 23 ft. from the wall. It was composed of a double row of columns; but of this peristyle only one column remained in its place. Exactly facing the portal or entrance before described, and at a distance of about 250 feet from it, therefore on the eastern side of the quadrangle, were some ancient foundations, and upon them a church of barbarous construction called *ee megále Panagía*, or Great St. Mary's. In this church were some excellent remains of ancient masonry.

There can be no doubt that this was a Roman building, and most probably of the time of Hadrian, for Mr. Wilkins discovered a marked

---

[1] Ant. of Athens, vol. i. ch. 5.

resemblance between the details of the western colonnade and those of Hadrian's arch.[1] But the question still remains, which of Hadrian's buildings was it? Among those attributed to him by Pausanias, the choice lies between a gymnasium, which it is usually called by German topographers, and a hierum or sacred enclosure, consecrated to all the gods, with a temple of Zeus Panhellenius, and other buildings,[2] including a library; the whole surrounded with a colonnade or portico. There is no authority to be found in Pausanias for speaking about a stoa of Hadrian as an independent building, though Leake and others give one of his buildings that name. The στοαὶ which Pausanias mentions[3] are only the colonnades or porticoes which surrounded the interior of the enclosure in question. We think it very probable that the building on the new agora was this *Hierum* or Pantheon, as it evidently contained a large open space with buildings upon it. This was also the opinion of Sir William Gell, who writes: "Near the Bazaar are the remains of

---

[1] Atheniensia, p. 165.

[2] May this have formed the ἀγορὰ θεῶν, or Forum of the Gods, which we sometimes find mentioned, but only by writers of a late date? Pausanias gives it no name, and in his time it must have been a recent work, if, indeed, entirely finished. Thus Hesychius : Θεῶν ἀγορά · τόπος Ἀθήνησιν, ἀπὸ τοῦ συναγερθῆναι προσαγορευόμενος. Cf. Aristeid. in Cyzicena, p. 239, Jebb. A Pantheon, that is an enclosed space with statues and altars of all the gods, might very well be called an ἀγορὰ θεῶν ; a name much more applicable to this place than, as Curtius strives to make out, to the Pnyx (Att. St. i. 40 sqq.).

[3] As the passage is somewhat obscure, we here give it entire: Ἀδριανὸς δὲ κατεσκευάσατο μὲν καὶ ἄλλα Ἀθηναίοις (i.e. besides the Olympium), ναὸν Ἥρας καὶ Διὸς Πανελληνίου, καὶ θεοῖς τοῖς πᾶσιν ἱερὸν κοινόν · τὰ δὲ ἐπιφανέστατα ἑκατὸν εἴκοσι κίονες Φρυγίου λίθου. πεποίηνται δὲ καὶ ταῖς στοαῖς κατὰ τὰ αὐτὰ οἱ τοῖχοι · καὶ οἰκήματα ἐνταῦθά ἐστιν ὀρόφῳ τε ἐπιχρύσῳ καὶ ἀλαβάστρῳ λίθῳ, πρὸς δὲ ἀγάλμασι κεκοσμημένα καὶ γραφαῖς · κατάκειται δὲ ἐς αὐτὸ βιβλία · καὶ γυμνάσιόν ἐστιν ἐπώνυμον Ἀδριανοῦ · κίονες δὲ καὶ ἐνταῦθα ἑκατὸν λιθοτομίας τῆς Λιβύων.—c. 18, 9. We hold with Siebelis that the whole of the first part of this passage, down to βιβλία, refers to one and the same building. It was a *hierum*, or place consecrated to all the gods, containing a temple of Hera and Zeus Panhellenius. The most striking part was the 120 columns of the stoæ, or porticoes, which surrounded the interior of the enclosure. The walls of the porticoes were of the same material (Siebelis shows that the use of the dative for genitive is frequent with Pausanias). In the enclosure were other buildings, besides the temple, containing a picture gallery, a sculpture gallery, and a library. The library is mentioned by Hieronymus in Chron. Eusebii Ol. ccxxvii.

many ancient edifices. The palace of the Vaivode, or Turkish governor, occupies the site of a building which was once imagined to be the Pœcilë, or Painted Portico, but is now with better reason termed the Pantheon of Hadrian; particularly as on excavation columns of Phrygian marble, which distinguished this building, have been found by Lord Guildford. The pavement is in some parts more than thirty feet below the soil. The order is Corinthian, and by no means comparable to the Corinthian of the best age of Greece."[1] The gymnasium of Hadrian must, therefore, be sought elsewhere.

The HOROLOGIUM of ANDRONICUS CYRRHESTES, commonly called the Tower of the Winds, faced the propylæum of the Roman agora, as we have already observed. It is described by Vitruvius as a marble tower of an octagon form, having on each of its sides a sculpture representing the wind which blew from the quarter it faced; that is, the four cardinal points and the intermediate ones between each. On the top, he says, was a marble meta, or pedestal, on which stood a bronze Triton, so constructed as to turn with the wind, and to point out, with a wand which he held in his hand, the quarter whence it blew.[2] The Triton has vanished, but the sculptures still remain in good preservation.

The tower, up to the cornice adorned with lions' heads, and excluding the roof, is about 40 feet high and 27 feet in diameter. Each of its eight sides is between 10 and 11 feet broad, and round the top of them runs a frieze upwards of 8 feet in height including the cornice. In each of the eight compartments of the frieze is sculptured, in high relief and of colossal size, the figure of the Wind to whose quarter it is turned, in a horizontal posture and a bold but somewhat rude style. The figures are all winged, and their character is typified by the objects which they bear. Thus Boreas, the north wind, has a conch in his hands from the noise he is supposed to make; Notus, the south wind, being a rainy one, is represented emptying a jar of water; Zephyrus, the west wind, has his mantle filled with flowers, and so forth. All the figures are more or less clothed; Libs and Zephyrus are the only ones without boots. The latter, by far the most graceful of the figures, is

---

[1] Itinerary, p. 37.   [2] Vitruv. lib. i. c. 6, s. 4.

almost naked, having only the scanty mantle in which he carries his flowers. The sculptures certainly show a decadence in art; and this perhaps may have been the reason why Pausanias, amidst such a multitude of finer objects, considered them not worth seeing, and left the building unnoticed. The name of each Wind is engraved on the cornice over it. Under each figure is a sun-dial, and the floor was so constructed as to form a water-clock, which was supplied with water by an

THE TOWER OF THE WINDS.

aqueduct from the fountain called Clepsydra at the Acropolis. Some arches of this aqueduct still remain. Thus besides showing the quarter from which the wind blew, this ingenious building likewise indicated the hour by night or day.[1]

[1] For a very complete description of this building, see the third chapter of Stuart's first volume. M. Palasca, a Greek and an officer of the French navy, has given the

At the time of Stuart's visit, and also of Gell's subsequent one, early in the present century,[1] this tower was a *teke*, or chapel of dancing dervishes. The surface of the ground on which it stands has been buried to a depth of 15 or 16 feet by an accumulation of soil and rubbish, as shown by the excavation made round its base. In its original state, therefore, it must have stood at a considerably lower level than the propylæum of the agora, of which the basement stands clear ; thus showing that this gateway stood on the summit of a ridge which sloped down to the Cerameicus, or ancient agora, on the west, as well as towards this building, and the lower parts of the city, on the east.

We will now accompany Pausanias further on his walk. He comes next to the PTOLEMÆUM (c. 17, 1), a gymnasium so called after its founder, probably Ptolemy Philadelphus.[2] He says that it lay not far from the agora ; and probably to the eastward of the Horologium of Andronicus, as will appear presently when we come to speak of the Theseium ; but its precise site cannot be determined either from existing remains, or from any passages in ancient authors. In the Ptolemæum were some stone Hermæ worth seeing. Also several statues ; as a bronze one of Ptolemy himself, and one of Joba, or Juba, called by some his descendant. Here also was a statue of Chrysippus, which appears to have been a different one from that in the Cerameicus. Cicero mentions having heard Antiochus in this gymnasium.[3] It seems to have

---

following interesting account of the dials :
" Bien que la tour ne soit plus exactement orientée, l'arrangement des lignes horaires prouve qu'à l'époque où elles furent tracées, les Athéniens divisaient le jour solaire en douze heures. Dans ce système les heures n'avaient pas une durée invariable comme aujourd'hui, mais elles croissaient et décroissaient avec le jour lui-même selon les saisons. Égales entre elles pendant une même journée, dont elles représentaient la douzième partie, elles étaient plus longues en été, plus courtes en hiver. Le lever du soleil (douzième heure de la nuit) était le point de départ des heures du jour ; la sixième heure (notre midi) était marquée par le passage du soleil au méridien, tandis que la douzième heure correspondait au coucher de cet astre. Quelques aiguilles placées d'après les conclusions de M. Palasca indiquent les heures anciennes facilement réductibles en heures modernes. '
—Revue des deux Mondes, 1851, p. 652.

[1] Itinerary, p. 37 ; cf. Dodwell's Tour, vol. i. p. 374 sq., where the reader will find a description of the dance, called *semá*.

[2] Leake, vol. i. p. 124, note 2.

[3] De Fin. v. i. 1.

been the most famous one within the walls, and hence was sometimes simply called τὸ γυμνάσιον. It was therefore probably this place that Pliny means, when he says that the Athenians erected " in gymnasio " a statue with a gilt tongue to Berosus the historian and astronomer.[1]

Close (πρὸς) to the gymnasium of Ptolemy lay the THESEIUM. The juxtaposition of these two buildings is confirmed by Plutarch ; who says that the bones of Theseus, when brought by Cimon from the island of Scyros, were interred near where " the gymnasium now is," in the middle of the city ; a description which suits this site accurately enough.[2] And the word νῦν in this passage applied to the gymnasium, indicates that it was built after the Theseium, as the Ptolemæum of course would have been. About 200 yards to the east of the Horologium of Andronicus, near the church of St. Demetrius Katephori, are some considerable ruins which Curtius and Bursian assign to the gymnasium called DIOGENEIUM ; but as a marble group of Theseus and the Minotaur was found at this spot,[3] and as the site answers so well to the route of Pausanias, we should be inclined to place the Theseium here. The Ptolemæum, therefore, would have lain between these ruins and the Horologium. A Diogeneium is mentioned by Plutarch as a place of education,[4] and in an inscription to which we have already alluded when speaking of the Eleusinium. This spot has been thought the site of the Diogeneium, because an inscription was found near it directing the placing of a psephisma in that building.[5] However, the Theseium and Diogeneium may have been adjacent.

The temple dedicated to Theseus was additionally sanctified by being the resting-place of his remains, and hence Pausanias (i. 17, 6)

---

[1] N. H. vii. 123.

[2] καὶ κεῖται μὲν (ὁ Θησεὺς) ἐν μέσῃ τῇ πόλει, παρὰ τὸ νῦν γυμνάσιον.—Plut. Thes. cap. ult. ; cf. schol. Aristoph. Plut. 627.

[3] Pervanoglu in Philol. xxvii. p. 671.

[4] Sympos. ix. 1, 1.

[5] This inscription, to which we have already adverted when speaking of the Eleusinium (supra, p. 223), runs thus : ἀνα-

γράψαι δὲ τὸ ψήφισμα τοῦτο τὸν ταμίαν τοῦ γένους τῶν Εὐμολπιδῶν ἐν τρισὶν στήλαις καὶ στῆσαι τὴν μὲν ἐν Ἐλευσινίῳ τῷ ὑπὸ τῇ πόλει, τὴν δὲ ἐν τῷ Διογενείῳ, τὴν δὲ ἐν Ἐλευσῖνι ἐν τῷ ἱερῷ πρὸ τοῦ βουλευτηρίου.—Philistor, ii. p. 238 sq.; cf. Bursian, Geogr. p. 295, note[3] ; Mommsen, Heortol. p. 228 ; Beulé, L'Acropole, t. i. p. 321 ; Boeckh, C. Inser. Græc. 427.

calls it a σηκός, or mortuary chapel.[1] He was worshipped there on the
8th day of each month, and with more particular solemnity on
the 8th of Pyanepsion, on which day it was related that he returned
with the youths from Crete. Hence the group before mentioned would
represent an act which particularly connected him with the life and
history of the Athenians, and chiefly entitled him to their veneration.
Agreeably to the philanthropic character of Theseus, and indeed of the
Athenians themselves, the Theseium afforded a refuge for slaves and
others who sought a shelter from powerful oppressors.[2] Hence in the
' Equites ' of Aristophanes, the aggrieved triremes are represented as
resolving to sail thither or to the Semnæ, whose temple served the same
purpose :

> ἦν δ' ἀρέσκῃ ταῦτ' 'Αθηναίοις, καθῆσθαί μοι δοκεῖ
> εἰς τὸ Θησεῖον πλεούσαις ἢ 'πὶ τῶν σεμνῶν θεῶν.—v. 1311.

> "If the will of Athens be such, then I think we'll sail away
> And sit down at the Theseium, or by the Eumenides."

In the Theseium was depicted the combat of the Athenians and
Amazons; a subject, remarks Pausanias, also found on the shield of
Athena, and on the base of the statue of the Olympian Jove, viz. at
Elis, whose statue there is described by Pausanias in his Eliacs.[3] Hence '
we see the popularity of this subject with artists—we have met it before
at the Pœcilë—and may we not hence infer that we should not too
closely press it, or its cognate one of the battles of the Centaurs and
Lapithæ, as a means for determining to what hero or deity any particular building was dedicated, as has been done with the so-called
Theseium at Colonus Hippios? The Centaurs and Lapithæ were also
depicted in the Theseium ; Theseus had killed the Centaur opposed
to him ; but among the rest, the combat was still equal. Those who
hold the commonly-received opinion about the Theseium being the still
extant temple, contend that Pausanias is here referring to the bas-
reliefs upon it, and that these were coloured.[4] But the words used by

---

[1] σηκός · (ἄλλοτε) τὸ ἡρῷον τῶν σωμάτων.
—Lex. Rh. MS. ap. Ruhn. ad Tim. Lex.
Plat. in voc.

[2] Plut. Thes. c. 36.

[3] lib. v. 11, 2.

[4] See Dodwell's Travels, i. 2, 191, &c.

Pausanias, γραφή, γέγραπται, as well as his whole description, too plainly refer to pictures to admit such a view.

The picture on the third wall, continues Pausanias, is not very clear to those unacquainted with the legend; partly because some of it is effaced through the effects of time, and partly because Micon, who painted it, has not represented the whole story. Minos, when he caused Theseus and his band of youths and maidens to come to Crete, became enamoured of Periboea, and when Theseus opposed his desires, loaded him with abuse, telling him, among other things, that he was no son of Poseidon; then, flinging his ring into the sea, affirmed that Theseus would not be able to recover it. But Theseus dived and came up not only with the ring, but also with a golden diadem, the gift of Amphitritë. It was this part of his adventure, apparently, that was but imperfectly represented. In the last three sections of this chapter, Pausanias states various opinions about the death of Theseus, of which we have treated elsewhere. And he confirms the account of Plutarch, that his bones were brought from Scyros by Cimon after the battle of Marathon.

The Theseium was regarded with so much veneration that Plutarch places it in that respect on a level with the Parthenon and the Eleu-sinium.[1] And yet when some Lacedæmonians were marching against the Bœotians, and crossing the Isthmus, a body of armed citizens appears to have slept in it.[2] And on this occasion Thucydides is careful to say that it was the Theseium in the city (ἐν Θησείῳ τῷ ἐν πόλει), for there was another one, but of course not so sacred, within the Long Walls. In the Theseium, certain of the magistrates were elected by lot by the Thesmothetæ.[3] It appears also to have been a court of justice and a prison.[4] According to Demosthenes, Tromes, the father of Æschines, was slave to one Elpias, who kept a low school near the Theseium.[5]

Pausanias next arrives at the temple of the Dioscuri or Castor and

[1] De Exsil. p. 395, Reiske.

[2] Thucyd. vi. 61.

[3] Æschin. c. Ctesiph. p. 399, Reiske.

[4] Phot., Hesych. in voc.; Et. M. in Θη-σειότριψ.

[5] De Cor. p. 270, Reiske.

Polydeuces (c. 18, 1). This was also called the ANACEIUM and Anactoron; for Menestheus, son of Theseus, gave the Dioscuri the title of ἄνακες (=ἄνακτες), for having restored him to his kingdom.[1] The site of the Anaceium under the northern side of the Acropolis, and about its centre, is well ascertained, since it is known to have lain under the grotto of Aglaurus, which was just under, but a little westward, of the Erechtheium. Pausanias, therefore, has now returned to the line of road which he was pursuing when he quitted the Eleusinium and temple of Eucleia, in order to go back to the Stoa Basileios. The Anaceium must have been an ancient foundation. It was here that, by a stratagem, Peisistratus disarmed the Athenians, as we have already related. We may infer from this story, that the temple and its temenos must have occupied a considerable space. The strength and size of it are also shown by the fact of Theramenes and his hoplitæ having taken possession of it in the twenty-first year of the Peloponnesian war, during the revolution which ended in the deposition of the Four Hundred.[2]

In the Anaceium were statues of the Dioscuri on foot, and of their sons, Anaxis and Mnasinus, on horseback. Polygnotus and Micon, who seem often to have worked together, were fellow-painters at this building, as at the Pœcilë. Polygnotus painted the marriage of the sons of the Dioscuri with Hilæira and Phœbë, daughters of Leucippus; while Micon painted the crew that sailed with Jason to Colchis. The part of the picture most carefully executed was Acastus and his horses.

Above the Anaceium lay the TEMENOS OF AGLAURUS.[3] The proximity of the two sanctuaries is shown by the anecdote about Peisistratus; and the communication between them still exists. At the back of the grotto consecrated to Aglaurus—which is one of those natural ones of which there are several on the sides of the Acropolis—there is a

---

[1] Harpocr. in voc.; Ælian, V. H. iv. 5; Plut. Thes. 33.

[2] Thucyd. viii. 93.

[3] ὑπὲρ δὲ τῶν Διοσκούρων τὸ ἱερὸν Ἀγλαύρου τέμενός ἐστιν.—Paus. i. 18, 2. Here

is another unmistakeable example of ὑπὲρ with an acc. denoting above; for there can be no doubt that the temenos of Aglaurus was on the cliff.

fissure in the rock, forming a winding passage which seems to close. But further onwards the light is seen descending through an oblique shaft or well, with rugged sides, and to all appearance inaccessible. On the summit of the Acropolis, west of the Erechtheium, and about 12 feet below the surface of the ground, is found a descent to this opening; to which a modern staircase conducts, cut in the thickness of the wall of the Acropolis. Here the fissure begins, consisting at first of a perpendicular shaft about 22 feet to 26 feet deep, without a stair, and therefore requiring a ladder; but the steps recommence at the bottom. Thus it could have been used only in extraordinary circumstances; and M. Beulé, who explored it, thinks that the guards of Peisistratus must have hauled up the arms with a rope.[1] Herr Bötticher, however, is of opinion, that originally there were at this part steps cut in the rock, but that they have been carefully destroyed.[2] It was through the same aperture, apparently, that the Persians made their way into the Acropolis.[3]

It was in the temple of Aglaurus, which seems to have been the grotto with a temenos before it, that the Athenian ephebi took an oath to die in defence of their country, never to desert their comrades, and to defend all the cultivated parts of Attica.[4] The gods invoked to witness this oath (ἵστορες θεοί) were Aglaurus, Enyalius, Ares, Zeus, Thallo, Auxo, and Hegemonë.[5] It was here that Aglaurus and her sister Hersë were supposed to have precipitated themselves from the Acropolis. Dr. Wordsworth ('Athens,' p. 34), adopting that version of the myth which represents Aglaurus as precipitating herself from the rock in order to deliver her country from a war, which patriotic deed occasioned the military oath to be taken at her shrine, adds that the ascent of the Persians here may have contributed to its selection for that purpose.

[1] Beulé, L'Acropole, t. i. p. 157; cf. Rangabé, Ant. Hell. ii. 739.

[2] Bericht, p. 221.

[3] ἀνέβησάν τινες κατὰ τὸ ἱρὸν τῆς Κέκροπος θυγατρὸς Ἀγλαύρου, καίτοι περ ἀποκρήμνου

ἐόντος τοῦ χώρου.—Herod. viii. 53.

[4] Demosth. de fals. leg. p. 438, Reiske: Philostr. V. Apoll. iv. 7; Plut. Alc. 15.

[5] Pollux, viii. s. 106.

Pausanias next comes to the PRYTANEIUM (c. 18, 4), which lay near the Agrauleium, and must therefore have been situated between that temple and the eastern extremity of the Acropolis. He says that the laws of Solon were preserved in it; that there were statues of Peace and Hestia, and several statues of men, among whom he names Autolycus the Pancratinst, Miltiades, and Themistocles; but the two latter had been reinscribed to a Roman and a Thracian. Among those which he leaves unnamed was a statue of Demochares, nephew of Demosthenes, which stood at the entrance, on the right hand of the statue of Hestia. It was clothed and girt with a sword, in which habit he is said to have addressed the people when Antipater demanded the orators.[1] Near the Prytaneium stood a statue of Good Fortune, of such exceeding beauty that a young Athenian is said to have become enamoured of it.[2] Plutarch had seen the laws of Solon here, or at least a few remains of them. They were written on square blocks of wood called ἄξονες, because, being enclosed in wooden cases of greater length than breadth, they could be turned round. They had been originally placed in the Acropolis, but were brought down here in order that they might be open to the inspection of all.[3]

A Prytaneium was by no means peculiar to Athens, but was common to most or all Grecian cities. Aristeides, indeed, asserts that Athens was the only city, or at all events one of the few, which preserved a fixed and immovable Hestia in its Prytaneium;[4] and Plutarch[5] mentions only two—Delphi and Athens—that enjoyed the privilege, but not in a way to exclude others. Casaubon, however, has shown[6] that there were Prytaneia at Syracuse, Tarentum, Corinth, Elis, Megara, Rhodes, Miletus, Tenedos, Argos, Mitylene, Ephesus, &c. Rome also, a city of Greek origin, had its public hearth and eternal fire. Every

---

[1] Vit. X. Orat. in Demosth. ix. 369, Reiske.

[2] Ælian, V. H. ix. 39. See also the Epistles ascribed to Demosthenes, Ep. 4.

[3] Plut. Sol. 25; Pollux, viii. s. 128; Harpocr. in voc.

[4] καὶ μόνη πόλεων, ἢ κομιδῆ γε ἐν ὀλίγαις, Ἑστίαν ἀκίνητον Πρυτανείου δικαίως νέμει. —Orat. Panath. t. i. p. 103, Jebb.

[5] In Numa, 9.

[6] See his note on Athen. xv. 60.

Prytaneium had its Hestia, who was the guardian of cities, as Rhea, her mother, was supposed to be their founder. Hence Pindar:

Παῖ 'Ρέας, ἅτε Πρυτανεῖα λέλογχας, 'Εστία.

Nem. xi. 1.

where the scholiast remarks, that the public hearths with the sacred fire burning upon them were erected in the Prytaneia. This perpetual fire appears, however, to have been only a lamp, whence the proverb τὸ λύχνιον ἐν πρυτανείῳ, of anything that never failed.[1] We shall see further on that there was also a lamp continually burning in the temple of Athena at the Erechtheium; for in the earlier days of Athens, when the Acropolis comprised the city, Athena seems to have supplied the place of Hestia as guardian of it. The Prytaneium was first founded when Athens became the metropolis of Attica, according to tradition under Theseus, as we are told by Thucydides;[2] and Plutarch adds that this general Prytaneium was built in the place which it continued to occupy in his time; on which occasion Theseus gave the name of Athens both to the asty and the polis—that is, the Acropolis and the town which had sprung up around it.[3]

Curtius maintains that the Prytaneium described by Pausanias was built by the Romans and belonged to the new agora; that the Prytaneium of the Thesean city lay on the south side of the Acropolis, in an ancient market there, but that the business transacted in it was afterwards transferred to the Tholus, near the Bouleuterium, on the north side of the Acropolis, which we have before described.[4] But, as we have seen, there is little authority for the market assumed by Curtius, and still less for a Prytaneium there, which is a mere conjecture; and its transference to the Tholus at the Bouleuterium is directly contrary to the evidence of Plutarch, quoted above, that it always stood in the same place. It is not likely that the Romans, who respected the national and superstitious feelings of the Athenians, should have done

---

[1] Casaubon, loc. cit.

[2] lib. ii. c. 15.

[3] ἐν δὲ ποιήσας ἅπασι κοινὸν ἐνταῦθα πρυτανεῖον καὶ βουλευτήριον, ὅπου νῦν

ἵδρυται, τὸ ἄστυ τήν τε πόλιν 'Αθήνας προσηγόρευσε.—Plut. Thes. 24.

[4] See Att. Stud. ii. 62 sqq.

violence to them by removing so sacred and ancient a foundation, and
the antiquities in it which Pausanias saw, such as the image of Hestia,
the laws of Solon, &c. And it is hardly possible that, if there had been
such a change, Pausanias should have passed it over unnoticed, especially
when he remarks that the statues of Miltiades and Themistocles in it
had been re-inscribed to a Roman and a Thracian. In early times the
Prytaneium was also the Bouleuterium, or council house for the tribes;
but when the Senate of Four Hundred was instituted, a new senate
house would have been required, and this was the Bouleuterium near
the Areiopagus, already described. At the same time was probably
built the adjoining Tholus for the accommodation of the Prytanes,
whose duties were intimately connected with the deliberations of the
senate. Hence the Tholus appears also to have been called Prytaneium,
but perhaps only by a confusion in the later writers.[1] For the same
reason the scribes, or clerks, of the senate seem to have lived in the
Tholus.[2] It is evident, from Pausanias' slight notice of it, that the
Tholus was a much inferior building to the Prytaneium. At the Tholus
he mentions only a few little silver images; whilst at the Prytaneium
he finds two statues of divinities, besides several statues of men. And
this agrees with what we hear about them. For the scholiast on Thucydides says that the Prytaneium founded by Theseus was a large building ($οἶκος$ $μέγας$, ii. 15); whilst the scholiast on the 'Knights' of
Aristophanes (loc. cit.), evidently mistaking the Tholus for it, calls it
a small one ($οἰκίσκος$), a mistake which has been animadverted on by
Meursius.[3]

Those who had deserved well of their country were entitled to
partake of the public dinner given daily in the Prytaneium, and in
some cases the privilege was extended to their posterity. The first who
enjoyed it appear to have been the descendants of Harmodius and
Aristogeiton.[4] Among others entitled to it we also hear of Hippocrates

---

[1] Harpocr., Phot., Tim. Lex. Plat. in
voc.; schol. ad Aristoph. Eq. 167.
[2] Demosth. De fals. leg. p. 419.
[3] Athen. Att. i. 8.

[4] Deinarch. c. Demosth. p. 69, Reiske;
cf. p. 33, and Isaeus, de Dicæog. hered.
p. 118, Reiske; Lycurg. c. Leocr. p. 196,
Reiske.

the physician, and his posterity.[1] Socrates affirmed that he deserved it, an assertion which appears to have been a cause of his condemnation.[2] The fare, however, as regulated by a law of Solon, seems not to have been very luxurious, being barley bread for ordinary days, and wheaten bread on festivals. On the festival of the Dioscuri, however, there was cheese, physta (a kind of barley cake), ripe olives, and leeks.[3] Probably, however, the fare grew better as the manners of the Athenians became less simple, for we find that the Prytaneium was entitled to the tenth part of the entrails of all victims sacrificed. Hence in the 'Knights' of Aristophanes, Cleon threatens the sausage-maker that he will denounce him to the Prytanes for having in his possession the sacred entrails untithed :

> καί σε φαίνω τοῖς πρυτάνεσιν,
> ἀδεκατεύτους τῶν θεῶν ἱ-
> ρὰς ἔχοντα κοιλίας.—v. 301, et ibi schol.

> " I'll peach about you to the Prytanes
> And show you've got the holy guts untithed."

A passage whence we may infer that the priests converted these perquisites into ready money. The Prytanes and higher magistrates appear also to have been entitled to sleep at the Prytaneium. Thus Cnemon relates of his father Aristippus, an Areiopagite (τῆς ἄνω βουλῆς), that after a feast and public potation he was going to pass the night there.[4] A passage, by the way, which shows that there must have been good drinking as well as good eating. Cimon, father of Miltiades, was probably proceeding to it when he was murdered near it in the night time by assassins hired by the sons of Peisistratus, out of envy at his having thrice carried off the Olympic prize with his quadriga.[5] By the Theseium was a place called HORCOMOSIUM, where Theseus was reputed to have ratified the treaty with the Amazons.[6]

[1] Soranus, Vit. Hipp. ap. Meurs. Ath. Att. i, 8.

[2] Diog. Laërt. ii. 42 ; Cic. de Orat. i. 54.

[3] Athen. iv. 14.

[4] Heliod. lib. i. ap. Meurs. Ath. Att. i. 8.

[5] Herod. vi. 103.

[6] Plut. Thes. 27.

At the Prytaneium was held one of the four courts for trying cases of homicide ; the others being the Areiopagus, which was the principal one, the Palladium, and the Delphinium.[1] Here, too, foreign ambassadors appear to have been received :

> τὸν βασιλέως ὀφθαλμὸν ἡ βουλὴ καλεῖ
> εἰς τὸ πρυτανεῖον.—Aristoph. *Acharn.* 124.

> " The senate summons to the Prytany
> The great king's Eye."

Because, apparently, as the scholiast adds, the Athenian ambassadors who had been sent to Persia were there.

Behind the Prytaneium, and towards the Acropolis, appears to have been a place called the FIELD OF HUNGER (λίμου πεδίον), of which, however, nothing more than the name seems to be known.[2] We also hear of a place called Boucoleium (βουκόλειον), near the Prytaneium, where the archon basileus had his tribunal before Solon forbad the archons to sit in judgment together. At the same early period the archon polemarch took his seat at the Lyceium, the archon eponymus at the statues of the Eponymi, and the six thesmothetæ at a place called Thesmotheseium.[3] But we are not aware that the Boucoleium and Thesmotheseium are mentioned by any other writer, and their sites cannot be determined.

---

[1] τέταρτον τοίνυν ἄλλο πρὸς τούτοις δικαστήριον.—Demosth. c. Aristocr. p. 645, Reiske; Plut. Solon, 19.

[2] Hesych. in voc.

[3] Suidas in Ἄρχων.

•

CHAPTER IX.

A LITTLE to the eastward of the Prytaneium the road divided into two
branches, one of which proceeded almost straightforwards to the Olympium and what Pausanias calls the lower parts of the city (τὰ κάτω τῆς
πόλεως), while the other turned to the south round and under the
eastern foot of the Acropolis towards the Lenæum and Dionysiac
theatre. Pausanias now takes the former of these roads, and after
traversing these lower parts in the region about and beyond the Ilissus,
returns again to the Prytaneium and proceeds to describe the objects
on the latter route. Each of these may therefore be considered as
forming a separate tour or journey.

The first object met with after quitting the Prytaneium was the
TEMPLE OF SARAPIS, which must, therefore, have lain near the eastern
foot of the Acropolis (xviii. 4). The worship of Sarapis was introduced
by Ptolemy. The Athenians readily admitted foreign deities. Their
native gods, public and private, were called πάτριοι and πατρῷοι; the
foreign ones, θεοὶ ξενικοί. Such were Genetyllis, Corythalia, Hyes, &c.[1]
But especially they had admitted a vast multitude of Egyptian gods;
so that Aristophanes, long before the time of Ptolemy, complained that

---

[1] Hesych. voc. ξενικός with note of Hemsterhuis.

Athens had been converted into Egypt.[1] To admit such gods a decree of the people was necessary. Strange that so lax a theology should have been combined with a high degree of intolerance, and that such a people should have entertained a deadly enmity against freethinkers, astronomers, and philosophers, like Anaxagoras or Socrates.[2]

In the time of Stuart three Ionic columns supporting an architrave were to be seen at an oil mill about midway between the monument of Lysicrates and the arch of Hadrian, consequently on the line of road which Pausanias is now pursuing; and Leake is of opinion[3] that they may possibly have belonged to the Sarapeium. But it seems to us that they would have been too far to the east to have belonged to that temple, which must have been nearer the foot of the Acropolis; and that if they formed part of any temple mentioned by Pausanias, it would rather have been that of Ileithyia. Though the images within were ancient, the building itself might have been more modern, and a *rifaccimento*.

Not far from the Sarapeium was a place (χωρίον) where Theseus and Peirithoüs were said to have agreed on their expeditions, first to Lacedæmon, and afterwards to Thesprotia. We read in the 'Œdipus at Colonus' of Sophocles:

> ἔστη κελεύθων ἐν πολυσχίστων μιᾷ,
> κοίλου πέλας κρατῆρος, οὗ τὰ Θησέως
> Περίθου τε κεῖται πίστ' ἀεὶ συνθήματα.—v. 1591.

> "He stood in one of many branching roads
> Near to a hollow basin, which recalls
> The plighted faith of Theseus and his friend."

Meursius[4] refers these lines to the place here mentioned by Pausanias; while Leake observes[5] that Sophocles seems to fix the meeting near the Colonus Hippios. The death of Œdipus took place at Colonus, and

---

[1] Αἴγυπτον αὐτῶν τὴν πόλιν πεποίηκας ἀντ' Ἀθηνῶν.—Frag. of the Horæ, ap. Athen. ix. 14. In the 'Birds' also the barbarous gods admitted by democracy are alluded to, v. 1520.

[2] See the decree of Diopeithes against Anaxagoras, Plut. Pericl. 32.

[3] vol. i. p. 272.

[4] Ath. Att. i. 9.

[5] vol. i. p. 129, note 2.

not at Athens. Theseus and Peirithoüs also made an agreement at
Colonus, but for a very different purpose from that mentioned by Pausanias, namely, their descent into Hades ; and Meursius and Leake have
confounded those treaties. At Colonus were some ancient copper mines,
the gaping orifice or threshold of which (χαλκόπους ὁδός, Œd. Col. v.
57) was supposed to form an entrance into Hades, through which,
according to some accounts, Persephonë was carried off, and which was
also used by Theseus and Peirithoüs for their descent ; and here, also,
was some memorial of the agreement they had made on that occasion.[1]

Near this place, continues Pausanias, is a TEMPLE OF EILEITHYIA
(Lucina). Plato remarks that there was every day a posse of women
about it.[2] But let us observe that there seems to have been another
temple of Eileithyia at the place called Agræ on the further side of the
Ilissus, which Pausanias describes further on, without, however, mentioning such a temple there.[3] He proceeds to relate some anecdotes of
Eileithyia. She came from the Hyperboreans to Delos to assist at the
accouchement of Leto, and the Delians sing to her the hymn of Olen
('Ωλῆνος).[4] But the Cretans also claimed her, as born at Amnisus, and
said that she was the daughter of Hera. The Athenians had three
wooden images of her (ξόανα), and they were the only people who
clothed her to the feet. Two of these images, the women said, were
Cretan, and dedicated by Phædra, whilst the third and most ancient
one was brought by Erysichthon from Delos.

Pausanias next comes to the Olympium, or temple of the Olympian
Zeus. But he leaves altogether unnoticed the ARCH OF HADRIAN, which
must have been a conspicuous object in approaching the temple. It is

---

[1] Thus the scholiast on v. 1593 : ξυν-
θήματα, οἷον ὑπομνήματα τῆς πίστεως ἧς
ἔθεντο πρὸς ἀλλήλους πρὸ τῆς εἰς "Αιδου
καταβάσεως. The existence of the copper
mines is testified by the scholiast on v. 57.

[2] γυναῖκες ... πρὸς τὸ τῆς Εἰλειθυίας ἱερὸν
ἑκάστης ἡμέρας ξυλλεγόμεναι.—De Leg. vi.
p. 784 A (iii. ii. 474, Bekk.).

[3] The authority for this is the Anecdota
Græca of Bekker, p. 326, where, in an

article on Agræ, we read : τὰ μὲν οὖν ἄνω
τὰ τοῦ Ἰλισσοῦ πρὸς 'Αγορὰν Εἰληθυῖα. It
is evident from the whole context that we
should here read "Αγραν for 'Αγοράν. The
place was called indifferently Agra and
Agræ. There is a similar error in Plutarch's
Demetrius, c. 26 : ἐτέλουν τῷ Δημητρίῳ τὰ
πρὸς ἀγοράν, where Salmasius and others
have corrected "Αγραν.

[4] Cf. Pausan. viii. 21, 2 ; ix. 27, 2.

possible, however, that this arch, which is still pretty perfect, may have been erected subsequently to Pausanias' visit. It does not form an entrance to the peribolus of the temple, nor indeed to any enclosure, as it seems to be quite unconnected with any wall. The design of it appears to have been to mark, by a sort of triumphal arch, the boundary between ancient Athens, or the city of Theseus, and that quarter which obtained the name of Hadrianopolis, from the munificence of Hadrian in adorning it. That a part of Athens bore that name we know from the life of Hadrian by Spartianus;[1] and that it must have been the quarter which lay to the eastward of this gate we learn from the inscriptions on the gate itself. For on the frieze of the architrave on the north-western front is written: αἵδ' εἰσ' Ἀθῆναι Θησέως ἡ πρὶν πόλις; and on the south-eastern front, αἵδ' εἰσ' Ἀδριανοῦ καὶ οὐχὶ Θησέως πόλις.[2] The arch, therefore, probably marked the boundary of the ancient city of Theseus, as handed down by tradition or still recognisable at the period of its erection by some ancient remains; thus serving a similar purpose to that of the pillars which stood at the Isthmus on the confines of Peloponnesus and Ionia, with the following inscriptions : τόδ' ἐστὶ Πελοπόννησος οὐκ Ἰωνία, and τάδ' οὐχὶ Πελοπόννησος, ἀλλ' Ἰωνία.[3] Gell conjectures that it may possibly have been built on the spot where there once stood in the ancient enclosure a gate called the gate of Ægeus.[4] The arch stands in an oblique position as regards the plan of the temple, which lies due east and west, whilst the arch faces south-east and north-west. Leake, who erroneously thought that it formed an entrance to the peribolus, considered that this obliquity was purposely adopted in order to afford a better view of the temple;[5] but the true entrance of the peribolus has been recently discovered at a distance of nineteen or twenty yards from

---

[1] " Multas civitates Adrianopolis appellavit, ut ipsam Carthaginem, et Athenarum partem."—Spart. Adrian. c. 20.

[2] These inscriptions have been frequently published, and will be found in Wheler (but imperfect), in Stuart, and in Boeckh,

Corp. Inscr. No. 520 ; and, in their present condition, in the Ἀρχαιολογικὴ Ἐφημερίς for February, 1862, p. 34.

[3] Strab. ix. p. 392 ; Plut. Thes. 25.

[4] Itinerary, p. 40.

[5] vol. i. p. 516.

the gate. The oblique position of the arch was no doubt occasioned by the circumstance that, with such bearings, it would have spanned a street running in a south-easterly direction from the Prytaneium to the Olympium.

The archway of this gate, about twenty feet wide, is situated between square piers, each about fifteen feet broad, making in all a breadth of about fifty feet, with a height of about thirty-four feet to the top of the cornice. Before each pier stood two Corinthian columns on lofty bases; at each end are composite pilasters, and the arch springs from two shorter pilasters of the same order. Above is an attic about twenty feet in height, consisting of four Corinthian columns, with a pediment over the two middle ones. Both sides of the arch are similar. A full description of it, with a view and plans, will be found in Stuart's 'Antiquities of Athens.'[1] The lowness of the arch, in comparison with its width, gives the structure a mean and heavy appearance; and it must have contrasted very unfavourably with the magnificent temple to which it led, when the temple was in a perfect state.

Pausanias now arrives at the OLYMPIUM;[2] but though this was one of the most magnificent temples in the world, his description of it is very meagre and unsatisfactory. We will first of all say a few more words about its history.

That there was at this spot a very ancient temple of Zeus, which tradition carried up to the fabulous times of Deucalion, formed a part of the Athenian creed; and in proof of Deucalion's residence at Athens, they appealed to his tomb, which lay not far from the temple.[3] But as we have already observed, the Pisistratids were the founders of the magnificent temple by which it was superseded, the architects being

---

[1] vol. iii. ch. 3.

[2] The name is found written in five different ways, viz.: 'Ολύμπιον, 'Ολύμπειον, 'Ολυμπεῖον, 'Ολυμπίειον, and 'Ολυμπιεῖον; but the forms 'Ολυμπίειον and 'Ολύμπιον seem to be the only genuine ones. The former is the old Attic form, and is used by Thucydides, vi. 64, &c.; whilst later writers have the form 'Ολύμπιον. — See Aristot. Polit. v. 11, p. 407 E; Plut. Phædr. init.; Strabo, ix. 396 and 404, &c. &c. Pausanias appears to have used both forms. See Wesseling ad Diod. Sic. xiii. 6, p. 546, 52; Lobeck ad Phryn. p. 371.

[3] Pausan. i. 18, 8.

Antistates, Callaeschrus, Antimachides, and Porinus.[1] They left it, however, very imperfect, and so it continued for many centuries amid all the glories of the Acropolis, which had sprung up in its neighbourhood. Hence Plutarch observes that as among many fine works Plato had left only his 'Atlantis' incomplete, so Athens was in a like predicament with regard to this temple.[2] We have already adverted to some additions by Antiochus, perhaps also by Augustus,[3] and to its final completion by Hadrian, about seven centuries after its foundation by Peisistratus, viz. in the third year of the 227th Olympiad, or A.D. 130. In honour

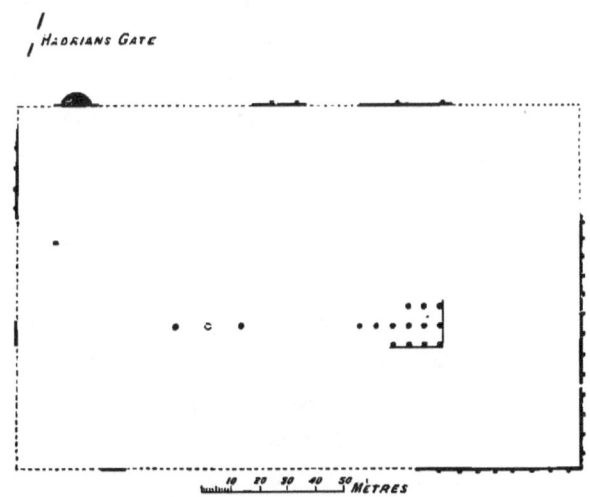

PLAN OF PERIBOLUS OF OLYMPIUM.

of this χρόνου μέγα ἀγώνισμα, or in Bacon's phraseology, great birth of time, Polemo was ordered to deliver an appropriate discourse, or hymn of praise, which he did ex tempore, during the usual sacrifice.[4]

Pausanias says that the peribolus of the temple is about four stades in circumference. The northern wall, the only doubtful boundary, was traced by excavations made in the summer of 1861, when the dimensions

---

[1] Aristot. Polit. v. 11; Vitruv. vii. Praef. s. 15; Strabo, ix. p. 396. But it seems uncertain whether in the last passage the word βασιλεὺς is to be referred, with Meursius, to Peisistratus; for Casaubon, ad loc. refers it to Perseus.

[2] Vit. Solon. c. 32.

[3] See above, p. 158 and 170.

[4] Dio Cass. lxix. 16; Spart. Hadr. 13; Philostr. Vit. Soph. i. 25, 3.

T

of the enclosure were found to be 204 Fr. mètres (223 yards) in length from east to west and 130 (142 yards) in breadth, from north to south, giving a circumference of 668 mètres (730 yards) or 3¾ Olympic stades.[1] The wall or substruction of the peribolus at the south-east angle and part of the eastern and southern sides, rises more than 20 feet above the level of the surrounding soil, and the boundary wall on the western side can also be easily traced. The discovery of the northern wall showed that the temple was built exactly in the centre of the peribolus. On the north wall, 20 yards from its western angle, a circular building was discovered about 12 yards in diameter, built of the same materials, and therefore of the same age as the peribolus itself. This formed the entrance into the peribolus, and afforded a view of the temple from the north-west, embracing its western front and northern side, just in the same manner as the Parthenon was beheld on entering by the Propylæa; though in both cases the principal front was on the east, and therefore at first unseen.[2] Leake conjectured[3] that the Arch of Hadrian had been placed in the position which it occupies for the purpose of affording this angular view of the temple, which no doubt it would have done; but it is not the real entrance, and stands some 20 yards to the north-west of it. "The walls of the peribolus," says Gell, "are built of stones which have been taken from other more ancient edifices, and remains of *very ancient* inscriptions in large characters may be discovered on them."[4]

The whole length of this magnificent temple was 359 feet, and its breadth 173. Thus, with the exception of the temple of Artemis at Ephesus, which according to Pliny was 425 feet long by 225 broad,[5] the Athenian temple of Zeus was the largest on record of the dipteral construction. The temple of the Didymæan Apollo at Branchidæ, near Miletus, was only 304 feet by 165 feet; but its Ionic columns were almost as numerous, and a trifle larger, than the Corinthian ones of the

[1] Rousopoulos in the Athenian 'Εφημερίς for February, 1862, p. 28.

[2] Gerhard, Arch. Anzeiger, March, 1862, p. 295 sq.

[3] vol. i. p. 516.

[4] Itinerary, p. 43.

[5] H. N. xxxvi. 95.

Olympium. The cella of the temple of Zeus at Agrigentum was only a little smaller than the whole of the Athenian temple; but it was not peripteral, the columns being *engaged*, or encased in the wall; and it was partially ruined by the Carthaginians before it had been completed.[1]

The Olympium at Athens was dipteros decastylos; that is, had a triple range of ten columns at each front, and a double range of twenty at the sides, making 116 in all; the side columns at each end were parallel with those of the fronts, and thus twenty-four in number, being

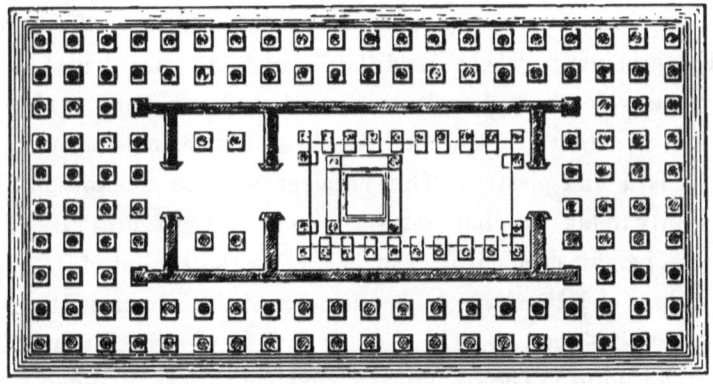

PLAN OF TEMPLE OF ZEUS OLYMPIUS.

counted twice over. Besides these, there were four columns between the antæ at each front, making the total number 124.[2] Fifteen columns, all on the south side, are all that now remain of this magnificent structure. Of these, thirteen in one group formed the south-east angle; four belonging to the outer line on the south side; six to the inner or second line; and three to the façade before the east front of the cella.

---

[1] Diodor. Sic. xiii. 82, who gives the dimensions as follows : ἔστι δὲ ὁ νεὼς ἔχων τὸ μὲν μῆκος πόδας τριακοσίους τεσσαρά-κοντα, τὸ δὲ πλάτος ἑξήκοντα, τὸ δὲ ὕψος ἑκατὸν εἴκοσι, χωρὶς τοῦ κρηπιδώματος. Here the breadth and height are evidently interchanged. Diodorus must mean 120 feet broad and 60 high. Modern measure-ments give the length 344 feet, breadth 172, height of columns 52. Baedeker's

Italy, iii. p. 239.

[2] Leake (i. 515) says 120. He allows indeed only 3 columns between the antæ; but still on his own showing there must have been 122. For a treble row of 10 columns at each front will give 60; and a double row of 20 on each side 80; from which, however, 24 columns counted twice must be deducted, leaving 56; and $60 + 56 + 6$ (between antæ) $= 122$.

The other two, which stand at a considerable distance and towards the western end of the temple, belong to the second or inner row, and are of course on a line with the six before mentioned. In the annexed plan, these fifteen columns are shaded black. In the time of Stuart two more were extant; one between the two now standing on the south-western side and one on the western front, the fourth from the north. This last was removed about a century ago by the Turkish governor of Athens, for the use of a mosque which he was building at the Bazaar;[1] the middle one of the three was thrown down in 1852 by an earthquake which overthrew at the same time the columns of the western wall of the Erechtheium.[2] There it still lies with its vast drums of solid Pentelic marble shuffled under one another like so many cards spread to choose a partner; a sight well fitted to excite astonishment in these days of lath and plaster. This accident afforded M. Rousopoulos an opportunity to take its dimensions accurately. It measures 27·25 French mètres in height, or about 57 feet, including the capital of 2·02 mètres and the base of 1·16 mètres. The diameter of the column is 1·70 mètres, or very nearly 6 feet, above the base, and 1·49 mètres, or nearly 5 feet, under the capital. The column is channelled with twenty-four flutings, each the fifth of a mètre (or about 8 inches) wide in the middle of the column.[3] It is the fifth from the west front, and belongs, as we have said, to the inner row, the columns of which were rather smaller than those of the outer one; but even so it appears to be rather below the dimensions given by Stuart, Leake, and Gell. The last two writers made the diameter of the exterior columns 6 feet 6 inches, or more (Stuart's measurement is nearly 6 feet 7 inches); and the height rather more than Rousopoulos; but they appear to include the architrave.[4] Most of the columns that remain erect have preserved their epistyle. In the middle ages the architrave over two of them was chosen by a stylites, or hermit of the columns, for his aërial abode.

The statue of the god within, says Pausanias, was well worth seeing,

[1] Stuart, vol. iii. ch. 2; Chandler, 13.

[2] Beulé, L'Acropole, t. ii. p. 274.

[3] Ἀρχαιο. Ἐφημερίς, 1862, p. 31.

[4] See Stuart, vol. iii. ch. 2; Leake, vol. i. p. 515; Gell, Itinerary, p. 43.

not so much on account of its size - for the other images of the god are about as large, except the colossal ones at Rhodes and Rome—as for its materials, which are ivory and gold, and for the beauty of its workmanship, considering its magnitude. There were also four statues of Hadrian, two of Thasian, and two of Egyptian marble.[1] Before the pillars stood bronze statues of the cities that were colonies of Athens.[2] These statues were probably fixed close to the columns like that of Athena Hygieia at the Propylæa.[3] The whole peribolus indeed was full of statues; for each of the before-mentioned cities dedicated to Hadrian one of himself;[4] while the Athenians outdid them by erecting behind the temple—that is, at the west front, where it must have immediately struck anybody entering the peribolus—a colossus of him, which was well worth seeing, says Pausanias; whence we may conclude that it was really a fine work of art. Some of the statues of Antinoüs show that sculpture still flourished in the time of Hadrian. Many of the bases of these statues have been found with their dedicatory inscriptions, which have been published from time to time by various authors, and are collected by Boeckh in his 'Corpus Inscriptionum Græcarum.'[5] They seem to have stood round the sides of the enclosure. When its northern wall was discovered in 1861, while making a road, one of these bases was found with an inscription purporting that the statue had been dedicated by Laodiceia on the Sea. A dedicatory inscription, seemingly either of Ephesus or Smyrna, published by Chandler, but afterwards lost, was also rediscovered.[6]

---

[1] On these stones see Winckelmann, Op. iii. 34.

[2] χαλκαῖ δὲ ἑστᾶσι πρὸ τῶν κιόνων ἃς Ἀθηναῖοι καλοῦσιν ἀποίκους πόλεις.—Paus. i. 18, 6. Leake (p. 129 sq.), following Facius, translates : "Before the columns stand brazen statues (of Hadrian, presented by those) cities which the Athenians call colonial." But the statues of Hadrian are mentioned by Pausanias a few lines further on. The old version of Romulus Amasæus, adopted by Siebelis (ad loc.) and by

Meursius (Ath. Att. i. 10) is more correct : "ad templi vero columnas urbium, quas colonias Athenienses appellant, ex ære erecta sunt simulacra." Each of the colonial cities presented a bronze statue of itself (personified), and also a statue of Hadrian.

[3] Ross, Aufs. i. 192. See below.

[4] εἰκών—a portrait statue.

[5] Nos. 321 to 346.

[6] Gerhard's Arch. Anz. March, 1862, p. 295 sq.; Boeckh, C. Inscr. Gr. No. 335

Besides these statues, the peribolus or enclosure contained other objects of a more ancient character. Such were a bronze Zeus; a TEMPLE OF CRONOS AND RHEA; and a TEMENOS OF GË, or Gaia, called the Olympian.[1] It does not appear from the account of Pausanias, that Gaia had any temple here. What he calls a τέμενος, indeed, Plutarch and Thucydides call a ἱερόν,[2] but which there stands only for τέμενος. As the statue of the Amazon mentioned by Plutarch in the passage just referred to, stood near to the Itonian Gate as well as to this sanctuary of Gaia, we must conclude that the latter was at the south-west extremity of the peribolus, or rather, perhaps, that the enclosure called Olympium, extended in this direction beyond the artificial quadrangular terrace on which the temple stood. Gaia, with the title of Olympia, was considered to be the mother of the gods and enthroned in heaven. In her temenos was a chasm in the earth about a cubit wide, through which the waters of Deucalion's flood were said to have escaped. Every year, wheaten cakes mixed with honey were thrown into it, apparently on the first of the month Anthesterion.[3]

We have seen that Cronos had a temple at the Olympium; and according to a passage in Bekker's 'Anecdota Græca,' he had also a temenos which reached as far as the Metroum at Agræ.[4] This is rather perplexing, as the city wall and the Ilissus must have intervened, as

[1] The text has (c. 18, 7) καὶ τέμενος τὴν ἐπίκλησιν 'Ολυμπίας, which is evidently corrupt, there being no deity called Olympia. Again, the article τὴν is not wanted before ἐπίκλησιν, and Letronne has shown that Pausanias never uses it. See i. 19, 1; 26, 4; 38, 5; 40, 2; ii. 2, 4; 10, 11, and many other places. Wherefore for τὴν we should read Γῆς—καὶ τέμενος Γῆς ἐπίκλησιν 'Ολυμπίας. Leake (i. p. 131, note 1) would read τέμενος τῆς Γῆς ἐπίκλησιν 'Ολυμπίας. But the article is not necessary before Γῆς, and Pausanias generally omits it. See i. 22, 3; 31, 4; iii. 11, 9; 12, 8, &c.

[2] τὸ τῆς Γῆς τῆς 'Ολυμπίας ἱερόν.—Plut. Thes. 27. τὸ τῆς Γῆς (ἱερόν).—Thuc. ii. 15. But ἱερὸν does not necessarily mean a temple, and is sometimes expressly distinguished from it, as in the following passage: τάφρον μὲν κύκλῳ περὶ τὸ ἱερὸν καὶ τὸν νεὼν ἔσκαπτον.—Thucyd. iv. 90. Where ἱερὸν must mean the enclosure in which the temple stood.

[3] Pausan. i. 18, 7; Plut. Sull. 14.

[4] Κρόνιον τέμενος · τὸ παρὰ τὸ νῦν 'Ολύμπιον μεχρὶ τοῦ Μητρῴου τοῦ ἐν ἀγορᾷ.—p. 273, 20. It is evident that we have here an error that we have before noted of ἀγορᾷ for Ἄγρᾳ (supra, p. 270, note [3]). There was indeed a Metroum in the agora, as we have seen; but it would be quite preposterous to think that a temenos could have reached thither from the Olympium.

TEMPLE OF ZEUS OLYMPIUS AND ACROPOLIS.

well as the sanctuaries of other gods. And even allowing that Agræ extended on both sides of the Stadium, yet the distance would have been very considerable for a temenos.

In the Olympian peribolus was also a statue of Isocrates, erected on a pillar. Pausanias takes this occasion to relate (c. 18, 8) three anecdotes illustrating his indomitable perseverance, his excessive modesty, and his greatness of soul; first, that though he lived to be ninety-eight years old he never gave over teaching; second, that he abstained from politics and took no part in public life; third, that he committed suicide from grief at the news of the battle of Chæroneia. The statue was erected to him by his adopted son Aphareus, and according to the inscription on it, dedicated to Zeus;[1] which indeed would have been necessary for its admission into the enclosure. There was also an elegant group in Phrygian marble, of Persians supporting a bronze tripod; both the men and tripod were deserving of close inspection. The tomb of Deucalion was shown at no great distance from the present temple. The Parian marble also records that Deucalion sought refuge from the flood at Athens in the reign of Cranaos, and founded the original temple.

In the last section of his 18th chapter, Pausanias enumerates the other buildings erected by Hadrian for the Athenians; but as he neither mentions them in their topographical order, nor indicates the place where they stood, it is difficult to fix their sites. The Corinthian façade near the Bazaar appears, as we have already said (supra, p. 253 sq.), to have belonged to the Pantheon; including under this name all the separate buildings that Pausanias here mentions, except the Gymnasium; to the site of which we have no clue.

On leaving the Olympium, Pausanias proceeds in an easterly direction. Close to it he finds an image of the Pythian Apollo; and another ἱερόν, or temple, with a temenos of the Delphinian Apollo (c. 19, 1). Hence though with regard to the Pythium he only mentions the image; yet as he uses the words ἄλλο ἱερὸν of the Delphinium, we must conclude that they were both sanctuaries of much the same

---

[1] Vit. X. Orat. Isocr. (Plut. Op. ix. p. 337, Reiske).

kind. This is all he tells us about them; and we must therefore endeavour to supplement his account from other sources.

The first of these sanctuaries was called the PYTHIUM, as we learn from Strabo.[1] According to Hesychius and other lexicographers, the temple in it was erected by Peisistratus.[2] By Peisistratus, however, they mean not the tyrant but his grandson, the son of Hippias; as appears from Thucydides, who says that Peisistratus set up the altar in the Pythium in his archonship, and that the inscription on it was legible in his time to the following effect:

$$\mu\nu\tilde{\eta}\mu\alpha \ \tau\acute{o}\delta' \ \tilde{\eta}s \ \dot{\alpha}\rho\chi\tilde{\eta}s \ \Pi\epsilon\iota\sigma\acute{\iota}\sigma\tau\rho\alpha\tau\sigma s \ ^{\prime}I\pi\pi\acute{\iota}\sigma\upsilon \ \upsilon\acute{\iota}\grave{o}s$$
$$\theta\tilde{\eta}\kappa\epsilon\nu \ ^{\prime}A\pi\acute{o}\lambda\lambda\omega\nu\sigma s \ \Pi\upsilon\theta\acute{\iota}\sigma\upsilon \ \dot{\epsilon}\nu \ \tau\epsilon\mu\acute{\epsilon}\nu\epsilon\iota.[3]$$

" Peisistratus, son of Hippias, erected this monument of his government in the temenos of the Pythian Apollo."

The passage in Strabo just cited, may help to determine its locality; for he there says that the sacrificial altar of Zeus Astrapæus was at the city wall between the Pythium and the Olympium; and as we know that the Olympium was just within the walls, it follows that the Pythium must have been just without. And the reason for this site appears from the same passage. For Strabo there tells us that certain priests, called Pythaïstæ, having taken their station at this altar, watched during three consecutive days and nights in three consecutive months, for the lightning[4] at Harma, near Phylë, which was the signal for sending the sacrifice to Delphi. Harma lay on Mount Parnes, at a distance of about twenty miles north of Athens; and hence if the Pythium and the altar had lain within, instead of without, the city, the view would have been interrupted by the wall. Forchhammer indeed contends[5] that Strabo means not the city wall, but a boundary wall between the Pythium and Olympium. But τεῖχος used absolutely

---

[1] ἔστι δ' αὕτη (ἡ ἐσχάρα) ἐν τῷ τείχει μεταξὺ τοῦ Πυθίου καὶ τοῦ Ὀλυμπίου.—lib. ix. p. 404.

[2] ἐν Πυθίῳ χέσαι · Πεισίστρατος ᾠκοδόμει τὸν ἐν Πυθίῳ ναόν. Cf. Photius and Suidas, voc. Πύθιον.

[3] lib. vi. c. 54.

[4] These lightnings are alluded to by Euripides :

τιμᾷ σφε Πύθιος, ἀστραπαί τε Πύθιαι;—
Ion, 288.

[5] Topographie, p. 295.

as in this place can mean only the city wall. Forchhammer had a completely untenable and now exploded theory about the course of the wall; but we have already shown that it must have run close under the Olympium. Strabo might perhaps mean that the altar whence the observations were made was actually *upon* the wall (ἐν τείχει - as ἐν κορυφῇσι, ἐν οὔρεσι), whence there would have been a still clearer prospect. The altar was no doubt sacred to Zeus under his titles of Παρνήθιος and Σημάλεος—the Parnethian and the Sign-giver—as well as Ἀστραπαῖος; for Pausanias writes that there was on Mount Parnes a bronze image of Parnethian Zeus, and an altar to him as the sign-giver.[1]

It may be objected that Pausanias does not mention having passed through any gate in going to the Pythium, which he must have done had it lain outside the walls. To this it may be answered that in the present tour he visits places which must undoubtedly have lain outside the walls, as the Lyceium, Cynosarges, &c.; yet he does not once mention a gate; though when he goes to the Academy he signifies that it is without the walls (c. 29), and also indicates when he enters the city (εἰσελθόντων δὲ ἐς τὴν πόλιν, c. 2, 4). Hence we must conclude with Wachsmuth and Curtius that, as we have before remarked, the wall in this quarter had been pulled down when Hadrianopolis, or New Athens, was built; and that its materials were probably used in the construction of the numerous Roman villas in this neighbourhood; of which there are many remains north of the Olympium and south of the Stadium bridge.[2] The altar of Zeus Astrapæus, which existed in the time of Strabo, seems to have vanished with the wall; at all events, Pausanias does not mention it.

We learn from the lexicographers that the tripods gained as prizes by the cyclic chorus on the festival of Thargelia in honour of Apollo, were deposited in the Pythium;[3] probably, as A. Mommsen says, not in

---

[1] i. 32, 2; cf. Bekk. An. Græc. p. 212; Ἀστραπὴ δι᾽ Ἅρματος· τόπος Ἀθήνῃσιν ἐν τῇ Πάρνηθι, ὅπου Διὸς ἀστραπαίου ἐστὶ βωμός. Which seems to be the altar mentioned by Pausanias. Observe too ἐν τῇ Πάρνηθι, 'on Parnes.'

[2] Wachsmuth, Rh. Mus. 1868, p. 18; Curtius, Att. St. i. p. 69.

[3] Πύθιον· ἱερὸν Ἀπόλλωνος . . . εἰς ὃ τοὺς τρίποδας ἐτίθεσαν οἱ τῷ κυκλίῳ χορῷ νικήσαντες τὰ Θαργήλια.—Phot. Lex.; cf. Suidas in voc.

the temple, but in the temenos, just as the Dionysiac tripods were placed in the open air.[1] Hence it is probable, as Leake inferred,[2] that the Thargelia were actually celebrated in this enclosure, and that the cyclic chorus danced round the altar erected by Peisistratus.

The adjacent DELPHINIUM is said to have been in the course of erection when Theseus arrived at Athens, as we have already related (supra, p. 59) from the account given by Pausanias here. The temple was dedicated by his father Ægeus, and was sacred also to Artemis Delphinia.[3] Courts for trying cases of homicide were held in the Delphinium, and here Theseus was related to have been arraigned for slaying the robbers and the Pallantidæ.

The Delphinian Apollo seems to have been originally worshipped in Crete, and was probably introduced at Athens through its connection with that island in the time of Ægeus. The name Delphinian, derived from the dolphin, appears to have some reference to the power of the god over the sea and its storms; but of its mythical origin there are various accounts. According to the scholiast on Lycophron (v. 208), it came from Apollo's slaying of a dragon in the shape of a dolphin. Plutarch says that the favourite seat of the Delphinian Apollo was Cirrha or Crissa, the port of Delphi founded by the Cretans, to which the god had directed them by sending a dolphin to guide their course.[4] This version was no doubt derived from the name of Delphi. According to another account, Apollo, in the shape of a dolphin, preserved some tempest-tossed Cretans, and brought them to Attica.[5] Another shape of the myth is founded on the supposed musical taste of the dolphin, which is said to be attracted by the sound of the flute. Hence Pindar:

$$\text{'Αλίου δελφῖνος ὑπόκρισιν,}$$
$$\text{τὸν μὲν ἀκύμονος ἐν πόντου πελάγει}$$
$$\text{αὐλῶν ἐκίνησεν ἐρατὸν μέλος.}^{6}$$

---

[1] Heortologie, p. 423, note. Meursius, Ath. Att. ii. c. 10, erroneously says that the golden statue of Gorgias was erected in the Athenian Pythium, instead of at Delphi. See Cic. de Orat. iii. 32, 129; Philostr. Vit. Soph. i. 9, 2.

[2] vol. i. p. 132, note 2; cf. Lysias, De muner. acc. p. 698, Reiske.

[3] Pollux, viii. 10, s. 119.

[4] De solertia anim. p. 93, Reiske.

[5] Etym. M. in ἐπὶ Δελφινίῳ.

[6] Fragm. Incert. xlix.; cf. Plut. loc. cit.

> " Like as the dolphin, when the flute
> Utters its pleasing melody
> And winds are mute,
> Sports on the bosom of the waveless sea."

The worship of the Delphinian Apollo was common to all the Ionian race, and his temples might be seen on many an island and promontory of the Mediterranean.[1] The Delphinian Artemis was probably the same as Dictynna, a name derived from the net in which she was fabled to have been caught after springing into the sea, to escape the pursuit of Minos.

It was to the Delphinian Apollo that Theseus sacrificed the Marathonian bull. Here, also, before proceeding to Crete, he deposited the suppliant bough (ἱκετηρία) on behalf of his allotted companions; a twig of the sacred olive, bound about with white wool. Then after making his vows to the deity, he descended to the sea in the eighth month, or Munychion, and commenced his voyage. Hence even in Plutarch's time, the Delphinia continued to be celebrated here, and young maidens resorted to the temple to supplicate the deities.[2]

The palace of Ægeus must have been close to the Delphinium ; nay, even the temple itself seems to have been regarded as the place where the banquet was given when Theseus arrived at Athens ; for in the time of Plutarch it contained an enclosed space on which, according to tradition, the poison had fallen when the cup was dashed from his hand. (Above, p. 59.) For here, says Plutarch, Ægeus dwelt ; and a Hermes which stood on the east of the temple was thought to mark the gate of his palace.[3]

Pausanias next comes to a district (χωρίον) called Kepoi (κῆποι), or the GARDENS, where there was a temple (ναός) of Aphroditë, and near it

and Sympos. vii. 5, p. 816 ; Eurip. Helen. 1454.

[1] Strabo, iv. p. 179.

[2] Plut. Thes. c. 14 and 18.

[3] Ibid. c. 12. Meursius, Ath. ii. c. 1, erroneously places in the Delphinium the celebrated tripod dedicated to this god by Thales, referring to Diog. Laërt. i. 29. But Diogenes speaks there of a phial (φιάλη) not a tripod ; and Ménage has shown that we should read Διδυμαίῳ for Δελφινίῳ.

an image of the goddess, of a square form, like the Hermæ. The inscription on it showed that it was the heavenly Aphroditë, the eldest of the Mœræ, or Fates; but there was no legend connected either with the temple or the statue. The statue of Aphroditë, on the other hand, which stood in the garden, was the work of Alcamenes, and among the celebrated statues at Athens, the most worth seeing. That this was a very fine statue appears also from the notice of it by Lucian,[1] and by Pliny, who notes it as one of the best works of Alcamenes, and adds that his master Pheidias was thought to have put the finishing hand to it.[2] Aphroditë Urania and the Fates are said to have been the offspring of Cronos and Euonymë.[3] The victim sacrificed to the heavenly Aphroditë and her of the gardens, was a heifer to each.[4]

Siebelis in a note on this passage says that the Kepoi must have been within the walls; founding this inference on another passage where Pausanias seems to speak of them as being in the city.[5] But we have seen that the wall in this quarter had been destroyed in the time of Pausanias, and therefore the ancient boundary of the city was difficult to discover, and consequently he speaks of all this east quarter as being within it. Any such vague phrase as this in his mouth cannot therefore weigh for an instant against the direct testimony of Pliny, who says that the Aphroditë in the gardens was *outside the walls ;*[6] where indeed it was most probable that gardens would be found. Forchhammer has of course seized upon this passage of Pausanias, and contends that Pliny wrote ' extra muros,' merely by induction from the gardens (p. 96). But his argument drawn from Pausanias not mentioning any wall or gate falls to the ground on his own showing; for he admits that Cynosarges and the Lyceium were outside even *his* walls, and yet Pausanias arrives at them without alluding to any gate. Forchhammer's explanation of that fact, namely, that these two gym-

---

[1] Imagin. c. 4 & 6.

[2] H. N. xxxvi. s. 16.

[3] Fragment of Epimenides in schol. to Lycophr. p. 406 (Müller).

[4] Lucian, Dialog. Mer vii. 1 : τῇ Οὐρανίᾳ δέ, καὶ τῇ ἐν κήποις δάμαλιν ἑκατέρᾳ (θῦσαι).

[5] ἔστι δὲ περίβολος ἐν τῇ πόλει τῆς καλου-μένης ἐν κήποις 'Αφροδίτης οὐ πόρρω.— c. 27, 4.

[6] " Præclarumque (opus) Veneris *extra muros* quæ appellatur Aphroditë *ἐν κήποις.*" —H. N. xxxvi. 16.

nasia were mere adjuncts to the city walls, like the Prætorian camp at Rome, requires no serious refutation.

Pausanias next arrives at the gymnasium of CYNOSARGES (c. 19, 2, 3). He is proceeding along the right bank of the Ilissus in a northerly direction, and as Cynosarges is the next object that he comes to after the gardens, we may infer that it stood nearly opposite the Stadium, or perhaps a little lower down. There is here room enough between the walls and the river for the site of a gymnasium; for we know that it stood at no great distance from a gate that lay here;[1] and therefore could not have adjoined the wall, as Forchhammer asserts. Pausanias does not mention its being a gymnasium. He speaks of it only as an enclosure sacred to Heracles, and says that it had altars of that hero, of Hebë, daughter of Zeus, whom he was said to have married; also of Alcmenë, and of Iolaüs, who was the companion of many of his labours. And he just adverts to the legend of its origin, which ran as follows, and seems to have been taken from an oracle inscribed in the temple: as Diomus was sacrificing to Heracles, a white bitch seized the thigh of the victim and ran off with it. On consulting the oracle, Diomus was ordered to erect an altar to Heracles at the spot where the bitch had deposited her prey. Thus arose the Cynosarges, from κύων and ἀργός, either *white* or *swift of foot;* or rather, perhaps, thus was concocted the legend from the name.[2]

It seems probable that it had anciently been only a temple of Heracles, and that the gymnasium was a later addition. Thus we frequently find it called a Heracleium.[3] But we learn also from other passages that there was a gymnasium connected with it, and a grove.[4] It must have existed as a gymnasium at least as early as the time of Solon; for he made a law that whoever stole the most trifling

---

[1] μικρὸν ἄπωθεν τῶν πυλῶν.—Diog. Laërt. vi. s. 13. εἰς Κυνόσαργες . . . τοῦτο δ᾽ ἐστὶν ἔξω πυλῶν γυμνάσιον Ἡρακλέους.—Plut. Them. 1.

[2] Hesych. in voc.; schol. ad Demosth. adv. Timocr. 736 (t. ii. p. 182, Reiske).

[3] Herod. vi. 116; Athen. vi. 26, &c.

[4] " Castra ad Cynosarges (templum Herculis gymnasiumque, et lucus erat circumjectus) posuit (Philippus)."—Liv. xxxi. 24; also the passages cited above from Plutarch and Diogenes Laërtius.

thing from it, or from any other gymnasium, should be capitally punished.[1]

Cynosarges being just outside one of the gates—and as we have before observed (p. 106), probably the Diomeian Gate, from the legend respecting the foundation of the temple—was used as a place of sepulture, or rather, it would seem, the road which led to it. Thus we learn from the ' Lives of the Ten Orators,'[2] that Isocrates and his relatives were buried near it, on a rising ground on the left hand. On these tombs were once six trapezæ or tables, intended apparently for inscriptions or painted portraits; but they had perished before the time of the writer of the Lives. On the tomb of Isocrates himself, was a colossal ram of 30 cubits, having on it a siren of 7 cubits, typical of his eloquence. Near it was a trapeza, having a picture of certain poets, and of the teachers of Isocrates; among whom was Gorgias surveying an astrological sphere, and Isocrates standing by him. But these also had perished, and were probably destroyed by Philip V. of Macedon, when he committed such wanton havoc in the Athenian suburbs,[3] and destroyed not only the buildings and groves but even the tombs. His ravages appear to have been made principally on this eastern side of the city, where indeed he had pitched his camp, as Livy specifies more particularly Cynosarges and the Lyceium. Herodotus alludes to a tomb of Anchimolius here, in a passage from which we also learn that Cynosarges was in the deme of Alopecæ.[4] That deme must have extended at least a mile or two from the city; for Æschines speaks of a farm in it 11 or 12 stadia from the walls.[5] Socrates belonged to the deme

---

[1] Demosth. c. Timocr. p. 736, Reiske; cf. Aristot. Probl. xxix. 14.

[2] tom. ix. p. 333 sq. Reiske.

[3] "Cynosarges et Lyceum et quidquid sancti amœnive circa urbem erat, incensum est, dirutaque non tecta solum sed etiam sepulcra."—Liv. xxxi. 24.

[4] καὶ Ἀγχιμολίου εἰσὶ ταφαὶ τῆς Ἀττικῆς Ἀλωπεκῆσι, ἀγχοῦ τοῦ Ἡρακληίου τοῦ ἐν Κυνοσάργει.—v. 63.

[5] τὸ δ' Ἀλωπεκῆσι χωρίον, ὃ ἦν ἄπυθεν τοῦ τείχους ἕνδεκα ἢ δώδεκα στάδια.—adv. Timarch. p. 119. Reiske takes Æschines to mean from the walled town or fortress of Alopecæ, not from the city wall. But we have seen that Cynosarges was close to the gate. Leake (vol. ii. p. 31) erroneously places the deme a mile and a half from the city walls, from misinterpreting this passage of Æschines.

of Alopecæ, and hence he is frequently represented going out on this side of the town.

Leake places Cynosarges at the foot of Lycabettus, and is followed by Wachsmuth;[1] who thinks that Cynosarges was the furthest point to the north-east visited by Pausanias, and that he describes the Lyceium, which he must have passed on the road thither, on his way back. But this is contrary to the usual practice of Pausanias, who takes things in their regular order. Thus he describes all the south side of the agora, and then returns at one jump to the Stoa Basileios, whence he had started. In like manner in the present route, he describes the objects first on the right bank of the Ilissus, then on the left bank; after which he goes back at once to the Prytaneium, his starting point. Wachsmuth's reason for placing Cynosarges here appears to be because he fancies that the Athenian encampment there, after the battle of Marathon, might have been seen by the Persians when they sailed to Phalerum with the view of surprising Athens, and thus have caused them to abandon the enterprise. But Herodotus assigns no such reason for their retreat, and leaves it quite uncertain by what method they learned the return of the Athenians.[2] That from the Bay of Phalerum they should have been able to descry an encampment five or six miles off, at the foot of Lycabettus, we hold to be a physical impossibility. Between the Bay of Phalerum and Athens, the ground rises from 100 to 200 feet and more, as may be seen from Curtius' map, not to mention the intervening buildings and walls.

Antisthenes, the founder of the Cynic philosophy, lectured in this gymnasium, and according to some the name of the sect was derived from it; but others thought that it came simply from the dog, an appellation which appears to have been given to Antisthenes himself. Such was the opinion of Lactantius, Moschopulus, Ammonius, and Nonnus.[3] We may add here that the superintendents of the gymnasia, called σωφρονισταί, ten in number, were chosen by the tribes, and received a

---

[1] Rh. Mus. 1868, p. 20.
[2] lib. vi. c. 116.

[3] See Diog. Laërt. vi. 13, with the note of Ménage.

drachm a day from the state.[1]   There are many busts of gymnasiarchs, represented like Hermæ, in the Barbakeion at Athens.

A still more celebrated gymnasium was the LYCEIUM, which Pausanias next arrives at.   It must have lain therefore pretty near the Cynosarges, and a little to the north of it.   That it was at no great distance from the city we know from the scholiast on the ' Peace ' of Aristophanes,[2] where we see that it served as a place of exercise for the soldiery.   It was probably near the present Rizarion, or seminary for priests.   A broad road led to it along which they were marched in and out of the gymnasium :

> καὶ γὰρ ἱκανὸν χρόνον ἀ-
> πολλύμεθα καὶ κατατε-
> τρίμμεθα πλανώμενοι
> ἐς Λύκειον κἀκ Λυκείου σὺν δόρει σὺν ἀσπίδι.[3]

> " Pretty long we've been plagued and kept knocking about
> At that horrid Lyceium, marching in, marching out,
> With spear and with shield."

After the departure of the Thirty, this road was strewn with large stones to prevent the bringing-up of military engines.[4]   The cavalry also was exercised in the Lyceium,[5] whence we must conclude that it was of considerable extent.   The δρόμος, or road to it, seems to have issued from the Gate Diocharis, which we know from Strabo to have been near the Lyceium.[6]   This, as we have said, we take to have been the gate near the palace gardens, where the wall, after running north-east, makes an angle to the north-west.[7]   A passage in the ' Lysis ' of Plato contributes to fix the locality.   Socrates is there represented as walking from the Academy towards the Lyceium under, and outside, the walls, when he meets with Hippothales and others at a postern gate (πυλίς) where there was a fountain named after the Attic hero PANOPS.[8]   This fountain is not mentioned by Pausanias, but it seems to be the same as that

[1] Bekker, An. Græc. p. 301, line 7.

[2] ἐξοπλίσεις τινὲς ἐγίνοντο ἐν τῷ Λυκείῳ διὰ τὸ παρακεῖσθαι τῇ πόλει.—ad v. 352.

[3] Pax, loc. cit.

[4] Xenoph. Hell. ii. 4, 27.

[5] Id. Mag. Eq. iii. 6.

[6] lib. ix. p. 397.

[7] See the Plan of Athens. Leake also places the Porta Diocharis here.

[8] Lysis, init.

alluded to by Strabo in the passage just cited, where he describes it as
being near the Gate Diocharis. The πολὶς mentioned by Plato seems
to have been an unimportant one, as he gives it no name; and it was
perhaps for this reason that Strabo preferred to indicate the site of the
fountain by the better known Gate Diocharis. Some 200 yards to the
north of its supposed site, traces of a small gate were observed by
Fauvel; and here Leake has placed the fountain of Panops.[1] His site
for the Lyceium appears therefore to be the true one; only he has put
Cynosarges on the wrong side of it, and thus given an unreasonable
extension of nearly half a mile to the Kepi or Gardens.

The foundation of the Lyceium was attributed to Lycus, a son of
Pandion; from which we merely infer that it was of high antiquity.   It
was from the first sacred to Apollo, and Pausanias says that the god
derived from it his name of Lycius (c. 19, 4).   The scholiast on
Demosthenes, however, says that the place was sacred to Apollo as the
wolf-slayer (λυκόκτονος), and the same etymology is assigned to the
Lyceium at Argos by a scholiast on the 'Electra' of Sophocles.[2] As at
Cynosarges, there was at first only a temple here; and the accounts
about the erection of the adjoining gymnasium are very various.
According to Theopompus, it was founded by Peisistratus; Philochorus
attributed it to Pericles; while according to the author of the 'Lives
of the Ten Orators,' it was the work of Lycurgus.[3] We have seen,
however, that it was used as a place for drill in the time of Aristophanes, who flourished the greater part of a century before Lycurgus;
and when applied to such a purpose it was most probably already a
gymnasium.   The polemarch, moreover, as we have already said (supra,
p. 267), took his seat there in very early times, which is hardly consistent with its being a mere sanctuary.   Perhaps, therefore, Lycurgus
only made some improvements in it.

What gave the Lyceium its chief renown was its being the seat of the

---

[1] See his plan. Also vol. i. p. 448.
[2] Schol. ad Timocr. p. 736, Reiske
(t. ii. p. 182); Schol. ad Soph. El. v. 6.
Cf. Pausan. ii. 19, 3.

[3] Harpocr., Phot., Suid. voc. Λυκεῖον;
Vit. X. Orat.: τὸ ἐν Λυκείῳ γυμνάσιον
ἐποίησε καὶ ἐφύτευσε (sc. Lycurgus).—
t. ix. p. 346, Reiske.

Peripatetic philosophy. Aristotle deserted the Academy, when he found, on returning from his embassy to Philip, that Xenocrates had been succeeded, as principal of that school, by another philosopher. He then resorted to the Lyceium, and walked about with his disciples till the time of anointing.[1] Hence the name of *peripatetic;* not however from the action of walking, but from the promenade (περίπατος, 'ambulatio') on which it was accomplished.[2] Aristotle, however, was not the first to whom the name was applied, for Plato also appears to have been so called from his custom of promenading in the Academy,[3] and after him Xenocrates. Hence there appears at first to have been a distinction between the Peripatetics of the Academy and those of the Lyceium; but ultimately the former came to be called Academics, while the latter retained the name of Peripatetics.[4] The shady walks in these gymnasia invited to such promenades. The Lyceium was distinguished by a magnificent plane tree, which Theophrastus mentions as having attained a vast size when still quite young.[5] It is also alluded to by Maximus Tyrius.[6]

Both the Lyceium and the Academy, though of such celebrity as seats of learning, were also sometimes the scenes of more sensual entertainments, at all events in the later times. In a supper at the Academy, the cook having brought in an earthenware dish of foreign manufacture, the hieropoioi broke it in pieces. At another, at the Lyceium, the cook was punished for a gastronomical offence. Having served up a sauce made of salt meat and passed it off as a fish-sauce, he was ordered to be whipped as a roguish culinary sophist.[7]

Lucian has described the statue of Apollo. He was represented leaning upon a pillar, with his bow in his left hand and his right bent

---

[1] Diog. Laërt. Vit. Aristot. v. s. 2.

[2] See Ménage at Diog. Laërt. loc. cit.; Suidas, in Ἀριστοτέλης and Σωκράτης. Thus: Ἀθηνίων δέ, ἐπιλαβόμενος τῶν δογμάτων τῶν τοῦ Περιπάτου.—Athen. v. 53.

[3] "Platonis auctoritate una et consentiens duobus vocabulis philosophiæ forma instituta est, Academicorum et Peripateticorum : qui rebus congruentes, nominibus differebant."—Cicero, Acad. Post. i. 4, 17.

[4] Ammon. ap. Casaubon. ad Diog. Laërt. l. c.

[5] Hist. Plant. i. 11.

[6] Dissert. viii.

[7] Athen. iv. 14.

over his head, as if resting after some long labour.[1] Plutarch says that
the gymnasium was dedicated to Apollo as the god of health.[2] Behind
the Lyceium was a monument to Nisus, King of the Megarenses—him
of the purple lock[3]—who was allied with the Athenians against Minos
and the Cretans; for Megara was invaded by them as well as Attica.
Nisus appears to have been put to death in Crete; but the Athenians
carried home his remains and buried them here. Before the gymnasium,
which he had either erected or improved, Lycurgus caused to be
engraved on a pillar for public perusal an account of all that he had
done in his administration.[4]

Pausanias now prepares to cross over the Ilissus to Agræ and the
Stadium, but before doing so, he gives an account of that river and its
tributary the Eridanus, which we here omit as we have adverted to this
subject in the introductory chapter. We may note this, however, as a
proof that all the objects he has hitherto mentioned were on the right
bank of the river. Before passing the stream he notices one or two
objects which seem also to have been on the right bank. One of these
was an altar of the Musæ Ilissiades, or Muses of the Ilissus. Vestiges
of this monument seem to have been extant in the time of Wheler, who
says: " Advancing a little higher upon the river Ilissus [i.e. from the
Stadium, which he has just described], on the left hand, we saw the
foundations of a little round temple, discovered not long since by an
inundation, which did a great deal of mischief to the Athenians, throwing down their country houses, trees, and walls, and quite destroying
all their gardens in its passage. This probably was the temple of the
Musæ Ilissiades, being seated upon the banks of this river, according as
Pausanias informs us. From whence Boreas in a whirlwind took away
the nymph Orithyia, whom he found sporting upon these banks." [5]

Pausanias also alludes to this fable, and adds that through the
affinity which Boreas had thus contracted with the Athenians, he aided
them by destroying the greater part of the triremes of the barbarians.

[1] Anacharsis, c. 7.
[2] Sympos. viii. Q. 4, p. 889, Reiske.
[3] Tibull. i. 4, v. 63.
[4] Vit. X. Orat. p. 355, Reiske.
[5] Journey, &c. p. 377.

The effects of the north wind are indeed sometimes terrible at Athens. At this spot there was also an altar of Boreas, as we learn from Plato's 'Phædrus.'[1] In that dialogue, Socrates is represented as meeting Phædrus near the Olympium, as appears from Phædrus indicating a house close to that temple as the abode of Lysias. They then walk down to the river, and on Phædrus inquiring whether it was not here that Orithyia was carried off by Boreas, Socrates replies, " No, but at a spot about two or three stades further, at the place where we cross over to the temple of Artemis at Agræ; and there is an altar of Boreas there." Two stades and a half from the angle described by the Ilissus opposite the eastern side of the Olympium, would bring us precisely to this spot. In this neighbourhood Cicero's friend Atticus once resided.[2] Near here, also, was the place where the Athenian king Codrus was said to have been slain by the Lacedæmonians.[3]

Pausanias does not mention whether he crossed a bridge in going to Agræ, or walked through the stream, which is easily fordable here, except in seasons when it becomes a torrent. That there was an ancient bridge here we know from the accounts of travellers who saw it when perfect. Wheler describes it as consisting of three arches of large hewn stone, laid firmly together without mortar and about 40 feet long. He adds, that there was a monastery upon it before Athens was taken by the Turks.[4] It appears to have been destroyed in 1780;[5] but there are still some vestiges of it left. Wachsmuth is of opinion[6] that the bridge was a Roman work, and that there was none here before the time of Herodes Atticus; but one a little higher up, alluded to by Plato in the passage of the 'Phædrus' before cited, as

---

[1] See the beginning of that Dialogue.

[2] " Athenis, non longe item a tua illa antiqua domo, Orithyiam Aquilo sustulerit."—De Leg. i. 1, 3.

[3] Pausan. i. 19, 6 : so πρὸ τῆς πόλεως.— Lycurg. c. Leocr. p. 196, Reiske. πρὸ τοῦ τείχους.—Bekk. An. Gr. p. 193, 2. Both which passages show that these places, on the right bank of the river, were out-side the gates, though Pausanias has not mentioned passing any. An inscription relating to the death of Codrus, of course of a later period, was found a few years ago.—Arch. Zg. 1866, p. 183.

[4] Journey, p. 375. Cf. Babin, in Laborde's Documens Inéd. p. 79.

[5] Dodwell, vol. i. p. 408.

[6] Rh. Mus. 1868, p. 22.

leading to the temple of Artemis. But the description of the bridge by Wheler seems rather to show a Grecian origin; and it is incredible that there should have been none to so frequented a place as the Stadium must have been long before the Roman times.

On crossing the Ilissus, continues Pausanias, one arrives at the district called Agræ, where there is a temple of ARTEMIS AGROTERA.[1] This temple Wheler identifies with the church dedicated to St. Peter crucified (Stauromenou Petrou), the floor of which he says was paved with ancient mosaic work, and the whole fabric of white marble.[2] This view has been adopted by modern topographers.[3] The church of St. Peter lies about 200 yards north-east of the Stadium and the same distance from the river. The statue of Artemis was represented holding a bow, from a tradition that it was here she first hunted, after her arrival from Delos. Before the battle of Marathon, Miltiades is said to have vowed that he would sacrifice to Artemis Agrotera as many she-goats as he should kill enemies; but as a sufficient number could not be found, it was resolved to sacrifice 500 yearly; a custom which still continued in the time of Xenophon.[4] Aristophanes alludes to these enormous sacrifices in his 'Knights':

$$\tau\tilde{\eta} \ \delta' \ '\mathrm{A}\gamma\rho\sigma\tau\acute{\epsilon}\rho\alpha \ \kappa\alpha\tau\grave{\alpha} \ \chi\iota\lambda\iota\tilde{\omega}\nu \ \pi\alpha\rho\acute{\eta}\nu\epsilon\sigma\alpha$$
$$\epsilon\grave{\nu}\chi\grave{\eta}\nu \ \pi\omega\acute{\eta}\sigma\alpha\sigma\theta\alpha\iota \ \chi\iota\mu\acute{\alpha}\rho\omega\nu \ \epsilon\grave{\iota}\sigma\alpha\acute{\nu}\rho\iota\nu.—\mathrm{v}. \ 660.$$

"'T' Agrotera I bade them vow
Some thousand goats to-morrow."

Where the scholiast attributes the vow to the polemarch Callimachus, instead of Miltiades, and says that the victims were to have been oxen; but as so many could not be found, she-goats were substituted. In after times it was the polemarch who conducted the sacrifice.[5]

---

[1] There were three forms of the name: Ἄγρα, Ἀγραία, and Ἀγροτέρα. See Ruhnken ad Tim. Lex. (πρὸς τὸ τῆς Ἄγρας).

[2] Journey, p. 378.

[3] See Curtius' map of Athens, and Erl. Text, p. 51; Wachsm. Rh. M. 1868, p. 23.

[4] Exped. Cyri, iii. 2, s. 12; cf. Plut. de Herod. Malign. t. ix. p. 421; Æl. V. H. ii. 25, who, however, says 300.

[5] Pollux, viii. s. 91.

The district in which this temple was situated was called indifferently either in the singular or plural, Agra and Agræ.[1] We have
already observed that in early times the hill of Agræ had the name of
Helicon, and on its summit was an altar for burnt-offerings to the
Heliconian Poseidon.[2] At Agræ was also a Metroum, or temple of
Demeter.[3] For the temples of this goddess, as well as Rhea, were
sometimes called Μητρῷα, and she herself simply Μήτηρ.[4] We may
observe that Pausanias takes no notice of this last temple. Indeed he
seems always to have avoided this subject with a sort of superstitious
awe. Thus we have seen above that he declines to speak of the Eleusinium near the agora, in consequence of a dream; and what is still
more marked and singular, he does not even mention the celebrated
temple at Eleusis (ch. 38), except to say that he refuses to describe
its interior, under the influence of the same dream. If we followed his
authority only, we might suppose that Agræ was sacred entirely to
Artemis; but, though he says not a word about Demeter, we know
from other authorities that she was the chief deity of the place. This
omission need not surprise us, considering the aversion which, as we
have pointed out, Pausanias entertained against speaking of Demeter
and her mysteries; and likewise the many objects which he has left out
in all parts of the town. He also omits here the altar of Poseidon,
though that was certainly an important object. The omission cannot
therefore serve as an argument for those who hold that Pausanias has
already spoken of this temple in his 14th chapter, in that eccentric
deviation which has been attributed to him from the agora to the banks
of the Ilissus. Nobody, we suppose, will contend that Agræ could have
been at Callirrhoë. Pausanias does not mention its name on that occasion (in his 14th chapter), and not until this 19th chapter, where he

[1] Ἄγρα καὶ Ἄγραι, χωρίον, ἑνικῶς καὶ
πληθυντικῶς.—Stephan. Byzant.

[2] Pausan. vii. 24, 4; supra, p. 18.

[3] τῷ δ' ὄχθῳ πάλαι ὄνομα τούτῳ, ὃς νῦν
Ἄγρα καλεῖται, Ἑλικών. καὶ ἡ ἐσχάρα τοῦ
Ποσειδῶνος τοῦ Ἑλικωνίου ἐπ' ἄκρου
(Κλειδῆμος ἐν πρώτῳ Ἀτθίδος ... καὶ ἐν τῷ

τετάρτῳ)· εἰς τὸ ἱερὸν τὸ Μητρῷον τὸ ἐν
Ἄγραις. Where we see the sing. and plur.
used as equivalent (Bekker, An. Græc.
p. 326 sq.).

[4] As by Herodotus, viii. 65: τῇ Μητρὶ
καὶ τῇ Κούρῃ.

expressly says that it is on the further side of the Ilissus.[1] And that this was the first time that he crossed it is plain from his giving an account of that river and its tributary.

The existence of a METROUM, or TEMPLE OF DEMETER, at Agræ, is shown from a host of authorities. It was here that the Lesser Mysteries were celebrated, a necessary preliminary to initiation in the Greater, which required an interval of a year. Thus Demetrius was initiated in the Lesser Mysteries at Agra, but the interval was shortened in his favour. The text of Plutarch indeed has τὰ πρὸς ἀγοράν;[2] and it might be thought that he was alluding to the Eleusinium on the agora which we have already described. But though this is not the sole instance where, in such a connexion, we find ἀγορὰν where we should expect Ἄγραν, yet we are not aware that the celebration of the mysteries at the temple on the agora can be established on any good authority. At the same time we do not think it impossible that the Lesser Mysteries might sometimes have been celebrated there, or in any temple of Demeter; for, as we have already seen, Heracles was related to have been initiated in them, in a temple in Melitē (supra, p. 51). But the existence of a Metroum, and the celebration of the Lesser Mysteries in it, at Agræ on the Ilissus, are so well established as to admit of no doubt. We give some of the principal authorities on the subject in a note.[3] To the site of the temple we have no clue. There are considerable remains of masonry on the top of the hill, on the south side of the Stadium, which Leake and others have attributed to Herodes' temple of Fortune, but which may not improbably have belonged to the Metroum.

[1] διαβᾶσι δὲ τὸν Εἰλισσόν, χωρίον Ἄγραι καλούμενον καὶ ναὸς Ἀγροτέρας ἐστὶν Ἀρτέμιδος.—i. 19, 7.

[2] ἐτέλουν τῷ Δημητρίῳ τὰ πρὸς ἀγοράν.—Demetr. c. 26.

[3] Ἄγραι· χωρίον ἔξω τῆς πόλεως Ἀθηνῶν, οὗ τὰ μικρὰ τῆς Δήμητρος ἄγεται μυστήρια, ἃ λέγεται τὰ ἐν Ἄγραις, ὡς ἐν Ἀσκληπίου.—Bekk. An. Gr. 326. And at the end of the same article, from Cleide-mus: εἰς τὸ ἱερὸν τὸ Μητρῷον τὸ ἐν Ἄγραις (which shows that this Metroum belonged to Demeter). παρ᾽ Ἰλισσοῦ μυστικαῖς ὄχθαις.—Himer. ap. Phot. Bibl. p. 1120 (369 A, Bekk.). ταῦτα μὲν δὴ συνέθεντο παρὰ τὸν Ἰλισσόν, οὗ τὸν καθαρμὸν τελοῦσι τοῖς ἐλάττοσι μυστηρίοις.—Polyæn. Strat. v. 17; cf. Dionys. Perieg. 424. Ἄγραι· χωρίον Ἀττικὸν ἔξω τῆς πόλεως, ἱερὸν Δήμητρος.—Hesych.; cf. Suid. in voc. &c.

The hill of Agræ had naturally the form of a crescent or amphi-theatre, the horns of which ran down to the river, whilst the centre of it was occupied by the bed of a torrent. It is a moot point whether the place served for a STADIUM before the time of the orator Lycurgus. Leake[1] is of opinion that it might possibly have been so used; but we are rather inclined to agree with Wachsmuth,[2] who infers from the life of Lycurgus, that as the place was previously the private property of Dei-nias, it could not have been used for gymnastic contests till it had been purchased of him and the ground properly levelled. The scene of these agones had been previously, he thinks, at Echelidæ.[3] Lycurgus, how-ever, left it in a comparatively rude state; and it was not perfected till some centuries after, when, as we have said (above, p. 179), Herodes Atticus completed it with great magnificence. Pausanias relates that Herodes almost exhausted for it the quarries of Pentelicus, and seems to have despaired of conveying to his readers by words the impression which the sight of it was calculated to produce (c. 19, 7).

The whole length of the Stadium is 680 feet; but there was pro-bably a platform or portico between it and the river, which would reduce its actual length to about 630 feet. The breadth of the arena is about 130 feet, or nearly double that of the ordinary Greek stadium.[4] It is doubtful whether the marble seats reached to the summit; but even if they went only halfway up, they would have been between thirty and forty in number, and capable of accommodating some 40,000 spectators, whilst as many more might have found standing room above. The seats have now for the most part disappeared, having probably been used as building materials. The place was being excavated when the author was there in 1869, and the whole of the κρηπίς or skirting wall had been laid bare.[5] At the beginning of the semicircular extremity on the north-east side, a tunnel about twelve feet broad and ten high runs through the hill, and was probably used, in the Roman times, for

[1] vol. i. p. 192.

[2] Rh. Mus. 1868, p. 22.

[3] Ἐχελίδαι· δῆμος Ἀττικῆς . . . ἐν ᾧ τοῖς γυμνικοὺς ἀγῶνας ἐτίθεσαν τοῖς Παν-αθηναίοις.—Steph. Byz. sub voc.

[4] Gell, Itinerary, p. 43; Leake, i. p. 193.

[5] I am informed by Dr. Finlay that these excavations were abandoned soon after, as everything was found to have been completely destroyed (1872).

venationes or combats with wild beasts. Hadrian gave one of these spectacles in which, it is said, a thousand were slaughtered.[1] Gladiatorial combats were also probably exhibited here, to whose introduction at Athens by the Romans we have before adverted; but the more usual place for them seems to have been the Dionysiac theatre.

Herodes also erected a TEMPLE OF FORTUNE near the Stadium, with an ivory image of the goddess. He died at his villa at Marathon, and directed that his remains should be buried there; but they were forcibly carried off by the Athenians, and interred at his Panathenaïc Stadium.[2]

Pausanias, having completed his survey of the lower parts of the city by the description of the Stadium, returns to the Prytaneium, whence he had started, and begins another tour. But before we accompany him on it we must advert to one or two things which he appears to have omitted in the present one.

We may infer from Plutarch's description of the battle with the Amazons that the places called ARDETTUS and PALLADIUM lay not far from the Lyceium, since he mentions them all in connection when he describes the Athenians as marching from that quarter.[3] And this inference is confirmed by other accounts. Harpocration and Hesychius (sub voc.) describe Ardettus as near the Ilissus and Panathenaïc Stadium; Harpocration, in particular, states that it was *above* the Stadium, and near the deme of Agrylë, which lay below it.[4] This deme most probably lay towards Hymettus,[5] and hence we should have to place Ardettus on the southern side of the Stadium. Harpocration adds, it was said that the heliastic oath was formerly taken here, and that the place was named after an ancient hero, Ardettus, who first administered the oath; but Theophrastus had recorded, in his book on the laws, that the custom had been abolished.

It is one of the arguments of Forchhammer for extending the city walls beyond the Ilissus, that the heliastic oath would hardly have been taken outside of them. But we see from this passage that the custom

---

[1] Spartian, Adr. c. 19.
[2] Philostr. Vit. Herod. s. 15.
[3] Thes. c. 27.

[4] ὑπὲρ τὸ στάδιον τὸ Παναθηναϊκόν, πρὸς τῷ δήμῳ τῷ ὑπένερθεν Ἀγρυλέων.—in voc.
[5] See Leake, i. 281.

was a very ancient one, and must have existed long before the walls of
Themistocles were built; and we suppose that Forchhammer would
hardly contend that Ardettus was comprehended within the walls
attributed to Theseus.   Of the site of the PALLADIUM we know nothing
more than that it must have been somewhere in this neighbourhood.
There was a court at it for the trial of involuntary homicides.   Its
origin is referred to a story of Diomedes having brought with him the
Palladium, which he was carrying off from Troy, to Phalerum, when
his sailors, not knowing where they were, having landed and committed
some devastations, were repulsed by Demophon, who carried off the
Palladium.   His horse having accidentally killed a man on his road
back to Athens, Demophon was the first who was tried in the court.[1]

We shall only further observe about this neighbourhood, that at the
time of Stuart's visit to Athens, about a century ago, there existed on
the right bank of the Ilissus, near the cascade called Callirrhoë, a small
church called e *Panaghia eis ten Petran*, or St. Mary on the Rock, which
still exhibited many remains of its former state as a temple of the
Ionic order.   It was considered a fine example of that order, which is
somewhat rare at Athens, the Erechtheium and the reconstructed temple
of Nikë Athena being the only other instances of it extant.   It has now
completely disappeared.   Various attempts have been made to identify
it, but they rest only on conjecture.[2]

[1] Pausan. c. 28, 9.

[2] For a full description of this building

see Stuart's Antiquities of Athens, vol. i.
ch. 2 ; and Ross, Nikë Tempel, p. 11.

CHAPTER X.

HAVING returned from the Stadium to the Prytaneium, Pausanias takes on his next tour (c. 20) the street to the right, which, he says, was called the Street of the Tripods,[1] because, as he explains, there were in it several temples on which stood large bronze tripods, serving as a sort of frame to some exquisite statues which they contained between their legs. Among these was the Satyr which Praxiteles considered to be one of the finest of his works. Pausanias here relates the well-known story how Phrynë discovered his estimation of it by telling him that his house was on fire; on which he exclaimed, that if his Satyr or his Cupid had perished he was undone.[2] The Satyr seems to have been the statue which obtained among the Greeks the name of ' Periboëtos,' or the renowned.[3] In a neighbouring temple was also a young Satyr offering a cup to Dionysus. The statue of the god and the Cupid standing by were the work of Thymilus. These temples, adorned with the masterpieces of Greek sculpture, seem to have rendered the Street of Tripods a favourite lounge; and thus we are told, that whoever wanted to

---

[1] This street is also mentioned by Athenæus, xii. 60.

[2] Cf. Athen. lib. xiii. c. 59.

[3] See Winckelmann, Stor. delle Arti, ii. 224. The Satyr was of bronze. Plin. H. N. xxxiv. 69.

attract the notice of Demetrius Phalereus, when governor of Athens, would be sure to find him taking his morning walk there.[1]

In the name of this street we perceive that it was an Athenian custom to call the streets after some objects in them, or trades carried on there. Thus we hear of the street of the sculptors' shops (ἡ τῶν Ἑρμογλυφείων).[2] As the carving of Hermæ, which were in great demand, was the principal occupation of the statuaries, ἑρμογλυφεύς came to be a generic name for a sculptor. For, as we have seen, they were as common objects at Athens as posts in a modern city. They were often double-headed, and sometimes triple-headed, where they served for finger-posts at the meeting of three roads. In like manner, we hear of the street of the cabinet-makers (ἡ τῶν κιβωτοποιῶν).[3] Sometimes, again, they were called after a temple in them, as ἡ Ἑστίας ὁδός, the street of Hestia or Vesta.[4] They seem, also, to have been sometimes known by numbers, as we hear of Third Street.[5]

Fortunately, one of the small temples which supported the tripods in this street has been preserved to us in the well-known MONUMENT OF LYSICRATES. It stands between 130 and 140 yards from the eastern cliff of the Acropolis, thus showing that the Street of the Tripods must have been quite on the plain; and as the front with the inscription faces the south-east, the temple must consequently have lain on the north-west side of the street. Recent excavations at the theatre of Dionysus show that the street terminated at its eastern entrance.[6] It must thus have formed the principal and most convenient approach to the theatre from the agora, avoiding the hill on the road to the Pnyx between the Acropolis and Areiopagus. The monuments which lined it would have reminded the spectator on his way of the

[1] Carystius ap. Athen. xii. 60.

[2] Plut. De genio Socr. p. 580 (t. viii. p. 294, Reiske).

[3] Ibid.

[4] Isæus ap. Harpocr. voc. τρικέφαλος.

[5] If the following line of Philippides, as emended by Dobrée, be correct:

Πλάτην ὑφοδώσεις παιδίοισιν ῥύμην :
τρίτην.—Ap. Poll. ix. 38.

The word Ῥύμη to signify a *street* was a barbarism introduced in the Macedonian times, to which Philippides belonged. See Phrynich. in voc. p. 404, Lobeck. About the Athenian streets, see Meursius, Ath. Att. iii. 8.

[6] Pervanoglu, Philologus, xxiv. 459 ; Bötticher, ibid. Suppl. Bd. p. 308.

triumphs of that scenic art which he was about to assist at. About
the year 1669 there existed opposite to the monument of Lysicrates,
then called the lantern of Demosthenes (τὸ φανάρι τοῦ Δημόσθενι),
another similar building called the lantern of Diogenes (τὸ φανάρι τοῦ
Διογένη), thus further proving the direction of the street; but the
latter monument had entirely vanished when Athens was visited by

VIEW OF MONUMENT OF LYSICRATES.

Spon and Wheler in 1676.[1] The monument of Lysicrates then formed
part of a Capuchin convent,[2] and continued to do so when seen by
Stuart, who describes it as enclosed in a wall, so that of the six columns
only two and part of another were visible.[3] It was still part of a
convent at the beginning of the present century, when Athens was
visited by Dodwell and Lord Broughton. The former writer attributes

[1] Voyage, ii. 128; cf. Ross, Aufsätze, i. 264, note 51.

[2] See Wheler's Journey, p. 397.

[3] Antiq. of Athens, vol. i. ch. 4.

its preservation to this circumstance (i. 291). At present, the convent having been pulled down, it stands entirely isolated; and the soil which had accumulated round the base to the depth of eleven feet in Stuart's time, having been excavated, the whole monument is exposed to view.

This little temple is composed of three parts; a quadrangular basement, a circular colonnade, of which the intercolumniations were closed, and a tholus or cupola, with a triangular ornament upon it, on which the tripod stood. Only three of the marble panels which filled the intercolumniations were entire when seen by Stuart; and on each of them, just under the architrave, two tripods with handles were carved in bas-relief; two of the other sides had been walled in with brick, whilst the sixth formed a door, giving entrance to a sort of closet, but so narrow that a man could hardly stand upright in it. Originally there was no aperture in any part of the temple, so that it was never meant to be entered; and thus, in fact, it served for little more than a magnificent pedestal for the tripod and statue. The height of the whole building to the top of the ornament bearing the tripod is very nearly thirty-four feet—of which the base occupies nearly fourteen feet; the fluted Corinthian columns, with their stylobate and entablature, rather more than fourteen; the cupola between one and two feet; and the ornament four. From this ornament it would appear that the legs of the tripod formed an equilateral triangle, of which each side was about three feet in length. The diameter of the circular part is less than six feet in the clear. Round the frieze, which is hardly ten inches high, is sculptured in bas-relief, with great vigour and elegance, though in diminutive form, the story of Dionysus and the Tyrrhenian pirates. These figures, of almost the original size, will be found engraved in Stuart's work. Beneath, on the architrave, was an inscription recording that "Lysicrates of Cicyna, son of Lysitheides, was choragus; the tribe Acamantis gained the victory with a chorus of boys; Theon played the flute; Lysiades, an Athenian, taught the chorus; Euænetus was archon."[1] The archonship of Euænetus

---

[1] Λυσικράτης Λυσιθείδου Κικυνεὺς ἐχορήγει, Ἀκαμαντὶς παίδων ἐνίκα, Θέων ηὔλει, Λυσιάδης Ἀθηναῖος ἐδίδασκε, Εὐαίνετος ἦρχε.

fell in the year B.C. 335; so that the absurd story of Demosthenes having his study here was, at all events, not inconsistent with chronology. As we shall see a little further on, the custom of erecting tripods as choragic prizes had begun at least in the time of Aristeides and Themistocles, a century and a half before this date, and they were then placed in the precincts of the theatre, as they continued to be a great deal later. We know not when the custom began of erecting them in the street leading to the theatre; at first, probably, in its immediate vicinity, and then gradually extending themselves along the street.

As we shall have to advert again to the tripod as a choragic prize when we come to describe the theatre and the monument of Thrasyllus, we will here say a few words about its origin and purpose. Originally it was the kettle of the domestic hearth, the τρίπους ἐμπυριβήτης, and is mentioned by Homer among the other prizes given by Achilles at the funeral games in honour of Patroclus.[1] The custom, therefore, appears to have been of high antiquity. Herodotus (v. 60 sq.) records some very ancient inscriptions, in what he calls Cadmeian letters, on tripods dedicated to the Ismenian Apollo at Thebes. In early times the tripod was the reward of victors in the Olympic contests, and hence formed part of the anathemata in the temple of Apollo at Delphi, by which custom an impulse was given to the improvement of its form, and to the art of working in bronze. An inscription on one of those said to have been given by Achilles and dedicated to the Pythian Apollo, purported it to be an anathema of Diomedes. In the Homeric times, some of these tripods were colossal and meant only for show. Such were called ἄπυροι, 'fireless.'[2] The Lydian king Gyges is said to have been the first who dedicated a golden one in the temple of Apollo. After Olympiad 48.3, the tripod appears to have been discarded as a reward in gymnastic contests, and the chaplet substituted for it.[3] But

---

[1] τῷ μὲν νικήσαντι μέγαν τρίποδ' ἐμπυρι-
βήτην.—Il. xxiii. 702; cf. vii. 699, &c.
[2] One of these tripods, with ears, is said to have been 22 metra :

καὶ τρίποδ' ὠτώεντα δύω καὶ εἰκοσί-
μετρον.—Il. xxiii. 264.

From this we must infer a large size, though we do not know the measure of the metron. It appears to have expressed capacity.—See Paley, ibi.

[3] στεφανίτης ἀγών.—Pausan. x. 7, 3.

the more elegant form of it had been adopted as a choral prize at Athens, where it continued in use for that purpose till a late period. The victorious choragus received from his tribe a bronze tripod, which, if he pleased, he might plate with gold or silver and place in some conspicuous situation.[1] In the earlier times these choragic monuments were very simple. When Themistocles gained the prize with a tragic chorus, his victory was recorded by a simple slab with the inscription, "Themistocles the Phrearian was choragus, Phrynichus was chorus-master, Adeimantus was archon"[2] (B.C. 477). Aristeides, on a like occasion, placed tripods in the theatre, which were still to be seen in the time of Plutarch;[3] and this, we believe, is the first instance recorded of their use on such occasions. No archonship is given in the inscription, but Aristeides was contemporary with Themistocles. It is possible, however, as we shall see presently, that this was not the great Aristeides, but a later namesake. Nicias, who lived about half a century later than Themistocles, appears to have been the first who made choragic monuments more splendid;[4] and, as is not unfrequently the case, their magnificence appears to have increased as the talent which they illus-trated declined. Nicias and his brothers appear to have placed a whole row of tripods in the Dionysiac peribolus, to which Plato alludes in his 'Gorgias.'[5] These tripods were not only an ornament to the city, but the inscriptions on them were sometimes also useful in illustrating points of history. Heliodorus wrote a work upon them, and Harpo-cration quotes it to show that Onetor had been a choragus (in voc.). And thus Demetrius Phalereus, in his book called 'Socrates,' appealed to the tripods of Aristeides in proof that he must have been a rich man; while Panætius, who took the opposite side of the question, maintained that from the Persian times down to the end of the Pelo-ponnesian war there had been only two choragi named Aristeides; of whom one was the son of Xenophilus, and therefore not the great Aristeides; whilst the other one must have been considerably younger,

[1] See Athen. vi. 20 sq.
[2] Plut. Them. 5.
[3] Id. Arist. 1.
[4] Id. Nic. 3.
[5] Νικίας ὁ Νικηράτου καὶ οἱ ἀδελφοὶ μετ' αὐτοῦ, ὧν οἱ τρίποδες οἱ ἐφεξῆς ἑστῶτές εἰσιν ἐν τῷ Διονυσίῳ.—p. 472 (ii. i. 55, Bekk.).

as appeared from the inscription on the tripod, the characters of which were posterior to the time of Eucleides.[1] They have served the same purpose of illustration in modern times. Thus Dr. Wordsworth has shown, from a choragic inscription on the west side of the theatre, that Ctesippus, the son of Chabrias, had discharged the office of choragus; whence he infers that Demosthenes must have failed in the attempt which he made, in his speech against Leptines, to secure for Ctesippus an immunity from public burdens; although Dion Chrysostom says he was successful. But may not the inscription be reconciled with Chrysostom's testimony as follows? Leptines had in the first instance carried his law, and it had been in force more than a year (see the second Argument), during which we may suppose it was that Ctesippus was obliged to provide a chorus. Next year he, with the aid of Demosthenes, got the law repealed. It cannot be supposed that the law of Leptines was permanently successful. (See Boeckh, 'Public Economy of Athens,' bk. iii. ch. xxi. end.[2])

The Street of Tripods led to the peribolus or enclosure called the LENÆUM, which was sacred to Dionysus, and derived its name from the ληνός, or winepress. It contained two temples and two statues of Dionysus, one of which appears to have been the ξόανον, or rude wooden image of the god, brought from Eleutheræ when the Dionysiac worship was first introduced at Athens; the other was a fine statue of ivory and gold, the work of Alcamenes (Paus. 20, 2, cf. 38, 8). The older temple is no doubt that mentioned by Thucydides[3] as lying under the south side of the Acropolis, in the district called Limnæ or the Marshes, where the more ancient Dionysia were celebrated on the 12th of Anthesterion. The older temple was opened only once a year, on this occasion.[4] The sacred rites in it were performed by fourteen

---

[1] Plut. Arist. 1.

[2] The inscription (restored) is thus given by Dr. Wordsworth, ch. xvii. p. 119:—

κεκΡΟΓΙΣΓΛΙΔων ενικα
κτηΣΙΓΓΟΣΧΑΒΡιου εχο
PHΓΕΙ ΔΑ.

It is rather differently given by Rangabé,

(t. ii. No. 2352); but it is plain from both that Ctesippus was choragus.

[3] lib. ii. c. 15.

[4] καὶ διὰ ταῦτα ἐν τῷ ἀρχαιοτάτῳ ἱερῷ τοῦ Διονύσου καὶ ἁγιωτάτῳ τῷ ἐν Λίμναις, ἔστησαν (τὴν στήλην), ἵνα μὴ πολλοὶ εἰδῶσι τὰ γεγραμμένα· ἅπαξ γὰρ τοῦ ἐνιαυτοῦ ἑκάστου

priestesses called Geraræ (Γεραραί).[1] It was probably, therefore, the more modern temple, with the statue by Alcamenes, which contained the three pictures described by Pausanias. One of these represented Hephæstus conducted to heaven by Dionysus in order to liberate Hera from the throne to which he had contrived to enchain her. The subject of another was the punishment of Pentheus and Lycurgus for the insults which they had offered to Dionysus. The third represented Ariadnë sleeping, Theseus deserting her and putting out to sea, while Dionysus approached to carry her off. This subject seems to have been frequently repeated, and occurs in some of the paintings at Pompeii.

We may fix the site of one of these temples with tolerable accuracy from what Marinus says about the house of Proclus. He describes it as lying between the temple of Asclepius and that of Dionysus, near the theatre;[2] and as the Asclepieium, as we shall see further on, lay a little to the west of the theatre, it follows that this temple of Dionysus must have been close to the western side of the theatre. This was probably the more modern temple; the site of the ancient one cannot be so accurately determined. M. Rousopoulos in the ' Archæological Ephemeris ' (1863, p. 287) places both close to the scene of the theatre, one on its eastern, the other on its western side; and A. Mommsen[3] very near the same spots, a little further south, though still within the boundary walls of the theatre. But the passage we have cited from Marinus shows, we think, that one of the temples at least must have lain beyond its western wall. The other we should be inclined to place between the monument of Lysicrates and the eastern wall of the theatre. For the ODEIUM OF PERICLES undoubtedly lay on the east side of the theatre, and Pausanias (20, 3) describes it as being near both the theatre and the temple of Dionysus.

Pausanias does not mention the name of Odeium, but calls it a structure (κατασκεύασμα) built in imitation of the tent of Xerxes;

ἀνοίγεται, τῇ δωδεκάτῃ τοῦ ἀνθεστηριῶνος μηνός.—Demosth. c. Neær. p. 1371, Reiske.
  [1] Harpocr. and Hesych. in voc.; Demosth. loc. cit.

[2] (οἴκησιν) γείτονα μὲν οὖσαν τοῦ 'Ασκληπιείου, καὶ τοῦ πρὸς τῷ θεάτρῳ Διονυσίου. —s. 29, p. 74.
  [3] Heortologie, p. 353, note.

though he says that the building he saw was a restoration, the original having been burnt by Sulla when he took Athens. He then gives an account of the Mithridatic war, into which it is not necessary to follow him. Appian, on the contrary,[1] says that it was burnt by Aristion, in order to prevent Sulla from using the materials for the assault on the Acropolis. We have touched on this subject before (supra, p. 163). Near the theatre was found a *stelë*, with an inscription by the Athenian people to Ariobarzanes, their benefactor, with regard doubtless to his restoration of it.[2] The restored building was no doubt an exact copy of the original, since the form of it, as seen by Plutarch, answers to a joke attributed to Cratinus about Pericles' head. That author says,[3] that it contained many seats and many columns; that its peaked or conical roof was an imitation of the tent of Xerxes, thus resembling the head of Pericles (supra, p. 113). Dicæarchus, who must have seen the original, considered it the finest building of the sort in the world.[4] Its site may be identified by the passage cited from Vitruvius, in which it is said to have been on the left hand on going out of the theatre, where Stuart saw foundations; and by a passage in Andocides, where he says,[5] that by the light of a full moon, men were seen descending from the Odeium to the orchestra of the theatre.

Pausanias now arrives at the great or DIONYSIAC THEATRE;[6] but his account of it is very meagre and unsatisfactory. He gives no description of the building itself. He merely says that there were in it statues of tragic and comic poets; but, except Menander, the basis of whose statue was recently found near the western entrance, the comic poets were of little renown. Hence we may conclude that Aristophanes was unrepresented. Among the tragic writers there were statues of Sophocles and Euripides. These, we may conclude, had been taken from life; for he proceeds to add that there was also a statue of Æschylus, but executed probably long after his death, and after the

---

[1] Bell. Mithr. c. 38 (p. 331).

[2] Vitruv. v. 9; Boeckh, C. Ins. Gr. No. 357; Ἀρχαιολ. Ἐφημ. July, 1862, p. 166, No. 167.

[3] Vit. Pericl. c. 13.

[4] Ap. Müller, Fr. Hist. Græc. ii. 254, note 59, 1.

[5] De Myster. p. 19, Reiske.

[6] cap. 21, 1.

picture of the battle of Marathon in the Pœcilē. Whence we may infer that there was a portrait of Æschylus in that picture, although Pausanias says nothing about it in his description of the painting. Above the theatre, on the south wall of the Acropolis, was a gilt head of the Gorgon Medusa, enveloped in an ægis. From another passage of Pausanias,[1] we learn that the ægis also was gilt, and that the whole was an anathema of King Antiochus. At the very summit of the theatre was a cave, or grotto, and over it a tripod. Within the cave were statues of Apollo and Artemis slaying the children of Niobë.

COIN, SHOWING DIONYSIAC THEATRE.

The site of the Dionysiac theatre seems easy to identify. We know that it lay at, or under, the Acropolis,[2] in the district called Limnæ. The order of the route of Pausanias, who arrives at it in the regular course of his peregrination through the Street of the Tripods, and who, after describing it, mentions objects which we know to have lain to the west of it, as well as the grotto at its summit which still exists, might, one would think, have indicated its situation clearly enough. Again: an Athenian coin, formerly in the collection of R. P. Knight, and now in the British Museum, of which we annex a cut, shows the theatre surmounted by the grotto, with the Parthenon and Propylæa

[1] lib. v. c. 12, 2.

[2] Philostrat. Vit. Apoll. Tyan. lib. iv. c. 22; Dion Chrys. Orat. Rhod. t. i. p. 386 (Teubner). There seems no necessity to substitute ὑπό for ἐπὶ in the former pas-

sage (τὸ θέατρον τὸ ἐπὶ τῇ ἀκροπόλει) with Dr. Wordsworth (Athens, p. 75, note 2). As the theatre occupies the side of the hill nearly to the top, it may justly be said to be at it.

above, and is no bad representation of it as it exists at the present day.[1] Nevertheless it is only in comparatively recent times that its identity has been universally recognised. Wheler took the Odeium of Herodes Atticus to be the large theatre; and though he visited the grotto above the latter, and copied the choragic inscriptions upon it, yet he fancied it to belong to some gymnasium, and does not even notice the vast concavity beneath it; which yet must have existed in his time, and from its form was eminently calculated to suggest the idea of a theatre.[2] It may be alleged in his excuse that even Lord Broughton, in 1810, observes that " the circular sweep of the seats, indented into the side of the hill, is scarcely perceptible."[3] Yet it did not escape the attention of Stuart, who, however, took it to be the Odeium of Pericles, and, like Wheler, imagined the Odeium of Herodes to be the Dionysiac theatre.[4] Leake and other more recent topographers have given to the spot its right appellation. But whatever doubts might have existed on the subject, must have been dispelled by the late excavations, which have discovered the theatre in all its dimensions, and with some of its fittings in a more perfect condition than could have been reasonably hoped after the lapse of so many centuries.

Some excavations at this spot were begun by the Archæological Society of Athens; but, after having been carried to some depth, were abandoned in despair; having produced, says M. Rangabé, the sad conviction that the theatre, with its immortal recollections, had been destroyed for the sake of the white marble of which its seats were constructed.[5] Success, however, was reserved for a more enterprising discoverer. In 1862, a German architect, Hofbaurath Strack, the author of an esteemed work on Greek theatres,[6] visited Athens with the design of excavating that of Dionysus. He was accompanied by

---

[1] There is a still better representation of it in a plate from an ancient vase in Millin, ' Peintures de vases antiques,' t. ii.

[2] See his Journey into Greece, p. 369.

[3] Hobhouse's Journey, vol. i. p. 320.

[4] See his Antiquities of Athens, vol. ii.

[5] Antiquités Helléniques, t. i. Préf. p. 10.

[6] Das altgriechische Theatergebäude, Potsdam, 1843. Strack was a member of a commission, which included Bötticher, despatched from Berlin to examine the Athenian monuments.

Dr. William Vischer, of Basle, the editor of the ' Neues Schweitzerisches
Museum ;' who has given some account of the proceedings in that pub-
lication for the year 1863. The orchestra and lower part of the
theatre was at that time covered with soil to the depth of about 20 feet,
on which was growing a crop of corn, whilst below were some remains
of foundations of houses. The spot seems to have remained in this condition for at least about two centuries, for Wheler also describes it as
uninhabited and turned into cornfields. After some trouble with the
owners and lessee of the soil, Strack set to work at his own expense, and
after some days of fruitless labour, which occasioned many exhortations
to relinquish the enterprise, was at length rewarded by the discovery
of some seats in the central part of the theatre. The work was now
pushed with fresh vigour, the King of Prussia engaging to defray the
expenses, and the Athenian Archæological Society supplying twenty
labourers. After a residence of two or three months, during which he
excavated a large part of the theatre, Strack left Athens, and the work
was brought to a conclusion under the direction of the society just
named.

We will now describe its present appearance. The scene is
destroyed, but its foundations may be traced and also the λογείον, or
stage. Along the front of this, and separating it from the orchestra,
runs a parapet wall about three feet high ; in the middle of which is a
flight of five steps of white marble leading up to the logeium, the height
of which is 1·40 mètres, or rather more than 4 feet 6 inches. On the
topmost step is the following somewhat barbarous inscription :

σοὶ τόδε καλὸν ἔτευξε, φιλόργιε, βῆμα θεήτρου
Φαῖδρος Ζωΐλου, βιοδώτορος Ἀτθίδος ἀρχός.

That is : " Phædrus, son of Zoïlus, governor of life-giving (or fruitful)
Attica, erected for thee, O revel-loving Dionysus, this handsome stage
(or rostrum) of the theatre."

The letters of this inscription belong to a late period, and M. Rousopoulos, who watched the excavation, and recorded its progress in the
' Journal of the Athenian Archæological Society,' is inclined to ascribe it

to the reign of Diocletian.[1] The name of Phædrus, son of Zoïlus, with the addition of Pæanieus (Παιανιεὺς of the demos Pæania), was already known from a marble dial brought to London by Lord Elgin;[2] of which, from the inscription, he appears to have been the maker. From the character of the letters, some critics are inclined to assign this last inscription to the time of the Antonines, and others to that of Septimius Severus. Even between this last emperor and Diocletian there is an interval of three quarters of a century; and therefore, if both inscriptions are not to be referred to the same person, we must infer, with M. Rousopoulos, that the restorer of the scene was the grandson of the maker of the dial. M. Rousopoulos' reasons for placing the latter so late are, first, some trifling differences in the characters of the inscriptions, and especially the small *o* in that in the theatre; which in that on the dial, is equal in size with the rest of the letters. Whether this is decisive must be left to those well skilled in palæography. We shall only observe that in these changes of character we do not find any very strict line of demarcation; and that, even in so marked an epoch with regard to this matter as that of Eucleides, we find before his time, the custom varying, and some of those innovations occasionally presenting themselves which, as a general rule, are said to belong to the post-Eucleidan period. And with regard more particularly to the small *o*, it appears' to have been in use, partially at least, before the time of the Antonines; for it occurs in an inscription on the base of a statue dedicated to Hadrian, also found in the theatre, and published by M. Rousopoulos himself only a few pages after the one in question.[3]

M. Rousopoulos' second reason is that the maker of the dial was an artist (τεχνίτης), as appears from the word ἐποίει in the inscription;

---

[1] The following is a copy of the original:—

$$C^O IT^O \Delta EKA\Lambda^O NETEY\Xi E\Phi I\Lambda^O P\Gamma IEBHMA\Theta EHTP^O Y$$
$$\Phi AI\Delta P^O CZ\omega I\Lambda^O YBI^O \Delta\omega T^O P^O CAT^\Theta I\Delta^O CAPX^O C$$

See Ἀρχαιολ. Ἐφημερίς, July 6, 1862, p. 163.

[2] See Corp. Inscrr. Græc. No. 522; Pauly, Real-Encycl. t. v. p. 1417; Account of Elgin Marbles, in Library of Entertaining Knowledge, vol. ii. p. 111

[3] Ἀρχαιολ. Ἐφημ. ibid. p. 179. Where we read: $TPAIAN^O Y — YI\omega N^O N — APEI^O Y.$

while the restorer of the stage is characterised as ἀρχός; whether that word may be used, poetically, to signify the archon eponymous, and therefore a political man; or, as M. Rousopoulos is more inclined to think, a στρατηγός, or magistrate.[1] But let us observe that the dial in question was a very curious piece of workmanship. It had four faces, and is supposed to have shown the hour at a crossway between several diverging streets. Its maker, therefore, was no common workman, but a mathematician, and needed not have been ashamed to put his name upon it had he been even an eponymous archon.

The parapet wall to which the steps with this inscription belong, and which must therefore have been coëval with it, gives *primâ facie* evidence of an earlier date than the time of Diocletian. For along the side of it which faces the orchestra there still remain some well-executed groups in high relief, which, though probably of the Roman times, could hardly have been of so late a date as Diocletian. These statues, of the height of the parapet, agree with the account of Pollux,[2] that the under part of the stage, towards the audience, was adorned with small figures. On the left, or eastern side of the steps, these groups have shared the ruin which is general at that side of the theatre; whilst on the western side they are pretty perfect, except that all the figures have lost their heads. The subjects are Bacchanalian scenes, and one of the slabs evidently represents a sacrifice to Dionysus. The western side of the parapet is broken about the middle by a square recess containing, in comparison with the other figures, a colossal Silenus; whose head, which is perfect, is, from his kneeling posture, brought on a level with the top of the parapet. This figure seems quite out of keeping with the rest of the wall, as it now exists; but we are hardly in a position to judge of its effect when the scene was entire. Originally, perhaps, it may have supported a pillar, or a base with a statue. It can hardly be doubted that there was a corresponding one on the eastern side.

---

[1] The term στρατηγὸς in later ages had come to signify a civil magistrate.

[2] ἀγαλμάτιοις.—lib. iv. s. 124. Pollux appears to be speaking of the theatre at Athens, as he alludes to it at the beginning of the chapter (c. ix.), and observes further on (s. 122), that the nine archons were entertained in the portico attached to it.

The connection of this wall with the flight of steps, as well as the epithet καλὸν in the inscription, implying an ornamental work, afford reasons for believing that the sculptures were placed there by Phædrus. Allowing, however, that they are of an earlier date than Diocletian, it does not necessarily follow that the wall is also. M. Rousopoulos, who ascribes the relief to the time of Hadrian,[1] observes that it may have been taken from an older proscenium, of which there are remains at a considerable distance behind that of Phædrus. The latter, it appears, advanced the logeium considerably into the orchestra. Hence the proscenium and its inscription afford no certain data from which to determine at what time the theatre, as we now see it, was restored. On the whole, however, they raise a presumption of an earlier date than Diocletian. And this presumption is somewhat confirmed by the fact that, so far as we are aware, no inscriptions have been found in the theatre of a later date than M. Aurelius Antoninus. There is a pedestal inscribed to that emperor as προστάτης ’Αθηναίων, which we have already mentioned.

We have entered at some length into these points, because it would be interesting to discover, with a view to the manner in which the ancient Greek dramas were presented, at what period the theatre was arranged as it now exists. The earlier its date, the more likely are we to see it as it still served for the representation of the pieces of Æschylus, Sophocles, or Aristophanes. On the whole, and excluding the scene, M. Rousopoulos considers the restoration to have been the work of Hadrian. There are some strong grounds for this opinion. The munificence of that emperor in adorning Athens is well known. That some part of it was bestowed on the theatre appears to be attested by the numerous statues of him which it contained, of which several of the inscribed bases are still extant. Yet we are not aware that any inscription, or any passage of an ancient author, records that he devoted part of his attention to this object. It is supposed that there were thirteen statues of him in the theatre, one in each of the cunei, or sections, into which the audience part was divided, and that each was dedicated by one of the

[1] Ephemeris, 1862, p. 209 sq.

thirteen tribes. It is from these thirteen *cunei* that M. Rousopoulos has derived one of the arguments in favour of his view.[1] The Attic tribes were increased from twelve to thirteen, by the addition of the Hadrianis; and it was, he thinks, to accommodate this new tribe, that the theatre was divided into thirteen sections. But, first, we have no evidence that the spectators took their seats in the theatre according to their tribes. Again, though the pedestals discovered record that the statues upon them were dedicated by one of the tribes — except one in the middle, which mentions no tribe — yet, as Dr. Vischer observes,[2] they also record that they were erected by the Senate of *Six Hundred*; and it is well known that, after the creation of the thirteenth tribe, the senate was reduced to its ancient number of *Five Hundred*.[3] It follows that the dedications of these statues were *previous* to the creation of the thirteenth tribe; and as they must have been placed in the theatre after it was finished, it could not have been laid out to accommodate a number of tribes which did not exist. This also negatives a perhaps more plausible conjecture, that the thirteen *cunei* were meant to accommodate the tribes when they met in the theatre in their political capacity.

But, though the theatre may have been re-arranged and considerably altered in the time of Hadrian, there are reasons for thinking that the old plan was in the main adhered to. One argument for this view may be drawn from the marble thrones for the priests and chief magistrates still in existence, and forming the first circle, which we shall describe presently. It is certain that these thrones were in the same position before the time of Hadrian; since Dion Chrysostom, who flourished considerably before that emperor, mentions them in a passage which we have already cited (supra, p. 177), respecting the gladiatorial combats in the theatre. These seats, as we have seen, were

---

[1] See Ephemeris, Dec. 12, 1863, p. 287.

[2] Neues Schweitzerisches Museum, 1863, p. 66.

[3] The following is one of these inscriptions: αὐτοκράτορα Καίσαρα θεοῦ Τραιανοῦ Παρθικοῦ υἱόν, θεοῦ Νερούα υἱωνόν, || Ἀδρι-

ανὸν Σεβαστόν, ἡ ἐξ Ἀρείου πάγου || βουλή, καὶ ἡ βουλὴ τῶν χ, καὶ ὁ δῆμος || ἐπιμελουμένης τῆς Οἰνηΐδος φυλῆς. They were accompanied by a Latin inscription, giving the emperor's Roman titles. Pausanias knows only a senate of 500 (i. 3, 4).

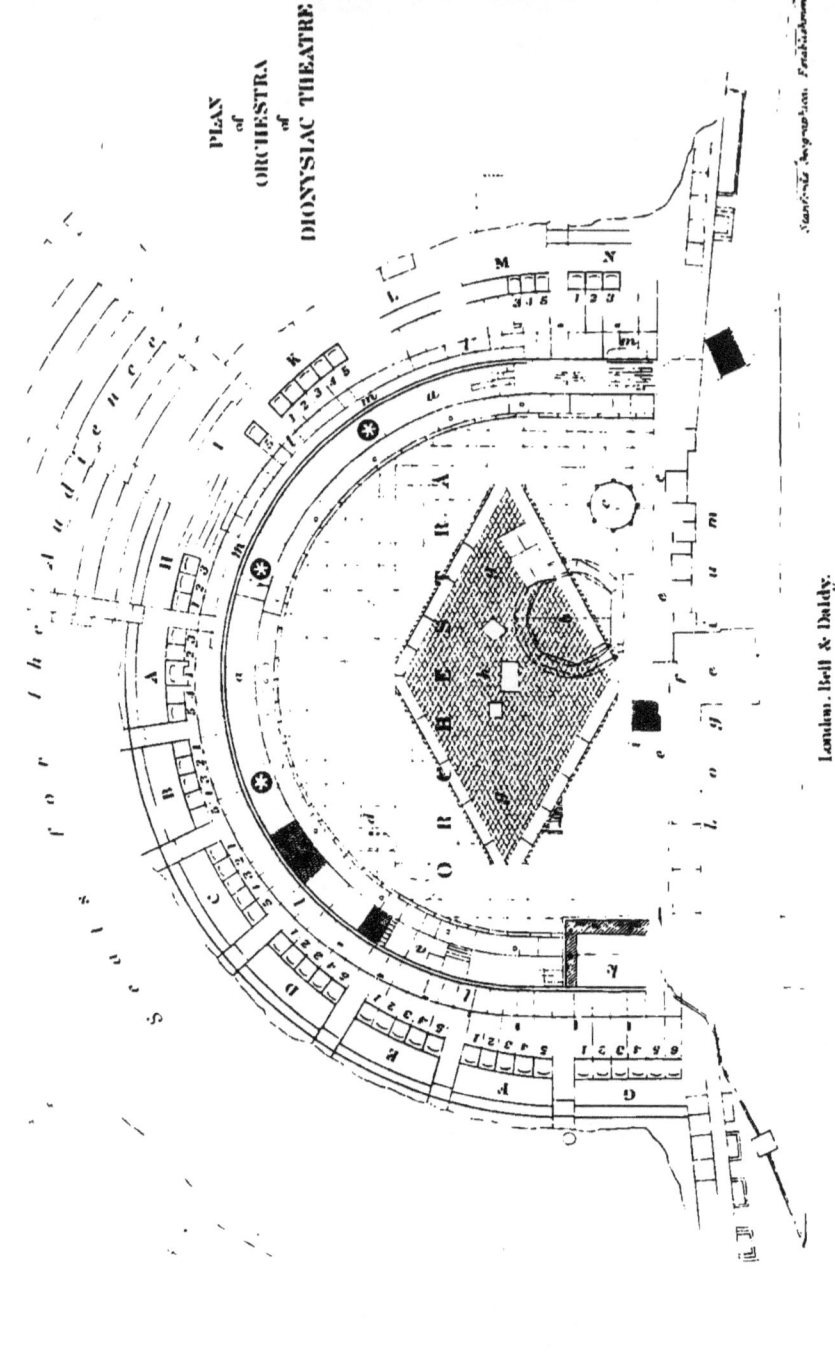

PLAN
of
ORCHESTRA
of
DIONYSIAC THEATRE

Stanford's Geographical Establishment.

London, Bell & Daldy.

separated from the orchestra only by a parapet wall about three feet high, easily overleapt by a man contending for his life. And, indeed, this wall may not have existed in the time of Dion, but have been subsequently erected in order to prevent such accidents. It is no improbable supposition that some of the thrones in question are as old as the time of Lycurgus, who first completed the theatre, and adorned it in a suitable manner; for some of the inscriptions appear to be much older than others; and in a few cases the ancient inscription has evidently been obliterated, in order to make room for a new one. It is probable that the κοῖλον, or audience part, in its general outline, still presents the original construction, or at all events the restoration, of Lycurgus. The chief alterations appear to have been made about the scene; the ancient one, as we have already remarked, having evidently lain considerably further to the south than the more recent one. That of Phædrus is built of brick, and of bad workmanship, while the older one behind it is constructed of Hymettian marble.[1]

We will now proceed to describe the orchestra. Its width along the parapet wall in front of the stage (*e, e, e, e* in plan) is 24 French mètres, or about 78 ft. 6 in. English. Its measure from the steps of Phædrus (*f*) in the middle of the boundary wall to the boundary in front of the. throne of the priest of Dionysus, in the centre of the first circle of spectators, is 17·96 mètres, or about 58 ft. 6 in. A great part of this semicircular area is occupied by a rhomboidal or lozenge-shaped figure (*g, g*), with two obtuse and two acute angles, lying nearer to the stage than to the spectators. It is formed of Hymettian marble, and appears to be of Roman workmanship, with some barbarous reparations. In order to understand the form and situation of this figure, as well as the general arrangement of the orchestra, and the objects which immediately surround it, the reader is referred to the annexed plan, taken from the Athenian 'Ephemeris.' The figure in question is level with the floor of the rest of the orchestra, from which it is distinguished by its being formed of marble, in small squares, and by a border; while the remaining portion of the orchestra is paved with square stones of a

---

[1] Ephemeris, June 1862, p. 135.

larger size. It can hardly be doubted that the figure in question marked out the station for the chorus, which has commonly been called the *thymelē* (θυμέλη), and by most modern writers is considered to have been a raised platform, including an altar in the middle of the orchestra, upon which the choreutæ were stationed.[1]

In the plan will be observed a round hole (*h*) about 18 inches in diameter, in the middle of the rhomboidal figure, in which, probably, by means of a shaft, was fixed the altar of Dionysus. Among the remains which lie before the theatre is perhaps this altar, a circular one of solid white marble 1·20 mètres, or a little less than four feet, high, and of about the same diameter. Around it, in bas-relief, are four bearded masks, apparently of Sileni, from which hang festoons of leaves and grapes. In the middle of the semicircle described by each festoon, is a flower, apparently a rose. At the top and bottom of the altar is an Ionic border. On one side is a nearly obliterated inscription, of which only the following words are legible :

Πιστοκράτης καὶ Ἀπολλόδωρος . . . Ἄρχοντες . . . ἀνέθηκαν.

Round the arc of the orchestra runs a border marked by the different colour and arrangement of the stones (*a, a, a,* in plan). This was a drain which had its exit on the eastern side of the theatre. The portion where three asteroids are still visible, is perfect. The floor of the orchestra is somewhat elevated towards the middle, to allow the water to flow towards the drain, which has holes for its reception. The imperfect circle, which is marked (*b*), and the smaller circle (*c*), are engraved on the stone floor on the eastern side of the orchestra, near the stage. M. Rousopoulos is of opinion (p. 289) that one represents the theatre and the other an odeium. The use of such representations it is difficult to discover, and it seems more probable that they were meant to guide some of the evolutions of the chorus, as, for instance, the parabasis ; but in what way, we will not venture to conjecture. The

---

[1] We have examined, in an Appendix, No. II., how this construction may have affected the dramatic representations.

engraving at the upper western side of the orchestra (*d*) shows the form of a gate. Near the stairs of Phædrus (*f*), on the western side, is a deep hole (*i*), which may perhaps have been that through which the ghosts ascended. The square wall (*k*) at the western corner of the orchestra, is of late Byzantine, or even of Frankish or Turkish construction, and may have marked out the seat of an emperor or great magistrate.

We will now proceed to the audience part of the theatre. The marble wall (*l, l, l, l*) which separates it from the orchestra is thought to be of the Roman times, and is pretty complete except towards the eastern side. Behind it was another wall of about the same height, but of ruder construction, of which there are some remains at the eastern side of the orchestra (*m, m, m*). M. Rousopoulos is of opinion that it served to keep the orchestra water-tight when flooded for the exhibition of naumachiæ. Between the parapet wall and the first circle of seats are some square holes marked black in the plan, which served perhaps for poles for velaria, or awnings.

The proëdria, or first circle of seats, marked by the capital letters at the back of it, consisted of marble thrones, and the plan shows those which are preserved and those which are deficient. They are separated into compartments by the fourteen staircases which divide the theatre into thirteen κερκίδες, or *cunei*. Each compartment contained five thrones, except the two at the extremities next the scene, which held six. The whole number of thrones in the proëdria was consequently sixty-seven. They are made of solid blocks of marble, which form sometimes three thrones, sometimes two, and sometimes only one throne.

These marble seats, and probably also the stone seats behind, were furnished with cushions or pillows, and carpets; for we find Æschines animadverting on the obsequiousness of Demosthenes, in providing these appliances for Philip's ambassadors, and procuring for them by a psephisma, a seat in the proëdria (on which occasion, we must suppose that some of the magistrates, or priests, had to vacate their seats in favour of the ambassadors), adding with spontaneous complaisance, the cushions, &c.[1] In like manner, the Flatterer, in the 'Characters' of Theophrastus, takes away the cushions from the servant in the theatre, and places them himself under his patron.[2] From Æschines we also learn that the dramatic performances, like the assemblies in the Pnyx, began with the break of day.

We will describe the thirteen compartments of the proëdria, or first circle, separately, marking them by the capital letters A, B, C, &c.; and the separate seats in each compartment by figures. We will call the middle compartment, in which sat the priest of Dionysus, A, and his throne No. 1. And we will first of all give the inscriptions on all the thrones that still exist, and then discuss any points connected with them which may require explanation. It will be observed that they contain many barbarisms.

Exactly in the centre of the half circle, and opposite the steps of Phædrus, was the seat of the priest of Dionysus, A, No. 1, inscribed with his name, ἱερέως Διονύσου 'Ελευθερέως—seat of the priest of Dionysus of Eleutheræ; that is, of the older Dionysus, to whose history we have already adverted. It is more magnificent than the rest, as became the chief priest of the festival, projecting a few inches in front of the other four in the same compartment, and being more elaborately sculptured. The feet are carved like the claws of a lion, or rather, perhaps, a panther. On the back are two sturdy satyrs, supporting with difficulty a vine branch with huge bunches of grapes.[3] On the outside of each arm, a youthful Nikë, or Victory, with spread wings, stoops apparently towards the thunderbolts of Zeus, typifying the birth of Dionysus. Beneath, is an ornament terminating in a swan's head. At the back of the Nikë is a branch and leaf. The sculpture under the abacus shows the Asiatic conquests of the god. A mon-

---

[1] καὶ τὸ περὶ τῆς προεδρίας τῆς εἰς τὰ Διονύσια τοῖς πρέσβεσι τοῖς Φιλίππου ψήφισμα, καὶ προσέθηκε τὴν ἐπιμέλειαν τὴν αὐτοῦ, καὶ προσκεφαλαίων θέσιν, κ.τ.λ. Æsch. de f. Leg. p. 281, Reiske. καὶ πρέσβεις εἰς προεδρίαν ἐκάλεσε, καὶ προσκεφάλαια ἔθηκε, καὶ φοινικίδας περιεπέτασε, καὶ ἅμα τῇ ἡμέρᾳ ἡγεῖτο τοῖς πρέσβεσιν εἰς τὸ θέατρον.—Id. c. Ctesiph. p. 466.

[2] καὶ τοῦ παιδὸς ἐν τῷ θεάτρῳ ἀφελόμενος τὰ προσκεφάλαια αὐτὸς ὑποστρῶσαι.—Περὶ κολακείας, c. 2.

[3] Figured in the Athenian 'Ephemeris' for June 1862, p. 142.

strous lion-shaped, but winged, beast symbolizes his power; kings in Asiatic costume, with diadems on their heads and scythe-like swords, oppose his progress. The dimensions of this throne, which is rather larger than the others, are as follows: height 2 ft. 9 in.; breadth, 1 ft. 11 in.; depth, 1 ft. 7 in. We may remark that a cast of this chair has been placed in the Athenian room of the British Museum, through the munificence of Miss Wyse.

The throne next to that of the priest of Dionysus, on his left, A, No. 2, is inscribed ἱερέως Διὸς πολιέως, seat of the priest of Zeus Polieus, or guardian of the city. No. 3, θυηκόου,[1] seat of the sacrificer. No. 4, next throne on the right of the priest of Dionysus, ἱερέως Πυθοχρήστου ἐξηγητοῦ, seat of the expounder appointed by the Pythian deity. No. 5, ἱερέως Διὸς Ὀλυμπίου, seat of the priest of the Olympian Zeus. These seats complete the middle *pempas*, or group of five.

In the next compartment, B, on the right hand of the priest of Dionysus, as also in the following ones, we shall number the seats in consecutive order, that is, from east to west. No. 1 is inscribed ἱεροφάντου, seat of the hierophant, or chief priest of the Eleusinian mysteries.[2] No. 2. ἱερέως Ἀπόλλωνος Δηλίου, priest of the Delian Apollo. No. 3. ἱερέως Ποσειδῶνος φυταλμίου, priest of Poseidon, the nourisher. No. 4. ἱερέως Χαρίτων καὶ Ἀρτέμιδος ἐπιπυργιδίας πυρφόρου, priest of the Graces, and of the fire-bringing Artemis Epipurgidia, or Hecate.[3] No. 5. ἐξηγητοῦ ἐκ εὐπατριδῶν χειροτονητοῦ ὑπὸ

---

[1] This word is also found written θυηχόος, which form, though doubtful, is retained by Porson in his edition of Photius, pp. 96, 689. In inscriptions it occurs in both forms. An altar of the θυηχόος is mentioned in Chandler's inscription respecting the Erechtheum, and in an inscription given by Rangabé, t. i. p. 53, line 63. Cf. Boeckh, Corp. Inscr. Gr. No. 160 (vol. i. p. 281). See above, p. 143, note [1].

[2] The hierophant may be considered as the head of the Athenian hierarchy. Dion Chrysostom, speaking of these thrones, names only him (οὗ τὸν ἱεροφάντην καὶ τοὺς

ἄλλους ἱερεῖς ἀνάγκη καθίζειν. Orat. xxxi. p. 348 (386, Teubner); and he is generally named first in inscriptions (Boeckh, C. In. Gr. No. 184 sq. No. 190). But here he is the third on the right hand of the priest of Dionysus, who, of course, was the chief personage in this place. See Vischer, in Schweitz. Mus. iii. p. 37. The priests of the Eleusinian mysteries appear to follow in order thus: Hierophantes, Daduchus, Hierokeryx, and the ἐπὶ βωμῷ. C. Inscr. No. 185.

[3] Or perhaps it may mean of the sacrificial priest of Artemis Epipyrgidia, that

τοῦ δήμου διὰ βίου, the expounder chosen for life by the people from among the Eupatrids, or nobles.

Compartment C. No. 1. ἱερέως Ποσειδῶνος γαιηόχου καὶ Ἐρεχθέως, seat of the priest of earth-surrounding Poseidon and Erechtheus. 2. ἱερέως Ἀρτέμιδος Κολαινίδος, priest of Artemis Kolainis. 3. ἱερέως Μελπομένου Διονύσου ἐξ Εὐνειδῶν, priest of Dionysus Melpomenos of the race of the Eunēidæ. 4. Βουζύγου ἱερέως Διὸς ἐν Παλλαδίῳ, priest of Zeus in the Palladium, of the race of the Bouzygæ. 5. ἱερέως Διὸς Βουλαίου καὶ Ἀθηνᾶς Βουλαίας, priest of Zeus Boulaios, or the counsellor, and Athena Boulaia.

Compartment D. No. 1. ἱερέως Διὸς Διὸς (sic) σωτείρου (σωτῆρος) καὶ Ἀθηνᾶς σωτείρας, priest of Zeus and Athena in their character of saviours or defenders. 2. ἱερέως Ἀντινόου χορείου ἐκ τεχνειτῶν, priest of Antinoüs the choral, elected from the artists. 3. ἱερέως Ἀπόλλωνος Πατρῴου, priest of Apollo Patrous, or the founder. 4. ἱερέως Διονύσου Μελπομένου ἐκ τεχνειτῶν, priest of Dionysus Melpomenos, chosen from among the artists. 5. ἱερέως Εὐκλείας καὶ Εὐνομίας, priest of Eucleia and Eunomia.

Compartment E. No. 1. ἱερέως Ἀσκληπίου, priest of Asclepius. 2. ἱερέως Μουσῶν, priest of the Muses. 3. ἱερέως Διὸς φιλίου, priest of the friendly Zeus. 4. ἱερέως δώδεκα θεῶν, priest of the Twelve Gods. 5. φαιδυντοῦ (sic) Διὸς ἐκ Πείσης, seat of the cleaner of the statue of Zeus at Pisa.

Compartment F. No. 1. ἱερέως Ἀπόλλωνος Λυκήου,[1] seat of the priest of the Lycian Apollo. 2. φαιδύντου (sic) Διὸς Ὀλυμπίου ἐν ἄστει, cleaner of the statue of Olympian Zeus at Athens. 3. ἱερέως Ἀνάκων καὶ ἥρωος Ἐπιτεγίου, priest of the Anakes, or Dioscuri, and of the hero Epitegius. 4. ἱερέως οὐρανίας Νεμεσέως, priest of the heavenly Nemesis. 5. ἱερέως Ἡφαίστου, priest of Hephæstus.

Compartment G. No. 1. ἱερέως Ἀπόλλωνος δαφνηφόρου, seat of the priest of Apollo, crowned with laurel. 2. ἱερέως Αὐλωνέως Διονύσου,

---

office being combined with the priesthood of the Graces.

[1] This seems to be a late mode of spelling Λυκείου.

priest of the Aulonean Dionysus. 3. ἱερέως λιθοφόρου, priest who carried the stone. 4. ἱερέως Θησέως, priest of Theseus 5. ἱερέως Διὸς τελείου βουζύγου, priest of Zeus Teleios, or the perfecter, of the race of the Bouzygæ. 6. ἱερέως Δήμητρος καὶ Φερεφάττης, priest of Demeter and Persephonë.

This is the last compartment on the western side of the theatre, and completes the number of thirty-three seats, counting from the right hand of the priest of Dionysus. We will now specify those that remain on his left hand; of which we have already mentioned those of Zeus Policus, and of the Sacrificer, who sat in the same pempus or compartment as the priest of Dionysus.

The next compartment on his left, which we will mark H, has only the first three seats remaining, viz. No. 1. ἱερομνήμονος, seat of the hieromnemon. 2. ἱερέως καὶ ἀρχιερέως Σεβάστου Καίσαρος, priest and chief priest of Augustus Cæsar. 3. ἱερέως Ἀδριανοῦ ἐλευθεραίως (sic), priest of Hadrian, the deliverer, or saviour. Nos. 4 and 5 are missing, and also the first four of the next compartment, I. No. 5 in this compartment is inscribed Πολεμάρχου, seat of the polemarch.

The following compartment, K, is perfect. The first four thrones were appropriated to thesmothetæ, having each the inscription Θεσμοθέτου. The thrones of the remaining two thesmothetæ were probably among the missing ones. The last seat, No. 5, in this compartment is inscribed ἱεροκήρυκος, seat of the holy herald.

The thrones of the next compartment, L, are entirely gone; and of the following one, M, only the last three remain: viz. No. 3. ἱερέως Ἀπόλλωνος Ζωστηρίου, priest of Apollo at Zoster; No. 4. ἱερέως Ἰακχαγωγοῦ, seat of the priest who carried the image of Iacchus, or infant Dionysus; and No. 5. ἱερέως Ἀσκληπίου, priest of Asclepius. We must observe that the throne of the priest of the Zosterian Apollo was not *in situ* when the theatre was excavated. It was found some years before the excavation was begun, in 1853, in what is called the *metropolis*; but as it evidently belonged to the theatre, it has been restored to it.[1]

---

[1] See the 'Ephemeris' for 1862, p. 218.

Of the six thrones which filled the last compartment on the east, N, only the first three remain. They are inscribed as follows: No. 1. ἱερέως πυρφόρου ἐξ ἀκροπόλεως, seat of the sacrificial priest from the Acropolis. 2. ἱερέως Δήμου καὶ Χαρίτων, καὶ Ῥώμης, priest of Demos and the Graces, and Rome. 3. κήρυκος παναγοῦς καὶ ἱερέως, seat of the all-holy herald and priest.

Besides these thrones, which still remain in situ, and amount to fifty out of the whole number of sixty-seven, there are some further back in the audience part of the theatre, which may perhaps have been thrust by violence from the first row; though it is not improbable that some such chairs may also have originally stood further back. In the second row, immediately behind the seats of the sacrificer and of the priest of Zeus Polieus: 1. δᾳδούχου, seat of the torch-bearer in the mysteries. 2. ἱερέως Ἀπόλλωνος Πυθίου, seat of the priest of the Pythian Apollo. Further back still, and scattered, are the following: 3. στρατηγοῦ, seat of the strategus (probably the στρατηγὸς ἑξαπέλεκυς, or Roman praetor). 4. κήρυκος, of the herald. 5. Διογένους εὐεργέτου, throne of Diogenes, a benefactor. And cut out of the same block of marble, 6. ἱερέως Ἀττάλου ἐπωνύμου, seat of the priest of Attalus the Mysian king, the eponymous hero of the tribe Attalis. 7. ἱερίας (sic) Ἀθηνᾶς Ἀθηνίου, seat of a priestess of Athena. 8. ἱερέως Ὀλυμπίας Νίκης, priest of Olympian Victory. 9. βασιλέως, seat of the archon basileus. 10. αρχον[τος (imperfect), probably seat of the archon eponymous.

These thrones, added to those still existing in the first circle, make sixty, leaving only seven in that circle to be accounted for, supposing that all these at the back had originally stood there. But, as we have said, some of them may possibly occupy their original places. A few inscriptions may also be traced on the ordinary stone seats of the κοῖλον. Among those that may still be deciphered are ἱερείας Ἡλίου, priestess of the Sun: . . Διονύσου, priest of Dionysus. Also Δήμητρος and Μοιρῶν. These may have been the seats of some of the smaller or provincial hierarchy, not entitled to a throne in the proëdria.

We will now make a few remarks that may be necessary to explain some of the inscriptions which do not speak for themselves.

We find in them two exegetæ (A 4, B 5). The exegetæ, in this special signification, were expounders of sacred law and custom. Besides the two here mentioned, we also hear of a third, of the race of the Eumolpids.[1] Timæus[2] says that there were three, and calls them all πυθόχρηστοι, or declared by the Delphic oracle. But this does not seem to agree with what we read on the second throne of an exegetes chosen by the people for life; unless, indeed, the election was subject to the approval of the Pythian god. The Eupatrids at Athens, like the Patricians at Rome, had the care of sacred things, with which they had been intrusted by Theseus.[3] According to some authorities the office of exegetes was confined entirely to the race of the Eumolpids.[4] If that was the case, we do not see the necessity for using the word εὐπατριδῶν in the inscription on the throne, or Εὐμολπιδῶν in the passage from the Lives of the Ten Orators. In the latter case, if they were all Eumolpids, it is a tautology; in the former case it is a vague term for the preciser one Εὐμολπιδῶν, if it was necessary to use any definition at all. From what we can gather from a comparison of these inscriptions and passages, it would seem most probable that the exegetæ being all Eupatrids, one was named by the Pythian oracle, one was chosen by the people, and the third was a Eumolpid, either claiming the office hereditarily, or being chosen by his family. The two last may possibly have been subject to the approval of the oracle, if the account of Timæus be correct.

In compartment B, No. 3, we find a priest of Poseidon with the epithet φυτάλμιος, or the nourisher. Poseidon was the god of humidity in general, one of the principles of generation and growth.[5] The Artemis Epipyrgidia mentioned on the fourth throne of this compartment is the three-headed Artemis or Hecaté, who had a shrine on the Acropolis, near the temple of Niké Athena. Pausanias alludes to this statue and name in

[1] Μήδειος, ὁ καὶ ἐξηγητὴς ἐξ Εὐμολπιδῶν γενόμενος. Vit. X. Orat. t. ix. p. 352, Reiske.

[2] Lex. Platon. in voc.

[3] Plut. Thes. 25. An exegetes of the Eupatrids is named in the Corp. Inscr. Græc. No. 765; an exegetes of the Eu-

molpidæ in No. 392.

[4] Smith's Dict. of Antiquities in Exegetæ and Eumolpidæ.

[5] See Plutarch, Sympos. v. 8, and viii. 8, pp. 688 and 914, Reiske.

his Corinthiaca,[1] though he does not mention her in his description of the Athenian Acropolis. According to that writer, Alcamenes was the first who made these triple images. Siebelis, in a note on this place, thinks that ἐπιπυργιδία is equivalent to guardian of the Acropolis, citing the dictum of Phavorinus that πύργος has a metaphorical meaning of ἀσφάλεια and φυλακή. But surely Athena was the proper guardian of the Acropolis; and it seems more probable that the epithet ἐπιπυργιδία was derived from the statue standing on a small tower, or rather, perhaps, the abutment of Cimon's wall, which resembled a tower. And the preposition ἐπὶ seems to support this meaning, whilst it is worse than superfluous in that proposed by Siebelis. We often find the Graces associated with other deities. The group here mentioned was probably that executed by Socrates standing near the entrance of the Acropolis, which we shall have occasion to describe when we come to that district.

In compartment C, No. 1, we find Erechtheus associated with Poseidon, and both having a common priest. We have adverted to this identification in chap. ii. (p. 36), and shall have to speak of it again when we come to describe the Erechtheium. In throne No. 2 of this compartment we find the epithet Κολαινὶς applied to Artemis, under which name she is mentioned by Aristophanes.[2] The chief seat of her worship seems to have been in the Attic deme of the Myrrhinusii, where there was an ancient wooden image (ξόανον) of her. Her surname is said to have been derived from Colainos, a mythical king older than Cecrops and a descendant of Hermes, who, in obedience to an oracle, built a temple to Artemis Colainis.[3] Myrrhinus was probably the present Merouda, south-east of Athens and south of Brauron, where an inscription was found in which the temple is mentioned.[4] On the other hand, Euphronius, cited by the scholiast on the 'Aves,' says that she got the name of Colainis at Amarynthus in Euboea, because Agamemnon sacrificed to her there a stump-horned ram (κριὸν

---

[1] ii. 30, 2.

[2] οὐκέτι Κολαινὶς ἀλλ' Ἀκαλανθὶς Ἄρτεμις.—Aves, 874.

[3] Scholia in Av. 873; Pausan. i. 31, 3.

She is also mentioned in a fragment of the comic poet Metagenes; schol. loc. cit. and Meineke, p. 424.

[4] Boeckh, Corp. Ins. Gr. No. 100.

κῶλον). It is certain that there was at that place a famous temple and festival of Artemis;[1] and hence she was called also Amarynthis, or Amarysia. This last was the name of a festival to her celebrated at Athens; or rather, perhaps, in the deme of the Athmones, the modern Marusi, where was found an inscription in very ancient characters indicating the boundary of the temenos of the Amarysian Artemis.[2] Before quitting this inscription we will observe that it affords an instance—and we shall meet with several more—that the priests of the Attic demes were admitted to equal honours in the theatre and the Acropolis with those of the capital.[3]

In No. 3 of the same compartment we meet with a priest of Dionysus Melpomenos of the race of the Euneidæ. The title of Melpomenos we have already had occasion to explain. The Euneidæ were one of those Attic families who had an hereditary right to certain sacred functions. They were the prescriptive citharœdi in solemn festivals, and from the inscription on this throne we may infer that a priest of Dionysus Melpomenos was chosen from among them. They were said to be descended from Euneus, son of Jason and Hipsipylë, and to have had their origin in Lemnos; but how they came to settle in Attica seems to be unknown.[4]

The Buzygæ mentioned in the inscription on the next seat, No. 4, were also one of these families with hereditary rights. The founder of it was an Attic hero named Epimenides, who first yoked oxen to the plough under the tuition of Athena. Hence the name of βουζύγης, which descended to his successors. The Athenians instituted three sacred ploughings: one at Sciron, another on the Rharian plain near Eleusis, and a third under the Acropolis. This last, called Buzygia, seems to have been conducted by the Buzygæ. With this office they appear to have united the priesthood of Zeus at the Palladium. An

---

[1] Strabo, x. 448; Liv. xxxv. 38.

[2] Hesych. in 'Αμαρυσία; Pausan. i. 31, 3; Leake, vol. ii. p. 41.

[3] On the wall of the Pinacotheca in the Propylæa was found scratched in ill written characters of the second century of our era the following invocation of this deity :

ΔΕCΠΟΙΝΑ ΑΡΤΕΜΙ ΚΟΛΑΙΝΙ.—Ross, Archäol. Aufs. i. 120.

[4] Harpocr. and Etym. M. in voc.; schol. in Iliad, vii. 468, &c.

inscription records that a priest of Zeus at the Palladium, the same being Buzyges, dedicated a new image to Pallas.[1] Pericles seems to have been of the race of the Buzygæ.[2]

We shall see from an inscription on another throne (compartment G, No. 5), that a Buzyges was also priest of Zeus Teleios, or the perfecter. Of the Palladium we have spoken elsewhere. The remaining seat in this compartment requires no explanation.

Why the name of Zeus should have been repeated on the first throne of the next compartment, D, we are unable to explain. Sacrifices were made to Zeus Soter on the last day of the year.[3] We here find Zeus and Athena again united as protecting deities of the city, and served by the same priest. As father and daughter, they were always inseparably connected. Pindar described her as sitting on the right hand of Zeus and receiving his commands to the gods.[4] The deification of Hadrian's favourite, Antinoüs, whose priest occupied the next throne in this compartment, is well known. Pausanias describes a temple dedicated to him at Mantineia, and says that the pictures and statues of him generally resembled Dionysus.[5] Hence the epithet χορεῖος, which was also proper to the wine god.[6] We see, also, that his priest was chosen ἐκ τεχνειτῶν (τεχνιτῶν), in the same manner as the priest of Dionysus Melpomenos in the same compartment, No. 4. The οἱ περὶ τὸν Διόνυσον τεχνῖται were the artists connected with the theatre, *artifices scenici*, musicians, singers, actors, and so forth, who appear to have been enrolled in a guild or corporation called σύνοδος τεχνιτῶν. A long inscription records their erecting a sanctuary at Eleusis.[7] It may be inferred from the inscription on the throne that from among

[1] Corp. Inscr. Græc. No. 491.

[2] See Plut. Conj. Præcepta, p. 544, Reiske; Aristid. Orat. in Min. t. i. p. 13; Orat. in Plat. t. ii. p. 130, and scholia (Jebb).

[3] Lysias, Euandr. Docim. p. 790, Reiske; cf. Plut. Demosth. 27.

[4] Aristid. Orat. in Min. t. i. p. 9 and 10; Pind. Frag. Incert. lxxviii. t. iii. p. 119,

Heyne.

[5] lib. viii. 9, 4. From the same passage it appears that Pausanias was contemporary with him, since he observes that he had never seen him alive.

[6] Plut. De ira cohib. t. vii. p. 811, Reiske; cf. Sympos. lib. i. Q. v. p. 465.

[7] Rangabé, Ant. Helléniques, t. ii. p. 436 sq. See above, p. 250, note [1].

this body was chosen a priest of the god who was their especial patron.[1] Of the remaining seats in this compartment we may only remark of the fifth, that a priest of Eucleia and Eunomia is frequently mentioned in inscriptions. We have already noticed a temple of Eucleia in the agora, near the Eleusinium (supra, p. 225). Eunomia, one of the Horæ, appears to have been worshipped at Athens along with her sisters Thallo and Carpo; but little seems to be known about her. To Thallo were accorded the same honours as to Pandrosos.[2]

Of the priest of the Muses, to whom the second throne of the next compartment, E, was appropriated, we are unable to give any precise account. The Muses had temples on the Ilissus and in the Academy; the hill called Museium was dedicated to them, and in every school was a place containing images of them.[3] Thus they were perhaps even more popular than the Graces. The epithet of φίλιος applied to Zeus on throne No. 3 is equivalent to ἑταιρεῖος, and characterizes him as the god of friendship and good fellowship.[4] In this character he is found represented with the attributes of Dionysus; and Pausanias describes an image of him in which he had on cothurni, and held in one hand a cup, in the other a thyrsus, on the top of which, however, sat an eagle.[5] The word φαιδυντής, which we find inscribed on throne No. 5 of this compartment, occurs only in inscriptions; in codices it is always written φαιδρυντής. We find the form φαιδυντὴς again on throne No. 2, compartment F; also in an inscription contained in the Athenian Philistor[6] —ὁ φαιδυντὴς τοῖν θεοῖν; and in another in Boeckh's 'Corpus Inscriptionum Græcarum,' where the editor would insert a ρ;[7] and in spite of these repeated instances, it is probably an error of the stone-cutter. The Eleans conferred upon the descendants of Pheidias the care of cleansing the statue of Zeus at Olympia, whence they were called φαιδρυνταί. Before beginning the task, they sacrificed to Athena Erganë. As the

---

[1] Cf. Polyb. xvi. 21, 8 (t. iii. p. 299).

[2] Pausan. ix. 35, 1.

[3] Æschin. c. Timarch. p. 35, Reiske, and scholia.

[4] See his attributes described in Aristides, Orat. i. in Jovem, end: φίλιος δὲ καὶ ἑταιρεῖος ὅτι πάντας ἀνθρώπους ξυνάγει καὶ βούλεται εἶναι ἀλλήλοις φιλίους. Dio Chrys. Orat. i. p. 9 (Teub.); cf. Orat. xii p. 237.

[5] Paus. viii. 31, 2.

[6] t. ii. 238, line 13.

[7] No. 446.

descendants of Pheidias they would be entitled to much honour at Athens, and hence the throne assigned to them in the proëdria. Was the Phaidryntes of the statue of Olympian Zeus at Athens (F, No. 2) of the same family? It would seem not, as in that case it would hardly have been necessary to provide a separate throne for him. The statue at Athens was dedicated by Hadrian (see above, p. 276), and therefore must have been a recent one; and though the descendants of Pheidias may have been equal to the mere technical detail of cleansing a statue, it is probable that they were not able to make one. The statue of Athena in the Parthenon being, like those of Zeus just mentioned, made of ivory and gold, would also, we may presume, require a Phaidryntes, but we do not find a throne for one in the theatre. The cleaners of this statue appear to have been called Praxiergidæ, who also clothed the primitive statue ($\xi \acute{o} a v o v$) of Athena Polias at the festival called Plynteria.[1]

Who the hero Epitegios may have been, coupled with the Anaces or Dioscuri on the third throne of compartment F, we are unable to explain. With regard to throne No. 4, set apart for the priest of the heavenly Nemesis, we may observe that the Attic deme Rhamnus was celebrated for her worship, and that the statue of her there was the work of Pheidias;[2] but he allowed his beloved Agoracritus, the Parian, to put his name upon it. This is the name of the artist, according to Pliny,[3] who says that the statue was first meant for a Venus, but afterwards called Nemesis. The Athenians seem sometimes to have considered Erechtheus as her son,[4] and as having founded her worship. She was thought to be the daughter of Oceanus; and hence, perhaps, having risen like Aphroditë from the sea, she was sometimes confounded with her, for Suidas says[5] that Nemesis was first worshipped under the form of that goddess.

Of the six seats in the last compartment on the west, G, No. 1, is inscribed to the priest of Apollo the laurel-bearer. The story runs

---

[1] Plut. Alcib. 34; Hesych.; voc. Πρα-
ξιεργίδαι.
[2] Pausan. i. 33, 2, sq.

[3] H. N. xxxvi. s. 17.
[4] Phot. Lex. voc. Ῥαμνουσία Νέμεσις.
[5] voc. Ῥαμνουσία.

that Apollo, after slaying the Python, crowned himself with laurel.[1] This title does not often appear, but it is mentioned by Plutarch;[2] and there was a δαφνηφορεῖον, or fane of Apollo Daphnephorus at Phylè, if we should not rather read Phlya.[3] With regard to Dionysus Auloneus, throne No. 2, this is, we believe, the only instance in which that epithet occurs. There was a place called Aulon,[4] in the district of Laurium, but we are not aware that it was celebrated for the worship of Dionysus. The form αὐλωνεύς, however, can hardly come from anything else. We have already seen several instances, and we shall meet with more, of rural priests being admitted to the same honours as the metropolitan. Such were the priests of Artemis at Myrrhinus, of Nemesis at Rhamnus, and apparently also the Apollo just mentioned at Phylè. Of the stone-bearer who occupied throne No. 3 in this compartment we can give no account. He probably bore a sacred stone in some procession. In seat No. 5 one of the Buzygæ again appears as the priest of Zeus Teleios, or the perfecter. In a more special sense this epithet referred to Zeus as bringing marriage to a happy conclusion.[5] Plutarch, in his 'Conjugal Precepts,' after mentioning the three sacred ploughings to which we have before alluded when explaining the inscription on the throne of the priest of Zeus in the Palladium,[6] adds: "But of all these the most sacred is the marriage ploughing for the sake of children."[7] Whence we may infer, as Otto Jahn observes,[8] that this priest was also concerned in the ceremony of marriage. The other seats in this compartment require no explanation.

Proceeding now to the left hand of the priest of Dionysus, we find in compartment H, No. 1, the seat of a hieromnemon. The hieromnemones, according to Plutarch,[9] were priests of Poseidon. The Amphictyonic Assembly, as we have already observed (p. 176), continued to

---

[1] Tertull. De Corona, 7; supra, p. 217.

[2] In Them. 15.

[3] Athen. x. 24.

[4] Bekk. An. Gr. p. 206; Æsch. c. Timarch.

[5] Schol. Aristoph. Thesm. 973.

[6] Supra, p. 325.

[7] τούτων δὲ πάντων ἱερότατός ἐστιν ὁ γαμήλιος σπόρος καὶ ἄροτος ἐπὶ παίδων τεκνώσει.—t. vi. p. 544, Reiske.

[8] Nuove memorie dell' Instituto, 1865, p. 5, n. 5.

[9] Sympos. vii. p. 914, Reiske.

exist in the time of the Antonines. From the inscription on No. 2 it
would appear that Augustus Cæsar had a chief priest, from which we
may infer that he had many shrines in Attica. The priest mentioned
here was probably he who ministered at the temple of Roma and
Augustus on the Acropolis, which we shall have to describe further on,
and that by virtue of this office he was arch-priest over the others. On
the next seat, No. 3, we find Hadrian with the title of ἐλευθεραίως,
apparently for ἐλευθερέως, genitive of Ἐλευθερεύς, the stone-cutter
having followed the pronunciation of the αι like ε.[1]   But this would
identify Hadrian with Dionysus as springing from Eleutheræ; whereas
it is more probable that it was meant for ἐλευθερίου, the saviour or
deliverer, an epithet of Zeus as well as of Dionysus.   Had Ἐλευθερεύς, the gentile name of a citizen of Eleutheræ, now come to be
confounded with ἐλευθέριος?   Which it probably might, from both
being epithets of Dionysus.

The following inscriptions down to that on throne No. 3, M, require
no explanation; for of the hieroceryx at No. 5, K, we shall have occasion
to speak when treating of the ceryx panages.   The Apollo mentioned
on No. 3, M, with the title of Zosterius, was the god who had a shrine
at Cape Zoster, a promontory midway between Sunium and Phalerum.
Its name was said to be derived from Leto having there loosed her
girdle in preparing for the birth of Apollo and Artemis, which however
did not happen at this place.   But Leto and her offspring had an altar
here; and there was also another to Athena, who has sometimes the same
surname.   Thus, in an ancient inscription found in the wall of a modern
substruction in the Erechtheium relating to loans from different temples,
we find: Ἀθηναίας Ζωστηρίας.[2]   Another form of the adjective was
Zostrius (Ζώστριος).[3]   Euripides was pyrphorus (πυρφόρος)—that is, the
sacrificial priest at the altar of Apollo Zosterius.[4]   Conspicuous headlands were generally the seat of the worship of some deity.   We need
only further remark that this is another instance of the honour paid to

---

[1] Which is the modern pronunciation.
Geldart, Mod. Greek Language, p. 25.

[2] Ap. Rangabé, Ant. Hell. t. ii. No.
2253, line 23, p. 945.

[3] Etym. M. voc. ζωστήρ; cf. Bekk. An.
Græc. p. 261, &c.

[4] Anon. life prefixed to his works.

provincial priests. Of the Iacchagogos (No. 4) we have already spoken when describing the temple of Demeter, near the Peiraïc Gate. The inscription on the fifth chair, which has by some been read ἱερέως Ἀσκληπίου, is imperfect, thus:[1]

ΙΕΡΕΩΣ
ΛΣ ΚΛΙΠΟΥ
ΙΙ ΩΟ⸦ .

We have already had a priest of Asclepius, E, No. 1, and it is not likely that there should have been two thrones for the priests of so subordinate a deity. Nor do the letters as they exist form the name of that god. The fragment of the word ἥρωος underneath is evidently of a much older period; still, as it has been left, we must infer that it was meant to apply to the new occupant of the throne; and the god Asclepius would hardly have been called a hero, not at least in the later times, though Homer seems to have considered him a mortal. The throne, therefore, probably belonged to the priest of some deified hero, whose name we cannot decipher. This throne, as well as some others, appears to have been covered by the Turks with lime or plaster, a common way of obliterating inscriptions among that people.[2]

The πυρφόρος (N 1), as we have already observed under M 3, was the sacrificial priest.[3] But may we not surmise that as this one is designated as belonging to the Acropolis, he may have brought the fire for the sacrifice to Dionysus, from that which eternally burnt in the temple of Athena Polias? The inscription on the next throne, recording a priest of Demos, the Graces, and Rome, may probably have allusion to the temple of Rome on the Acropolis which we have already mentioned. From an inscription[4] we learn that Rome, as a deity, was associated with Augustus in a sanctuary on the Acropolis. M. Rousopoulos thinks that the whole is typical of the thankfulness of the Athenians for the favours received by the demos from Rome; referring for the idea of the Charites, as representing Gratitude, to Aristotle, Eth.

---

[1] See Athenian 'Ephemeris,' 1862, p. 157.
[2] Ephemeris, loc. cit.
[3] Phot. Lex. in voc.
[4] Corp. Inscr. Graec. No. 478.

Nicom. v. 8. Of the deification of the *Demos*, and its union with the Graces, we have already spoken (p. 194) when treating of the Peiræeus, as described by Pausanias. Seat No. 3 is appropriated to the all-holy herald and priest. We have already had two other heralds, viz. the ἱεροκῆρυξ (K 5), and simply, the herald (scattered thrones, No. 4). The last no doubt was the state, or political herald, and the hieroceryx, the herald of the mysteries, or of the mystæ.[1] But it is difficult to distinguish from this last the κῆρυξ παναγής. There is the difference, indeed, that the παναγής is also characterized as a priest, which the ἱεροκῆρυξ is not; and Pollux[2] mentions them separately from κήρυκες as ministers in the mysteries, but he does not explain in what the difference consisted.

It may be observed in general of the seats *in situ* on the left or eastern side of the theatre, that a considerable proportion of them were assigned to civil magistrates, as the thesmothetæ, polemarch, &c., while the right side of the circle was appropriated entirely to the hierarchy. Let us observe that we find no throne of the eponymous archon, unless indeed it be No. 10 among those not remaining *in situ* (supra, p. 322). Even the thrones of the priests of Augustus and Hadrian, on the left side, partake as much of a political as of a religious character.

Of the scattered seats, we are unable to explain who was the Diogenes mentioned as a benefactor in the inscription No. 5. May he not have been the founder of the gymnasium called Diogeneium, to which we have before adverted (supra, p. 258)? That on No. 7 relating to a priestess of Athena is also perplexing. What is the genitive Ἀθηνίου? Vischer[3] translates: seat of the priestess Athena Athenion, thinking that it was appropriated as a mark of honour to this particular lady called Athenion; and states that her name also occurs, as priestess of Athena, on the base of a statue to one Claudius Atticus. But, first, is it probable that a seat of honour would be assigned to a particular individual, and not to the holder of the office in general? There is no example of such a thing among the sixty thrones which we have

---

[1] ὁ τῶν Μυστῶν κῆρυξ.—Xenoph. Hell. ii. 4, 20.

[2] lib. i. s. 35.

[3] Neues Schweitz. Mus. p. 60.

examined. That the names of the priestesses of Athena Polias sometimes appear in inscriptions when used to denote an epoch we know,
as in the following found upon the Acropolis: ἐπὶ ἱερείας Ἀλεξάνδρας τῆς
Λέοντος ἐκ Χολλειδῶν.[1] But that is a different thing from putting the
name of an individual on an official chair. Again, is Athenion really
a female name? and if it is, how can it have a genitive Ἀθηνίου? It is
probably a blunder. It may be observed that this seat is very different
from the rest, being adorned with Gorgons' heads and snakes, and
Dr. Vischer is inclined to agree with Kumanudes, that it has been
brought into the theatre from some other place. The Olympia Nikë
(No. 8) refers probably to some Victory at Olympia, to which deity there
were several altars there. Thus, she had an altar at Olympia in conjunction with Ζεὺς καθάρσιος, or the purifier; another erected by the
Messenians on the occasion of the capture of the Spartans at Sphacteria,
when the Athenians also erected one in the Acropolis; and one in imitation of the Nikë Apteros at Athens, an anathema of the Mantineans.[2] It
may probably have been the priest of one of these two last, to whom the
seat in the Dionysiac theatre was assigned. As the Olympic contests
were open to all Greece, and as the prizes had often been carried off by
Athenians, it was natural enough that the priest of Olympic Victory
should have been honoured with a seat in the Athenian theatre.
M. Rousopoulos thinks[3] that it was the seat of the priest appointed to
receive the Olympic visitors; but it should be shown that there was
such an office, and the words of the inscription yield no such meaning.

With respect to the inscriptions on the ordinary seats of the κοῖλον,
we need only say a few words respecting that of the *priestess* of the
Sun. We are not aware that such a priestess is mentioned anywhere
else, or indeed that female priests were attached to male deities, though
we hear of a *priest* of Helios. Harpocration says (voc. σκίρου) that in
the festival called σκίρα, the priestess of Athena, the priest of Poseidon,
and the priest of Helios, walked under a canopy from the Acropolis to
a place called Sciron, on the road from Athens to Eleusis.[4] The canopy

---

[1] Ap. Beulé, Acrop. d'Athènes, t. i. p. 324.
[2] Pausan. iv. 26, 1; v. 14, 6, and 26, 1 and 5.
[3] Ephemeris, 1862, p. 100.
[4] Pausan. i. 36, 3.

was borne by the Eteobutadæ; whence we may infer that the priestess who walked under it was the priestess of Athena Polias. It was probably to this *priest* of the Sun that the inscription refers; for it is written in indistinct characters,[1] and ἱερέως may have been mistaken for ἱερείας.

We shall have occasion to remark in Appendix II. that the dramatic contests must have existed at least till the times of the Antonines, and the same thing may be inferred from a marble base inscribed to Marcus Aurelius, son of Antoninus,[2] found on the western side of the theatre. Dr. Wordsworth[3] has drawn the same conclusion from some inscriptions relating to choragic victories, cut on the face of the rock, near the cave, the characters in which they are engraved being of a late Roman period. The same arrangement of the theatre which we see at present must have existed in the days of the Antonines; and hence we may conclude that the most ancient forms of Attic paganism must have still continued to flourish in full vigour. The priest of Dionysus, the hierophant and other priests connected with the Eleusinian mysteries, the priest of Poseidon Erechtheus, the interpreters appointed by the Delphic oracle, the ancient priestly families of the Buzygæ and Euneidæ, have still their appointed seats, attesting the existence of their functions. We may infer, also, that some of the great political magistrates, as the archons, the thesmothetæ, &c., still nominally existed, though their functions could have been little more than a shadow of their former ones.

We have already remarked that the κοῖλον, or audience part of the theatre, is divided into thirteen κερκίδες or *cunei*, each of which appears to have had a statue of Hadrian. On a pediment in the centre *cuneus*, which must have belonged to one of these statues, there is no record that it was erected by a tribe, as there is on the other pediments, and this may afford another argument that the theatre was laid out before the thirteenth tribe was created. It was probably in this central place that Hadrian, having finished and dedicated the Olympium, celebrated,

[1] ἀμυδρὰ ἔχουσι τὰ γράμματα.—Ephemeris, 1862, p. 163. I did not observe the inscription myself.

[2] Ephemeris, June 1863, p. 271.

[3] Athens and Attica, p. 77 (ed. 1869).

in Attic attire,[1] the Dionysiac festival, and beheld the dramatic contests.
It is said that he had previously been archon at Athens in A.U.C. 865
(A.D. 112), five years before he had attained the imperial dignity (supra,
p. 172), and that he now again took the office of archon for the purpose
of conducting the Dionysia. On this subject the words of Dion Cassius,
or his epitomator, are ambiguous.[2] Some have thought that Hadrian
must now have had a second archonship, because, as the direction of the
Dionysia and Thargelia was one of the prerogatives of the archon, he
would otherwise have deprived the true archon of the honour of being
agonothetes : which Spartianus tells us Hadrian was on this occasion. Let us further observe that this passage of Dion Cassius confirms
what we have just observed respecting the at least nominal continuance
of the Athenian constitution ; and indeed Gallienus was archon at Athens
more than a century afterwards.[3] But we have already touched upon
this subject, and only revert to it because the excavation of the theatre
has brought to light ocular proofs of the testimony of historians.[4]

The seats in the middle and upper part of the κοῖλον are cut out of
the solid rock; the others were made of Peiraïc limestone, which
accounts for their disappearance.[5] We have already observed (supra,
p. 83) that the men were seated separately from the women, and it

---

[1] ἐν τῇ ἐσθῆτι τῇ ἐπιχωρίῳ. — Dion
Cassius, lxix. 16.

[2] τὴν μεγίστην παρ᾽ αὐτοῖς ἀρχὴν ἄρξας.—
Ibid. Where Casaubon translates ἀρχὴν
ἄρξας, 'cum magistratum cepisset;' Salmasius, 'cum magistratum gessisset.' It is
said that an ex-archonship would not have
given him the right to be agonothetes,
and that Hadrian's being dressed in the
national costume obviously means the
archon's dress. See Casaubon's note on
Spartian. Adrian. c. 13, Hist. Aug. t. i.
p. 122, where several examples are adduced of the use of the aorist in a perfect-
present sense for ἀρχὴν ἄρχων. But see
also there the note of Salmasius. And
it must be confessed that Spartianus

mentions only one archonship—Athenis
archon fuit, c. 19 ; not, bis fuit. And
a second archonship would have been a
greater violation of the Athenian constitution than Hadrian's usurping the functions of the archon as agonothetes. This
might have been conceded to him on the
strength of his former archonship; and
especially the imperial power would not
have been questioned, and the assumption
of the dress would only have been a
natural consequence of the temporary re-
sumption of the office.

[3] Treb. Pollio, Gallieni duo, c. 11.

[4] See above, p. 176.

[5] See account of the excavation in
Neues Schweitzer. Museum, 1863.

also appears that the female citizens sat apart from the Hetairæ; not so much, however, because the latter were regarded with abhorrence on account of their immorality—for in that case why should they have been admitted to the theatre at all?—as because they belonged to the servile class.[1] Foreigners, or at all events female foreigners, appear from some lines of the Γυναικοκρατία of Alexis,[2] to have been placed in one of the end or side cunei, whence of course there would not have been so good a view of the stage as from the centre. Only nineteen rows of the lower seats can now be traced, and those are imperfect. The height of the seats is about 1 ft. 2 in.; their horizontal breadth about 2 ft. 8 in. In this breadth is an excavation or depressed place, for the feet of those in the row above. The two lowest rows are rather broader than the others. The stairs which divide the seats into cunei are about 2 ft. 4 in. broad. There are traces of only one broad diazoma, about two-thirds of the ascent towards the summit of the theatre, as represented in the coin. In the lower part of the κοῖλον, rather to the east of the centre, was found the inscription, evidently of the Byzantine times, ΛΙΘΟ-ΚωΠωΝ Ο, i.e. apparently λιθοκόπων ὅρος, or boundary of the quarriers. Hence this eastern side of the theatre would appear to have been used as a stone quarry; a fact which would account for its having been more destroyed than the western. The inference is strengthened by the discovery of a limekiln at this part.

It is probable that the whole of the κοῖλον belongs to the original construction. The wall which bounds it on the west is still preserved. The upper part of it, above the diazoma, trending in a north-eastern direction towards the grotto, is of a later date. Just above the diazoma, a little to the west, or left, of the centre, are bases for seats formed of large bricks. Similar appearances may be observed at the west wall, and at the south-eastern angle of what remains of the east wall. Quite up to the grotto are seats or steps cut out of the natural rock.

At the very top of the theatre, not however exactly in its centre, as

---

[1] ὁ δὲ Σφυρόμαχος ψήφισμα εἰσηγήσατο, ὥστε τὰς γυναῖκας καὶ τοὺς ἄνδρας χωρὶς καθέζεσθαι καὶ τὰς ἑταίρας χωρὶς τῶν ἐλευθέρων.—Schol. ad Aristoph. Eccles. 22.

[2] Ἐνταῦθα περὶ τὴν ἐσχάτην δεῖ κερκίδα ὑμᾶς καθιζούσας θεωρεῖν ὡς ξένας.
Apud Polluc. ix. 44.

Leake[1] and other topographers have described it, but some way to the east of it, is the grotto or cavern which was converted into the CHORAGIC MONUMENT OF THRASYLLUS. It is alluded to by Pausanias only in a few passing words.[2] The cavern itself, like others on the Acropolis, is probably Pelasgic. We learn from Plutarch that Nicias converted it into a shrine or temple.[3] At a later period, in the archonship of Neæchmus, B.C. 320, Thrasyllus made it into a choragic monument. In the Byzantine times it was converted into a chapel of the Virgin, under the title of Panaghia Spilotissa, or Our Lady of the Grotto. About two centuries ago, when Wheler saw it, and even a century later, when visited by Stuart, the façade of the little temple appears to have been perfect; and both have given views of it. It consisted of a plain wall with three pilasters, and an architrave with inscriptions. We may, however, note some differences in the views of it as given by those travellers. Wheler places the door on the east side of the façade, and indicates no window; which indeed it is just possible may have been made after his time; whilst Stuart places the door on the west side, and adds a small window over it. The wall, however, and consequently the door and window, appear to have been made when the cavern was converted into a church. In ancient times the front seems to have been open, but the pilasters and architrave were there. In the middle of the architrave were three steps, and on the top of them a sitting figure, clothed, according to Stuart, in a lion's skin.[4] The figure was without head and arms in the time of Wheler. The head had no doubt been cut off centuries before, probably by the Christian iconoclasts; who perhaps defaced in the same barbarous manner the figures in the orchestra, and the metopes of the Parthenon. Wheler ventures no opinion about the figure, and does not even indicate whether it is male or female. Stuart called it a female, and supplied in his cut a female head; taking it to be a personification either of the deme Deceleia or of the tribe Hippothoöntis, which are mentioned in the inscriptions. It is now in the British Museum, and has been recognised as a statue of Dionysus. It is indeed surprising

[1] vol. i. p. 188.
[2] Above, p. 308.
[3] Plut. in Nic. 3.
[4] vol. ii. p. 31.

z

that Stuart should have taken it to represent a female, for there are not the slightest indications of the female bosom. The figure, no doubt, is delicate and feminine, and the dress might also appear to be that of a woman. But a beautiful and somewhat feminine form was one of the attributes of Dionysus:

> "Tibi enim inconsumpta juventas;
> Tu puer æternus, tu formosissimus alto
> Conspiceris cælo ; tibi, quum sine cornibus adstas,
> Virgineum caput est." [1]

Hence we see the reason why Antinoüs was represented as Bacchus. The lion's skin, says Visconti, was as appropriate to Dionysus as that of the panther or the roebuck, for they were all comprehended under the common name of *Nebrides*.[2] The broad belt which girdles the dress was also characteristic of Dionysus:

> Εἶτα δ᾽ ὕπερθε νεβρῆς χρύσεον ζωστῆρα βαλέσθαι
> παμφανόωντα πέριξ στέρνων φορέειν μέγα σῆμα.[3]

> "Then o'er the fawn-skin let a gold belt shine,
> Circling his bosom, a distinguished sign."

In the lap of the figure appears to have been a tripod, the choragic prize ; and there are still holes which show that something stood there. This must have been the tripod mentioned by Pausanias, who speaks of only one ; but he does not mention the statue, nor advert to the tripods on the neighbouring columns, which we shall describe further on.

The architrave had three inscriptions. The centre one, according to the translations both of Wheler and Stuart, records that Thrasyllus, son of Thrasyllus, of Deceleia, dedicated *the building*, having gained the prize, as choragus, with the men of his tribe, Hippothoön ; that

---

[1] Ovid, Met. iv. 16 sqq. See the whole passage for the history and attributes of Bacchus. Compare the beautiful figure of the deity given by Stuart from the monument of Lysicrates, vol. i. ch. iv. pl. x.

[2] See his Memoir, quoted in the Libr. of Entert. Knowledge, t. ii. p. 91 sq. But I find no authority for his assertion in Servius, whom he quotes. Perhaps it is a panther's skin. Dionysus in the lion's skin is an object of ridicule in the ' Frogs.'

[3] Orphic verses, quoted by Macrobius, Sat. i. 18.

Evius of Chalcis was the musician; Neaechmus was archon; and Carchidamus, son of Sotis, composed the piece. But let us observe that the inscription says nothing about the building.[1] It was in its place when Stuart saw it; and stood in the centre of the architrave, consequently immediately under the statue with the tripod. It is true that Wheler in his cut does not place this inscription, but one of the others, relating not to Thrasyllus as choragus, but to Thrasycles, his son, or grandson, as agonothete, in the centre.[2] But, first, Wheler does not, like Stuart, give all three inscriptions in his cut of the building, but only one, so that it is evidently more carelessly done; secondly, the word ἀνέθηκεν is more appropriate to a statue and a tripod than to a building;[3] thirdly, as the inscription relating to Thrasyllus, as choragus, was many years older than the other two relating to Thrasycles, as agonothete, it is natural to suppose that it was placed in the middle of the architrave, and the two later ones, which both relate to the same epoch, on each side of it. This being so, the centre inscription, we think, refers not to the dedication of the building, but to the dedication of the choragic prize, that is, the statue with the tripod, which stood immediately over the inscription. The building, as we have seen, was the work of Nicias, long before the time of Thrasyllus. It is possible, however, as Leake suggests,[4] that Thrasyllus made some embellishments in the architecture, and especially he may have altered the architrave in order to suit his anathema.

The other two inscriptions relate, as we have said, to choragic contests in the archonship of Pytharatus, which was in the year B.C. 271,[5] and, consequently, forty-nine years later than the monument of Thrasyllus. In both these latter contests the people supplied the chorus, an office which it appears to have taken upon itself in the interval between

---

[1] It runs as follows: Θράσυλλος Θρασύλλου Δεκελεὺς ἀνέθηκεν | χορηγῶν νικήσας ἀνδρασὶν Ἱπποθοωντιδὶ φυλῇ | Εὖιος Χαλκιδεὺς ηὔλει Νεαιχμος ἦρχεν | Καρχιδαμος Σώτιος ἐδίδασκεν.

[2] See Wheler's Journey, p. 368; Stuart's Athens, vol. ii. ch. iv. and pl. iii.

[3] καθιερόω would be more appropriate to the dedication of a temple than ἀνατίθημι, though the latter may be sometimes used for it.

[4] vol. i. p. 186.

[5] Clinton, F. II. iii. 6.

the archonship of Neœchmus and that of Pytharatus. Thrasycles, instead of being choragus like his father or grandfather Thrasyllus, was merely agonothete, or president. The right hand inscription records the victory of a chorus of men of the tribe Pandionis; on which occasion Nicocles, an Ambracian, played the flute, and Lysippus, an Arcadian, composed the piece. The left hand inscription[1] purported that the boys of the tribe Hippothoöntis obtained the victory; that the flute was played by Theon, a Theban, and that Pronomos, also a Theban, composed the piece. It will be observed that the musicians mentioned in all these inscriptions were foreigners, and it has been sometimes said that the Athenians, like their patron goddess, disdained to play upon the flute. This, however, does not seem to hold universally good, at all events in the later times; for a choragic inscription found at Athens records that on that occasion the flute was played by an Athenian.[2] The Thebans were distinguished as flute players. Pronomos, a Theban, had been the music-master of Alcibiades;[3] and an inscription of the time of the archonship of Diotrephes, B.C. 384, records that his son Œniades played the flute in a choral victory.[4] The Pronomos mentioned in the third inscription over the grotto may not improbably have been a descendant of the same family.

Pausanias, as we have already said, mentions that within the cavern was a group of statues representing Apollo and Artemis slaying the children of Niobë. It is difficult to trace any connection between this story and a choragic victory; yet we may probably assume that this group was an anathema not of Thrasyllus, but of his predecessor Nicias in commemoration of the many victories which he had gained. Pausanias takes no notice of the two Ionic columns with tripods, which stand above the cavern. Yet they must have been there in his time; for Plutarch, who flourished about a century earlier than he, alludes to

---

[1] This inscription, beautifully cut on a block of grey marble, still lies with the wrong side upwards before the cavern, where the writer saw it. Cf. Boeckh, C. Ins. Gr. Nos. 224–226.

[2] ὁ δῆμος ἐχορ(ήγει) . . ἀγωνοθέτης . . π)αίδων ἐνίκα . . 'Α)θηναῖος ηὔλει. See Rangabé, Ant. Hell. t. ii. p. 703 (No. 983).

[3] Athen. iv. 84.

[4] Rangabé, ibid. p. 700 (No. 972).

them as being over the temple of Nicias.[1] They are supposed to be of the Roman times, which of course does not prevent them from being older than the time of Plutarch. The taller and more eastern one has an imperfect inscription on its base, which is given in the Corpus Inscript. Græc. No. 227 b. Tripods seem to have been placed in the upper part of the theatre without pillars. Thus Aischræos, of the deme Anagyrsus, placed a silver-plated tripod above the theatre, having been victorious the year before with a chorus of boys; while he inscribed his victory on that part where the rock is cut away.[2] On the eastern side of the cavern, and level with its roof, are the remains of a sun-dial. The perpendicular rock under it, which seems to have been made so by art, is full of inscriptions; and it has been supposed that this was the part called κατατομή in the passage just cited from Harpocration, and by other ancient writers.[3] On the west side of the cavern are two niches, probably also destined for choragic anathemata.

The southern front of the theatre appears to have had a magnificent propylæum, or screen. Andocides relates the statement of Dioclides, that on the night when the Hermæ were mutilated, it being a full moon and having mistaken the hour, he walked about till he found himself at the propylæum of the theatre; when perceiving many men descending from the Odeium into the Orchestra, he was alarmed, and, entering the propylæum, sat down in the shade between the column and the stelë, on which was a brazen statue of a strategus.[4] This part of the theatre was no doubt adorned with many statues. Fronting the entrance on each side were statues of Miltiades and Themistocles,[5] each

---

[1] καὶ ὁ τοῖς χορηγικοῖς τρίποσιν ὑποκείμενος ἐν Διονύσου νεώς. — Nic. 3. The phrase ἐν Διονύσου does not here mean in the *theatre* of Dionysus, but in the *peribolus* sacred to that god. The temple was not *in* the theatre but *above* it. The theatre itself is sometimes spoken of as ἐν Διονύσου: τὸ ἐν Διονύσου θέατρον.—Eustath. ad Odyss. iii. 350. Sometimes however it seems to mean the theatre, as in the law quoted by Demosthenes (in Mid. p. 517): τοὺς πρυ-

τάνεις ποιεῖν ἐκκλησίαν ἐν Διονύσου τῇ ὑστεραίᾳ τῶν Πανδίων.

[2] ἐπὶ τὴν κατατομὴν τῆς πέτρας. Philochorus ap. Harpocr. voc. κατατομή. But the word is variously applied. See Bekk. An. Gr. p. 270.

[3] See M. Rusopulos in the Ath. Ephemeris, 1862, p. 293.

[4] Andoc. De Myster. p. 19, Reiske.

[5] Schol. in Aristid. ap. Leake, vol. i. p. 628.

attended by a Persian captive. The statues of Æschylus, Sophocles, and Euripides, mentioned by Pausanias as inside the theatre, were probably, as we have said, those which Lycurgus the orator had caused to be executed in bronze. Pausanias, as before related (p. 307), tells us that among some statues of comic poets was one of Menander. The pedestal of this still exists, and is inscribed, besides his name, with the names of the artists, Cephisodotus and Timarchus. These were the sons of Praxiteles, and the statue therefore was probably erected about B.C. 300. The basis is said to correspond with the celebrated statue of Menander, in a sitting posture, in the Vatican, which Visconti suspected to have come from the theatre at Athens.[1] Near this great poet was placed the statue of a very common poet indeed, and that too in bronze.[2] His name is not mentioned. Pedestals inscribed to Dionysius and Diomedes have also been found; the former a mediocre, the latter an utterly unknown writer. Besides these we can only mention a slab inscribed with the name of Thespis. A decree in honour of the comic poet Philippides, found not in the theatre but at S. Demetrius, is interesting for the history of the period.[3]

The excavation of the theatre has shown that Socrates need not be accused of much exaggeration when he slily taunts the tragic poet Agathon with having displayed his wisdom before 30,000 spectators.[4] The peculiar form of the Dionysiac theatre, and the difficulty of ascertaining the exact curve of the seats, which have for the most part perished, make it hard to determine the precise number of persons that it would accommodate; but it may be safely asserted that it would have held considerably more than 20,000. Its length from the first row of seats to the topmost row is 75 French mètres, or about 82 yards. Twenty rows of seats still existing at the lower part of the κοῖλον

[1] See Mus. Pio Clement. iii. 70 sq.; Vischer, N. Schweitz. Mus. 1863, p. 75.

[2] Dion Chrys. Orat. Rhod. t. i. p. 384 (Teubner).

[3] Ephemeris, June, 1862, and plate xvii.

[4] ἥ γε σὴ σοφία . . . ἐκφανὴς ἐγένετο πρώην ἐν μάρτυσι τῶν Ἑλλήνων πλέον ἢ τρισμυρίοις.—Conviv. p. 175, extr. (ii. ii. p. '376, Bekk.).' Where let us observe that Socrates speaks not of Athenian citizens alone, often computed in round numbers at 30,000, but of a mixed audience of all manner of Greeks (Ἑλλήνων).

occupy 15 mètres; consequently 75 mètres would contain 5 times as many, or 100. But from these must be deducted the space occupied by the diazoma, which has a breadth of about 4 mètres, and would therefore contain 5 rows of seats; leaving the actual number of rows at 95. The breadth of the seats is about 2 ft. 7 or 8 in. The annexed plan, reduced from Ziller's, will enable the reader to form some idea of the arrangement and capacity of the theatre.

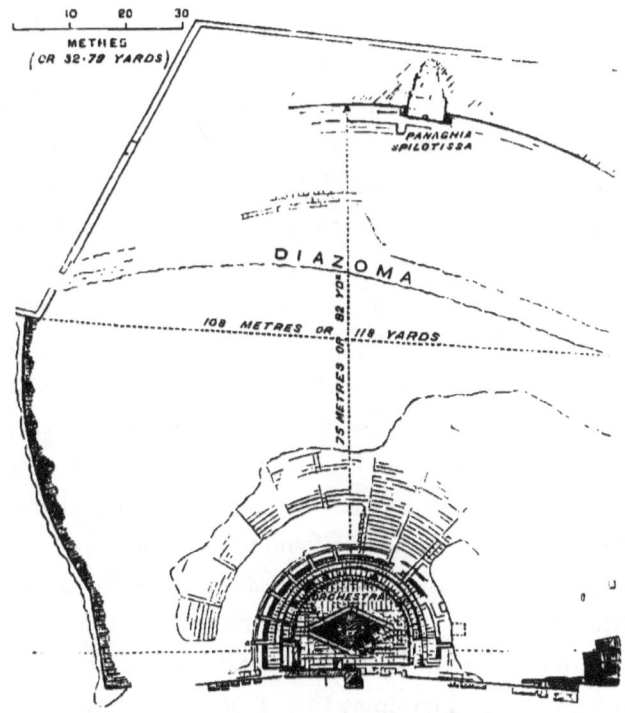

PLAN OF DIONYSIAC THEATRE.

Pausanias, after describing the Dionysiac theatre—if his brief account of it deserves that name—proceeds on his route westwards towards the entrance of the Acropolis (ch. 21, 6). In order to do this he needed not to have descended to the bottom of the theatre and taken the road quite at the foot of the Acropolis, from which indeed he would have found no access to the sanctuaries lying on its side. After visiting the cavern and the choragic monument of Thrasyllus he would have left the theatre at the diazoma, at which height there was a road, or path, which encircled the whole hill, and which appears to have given access to all the shrines and sanctuaries situated ὑπὸ πόλιν, or on the sides of the cliffs, the Anaceium, Aglaurium, &c., on the north side as well as those on the south. In 1862 was discovered on the north-east side of the Acropolis, on the cliff above the spot where the Prytaneium is commonly placed, an imperfect inscription interpreted to mean that this encircling road measured 5 stades and 18 feet, or about 3052 English feet; which measure agrees with the circumference of the hill at this height.[1] The first object which Pausanias mentions after leaving the theatre is the tomb of Talus.[2] He does not say on which hand it lay; but it must have been close to the cliff, as the story ran that Dædalus, before his flight from Athens, fearing that his sister's son, Talus, would excel him in art, precipitated him from the Acropolis. The body was found; Dædalus was tried for the murder and condemned by the Areiopagus; whereupon he fled to Crete.[3] We may presume that Talus was buried at the spot where his body was found, and this is confirmed by Lucian, when he makes the tomb of Talus one of the points from which the philosophers attempt to scale the Acropolis.[4]

The next object mentioned by Pausanias, is a TEMPLE OF ASCLEPIUS, worth seeing, he observes, for several statues of the god and his sons, and for some pictures.[5] In it is a fountain at which Hallirrhotius, son of Poseidon, is said to have been killed by Ares, for an outrage on his daughter Alcippë.[6] This was the subject of the first trial for murder. Here also was a Sarmatian breastplate, of as good workmanship as any Grecian. Pausanias then proceeds to describe the warlike

---

[1]
    T]ΟΥΓΕΡΙΓΑΤΟ[Υ
    ΓΕΡΙΟΔΟC
    [Ε[ΓΟΔΕC
    ΔΓΙΙΙ

i.e. τοῦ περιπάτου περίοδος στάδια πέντε πόδες ὀκτωκαίδεκα. See Ἐφημ. Ἀρχ. June, 1862, p. 146, and pl. III. 1.; cf. Pervanoglu in Philol. B. xxiv. s. 460; C. Wachsmuth, in Rh. Mus. 1868, s. 14, 25.

[2] Sometimes written Kalos, but more

correctly Talos. Cf. Talaus and Kalaus ap. schol. ad Soph. Œd. Col. 1320.

[3] Apollod. iii. 15, 9.

[4] Piscator, 42.

[5] Leake translates: "worthy of inspection for the statues of Bacchus and his children and for the pictures which it contains."—vol. i. p. 141. Where Bacchus is probably a slip of the pen for Asclepius.

[6] Demosth. c. Aristocr. p. 641, Reiske.

equipment of the Sarmatians, and mentions that the breastplates were made of horses' hoofs. It is probable, therefore, that this was a recent anathema, the produce of Trajan's wars. The Sarmatian armour is shown on that emperor's column at Rome.

Leake, after observing that the fountain in this temple was one of the few sources of water which Athens possessed, says, that it could not have been drinkable, and therefore identifies it with a stream of brackish water which rises at the south-western angle of the Acropolis. But there are several reasons why the temple could not have lain so far westward as he places it; viz. between the summit of the Odeium of Regilla and the temple of Nikë Apteros. For, first, there would not have been room for several objects which Pausanias mentions, as intervening between the temple of Asclepius and the entrance to the Acropolis. It is true that several dedicatory inscriptions to Asclepius have been found near the south side of the Propylæa;[1] but these were, in all probability, moved from their original situation in the course of the many vicissitudes which Athens has undergone. How much scattered they have been appears from the fact that several have been found in the interior of the Acropolis; and one again far away to the eastward, near the Street of Tripods.[2] But more recently, during the excavations at the theatre, there was found near its western wall the fragment of an epistyle with an inscription recording the rebuilding of the temple by the priest Diophanes.[3] This was probably at or near the spot actually occupied by the temple. From the length of this fragment, which from its bearing the inscription must have been the centre-piece, M. Pervanoglu has calculated that the whole breadth of this little temple was 5·25 mètres, or rather more than 17 feet.[4] And with regard to the spring, it appears that about fourteen paces from the western wall of the theatre, and fifty from the cliff, are traces of a well now filled up, which was probably the spring seen by Pausanias in the peribolus of the temple.[5] Most recent topographers, Ross, Curtius,

---

[1] See Rangabé's Ant. Hell. t. ii. Nos. 1047–1049.

[2] Ibid. Nos. 774, 1050, 1052, 1053.

[3] Διοφάνης ἱερεὺς γενόμενος Ἀσκληπίῳ

καὶ Ὑγείᾳ, κ.τ.λ.—Pervanoglu, in the Philologus, t. xxiv. p. 462.

[4] Ibid. 464.

[5] Ibid. 459.

Bursian, have placed the temple at this spot; whence there would have been a view towards Epidaurus, the original seat of the god, from which place his worship was introduced into Attica.

A passage in Marinus' life of Proclus also fixes the temple near the theatre.[1] The Asclepicium was perfect in the time of Proclus, who resided at Athens about the middle of the fifth century.[2] In those days of expiring paganism, he secretly offered up in it his prayers for the daughter of a friend. But towards the latter part of that century, and during the lifetime of his pupil and biographer Marinus, it appears to have been destroyed. Marinus, as we see, also alludes to the Asclepicium as having been rendered famous by Sophocles; apparently by a pæan which he composed in honour of the god.[3]

After the temple of Asclepius, Pausanias proceeds to mention (c. 22, 1) a TEMPLE OF THEMIS, having before it a monument to Hippolytus. Poseidon had promised Theseus to accomplish three of his vows; and the Athenian king, suspecting that his son Hippolytus had conceived a passion for his wife Phædra, employed one of these promises for his destruction; which Aphroditë thus accomplished:

κaὶ τὸν μὲν ἡμῖν πολέμιον πεφυκότα
κτενεῖ πατὴρ ἀραῖσιν, ἃς ὁ πόντιος
ἄναξ Ποσειδῶν ὤπασεν Θησεῖ γέρας,
μηδὲν μάταιον ἐς τρὶς εὔξασθαι θεῷ [4]

"a paternal curse
Will slay mine enemy, Hippolytus;
For the sea-king, Poseidon, promise t Theseus,
That thrice he would accomplish what he pray'd."

Close by was a TEMPLE OF APHRODITË, which was often connected with the same story. Phædra, it was said, had first become enamoured of Hippolytus, when he came from Trœzen to Athens, for the purpose of

---

[1] οἴκησιν . . . γείτονα μὲν οὖσαν τοῦ ἀπὸ Σοφοκλέους ἐπιφανοῦς 'Ασκληπιείου, καὶ τοῦ πρὸς τῷ θεάτρῳ Διονυσίου.—sect. 29.

[2] καὶ γὰρ ηὐτύχει τούτου ἡ πόλις τότε, καὶ εἶχεν ἔτι ἀπόρθητον τὸ τοῦ σωτῆρος ἱερόν—

i.e. τὸ 'Ασκληπιείον.—Ibid.

[3] See Philostratus, Vit. Apollon. Tyan. iii. 17, p. 109.

[4] Eurip. Hippol. 43 sqq.

being initiated; and on his departure erected on this spot, in the name
of Hippolytus, the temple, which had a prospect towards the land of her
beloved:

κοὶ πρὶν μὲν ἐλθεῖν τῆνδε γῆν Τροιζηνίαν,
πέτραν παρ' αὐτὴν Παλλάδος κατόψιον
γῆς τῆσδε ναὸν Κύπριδος ἐγκαθείσατο,
ἐρῶσ' ἔρωτ' ἔκδημον· Ἱππολύτῳ δ' ἔπι
τὸ λοιπὸν ὠνόμαζεν ἱδρῦσθαι θεάν.[1]

"Before she came to this Trœzenian shore,
Phædra, enamoured of Hippolytus,
Upon the rock of Pallas raised a temple
Which viewed his foreign land, and did ordain it
Unto the Cyprian goddess consecrate
For ever, in the name of him she loved."

The temple was also sometimes called the Hippolyteium. Of all
the Athenian temples of which there are no remains, the site of none
can be more surely fixed than this; for only from a small tract about
midway between the theatre and the Odeium of Regilla, and nearer to
the former, can a view be obtained towards Trœzen, which is mentioned
in the lines just quoted, and is indicated by the heights of Methonë.
Further westward, as Leake places it, the view is intercepted by the
Museium Hill. Here also was found an inscription relating to Aphroditë.[2] Pausanias, however, adopts quite a different view respecting it,
and takes it to have been dedicated by Theseus to Aphroditë Pandemos
when he united the Attic demi. This is a more probable story than
that a temple in honour of Hippolytus should have been suffered to
exist close to the monument which recorded his disgrace and destruction.
Here in the time of Pausanias, was a statue of Aphroditë and another
of Peitho, or Suadela, her usual attendant; not the ancient ones,
indeed, for those had disappeared, but a great deal finer ones, and the
work of no common artist.

In connexion with the story of Phædra and Hippolytus, we hear also
that Theseus set up statues of Hermes ψιθυριστῆς, or the whisperer, and

---

[1] Eurip. Hippol. 29 sqq. See on this   Att. St. i. 48; C. Wachsmuth, Rh. Mus.
temple Boeckh, C. Inscr. Gr. i. p. 470.   1868, p. 26.

[2] See Ross, Theseium, p. 39; Curtius,

of Eros and Aphroditë under the same appellation ; because it is said Phædra had whispered calumnies against Hippolytus. Leake appears to assume [1] that these statues were in the temple of Aphroditë, but we know not on what grounds. Pausanias does not mention them ; and in the Λέξεις Ῥητορικαὶ [2] they are merely said to have been "at Athens." The Hermes Psithyristes mentioned by Demosthenes [3] must, as Leake himself observes, have stood in a different part of the city ; yet it is not likely that there was more than one such statue. The statues of Eros and Aphroditë to which the same epithet (ψιθυρὸς), "the whispering," was applied,[4] no doubt formed a group with it. The origin of the epithet was evidently lost in obscurity ; for in the Anecdota it is said that the Hermes got the name because the passers-by whispered things not to be spoken aloud.

The only other temple mentioned by Pausanias on the south side of the Acropolis before arriving at the Propylæa is a joint one of GÆA, surnamed κουροτρόφος, or the nourisher of children, and of DEMETER CHLOË (Χλόη, i.e. Verdure). These names were doubtless connected with the Eleusinian Mysteries, since Pausanias, as is his custom on such occasions, declines to explain them, and refers to the priests. Demeter and Gæa were often considered identical,[5] and indeed the name of Δημήτηρ is equivalent to Γῆ μήτηρ, or mother earth, γῆ being called δᾶ in the Doric dialect. Erichthonius was said to have established the worship of Gæa Courotrophos on the Acropolis, where he erected an altar to her and appointed that a sacrifice should first be made to her when other sacrifices were performed.[6] Women alone were allowed to sacrifice to her, and even the presence of men was forbidden.[7]

The temple of Demeter Chloë at the Acropolis is also indicated in a fragment of the 'Marikâ' of Eupolis, preserved by a scholiast on Sophocles :[8]

---

[1] vol. i. p. 142, note 1.
[2] Bekk. An. Græc. p. 317.
[3] con. Neær. p. 1358, Reiske.
[4] Harpocr. in ψιθυριστῆς Ἑρμῆς ; Bekk. An. Gr. l. c.
[5] Proclus in Tim. ap. Menrs. Ath. Att.

ii. 7.
[6] Suidas, in Κουροτρόφος Γῆ.
[7] See life of Homer, attributed to Herodotus.
[8] Ad Œd. Col. 1600. Δημήτηρ Χλόη is an apposition, like Ἀθήνη Νίκη, &c.

ἀλλ' εὐθὺ πόλεως εἶμι · Θῦσαι γάρ με δεῖ
κριὸν Χλόῃ Δήμητρι.

" I will to th' Acropolis, for I must
Offer a ram unto Demeter Chloë."

Where πόλις is used for ἀκρόπολις, as is very frequently the case. But the scholiast himself seems here to have confounded this temple of Demeter Chloë with another of Demeter εὔχλοος, under which epithet it is, and not Χλόη, that Demeter is really alluded to by Sophocles; and the opinion of Elmsley and Hermann seems a probable one, that he meant a sanctuary near Colonus. Another similar name of Demeter was 'Ιουλώ,[1] referring to the yellow colour of the wheatsheaves.

On approaching the Propylæa in the same direction as Pausanias, two niches may be perceived in the ancient wall under the temple of Nikë Apteros. They are separated from each other by a pillar, and are between 7 ft. and 8 ft. high, but vary in depth and breadth; the first, or southern one, being about 4 ft. 4 in. deep, and 5 ft. 6 in. broad; the northern one rather smaller both ways.[2] These have been taken for the sanctuaries of Demeter Chloë and Gæa Courotrophos. From their smallness they can have contained no statues, and, indeed, Pausanias mentions none; they would have sufficed only for altars; and that is all Erichthonius is said to have founded. Myrrhinë, in the ' Lysistrata ' of Aristophanes (v. 835), spies her husband Cinesias coming towards the Acropolis, where she and the other women are assembled, and passing the sanctuary of Chloë. M. Beulé disputes Leake's view, which is also held by Ross and others, that the niches in question were the sanctuaries mentioned by Pausanias. He argues that the word ἱερὸν is not appropriate to the objects in question, and thinks that Pausanias must be alluding to a large temple of Gæa mentioned by Thucydides (ii. 15), as lying to the south of the Acropolis. But ἱερὸν is a word of universal application to any sanctuary or holy place. The object mentioned by

[1] Athen. xiv. 10. It should, however, be mentioned that near the spot indicated, under the temple of Victory, a marble base was found with an inscription to Demeter εὐχλόη. See Rangabé, Ant. Hellen. t. ii. p. 1015, No. 2370.

[2] See Beulé, L'Acropole, t. i. p. 267.

Thucydides was sacred not to Græa Courotrophos but to Gæa Olympia; and, as we have already said,[1] it may even be doubtful whether there was any temple there at all. That the scholiast on that passage of Thucydides identifies Gæa with Demeter is of no importance. We will only further remark about these sanctuaries that they must have been remade by Cimon, as they are within his wall; and it is not improbable that the original ones were destroyed in its construction.

Pausanias now prepares to enter the Acropolis; but before we accompany him thither, we must advert to two objects which he has omitted to notice in his walk along the south side of the Acropolis. These are the so-called PORTICO OF EUMENES and the Odeium of Herodes Atticus, called after his wife Regilla.

The arches which still remain of the portico, running from the Dionysiac theatre to the Odeium, may be traced in the frontispiece to this volume. Those nearest the Odeium are ruined. The portico is attributed to Eumenes II., son of Attalus, on the strength of the following passage in Vitruvius: "Post scenam porticus sunt constituendæ . . uti sunt porticus Pompeianæ, itemque Athenis porticus Eumenia, Patrisque Liberi fanum."[2] But it may be observed that the definition "post scenam" does not agree very well with the position of these arches. We should rather expect, on the authority of Vitruvius, to find the portico at the southern front of the theatre than at its side. The remains of it, too, favour an opinion advanced by M. Breton,[3] that it must at all events have been rebuilt at the time when the Odeium of Herodes was erected. For not only is it in a similar style of architecture, but the materials also of which it is built are of the same sort. M. Pittakis, in his 'Antique Athènes' also adverts to this striking resemblance, but thinks that the Odeium was an imitation of the portico. It seems more probable that the portico was built after the Odeium, or at the same time with it; since Pausanias omits all mention of both. Curtius remarks, in the Explanatory Text to his 'Seven Maps of Athens' (p. 42), that no certain remains of the portico of Eumenes have yet been found.

[1] See above, p. 258. [2] lib. v. c. 9. [3] Athènes, p. 285.

Pausanias himself accounts for his silence about the Odeium. He says in his Achaica that he had passed it over in his Atthis, because the building was not begun before he had finished that book.[1] In the same place he calls it the finest Odeium in Greece, and says that it was built by Herodes in memory of his departed wife, Regilla, whose name it commonly bore. Of Herodes and his works at Athens we have already spoken.[2] Philostratus, in his life of Herodes,[3] says that his Odeium at Athens was much superior to the roofed theatre which he built at Corinth. It was principally the roof, as we have before observed, which distinguished an Odeium from a theatre. The roof of that of Herodes was of cedar, beautifully carved.

From the time of Spon and Wheler down to that of Chandler, the ODEIUM OF REGILLA was thought to be the Dionysiac theatre. Even Stuart and Revett adopted this error. The opinions of earlier topographers were still more absurd. The Anonymous who visited it in 1460 called it the palace of Leonidas and Miltiades, and the school of Aristotle. Theodore Zygomalas, in a letter to Crusius in 1575 also calls it the school of Aristotle and Miltiades; Babin in 1665 took it for the Areiopagus. In the reign of Valerian it had been converted into a fortress;[4] and when excavated in 1857, under the superintendence of M. Pittakis, was found covered with rubbish to a great depth. This débris, among which was a mass of shells whose presence it is difficult to account for, showed, by the coins found in it, five different strata, from the Byzantine times down to the Turkish. It contained a great many other remains, such as vases, and other earthenware, sculptures, rings, &c.;[5] also pieces of calcined cedar, which must have belonged to the roof. A bomb still full of powder was also discovered, probably one of those discharged by Morosini and Königsmark. The scene must have extended upwards of seventy feet to the south of what is still seen, as indicated by several large stones, which must have belonged to the foundations of the façade.

[1] See lib. vii. 20, 3.
[2] See above, p. 178.
[3] cap. 5.
[4] Zosimus, i. 29; Zonaras, xii. 23.

[5] See M. Christopulos' Report to the King, ap. Breton, Athènes, p. 289. In 1825 General Fabvier got into the Acropolis through one of the arches of this Odeium.

The Odeium of Regilla lies under the south-west angle of the Acropolis; and as in the Dionysiac theatre at the opposite extremity, the κοῖλον, or audience part, leant in a great measure upon the rock. It was separated into two hemicycles by a diazoma, or belt, about 7 ft. 6 in. broad. The lower hemicycle was divided by six staircases into five κερκίδες or cunei. The upper hemicycle, being of course much larger, had eleven staircases, and consequently double the number of cunei, or ten. The number of rows of seats in the first hemicycle was eighteen; those in the second have almost entirely disappeared, but there do not seem to have been more than half that number. The first rank of seats round the orchestra was, as in the Dionysiac theatre, the place of honour. Behind it was a passage about 2 feet wide and a step about 16 inches broad and 8 high, for the feet of the next row of spectators. A gallery ran round the top of the building, enclosed by a thick semicircular wall, on which, no doubt, the roof of cedar-wood rested. The greatest diameter within the walls is only 240 feet, and Leake is therefore of opinion that it could not have contained more than 6000 spectators.[1] M. Pittakis, however, reckons the number at 10,000.[2] It does not belong to our plan to enter any further into the architectural details of a monument which, after all, is not very interesting for Athenian art and literature; and we shall content ourselves with observing that it is in the Roman style of the time of Hadrian, and that its principal feature is the arch.

[1] vol. i. p. 189. M. Le Roy made it 247 French feet.   [2] L'ancienne Athènes.

CHAPTER XI.

WE have now made the circuit of the Acropolis, and have seen that even its sides contained some of the most ancient and venerable of the Attic sanctuaries; as the temple of Aglaurus, the Eleusinium, the temples of Dionysus, of Themis, of Asclepius, and others. How great, then, the veneration with which the sacred enclosure itself must have been regarded! That small isolated rock, whose plateau is about 1000 feet in length, and 450 in its greatest breadth, had not only been the cradle of Athens, the ancient Cecropian city, but had also obtained so sacred a character as to be regarded as one vast temple, or temenos. In the eyes of its most fervent admirers it appeared to be the very centre of the world. Thus, Aristeides[1] fancifully compares it to the innermost circle of a shield, surrounded by four others; the world being the outermost, of which Greece was the centre, Attica the centre of Greece, Athens the centre of Attica, and the Acropolis the centre of Athens. By a similar metaphor, Pindar, as usually interpreted, calls it the navel of the city; for it was almost the only Greek city whose Acropolis lay in the centre of it:[2]

[1] Or. Panath. t. i. p. 99 (Jebb).　　　[2] Leake, vol. i. p. 303, note.

"Ἴδετ' ἐν χορὸν Ὀλύμπιοι,
ἐπί τε κλυτὰν πέμπετε Χάριν, θεοί,
πολύβατον οἵτ' ἄστεος ὀμφαλὸν θυόεντα
ἐν ταῖς ἱεραῖς Ἀθήναις
οἰχνεῖτε, πανδαίδαλόν τ' εὐκλέα ἀγοράν.[1]

When Pindar here calls the Acropolis " much trodden " or " frequented," he must either mean much visited by the gods, or by mortals for purposes of devotion; for, with regard to profane uses, we find the exactly contrary epithet of ἄβατος, "untrodden," or "not to be trodden," applied to it. Thus Aristophanes:

(βασανιστέον) ἐφ' ὅ τι τε μεγαλόπετρον ἄβατον ἀκρόπολιν
(κατέλαβον) ἱερὸν τέμενος.—Lysistr. 482.

" We must examine wherefore they have seized
This sanctuary, this huge, untrodden rock,
Th' acropolis."

Here the name of τέμενος is applied to the whole rock. In the same play, one of the women assembled on the Acropolis pretends to be taken in labour, as a pretext for leaving it, and exclaims:

᾽ ὦ πότνι' Εἰλείθυι', ἐπίσχες τοῦ τόκου
ἕως ἂν εἰς ὅσιον μολῶ 'γὼ χωρίον.—v. 742.

" O honoured Eilythuia, check the b'rth
Until I reach some proper place profane."

The place was too sacred (ἱερὸν) for a profane (ὅσιον) act.[2] In the same

---

[1] " Look at our chorus, O Olympic gods, and send also the far-famed Grace, ye who frequent in holy Athens the much-trod navel of the city, redolent of sacrifice, and the glorious Agora, abounding with works of art."—Fragm. Dithyr. iii. ap. Heyne, t. iii. p. 67. δεῦτ' for ἴδετ' is the reading of Hudson (Dion. Hal. Op. t. ii. p. 41), of Heyne, and of Boeckh. It is said, however, that all or most codd. have ἴδετ', which is adopted by Bergk (Poet. Lyr. Gr. p. 226), and it is urged that Dionysius

calls the first word a *verb* (Op. ib. 42). ἐν Dor. for ἐς or εἰς. For οἰχνεῖτε conf. Soph. Electr. 165, ἀνύμφευτος αἰὲν οἰχνῶ : where the scholiast : οἰχνῶ · ἀναστρέφομαι, περιέρχομαι (t. ii. p. 249, ed. Oxon. 1852).

[2] So the scholiast here : ἀντὶ τοῦ εἰς βέβηλον καὶ μὴ ἱερόν, ἀλλ' ὅσιον εἰς τοκετάν. For ὅσιος, often misunderstood, see Taylor ad Aeschin. c. Timarch. p. 48 sq., Reiske ; Bekk. An. Graec. p. 288 ; Timaei Lex. Plat. in voc.

manner Demosthenes calls the whole Acropolis "sacred;"[1] and Pausanias characterises all the objects upon it as offerings (ἀναθήματα).[2] Aristeides, in the oration before cited, gives the same appellation to the Acropolis itself; or rather, he adds, correcting himself, not an anathema, but a divine image.[3] Hence probably the opinion of Petersen (Zwölf-göttersystem, p. 39) is preferable, that Pindar, in the fragment just quoted, by ὀμφαλὸς does not mean the Acropolis, but the altar of the Twelve Gods near it, from which all Attic distances were measured. For the poet summons the Olympic gods as if to the spot consecrated to them; and the epithets θυόεντα and πολύβατον are more appropriate to an altar than the Acropolis.

From the sacred character of the Acropolis Leake's opinion,[4] that there were no houses upon it, seems preferable to that of Chandler. And this view seems to be confirmed by the account of Thucydides, who says[5] that the Acropolis, the Eleusinium, and one or two other places, were the only ones which the rural population were not permitted to inhabit when they took refuge at Athens at the breaking out of the Peloponnesian war; though they appear to have been admitted into most of the temples, and even into the Pelasgicum, though forbidden by an oracle. This sacred character, however, should be restricted to the later times of Athens; for, when the Acropolis formed the whole city, it must of course have been inhabited. May it not have assumed the character of a temenos after the Persian wars? In the 'Knights' of Aristophanes the Propylæa are opened, and Demos is displayed dwelling in the ancient violet-crowned Athens (ἐν ταῖσιν ἰοστεφάνοις οἰκεῖ ταῖς ἀρχαίαισιν Ἀθήναις) in the same costume as when he feasted with Aristeides and Miltiades.[6] From this passage we see that the gates of the Acropolis were kept shut; and, indeed, there were proper officers called thyrori (θυρωροί) whose office it was to open and close them. Thus, when Proclus first visited the Acropolis, he found the thyroros in the

---

[1] ὅλης οὔσης ἱερᾶς τῆς ἀκροπόλεως ταυτησί.—De fals. legat. p. 428, Reiske.

[2] lib. v. 21, 1.

[3] ὥστ' εἶναι πᾶσαν ἀντ' ἀναθήματος, μᾶλλον δὲ ἀντ' ἀγάλματος.—t. i. p. 149, Jebb.

[4] vol. i. p. 308.

[5] lib. ii. c. 17.

[6] Eq. 1321 sqq. May not a statue of Demos have been set up in the Acropolis about this time?

2 A 2

act of closing them.[1] The care bestowed upon the adornment of the Acropolis after the Persian wars had not only converted it into a holy precinct but also into a sort of national museum. There was so much to be seen there that, as we have before remarked, Heliodorus had devoted fifteen books to the description of it,[2] whilst Polemo wrote four books on the anathemata it contained.[3] An inventory of these was made out in the archonship of Alcibiades.[4] Probably, however, as the commentator on this passage remarks, this was done in every archonship; and the list of Alcibiades is only more particularly adverted to because it contained the brazen weights. In short, so much was there to be seen, that Strabo fears to enter into any description, lest he should be led away from his proper subject, and we learn from Horace that some poets had devoted their whole labours to the celebration of its treasures.[5]

For many a century, under the rule of the Byzantine, the Frank and the Turk, this glorious spot, the cradle of European art and literature, had been a prey to the accidents of war, the ruthless hand of the spoiler, and the slower but no less certain ravages of neglect and decay. At length the establishment of Greek independence has arrested, for a while at least, the progress of these calamities, and even in some degree repaired the mischief that had been done. On the 20th of March, 1833, the Turks evacuated the Acropolis, and a few months afterwards an excavation was begun by private subscription on a small scale under the superintendence of M. Pittakis, who was rewarded by the discovery of part of the frieze of the Parthenon, and of several inscriptions.[6] In the following year, the matter was taken up by the Bavarian government; a credit of 72,000 drachms (about £2000) was opened to restore the Parthenon, so far as might be practicable, under the direction of

[1] Marin. Vit. Procl. c. 10.

[2] Athenaeus, vi. 16 (Schweigh.).

[3] Strabo, lib. ix. p. 396.

[4] Pollux, x. s. 126.

[5] " Sunt quibus unum opus est intactae
        Palladis arcem
   Carmine perpetuo celebrare."—Od. i. 7, 5.

[6] The following sketch of the excavations is taken from the Introduction to M. Rangabé's ' Antiquités Helléniques,' and from the accounts published by Professor Ross, at various times, in the Kunstblatt, and collected in his Archäologische Aufsätze, 1te Sammlg. S. 72-142.

Geheimrath Von Klenze. In 1835 the superintendence of the work was intrusted to Professor Ludwig Ross, with the architects Schaubert and Hansen as coadjutors. Their first care was to break up the modern fortifications on the west side of the Acropolis; and about the same time an excavation was begun around the Parthenon. It is to be regretted that it was considered necessary, we suppose for economical reasons, to shoot the rubbish thus turned up over the side of the Acropolis. It may be true, as Professor Ross alleges, that no actually existing monument was overwhelmed by this process; nevertheless, it may have obliterated the sites of some, such as the temples of Asclepius or Themis; and it has at all events destroyed the original contour of the rock. During these operations, the greater part of the plateau of the Acropolis was excavated as deep as, and even below, the ancient level, and the surface of the primitive rock laid bare. In these researches many interesting objects were discovered, such as fragments of statues and sculptures, pieces of coloured terra-cotta, belonging to the frieze or other parts of the old Hecatompedon, or some other building; and, especially, before the east side of the Parthenon, unfinished drums of columns as large as those still existing at that temple, which appear to have been rejected by the architects on account of their imperfections. On the south-west side of the building the substruction was found to be no less than 5·50 mètres, or between eighteen and nineteen English feet, high. On the opposite side the primitive rock rises to a much greater height, and the substruction is comparatively low. Before the west front of the Parthenon, at a depth of five or six feet, the ground was filled with the foundations of modern houses. It may be seen from Stuart's view[1] of the eastern façade that there were also houses on that side, and indeed apparently all round the temple.

Perhaps the most interesting discovery in the course of these excavations was that of almost all the parts of the little temple of Nikë Athena, commonly called Victory without wings, by which the German architects were enabled to reconstruct it. But of this we shall speak further on. In 1836 Professor Ross was succeeded as

[1] The Antiquities of Athens, vol. ii. ch. i. pl. i.

superintendent by M. Pittakis, who discovered the Propylæa, then
entirely masked by walls and batteries. He excavated the Pinacotheca,
and discovered the steps of the Propylæa, as broad as that building
itself. The walls and columns of the Erechtheium were now repaired;
many antiquities were discovered in other parts of the city, and many
tombs were opened in the Peiræus. After the exhaustion of the sum
assigned by the government, an Archæological Society was instituted,
under whose auspices the Tower of the Winds was excavated, at that
time buried up to the middle in rubbish. This society also repaired
the so-called Theseium and parts of the Parthenon, and attempted
the excavation of the Dionysiac theatre, which however, as we have
said, it abandoned in despair. Nor did it confine its efforts to Athens,
but among other things uncovered the lions at Mycenæ.

One of the most curious discoveries at the Acropolis was however
reserved for a Frenchman. In 1852 M. Beulé, a member of the French
school of Archæology and Philology at Athens, suspecting that there
was an entrance at a lower level, undertook the search for it, being
supplied by his government with the necessary funds.[1] At a depth of
16 mètres, or about 17½ yards, below the Propylæa, and 36 mètres, or
about 39 yards 1 foot, in advance of them, he found another façade
parallel with the grand one above, and rather broader. It consisted of
a marble wall of Doric architecture, having in the middle of it a gate
exactly in the axis of the central gate of the Propylæa. On each side
were two square towers to protect it, projecting 5·20 mètres, or more
than 6 yards, beyond the line of the wall. The length of the wall
between the towers is 7·20 mètres, or nearly 8 yards; its height
6·74 mètres, or about 7 yards 1 foot. The gateway is 3·87 mètres, or
about 13 feet high; 1·89 mètres, or upwards of 6 feet, broad at the base;
and, being of the Doric order, narrows towards the top to 1·63 mètres,
or about 5 feet. The wall is composed of marbles taken from various
monuments. The entablature appears to have belonged to some Doric
edifice, and is built in like that in the wall of Themistocles on the north

---

[1] The following account of his labours is taken from his L'Acropole d'Athènes, t. i.
p. 99 sqq.

side of the Acropolis. The marble cornice does not correspond with it, and has been taken from a different edifice. The metopes are of white marble, without any traces either of sculpture or painting. The wall shows marks of having been struck with cannon balls, so that it must have served after the invention of fire-arms. The antique frieze might have belonged to a temple destroyed by the Persians; while the architrave is more modern, and has an inscription in well cut letters recording a choragic victory of boys in the archonship of Neæchmus, consequently in the same year as that of Thrasyllus, or B.C. 316.[1]

M. Beulé is of opinion that the towers may be coeval with the Propylæa, and the work of Mnesicles; but he thinks that their foundations have been restored at a later period, and perhaps in the reign of Valerian. This, he says,[2] would not be the only example of foundations being younger than the superstructure which they supported, and adduces several instances of buildings thus underpinned. After passing the gate there are seven rude steps of a late construction leading to the ancient level of the entrance, whence the Propylæa may be seen in all their magnificence. At this point begins a staircase of 70 ft. in breadth, and consequently of the same dimensions as the front of the Propylæa. The base of it is 45 ft. lower than the base of the Propylæa, and in ascending length it exceeds 100 ft. The side walls were lined with white marble. Towards the top the pedestal of Agrippa breaks in upon it. In later ages this part had been turned into a cemetery, and in it were discovered heaps of bones. We cannot, however, agree with M. Beulé that this is the staircase represented on a coin in the British Museum.[3] He admits that there was an ascent on the north side of the Acropolis, near the cave of Pan, with an entrance under the

---

[1] M. Beulé (p. 103) seems to regard this as the sole choragic monument besides those of Lysicrates and Thrasyllus; but there are at all events several other inscriptions belonging to such monuments. See Rangabé, and other collections. The inscription in question runs as follows:

. . . . ἥτου [Εὐπετ]αιὼν ἀνέθηκε νικήσας χορηγῶν Κεκροπίδι παίδων . . . [α . σάων

Σικυών](ιος) ηὔλει ᾷσμα 'Ελπήνωρ Τιμοθέου. Νέ(αι)χμος ῆρχε.—Rangabé, Ant. Hell. t. ii. p. 704.

[2] vol. i. p. 112.

[3] See cut in next chapter (Grotto of Pan). The coin is thought to commemorate the restoration of some of the objects displayed, and to be later than the time of Hadrian.

Pinacotheca; and this, it seems to us, is the staircase represented on the coin. M. Beulé allows that, if it was intended to represent his newly-discovered staircase, the perspective would be false; and as there was another flight, which it truly represented, we can hardly accept his excuse for the die-sinker, that the necessity of so small a space compelled him to violate the laws of perspective.

M. Beulé's discovery is no doubt a most valuable and interesting one; but we can hardly agree with him that any part of this work belonged to the design of Mnesicles. Had this exterior fortification existed in the time of Aristophanes, the amusing scene between Cinesias and his wife, which he has pictured in his 'Ecclesiazusæ,' and to which we shall advert when we come to speak of Pan's grotto, would, as M. Rangabé has pointed out, have been impossible.[1] It is evident that the Propylæa then formed the first and only entrance to the Acropolis; and, indeed, the plan and construction of them shows that such was their destination. Nor, when the walls of the city were perfect, as they must have been when the Propylæa were built, would the entrance of the Acropolis have required any stronger fortification. M. Rangabé infers,[2] from an inscription in the Acropolis, that the staircase was added by Augustus and Agrippa, in the archonship of Rhœmatalces; and that the statue of Agrippa on the pedestal was erected in commemoration of the work. But even so, it seems surprising that Pausanias should have taken no notice of this staircase. It is evident that he entered the Acropolis at once and immediately by the Propylæa. With regard to the inscription, M. Beulé is of opinion[3] that two different ones have been confounded, viz. one relating to the staircase, and the other to the archonship of Rhœmatalces, which, however, is a Thracian name; while Ross gives to the word ἀνάβασις in the former a different sense from staircase.[4] On the whole, we are inclined to think that it must have been as late as the time of Valerian at least.

---

[1] Nuove mem. dell' Instituto, 1865, p. 362.

[2] Ant. Hell. t. ii. p. 70.

[3] L'Acropole, i. 129.

[4] The inscriptions are published by Ross, Demen von Attika, p. 35, and by the Archæological Society of Athens, Inscriptions, 1852, part ii.

Bursian is of opinion that the gate and towers may have been of the time of Justinian (Geogr. v. Griechenland, i. p. 306).

It would have been as well if M. Beulé had not thought fit to record his achievement, and that of France, however valuable, by a somewhat vainglorious inscription inserted at the side of the new entrance.[1] The Germans have done more than the French for the restoration of the Acropolis, and their doings will not be the less remembered because they have not inscribed their names among those of the ancient Greeks. However, in spite of this little outburst of national and personal vanity, M. Beulé's book on the Acropolis is remarkable not only for ingenuity and good taste, but also for sobriety of judgment, although he has not gone into the subject in the exhaustive, and occasionally somewhat tedious, manner of the Germans.

Before quitting this subject we may mention that, in the course of these excavations M. Beulé found in the bastion which masked the Propylæa on the west a bas-relief commemorating, as appears from the inscription,[2] some victory in a Pyrrhic dance, in which are represented eight children engaged in one. M. Rangabé thinks, from the characters of the inscription, that it belonged to the period between the 120th and 130th Olympiad (B.C. 300—360). The children are naked, except that they have a helmet and a buckler fastened with a strap to the left arm, which is extended. The dance is represented by ancient writers as an armed one.[3] There was a very similar bas-relief in the Museo Pio Clementino, where the children, though in a somewhat different position, have on only a helmet and buckler.[4] From an inscription found near the Parthenon in 1839, it appears that children and youths, as well as men, gained an ox for a victory in the Pyrrhic dances.[5] At Sparta[6] the children began to be instructed in them at the

---

[1] Ἡ Γαλλία τὴν πύλην τῆς ἀκροπόλεως, τὰ τείχη, τοὺς πύργους καὶ τὴν ἀνάβασιν κεχωσμένα ἐξεκάλυψεν. Βεϋλὲ εὗρεν.

[2] Πυρρι]χισταῖς νικήσασ(ιν) "Αταρβος.— Rangabé, An. II. t. ii. p. 705. A cut of the bas-relief will be found there, and also at the end of M. Beulé's second volume.

[3] Strabo, x. 467; Lucian, De Salt. 20.

[4] Visconti, Mus. Pio Clem. t. iv. 9.

[5] Rangabé, ibid. p. 668, Inscr. No. 960.

[6] Athen. xiv. 29.

age of five. A draped figure on the left of the relief appears to be
their teacher, but it is difficult to make out whether it is a man or
woman. These two reliefs are, we believe, the only existing representations of the dance.

Pausanias does not notice the PEDESTAL OF AGRIPPA standing before
the northern wing of the Propylæa, to which we have just adverted.
It must, of course, have been there at the time of his visit, and from
its size it could not have escaped his observation; but it would be
useless to inquire after the reasons for his silence. He passes over
many still more remarkable objects, either because he did not think
them of much value as works of art, or because he had nothing new or
interesting to say about them. This huge pedestal of 27 ft. in height
and 12 ft. square does not stand exactly on the square with the front
of the Propylæa, but faces a little to the north; and, as M. Beulé
observes, is not in very good keeping with the building before which it
stands. We do not think that Pausanias makes any allusion to it when
he speaks of two equestrian statues at the entrance to the Propylæa.
We agree with Ross[1] that he alludes to two distinct statues on each
side of that building. They could hardly have stood, as some have
thought, on Agrippa's pedestal, the inscription on which excludes such
an idea. "I cannot tell," says Pausanias (c. 22, 4), "whether these
statues are the sons of Xenophon, or were merely placed there for
ornament." It is not improbable, as Leake says,[2] that they did
represent Gryllus and Diodorus; and, according to an Athenian, and
indeed Grecian, practice, had been converted into two Romans; wherefore Pausanias affected to ignore them, or ventured merely to give a
hint of what they really were. M. Beulé thinks it a mistake to suppose
that Greek statues were made to represent Romans, and that from many
of the pedestals whose inscriptions have been altered the statues had
been carried off, and the pedestals afterwards used for new statues.
In some cases this may perhaps be true; but the evidence respecting
the conversion of the statues themselves is too strong to be lightly

---

[1] Nikē Apteros, p. 7. The pedestal is inscribed: ὁ δῆμος Μάρκον Ἀγρίππαν Λευκίου

υἱόν, τρὶς ὕπατον τὸν ἑαυτοῦ εὐεργέτην.
[2] vol. i. p. 329.

rejected. We know from Plutarch[1] that colossal statues of Attalus
and Eumenes had been inscribed to M. Antony. The author of the
lives of the Ten Orators mentions that the inscription on the pedestal
of the statue of the mother of Isocrates had been altered.[2] Dion
Chrysostom denounces the practice in his Rhodiac oration,[3] and the
custom has also been branded by Cicero.[4] A statue of Orestes at
Mycenæ had been converted into one of Augustus Cæsar.[5] A marble
found near the pedestal of Agrippa had an inscription to the Roman
proconsul Cn. Acerronius Proclus, below which, in more ancient characters, the words Πραξιτέλης ἐποίει proved its misappropriation.[6] It
was probably from disgust at this practice that Pausanias affected to
ignore the new owners of the statues of Poseidon near the Peiraïc Gate,
and of Miltiades and Themistocles at the Prytaneium.

Pausanias observes (c. 22, 4) that in his time nothing surpassed the
PROPYLÆA of the Acropolis, whether for the size of the stones or the
beauty of the workmanship. They were the greatest achievement of
Pericles and his architects, and attracted more admiration even than
the Parthenon. The works of the ancients abound with allusions to
them. The comic poet, Phœnicides, in a fragment preserved by
Athenæus,[7] mentions among the four most celebrated things at Athens,
the myrtles, the honey, the Propylæa, and the figs. Epaminondas
wished to carry the Propylæa to Thebes, and place them before the
Cadmeia, its Acropolis.[8] Cicero enumerates them amongst the most
glorious buildings of Athens.[9] The idea of the Propylæa seems to be
of Egyptian origin. Amasis had erected at Saïs some admirable propylæa in honour of Athena; and Herodotus[10] admired in them the size

---

[1] M. Ant. c. 60.

[2] Plutarch, t. ix. p. 339, Reiske.

[2] εἶτα τῆς μὲν πρότερον οὔσης ἐπιγραφῆς
ἀναιρεθείσης, ἑτέρου δ' ὀνόματος ἐγχαρα-
χθέντος, πέρας ἔχει τὸ τῆς τιμῆς, καὶ λοιπὸν
τέτευχε τῆς εἰκόνος ὁ δόξας ὑμῖν ἄξιος, κ.τ.λ.
—p. 312, Mor. (i. 346, Teubner).

[4] "Odi falsas inscriptiones statuarum
alienarum."—Ad Att. vi. 1, sub fin. Where
he is talking about erecting some monument of himself at Athens.

[5] Pausan. ii. 17, 3.

[6] Leake, vol. i. p. 329, note.

[7] xiv. 67, Meineke, p. 1140.

[8] Æschin. Παραπρ. p. 277, Reiske.

[9] De Rep. iii. 32, 44.

[10] lib. ii. c. 175. Many of the older
Egyptian temples had propylæa.

and quality of the stones, the largest being brought from Elephantinë, just as Pausanias admired those at Athens. There was a propylæum before the temple of Demeter at Eleusis, which may perhaps be that alluded to by Cicero as building, or at all events designed, by Appius Claudius. Cicero had entertained the idea of erecting a propylæum at the Academy by way of an Attic monument to himself.[1] Such structures, therefore, must be regarded rather as entrances to some sacred

VIEW OF THE PROPYLÆA.

precinct than fortifications, as Leake[2] and other topographers have thought. As M. Beulé observes, the elegance of the Athenian structure, and the statuary and paintings with which it was adorned, show that it was not meant for such a purpose. *Propylæa* differed from *pylæ* (πύλαι, gates), in being complex buildings and having *pylæ* of their own. In that at Athens there were no fewer than five gates. These, though not

[1] Epp. ad Attic. vi. 1, 26.   [2] vol. i. p. 317.

intended for defence against foreign enemies, were still kept strictly
guarded; for they not only gave admission to the most sacred precinct
of Athens, but also locked up the treasure of the state deposited in the
Opisthodomos, or western cell of the Parthenon. The gates appear to
have been of wood, as the old men in the 'Lysistratë' of Aristophanes
threaten to burn them.[1] The keys were intrusted, for one day only,
to the epistates, one of the ten proëdri, in order that he might not be
tempted to seize the state treasure and make himself tyrant.[2] We
have before adverted to the building of the Propylæa (supra, p. 132).
We may here mention that our countryman, Wheler, was the first to
give them their right name.[3] By the older topographers, as Babin
and Guillet, they had been called the Arsenal of Lycurgus.

Pausanias particularly adverts to the ceiling of the Propylæa. In
excavating the Turkish battery a great quantity of ornaments were found
which are thought to have belonged to this ceiling;[4] but as they bear
traces of colour, blue, green, and red, this fact seems rather to militate
against the assumption, since Pausanias speaks of the roof as being of
white stone or marble (λίθου λευκοῦ, c. 22, 4). Nor does it correspond
with the description of Wheler, in whose time the roof seems to have
been entire, who says that it consisted of two great marble beams
covered with large marble planks.[5] But what chiefly attracted the
attention of Pausanias was the picture gallery, or pinacotheca (οἴκημα
ἔχον γραφάς), on his left as he entered, the still existing contents of
which he proceeds to describe (c. 22, 6). His description of the first
picture contains a somewhat unusual, though not unexampled,[6] construction of the particles μέν and δέ, in which μέν is made to refer to
the latter of two antecedents and δὲ to the former, contrary to the more
general practice, which is the reverse. We should not have mentioned
this, had it not led Leake into a curious error, who translates: "Those
(pictures) which are not obliterated by time represent Diomedes bringing

[1] See v. 310.

[2] See argument to the speech of Demosthenes against Androtion, p. 590, Reiske.

[3] Journey, &c. p. 359.

[4] Ross, Arch. Auf. i. p. 97.

[5] Journey, p. 359.

[6] See the examples collected by Hoog-
even under these particles, s. 2.

from Lemnos the bow of Philoctetes, and Ulysses carrying off the statue of Minerva from Troy."[1] It is hardly necessary to remind the reader that the facts were exactly the reverse, that Ulysses carried off the bow and Diomedes the palladium.

The next picture represented Orestes slaying Ægisthus, and Pylades despatching the sons of Nauplius, who had come to his aid. There also was Polyxena about to be sacrificed at the tomb of Achilles; a barbarous act, which, says Pausanias, Homer has properly omitted. In fact, however, it lay beyond his subject. Next, two pictures by Polygnotus: one of the taking of Scyros by Achilles, where also Homer (Il. ix. 664) differs from other poets in not describing his life there with the maidens. The other represented Odysseus appearing to Nausicaä and her companions at the river. Also a picture of Alcibiades, in which his equestrian victory at Nemea is indicated. This picture appears to have been by Aglaophon, and the indication of the victory was Nemea personified, bearing on her knees Alcibiades, who had a face of more than feminine beauty.[2] There also was Perseus at Seriphus bringing the head of Medusa to Polydectes. But, continues Pausanias, I will say nothing about Medusa in this book upon Attica; reserving the subject as more proper for his next book, where, in treating about Argos, he tells the story.[3] Passing over the boy carrying the hydriæ, and the wrestler painted by Timænetus, there was among the rest a picture of Musæus. I have read an epic poem, says Pausanias, which I think was written by Onomacritus, in which it is said that Musæus was endowed by Boreas with the faculty of flying. Of Musæus himself, he says, we have nothing certain but a hymn to Demeter, composed for the Lycomidæ.

There are at present no traces of any paintings on the walls of the Pinacotheca, or of nails by which they might be suspended; and it is a subject of dispute whether they were done on the walls or suspended

---

[1] vol. i. p. 143. The translation in Siebelis' edition, who has no note on the passage, is as bad: "Diomedes erat e Lemno Philoctetæ sagittas reportans, et Ulysses ex Ilii arce Palladium surripiens." We subjoin Pausanias' words: ὁπόσαις δὲ

μὴ καθέστηκεν ὁ χρόνος αἴτιος ἀφανίσιν εἶναι, Διομήδης ἦν καὶ 'Οδυσσεύς, ὁ μὲν ἐν Λήμνῳ τὸ Φιλοκτήτου τόξον, ὁ δὲ τὴν 'Αθηνᾶν ἀφαιρούμενος ἐξ 'Ιλίου.—c. 22, 6.

[2] Athen. xii. 47 (Schweigh.).

[3] ii. 21, 6.

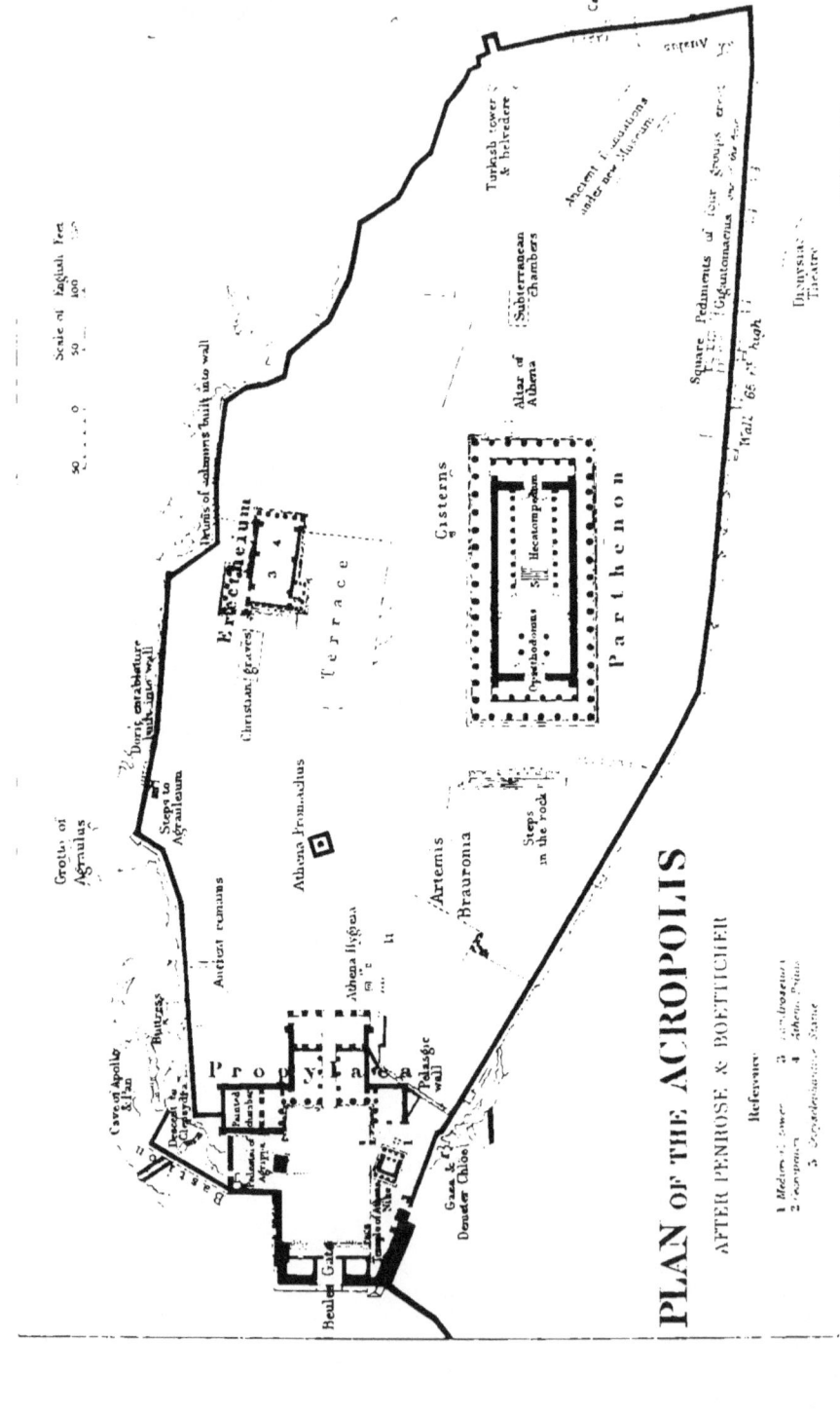

PLAN OF THE ACROPOLIS

AFTER PENROSE & BOETTICHER

Reference

1 Medieval tower   3 Artropoleion
2 Propylaea   4 Athena Polias
5 Lenaukephoros Statue

Beulé Gate

Cave of Apollo & Pan

Buttress

Descent to Clepsydra

Pelasgic wall

Propylaea

Athena Hygeia

Grotto of Agraulus

Doric entablature built into wall

Ruins of columns built into wall

Steps to Agraulium

Erechtheium

Christian graves

Terrace

Athena Promachus

Antient remains

Artemis Brauronia

Steps in the rock

Cisterns

Altar of Athena

Subterranean Chambers

Hecatompedon

Opisthodomus

Parthenon

Square Pediments of four groups each Gigantomachia

Wall 65 ft high

Turkish tower & belvedere

Ancient foundations under new Museum

Cavern

Dionysiac Theatre

Scale of English Feet
0   50   100

in wooden tablets. We have no means for deciding this question, and shall only add that in the opinion of Professor Ross the pictures were done on the wall.[1]

Leake observes (vol. i. p. 326) that Pausanias "confined the name Propylæa to the gates opening into the Acropolis with their vestibules, although in truth the wings were contemporary buildings and component parts of the Propylæa, and he omitted all notice of the southern wing of the Propylæa, a neglect which, according to the usual method of this author, was justified by the inferior importance of that wing, which seems to have been little more than a place of arms," &c. But, in fact, Pausanias mentions neither wing, probably because he did not consider that there was anything in them that required description; yet that he considered them to be parts of the Propylæa is evident from his saying that the Pinacotheca is on the left *of the Propylæa,* when in reality it is on the left *of the north wing* of that building.[2] He comprehended, therefore, under the name of Propylæa, the gateway with its two wings, and regarded only the Pinacotheca as a separate and distinct building, though by other authorities this also has been included in the Propylæa.[3]

The following description, with the aid of the annexed plan of the Acropolis, may suffice to convey to the general reader a tolerably accurate idea of the Propylæa.[4] The breadth of the western ascent to the Acropolis was at its summit 160 feet, and this space Mnesicles, the architect of Pericles, filled up with a single building, consisting of a grand hall, or megaron, with wings on each side. The megaron is about 60 feet broad from north to south. Towards its eastern end, at a distance of 36 or 37 feet from its commencement, it is crossed by a wall having five doors. On each side of the megaron are Doric hexastyle porticoes. Its roof is supported by a double row of Ionic columns, flanking

---

[1] Archäol. Aufsätze, i. 119, note; cf. Beulé, L'Acropole, i. 211.

[2] ἔστι δὲ ἐν ἀριστερᾷ τῶν προπυλαίων, οἴκημα ἔχον γραφάς.—i. 22, 6.

[3] Thus the title of one of Polemon's books on the Acropolis was, Περὶ τῶν ἐν τοῖς προπυλαίοις πινάκων.—Harpocr. voc.

Λαμπάς.

[4] It should be mentioned here that the measurements of all the monuments on the Acropolis are very accurately given by Mr. Penrose in his 'Principles of Athenian Architecture,' London, 1851.

each side of the road which runs through its centre. The western portico, which projects about 12 feet, has entrances into the wings on each side. The north wing projects about 20 feet westward of the columns of the portico, while the south wing is considerably shorter— in order apparently, as we have before remarked, not to encroach upon the temple of Nikë Apteros. Each wing was fronted with three Doric columns of smaller dimensions than those of the main porticoes. The modern Frankish tower which surmounts the south wing was probably built by Neri di Acciajuoli, first Duke of Athens (d. 1393), who erected many sumptuous edifices at Athens.[1] The breadth of the wings is about 27 feet, though the southern one is a trifle broader than the northern. The breadth of the Pinacotheca is about 30 feet, and it is of the same length as the northern wing. These buildings, therefore, allowance being also made for the thickness of the walls, completely filled up the breadth of the access to the Acropolis. The Propylæa were originally crowned with a pediment called aëtoma (ἀέτωμα), because it resembled in form an eagle with moulted wings.[2] Of this there are now no remains. The middle gate of the wall of the megaron, and the intercolumniation between the two middle columns of each portico, which correspond with it, are considerably broader than the rest in order to admit through them a road about 13 feet broad, intended for the passage of animals and chariots. This road is paved with slabs of marble, notched or roughed in order to prevent the animals from slipping. The steps leading to the Propylæa are as broad as the megaron, and the roadway in question cuts them in the middle on an inclined plane. Whether the whole Panathenaïc procession ascended the Acropolis is a disputed point, which we shall consider further on when we come to speak of the Erechtheium. The victims at all events must have ascended by this road, and perhaps some of the chariots also.

Pausanias, before describing the Pinacotheca, briefly adverts to a temple of Victory without wings, which he indicates as being *on his*

---

[1] Fanelli, Aten. Att. iii. s. 588; Beulé, i. 60.

[2] ἡ γὰρ ἐπὶ τοῖς προπυλαίοις κατασκευὴ

ἀετοῦ μιμεῖται σχῆμα, ἀποτετακότος τὰ πτερά.—Bekk. Anecd. Græc. 348, 3.

right before entering the Propylæa.[1] Hence, he says, the sea may be descried; and it was from this place that Ægeus is said to have precipitated himself when he beheld his son's vessel returning with the black sail. He then proceeds to sketch that well-known story, to which we have already adverted.[2]

The name of Victory without wings seems to have been a later one for the deity of this temple, which appears to have been originally dedicated to Nikō Athena. Thus Heliodorus, in his *first book*, and therefore, we may presume, in describing the entrance of the Acropolis,[3] said that the Athenians had an image of Nikē Athena, without wings, holding in her right hand a pomegranate, and in her left a helmet. The two names belong only to one goddess—Victory and Athena in one. Thus Aristeides remarks that Athena is not *eponymous* of Victory, but *homonymous*.[4] And under this homonym we find her invoked by Creüsa in the 'Ion' of Euripides:

μὰ τὴν παρασπίζουσαν ἅρμασίν ποτε
Νίκην Ἀθάναν Ζηνὶ γηγενεῖς ἔπι.—v. 1528.

" I swear by her who from her chariot once
Assisted Zeus against the Titan-brood,
Nikē Athena."

We have other examples of homonymous deities in Poseidon Erechtheus, &c. In this character, then, Victory appears never to have had wings, which were a later attribute of her, regarded as a substantive deity. And thus in Ptolemy's pageant at Alexandria we find them separated,

[1] τῶν δὲ προπυλαίων ἐν δεξίᾳ.—c. 22, 4. This passage, as well as his specifying that the Pinacotheca was on the left of the building (ἐν ἀριστερᾷ τῶν προπυλαίων, ib. 6), shows that Pausanias used the words *right* and *left* with regard to his own position. Leake (vol. i. p. 324, note) has collected many instances of this, and can find only two examples to the contrary, for which he accounts. This is important for the position of objects.

[2] See above, p. 61. Leake has very satisfactorily proved the site of the temple. —vol. i. p. 322 sqq.

[3] Ap. Harpocr. voc. Νίκη Ἀθηνᾶ.

[4] ἡ μόνη μὲν ἁπάντων θεῶν, ὁμοίως δὲ πασῶν, οὐκ ἐπώνυμος τῆς νίκης ἐστίν, ἀλλὰ ὁμώνυμος.—Orat. in Min. p. 16, Jebb. He had observed just before (p. 13) that he could say nothing greater of her power than that she always conquered; and that Victory was not mistress of Athena, but Athena of Victory (οὐ γάρ ἐστιν Ἀθηνᾶς νίκη κυρία, ἀλλ᾽ Ἀθηνᾶ νίκης ἀεί).

on which occasion on one hand of Alexander's car stood a Nikē, on the other an Athena.[1] Hence in after-times her wingless state came to be regarded as a peculiarity, and conjectures were made as to the cause of it. Wheler's solution, that she was called ἄπτερος because the fame of Theseus' victory arrived not at Athens before Theseus himself, is a mere guess, unsupported by any authority. Pausanias (iii. 15, 5) says that the Athenians made her so that she might always remain with them, just as the Spartans, with the same view, bound Enyalius in chains. We know not whether there is an instance of Victory, as a substantive goddess, without wings. That they were a comparatively modern addition may be inferred from a scholium[2] on the 'Birds' of Aristophanes :

αὐτίκα Νίκη πέτεται πτερύγοιν χρυσαῖν.—v. 574.

" Now Victory flies with golden wings."

Here αὐτίκα is usually rendered ' for example ;' but the scholiast indicates a recent innovation (νεωτερικὸν) which some attributed to Archennus, father of Bupalos and Athenis, and others to Aglaophon, the Thasian animal painter. As the 'Birds' of Aristophanes were represented in the year B.C. 414,[3] and as Aglaophon the Thasian flourished seventy or eighty years before that time, some writers[4] have thought it probable that the innovation in question was introduced by Aglaophon, the painter of the Nemean victory of Alcibiades, who, according to Pliny,[5] flourished about the 90th Olympiad (B.C. 420–417), and who may have been the grandson of the Thasian, and the son of Aristophon, to whom indeed the picture of Alcibiades is attributed by Plutarch,[6] though no doubt erroneously; but there is no authority to establish this view. The scholiast is very precise in attributing the innovation to the Thasian, and his alternative of Archennus, or Archeneus, would land us at the same or a rather earlier date.[7] And if the coin figured by Stuart at the

---

[1] Athen. v. 34 (Schweigh.).

[2] νεωτερικὸν τὸ τὴν Νίκην καὶ τὸν Ἔρωτα ἐπτερῶσθαι.

[3] Clinton, Fasti Hell. sub an.

[4] See the life of Aglaophon in Smith's Dictionary.

[5] H. N. xxxv. s. 60.

[6] Alcib. c. 16.

[7] Or Archermus, Plin. xxxvi. 11. Cf. Boeckh, Corp. Ins. i. p. 38 ; Sillig, Catal. Artif.

head of the first chapter of his second volume is, as has been thought, a representation of the Athena of Pheidias, then, since she holds a winged Victory in her hand, the innovation must have been at least as early as the time of Pericles. Wherefore, perhaps, some latitude must be allowed to the words of the scholiast. The original image of Nikë Athena appears to have been a rude wooden one (ξόανον).[1] The Athenians consecrated a bronze image of Victory in the Acropolis after the battle of Sphacteria, B.C. 425, and this was probably represented in the newer fashion.[2] Dr. Wordsworth is not quite accurate in stating on the authority of this passage of Pausanias, that the temple of Victory without wings was then erected.[3] The bronze image in question may probably be that alluded to by Aristophanes in the passage of the 'Birds' before quoted, as having golden or gilded wings, which appear to have been subsequently stolen.[4] Here let us observe that artists, as well as poets, had a share in modifying the mythology of Greece; and we learn from the scholiast on the 'Birds' before cited, that Eros also was first furnished with wings about the same time as Nikë. According to Aristophon's account, Nikë was furnished with the wings of which Eros had been deprived when he was expelled from heaven.[5] Sophocles identifies Athena Nikë with Athena Polias:

Ἑρμῆς δ' ὁ πέμπων δόλιος ἡγήσαιτο νῷν
Νίκη τ' Ἀθάνα Πολιάς, ἣ σώζει μ' ἀεί.—Philoct. 133.

"And now deceitful Hermes be our guide
And she who is my constant guardian,
Nikë Athena Polias."

---

[1] Κάλαμις δὲ οὐκ ἔχουσαν πτερὰ ποιῆσαι λέγεται, ἀπομιμούμενος τὸ Ἀθήνησι τῆς Ἀπτέρου καλουμένης ξόανον.—Pausan. v. 26, 5.

[2] Pausan. iv. 36, 4. As Pausanias here uses merely the term Νική, we may conclude that it was a winged Victory; and at all events certainly not a Νίκη Ἀθηνᾶ.

[3] Athens and Attica, p. 90, note 1.

[4] Demosth. c. Timocr. p. 738, Reiske.

The word used by Demosthenes is ἀκρωτήρια, which the scholiast (t. ii. p. 183) explains by πτερά. The same scholiast says they were taken from the image of Nikë Athena; in which he can hardly be correct. But they were probably taken out of her temple, when this new image had been consecrated.

[5] Apud Athen. xiii. 14.

Which invocation seems an anomaly in the mouth of Odysseus, especially as it is uttered in Lemnos. But the poet doubtless intended a little compliment to the Athenians, and alluded probably, as Dr. Wordsworth suggests, to a custom which obtained among them of invoking her aid when starting on any dangerous enterprize. So likewise the chorus of old men in the 'Lysistratë' of Aristophanes appeal to her for assistance when about to attack the women in the Acropolis, of which she seemed from her position to guard the very entrance.

The temple of Victory was extant in the time of Wheler, who describes it as built of white marble, and gives its dimensions as fifteen feet in length and eight or nine in breadth;[1] which are pretty nearly accurate, but rather too small. It had disappeared in the time of Stuart, who took the Pinacotheca for it, and he wrongly accuses Spon and Wheler of error, asserting that the temple which they took for that of Nikë Apteros was in fact the temple of Aglaurus.[2] Professor Ross is of opinion that it must have been pulled down by the Turks after the date of Wheler's visit in order to strengthen their fortifications, which is probable enough. But his conjecture that their upper battery must have been in existence in Wheler's time, because he does not mention the pedestal of Agrippa, seems hardly correct, for the pedestal was certainly visible in the time of Stuart, who mentions it and its inscription.[3] The late Lord Broughton says of the temple, "The last memorial of its existence was carried away by Lord Elgin."[4] This was part of the frieze, which had been built into a wall, and is now in the British Museum. All the other fragments of the temple were discovered by Professor Ross and his coadjutors in the excavations of 1835; they had been

---

[1] Journey, p. 358. Leake (vol. i. p. 320, note 2) accuses Wheler of error in these dimensions. But it is evident that he was not alluding to the stylobate but to the cella; which is really only one foot longer than the measure given by Wheler. The latter however was wrong in calling the architecture Doric, and in assigning the sculptures to the architrave instead of the frieze.

[2] See his plan of the Acropolis in vol. ii. Also ch. v. p. 39 sq., and the plan of the Propylæa, pl. ii.

[3] Ibid. p. 38 sq. See Ross, Tempel der Nikë Apteros, S. 2.

[4] Hobhouse's Journey through Albania, &c., vol. i. p. 337.

built into a Turkish battery, which had in fact preserved them, and the temple was re-erected, chiefly under the superintendence of Herr Laurent, an architect of Dresden.[1] At a later period were discovered some bas-reliefs which evidently belonged to the temple, having been found in its neighbourhood. They represented winged Victories; one, in which the goddess is stooping to loose her sandal, is of supreme beauty. The others are in more questionable taste, and connoisseurs are generally of opinion that all of them are of a much later date than the temple itself, and probably of the time of Lysippus. As they are too large to have found a place in the temple itself, Ross is of opinion that they probably formed a sort of balustrade around it, and M. Beulé coincides in this view.[2]

The TEMPLE OF NIKÉ APTEROS, as it is commonly called, stands on the western abutment of the Cimonian, or southern, wall of the Acropolis; a gigantic structure of poros stone, varying in thickness from nearly 20 feet to more than 30. The temple is of the Ionic order, and technically an amphiprostylos tetrastylos, that is, having a portico of four columns at each front. It is approached by three steps, the upper stylobate being 27 ft. 2 in. long, and 18 ft. 3½ in. broad. The height of the columns, including base and capital, is 13 ft. 4 in.; the intercolumniation, from the middle of the columns, 5 ft. 2½ in.; the length of the cell, 16 ft.; the height of the entablature (architrave, frieze, and cornice), 3 ft. 8½ in.[3] It bears a considerable resemblance to the little Ionic temple on the Ilissus described by Stuart, but no longer existing, to which we have before adverted.[4] The frieze which ran round the temple is 1 ft. 5 in. in height, but so mutilated that the subjects of the sculptures, which are in high relief, cannot be determined with certainty. The part of the frieze already alluded to as carried off by Lord Elgin, had been previously drawn by Pars, and is engraved in Stuart's work on Athens.[5] The relief on the eastern façade must have contained 28

[1] Ross, ibid. S. 3. For the architectural details of the temple the reader is referred to that work.

[2] Ross, ibid. S. 17; Beulé, L Acropole,

t. i. p. 261.

[3] Ross, Niké Tempel, S. 11.

[4] Above, p. 298.

[5] vol. ii. ch. v. pl. xii. and xiii.

or 30 figures, and seems to represent an assembly of the gods. As this is mythological, so the other three sides appear to be historical, and to represent combats between foot and horse, foot and foot, Greeks and Greeks, and Greeks and Persians. The last have by some writers been taken to be Amazons, but Ross agrees with Leake in considering the figures on horseback to be Persians. The style of the sculpture bears some resemblance to that of the temple of Apollo at Phigalia.[1]

Close to the temple of Nikë Athena stood a statue of Artemis Epipyrgidia, or the triple Hecatë; which Pausanias does not mention in the regular course of his itinerary, but casually in his Corinthiaca (ii. 30, 2). This deity, he says, was principally worshipped by the Æginetans; but their statue of her, which was of wood, and made by Myron, had only one face and one body. We have already spoken of this deity when describing the throne of her priest.[2] A medal on which she is figured with three heads and three bodies has been engraved by Stuart (vol. ii. ch. 5, init.), and the inscription on it, Ἀθηνᾶς νικηφόρου, seems to indicate her proximity to the temple.

There seems also to have stood at the entrance of the Acropolis, though Pausanias does not mention it, a statue of Athena, surnamed Cleidouchos, or the Keeper of the Keys. It is alluded to by Aristophanes, in the following verses of the 'Thesmophoriazusæ':

(Παλλὰς) ἣ πόλιν ἡμετέραν ἔχει,
καὶ κράτος φανερὸν μόνη,
κλῃδοῦχός τε καλεῖται.—v. 1140 sqq.

"'Tis Pallas keeps our city,
Our only open strength,
The key-holder she's called."

It was said to be the work of Pheidias.[3] But Cleidouchos might perhaps be a *sobriquet* of the Lemnian Athena, of which statue, standing near the Propylæa, we shall have to speak further on.

At the very entrance into the Acropolis, says Pausanias (c. 22, 8),

[1] There is an elaborate account of the frieze in Ross, Nikë Tempel, 4ᵗᵉʳ Abschnitt. See also Leake, vol. i. App. xv.

[2] Above, p. 323.

[3] See Preller in the Hall. A. Encycl. p. 195.

stands a Hermes Propylæus and the Graces. It is evident, not only
from the words of Pausanias here,[1] but also from what follows, that he
has now passed the gates in the wall of the megaron, and is on the
eastern side of it. We mention this because Meursius, who had no
local knowledge of Athens, places these statues on the western side,[2]
and so in the following chapter goes on to describe the Temple of
Victory and the Pinacotheca. From the words of Pausanias it very
clearly appears that he considered Socrates to have executed the Hermes
Propylæus as well as the Graces;[3] though in general only the latter are
spoken of as his work. It is true that when he reverts to this group in
his Bœotica, in the passage quoted in note [1], he mentions only the
Graces; but this is natural enough, as he is there speaking particularly
of these deities. Diogenes Laërtius also mentions only the Graces as
the work of Socrates;[4] and no doubt they formed the most striking part
of the group; as, according to the ancient fashion they were clothed,
whilst in more modern times they were represented naked. Pausanias
did not know who had introduced this innovation, which in his time was
universally adopted. Let us observe that Diogenes Laërtius speaks
with no certainty of this group being the work of Socrates; he mentions
it only as a partial report. That Socrates executed some such group
may be pretty certainly inferred from the general testimony to that
effect. Aristophanes appears to have a sly allusion to it when he
makes Socrates swear by the Graces.[5] But according to the scholia
on that passage, they seem to have been sculptured on a wall—therefore a bas-relief—behind the Parthenon.[6] As the Graces at the Propylæa were clothed, they must at all events have been an ancient work.

---

[1] κατὰ δὲ τὴν ἔσοδον αὐτὴν ἤδη τὴν ἐς
ἀκρόπολιν. That this is the meaning also
appears from another passage where he
alludes again to these Graces, and mentions
them as being πρὸ τῆς ἐς τὴν ἀκρόπολιν
ἐσόδου (ix. 35, 2) in front of the entrance
to the acropolis, that is, its eastern front.

[2] Cecropia, cap. 7.

[3] Ἑρμῆν, ὃν προπύλαιον ὀνομάζουσι, καὶ

Χάριτας Σωκράτην ποιῆσαι λέγουσιν.—loc.
cit.

[4] εἶναί τε αὐτοῦ καὶ τὰς ἐν ἀκροπόλει
Χάριτας ἔνιοι φασίν, ἐνδεδυμένας οὔσας.—
Vit. Socr. ii. 19.

[5] Nubes, 773.

[6] ὀπισὼ τῆς Ἀθηνᾶς γλυφεῖσαι ἐν τῷ
τοίχῳ.

The Athenians, as is well known, repented of their injustice to Socrates, and erected a small shrine to him in the street leading from the Peiraïc Gate to the Acropolis. It seems to have contained a pillar with a bust of the philosopher.[1] We need only further observe that the Graces were very commonly associated with some other divinity, as here with Hermes, and especially with Aphroditë; and not only the unclothed and more wanton Graces, for they are represented in the Homeric hymn to Aphroditë, and therefore before they had obtained that character, as accompanying the goddess of love.[2]

The next object to the Hermes Propylæus was a statue of a lioness (Paus. c. 23, 1).   It was said to have been erected by the Athenians in honour of a courtezan named Leæna, beloved by Aristogeiton, as we have before related, and that Hippias caused her to be put to death with tortures because she would not reveal the associates of that con- spirator.   By the side of the lioness was a statue of Aphroditë, dedicated by Callias, and said to be the work of Calamis.   Near the spot indicated by Pausanias has been found the base of a statue bearing the name of Callias.   The characters of the inscription belong to about the 85th Olympiad.[3]   Pliny attributes the statue to Amphicrates.[4] Plutarch says that Leæna was represented without a tongue, to denote her taciturnity;[5] whilst according to Polyænus, she had bitten it off.[6] He describes her statue as being *in* the Propylæum ($\dot{\epsilon}\nu \ \tau\tilde{\omega} \ \pi\rho o\pi\upsilon\lambda a\acute{\iota}\omega$), whilst Plutarch says that it was in *the gates* of the Acropolis ($\dot{\epsilon}\nu \ \pi\acute{\upsilon}\lambda a\iota\varsigma \ \tau\tilde{\eta}\varsigma \ \dot{a}\kappa\rho o\pi\acute{o}\lambda\epsilon\omega\varsigma$).   From these indications we may infer that it was on the eastern side of the wall, but under the portico, like Hermes and the Graces; which Pliny also describes as being *in* the Propylæum (in Propylæo Atheniensium).[7]   Demochares[8] mentioned a sanctuary ($\iota\epsilon\rho\grave{o}\nu$) of Leæna Aphroditë at Athens, and Leake[9] thinks that it is the same here mentioned by Pausanias.   But the Leæna mentioned in Athenæus was a concubine of Demetrius Poliorcetes; besides, the objects described

[1] Marin. Vit. Procl. c. 10.
[2] Hymn to Aphroditë.
[3] Rangabé, Ant. Hell. t. i. No. 59; Boulé, L'Acropole, t. i. p. 280.
[4] H. N. xxxiv. s. 72.
[5] De Garrul. t. viii. p. 13, Reiske.
[6] Stratag. viii. 45.
[7] Ibid. xxxvi. 32.
[8] Ap. Athen. vi. 62.
[9] vol. i. p. 145, note 2.

by Pausanias appear to have been only statues, without any sanctuary or temple; which, indeed, as standing under the porch, they could hardly have had.

Close to Leæna was a statue of Diitrephes, pierced with arrows. Pausanias here tells his story, which is also related by Thucydides.[1] Leake (vol. i. p. 145, note 4) has mentioned the discovery of the basis of this statue, bearing the inscription, in characters of the 5th century, B.C.

HERMOLYKOΣ
ΔΙΕΙΤΡΕΦΟΣ
ΑΓΑΡΧΕΝ

KREΣΙ ΛAΣ
ΕΓΟΕΣΕΝ

(i.e. Ἑρμόλυκος Διειτρέφους ἀπαρχήν—Κρησίλας ἐποίησεν);[2] showing that the statue of Diitrephes was dedicated by his son Hermolycus. Leake gives only the first three words; but the name of the artist was also inscribed in equally ancient characters. According to Rangabé,[3] the inscription belongs to the 92nd Olympiad; and the expedition of Diitrephes, in which he appears to have been killed, was in the third year of the preceding Olympiad (B.C. 414). The basis in question was discovered in a cistern before the west front of the Parthenon, which agrees with the progress of Pausanias.

Passing over some statues of persons of small note, Pausanias next mentions one of Hygieia, said to be the daughter of Asclepius, and another of Athena Hygieia. Of the latter goddess there had only been an altar here before the time of Pericles, who set up a bronze image of her, because, it is said, she had instructed him in a dream how to cure a workman who had fallen from the roof of the Propylæa when that edifice was building. The remedy is said to have been an herb which grew upon the Acropolis, and which from that circumstance obtained the name of Parthenion. During the siege by Sulla, the garrison lived upon it, as we have already remarked (above, p. 164).[4] Athena was also

---

[1] vii. 29.

[2] Ross, Arch. Aufs. i. 168.

[3] Ant. Hell. t. i. No. 42.

[4] Plut. Pericl. 13; Sull. 13; Plin. N. H. xxii. 17, 44.

found united with Hygieia in the deme of Acharnae, and at Oropus.[1] We have already seen her as Παιωνία, in the street leading from the Peiraïc Gate to the Cerameicus.[2]

According to Plutarch, this statue was the work of Pheidias, and of gold ; but it was more likely gilded, for just before, as we have seen, he says it was of bronze. Unless, indeed, as is more probable, he be speaking of two different statues ; one of bronze at the Propylæa, and another of gold, or gilt, in another part of the Acropolis, and perhaps in one of the temples. Of the latter statue—if it was a separate one—Plutarch uses the word ἕδος,[3] which some critics have interpreted to mean the throne, or seat, on which the statue was seated.[4] But the absurdity is glaring of a golden pedestal for a bronze statue, and that too made by Pheidias for the statue of an inferior artist. Wherefore we think there can be little doubt that he is alluding to two different statues. The term ἕδος seems originally to have signified a seated statue. Many of the more ancient statues of Athena were in that posture. Thus Strabo says that the statue of that goddess described by Homer as seated, had in his time been exchanged for one standing upright ; and he goes on to enumerate many seated ones of ancient workmanship (ξόανα) in Phocæa, Massilia, Rome, Chios, and other places.[5] Such statues frequently carried something in their laps, and it was a convenient posture for receiving the supplications of worshippers. Hence probably the term γουνάζεσθαι, ‘ to clasp the knees,’ to denote the act of supplication ; transferred also to abject entreaties of mortals. The waxen tablets of the Romans were placed upon the knees of the gods, thus indicating that they were seated.[6] But ἕδος came at last to denote any statue of a god, and to be used as equivalent to ἄγαλμα.[7]

---

[1] Pausan. i. 31, 3 ; 34, 2.

[2] i. 2, 4. Above, p. 198.

[3] ὁ δὲ Φειδίας εἰργάζετο μὲν τῆς θεοῦ τὸ χρυσοῦν ἕδος, καὶ τούτου δημιουργὸς ἐν τῇ στήλῃ εἶναι γέγραπται.—Per. 13.

[4] Thus Sillig in his Catalogus Artificum, voc. Pheidias : “ Pericles aëneum Minervæ Hygiæ signum, et aureum ejus solium, hoc quidem a Pheidia faciendum curavit.”—

See Ross, Arch. Aufs. i. 187.

[5] lib. xiii. p. 601.

[6] Propter quæ fas est genua incerare deorum.—Juv. x. 55.

[7] Ἕδος · αὐτὸ τὸ ἄγαλμα.—Bekk. Anecd. Gr. 246, 3. Thus Isocrates : τὰ τῶν θεῶν ἕδη καὶ τοὺς νεὼς συλᾶν καὶ κατακαίειν.—Paneg. 74 b. Where ἕδη evidently means *statues.* Most probably also in the

Is it not possible that by χρυσοῦν ἕδος Plutarch meant the gold and ivory statue of Athena in the Parthenon? Though that statue was an erect one, the application of the word ἕδος to it would not, as we have seen, be incorrect; and, indeed, if we are right, Isocrates employs it of this very statue.[1] Plutarch says further on, that he has mentioned this statue;[2] but he has not done so, unless he means that to which he has alluded in conjunction with Athena Hygieia. In that case he has expressed himself very obscurely; for the words τῆς θεοῦ would naturally relate to some statue of Athena Hygieia, which that in the Parthenon was not. But to return to the statue mentioned by Pausanias.

Its base was discovered in excavating the Acropolis some thirty or forty years ago. It was of white marble,[3] rather more than semi-circular, and adjoined the last column, to the south, of the eastern portico of the Propylæa; the exact place where, following the footsteps of Pausanias, we should expect to find it. The feet of the statue might be traced on the top of the base, and from the marks it appeared that the right foot was advanced. It was about 13 inches in length, from which it may be inferred that the statue rather exceeded the size of life. The inscription on the base recorded that it had been erected by the Athenians to Athena Hygieia, and that it was the work of Pyrrhus, the Athenian. This is at variance with the tale of Plutarch, that it was dedicated by Pericles. Pliny seems to have heard the same story; but Pausanias says nothing about it, and most probably it was an idle fiction. Professor Ross[4] would conciliate matters by supposing that Pericles may have vowed it, but died before completing it; and that it was

---

Antidosis: Φειδίαν τὸν τὸ τῆς Ἀθηνᾶς ἕδος ἐργασάμενον (310 b); for though Pheidias may have *designed* the Parthenon, he can hardly be said to have *made* it, as he did the statue. Dionysius of Halicarnassus, of Æneas carrying off his household gods: παραλαβὼν καὶ τὸν πατέρα καὶ τὰ ἕδη τῶν θεῶν.—Ant. Rom. i. 47 fin. And Appian: τὸ τῆς Ἀθηνᾶς ἕδος ὃ Παλλάδιον καλοῦσι.—Mithr. p. 346, Toll. Cf. also Plut. Arist. 20. It also meant the place in which the

image was erected: Ἕδος · τὸ ἄγαλμα · καὶ ὁ τόπος ἐν ᾧ ἵδρυται.—Tim. Lex. Plat. Answering in this sense to the Latin word *sedes*.

[1] See preceding note.

[2] Φειδίας ὁ πλάστης ἐργολάβος μὲν ἦν τοῦ ἀγάλματος, ὥσπερ εἴρηται.—Pericl. c. 31.

[3] Another proof that it could not have been the second statue alluded to by Plutarch.

[4] Arch. Aufs. i. 191.

finally dedicated by the Athenians. But if they thought it necessary to perform his vow, surely they would have recorded his name. There can be little doubt that Pliny alludes to the same statue, when he says, " Pyrrus Hygiam et Minervam (fecit)." [1] The characters of the inscription belong to the transition period of the Greek Alphabet, between Olympiad 86–94, and therefore to the age of Pericles. [2] From the situation of the pedestal, it must have been erected after the finishing of the Propylæa in B.C. 431.

We have dwelt perhaps longer on this statue than its importance may seem to demand, because together with others which Pausanias mentions on the Acropolis, it not only confirms his general accuracy, but also more particularly, because from its well ascertained situation, it shows that he described what he saw in a regular and orderly manner, and thus confirms the confidence we feel in the rule which we have adopted, of taking the order of his narration as our guide for placing the objects which he mentions.

Close to this pedestal are traces of two others. The author of the ' Lives of the Ten Orators ' says at the end of that of Isocrates, [3] that a statue of the mother of that orator stood near the statue of Hygieia in the Acropolis, but that the inscription, according to a practice we have before adverted to, had been altered. This may probably be one of those which Pausanias passed over, and may have stood on one of the bases alluded to. A square marble pedestal was also found near this eastern portico of the Propylæa inscribed ΣΕΒΑΣΤΗΥΓΕΙΑ, " the august Hygeia ;" which may have been that other Hygieia mentioned by Pausanias, the daughter of Asclepius ; [4] though the epithet σεβαστὴ seems rather to refer to the imperial times.

[1] N. H. xxxiv. 80. Where Ross rightly proposes to omit the copula.

[2] The inscription will be found in Rangabé, t. i. No. 43 ; Ross, Arch. Aufs. i. 189 ; Beulé, L'Acropole, i. 284 ; and in Le Bas, Voyage Arch. i. 8, 4. But it is given differently in these authorities ; Rangabé, for instance, having the aspirate H before 'Υγιεία, which is not found in Ross. The latter also writes the θ and o in small characters, and observes that this fashion afterwards went out, but was revived in the Macedonian times (p. 191, note). See above, p. 311.

[3] t. ix. p. 339, Reiske's Plutarch. See above, p. 362 sq.

[4] Rangabé, Ant. Hell. i. No. 45 ; Ross, Aufs. i. 190.

The next object Pausanias mentions (c. 23, 6), is a stone of no great size, such as a small man might sit on, to which was attached a legend that Silenus reposed on it when Dionysus first came into Attica. He then gives an account of the Satyrs and Sileni, which we pass over. We may observe that Pausanias is now on his route from the Propylæa to the Parthenon. The path is not straight, but immediately makes a very decided curve to the right, along the different enclosures which occupied the south-west part of the Acropolis. He now meets on his right the statue of a brazen boy, holding a vessel of lustral water (περιρραντήριον), the work of Lycius, son of Myron; and close by Perseus slaying Medusa, executed by Myron himself.[1] The lustral water, as M. Beulé observes, clearly indicates the entrance to some temple, or sacred precinct, which could have been no other than that of ARTEMIS BRAURONIA, which Pausanias proceeds to describe. The goddess derived this name from Brauron, a port on the eastern coast of Attica, where Iphigeneia was said to have landed when flying from the Tauric Chersonese on her way to Athens and Argos,[2] and where she left the image of Artemis which she had brought with her. The shrine of Artemis at Brauron was visited in very ancient times by the Athenians. The Pelasgi, after they had been driven from Attica, and had occupied Lemnos, knowing that the Athenian women frequented Brauron on the festival of the goddess, sailed thither, and carried off many of them to be their concubines.[3] It may be remarked that the sanctuaries on the coast were more ancient than the inland ones. Such were that of Aphroditë at Cape Colias, of Poseidon at Sunium and Eleusis, and those of Artemis at Brauron and Munychia; which may probably be referred to a period before the migrations of the 12th and 11th centuries B.C.[4] A statue of Athena is indicated in the Iliad (vi. 273). The image of the Tauric Artemis still existed at Brauron in the time of Pausanias; but the statue of the deity in the temple on the Acropolis, was the work of Praxiteles. In this precinct, many small statues of

---

[1] This statue is mentioned by Pliny, H. N. xxxiv. 57.

[2] Paus. i. 33, 1 (supra, p. 17).

[3] Herod. vi. 138; cf. iv. 145.

[4] See Mommsen, Heortol. p. 19, note.

animals were discovered. M. Beulé observes [1] that this temple is a proof that provincial deities were admitted into the Acropolis. We have already observed that their priests were honoured with a throne in the theatre.

Near this temple stood the bronze horse called Doureios (δούρειος), an imitation of the Trojan horse made by Epeus. Menesthens and Teucer were represented looking out from it, and also the sons of Theseus: the Athenians, of course, wishing to see their own heroes in the foremost place, though without any warrant from Homer. While the Athenians were supposed to be forging Homer, in order to gratify their national vanity, might they not as well have put this incident into his text? The very subordinate part which they play in the Iliad, shows that they were at least very modest forgers. From the following line of Aristophanes:

ἵππων ὑπόντων μέγεθος ὅσον ὁ δούριος,[2]

we may infer that the horse was colossal. According to the scholiast on this passage, there was an inscription on the pedestal, stating that it was the anathema of Chæredemus of Cœlë, son of Euangelos. Early in 1841, two large slabs of white marble were found to the right of the path leading from the Propylæa to the Parthenon—and therefore about the spot indicated by Pausanias—having upon them *verbatim* the inscription given by the scholiast, with the addition of the name of the artist, ' Strongulion made it ; ' thus clearly showing that they formed part of

ΧΑΙΡΕΔΕΜΟΣΕΥΑΛΛΕΝΟΙ _ΚΚΟΙ ΛΕΣΑΝΕΘΕΚΕΝ
ΣΤΡΟΛΛΥΜΟΝΕΓΟΙΕΣΕΝ [3]

the base of the Trojan horse. Ross is of opinion that the characters show the inscription to have been later than the 86th Olympiad; the sigma having the form $\leq$ instead of $\nmid$; yet at the same time some

---

[1] L'Acropole, i. 298. On the custom of using lustral water when entering a temple see Athen. ix. 76 ; Eurip. Herc. Fur. v. 928 sq. ; Lysias, c. Andoc. p. 255, Reiske.

[2] " Drawn by horses as big as the Dou-

rian."—Aves, 1128. The penult is here short ; but long in Eurip. Troad. 13 :
δούρειος ἵππος, κρυπτὸν ἀμπίσχων δόρυ.

[3] i.e. Χαιρέδημος Εὐαγγέλου ἐκ Κοίλης ἀνέθηκεν · Στρογγυλίων ἐποίησεν.

Olympiads before the archonship of Eucleides, since it still retains the E for H, the Λ for Γ, and Ϡ for Λ.[1] As it is of the nature of comic poetry to allude to the freshest novelties, the line quoted from the 'Birds' of Aristophanes doubtless alludes to this horse, then recently erected; or a little before Olympiad 91.2 = B.C. 414, when that play was brought out (Clinton under the date). And this epoch agrees with the palæography of the inscription.

We know from another passage in Pausanias, that Strongylion was famed for making oxen and horses.[2] Professor Ross thinks that, as Pausanias uses the word μηχάνημα (c. 23, 10), the horse in question must have been an imitation of the original rude wooden machine. But μηχάνημα there applies only to the Trojan horse; and Strongylion in his bronze one was not obliged to follow the original model, which indeed existed only in imagination. And when Pausanias goes on to say that the bronze horse was made in the same manner (καὶ δὴ τοῦ χαλκοῦ τὸ σχῆμά ἐστι κατὰ ταὐτά), σχῆμα there refers to the words that immediately precede; viz. that the leaders of the Greeks were in its belly (λέγεται δὲ ἔς τε ἐκεῖνον τὸν ἵππον, ὡς τῶν Ἑλλήνων ἔνδον ἔχοι τοὺς ἀρίστους); and he means that the bronze horse was made in the same fashion, *in that respect.* For Strongylion would hardly have disfigured the Acropolis with so clumsy an animal as the wooden horse must have been, or have lost such a capital opportunity to display his art conspicuously.

We will only further observe, that in these days, when it is so much the fashion to depreciate the accuracy of the ancient writers, it is gratifying to find so striking and ocular a proof of the correctness of Aristophanes, of his scholiast, and of Pausanias.

Next to the horse was a statue of Epicharinus practising running in armour, the work of Critias. The common text has ἐπὶ Χαρίνου (though some MSS. have Ἐπιχαρῖνον), and was thought to mean in the archonship of Charinus, B.C. 308. This senseless reading was discarded by Meursius, who adopted that of Ἐπιχάρμου, found in one or two MSS.[3]

[1] There is a fac-simile of the inscription in Rangabé, Ant. Hell. t. i. No. 41; cf. Ross, Arch. Aufs. i. 194 sqq.   [2] ix. 30, 1.   [3] Cecropia, c. 11.

The basis of this statue also has been found in excavating the Acropolis, and what is legible of the name in the first line as deciphered by M. Pittakis, is the letters Eπι αριvo, which most probably mean 'Επιχαρῖνος. The rest of this line is too obliterated to be restored with confidence; but the second line is tolerably perfect and from it Ross corrects the text of Pausanias by reading Κρίτιος for Κριτίας, and adds that Nesiotes assisted him.[1] The name of Nesiotes is found, in another instance, in conjunction with that of Critias; and as Pausanias does not mention him either when speaking of this statue, or of those of Harmodius and Aristogeiton (i. 8, 5), which were also their joint production, it is probable, as Ross suggests (p. 165), that Critias was really the artist, and Nesiotes merely the caster or founder of the statues. This view will not be invalidated because Lucian couples their names together as the makers of statues of Harmodius and Aristogeiton :[2] as we see that they were so coupled in the inscriptions. A graver objection is, that the statues of the tyrannicides appear to have been erected in the year B.C. 478 ; and we can hardly place the anathema of Epicharinus on the Acropolis at a much earlier date than B.C. 436, when the Parthenon was finished and the Propylæa begun. This would make their joint labours extend over a period of more than forty years, which is barely within the limits of probability.

The next statue mentioned by Pausanias is interesting, from its being of some historical importance. It was that of Oinobios, who procured the decree for the return of Thucydides from exile. According to Pausanias, the great historian[3] was treacherously slain after he had

---

[1] ΚΡΙΤΙΟϟΚΑΙΝΈϟΙΟΤΕϟΕΓΟ . . . . ΑΤΕϟ. See Ross, Aufs. i. 164 ; Rangabé, A. H. t. i. No. 25. But Pliny also must be corrected, who wrote Critias before Pausanias. (H. N. xxxiv. 49 and 85). Vid. Sillig, ad loc. The characters are later than the 75th Olympiad. See two other inscriptions with their joint names.—ibid. Nos. 23, 24. In the first the name of Nesiotes is found alone ; which makes against the view of Ross, that he was merely a founder:

if the same Nesiotes is meant, for the characters seem older. See Beulé, L'Acropole, t. i. p. 285.

[2] ἐν οἷς καὶ τὰ Κριτίου τοῦ Νησιώτου πλάσματα ἕστηκεν, οἱ τυραννόκτονοι.— Philops. c. 18. Where no doubt we should read καὶ Νησιώτου for τοῦ ; though some have taken Νησιώτης to be the common noun, *islander*.

[3] ὡς κατῄει. The Attic writers use the word, 'to go *down*,' of going to Athens,

returned, and, as we have before mentioned, there was a monument to him before the Gate Melitides. It is hardly necessary to observe that this account of the death of Thucydides varies from that of other authorities.

Pausanias merely gives a few passing words to the statues of Hermolycus, the pancratiast, and Phormio, son of Asopichus, as they had been described by others. This Hermolycus is of course a very different person from the Hermolycus son of Dicitrephes before-mentioned; and it is not improbable that he may have been the pancratiast mentioned by Herodotus,[1] an Athenian, and son of Euythymus, who distinguished himself at the battle of Mycalë. Of Phormio, son of Asopichus,[2] Pausanias relates that being in debt, and having been chosen ναύαρχος, or admiral, he refused to serve, alleging, that in his situation, he should not have the spirit to command his men. Whereupon the Athenians discharged his debts.

Pausanias next mentions (c. 24, 1) a statue of Athena striking the Silenus, Marsyas, for picking up the pipes which she had thrown away. Further on was Theseus contending with the Minotaur. Then Phrixus, son of Athamas, sacrificing the ram which had carried him to Cholcis; Pausanias knew not exactly to what god, but thought it might be to him, whom the Orchomenians called Laphystius.[3] Having cut out the

---

when in general to approach a capital is expressed by going *up*. But especially is it used, as here, of the return of exiles. This remark may be deemed superfluous; but want of attention to this point has misled Leake, who, translating κάθοδος by *departure*, instead of *return*, draws from it a wrong historical inference. Thus he represents Philochorus (ap. Dionys. Hal. in Deinarch. c. 3) as interpreting the portent of a star seen from the sanctuary of Polias as portending "a departure of exiles (φυγάδων κάθοδον) not in consequence of any revolution, but from political considerations (οὐκ ἐκ μεταβολῆς πραγμά-των, ἀλλ᾽ ἐν τῇ καθεστώσῃ πολιτείᾳ). In

fact, soon after the restoration of liberty to Athens by Demetrius Poliorcetes, many citizens expatriated themselves in consequence of the part which they had previously taken."—vol. i. p. 579, note 3. Where "from political considerations" is another mistranslation for "under the existing government, or state of things."

[1] ix. 105.

[2] Thucydides and the scholiast on the 'Pax' of Aristophanes, v. 347, call him son of *Asopius*, Thucyd. i. 64; cf. Diod. Sic. xxxvii. 47. The name *Asopichus* occurs in Pindar, Ol. xiv. 25.

[3] See Paus. ix. 34, 4; cf. Müller, Orchomenos, s. vii. p. 156 sqq.

thighs, according to the Greek custom, he was seeing them burn. The story of Athamas and Phrixus is connected with the temple of Zeus Laphystius.

Other statues followed, and among them one of Heracles, strangling the serpents; of Athena issuing from the head of Zeus; also a bull, an anathema of the Areopagitic Council; but the occasion of it was a matter of conjecture. "I have already observed," says Pausanias, "that the Athenians have more zeal for religion than any other people. They were the first who gave Athena the name of Ἐργάνη ('operosa,' 'the worker') and who represented Hermes without limbs."

The surname ἐργάνη has a more special reference to the female arts of spinning and weaving, and such ἔργα Ἀθηναίης are frequently alluded to by Homer. Thus she spreads, in the chamber of Zeus, the peplus which she had made with her own hand, and she had also worked the robe of Hera.[1] She excelled in such works as much as Aphroditë did in beauty.[2] The Phaidryntæ at Pisa sacrificed to her before cleansing the statue of Zeus[3] as the presiding deity of the fine arts. And not only these, but the useful ones also, being the inventress of the plough, the chariot, the cultivation of the olive, &c. "Mille dea est operum," says Ovid;[4] and as the Athenian Acropolis was dedicated to her, it was natural that she should there be commemorated under her principal characteristics. We have already seen her as Victory and Health; we now behold her as the patroness of all the arts, and shall presently see her as the tutelary goddess of the city. As Erganë, the cock was sacred to her.[5]

That there was a temple to her here, between the Propylæa and the Parthenon, is not expressly stated by Pausanias, but it may be certainly inferred from his words,[6] as he goes on to say that there was *in the temple* an image of the dæmon Spoudaion, or, as we may say, the

[1] Il. v. 735; xiv. 178.

[2] Ib. ix. 390.

[3] Paus. v. 14, 5. See above, p. 327.

[4] Fast. iii. 833, where see her functions described.

[5] Pausan. vi. 26, 2.

[6] ὁμοῦ δέ σφισιν ἐν τῷ ναῷ.—i. 24, 3. Some critics have taken Σπουδαίων to be a common noun, and have translated, 'the dæmon of industrious men;' but it is better, we think, to take it as a proper name. See the note of Siebelis.

dæmon Stronuus. We sometimes find Erganë herself called *dæmon*, as by Ælian.[1] The existence of a temple at this spot may also be inferred from various objects found in the course of the excavations. Thus, under the south-west angle of the Parthenon was discovered a fragment of a marble statue of Athena, consisting of the breast with the Gorgoneium; also four dedicatory inscriptions to Athena Erganë, the letters of one of which belonged to the fourth century[2] B.C. And at about twenty-five paces from the south-west angle of the Parthenon, and a good deal deeper than that building, are the remains of an ancient pavement of white marble.

The objects preserved in the temple of Athena Erganë seem to have been remarkable rather for their antiquity than their beauty; and therefore Pausanias recommends to those who preferred the latter quality, the following objects: a man with a helmet, and finger-nails of silver, the work of Cleoitas, and an image of Gæa, imploring rain from Zeus. Then statues of Cimon and his son Timotheus; Procnë and Itys, dedicated by Alcamenes; Athena producing the olive, and Poseidon showing the sea; a statue of Zeus, by Leochares, and another of Zeus Polieus.

The collocation of the group of statues mentioned at this spot, showing Athena and Poseidon in the very act of contention, and Zeus standing by, could not have been without its significance. According to one version of the legend, the contending deities chose Zeus for their umpire,[3] and the votes of the Athenians being equal, Athena promised that if he would give her the casting vote, she would make to him the first sacrifice on his altar, as Polieus.[4] The spot at which the

[1] Ἐργάνης δαίμονος.—V. H. i. 2.

[2] Rangabé, Ant. Hell. t. ii. Nos. 1028, 1030; Ross, Aufs. i. 83; Beulé, i. 315. Probably the oldest inscription to Athena on the Acropolis is one of which only a word or two (σ Ἀθηναίᾳ μ' ἀνέθ[ηκεν) remain, written from right to left. It is in white marble, and the incised letters had been painted red.—See a facsimile in Rangabé, t. i. p. 17; and cf. Beulé, t. i. p. 333.

[3] "Jovem judicem sumpserunt." — Hygin. fab. 164.

[4] Διὸς θᾶκοι καὶ πεσσοί · τινὲς γράφουσι ψῆφοι. φασὶ δὲ ἐν τῇ τῶν Ἀθηναίων διαψηφίσει, ὅτε ἠμφισβήτει Ἀθηνᾶ καὶ Ποσειδῶν, τὴν Ἀθηνᾶν Διὸς δεηθῆναι ὑπὲρ αὐτῆς τὴν ψῆφον ἐνεγκεῖν καὶ ὑποσχέσθαι ἀντὶ τούτου τοῦ Πολιέως ἱερεῖον πρῶτον θύεσθαι ἐπὶ βωμοῦ.—Hesych. Another version says that Zeus left the decision to the family of

judgment was pronounced was called Διὸς ψῆφος;[1] and it can hardly be
doubted that it was here. Bergk has indeed arbitrarily transferred it to
the Pnyx Hill;[2] in which view he has been followed by Curtius, because
it favours his notion about the Pnyx; although he allows that there
is no authority for it.[3] We, however, who have no pet theories
to support, prefer the spot for which there is some authority; and
entirely agree with Otto Jahn, that the myth of Athena and Poseidon
is inseparably connected with the Acropolis.[4] And from the legend, as
given by Hesychius, we perceive the reason why Zeus Polieus, or, what
is the same, Zeus Hypatos, had an altar before the Erechtheium, as we
shall see further on; namely, on account of the promised sacrifice, and
as a pledge and symbol that both deities, Zeus Polieus and Athena
Polias, were guardians of the city. An Athenian coin figured by
Stuart, at the head of ch. ii. vol. ii., has been supposed to represent the
group in question. A fragment in the British Museum, of the stem of
an olive tree between two feet (Elgin Marbles, ii. pp. 27 and 31), has
by some been thought to belong to the group mentioned by Pausanias.
It could hardly have belonged to the *eastern* pediment of the Parthenon,
as Mr. Cockerell thought; but, as we shall see presently, it probably
formed part of the western pediment. Sir H. Ellis asserted that the
marble of the fragment was not Pentelic; but Michaelis recently affirms
that it is. (In N. Mem. dell' Inst. 1865, p. 16, note.)

I will describe, continues Pausanias, the accustomed sacrifice to
Zeus Polieus, but cannot tell the cause of it. Barley, mixed with wheat,
is put upon his altar, and left unguarded. The ox prepared for
sacrifice approaches the altar and eats. Then the priest called bouphonos (βούφονος) throws his hatchet that way, and runs off, for so it
is ordained; and the assistants, as if they knew not the man who did it,

---

Cecrops; in which the females predomi-
nated, and thus Athena carried the day.—
Schol. ad Aristid. t. iii. p. 60, Dind.

[1] ὁ γὰρ τύπος ἐν ᾧ ἐκρίθησαν, Διὸς ψῆφος
καλεῖται.—Suid. in Διὸς ψῆφος.

[2] Philologus, v. p. 579.

[3] "Ohne weitere Begründung, aber, wie

ich glaube, mit vollem Recht."—Att.
Studien, i. 45.

[4] "In ogni caso il mito di Minerva e di
Nettuno parmi che sia dal principio e
necessariamente congiunto coll' acropoli."
—N. Mem. dell' Instituto, 1865, p. 14,
note 3.

subject the hatchet to a trial, which is acquitted.[1] There was an
ancient law forbidding the labour ox to be slain.[2] The sacrifice in
question was said to have been instituted in the reign of Erechtheus,
and an imitation of it was repeated yearly at the Diipolia, called also
Bouphonia (above, p. 26).

The priest called here bouphonos was no doubt the same as the
priest of Zeus Policus, who, as we have seen, had a seat in the theatre.
He was of the race of Buzyges, who, as the founder of agriculture, and
consequently of civilization, was regarded at Athens as the guardian
and promoter of humanity, and his curse (ἡ βουζύγιος ἀρά) was supposed to rest on the violators of it; on those who refused to others the
use of fire or water; or to put wanderers in the right way, or to assist
in burying a neglected corpse; in short, on those who did not to others
as they would be done by.[3]

Pausanias seems to have passed over a temple or shrine of Zeus and
Athena, in their character of saviours (Ζεὺς σωτὴρ καὶ Ἀθηνᾶ σώτειρα)
which, there is reason to think, stood near the western front of the
Parthenon. It is alluded to by Lycurgus in his speech against
Leocrates.[4] Some are of opinion that Lycurgus may be alluding to a
temple of those deities at Peiræeus.[5] But we have seen that the priest
of such a temple had a throne in the theatre; and though the priests of
provincial sanctuaries were admitted to that honour, yet their locality
was recorded in the inscriptions on their seats; and as there is no such
record in that on the throne in question, we may safely conclude that
there must have been a shrine of Zeus and Athena, the saviours,
at Athens, and therefore, in all probability, the one alluded to by
Lycurgus. There is also reason to think that Plutus may have had an

[1] ἀφείθη κριθείς. See ch. xxviii. s. 11,
where he adverts to this sacrifice again.
But .Elian, on the contrary, says that it
was condemned.—V. H. viii. 3.

[2] Petit, Legg. Att. lib. v. tit. ii. 5; cf.
Plat. De Legg. p. 782 c (iii. ii. p. 471,
Bekk.); Varr. R. R. xi. 5, 4.

[3] Schol. Soph. Ant. 255; Clem. Alex.

Str. ii. p. 181; Æl. V. H. v. 14, &c. See
O. Jahn, in N. Mem. dell' Instituto, 1865,
p. 6.

[4] οὔτε τὴν ἀκρόπολιν καὶ τὸ ἱερὸν τοῦ
Διὸς τοῦ σωτῆρος καὶ τῆς Ἀθηνᾶς τῆς σωτεί-
ρας ἀφορῶν καὶ προδιδοὺς ἐφοβήθη.—p. 148,
Reiske.

[5] Vischer, in Neues Schweit. Mus. 1863.

image near this spot. Aristophanes, in the play of that name, intro-
duces the priest of Zeus Soter complaining that since Plutus had recovered his sight, and all had grown rich, sacrifices were no longer made
at the altar of his divinity, and that consequently he was dying of
hunger. Whereupon Chremylus comforts him, by promising that
Plutus should be re-established where he had stood before, always
guarding the opisthodomus of Athena.[1] Meursius[2] places here a statue
of Plutus by induction from these lines; but the allusion in the
' Icones ' of Philostratus, which he also quotes, seems to be rather to
the Acropolis of the Rhodians.

Pausanias now proceeds to the Parthenon (c. 24, 5); but according
to his usual custom, he says little or nothing about the building itself,
and confines his scanty notice almost entirely to the objects which it
contained. His route hitherto has been to the west front; but he
evidently enters the temple at the east front, which was the principal,
or rather, perhaps, only entrance.[3]

The σηκός, or cella, confining that name to the compartment in which
was the statue of the goddess, and which, as we have before observed,
was more specially called the Parthenon, was 98 ft. 7 in. long. The
back or western division was 43 ft. 10 in. long, and the breadth of both
chambers was the same, or 62 ft. 6 in. The back compartment was
called the opisthodomus; literally the back house or room, and was
used as the public treasury. The temple was of the Doric order, and
technically an octastylos peripteros; that is, it was surrounded on all
sides by a portico, which at the fronts had eight columns. The side
columns were seventeen in number, counting the corner ones of the
fronts twice; thus making in the whole forty-six columns. The
diameter of them was 6 ft. 2 in. at the base, and their height was 34 ft.
The walls of the building were prolonged at each end, between 17 ft.
and 18 ft., thus forming two prothyra, or vestibules, having before them

---

[1] Plat. v. 1173 sqq.

[2] Cecropia, cap. 27; cf. Philostr. lib. ii.
c. 27, p. 853.

[3] The following description of the temple
is taken from Stuart, Leake, and others.
The architectural reader will find a more
elaborate one in the recent work of Adolph
Michaelis (Leipsic).

six columns of 5 ft. 6 in. in diameter. There was the same distance between these columns as between the front columns of the portico. But the arrangement of the building will be best understood by a reference to its plan in the plan of the Acropolis (p. 367).

Outside and along the top of the wall of the building, that is, of the cella, opisthodomus, and two vestibules, and consequently under the outer portico, ran a frieze 3 ft. 4 in. in height, on which were sculptured figures in bas-relief representing the Panathenaïc procession. We shall not enter into any detailed description of this admirable work.

VIEW OF THE PARTHENON—WEST FRONT.

The variety and spirit of the figures, both horses and men, the grace of the females, the majesty of the gods represented in it, are well known to the public from the originals and casts preserved in the British Museum, and from the engravings in Stuart's and other works. We shall therefore content ourselves with indicating the general arrangement of the frieze. The march of the procession was directed towards the eastern, or principal, front of the temple. In the middle of this side of the frieze were seated twelve deities; not the Dii Consentes, for seven of them are male and five female. In the state of dilapi-

dation in which they are, it is difficult to identify them; but we may
pretty confidently assume that Zeus, Hera, Demeter, Dionysus, Poseidon, and Asclepius, were among them; while Ares may be recognized
by the fragments of a spear, and Hermes by the petasus which he bore.
These gods were divided by five intervening figures in a standing
posture, into two groups of six; one group looking towards the south,
the other to the north. The intervening figures, which occupied the
centre of the frieze, represented the priestess of the temple, taking
from two Errephoroi the objects which they had brought from the
temple of Aphroditë in the Gardens; and next to the priestess a male
figure, apparently the archon basileus, received the peplus from a boy.
On each side of the gods stood six magistrates and two or three others
somewhat separated from them; and then appeared the heads of the
procession, opened on both sides by females bearing different objects.
On turning the corner of the south-eastern angle appeared the oxen
led to sacrifice, followed by females and then by citizens on foot. Next
came quadrigæ and then horsemen in various costumes, who filled up the
remainder of this southern side. The procession on the north side was
also opened by victims, followed by men bearing offerings of bread,
wine, &c., and by four flute-players, leading apparently a chorus. The
remainder of this side, as on the south, was occupied by a procession
of quadrigæ and horsemen. The western frieze consisted principally of
youths preparing to mount their horses and join the train proceeding
along the north side, and consequently the figures faced the north.

The distance from the side walls of the building to the columns of
the outer peristyle, without including their diameter, was 9 ft. Round
the outside of the peristyle ran also a frieze, consisting of the triglyphs
characteristic of the Doric order, and the metopæ [1] between them,
on which were sculptured figures in high relief. Each front of the
peristyle had fourteen metopæ, each side thirty-two; making ninety-
two in all. In Carrey's time, those on the south side were the most
perfect; having been spared apparently by the Christian iconoclasts,

---

[1] ὀπή was a hole in the frieze to admit   with the triglyphs. The metopæ were the
the ends of the beams, which were adorned   square spaces between the triglyphs.

because they were less exposed to view than those on the other sides. Twenty-three out of the thirty-two metopæ on this side appear from the drawings of Carrey to have represented combats with centaurs. Fifteen of these have been destroyed by the explosion which shattered the centre of the temple after Carrey's visit; the remainder, with the exception of the last one on the west, have been carried off; fifteen to London and one to Paris. From Carrey's drawings, who paid more attention to this side than to the others, it appears that nine of its metopes were devoted to miscellaneous subjects of Attic mythology.

On the north side of the temple, twelve metopes only remain out of the thirty-two, and of these two are totally obliterated. Female figures often occurred upon them; whence it might be concluded that the war with the Amazons formed on this side a sort of pendant to the combats with the centaurs on the other. From drawings, however, discovered by M. Bröndsted in the National Library at Paris, it would appear that nine metopes on this side also represented centaurs, thus forming the same number of exceptions to the general subject as were found on the other side.[1] On this side also the last metope on the west is in good preservation and beautifully executed.

The fourteen metopes of the west front are still in place, but several of them are quite obliterated. The rest, so far as can be made out, seem to represent combats between horsemen and foot. The actions here represented were probably historical, being as it were on the profane side of the building, or that devoted to secular uses. The metopes, on the east front, on the contrary, are heroic and mythological, and seem to have related principally to the deeds of Athena herself. A description of them would be too long for our limits, and we may refer the general reader to the works of Stuart (vol. ii.), of Leake (vol. i. App. xvi.), and to the account of the Elgin Marbles in the Library of Entertaining Knowledge.

Under each metope in this eastern front, as will be seen in the view of it given by Stuart, are holes in the architrave, which were evidently made for pegs or fastenings on which shields might be hung; for the

[1] Bröndsted, Voyages et Recherches dans la Grèce, ii. 273.

marble which surrounds them has circular patches of a lighter hue than
the reddish tint which time has spread over the rest of the building:
thus showing that shields there suspended had screened the surface
they covered from the effects of sun and weather. From the contour
of these marks it may be inferred that the breadth of the shields must
have been about equal to that of the triglyphs. There are traces of
the same decoration having been applied to the other front and to the
sides of the temple. The shields or some of them were probably of gold
or gilt; for of such material were those suspended by the Athenians,
after the battle of Marathon, at the temple of Delphi, and by the
Ætolians, at the same sanctuary, after repulsing the Gauls.[1] But a
more direct proof is the anecdote already mentioned (p. 155), that
Lachares, when he fled from Athens, carried off the golden shields from
the Acropolis. The names of the persons who dedicated the shields
appear to have been inscribed beneath them.[2] Some, however, were
probably of less costly materials; since, in a fragment of Euripides
preserved in Stobæus,[3] the warrior expresses a wish to grow old in
peace, having crowned his grey hairs with a chaplet and hung up a
Thracian target at the peristyle of Athena's temple:

Θρηικίαν πέλταν πρὸς 'Αθανᾶς
περικίοσιν ἀγκρεμάσας θαλάμοις ·

where, as Dr. Wordsworth observes, the poet must be alluding to the
Parthenon, the eastern front of which would be visible from the stage
of the theatre, and probably suggested the allusion. These shields
must have had a striking effect from their contrast with the brilliant
colours of the painted architrave. Under the triglyphs on the south
side of the temple are also marks of bronze nails, probably for festoons
on festival days.

The crowning glory of the Parthenon must have been the sculptures of its pediments. These have now almost entirely disappeared;
and the only means we have of forming an idea of their grouping and
execution is afforded by some rather rude drawings made by the French-

[1] Pausan. x. 19, 3.　　　[2] See Dr. Wordsworth's ' Attica and Athens,' p. 98.
[3] ii. p. 403, Gaisford.

man Carrey, before mentioned, in 1674, and a description of them a little afterwards by the travellers Wheler and Spon. The groups of the western pediment were then tolerably perfect, and remained so till they were almost utterly destroyed a few years afterwards in a clumsy attempt of the Venetians to carry them off. The centre group of the eastern pediment seems to have been ruined many centuries before, probably when the Parthenon was converted into a Christian church.

Pausanias is the only ancient author who adverts to these sculptures; but unfortunately his account of them is a most meagre one, and consists only of a bare indication of the subjects. In his time there must have been so many descriptions of them extant, that he probably considered any lengthened notice of them superfluous; and thus his omission of what would have been a work of supererogation, is to us an irreparable loss. How invaluable would have been even so slight a description as he has given of the statues in the house of Polytion, or of the pictures in the Pœcilë! It is, however, a great point to know generally the subjects of the groups, and these he has indicated with sufficient clearness. In the pediment, he says, at the side by which we enter—that is, of course, at the eastern front—all the sculptures relate to the birth of Athena; while those on the back front represent the contention of Poseidon against Athena for the possession of Attica.[1] From this indication of the subjects, with the aid of Carrey's drawings, and of the few fragments that remain, several ingenious antiquaries— as Visconti, Müller, Leake, W. Lloyd, Welcker, and others—have endeavoured, with more or less success, to reconstruct the entire groups. What can be extracted from their speculations as absolutely certain forms but a very small portion of them.

In particular, from the paucity of materials for reconstructing the eastern groups, it is not surprising that the greatest diversity of opinion should have prevailed respecting them. In the time of Carrey only seven figures, besides the horses' heads, remained on that pediment;

---

[1] ἐς δὲ τὸν ναὸν ὃν Παρθενῶνα ὀνομάζου- σιν, ἐς τοῦτον εἰσιοῦσιν, ὁπόσα ἐν τοῖς καλουμένοις ἀετοῖς κεῖται, πάντα ἐς τὴν Ἀθηνᾶς ἔχει γένεσιν· τὰ δὲ ὄπισθεν ἡ Ποσειδῶνος πρὸς Ἀθηνᾶν ἐστιν ἔρις ὑπὲρ τῆς γῆς.—i. 24, 5.

four at the left or northern angle, and three at the southern. Subsequently a fourth figure was discovered on this last side, which had been overthrown, and was lying flat on the floor of the pediment, so that it escaped the observation of Carrey. It has been placed with the remainder of the group in the British Museum. The accuracy of Carrey's drawing of the western pediment may be tested by these remaining figures of the eastern one; and it will be found, we think, that, though coarsely executed, they present a tolerably faithful resemblance.[1] It is extraordinary that Wheler ('Journey,' p. 361) mentions only a horse's head in this pediment; for though he described the sculpture only from memory, he appears to have seen Carrey's drawings in the possession of M. de Nointel, the French ambassador at Constantinople; and the figures must have been there when he saw the temple, as they remained to be carried off by Lord Elgin.

It is a necessary preliminary in any attempt to reconstruct these groups to understand rightly and follow literally the words of Pausanias just quoted. He tells us that the eastern pediment represented, not the birth of Athena, but circumstances connected with it. The neglect of observing this has led to some singular mistakes. Thus Bröndsted, conceiving that the actual birth was represented,[2] supposed that Zeus sat enthroned in the middle of the group, as in the centre of the universe, between Day and Night, surrounded by the deities who preside over nativities and others—as the three Horæ or Seasons, the three Fates, Good Fortune, the Celestial Aphrodité, Ileithyia, Hephæstus, Prometheus, Ares, and Hermes. The goddess had just sprung from her father's head, and, brilliant in her golden arms, hovered above him, soaring to the top of the pediment. At the right hand angle the three Fates were turned towards the car of Night, whilst at the opposite one Cephalus was observing the ascent of the enamoured Aurora. The three figures which sat behind him were, he thought, the Horæ.[3]

This view Leake has characterised as an "ingenious hypothesis, the

---

[1] See the engravings at the end of the volume.

[2] This idea was also adopted by Gerhard and by Quatremère de Quincy.

[3] Voyages et Recherches en Grèce, t. ii. Pref. p. xi. note 3.

elegance and simplicity of which cannot be denied." [1] But later critics have discovered some fatal objections to it. First, contrary to the authority of Pausanias, it assumes the actual birth of Athena. Secondly, the Mœræ and other genethliac deities attending the birth of mortals are not appropriate to that of a goddess. [2] A third and still more fatal objection, founded upon considerations of art, and indeed of technical art, has been advanced by M. Beulé. [3] The principal divinities in the middle of the pediments, as we see by the drawing of the western one, were larger than the figures at the sides ; and we cannot, therefore, assign to Zeus a less stature than 11 or 12 feet, like the figure of Poseidon in the western pediment. [4] It is admitted that Zeus may have been seated ; but persons in that position lose only a third of their height, and something must be allowed for the throne and footstool. The space above his head, therefore, would not have admitted a figure above three feet long, which would have had a most absurd appearance among the surrounding deities of colossal size. The conception, moreover, is contrary to the myth ; for Athena had no childhood, but sprang in complete perfection from her father's head. Add the technical difficulty of making a statue hover in the air over the head of another. Such a thing would have been possible only in a bas-relief or a painting.

The names given by Bröndsted to the subordinate figures are as fanciful as his idea of the main group. Different appellations have been assigned to them by other critics and antiquaries, but for the most part they are probably no better founded. The noble recumbent figure next to the horses of the Sun, which has been called Theseus, Pan, and Bacchus, was designated by Visconti the elder Heracles, by Bröndsted, Cephalus, and by Welcker, Cecrops. The three female figures that follow were thought by Visconti to be Proserpine, Demeter, and Iris, while Bröndsted took them to be the Horæ, and Welcker, Thallo, Auxo, and Oreithyia. At the opposite angle the three females whom

---

[1] Topography, &c., vol. i. p. 538.

[2] See Welcker, in the Classical Museum, vol. ii. p. 376 sqq.

L'Acropole, t. ii. p. 63 sq.

[4] The extreme height of the pediments at their apex is 11 ft. 6 in. See Stuart's Athens, vol. ii. ch. 1, plate 3.

Visconti and Bröndsted agree in calling the Fates, Welcker styles Aglaurus, Hersë, and Pandrosus. These differences amongst the ablest writers show the difficulty of attempting to reconstruct from our present materials the conceptions of a Pheidias. One might as well attempt to re-write, with the aid of a few fragments, a tragedy of Sophocles. The myths concerning the birth of Athena are many and various, and it is impossible to say which of them Pheidias may have selected. The only objects in this pediment which speak for themselves, and about which there can be no difference of opinion, are the horses of Helios at the left hand corner, and those of Selenë, or Night, at the right; the first rising above the horizon, the second just sinking below it. They may suggest three hypotheses: 1. That they indicated what may be called the geography of the action. 2. That they showed the time in which it took place; or, the space of a day. 3. That, as Bröndsted supposed, the scene was supposed to take place in the centre of the universe. Against this last view it may be objected, that as Athena was so peculiarly an Attic deity, the subordinate figures of the groups may have had some reference to that country, but in what way we will not venture to determine.

The design of the western pediment, though fewer of its sculptures have come down to us, is better known than that of the eastern one, from the drawings of Carrey and the description by Wheler. This writer, however, mistook the western front, which is that first approached from the Propylæa, for the principal one; and thus, with an unaccountable perversity, which nevertheless found many followers, and may therefore serve as a caution against dogmatizing in such matters, interpreted the groups representing the contention of Poseidon and Athena as showing the birth of that goddess! And, though the error is so obvious and striking, it was only at a comparatively recent date, and after the time of Stuart, that M. Quatremère de Quincy discovered the real subject of this composition. Leake, in the first edition of his ' Topography of Athens,' still considered the central figure of this pediment to be Zeus. We will here insert Wheler's description, not only as a curious specimen of misapplied ingenuity, but also

as containing valuable notices by an eye-witness of the condition of
the sculptures when he saw them, and of the lively though erroneous
impression which they made upon him. The reader can compare it
with the copy of Carrey's drawing.

"There is a figure that stands in the middle of it (the pediment),
having its right arm broken, which probably held the thunder. Its
legs straddle at some distance from each other; where, without doubt,
was placed the *Eagle*. For its beard, and the majesty which the sculpture hath expressed in his countenance, although those other characters
be wanting here, do sufficiently show it to have been made for *Jupiter*.
He stands naked, for so he was usually represented, especially by the
Greeks. At his right hand is another figure, with its hands and arms
broken off, covered halfway down the leg, in a posture as coming
towards *Jupiter;* which perhaps was a Victory, leading the horses of
the triumphal chariot of *Minerva*, which follows it. The horses are
made with such great art, that the sculptor seems to have outdone
himself by giving them a more than seeming life; such a vigour is
expressed in each posture of their prancing and stamping, natural to
generous horses. Minerva is next represented in the chariot, rather as
the goddess of *learning* than *war*, without helmet, buckler, or a Medusa's
head on her breast, as Pausanias describes her image within the temple.
Next behind her is another figure of a woman sitting, with her head
broken off. Who it was is not certain. But my companion made me
observe the next two figures sitting in the corner to be the Emperor
Hadrian and his Empress *Sabina;* whom I easily knew to be so by the
many medals and statues I have seen of them.

"At the left hand of *Jupiter* are five or six other figures, my com-
rade taketh to be an assembly of the gods, where *Jupiter* introduceth
Minerva and owneth her for his daughter. The *Postick*, or *Hind Front*,
was adorned with figures expressing *Minerva's* contest with *Neptune*
about the naming of the city of *Athens;* but now all of them are
fallen down, only part of a *Sea Horse* excepted."[1]

Not the least singular of the misconceptions of Wheler and Spon

[1] Wheler's 'Journey,' p. 360.

was that the two figures near the left angle were those of Hadrian and
Sabina. They were too well informed to commit so gross an anachronism as to suppose that the Parthenon was a work of that reign ;
but they conceived that Ictinus only built the cella of the temple, that
the portico was added by Attalus, and that Hadrian repaired the
building and added the sculptures in both pediments, including among
them a statue of himself and of his empress ! Considering the age in
which they lived, they may, perhaps, be pardoned for thinking that the
works of Pheidias and his school could have been executed in the time
of Hadrian, as Stuart, in an age much more advanced in the knowledge
of art, held it possible that at least the two statues in question might
have been of Hadrian's time, grounding himself upon the statue of
Antinoüs at Rome.[1] He also considered them portraits of that emperor
and his wife, but suggested that the heads might have been added to
ancient statues.

Ottfried Müller attempted a restoration of this pediment at the end
of his life of Pheidias ; but he has made a great mistake in the figure
of Athena, in representing her head turned away from Poseidon,
whereas the position of the figure, and the fragment of the upper part
of the head preserved in the British Museum, show that she was
looking almost straight forwards, but with a slight inclination towards
Poseidon. He has also mistaken several of the figures in Poseidon's
train, and inserted among them Artemis, Latona, Apollo, and Ceres. It
is plain that the principal figures on this side are all connected with
the sea, as Mr. Watkiss Lloyd has well pointed out in a paper in the
' Classical Museum ;'[2] and the same view has been adopted, with more
or less variation, by several other writers. Not only does the subject
represented lead to such a conclusion, but it is also confirmed by the
unmistakable character of several of the figures. Thus, the second
figure on Poseidon's left, with a *cetus* at her feet, who, like the corresponding one on the opposite side, appears to be in the act of driving a

---

[1] See his ' Antiquities of Athens,' vol. ii.
p. 1, and plate ix.

[2] vol. v. p. 396 sqq. The reader will
here find, in a tabular form, a synopsis of
the views of nine different antiquaries
respecting this pediment.

chariot, is evidently Amphitritë. The animals attached to the car had disappeared before Carrey's drawing was made. They were probably hippocampi. Nor can there be any doubt respecting the nude female figure a little further on. It is evidently Aphroditë, reposing in the lap of her mother Dionë, and having her son Eros by her side. The remaining figures are not so plain. The female figure which stands between Poseidon and Amphitritë probably represented the sea, whose dominion Poseidon was striving to introduce, and may have been his granddaughter Thetis, for whom she has been also recognised by Müller and Leake. Mr. Lloyd calls her Thalassa. The figures on Amphitritë's left are styled Ino and Melicertes both by Welcker and Lloyd; and, as connected with the sea, these seem more appropriate to the group than Leto and Artemis, or Gë Kourotrophos, as they have been called by other writers. Welcker takes the statue next to Dionë to have been Peitho, and thus connects her with the group of Aphroditë; but it has the appearance of a solitary figure. Mr. Lloyd calls it Tethys, and this name may be as probable as any other. The two end figures on this side probably serve to connect the story with Attica. Leake and Lloyd take them to be Ilissus and Callirrhoë, whilst Welcker agrees as to the last, but names the male figure Theseus—an evident anachronism. It may, however, possibly have been Ægeus, who, as the father of Theseus, was sometimes reputed to have been identical with Poseidon, and who would thus have formed an appropriate link to connect the central group of the gods with the figures symbolising Attica.

The figures in the train of Athena are not so easy of identification from external signs as those on the other side; but if it has been shown that Poseidon's followers were connected with the sea, it seems almost a necessary inference that those of Athena represented the land. We have already observed (p. 33) that the basis of the myth was allegorical, having reference to the choice between a seafaring life and the pursuits of agriculture; and how much more significance must this allegory have derived from the strife of parties and the policy of Themistocles! We have seen (p. 75) that Peisistratus and the aristocratic party had endeavoured to make the Athenians agriculturists,

2 D

whilst Themistocles turned them into sailors ; a policy which resulted
in establishing a complete democracy.   In the time of Pericles and
Pheidias this circumstance must have lent an additional interest to the
group.   At the same time it was necessary to adhere to the original
myth, which represented Athena as victorious ; and the bitterness of
the contention, as we have already had more than one occasion to
observe, had been removed, and had sunk into oblivion, by the union of
the worship of Athena and Poseidon.

   If it be allowed that the deities in the train of Athena represented
the land, then it can hardly be possible that Demeter should be absent.
We take her to have been the seated female figure, the fourth from the
end ; whilst the naked boy on her left was probably Iacchus, and the
following female figure Persephonë.   This is also the interpretation of
De Quincy, Bröndsted, and Welcker.   Amongst the figures in this group
must surely have been Cecrops, who was either a judge or a witness of
the strife, and Erechtheus, who was so closely connected with the
worship of Athena.   Erechtheus we take to be represented by the figure
next to the last one, which appears to be seated on a huge snake.   From
this circumstance Mr. Lloyd has called this statue Cecrops,[1] and the
same name has been given to it by Müller and others.   But it seems to
us that the figure is too quiescent for the active part assigned by the
myth to Cecrops ; and we should therefore be inclined to give that name
to the figure which stands immediately behind the horses of Athena ;
a view for which we may plead the authority of Visconti, though no
other antiquary appears to have adopted it.   This figure is evidently
encouraging the female in the car in her onward course ; and if this
figure be Nikë, as almost every commentator has assumed, the group
would appropriately typify the victory of Athena as assigned to her by
Cecrops.   If there be any truth in this view, it would serve to confirm
the appellation of Erechtheus for the seated figure before mentioned ;
for he also was characterized by a snake, and indeed was worshipped
under that form in the Erechtheium (above, p. 32).   It naturally follows that the female next to him must be Pandrosus, who so faithfully

[1] Class. Mus. vol. v. p. 429.

preserved Athena's trust with regard to Erechtheus, became her original priestess, and, along with Erechtheus, shared her temple.[1] We have thus accounted for all the figures except the recumbent one in the northern angle. It is evidently a river god, and has been called Ilissus by Visconti, De Quincy, Müller, Millingen, and Welcker. But we agree with Mr. Lloyd in calling it the Cephisus, as we have placed the Ilissus on the other side of the pediment. Our reasons are, first : that to a spectator looking at this western front the Ilissus would really be on his right hand and the Cephisus on his left, as their images would also appear in the pediment : secondly, the Cephisus, being near Eleusis, would naturally be represented in the vicinity of Demeter and Corë.

Professor Ross saw on the western pediment several marble fragments of the stem of the olive-tree which Athena was reputed to have created.[2] Welcker had denied that any such fragments were to be found,[3] and Beulé observes that it would be difficult to find a place for the tree.[4] In a fragment in the British Museum, alluded to in p. 388, the stump of a tree is also seen between the remains of two feet in a striding attitude ; but this stump, as Welcker observes,[5] must have impinged upon the leg, and obviously only served as a support. We think, however, that it cannot be doubted that the feet in question belonged to the statue near the horses, which we have ascribed to Cecrops. They are too small to have belonged to Poseidon, but would have suited a statue eight or nine feet high, which would have been about the height of one in that part of the pediment ; and their position agrees well enough with the attitude of the figure as represented in Carrey's drawing. We shall only further remark about the pediments that the ground of them appears to have been painted blue.

Such was the exterior of the temple. With regard to the interior, we have already remarked that it was divided into two unequal portions,

---

[1] These two figures are the only ones still remaining on the pediment, but they have now lost their heads. Might not this support the inference that they were not the original heads, but put on by Hadrian ? He was quite barbarian enough to do it.

There are casts of the figures in the British Museum.

[2] Aufsätze, B. ii. S. 282.
[3] Alte Denkmäler, p. 111, 119.
[4] L'Acropole, t. ii. p. 83.
[5] Class. Mus. vol. ii. p. 390.

the eastern and largest of which formed properly the cella of the goddess, or the Parthenon strictly so called; whilst the western and
smaller one was the opisthodomus. The cella had at all events a partial
roof; but as to the number of columns which supported it, authorities
differ, for the traces of them are not very plain. Leake says[1] that there
were sixteen; yet in his plan he gives twenty-one, without counting the
two corner ones at the western end. It seems to be now pretty generally agreed that there were ten columns on each side, forming as it
were two aisles, and three at the western extremity.[2] It has also been
disputed of what order were the interior columns. This question appears
to have been settled by M. Paccard, who discovered that they were Doric
from traces of flutings on the slabs on which they rested.[3] These are
said to have been produced as follows: The Greeks did not begin to
flute their columns till all the drums had been put together, and the
column stood erect in its place. In the operation, the marks of the chisel
had been left upon the pavement, thus describing the contour of the
column and its flutings. It is believed that this lower order was
surmounted by another of smaller columns. Thus Wheler describes the
cella as having a gallery formed by two ranks of columns, twenty-two
below and twenty-three above.[4] A Corinthian capital was found in it,
and as the Corinthian order was invented about the time of its erection[5]
the upper columns may have been of that order. At the west end of
the cella, the place where the chryselephantine statue of the goddess
stood is marked by an oblong pavement of poros stone or tufa; which
was required to preserve a certain degree of moisture through its
porosity, in order to prevent the ivory from cracking. Pausanias tells
us[6] that, from the dryness of the Acropolis, it was necessary to use
water instead of oil for cleansing the statue, and that it wanted moist
exhalations. This pavement in a direction across the cella is 21 ft.
long, with a width of about 8 ft. But the pedestal itself was still
larger, as there are traces in the marble floor of the iron cramps which

[1] vol. i. p. 333.
[2] See Beulé, t. ii. p. 33.
[3] Ibid. p. 32.
[4] Journey, p. 363.
[5] Leake, i. p. 334.
[6] v. 11, 5.

secured it between two and three feet in advance of the pavement. This breadth of base was necessary because the goddess had on one side her shield, and on the other the serpent Erechtheus.

The roof of the opisthodomus was supported by four columns between four and five feet in diameter, and apparently of the Ionic order. Harpocration (in voc.) calls it an *οἶκος*, whence Ross infers that it was a covered building. It was separated from the Parthenon by a thick wall, which according to some writers was without a door.[1] Professor Bötticher, on the contrary, affirms[2] that he found traces of two folding-doors opening outwards from the cella towards the opisthodomus, each five feet wide. The first door opened into the wall, which is six and a half feet thick, while the second door opened into the opisthodomus. There is a passage in the scholia to the 'Plutus' of Aristophanes (v. 1194), of which Bötticher does not seem to have been aware, but which confirms his view in a remarkable manner.[3] The wall is here called a double one having a door; of which, however, there may have been two if the wall was very thick. The scholiast has indeed confounded the Athena of the Parthenon with Athena Polias, which, as we have before observed, is not unusual with the later writers; but that he is speaking of the Parthenon is evident from his mentioning the opisthodomus as a treasury. And indeed it can hardly be supposed that there was no communication between the two chambers. In the time of Demosthenes the opisthodomus caught fire, and the Hellenotamiæ were accused of having fired it.[4]

It has been disputed whether the Parthenon was a hypæthral temple—i.e. open to the air—or had a roof. This question we must leave to the decision of architects. All that we know respecting hypæthral temples is derived from Vitruvius (iii. 2, 8); and he mentions as the only example of them an octastyle temple at Athens, which, however, does not prove it to have been the Parthenon. At all events, it

---

[1] Ross, Archäol. Aufs. ii. 288.

[2] In Gerhard's Archäologischer Anzeiger, April, 1862, p. 322.

[3] *ὀπίσω τοῦ νεὼ τῆς καλουμένης Πολιάδος*

Ἀθηνᾶς διπλοῦς τοῖχος ἔχων θύραν, ὅπου ἦν θησαυροφυλάκιον.

[4] contra Timoer. p. 743, Reiske.

can hardly be supposed that a statue of such valuable materials as the Athena of Pheidias should have been left exposed to the vicissitudes of the atmosphere. Dr. Wordsworth suggests the employment of a velarium, an idea to which he was led by a passage in the 'Ion' of Euripides.[1]

The Parthenon owes its chief defacement to the Byzantine Christians. When the temple was converted into a church the pronaos became the apsis, and in order to admit light through windows of transparent stone, the roof of the eastern portico and the centre of the pediment were thrown down. Nine or ten statues, the chief ones of the group, now disappeared; and, as we have before observed, when Carrey made his drawing only seven remained. According to Leake[2] and others it was first dedicated as a church under the name of St. Sophia; but A. Mommsen[3] contests this, and contends that it was originally consecrated to the Virgin. It was probably also the Byzantines who, from religious scruples, defaced the metopes of the frieze; for those on the east, west, and north fronts bear evident marks of having been mutilated with the hammer.[4] We have already remarked, that those of the south side, which were less seen, escaped better. The Byzantines also adorned the interior with paintings, traces of which still remain. The Turks added a minaret at the western front. The western pediment seems to have suffered principally from the various sieges which Athens has undergone since the time of Wheler and Carrey. The most destructive of these sieges was that by the Venetians under Morosini and Königsmarck, in 1687. The Turks had stowed away their ammunition in the cella of the Parthenon, and an unlucky shell falling upon it caused an explosion, which destroyed a great part of the centre of the building. Eight columns of the peristyle on the northern side were thrown down or damaged, together

---

[1] Athens and Attica, p. 101; cf. Eurip. Ion, v. 1141 sqq. An elaborate account of the Parthenon, illustrated with plates, has recently been published, as we have said, by Adolph Michaelis at Leipzig, to which those readers are referred who may require a fuller notice of it than suits the object and limits of this work.

[2] vol. i. p. 480.

[3] Athenæ Christianæ, cap. vi.

[4] Beulé, ii. p. 112.

with their entablature; and on the southern, six. Only one column of the eastern pronaos was now left standing, though it is probable that two of the six may have been previously removed by the Byzantines in order to make room for the altar when the Parthenon was converted into a church. The opisthodomus and both pediments were but little injured, only two or three of the statues having been thrown down.

Although Morosini, the Venetian commander-in-chief, was not altogether a barbarian, and as a fellow-countryman of Titian could appreciate works of art, so that he had expressed his repugnance at the destruction of this beautiful temple,[1] yet as a monument of his achievement, and to grace his triumphal entry into Venice, he had resolved to carry off the car of Victory, with its admirable horses, which adorned the western pediment; but in the act of lowering, it was let fall by the awkwardness of his engineers and dashed to pieces.[2] It is probable that the other central figures of this pediment were destroyed at this time, either during or after the siege, but we have no account of their fate. The torso of the second figure in the southern angle, called by Leake Ilissus, was found in the excavations of 1835 almost under the place which it must have occupied. Other fragments of the sculptures on this pediment were also found,[3] especially pieces of a horse's head and parts of the chariot. The west façade suffered severely in the siege of the Acropolis by the Turks (1826–7), who bombarded it from the Philopappus. Large pieces of the columns were then chipped off. To answer the Turkish fire the Greeks had erected a rampart before the front of the temple.[4]

But though the Parthenon has suffered terribly from the ravages of

---

[1] See the letter quoted in Bröndsted, Voyage, &c., ii. p. 282.

[2] For an account of this siege, and its consequences, see Fanelli, Atene Attica, 4to, Venezia, 1707; Graziani, F. Mauroceni Gesta, 4to, Patav. 1698; Arrighi, De Vita et Rebus gestis F. Mauroceni, 4to, ib. 1749; Letter of a Venetian captain engaged in the siege, in Antonio Bulifon's Lettere Memorabili, Napoli, 1697, t. ii. p. 86; A Journal of the Venetian Campaigne, A D. 1687, translated from the original Italian, sent from Venice, and printed by the most Serene Republic, 1687 (in the King's Library, British Museum). Cf. Leake, vol. i. p. 80 sqq.

[3] Ross, Aufs. i. 84.

[4] Ib. i. 83.

war, it has been hardly less defaced in a peaceful manner and under the apology of a love of art. Early in the present century Lord Elgin, when English ambassador at Constantinople, procured a firman from the Sultan, which authorized him to take casts of the sculptures on the Parthenon, and to remove any pieces of stone having inscriptions or figures;[1] which seems to mean, any pieces that had fallen. That Lord Elgin exceeded his powers, appears to be sufficiently evident from the reluctance with which he was at last induced, on the representations of his agent, Lusieri, " to consent to the removal of whole pieces of sculpture."[2] Not only were the statues of the eastern pediment removed, but also many of the metopes and portions of the frieze. And this was done in so reckless a manner by Lord Elgin's workmen as to damage the building itself; for, in order to get at the metopes on the south side, the cornice also was damaged. Nor were Lord Elgin's scientific ravages confined to the Parthenon. From the Erechtheium were carried off a column of the eastern portico, and one of the canephoroi of the southern portico, the place of which was supplied by a rude pillar. From the theatre was taken the statue of Bacchus. The abstraction of the four pieces of the frieze of the temple of Nikë Apteros, which had been built into a Turkish house, was perhaps more excusable; but we hardly see what can be said in defence of the other depredations. The example of the French is pleaded, who had carried off one of the metopes, and, it was feared, would possess themselves of more. The apprehension of this, and the danger to which the sculptures were constantly exposed through the rapacity of travellers, the accidents of war or weather, and the carelessness and brutality of the Turks, form perhaps the best excuse for Lord Elgin's proceedings, and it must be allowed that it was impossible to foresee, at the time when these acts were committed, that the day would come when Athens should be placed under a civilized government, and the ravages of violence and decay in its beautiful monuments be not merely arrested, but repaired. It may be added that the removal of

---

[1] 'Elgin Marbles,' vol. i. p. 2; cf. Rangabé, Ant. Hell. t. i. Pref. p. 6.

[2] Ibid. p. 3.

these sculptures seems to have been recommended by Mr. William Hamilton. They were no doubt regarded as doomed irrevocably to perdition; and we may at all events congratulate ourselves that such numerous and beautiful specimens of them should have been secured in our own metropolis from the chance of further harm.

Having thus described the structure of the temple and its exterior ornaments, and briefly sketched the vicissitudes it has suffered, we will now accompany Pausanias in his description of what he saw in the interior. The principal object was, of course, Pheidias' chryselephantine statue of Athena, called by the Athenians ἡ Παρθένος, or the Virgin,[1] whence her cella obtained the name of ὁ Παρθενών, or the Abode of the Virgin. On the top of her helmet, says Pausanias (i. 24, 5), is the image of a sphinx, and on each side of it are engravings of griffins.[2] Griffins were beasts like lions, but with the wings and beak of an eagle. The statue of the goddess, he proceeds, is erect, and she wears a *chiton* reaching to her feet. On her breast is a head of Medusa worked in ivory, and she holds in one hand a statue of Victory four cubits high, and in the other hand a spear. We should here observe that, from the text of Pausanias, it would seem that the Victory also was carved upon her breast.[3] But we know from other sources[4] that she held the Victory in her hand, and in the text of Pausanias something is probably omitted. At her feet, he continues, rests a shield, and near the spear a serpent, which may perhaps be Erichthonius. The birth of Pandora is sculptured in relief on the pedestal of the statue. Hesiod[5] and others have related how she was the first woman.

---

[1] Pausan. lib. x. 34, fin.

[2] γρῦπές εἰσιν ἐπειργασμένοι. Leake has pointed out (vol. i. p. 109, note) that Pausanias employs the word ἐπεργάζομαι, or ἐξεπεργάζομαι, when speaking of works in relief: ἐπείργασται δὲ τῷ χαλκῷ πολλὰ μὲν τῶν ἄθλων Ἡρακλέους.—iii. 17, 3. And sometimes with τύπος: ἐπειργασμένοι δὲ ἐπὶ τύπων πρὸ τῆς εἰσόδου τῇ μὲν Ἄρτεμις, τῇ δὲ Ἀσκληπιός ἐστι καὶ Ὑγίεια.—viii. 31, 1. So ἐπὶ τύπου.—ix. 11, 2.

[3] καί οἱ κατὰ τὸ στέρνον ἡ κεφαλὴ Μεδούσης ἐλέφαντός ἐστιν ἐμπεποιημένη, καὶ Νίκη τε ὅσον τεσσάρων πηχῶν· ἐν δὲ τῇ χειρὶ δόρυ ἔχει.—c. 24, 7. See Leake, vol. i. p. 149, note 3.

[4] Epictetus in Arrian, ii. 8, 20. And she is so represented by Hesiod, Scut. Herc. 339; and on an Athenian coin, engraved by Stuart (vol. ii. ch. 1, frontispiece).

[5] See Theogon. 570; Op. et D. 60 sqq.

So far Pausanias, whose description even of this celebrated statue is very imperfect. For he says nothing here of the sculptures on the shield and the slippers, though he had indeed mentioned before (c. 17, 2) that on the shield was represented the battle with the Amazons. We must therefore supply his deficiencies from other sources. Pliny, who describes the statue in greater detail,[1] says that the battle with the Amazons was carved round the projecting border of the shield, and that in the concave part of it was represented the battle of the gods and giants. The statue, he says, which was made of ivory and gold, was twenty-six cubits high, or about thirty-nine English feet. On the slippers were carved the combats of the Lapithæ and Centaurs. The sculpture on the base represented the birth of Pandora, at which twenty deities were assisting.[2]

The slippers, or sandals, here mentioned were of the kind called Tyrrhenian, having gold thongs, and a wooden sole four dactyls or nearly three inches thick.[3] It was most probably on this sole that the combats of the Centaurs and Lapithæ were carved, a circumstance calculated to create astonishment at the versatile genius of Pheidias, who could conceive and execute so gigantic a statue, and yet condescend to adorn it with such minute specimens of the toreutic art.

Pheidias inserted in the shield a portrait of Pericles engaged in combat with an Amazon; his face was partly hidden by the spear he was hurling, but not so that he could not be recognised. According to Dion Chrysostom it was done without the knowledge of Pericles.[4] Pheidias had also inserted a portrait of himself, as a bald-headed man lifting a stone. This formed one of the charges against him, for which he was thrown into prison.[5]

---

[1] N. H. xxxvi. s. 18.

[2] The text of Pliny is almost hopelessly corrupt: In basi autem quod cælatum est Pandoras genesin appellant; di sunt nascentes xx numero. Böttiger's emendation among the many proposed appears to be the best: di adsunt nascenti (Andeutungen, p. 90). Panofka's (Annal. Inst. Archæol. ii. 108), though to the same

purpose, is rather more violent: nascenti adstantes. The next sentence also seems to be irretrievably corrupt, but as it offers no new feature, we pass it over.

[3] τὸ κάττυμα ξύλινον, τετραδάκτυλον.— Pollux, vii. s. 92.

[4] Orat. xii. De Dei cognitione, p. 195, Mor. (i. 214, Teubner).

[5] Plut. Pericl. 31.

We learn from Plato that the parts made of ivory were the eyes, face, feet, and hands; the pupils of the eyes were of stone,[1] probably of some grey colour. The gold on the statue, which might be removed, was reckoned by Pericles among the disposable property of the state, and weighed forty talents.[2] We have already adverted to the theft of it by Lachares. The breast-plate, or γοργόνειον, which, as we have seen, was of ivory, was also stolen by Philorgus.[3] But this, as well as the gold, appears to have been recovered or otherwise supplied, for Pausanias does not notice the absence of either. That author does not mention an owl that stood near the statue, also said to have been the work of Pheidias.[4]

The scholiast on the 'Pax' of Aristophanes[5] tells us that the statue was finished in the archonship of Theodorus (B.C. 438), and must therefore have been dedicated just before the commencement of the Propylæa. It was still the object of veneration towards the latter part of the fourth century of our æra, in the reign of Valentinian and Valens; for Nestorius, who was hierophant at that time, as admonished in a dream, consecrated a small statue of Achilles, and placed it under the image.[6] And, indeed, it existed about a century longer, for Proclus, who died A.D. 485, saw and lamented its removal, probably in the reign of Leo I., and of Anthemius on the western throne, when paganism received its final blow.[7] It must therefore have been in existence upwards of nine centuries.

The only portrait statues in the Parthenon which Pausanias recognised were one of Hadrian, and, near the entrance, one of Iphicrates. Pliny says[8] that Protogenes, the painter, had adorned the propylæum

---

[1] Hipp. Maj. p. 290 (ii. iii. p. 428, Bekk.).

[2] Thucyd. ii. 13. Diodor. Sic. xii. 40, says fifty talents; but Plutarch, De vitand. ære al. (t. ix. p. 292, Reiske) agrees with Thucydides, if indeed the great historian wants confirmation. The scholiast on the 'Pax' of Aristophanes, v. 604, gives, on the authority of Philochorus, 44 (μδ') talents.

[3] Isocrat. in Callim. p. 382 (547, Oxon. 1822).

[4] Dion. Chrys. loc. cit.

[5] loc. cit.

[6] Zosimus, lib. v.

[7] ὅπως δὲ αὐτὸς καὶ αὐτῇ τῇ φιλοσόφῳ θεῷ προσφιλὴς ἐγένετο . . . σαφῶς καὶ αὐτὴ ἡ θεὸς ἐδήλωσεν, ἡνίκα τὸ ἄγαλμα αὐτῆς τὸ ἐν Παρθενῶνι τέως ἱδρυμένον ὑπὸ τῶν καὶ τὰ ἀκίνητα κινούντων μετεφέρετο.—Marinus, Vit. Procli, s. 30, p. 24, Boissonnade.

[8] H. N. xxxv. 101.

of the temple, by which he must mean the east portico, with pictures of the triremes Paralus and Ammonias, and had added, in what the painters call the parerga or by-works, some small ships of war, in order to show from what paltry beginnings the Athenians had arrived at the highest pitch of ostentation in this matter. The Paralus and Ammonias were meant for state occasions, like the Venetian Bucentaur or the Lord Mayor's barge. There appears to have been five such ships —the Paralus and Salaminia, which date from the classic times of Athens; and the Antigonis, Demetrias, and Ammonias,[1] which were instituted at later periods, and the last probably at the Macedonian epoch. It carried the victims sent by the Athenians for the sacrifice to Jupiter Ammon. It appears also to have been sometimes called Nausicaa. Sillig's argument (ad Plin, l. c.), founded partly upon this, and partly upon grammatical grounds, that the Paralus and Ammonias mentioned by Pliny were not represented as ships, but as personifications of them under the form of a man and woman, seems quite untenable; for in that case, how could any contrast have been shown, as Pliny says there was, between the primitive trireme and these superb specimens of naval architecture? When Cicero alludes to the picture of Paralus as one of the notable works of art at Athens,[2] he appears to mean a man; but there is nothing to show that he was connected with this vessel.

Pausanias also passes over the silver-footed throne of Xerxes, from which the Persian monarch beheld the battle of Salamis, which under the name of ὁ αἰχμάλωτος, or 'the captive,'[3] formed one of the anathemata in the Parthenon. It had, indeed, been stolen by Glaucetes, when he was treasurer in the Acropolis, together with the acinaces, or scimitar, of Mardonius, worth 300 darics, or near £330;[4] which, however, appears from Pausanias to have been one of the ἀριστεῖα preserved in the temple of Athena Polias. The throne, indeed, may never have been recovered, and so mentioned by Harpocration only from tradition; but the scimitar certainly was, since, besides Pausanias, it is mentioned by

[1] Phot. Lex. voc. Πάραλος.
[2] In Verr. iv. 60, s. 135.
[3] Harpocr. in ἀργυρόπους δίφρος.
[4] Demosth. c. Timocr. p. 741, Reiske.

Dion Chrysostom[1] among the anathemata at Athens, together with the Spartan shields taken at Pylos. Alexander the Great, after the battle at the Granicus, sent 300 suits of Persian armour to the Parthenon.[2]

After quitting the temple, Pausanias proceeds to mention various objects on the Acropolis (cap. 24, 8; c. 25). Over against the Parthenon was a bronze statue of Apollo, surnamed Παρνόπιος, or the expeller of locusts, said to have been the work of Pheidias. Among other statues were Xanthippus, father of Pericles, who engaged the Medes in the naval action off Mycalë;[3] and Pericles himself; not, however, near his father, but on the other side of the temple, near the colossal statue of Athena Promachos, and the quadriga.[4] Near Xanthippus was a statue of Anacreon the Teian, the first, after the Lesbian Sappho, who composed chiefly amatory poems. He was represented in the posture of a drunken man, singing. The female statues near him, the work of Deinomenes, were Io, the daughter of Inachus, and Callisto, daughter of Lycaon. Both have a similar history; the love of Zeus, the hatred of Hera, and the metamorphosis of Io into a heifer, and of Callisto into a bear.

At the southern wall of the Acropolis were represented, in statues of about 2 cubits or 3 feet, in height, the legendary war of the giants, who at one time occupied Thrace and the isthmus of Pallenë; the war of the Athenians with the Amazons; the battle of Marathon against the Persians, and the rout of the Gauls in Mysia; the whole of them being the anathemata of King Attalus. The bases of these diminutive statues appear to have overtopped the parapet wall; which explains how that which represented Dionysus, in the war with the giants, could have been overthrown by a storm so as to fall into the theatre.[5] From this account, it follows that the group of the Gigantomachia must have stood immediately over the theatre; whereas Leake, in his plan of the Acropolis, has placed it too much to the east, while Beulé,

[1] Orat. ii. De regno, p. 26, Mor. (t. i. p. 27, Teubner).

[2] Arrian, Exp. Alex. i. 16.

[3] Herod. viii. 131; ix. 89 sqq.; Pausan.

[4] Pausan. i. 28, 2.

[5] Bötticher, Bericht, S. 68 sq.; Plutarch, Vit. M. Anton. c. 60.

on the contrary, puts it in his plan too much to the west. The same storm overthrew the colossal statues of Eumenes and Attalus, which probably stood near the same spot, though they are not mentioned by Pausanias; whence we may conclude that they were never restored. After the Roman fashion, they had been reinscribed to M. Antony; who also affected the name of Dionysus Junior, as Antinoüs did after him.[1] Here also was a statue of Olympiodorus, illustrious by his deeds, and especially by his courage in adversity, when others were cast down. He was especially famous for having liberated Athens from the Macedonians, and recaptured the Museium. Pausanias gives his history at length; but we need say no more about him here, as we have already spoken of him (above, p. 156).

Near the statue of Olympiodorus was a bronze statue of Artemis Leucophrynë, or Leucophryönë,[2] an anathema of the sons of Themistocles. Artemis Leucophrynë was worshipped by the Magnesians, of whom Themistocles had been made governor by the Persian king; she had a famous temple at Leucophrys, on the Mæander; which, though not so large as that at Ephesus, nor enriched with so many anathemata, was nevertheless considered to be the handsomer of the two.[3]

There was also an image of Athena in a sitting posture, with an inscription, recording that it was the work of Endœus, and consecrated by Callias. This statue must have been more ancient than the Persian wars; as may be inferred from the age of Endœus, and also from its posture. But when Pausanias says that Endœus was a pupil of Dædalus, and fled with him to Crete after the death of Talos, or Kalos, the assertion seems to be founded on an inference from the antique style of the art. The dedicator may possibly have been the Callias who opposed Peisistratus.[4]

Pausanias now approaches the Erechtheium. We have already given some account of the rebuilding or restoring of this temple (supra, p. 138 sqq.), from which it will have been seen that its history is somewhat

---

[1] Plut. Vit. M. Anton. c. 60.

[2] Pausanias in this place (c. 26, 4) and in another book (iii. 18, 6), calls her Leucophrynë; while Strabo (lib. xiv. p. 647) writes Leucophryönë.

[3] See Xenoph. Hellen. iii. 2, 19; Strabo, loc. cit.

[4] See Herod. vi. c. 121 sq.; cf. Thiersch, Epochen, &c. p. 124 sq.

obscure. Its internal arrangements are hardly less so, and we will therefore preface Pausanias' account with a short description, which will be
aided by a glance at the plan of the building. (See plan of Acropolis,
p. 367.) It is a quadrangular building of oblong form, being in length,
from east to west, about seventy feet, including the portico, and thirty-
two or thirty-three feet in breadth within the walls. This space seems to
have been divided into three by partition walls, forming two chambers of
the entire breadth of the building, each about twenty-four feet in length,

VIEW OF THE ERECHTHEIUM, FROM NORTH-WEST.

and a third at its western extremity, only about ten feet broad. But
the building has undergone such singular transformations in later times,
having been first converted into a Christian church, and then into a
Turkish harem, that it is doubtful whether the wall which separates this
last compartment from the central chamber be not of modern construction, and therefore, whether originally there were but two chambers, the
western one, consequently, being considerably longer than the other.
And indeed, this would agree with Pausanias' description of the building
as a *double* one. Moreover, we hear of its having formed only two shrines
or sanctuaries, those, namely, of Athena Polias and of Pandrosus. It is,

however, probable that the most westerly compartment was only a sort of corridor, connecting the two porticoes at the north and south sides of the building. On the eastern and principal façade it has also an Ionic portico of six columns. But it is chiefly the porticoes at the sides which distinguish this temple from other Grecian ones. That on the north side extends several feet beyond the western wall of the building, and also projects considerably; so that of its six columns, two are at the sides and four in front. The smaller prostasis, or portico, on the south side, and opposite to it, is arranged in the same manner; only for the columns six female figures are substituted, four in front and two at the sides. The west front had no portico, but consisted of a wall with four Ionic engaged columns, having three windows between them. It should be added, that the eastern chamber is about eight feet above the level of the rest of the building.

We shall now be in a position to follow the description of Pausanias (c. 26, 6). There is, he says, a building (οἴκημα) called Erechtheium. Before it is an altar of Zeus Hypatos, or the Most High, on which no living thing is sacrificed; cakes only are offered, and no wine.

We have already given an account of this worship in our second chapter. We must of course suppose that this altar of Zeus stood outside the temple. He was not associated with the worship of the deities within, Athena, Poseidon, Erechtheus, Pandrosus, and others, who had a story in common; but he was associated with Athena as guardian of the city, in which capacity she had promised the first sacrifice to him, as we have explained above.[1] And hence, perhaps, we may presume that every sacrifice to Athena Polias was preceded by one to Zeus Polieus, whose altar stood before her door; for, as we have shown, Zeus Polieus and Zeus Hypatos were the same.

On entering the Erechtheium, Pausanias continues, three altars are seen. One is that of Poseidon, on which, in obedience to an oracle, sacrifices are also made to Erechtheus. The second altar is that of the hero Butes, and the third is dedicated to Hephæstus. On the walls are pictures of the race of the Butadæ. He then proceeds to say, that

[1] Supra, p. 387.

there is in another part of the building some sea water, and makes a short digression respecting it ; to which he has been led, apparently, by the mention of Poseidon, Erechtheus, and their priests the Butadæ, with whom its history was connected ; although he had not yet finished his description of the eastern chamber, which was the temple of Athena Polias. But as this fact does not appear very clearly from the words of Pausanias, we must supplement his account with proofs drawn from other sources, and from his own context.

First, then, we have seen that he mentions altars of Poseidon and Erechtheus, and adverts to the Butadæ. Now we know that Poseidon shared the temple of Athena Polias ; that Poseidon and Erechtheus were identified by the Athenians ; and that the Butadæ were the priests not only of those united deities, but also at the same time of Athena Polias, in connexion with them. On the first of these points we have the testimony of Plutarch ; who says that at Athens[1] Poseidon possessed a temple in conjunction with Athena. That Poseidon and Erechtheus were identified by the Athenians we have before had occasion to remark, from Hesychius.[2] They thus formed a concrete divinity, much in the same way as Athena Nikë. The same fact appears from Lycurgus the orator, himself one of the Eteobutadæ, establishing, or rather perhaps regulating, their joint priesthood.[3] For, according to Apollodorus, the priesthood had been established in the very earliest times of Athens in the family of Butes, and included also the service of Athena[4] with that of Poseidon-Erechtheus. This union of worship is also displayed by the circumstance that the Athenians granted to the Epidaurians portions of the sacred olive, to make an image, on condition of their bringing a

[1] ἐνταῦθα γοῦν καὶ νεὼ κοινωνεῖ μετὰ τῆς Ἀθηνᾶς, ἐν ᾧ καὶ βωμός ἐστι τῆς Λήθης ἱδρυμένος.—Sympos. ix. Q. vi (t. viii. p. 955, Reiske). Where τῆς Λήθης is the certain correction of Xylander for the senseless reading ἀληθής.

[2] Ἐρεχθεύς · Ποσειδῶν ἐν Ἀθήναις.—Hesych. in voc. They are also identified in an ancient inscription found near the Erechtheium. Rangabé, Ant. Hell. t. i. p. 38.

[3] διετάξατο δὲ τὴν ἱερωσύνην τοῦ Ποσειδῶνος Ἐρεχθέως.—Vit. X. Orat. t. ix. p. 353, Reiske.

[4] καὶ τὴν βασιλείαν Ἐρεχθεὺς λαμβάνει, τὴν δὲ ἱερωσύνην τῆς Ἀθηνᾶς καὶ τοῦ Ποσειδῶνος τοῦ Ἐριχθονίου Βούτης.—Biblioth. iii. 15, 1. Where we have a not unusual confusion between Erechtheus and Erichthonius.

2 E

yearly sacrifice to Athena Polias and Erechtheus.[1] But, as a separate deity, Athena Polias was served by a female,[2] and Pandrosus appears to have been her first priestess.

Again, the image of the goddess was turned to the east; for Dion Cassius relates a prodigy that happened in the time of Augustus, when it is said to have turned suddenly towards the west, and to have spat blood.[3] It must therefore have been in the eastern chamber, for that alone has an aspect towards the east. Nor can Dion mean either the statue in the Parthenon or the Athena Promachos; for all such allusions must be to the more ancient and venerable one, unless the contrary be specified,[4] and the Promachos always looked to the west. The adjoining, or western chamber, that of Pandrosus, was entered from the north; and the relative position of the temple of Athena Polias and the Pandroseium, which two temples occupied the whole building, may be shown from Pausanias himself. For in his next chapter he describes the temple of Pandrosus as adjoining that of Athena; whence it follows that the latter must have been the eastern and the former the western chamber. For Pausanias would of course have visited the principal temple, which was that of Polias, first; and we know that the altars and pictures which he mentions were in it, and not in that of Pandrosus, to which he adverts afterwards. The situation of the Pandroseium is further proved from Chandler's inscription,[5] which specifies the wall with the four engaged columns, that is, the western wall depicted by Stuart, in whose time it appears to have been perfect, as being near it.[6] Bötticher, indeed, is of opinion that the building was divided into three cellæ, of which the easternmost was that of Polias, the westernmost that of Pandrosus, and the middle one a chapel of the Butadæ, containing Poseidon, Erechtheus, Hephæstus, and Butes.[7] But this collocation seems at variance with the description of Pausanias, who expressly states that the temple

[1] Herod. v. 82.

[2] Ibid. c. 72.

[3] (τὸ ἄγαλμα) πρὸς ἀνατολῶν ἱδρυμένον πρός τε τὰς δυσμὰς μετεστράφη καὶ αἷμα ἀπέπτυσεν.—liv. 7.

[4] See Meursius, Cecrop. c. 20.

[5] τῶν κιόνων τῶν ἐπὶ τοῦ τοίχου | τοῦ πρὸς τοῦ Πανδροσείου |||| κειμένων.—line 44 sqq. See Rose, Inscr. Gr. p. 189, note [1].

[6] vol. ii. ch. ii. pl. ii.

[7] Bericht, p. 193.

of Pandrosus was next to that of Athena;[1] and it is evident that the altars of Poseidon-Erechtheus, Hephæstus, &c., were at the eastern entrance, which was that of the temple of Polias.[2]

Having thus determined the relative sites of the temples of Athena Polias and of Pandrosus, we will, before proceeding with the description of Pausanias, offer a few remarks on what he has already said. We have seen that he calls the building an οἴκημα; and it is remarkable that Plato, in a passage already cited,[3] uses the same word of it; not, however, as the joint temple of Athena and Poseidon, but of Athena and Hephæstus, which deities seem also to have been united at Tyre,[4] as we have already seen that they also were in the Athenian Hephæsteium. It may not, indeed, be quite certain that Plato, in that passage of the 'Protagoras,' is alluding to the Erechtheium; but he certainly does so in his 'Critias,' where he says that the warrior race dwelt around the temple of Athena and Hephæstus, on the Acropolis.[5] In this view the temple would commemorate not so much the contention of Athena and Poseidon for the possession of Attica, as the more domestic story of the passion of Hephæstus for Athena, the birth of Erechtheus, the guardianship of him by Agraulus, Pandrosus, and Hersë, and the fate which they thereby incurred; thus connecting with the sacred spot a larger number of persons and legends, and regarding that of Athena and Poseidon as local and subordinate, or rather, ignoring it altogether. For Plato holds that the gods obtained the regions which they govern by choosing with mutual consent what was fittest for them; and rejects, as quite unworthy of them, the notion that they disputed for their presidencies.[6] A view which of course excludes the myth respecting the contention of Poseidon and Athena. It is clear, however, that Pausanias did not view the matter in this light, but considered the building to derive its chief importance from the strife of the god and goddess, or rather, perhaps,

[1] τῷ ναῷ δὲ τῆς Ἀθηνᾶς Πανδρόσου ναὸς συνεχής ἐστι.—i. 27, 3.
[2] Ibid. 26, 6.
[3] Protag. τὸ τῆς Ἀθηνᾶς καὶ Ἡφαίστου οἴκημα τὸ κοινόν.—p. 321. See above, p. 32.
[4] ἔνθ' Ἥφαιστος ἔχων χαίρει γλαυκῶπιν Ἀθήνην.—Achill. Tat. ii. 14.
[5] p. 112 (iii. ii. 156, Bekk.).
[6] Ibid. p. 109 (150, Bekk.).

2 F 2

their subsequent reconciliation. And we may perhaps feel satisfied that this was the more general view, when we reflect that the guardian deity of the city would be more appropriately honoured by the record of a victory by which she gained her presidency than that of a legend which could have been only distasteful to her. And this view is strengthened by two altars in the temple, which Pausanias has omitted to mention, but which seem to have reference to the contention. One of these was the altar of Oblivion, whose existence in the temple is attested by Plutarch, in a passage cited a little before,[1] and which appears to be typical of the reconciliation of the deities. The other was an altar of Dionë, several times mentioned in the inscription published by Rangabé as situated at the eastern portico.[2] That this marine deity was in some way connected with the ruling legend of the temple can hardly be doubted, but we are unable to point out in what manner.

Pausanias appears also to have omitted a sixth altar, that of the θυηχόος, or sacrificer, the existence of which is attested both by Chandler's inscription and that of Rangabé. On this subject Leake says: "In each of the two great porticos there appears to have been an altar for fumigation, styled ὁ βωμὸς τοῦ θυηχοῦ;" drawing his conclusion that there were two altars from the circumstance that such an altar is twice mentioned in the former inscription (lines 79 and 188).[3] But he has altogether mistaken its character. It was not intended for fumigation, but was the altar of the chief sacrificer, ὁ θυηχόος (κατ' ἐξοχήν), who must have been one of the magnates of the hierarchy, since, as we have seen,[4] he had a seat in the theatre next but one to the priest of Dionysus. He was no doubt the priest who performed the great public sacrifices, for which only one altar would have been required. In the first passage cited by Leake the inspectors found in the prostasis towards the entrance (θύρωμα) that the altar of the sacrificer was not set up;[5] but there is nothing to show that they are speaking of the

---

[1] Above, p. 417, note [1].

[2] ῥαβδώσεως τῶν κιόνων τῶν πρὸς ἔω · τὸν κατὰ τὸν βωμὸν τὸν τρίτον ἀπὸ τοῦ βωμοῦ τῆς Διώνης.—No. 57 A, line 35 sq. Cf. l. 65, and B. l. 49, 64.

[3] vol. i. App. xvii. p. 584.

[4] Above, p. 319.

[5] ἐν τῇ προστάσει τῇ πρὸς τοῦ θυρώματος τὸν βωμὸν τοῦ θυηχοῦ ἄθετον.

northern prostasis, as Leake asserts (p. 581, cf. p. 577). In the second passage, immediately after speaking of the hyperthyrum, or cornice over the lintel, *at the eastern entrance* (τῷ πρὸς ἕω), they proceed to say that there are stones of such and such dimensions for the altar of the Θυηχόος;[1] which accords very well with the notice in the first passage, that the altar had not been put together, and leads to the inference, therefore, that by θύρωμα, in the first passage, was meant the eastern entrance. The allusion to the altar of the Θυηχόος in Rangabé's inscription (No. 57 A, line 62) also shows it to have been in the eastern portico, since the whole passage, both what precedes and what follows, relates to the fluting of the pillars of that portico.

We have already explained what appears to us to be the reason why Pausanias, before he has finished his description of the temple of Polias, flies off at a tangent to speak of the sea water which was found in a different part of the building; viz. that he was led to do so rather by the connection of the subject, than by the connection of the parts of the building. M. Beulé explains his somewhat eccentric method in a rather different, and perhaps more ingenious, way, but substantially to the same effect; and makes him actually pay a visit to the objects which have attracted his attention. He supposes that Pausanias, after arriving under the portico of the temple of Athena, mentions the altars which decorated the façade and the pictures attached to the walls of the pronaos, but does not yet enter the temple. He alludes first of all to the well of sea water and to the marks of the trident. These two marvels were calculated more than anything else to interest the credulous piety of Pausanias; his first question to his guide was probably respecting them. On the north side of the hexastyle portico was a small staircase, the traces of which are still visible. By this he descends to the northern portico, where he is shown the rock pierced by Poseidon. At the same time this second portico naturally suggests to him the idea of a second temple; and in the words "the edifice is double," I think, says M. Beulé, that I recognize the answer of his cicerone. He does

---

[1] . . οἷς τῷ ὑπερθύρῳ τῷ πρὸς ἕω ἡμίεργον · τῷ βωμῷ τῷ τοῦ Θυηχοῦ λίθοι Πεντελει-κοὶ μῆκος τετράποδες, κ.τ.λ. Rose, p. 206.

not enter the Pandroseium, because the passage leading from it to the cave of Poseidon was a secret one; but after surveying the revered mark of the trident through an opening in the floor of the portico, he reascends by the same staircase, and again finds himself in the pronaos of Athena Polias.[1]

Pausanias proceeds to describe the phenomenon as follows: "The sea water in the well is no great wonder, as it occurs in other inland places; but it is worth recording that when the south wind blows there is a sound of waves in the well. There is also in the rock the form of a trident; which, with the well, are said to be evidences of the contention of Poseidon for the country." This sound of waves is not altogether improbable, as there might have been, perhaps, some subterraneous passage through which the south wind penetrated and caused an agitation of the water in the well; unless indeed, as M. Beulé suggests, the priests superseded the efforts of Nature, and produced the sound by some artificial contrivance.

M. Tétaz, a French architect, who made the Erechtheium his especial study, and wrote a paper on it which has been published in the 'Revue Archéologique,' 1851, claims to have discovered this cave of Poseidon; and the supposed marks of the trident at the bottom of it may, according to him, still be seen. They consist of two irregular holes joined by a sort of fissure, which he thinks were probably a lusus naturæ. A trident should have made three; but ancient credulity did not criticise so closely, and implicitly believed the words of the priest. In the same cavern, now partly filled by a ruined cistern, was, it is supposed, the sea water, or θάλασσα Ἐρεχθηΐς, alluded to by Pausanias.[2]

The view of Tétaz was adopted by Thiersch, and also by the Athenian savans. Bötticher, however, who examined the spot with great care, is of opinion that the chasm was made with great violence, in the Turkish times, for the purpose of inserting a powder magazine; after which the spaces between the columns were built up. The apartment thus made was subsequently converted into a harem of the aga; the powder magazine was then removed, and the place which it occupied turned into a

---

[1] Beulé, L'Acropole, t. ii. p. 239 sq.   [2] Breton, Athènes, p. 164 sq.

lakes. The supposed trident marks, or two deep holes, connected by a
fissure, are still visible in the rock.[1]

Whether this excursus of Pausanias was an actual or only a mental
one, we will now accompany him back to the pronaos of Athena Polias.
We learn from the Lives of the Ten Orators[2] that the picture of the
Butadæ, which he there indicates, was painted by Ismenias of Chalcis,
and that there were also wooden images of Lycurgus, and of his sons
Habron, Lycurgus, and Lycophron, which Pausanias omits to mention.
They were done by Timarchus and Cephisodotus, sons of Praxiteles.
The picture was dedicated by Habron, who, being the eldest, succeeded
to the priesthood, but ceded it to his brother Lycophron. Wherefore
Habron was represented as handing him the trident, which hence
appears to have been one of the insignia of the priest of Poseidon-
Erechtheus.

After his digression about the sea water, Pausanias appears to enter
the temple of Athena Polias (c. 26, 7). This fact, however, can only
be inferred from his short dissertation upon the superior holiness of
this Athena, and from his mentioning the lamp which burnt in her
honour ; and which we must conclude was within the building, as it was
so constructed as to carry off the smoke through the roof. But the
temple itself he does not name till the commencement of the following
chapter. We know, however, from the express testimony of Strabo,[3]
that this lamp was in the temple of Polias.

The whole city of Athens, says Pausanias, besides the Acropolis, nay,
the whole of Attica, is sacred to Athena ; and though other gods may
be worshipped in the various demi, that does not diminish their veneration for her. And the most holy image of her, common to them all
before they were collected together into one state, is that now in the
Acropolis, which was then called πόλις, or 'the city.' And this
supplies us with the reason for her surname of Polias. There is a tradition connected with the image, continues Pausanias, that it fell from
heaven ; but he prudently declines to inquire whether this was so or

---

[1] Bötticher, Bericht, p. 191 sq.   [2] Reiske's Plutarch, t. ix. p. 355.
[3] In a passage before cited, lib. ix. p. 396.

not. It may be added that the image was made of olive wood;[1] and it was for this, and not for Pheidias' splendid statue in the Parthenon, that the peplus was woven. Callimachus made the golden lamp for the goddess. It was replenished with oil on a certain day in every year, which sufficed till the same day recurred, though the lamp was kept burning day and night. It had a wick of Carpasian flax, which is the only sort that fire does not consume. The smoke was carried off through a bronze palm-tree over the lamp, which reached to the roof. This shows that the temple of Athena Polias was a covered one, while that of Pandrosus, as we shall see, appears to have been hypæthral.

Pausanias then proceeds to relate (c. 27, 1) that there was in the temple of Polias, which he now names for the first time, a wooden Hermes, said to have been an anathema of Cecrops. It could not be seen at the first glance, for the myrtle boughs round about it.[2] It was customary to deck the images of the gods with boughs, hair, garlands, &c.;[3] and the myrtle was sacred to Hermes as a χθόνιος θεός, or infernal deity. We cannot explain why he should have been placed in this temple, except that he appears to have been one of the original deities of the Cecropia, unless indeed he be here as conductor of the dead. For the whole building appears to have had a funereal character, as we shall see further on.[4] We may mention that near the Erechtheium is still seen a very archaic Hermes, bearing a calf on his shoulders. The original gods of Cecropia (ἀκραῖοι θεοί) appear to have been Zeus, Hermes, and Poseidon; to which were afterwards added Athena and Hephæstus. Apollo was a still later addition, and had no shrine on the Acropolis itself, but in the grotto under it (Ἀπόλλων ὑπακραῖος).[5] It seems probable that there was also a statue of Erechtheus in the temple, though Pausanias does not here mention it. For in another place he says that there was such a statue at Athens, and that it was one of the most famous works of Myron.[6]

---

[1] ἐξ ἐλαίας.—Demosth. c. Androt. p. 134, Reiske, and scholia, p. 597.

[2] The vulgate has εὐσύνοπτον, which makes no convenient sense; and we must therefore read, with Facius, οὐ for εὐ.

[3] See Paus. ii. 11, 6; iii. 26, 1; viii. 39, fin.

[4] See Siebelis, ad loc. and Mommsen, Heortologie, p. 15, note.

[5] Bötticher, in Philologus, B. xxii. S. 93.

[6] lib. ix. 30, 1.

Among the ancient anathemata in the temple worth mentioning, continues Pausanias, was a folding chair, the work of Dædalus. Such chairs appear to have been common enough among the Athenians,[1] and therefore we may suppose that this was remarkable only for its antiquity and some peculiarity of workmanship. From the Persian spoils was the breastplate of Masistius, who commanded the cavalry at Platæa, and a scimitar said to have belonged to Mardonius. Pausanias, however, appears to have entertained some doubts respecting the genuineness of the scimitar. Masistius, he observes, was killed, I know, by Athenian knights; but as Mardonius was opposed to the Lacedæmonians, and killed by a Spartan,[2] the Athenians could hardly have obtained the scimitar, nor would the Lacedæmonians have allowed them to carry it off. We have before adverted to this scimitar as stolen by Glaucetes,[3] and at all events, therefore, that seen by Pausanias may have been an imitation. Leake is of opinion[4] that the δίφρος ἀργυρόπους, or silver-footed throne of Xerxes, was also in the temple of Polias, referring to Demosthenes (in Timoc. p. 741, Reiske), and the scholia on the third Olynthiac (p. 35, rather 39). But Demosthenes only says that these objects were taken "from the Acropolis," which might embrace either temple, and the scholiast mentions no place whatever. These authorities therefore cannot invalidate the direct testimony of Harpocration and Suidas, that the throne was in the Parthenon; though it must be allowed that the later grammarians not unfrequently confound the two goddesses.

Pausanias next adverts to the sacred olive tree, which is a sign that he is approaching the temple of Pandrosus, though he has not yet entered it. All they tell us concerning it, he observes, is, that it is a proof of the goddess's contention for the country. They also say that when the Medes fired the city, the olive too was burnt; but that it sprouted two cubits on the same day; which is an illustration of the old maxim that a story loses nothing by the repeating of it. For in the account of Herodotus it sprouts only one cubit, and that on the

[1] See Ælian, V. H. iv. 22.
[2] By Acimnestus, Herod. ix. 64.
[3] Above, p. 412.
[4] vol. i. p. 154, note 3.

second day.[1] The olive appears to have been called ἀστή, or 'the citizen,' perhaps as an endearing appellation; also πάγκυφος, or 'the crooked,' from its dwarfed shape.[2]

Pausanias now appears to enter the temple, for he proceeds to describe its situation (27, 3). The temple of Pandrosus, he says, adjoins that of Athena; but that is all the information he gives us about it, for he again flies off to the legend of Pandrosus and her sisters. He probably entered the Pandroseium by means of an internal communication which it had with that of Polias. That there existed such a communication we know from a prodigy related by Philochorus; that a dog having entered the temple of Athena Polias, and penetrated (or descended) into that of Pandrosus, jumped upon the altar of Zeus Herceius, which lay under the sacred olive, though it is an ancient custom among the Athenians to exclude all dogs from the Acropolis.[3] From which few words we learn three things: that there was, as we have said, a communication between the two temples; that the olive was in the Pandroseium; and that under it was an altar of Zeus Herceius. This last circumstance corroborates the inference which might have been drawn from the presence of the olive alone, that the temple was hypaethral, for in such open places the altar of Zeus Herceius seems always to have stood.[4] The Pandroseium probably also contained a shrine of Thallo, one of the Horae; for Pausanias, in another place, informs us that she was worshipped by the Athenians in conjunction with Pandrosus.[5]

We will conclude Pausanias' account of the Erechtheium by quoting what he has to say of the Arrephoroi or Errephoroi, in connection with

---

[1] lib. viii. 55.

[2] ἔλεγον οὖν οἶον Ἀθηναῖοι . . . καὶ ἀστὴν ἐλαίαν, τὴν ἐκεῖθεν· καὶ μάλιστα τὴν ἐξ ἀκροπόλεως καὶ ἱεράν.—Eustath. ad Odyss. α', p. 1388; cf. Hesych. voc. ἀστή and πάγκυφος.

[3] κύων εἰς τὸν τῆς Πολιάδος νεὼν εἰσελθοῦσα, καὶ δῦσα εἰς τὸ Πανδρόσιον, ἐπὶ τὸν βωμὸν ἀναβᾶσα τοῦ Ἑρκείου Διός, τὸν ὑπὸ

τῇ ἐλαίᾳ, κατέκειτο· πάτριον δ' ἔστι τοῖς Ἀθηναίοις, κύνα μὴ ἀναβαίνειν εἰς ἀκρόπολιν. —Ap. Dionys. Hal. De Dinarcho, iii. (Rhet. et Critic. p. 181, ed. Oxon. 1704).

[4] Ὅμηρος δὲ τὴν αὐλὴν ἀεὶ τάττει ἐπὶ τῶν ὑπαίθρων τόπων, ἔνθα ἦν ὁ τοῦ Ἑρκείου Ζηνὸς βωμός.—Athen. v. 15.

[5] lib. ix. 35. 1.

it. He adverts to it as a subject not generally known, and which excited his surprise. Not far from the temple of Polias dwelt two young virgins, whom the Athenians called Arrephoroi. These remain with the goddess some time —that is, from one Arrephoria to another and when the festival has arrived, they do as follows :—They put on their heads during the night what the priestess of Athena gives them to carry, neither she nor they knowing what it is. The girls descend into an enclosure within the city,[1] not far from the temple of Aphroditë in the Gardens, which has a natural subterraneous passage through it. Here they leave what they had brought, and carry away instead a well wrapped-up parcel. After this, these virgins are dismissed, and others are brought into the Acropolis in their place (c. 27, 4).

Mœris is at variance with Pausanias about the Attic name for these damsels, and distinctly states that the Athenians called them 'Ἐρρηφόροι, as bearing the dew to Hersë.[2] Ludwig Ross denies that the etymology of the word is connected with Hersë;[3] and the aspirate in the latter seems to favour this opinion. But, in early times, this was very fluctuating; and in Homer we always find it written with the lenis (ἐέρση).[4] The substitution of the ῥ for the σ need not detain us; ἔρρη and ἔρση are the same word. The method in which the girls executed their mission seems to bear out the etymology of Mœris. Could there be a more striking indication of its nature than that they should set out before the sun was risen, and while the dew was falling, to gather it up from the bosom of the earth, thus carrying out the allegory connected with the early history of Athena Polias? We may perhaps therefore translate the word by 'the dew-bearers.' Ross admits[5] that ἐρρηφόροι is the form used in Attic inscriptions, and in support of ἀρρηφόροι only states that it appears to be the form commonly used

---

[1] We have already remarked (above, p. 281) that the walls on this side did not exist in the time of Pausanias, and therefore he calls the temple of Venus in the gardens, ἐν τῇ πόλει.

[2] ἐρρηφόροι Ἀττικοί, αἱ τὴν δρόσον φέ-

ρουσαι τῇ Ἔρσῃ, ἥτις μία ἦν τῶν Κεκροπίδων.—Mœris in voc.

[3] Archäol. Aufs. i. 86.

[4] Il. xxiii. 598; Od. xiii. 245, &c.

[5] loc. cit. note 4.

by writers. But what is the force of such a plea against the testimony of Mœris and the practice of inscriptions? And the word could hardly have been a compound from ἄρριχος, as he and others have supposed.

It is commonly said by writers on Athenian antiquities that there were four Errephoroi, and that two of them were employed in superintending the weaving of the peplus of Athena, whilst the other two performed the office just described.[1] But we have seen that Pausanias mentions only two; and this number is confirmed by Harpocration and the Etymologicum. It appears from these authorities that four Errephoroi were chosen by the people on account of their noble birth, but of these only two were selected; and it was these same two who were dismissed at the end of the year in the manner described by Pausanias. If there had been four, as is commonly supposed, then we have no account how two of them were employed, or in what manner they were dismissed. But as this is a new view, we must here state the grounds for our opinion. First, then, Pausanias says positively that only two virgins dwelt near the temple of Polias, and speaks only of two being dismissed; whereas if there had been four, he would surely have given some account of the other two whilst describing a custom that was quite new to him. Again, the article in the Etym. M., which is the fullest on the subject, runs as follows: Ἀρρηφορεῖν, τὸ χρυσῆν (l. λευκὴν) ἐσθῆτα φορεῖν, καὶ χρυσία· τέσσαρες δὲ παῖδες ἐχειροτονοῦντο κατ᾽ εὐγένειαν, ἀρρηφόροι, ἀπὸ ἐτῶν ἕπτα μέχρις ἕνδεκα· τούτων δὲ δύο διεκρίνοντο, αἳ [διὰ] τῆς ὑφῆς τοῦ ἱεροῦ πέπλου ἤρχοντο (l. ἦρχον) καὶ τῶν ἄλλων τῶν περὶ αὐτόν· λευκὴν δὲ ἐσθῆτα ἐφόρουν καὶ χρυσία.

The Etymologist is here explaining the word ἀρρηφορεῖν, which seems to have derived a secondary meaning of wearing white garments with gold ornaments, no doubt from this being the ordinary attire of the Errephoroi. But this dress was only worn by two, who superintended the peplus; and these must have been the same two mentioned by Pausanias as carrying the parcel, for he calls them ἀρρηφόροι. Had there been four actually employed, the Etymologist also leaves the

---

[1] See Preller, Greek Myth. i. 167; art. Arrephoria in Smith's Dict. of Ant. &c.

functions of the other two unexplained. The people returned four candidates, two of whom were selected for actual service.

The corrections in the above article, and the consequent suppression of the preposition διά, are taken from the article of Harpocration, which is much to the same purpose, only he does not state the age of the girls, and adds that the gold ornaments worn became sacred to the goddess. From an article in Bekker's 'Anecdota' (Ἀῤῥηφορεῖν, p. 202) we also learn that the Errephoroi served from the age of seven to eleven; that is, the four years which intervened between each great Panathenaïc festival. The women, or girls, who actually wove the peplus were called Ergastinæ (ἐργαστῖναι).[1] The web appears to have been begun at the festival of Hephæstus, called Chalceia.[2] One of the women in the 'Lysistrata' of Aristophanes (v. 641 sqq.) says that she was an Errephoros as early as the age of seven, that she was Aletris, or preparer of the cakes for Diana, at ten, and still a handsome young maiden when canephoros. The Errephoroi appear to have used a sort of cake, or bread, called ἀνάστατος.[3] We need only add that they seem to have had a playground near the temple,[4] in which was a statue of the orator Isocrates represented as a youth on a race-horse; his tomb, as we have already said, was at the Cynosarges. A sort of terrace of considerable size, recently discovered, on the south side of the Erechtheium, extending towards the Parthenon, and formed of polygonal blocks of limestone, is supposed to have been the sphæristra, or playground, of the Errephoroi, mentioned in the Lives of the Ten Orators.[5] The Errephoroi seem to have been regarded with distinguished honour, and the statue of one named Apollodora appears to have been dedicated by the senate and people to Athena Polias.[6]

Pausanias says nothing of the snake, which, as we learn from other authorities, was kept in the temple. At the time of the Persian war

---

[1] Hesych. in voc. Meursius (Att. Lect. ii. 12) seems to be wrong in saying that the Errephoroi wove it. They only superintended the work.

[2] Etym. M. voc. χάλκεια.

[3] Athen. iii. 80; Suidas, voc. Ἀνάστατος.

[4] ἐν τῇ σφαιρίστρᾳ τῶν Ἀῤῥηφόρων.— Vit. X. Or. t. ix. p. 338, Reiske. But the whole passage is doubtful.

[5] Bötticher, Bericht, p. 206 sqq.

[6] Boeckh, Corp. Ins. Gr. No. 431.

it deserted the cella, as appeared from the food not being touched, which, according to Plutarch, was offered to it every day. Themistocles, in one of his orations to induce the people to take to their ships, affirmed from this omen that Athena had left the city and was leading them to the sea.[1] Herodotus relates the story rather differently, and as if he doubted whether the snake were anything but a fiction. They offered it food, he says, consisting of honey cakes, *once a month*, as if it really existed.[2] But its reality is testified by several authorities. One of the women in the 'Lysistrata' says that she has not been able to sleep in the Acropolis since she saw the snake:

> ἀλλ' οὐ δύναμαι 'γωγ' οὐδὲ κοιμᾶσθαι ἐν πόλει
> ἐξ οὗ τὸν ὄφιν εἶδον τὸν οἰκουρόν ποτε.—v. 758 sq.

> " I have not had a wink of sleep up here
> After I saw the snake that guards the place."

Where the scholiast observes that this was the holy snake which guarded the temple of Athena. Demosthenes, when driven into exile, is said to have exclaimed, "O Polias, my mistress, how canst thou delight in three such horrible beasts, the owl, the snake, and the people!"[3] And Philostratus speaks of it as existing in his time.[4]

The singular arrangement of the Erechtheium, comprehending two temples under one roof, the beauty of its architecture, and the unusual style of the southern prostasis, or portico, with the canephoroi substituted for pillars, might, one would have thought, have drawn a word or two of observation from Pausanias; but he passes by with his usual reticence on architectural subjects, although the antiquity of the building, and especially the portico just named, might surely have afforded him a peg on which to hang some of those anecdotes in which he delighted. It appears from the inscriptions before cited recording the progress of the building, that the prostasis, or portico, in question was called the Cecropium. Thus in Chandler's inscription we find it stated that the south wall remained unpolished, except the portion of it in the prostasis at the Cecropium. Now, as there is only one prostasis

[1] Vit. Them. c. 10.   [2] lib. viii. 41.   [3] Vit. X. Or.
[4] Icon. ii. xvii. p. 837 ; cf. Etym. M. voc. δράκαυλος.

on the south side, this indication alone would suffice to fix the site of
the Cecropeium ; but, to put the matter beyond all doubt, it is stated
further on that at the prostasis at the Cecropeium the roofing stones
above the corœ wanted finishing : thus showing that the canephoroi,
which in the inscription are called simply corœ, belonged to the Cecropeium. This part of the building, as we have before observed, is also
mentioned in Rangabé's inscription.[1] It was entered by a flight of
steps from the western corridor. It can hardly be doubted that at this
spot was the traditionary tomb of Cecrops, who, as we learn from
several authorities, was buried near the shrine of Athena.[2] Erechtheus,
or Erichthonius, was also said to have been interred within the sacred
precincts of the temple,[3] and some writers are of opinion that the hall
of the corœ was his tomb.[4] But then what are we to call the Cecropeium mentioned in the inscription ? It seems not improbable that
the Erechtheium was originally the palace of the Cecropidæ. In the
ancient times of Athens it was customary to inter the master of the
house near his own door, and, as we have before had occasion to remark,
there are still traces of this custom among the remains of private
houses which cover the western hills of Athens. The traditions connected with the family communicated to the spot a sacred character ;
Erechtheus and his sisters had come to be regarded as divinities, and
at last the building (οἴκημα) was converted into a temple, including
the shrine of Athena, a goddess so closely connected with the history
of the race.

The substructure of the Cecropeium rises to a height of about 6 feet,

---

[1] τὸν τοῖχον τὸν πρὸς νότου ἀνέμου ἀκα-
τάξεστον, πλὴν τοῦ ἐν τῇ προστάσει τῇ πρὸς
τῷ Κεκροπίῳ.—Chandler's Inscr. line 56
sqq. ἐπὶ τῇ προστάσει τῇ πρὸς τῷ Κεκροπίῳ ἔδει τοὺς λίθους ὀροφιαίους τοὺς ἐπὶ
τῶν κόρων ἐπεργάσασθαι ἄνωθεν.—Ibid. 83.
sqq. Κεκρύπιον — Κεκροπικά, Rangabé's
Inscr. No. 56, line 24 sq. B.

[2] καὶ γὰρ Ἀθήνῃσιν, ὡς Ἀντίοχος ἐν τῇ
ἐννάτῃ γέγραφεν ἱστορίᾳ ἄνω γε ἐν τῇ ἀκροπόλει Κέκροπός ἐστι τάφος, παρὰ τὴν Πο-

λιοῦχον αὐτήν.—Theodoret. Therap. viii.
iv. "In historiarum nono Athenis in
Minervio memorat Cecropem esse manda-
tum terræ."—Arnob. adv. Gent. vi. p. 66.

[3] Ἐριχθονίου δὲ ἀποθανόντος, καὶ ταφέν-
τος ἐν τῷ τεμένει τῆς Ἀθηνᾶς.—Apollod. iii.
14, 7. τί δαί, Ἐριχθόνιος οὐχὶ ἐν τῷ νεῷ
τῆς Πολιάδος κεκήδευται.—Clem. Protrept.
p. 13.

[4] Mommsen, Heortologie, p. 15, note.

and is about 25 feet long and 12 deep. Upon this basis six coræ, or young women, four in front and one at each side, supported an entablature about 3 feet in height, composed only of an architrave and cornice; the frieze having been omitted, probably because it would appear too heavy for the supporting figures; hence they have the appearance of carrying a daïs. These figures, which are fine specimens of sculpture, were long called caryatides, but it is now the fashion to call them canephoroi, as supposed to be representations of the maidens who figured in the Pan-athenaïc procession. The inscriptions, as we have seen, simply call them κόραι, or 'the maidens.' At the time of Stuart's visit, five of these figures were still in their places;[1] the sixth was long supposed to have been carried off by the Venetians, and to have found its way into the Vatican. One of the remaining five was carried off by Lord Elgin, together with a column of the eastern portico, and these are now in the British Museum; another was overthrown in the Turkish bombardment of the Acropolis, in 1827, and the head lost. This, however, was subse-quently found, and the figure re-erected by M. Pittakys. The shattered remains of the figure supposed to be in the Vatican were also discovered during the excavations. The torso was tolerably perfect, but the lower limbs were so mutilated that they had to be remade before the statue could be set up in its place. It had probably been knocked over in the Venetian bombardment. The figure carried off by Lord Elgin was for some time replaced by a terra-cotta one sent from England; for which a marble statue, executed by a Greek artist, has since been sub-stituted.[2] The subjoined diagram represents the relative positions of the figures:

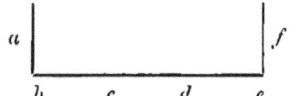

where the figures *a, b, c,* are in their original places; *e* is in England; *d* is the one overthrown in the Turkish bombardment; and *f* the one missing in the time of Stuart, but since found in fragments and restored.

[1] Ant. of Athens, vol. ii. ch. ii. p. 18.   [2] Breton, p. 174.

[3] Ross, Archäol. Aufs. i. 122.

The general appearance of the Cecropeium will be familiar to the Londoner from the imitation of it at the new St. Pancras Church.

Other portions of the Erechtheium also suffered severely during the siege by the Turks in 1827. On this occasion three columns of the northern portico, with their entablature, were overthrown, together with a large portion of the western wall, and three of the engaged columns. But this damage has been made good under the superintendence of M. Pittakys.[1] When we consider the vicissitudes which the building has undergone, it is almost surprising that so much of it should remain. It has been thought to have been converted by the Byzantines into a church; but it is objected to this view that, during the Frankish domination, the Duke appears to have lived in it.[2] In the time of Spon and Wheler it was a Turkish seraglio; the travellers, therefore, were not admitted into the interior, and Wheler could only conjecture that here might have been the temples of Minerva Polias and Pandrosus; but he seems to have had no notion that they were included in the Erechtheium. At that time the Cecropeium seems to have been converted into a chamber, into the wall of which the canephoroi were built, and Spon conjectured that they might be the Graces of Socrates.[3] About a century afterwards, in the time of Stuart, it had been converted into a military magazine. He describes it as follows: "These temples are now in a very ruinous condition. Those of Erechtheus and Minerva have at present no roof or covering of any kind. The wall which separated them, and that by which the pronaos, or passage to the Pandroscium (Cecropeium), was parted off from the temple of Minerva, are so demolished that hardly any traces of them remain, except where they joined the side walls. The pavements are so encumbered with large blocks of marble and variety of rubbish as to render the inside almost impassable, and a more particular disquisition there fruitless. The Pandroseium, though it has suffered least, is filled up to a great height in the same manner, and one of the caryatides is wanting. We found the portico of Minerva Polias (by which he means

[1] Rangabé, Ant. Hell. *préf.*   Laborde, Athènes, p. 6.
[2] Mommsen, Athen. Christ. c. vi. No. 37;   [3] Wheler's 'Journey,' p. 364 sq.

2 F

the northern portico) walled up, and being a magazine of military stores, all entrance into it was denied us."[1]

It will be seen from this description that Stuart took the temples of Erechtheus and Athena Polias to be separate buildings, and was consequently led to place the Pandroseium where the Cecropeium is now held to have been. In one respect he saw the building under more favourable circumstances than Wheler, since the Cecropeium, as shown in his view, had been restored to its original state, by the pulling down of the wall into which the canephoroi had been built. The roofless state of the Pandroseium, which he calls the temple of Minerva, might not have been the effect of dilapidation, if it was originally hypæthral. On the whole he appears to have seen the building, as to the exterior at least, in a tolerably perfect state, to judge from his view of it, and the restoration which he has given. From this last (pl. iv.) it will be seen, that though the two temples were on a different level this was compensated, so far as the porticos were concerned, by the superior tallness of the columns of the northern portico, so that the roof of the building was throughout of the same height. Consequently the frieze of black Eleusiniac marble was also carried round the building at the same level. The remainder of the building is of Pentelic marble. On the black frieze were fixed, as we have before had occasion to observe, small figures of Parian marble. Some of these are described in Rangabé's inscription before cited; in which we find mentioned, a young man near a breastplate, two horses, one with its back turned and kicking, a chariot, a youth, and two horses harnessing, a man beating a horse, a man near an altar leaning upon a staff, a girl prostrate before a woman, &c.[2] The holes in the frieze by means of which the figures were fixed are still visible; and in the recent excavations round the Erechtheium many fragments of the figures themselves have been discovered. They are 1 ft. 6 in. to 2 ft. high, corresponding with the height of the frieze, sculptured in bas-relief on one side, and on the other flat, to allow of their being fixed on the frieze.[3] From the custom of adorning a frieze

---

[1] vol. ii. ch. ii. p. 18. [2] Ant. Hell. vol. i. No. 57, lines 1—22.

[3] Beulé, L'Acropole, ii. 283 sq.

with such figures (ζῶα) it obtained the name of ζωφόρος. M. Beulé remarks that the frieze would have presented a sombre aspect unless the figures had been coloured. But this effect would only be a further confirmation of the opinion of some writers respecting the funereal character of the building. We find, however, a white κρηπίς to a wall of black marble in the temple at Olympia.[1] That the upper members at least of the architecture were coloured and gilded appears from the same inscription. Thus we find charges for painting the ceiling, the cornice of the architrave, for gilding the shells, the eyes of the volutes, &c.[2]

We will now accompany Pausanias in his further walk. There is, says he, at the temple of Athena a statue of an old woman named Euöris, calling herself, in the inscription, deaconess (διάκονος) to Lysimachë, about a cubit in height (c. 27, 4). This statue and the following ones appear to have been in the temenos which extended for a considerable distance before the west front of the temple. The Lysimachë here mentioned is probably she who was priestess of Athena sixty-four years.[3] From the same passage of Pliny the statue of Euöris appears to have been the work of Demetrius, whose portraits are said to have been more faithful than flattering.[4] The priestesses of Athena Polias, like the priests of Erechtheus, were of the race of the Eteobutadæ.[5] They appear to have been entitled to certain offerings; as a measure of wheat and barley, and an obol, on the occasion of deaths and births.[6] By a somewhat singular law, they were forbidden to eat new cheese, unless it were of home growth.[7] There were also two statues of men standing up as if to fight, and the ciceroni called one of them Erechtheus and the other Eumolpus; and yet, continues Pausanias, nobody acquainted with Athenian antiquities is ignorant that it was Immaradus, son of Eumolpus, whom Erechtheus killed. But, as Leake observes, according to the testimony of Apollodorus,[8] it was Eumolpus himself.

---

[1] Pausan. v. 11, 5.

[2] Rangabé, Ant. Hell. t. i. Nos. 56, 57.

[3] Plin. H. N. xxxiv. s. 76; Plutarch, t. viii. p. 114, Reiske. The text of Pausanias varies. We have followed Bekker.

[4] Quint. xii. 10, s. 9.

[5] Æschin. De falsa Leg. p. 313, Reiske.

[6] Aristot. Œcon. ii. 2, 4.

[7] Strabo, p. 394.

[8] Biblioth. iii. 15, 4.

At the threshold were other statues;[1] namely, Tolmides, a great Athenian captain, and the soothsayer who prophesied to him. Here also were some ancient images of Athena, which were burnt when the Persians captured the Acropolis; they must have been of bronze, as Pausanias proceeds to remark that the fire had not melted anything away from them, but had only rendered them of a darker colour and less able to bear a blow. Here also was a boar hunt, but he did not know whether it was the Calydonian boar; the combat of Heracles and Cycnos, whom Heracles slew near the river Peneus; Theseus removing the rock and carrying off the slippers and sword of his father Ægeus, the whole in bronze except the rock. Also another group, dedicated by the Marathonians, of Theseus sacrificing to Athena the bull of which he had delivered their country.

Pausanias could not tell why the Athenians should have set up here a statue of Cylon, who aimed at being their tyrant, unless it were on account of his beauty and the Olympic victory which he gained in the *Diaulos*, or from his having married the daughter of Theagenes, tyrant of Megara (c. 28, 1).[2] But might it not rather have been by way of expiation for the outrage committed on the goddess by the murder of Cylon, or at all events some of his followers, who had taken refuge at her altar? Pausanias himself relates further on how not only the murderers, but also their posterity, became accursed in the sight of the goddess (ἐναγεῖς τῆς θεοῦ).[3] Epimenides being sent for from Crete, among other methods of expiation, advised the erection of altars to Contumely and Impudence.[4] The spot where they stood

[1] Siebelis in his note on this probably corrupt passage, thinks that Tolmides and the soothsayer were carved in bas-relief on the base of the preceding group; but the term ἀνδριάντες seems hardly applicable to a bas-relief. Leake (i. 157) represents them as statues standing on this base; which would have presented a rather ludicrous appearance. It appears to me that the words ἐπὶ δὲ τοῦ βάθρου have no relation to the group previously mentioned, but

to the threshold, or perhaps stylobate, of the temple.

[2] For the affair of Cylon see above, p. 71 sq. [3] lib. vii. 25, 1.

[4] "Nam illud vitiosum Athenis, quod, Cylonio scelere expiato, Epimenide Crete suadente, fecerunt Contumeliæ fanum et Impudentiæ." —Cic. De Leg. ii. 11, 28. They seem to have been typical of the deed: Phot. Lex. in Θεὸς ἡ Ἀναίδεια; Diog. Laërt. i. 110.

appears to have obtained the name of the CYLONEIUM, from its having been the scene of the murder.[1] In the neighbourhood of the Erechtheium, several sculptures, bases, and inscriptions have been discovered, which however in general present nothing very interesting. One of the inscriptions bears the name of Sophocles, and seems to relate to some military achievement.[2]

Besides the objects already mentioned, there were also two other famous works of art in the Acropolis, made from the tithes of spoils taken in war (c. 28, 2). One of these, from the booty captured at Marathon, was the bronze Athena, the work of Pheidias. The battle of the Lapithae and Centaurs was engraved on the shield by Mys; but the designs for this and for the other ornaments of the shield were sketched by Parrhasius, the son of Euenor. The point of the spear and the crest of the helmet of this Athena might be seen at sea on approaching Athens from Cape Sunium.

Many of the interpreters of Pausanias make him say that these objects could actually be seen from Sunium; but Leake has pointed out that the Acropolis does not come into sight till Cape Zoster is passed; and even from there it would require good eyes to discern such small objects. It is evident, therefore, that Pausanias only means that they were visible when sailing up from Sunium. Leake also shows that in order to be seen over the roof of the Parthenon, the statue must have been at least 75 ft. high; the roof of that temple being 70 ft. higher than the platform of the statue.[3] These colossal proportions are alluded to by Demosthenes, who calls the statue the great bronze Athena. But he is at variance with Pausanias about the funds from which the expenses of it were defrayed, and says it was by contributions of the Greeks.[4] The

---

[1] οὗ ('Ησύχου) τὸ ἱερόν ἐστι παρὰ τὸ Κυδώνιον, ἐκτὸς τῶν ἐννέα πυλῶν.—Polemo, ap. schol. Soph. Œdip. Col. v. 489. For Κυδώνιον, O. Müller aptly reads Κυλώνειον in Rienäcke's German translation of Leake's work, p. 455.

[2] See Beulé, L'Acropole, ii. p. 299 sqq.

[3] Topography of Athens, vol. i. pp. 351

and 631.

[4] ταῦτα τὰ γράμματα . . . παρὰ τὴν χαλκὴν τὴν μεγάλην Ἀθηνᾶν ἐν δεξιᾷ ἕστηκεν· ἣν ἀριστεῖον ἡ πόλις τοῦ πρὸς τοὺς βαρβάρους πολέμου, δόντων τῶν Ἑλλήνων τὰ χρήματα ταῦτα, ἀνέθηκε.—De fals. leg. p. 428, Reiske.

colossal size of the statue may also be inferred from the traces of the pedestal which still remains on the pavement. These are between 22 ft. and 23 ft. in length, and rather more than 15 ft. in breadth.[1] They are situated about midway between the Erechtheium on the east, and the Propylæa on the west, and at a distance of about 120 ft. from the latter. The pedestal, however, did not lie exactly parallel with the line of the Propylæa, but a few degrees more to the south, so that the statue would have regarded the entrance in a slightly oblique direction.

ATHENA PROMACHUS. COIN FROM LEAKE.

This statue was called ATHENA PROMACHUS, as we learn from the scholiast on Demosthenes' speech against Androtion;[2] who enumerates the three statues of Athena on the Acropolis; and says that that of Polias, the most ancient one, was made of olive wood; the second one, about which we are now concerned, he calls Promachus, and says that it was made from the spoils captured at Marathon; the third, named Parthenos, of which the materials were gold and ivory, was executed after the battle of Salamis, when the Athenians had grown richer. The situation of the statue near the Propylæa, with the Parthenon in the background, is shown by the annexed engraving from a coin in the public library at Paris, which will also convey an idea of its colossal size. Ovid has alluded both to this statue and that of the Parthenos, as the work of Pheidias :

" Arcis ut Actææ vel eburna vel ænea custos
Bellica Phidiaca stat dea facta manu." [3]

Zosimus is sometimes cited to show that the Promachus still continued in existence in the time of Alaric; who is said to have seen

---

[1] Beulé, L'Acropole, ii. p. 307.   [2] p. 597, Reiske.   [3] Ex Pont. iv. 1, 32.

Athena, as represented by the statue, walking round and inspecting the fortifications. The words will hardly justify such an inference,[1] though there is no inherent improbability in the fact of the existence of the statue, since the gold and ivory one lasted longer. Dr. Wordsworth has pointed out that Aristophanes, in the ' Knights,' alludes to these three Athenæ by their different characteristics—the ivory hand, the spear and shield, and the peplus. The Promachus is there called Πυλαιμάχος, and her shield and spear are ludicrously converted into a porridge pot and ladle :

KΛ.   ἐγὼ δ' ἔτνος γε πίσινον εὔχρων καὶ καλόν ·
       ἐτύρυνε δ' αὖθ' ἡ Παλλὰς ἡ Πυλαιμάχος.
ΛΛΛ.   ὦ Δῆμ', ἐναργῶς ἡ θεός σ' ἐπισκοπεῖ,
       καὶ νῦν ὑπερέχει σου χύτραν ζωμοῦ πλέαν.—v. 1172 sqq.

CLEON.   " And I peas-porridge well complexioned, rich,
          Founded by Pallas the Pylæmachus.
SAUSAGE } O Demos, clear it is our goddess guards thee—
SELLER. } She wields a bowl above thee, filled with soup."[2]

The same writer observes that a following line which alludes to Athena Polias :

καλῶς γ' ἐποίησε τοῦ πέπλου μεμνημένη.—1180,

is a convincing proof that the peplus was dedicated to her, and not to any other Athena. In the name Πυλαιμάχος, for Προμάχος, M. Beulé thinks that, as it is Cleon who speaks, there may be some allusion to Pylos.[3]

The other anathema from warlike spoils alluded to by Pausanias was a bronze chariot erected after the victory of the Athenians over the Bœotians and Chalcidenses in Eubœa. It was on the same occasion, as we learn from Herodotus,[4] that the chains to which we have before adverted (supra, p. 132) were hung up before the ancient Propylæa. According to Herodotus this anathema, which was a quadriga of bronze, stood on the left hand side after entering the Propylæa. On the basis

[1] ἐπιὼν 'Αλάριχος πανστρατίᾳ τῇ πόλει, τὸ μὲν τεῖχος ἑώρα περινοστοῦσαν τὴν Πρόμαχον 'Αθηνᾶν, ὡς ἔστιν αὐτὴν ὁρᾶν ἐν τοῖς ἀγάλμασιν.—Zosim. lib. v.

[2] Athens and Attica, ch. 16.

[3] L'Acropole, ii. 307.   [4] v 77.

was an inscription in verse, alluding both to the chains and to the quadriga, which was dedicated by way of tithe to Pallas. As the victory over the Bœotians and Chalcidians was several years previous to the capture of Athens by the Persians, this anathema must have escaped the fury of the barbarian fires.

Pausanias mentions two other anathemata on the Acropolis: a statue (ἀνδριάς) of Pericles, and an image (ἄγαλμα) of Athena; the latter one of the finest works of Pheidias, and called the Lemnian, because it was dedicated by the people of Lemnos. The statue of Pericles seems to be the same that he has already mentioned in connexion with that of his father Xanthippus (c. 25, 1); but as it stood separate from it, and on the other side (ἑτέρωθι), that is, on his *left* hand as he entered, while he was then only describing the objects on his *right*, this is perhaps the reason why he mentions it again on leaving the Acropolis, when it would have stood, with the bronze chariot and other objects, on his right. And this may afford an additional proof of the methodical order of his descriptions. The Lemnian Athena was probably that to which Pliny alludes[1] as being of such exquisite beauty as to receive its name from it; viz. as Leake suggests, καλλίμορφος. It is also mentioned in terms of admiration by Lucian, who adds that Pheidias deigned to put his name to it, from which we may infer that this was not a common practice with him.[2] We have already remarked (supra, p. 374), that this may perhaps be the statue to which Aristophanes gives the name of κλῃδοῦχος, or 'keeper of the keys.'

[1] H. N. xxxiv. 54.   [2] Imagines, 4 & 6.

CHAPTER XII.

Grotto of Apollo and Pan—Clepsydra—Votive offerings on north cliff—The Pelasgicum —Areiopagus—Temple of the Eumenides—Athenian Courts of Justice—Panathenaïc Ship—Objects omitted—Musæum Hill—Philopappus—The Pnyx—Nymphs' Hill—Athenian customs—Public processions.

PAUSANIAS now quits the summit of the Acropolis ; he does not however descend into the city, but describes some objects on the side of the rock. Immediately under the Propylæa was a spring of water, and near it in a cavern a sanctuary of Apollo and Pan (c. 28, 4). Here it was that Apollo was supposed to have been intimate with Creüsa, daughter of Erechtheus, according to a passage of Euripides already cited.[1] We learn from the same passage that this northern side of the Acropolis was called μακραὶ πέτραι, or 'the high rocks.' The sanctuary of Pan was of much more modern date, namely, the time of the battle of Marathon. Philippides,'the Athenian messenger despatched to solicit help from the Lacedæmonians, returned with an answer that they would come at the full of the moon, according to their custom ; but he related how Pan met him at Mount Parthenium, told him that he loved the Athenians, and that he would come to their aid at Marathon. It was on this account that he was worshipped. The story is also told by Herodotus (vi. 105), who calls the messenger Pheidippides. He adds that the Athenians instituted an annual festival to Pan, with a torch-race (λαμπάδι).

Lucian also frequently alludes to the abode of Pan in this cavern, with which he represents him but ill content, as being nothing more than a metic, or domiciled stranger. In the 'Bis Accusatus,' or 'Double

_____
[1] Ion, 10 sq. ; see also below, p. 445.

Accusation,' he makes him utter the following complaint, which we quote as affording a glimpse of the mode in which he was worshipped in his grotto: "On the whole I do not live among the Athenians in a manner worthy of me; but much beneath my expectations; and this after delivering them from that terrible invasion of the barbarians. They come up indeed two or three times a year, and sacrifice a he-goat that smells terribly strong, and then banquet on the flesh, making me a witness of their joviality, and honouring me with a little cold applause. Nevertheless I find their jokes and laughter tolerably agreeable."[1]

The spring mentioned by Pausanias in this chapter was the CLE-PSYDRA. Aristophanes, in some lines to which we have already adverted, alludes to this spring and its vicinity to the cave of Pan.[2] The scholiast on that passage says that the original name of the spring was Empedo, and that it was called Clepsydra, that is, embezzling or concealing its waters, because though they sometimes overflowed, at other times they were deficient.[3] According to Istros, quoted by a scholiast on the 'Birds' of Aristophanes, the former phenomenon occurred when the Etesian winds blew; and when they subsided, the spring became dry.[4] We learn from the same scholiasts that the water ran under ground into the Phaleric Bay, as was proved by a bloody phial, which had fallen into the spring, being found in the sea there. But the name of the spring was derived not from this subterraneous passage, but from its waters being sometimes deficient, or, as it were, embezzled; and therefore Dr. Words-worth seems hardly to be correct when he remarks (loc. cit.) that the

---

[1] Bis Acc. c. 10.

[2] ΜΥΡ. .... ποῦ γὰρ ἄν τις καί, τάλαν,
δράσειε τοῦθ'; ΚΙΝ. ὅπου τὸ
τοῦ Πανός, καλόν·
ΜΥΡ. καὶ πῶς ἔθ' ἀγνὴ δῆτ' ἂν ἔλθοιμ'
ἐς πόλιν;
ΚΙΝ. κάλλιστα δήπου, λουσαμένη τῇ
Κλεψύδρᾳ.—Lys. v. 910.

[3] ἐν τῇ ἀκροπόλει ἦν κρήνη ἡ Κλεψύδρα,
πρότερον Ἐμπεδὼ λεγομένη· ὠνομάσθη δὲ
Κλεψύδρα, διὰ τὸ ποτὲ μὲν πλημμυρεῖν,
ποτὲ δὲ ἐνδεῖν· ἔχει δὲ τὰς ῥύσεις ὑπὸ γῆν,

φέρουσα εἰς τὸν φλεγρεώδη λειμῶνα. The last words are evidently corrupt, and Dr. Wordsworth corrects ('Athens and Attica,' p. 69, note 3), εἰς τῶν Φαληρέων λιμένα.

[4] κρήνη ἐν 'Ακροπόλει ἡ Κλεψύδρα, ἧς Ἴστρος ἐν τῇ ιβ´ μέμνηται .... οὕτως δὲ ὠνόμασται, ἐπειδὴ.ἀρχομένων τῶν ἐτησίων πληροῦται, παυομένων δὲ λήγει .... εἰς ταύτην δέ φησιν ᾑματωμένην φιάλην πεσοῦσαν ὀφθῆναι ἐν τῷ Φαληρικῷ.—ad Av. v. 1693.

Clepsydra was "so termed from its being supposed to secrete some of its waters in the summer months of the year, to be conveyed by a subterranean vein into the Athenian harbour Phalerum." For, on the contrary, this seems to have been the period, if we are to believe the testimony of Istros, when the spring was abundant, probably owing to the action of the Etesian wind on the sea. The deficiency of water observed in the months of July and August, during the siege of the Acropolis in 1826, must consequently have been an extraordinary phenomenon; or, what is more probable, the nature of the spring may have become entirely changed in the course of so many centuries; if, indeed, the Clepsydra, and the spring now existing on the Acropolis, be the same thing, which we very much doubt. The water-clock at the Tower of the Winds was supplied, as we have before remarked, from the Clepsydra. Dr. Wordsworth gives the following account of the spring on the Acropolis:

"The only access to this fountain is from the enclosed platform of the Acropolis above it, and the approach to it is at the north of the northern wing of the Propylæa. Here we begin to descend a flight of forty-seven steps cut in the rock, but partially cased with slabs of marble. The descent is arched over with brick,[1] and opens out into a small subterranean chapel, dedicated to the Holy Apostles, with niches cut in its sides; here is a well surrounded with a peristomium of marble: below which is the water, now at the distance of about thirty feet.

"The Clepsydra in ancient times was, as now, accessible from the citadel. This will explain why in the 'Lysistrata' of Aristophanes (v. 377) the particular mode of defence is selected, which is there adopted by the besieged women in the Acropolis. The local objects suggested it. It was this fountain which supplied the women with its water to extinguish the fire, and drench the persons of their veteran besiegers beneath the wall. The same fountain has since served to supply a Greek water-clock and a Turkish mosque."[2]

---

[1] This brickwork seems to be comparatively modern, for, as represented on the coin, the steps lie open to the view, and most likely were not those here mentioned.

[2] Athens and Attica, p. 69 sq.

Herr Bötticher says that the water here still wells out and flows away, and that it has no salt or mineral taste, but is perfectly pure and fresh.[1] But the water of the Clepsydra appears to have been brackish; and indeed it is expressly so characterized by the scholiast on the 'Birds.'[2] Hence it seems to us that this spring can hardly have been the Clepsydra; but it may have been the vein which supplied the Enneacrunus; which fountain, as we have endeavoured to show, lay in this neighbourhood (see above, p. 222). Bötticher describes the well as quadrangular and constructed of large slabs of marble; and says it can be proved that till towards the end of the sixteenth century the water had an issue in the rock, under the grotto of Apollo, and that the leaden pipes which conducted it were shut with cocks. In ancient times it may have trickled down the rock into the agora, and hence have obtained the name of Callirrhoë, till Peisistratus collected its waters in a basin and converted it into the fountain Enneacrunus. In this view the Clepsydra would have been a neighbouring but distinct source. At all events, the testimony of Bötticher proves the possibility of an ancient spring of fresh water in this neighbourhood, and is therefore an additional argument for the Enneacrunus having been here. There could have been no access to this spring from the platform of the Acropolis in ancient times; for the drinking water on it was then preserved in cisterns. Thus Cylon, when besieged there, was obliged to make his escape for want of water;[3] and the same cause compelled the surrender of Aristion.[4] Hence we may infer that the opening and descent to the spring, and the construction of the marble well, was a plan adopted later, probably in the Byzantine times, to obviate this inconvenience; on which occasion the water that supplied the Enneacrunus may have been cut off, and thus have occasioned the destruction of a fountain that had been rendered useless.

For these reasons, we cannot coincide in Dr. Wordsworth's view, that this spring was the Clepsydra, and was always accessible from the

[1] Bericht, &c. p. 221, and Philologus, xxii. 73.

[2] φασὶ δὲ αὐτὴν ἀπέραντον βάθος ἔχειν,

τὸ δὲ ὕδωρ ἀλμυρόν.—loc. cit.

[3] Thucyd. i. 126.

[4] Plut. Sull. 14. See above, p. 161.

Acropolis. Being a spring of fresh water, it could not have been accessible in the time of Cylon and Aristion, for in that case they might have endured a siege. Had it been the Clepsydra, that is, a brackish spring, it would hardly have been worth while to make a well for it. With regard to the scene in the 'Lysistrata,' there is nothing to show that the woman procured her pitcher of water within the precincts of the Acropolis. On the contrary, she appears to have got it outside, probably at the Enneacrunus. For she says that she procured it at early dawn (κνεφαία, v. 327), that is, we may infer, before she entered the Acropolis, and that in doing so she was pushed about by a crowd of female slaves with their jugs. Consequently she must mean a public fountain of fresh water, and outside the Acropolis, for such a scene could hardly have occurred within it. That the Clepsydra was also outside, is plain from v. 913, quoted above; where Cinesias tells his wife that she may re-enter the Acropolis in a state of purity by washing herself in it. The spring was re-discovered in 1822, when General Odysseus enclosed it in the fortifications, by erecting a new bastion.

We need only add about the Clepsydra, that it seems to have been regarded as sacred; for when Mark Antony left Athens to take the field, he provided himself with a chaplet from the sacred olive, and a vessel of water from this spring.[1]

According to ancient descriptions, Apollo and Pan had their shrines in one and the same grotto. Thus Euripides, in his 'Ion,' alludes to the cave of Pan as the same in which Creüsa became a mother by Apollo:

> ὅταν αὐλείοις συρίζῃς,
> ὦ Πάν, τοῖσι ooῖs ἐν ἄντροις,
> ἵνα τεκοῦσά τις
> παρθένος, ὦ μελέα, βρέφος Φοίβῳ, κ.τ.λ.
>
> v. 500 sqq.

> "When thou, O Pan,
> Pipest in thy lofty cave,
> Where once a maid,
> Unfortunate! a child to Phœbus gave."

---

[1] Plut. Ant. 34.

And so Pausanias speaks of it as only one cave. But some modern investigators assert that there are two distinct grottoes, and that one faced the west, the other the north.[1] There may have been alterations in later times, and this cavern, like others, seems to have been made into a Christian chapel. M. Breton says that it was a chapel dedicated to S. Athanasius;[2] which seems to rest only on the authority of M. Pittakys.[3] Bötticher says that the floor of the cave had been terribly mutilated by force, so that every vestige of the site of the altar had vanished.[4] Traces of mortar along one half of the front showed that it had once been partially closed. On the rock inside the grotto, Göttling found traces of the name of Apollo.[5] He had here the surname of Hypacraeos (ὑπακραῖος), that is, 'under the height,' or 'under the Acropolis:' for the gods on the summit of it were called ἀκραῖοι.[6] We borrow from Dr. Wordsworth the following description of the grotto:

"Here probably was an imitative grove. Here Pan's statue was enshrined. It was perhaps that which was dedicated by Miltiades, and for which Simonides wrote the inscription,[7] and that now stands in the vestibule of the Public Library at Cambridge. What an unexpected migration! How many thoughts does it suggest! The cave measures about six yards in length, ten in height, and five in depth. Niches are cut in its rocky interior for the reception of statues and votive tablets, which have now disappeared, but have left their hollow sockets in the rock."[8]

---

[1] Wachsmuth, in Rh. Mus. 1868, p. 27; Bötticher, in Philol. xxii. p. 69. The latter appeals to Eurip. Ion, 493, to show that Apollo's grot neighboured on that of Pan (παραυλίζουσα). But the allusion is to the vicinity of the cave of Pan to the sanctuary of Agraulus.

[2] Athènes, p. 186.

[3] Ancienne Athènes, p. 153; cf. Mommsen, Athenæ Christianæ, p. 41.

[4] Bericht, p. 222. He here speaks of only one grotto, that of Pan.

[5] Philol. ib. p. 70, note.

[6] Pollux, ix. 40. According to Le Bas, the following inscription was found in the grotto: Πολύβιος—πολεμαρχήσας—᾽Απόλλωνι ὑπακρίῳ ἀνέθηκεν.—Attiq. sect. i. No. 114, p. 16.

[7] Which ran as follows:

τὸν τραγόπουν ἐμὲ Πᾶνα, τὸν ᾽Αρκάδα,
  τὸν κατὰ Μήδων,
τὸν μετ᾽ ᾽Αθηναίων στήσατο Μιλτιάδης.
      Anthol. i. p. 131, Brunck.

[8] Athens and Attica, p. 69.

These niches are not confined to the grotto, but extend over the whole northern cliffs of the Acropolis. Bötticher counted eighty of them, without including those in the grotto; while he could discover none on the other three sides of the Acropolis.[1] He attributes the superior veneration in which these northern cliffs appear to have been held to the Pelasgicum; but hardly, perhaps, with adequate reason; though that place was no doubt regarded with a peculiar veneration. And as its site and purpose have been the subjects of much controversy, we will here say a few words about it.

When Pausanias is on the point of leaving the Acropolis, he remarks (c. 28, 3) that the Pelasgi, who at one time dwelt under the Acropolis, were said to have built the whole wall round about it except the part erected by Cimon, the son of Miltiades; and the builders of it were reported to be Agrolas and Hyperbios. But when Pausanias inquired about them, he could learn nothing more than that they were of Sicilian origin; whence they migrated to Acarnania.

We have here, then, only a very vague report, and moreover one evidently false; for the northern wall, in which are found columns and other architectural members, as well as stones with inscriptions upon them, was evidently not the work of the Pelasgi, and is with much better reason attributed to Themistocles. Yet that there were remains of some Pelasgic structure at the western end of the Acropolis, near the Propylæa, cannot admit of a reasonable doubt; and it was the sight of them, apparently, that suggested to Pausanias as he went forth from the Propylæa, the inquiries respecting the Pelasgi and their doings. We have seen before (supra, pp. 71 and 436), that Cylon, or some of his confederates, was stoned to death outside the Enneapylum, or Nine Gates, at a place called the Cyloneium, which lay between the entrance to the Acropolis and the Areiopagus. At that time, therefore, which was before the Persian wars, the Pelasgic fortification appears to have been perfect; and at this side, which, from the nature of the rock, must always have been the sole entrance, there were nine gateways; but how they were arranged, whether they were single ones or treble, there is

[1] Bericht, p. 219.

nothing to show. Being at the most assailable point, they seem to have formed a kind of fort, which Wachsmuth compares to the Hexapylum at Syracuse.[1] The Enneapylum could not have been an extended wall, for in that case the site of the Cyloneium and the shrine of Hesychus could not have been indicated by it.

We cannot, however, agree with Wachsmuth, that the whole Pelasgic fortification was confined to this western side of the Acropolis. The testimonies of ancient authors to the fact that the Pelasgic wall ran all round the Acropolis are too numerous and too distinct to be explained away. Thus Hecatæus, quoted by Herodotus, says that the Athenians assigned to the Pelasgi a tract under Hymettus as a reward for the wall which they had built around the Acropolis.[2] Cleidemus, Myrsilus, and lastly, Pausanias in the passage we are considering, all give evidence to the same effect.[3] We cannot escape the proof thus offered that the wall encircled the whole rock.

Let us observe, however, that the Enneapylum, as being near the Cyloneium, and the shrine of Hesychus, must have stood on the saddle, or neck, which connects the Areiopagus with the Acropolis, and therefore considerably below the Propylæa afterwards built by Pericles. It can hardly be supposed, however, that it was on a different level from the wall; and this would lead us to think that the latter was neither carried round the summit, nor yet quite at the base of the cliff, but somewhere on the ascent. And this agrees with Lucian's description of the cave of Pan, already quoted (supra, p. 442), where it is said to be only " a little above" the Pelasgicum; that is, substituting, with Leake, ὑπέρ for ὑπό, as the sense undoubtedly requires.[4] The existence

---

[1] In Rhein. Mus. xxiv. 47 sqq.

[2] μισθὸν τοῦ τείχεος τοῦ περὶ τὴν ἀκρόπολίν κοτε ἐληλαμένου.—Herod. vi. 137.

[3] ἠπέδιζον τὴν ἀκρόπολιν, περιέβαλλον δὲ ἐννεάπυλον τὸ Πελαργικόν.—Kleid. ap. Müller, Fr. Hist. Gr. i. 363. καὶ τοῖς Ἀθηναίοις τὸ τεῖχος τὸ περὶ τὴν ἀκρόπολιν, τὸ Πελαργικὸν καλούμενον, τούτους περιβαλεῖν.—Myrsilus, ap. Dion. Halic. A. R. i. 28.

τῇ δὲ ἀκροπόλει, πλὴν ὅσον Κίμων ᾠκοδόμησεν αὐτῆς ὁ Μιλτιάδου, περιβαλεῖν τὸ λοιπὸν λέγεται τοῦ τείχους Πελασγοὺς οἰκήσαντάς ποτε ἱπὸ τὴν ἀκρόπολιν.—Paus. i. 28, 3.

[4] οἰκεῖ μικρὸν ὑπὲρ τοῦ Πελασγικοῦ.—Bis Acc. 19; Leake, i. 315. To Leake's observations it may be added that one codex has ὑπέρ. Siebelis ad Paus. i. 28, 4.

of such a wall might help us to understand the account of Herodotus,[1]
that on the approach of the Persians, those Athenians who misunderstood the oracle about the wooden wall, placed stakes and planking
round the Acropolis; that is, round the summit of it; which would
have been absurd, if not impracticable, if the wall ran round the top.
The greater part of the Pelasgic wall was probably destroyed after the
capture of the Acropolis by the Persians had shown that it was useless
for defence, and the wall round the summit erected in its stead. It
may indeed have been destroyed by the Persians themselves, if we should
be disposed to construe literally the words of Herodotus; but it is
hardly probable that Mardonius should have undertaken so vast and
useless a labour concerning an obstacle he had so easily overcome; and
probably the passage conveys only that vague and general meaning of
terrible destruction, which we so often find in descriptions of this
nature.[2] The foundations of the wall would then have served to make
that road, or path, round the sides of the Acropolis to which we have
already alluded; just as in modern times ramparts are turned into
boulevards. But we offer these only as conjectures, and for what they
may be worth in helping to solve a very difficult problem in Athenian
topography. One thing at least appears certain, that part of the enclosure was known in later times by the name of the Pelasgicum (τὸ
Πελασγικόν). Lucian alludes to it not only in the passage just quoted,
but also in another in the dialogue of the 'Fisherman,' where Parrhesi-
ades is represented as perched on the wall of the Acropolis, and fishing
for philosophers by letting down his line into the Pelasgicum.[3]

We may observe, that we find the Pelasgic fortification mentioned by
ancient authors under two distinct appellations; namely, as the Pelasgic
wall, or rather fortress (τὸ Πελασγικὸν τεῖχος), and simply as the Pelasgicum (τὸ Πελασγικόν). But the former name appears to be used only
in passages relating to a period antecedent to the Persian wars, while
the latter refers to a subsequent time. Thus, Herodotus relates how

---

[1] lib. viii. 51.

[2] ἐμπρήσας τε τὰς Ἀθήνας, καὶ εἴ κού τι
ὀρθὸν ἦν τῶν τειχέων ἢ τῶν οἰκημάτων ἢ τῶν

ἱρῶν, πάντα καταβαλὼν καὶ συγχώσας.—
lib. ix. 13.

[3] Piscator, c. 47.

Cleomenes besieged the Peisistratidæ in "the Pelasgic fortress."[1] The Parian Marble uses the same expression concerning the same event.[2] We agree with Wachsmuth (*loc. cit.*) in thinking that these passages refer to the whole Acropolis, as fortified by the Pelasgians. In this view it is equivalent to 'Acropolis;' but it further indicates the Acropolis in its ancient state, as fortified by the Pelasgi. On the other hand, the term 'Pelasgicum' denotes either a part of this fortification, preserved after the remainder had been destroyed, or a tract of enclosed ground which, according to tradition, had been formerly occupied by the Pelasgi. The former, perhaps, is the more probable of these two hypotheses; but however this may be, there can be no doubt that the place so called, whatever it may have been, was under Pan's grotto, at the north-western extremity of the Acropolis, as we see it very exactly indicated in the passage before quoted from Lucian's 'Bis Accusatus' (p. 448). Strabo says, that part of the city, or rather of the Acropolis (τῆς πόλεως), was called Pelasgicum after the Pelasgi;[3] and Thucydides adverts to it in a passage which shows that, in pursuance of an oracle, it was regarded as sacred ground.[4] Aristophanes alludes to it in the following line, under the form Pelargicum:

τίς δαὶ καθέξει τῆς πόλεως τὸ Πελαργικόν;[5]

The form πελαργικὸς seems to have been current among the Athenians, and is said to have been adopted because the wanderings of the Pelasgi resembled those of the crane (πελαργός).[6] It was not, therefore, altogether a comic invention of Aristophanes, but was naturally employed by him in a play whose subject was the birds.

After adverting to the cave of Pan, Pausanias proceeds to the

[1] Κλεομένης . . . ἐπολιόρκεε τοὺς τυράννους ἀπεργμένους ἐν τῷ Πελασγικῷ τείχεϊ.—v. 64.

[2] ἐξανέστ[ησαν] τοὺς Πεισιστρατίδας ἐκ [του Πε]λασ[γι]κοῦ τείχους.—ep. 114. And so Aristotle, quoted by the scholiast on the 'Lysistrata' of Aristophanes, v. 1155: Κλεομένης . . . . εἰσῆλθεν εἰς τὴν Ἀττικὴν καὶ τὸν Ἱππίαν συνέκλεισεν εἰς τὸ Πελαργικὸν τεῖχος.

[3] ἀφ' ὧν (Πελασγῶν) ἐκλήθη μέρος τί τῆς πόλεως Πελασγικόν.—lib. ix. 401.

[4] τό τε Πελασγικὸν καλούμενον τὸ ὑπὸ τὴν ἀκρόπολιν, ὃ καὶ ἐπάρατόν τε ἦν μὴ οἰκεῖν καί τι καὶ Πυθικοῦ μαντείου ἀκροτελεύτιον τοιόνδε διεκώλυε, λέγον ὡς τὸ Πελασγικὸν ἀργὸν ἄμεινον.—ii. 17.

[5] "Who will occupy the Pelargicum of the Acropolis?"—Aves, v. 833.

[6] Strabo, v. 221: Myrsilus ap. Dion. Hal. loc. cit.

Areiopagus, or Hill of Ares. It was so called, he says, because Ares was the first who was arraigned upon it for killing Halirrhotius, to which myth we have already adverted (supra, p. 39). Orestes was afterwards tried there for the murder of his mother, and dedicated, on his acquittal, an altar to Athena Areia. We may remark, that in this case the surname of the goddess may have been derived from her altar being on the Areiopagus; but 'Αρεία was also a general epithet of Athena, as sharing the warlike attributes of Ares, in conjunction with whom she is often named. The Platæans had a sanctuary to her under that appellation.[1] Pausanias concludes his account of the Areiopagus by saying that there were on it two rude stones—one called the stone of Contumely (ὕβρεως), the other the stone of Impudence (ἀναιδείας); and in trials the accuser stood on one of them, and the accused on the other. These seem to have been distinct from the altars of those deities (if such they may be called) at the Cyloneium, to which we have already alluded; but it is probable that the altars may have given occasion to the names.

Most authors agree with Pausanias in attributing the name of the hill to Ares having been arraigned upon it for the murder of Halirrhotius before a council of the gods (supra, p. 39):

> ἔστιν δ' "Αρεώς τις ὄχθος, οὗ πρῶτον θεοὶ
> ἕζοντ' ἐπὶ ψήφοισιν αἵματος πέρι,
> 'Αλιρρόθιον ὅτ' ἔκταν' ὠμόφρων "Αρης.[2]

> " There is a Hill of Mars, where first the gods
> In council sat and voted about blood
> When cruel Mars slew Halirrhotius."

But Æschylus derives the name from the Amazons, who were the daughters of Ares, when they were besieging Athens, having taken possession of the hill, and offered sacrifice upon it to Ares:

> "Αρει δ' ἔθυον, ἔνθεν ἔστ' ἐπώνυμος
> πέτρα, πάγος τ' "Αρειος.[3]

> " They sacrificed to Mars, from which that rock
> Derived its name of Areiopagus;"—

---

[1] Pausan. ix. 4, 1.   [2] Eurip. Electr. 1258.   [3] Eum. 692.

2 G 2

in which he is followed by the author of the Etymologicum M. (in voc.), and by Eustathius in his commentary on Dionysius Alexandrinus. We have already mentioned that it was also occupied by the Persians when besieging the Acropolis. In the early times, at least, the Council of the Areiopagus appears to have assembled on the top of the hill, whence it was called ἡ ἄνω βουλή, or the Council above.[1] Like other tribunals for the trial of homicides, its sittings were held in the open air; the reason for which, according to Antiphon, was partly that the judges might not be in the same place with those whose hands were impure, and partly that the prosecutor might not be under the same roof with the perpetrator.[2] The Areiopagites assembled on the eastern and highest portion of the hill, where there still remain vestiges of an artificial platform, with seats cut in the rock. It may still be ascended from the south by a flight of sixteen rude steps. Vitruvius speaks of its having had a roof of clay, which seems to be at variance with the Greek authorities, that their judgments were given in the open air. Leake observes on this point: "As the Areopagitæ formed a council (βουλή), as well as a court (δικαστήριον), the building described by Vitruvius may have served for their use in the latter capacity" (p. 356), where *latter* seems to be a slip of the pen for *former*. They appear also to have met in the night, in order that they might not see those who were pleading before them, but only hear what they had to say; and thus also the faces, and even the number, of the judges remained unknown.[3] It is, however, hardly necessary to say, that their functions, at all events after the time of Solon, were not confined to the trial of murderers. Among these functions was the cognizance of innovations in religion; and if St. Paul was actually brought before the Council, it must have been on this account; but more probably it was only an assembly of philosophers and others on the hill.

The Areiopagitic Council would of itself have sufficed to throw an air of solemn awe over the hill on which it assembled; and this must

---

[1] Plut. Solon. 19; Heliodor. Æthiop. lib. i.

[2] Poll. Onom. viii. 10; Antiph. de cæde

Herodis, p. 709, Reiske.

[3] Lucian, Hermot. c. 64; De Domo, c. 18; Clearchus, ap. Athen. vi. 68.

have been immeasurably increased by the temple of the Semnæ, which formed a sort of adjunct to the court. "Near it," says Pausanias (28, 6), "is the sanctuary of the goddesses whom the Athenians call Semnæ; but whom Hesiod, in his 'Theogony,' styles Erinnyes. Æschylus first represented them with snakes in their hair; but the images of them have nothing horrible, nor have those of the other subterranean deities which stand here—namely, Pluto, Hermes, and Gæa. Those who are acquitted by the Court of Areiopagus sacrifice in this temple; and not only these, but others indiscriminately, both citizens and strangers. Within the peribolus there is a monument of Œdipus; and I found, after much inquiry, that his bones had been brought hither from Thebes. For, what Sophocles feigns respecting the death of Œdipus, Homer prevents me from believing, who relates that Mecisteus went to Thebes and contended in the funeral games at his tomb."

In this passage Pausanias says that the Attic name for the Furies was only Semnæ; and in his next book[1] he reiterates this assertion by saying that the goddesses whom the Athenians called Semnæ, the Sicyonians named Eumenides; by which, as Siebelis observes, he seems only to mean that this was the name for them publicly recognized in those countries respectively, and inscribed on their temples and altars; for that they were also called Eumenides at Athens is sufficiently certain,[2] though Æschylus does not use that name. (See Sophocles, Œd. Col. v. 42, &c.) According to some authorities, they obtained it when Orestes was acquitted by the Court of Areiopagus of the murder of his mother, because they had become lenient (εὐμενεῖς) towards him; though it must be allowed that Philemon, the comic poet, considered the Semnæ to be different deities from the Eumenides.[3]

A deep chasm in the cliffs at the north-east side of the Areiopagus, containing a spring of dark-coloured water, is supposed to have formed the adytum of the subterranean sanctuary of the SEMNÆ, as well as an entrance to Hades. According to a certain Argive writer named

[1] Corinthiaca, 11, 4.

[2] On this subject see Müller's 'Eume-

nides,' sect. 87.

[3] Schol. ad Soph. Œd. Col. 42.

Lobon, quoted by Diogenes Laërtius (i. 112), the temple of the Semnæ, or Furies, was founded in the time of Pisistratus by the Cretan Epimenides, whose name, as we have seen, is connected with other legends respecting the Areiopagus. This account, however, is at variance with the history of Cylon, to which we have before referred (p. 71). As Cylon was slain at the altar of the Semnæ, their sanctuary must have existed before the time of Epimenides, who was invited to Athens in order to devise some proper expiation of that deed. According to the poets, who followed perhaps an ancient tradition, the Semnæ were installed on the acquittal of Orestes. Æschylus, in the splendid passage which concludes his ' Eumenides,' represents Athena, who had given her casting vote in favour of the accused, as conducting them from the tribunal to their new abode with the light of torches; where we have another proof that trials of this kind were conducted by night. Euripides has also touched upon the same story in two of his dramas.[1]

According to Phylarchus,[2] the Eumenides were only two in number, and consequently had only two statues at Athens; but Polemo made them three, which agrees with Pausanias and the more commonly received account. One of their statues was the work of Calos, or perhaps, according to the reading of Osann, Calamis; the other two were done by Scopas.[3] Whether this circumstance occasioned the difference between Polemo and Phylarchus respecting the number of the Semnæ, as assumed by Müller,[4] seems very problematical. It should be mentioned that there was at Colonus another temple of the Eumenides.[5] The peribolus of that at Athens must have extended towards the Acropolis, since Valerius Maximus indicates the monument of Œdipus as lying between the Acropolis and the Areiopagus.[6] Near the same

---

[1] Electra, 1258 sqq.; Iphig. in Taur. 961 sqq.

[2] Ap. schol. ad Soph. Œd. Col. 39.

[3] Clem. Alex. Protrept. p. 30; cf. Annal. dell' Instit. 1830.

[4] Eumenides, p. 207, Engl. transl.

[5] See Soph. Œd. Col. 38 sqq.

[6] " Œdipodis ossa inter ipsum Areopagum et excelsam præsidis Minervæ arcem honore aræ decorata quasi sacrosancta colis."—v. 3.

spot and the Cyloneium already mentioned was an heroum of Hesychus, the fabled ancestor of the Hesychidæ, or priestesses who performed the sacred offices to the Semnæ. It can hardly be doubted that, as Müller has observed,[1] the name was derived from the stillness and silence (ἡσυχία) which characterised the worship.[2] The ceremonies were begun by the sacrifice of a ram to Hesychus.[3]

From the mention of the Court of Areiopagus, Pausanias takes occasion to enumerate the other Athenian courts of judicature (c. 28, s. 8 to end). Among these were the Parabystum and the Trigonum; the former so called from its being in an obscure part of the city, and from the trifling nature of the causes pleaded in it; whilst the latter derived its name from its shape. The courts called Batrachium and Phœnicium were so named from the colours of them—grass green and scarlet—and have continued to be so, he remarks, to the present day. The Attic courts, we may observe, were distinguished from one another by colours, as well as by letters, and the judges received a staff of the same colour as the court, to prevent their going to the wrong one.[4] Leake has pointed out (i. 359) that the names Batrachium and Phœnicium are not found in any other author, and therefore he considers these courts to be the Epilycum[5] and Metichium mentioned by Pollux (viii. 121), which are not found in Pausanias, and which complete the number of ten, designated by the letters α′ to κ′; and thus, leaving out the Ardettus, named by Pollux as an eleventh court, but which had long ceased to be one, the enumerations of Pausanias and Pollux agree.

But the greatest and most frequented court of all, continues Pausanias, is the Heliæa. Amongst other courts for the trial of homicide is that at the Palladium for cases of involuntary manslaughter; and all agree that the Athenian king Demophon was first tried here, but there is a difference as to the cause. According to some, Diomedes, when returning from Troy, mistook his course in the night and came to Phalerum; when the Argives who were with him invaded the

---

[1] Eumenides, p. 207, Engl. transl.
[2] Soph. Œd. Col. v. 130 sqq. and scholia on v. 489.
[3] Ibid.
[4] Bekk. An. Græc. voc. βακτηρία, p. 220; schol. ad Aristoph. Plut. 278; Vesp. 1105.
[5] Or rather, τὸ ἐπὶ Λύκῳ.

country, thinking it to be a hostile one, and not Attica. Demophon, in ignorance that it was an Argive fleet, attacked and killed some of the ravagers, and seized and carried off the Palladium, on which occasion his horse ran over and killed an Athenian in the darkness. Some say that he was arraigned by the relatives of the man, others by the Argive state. We may perhaps infer, that this story was invented to explain how there came to be a Palladium at Athens.

As this court was appropriated to cases of accidental homicide, so that called the Delphinium tried causes of justifiable homicide; and here, says Pausanias, Theseus was acquitted after he had put to death Pallas and his sons, who had risen against him. Before this acquittal, everybody who had committed homicide was obliged to fly the country, on pain of capital punishment if he remained. At the Prytaneium, swords and other instruments of murder were subjected to trial; a custom which seems to have begun with the slaughter of the ox at the altar of Zeus Polieus, as already related; a trial that was repeated every year. Anything occasioning an accidental death, as a piece of stone, wood, or iron, was also subjected to trial.[1] Another court of this kind was the Phreattys in the Peiræeus. Here those who had fled for homicide, if another accusation was brought against them during their absence, and they attempted to return, had to plead their cause from the ship before they landed, while their judges sat on the shore. The first instance of this kind is said to have been the defence of Teucer, before Telamon, of any participation in the death of Ajax.

The situation of most of the more famous of these courts has been already indicated; respecting that of the inferior ones we need not inquire. Only we must remark that the site of the Heliæa, the principal of them all after the Areiopagus, cannot be identified. It probably derived its name, as suggested by the scholiasts on Aristophanes,[2] from its assembling in the open air, and being thus exposed to the rays of the sun. Leake (i. 361) selects for it a site in the valley to the south of the Areiopagus, which is a probable one enough, as room could hardly

---

[1] Cf. Demosth. c. Aristocr. p. 645, Reiske; Æschin. c. Ctesiph. p. 636.

[2] Eq. 255; Nub. 860; Vesp. 88, 769.

have been found for it on the northern side, or that of the Agora. But his argument for the same site drawn from its being the *lower* court in contradistinction to the higher one of the Areiopagus (ἡ ἄνω βουλή), is hardly satisfactory; as the contrast seems rather to be between the Senate and the Areiopagus, as a council, than between two dicasteria.

Pausanias finishes his account of the interior of the city by saying that there was near the Areiopagus—apparently in the temenos of Apollo Patroüs—a ship made to be used in the Panathenaïc procession. It was of no great magnitude, and in this respect not at all comparable to the trireme at Delos, which had nine banks of oars (c. 29, 1). Pausanias then proceeds to describe objects which lay without the city; but before following him thither, we must advert to a few objects in the interior which he has omitted.

Of many of these objects we know only the names, and nothing of their site and history. Thus we read of a temple of the Hours, with a statue in it of Dionysus Ὀρθός (the upright, not reeling) and near it a temple of the Nymphs.[1] Sophocles is said to have erected a temple to Heracles Μηνύτης, the informer or indicator, because he had pointed out to the poet in a dream the house where either a golden crown or patera was hidden which had been stolen from one of his sanctuaries.[2] So also we hear of a temple, or rather perhaps a statue, of Hermes Ἡγεμόνιος, or leader of the blind,[3] another of Artemis Λυσίζωνος,[4] &c. But it would be useless to pursue a bare catalogue of names; and we will therefore turn to a few objects of more importance, and which can be better identified.

We may observe that Pausanias does not perambulate that range of hills which lies on the south side of Athens—viz. the Musæum, the Pnyx, and the Hill of the Nymphs—nor the district which extends beyond them, still so thickly covered with the vestiges of ancient dwellings. He does indeed mention the Musæum and the monument on the top of it (c. 25, 6), but only parenthetically, and in explanation of his account of the actions of Demetrius. He mentions a tradition that Musæus had

---

[1] Philochorus, ap. Athen. ii. 7.
[2] Schol. in Vit. Soph.; Cic. Div. i. 25, 54.
[3] Schol. ad Aristoph. Plut. 1160.
[4] Schol. ad Apollon. Rhod. i. 288.

died at Athens at an advanced age and been buried on the hill on which
he had sung; and that afterwards a monument had been erected there
to a certain Syrian. A little below the summit of the Musæum hill, on
its eastern side, is an entrance to a very ancient tomb, which tradition
asserts to be that of Musæus; but the means of verification are of course
wanting. Diogenes Laërtius, on the contrary, says that Musæus died
and was buried at Phalerum, and gives the epitaph on his tomb.[1] The
Syrian alluded to was Philopappus, grandson of Antiochus IV., last king
of Commagene. Epiphanes, one of the sons of Antiochus, appears to
have settled at Athens, where he became the father of Philopappus. The
monument is still extant, though very much dilapidated; but though
remarkable, from its elevated position, it has from its subject but little
interest for the student of Athenian antiquities. When perfect it consisted of a curved, or slightly concave front, or wall, between 32 and 33
feet in height, and about 30 in breadth, along the chord of the curve,
forming the façade of a quadrangular mausoleum, of which traces may
still be discerned behind it. It had what may be called two stories,
divided from each other by a cornice; the lower one or basement being
about 10 feet high; while the upper one occupied the remaining height
of the building. Each of these stories was divided perpendicularly
into three compartments, separated in the upper one by pilasters with
Corinthian capitals, the middle compartment being considerably broader
than the side ones. In each of these compartments was a niche for a
statue; the middle and larger one having a semicircular top, while the
other two were square. In the central niche was a seated statue, below
which a Greek inscription showed that it represented Philopappus, son
of Epiphanes, of the Attic demus Besa. In the square niche on his
right was another seated statue, purporting, from the inscription, to be
that of King Antiochus, son of King Antiochus. These statues are still
in situ, but much mutilated and headless. All the western side of the
building, with its niche and statue, is completely demolished, and was
so when Wheler was at Athens; but in the time of Ciriaco d' Ancona,
who visited Athens about two centuries earlier, it still existed.

[1] lib. i. s. 3.   [2] ap. Leake, vol. i. p. 491 sq.

On the basement, under the central statue, is sculptured in high relief the quadriga of a triumphal general, bearing much resemblance to that in the interior of the arch of Titus at Rome. Behind the car, beneath the pilaster on the left of the central statue, stands a single figure having the appearance of a barbarian prisoner. There were, no doubt, other figures to the west of this, which have vanished with this part of the building itself. They probably represented, as M. Breton conjectures, other prisoners following the car of the victor. On the other or eastern side, as appears from Stuart's engraving, which represents the monument in a considerably more perfect state than at present, is a person leading the horses, while another, under the east pilaster, precedes the car on foot, and forms a pendant to the prisoner under the western pilaster. In the eastern compartment of the basement, under the statue of Antiochus, are five more figures which face the spectator, and seem intended for persons viewing the triumph. It should be added that at the top of the still extant pilaster on the right hand of the statue of Philopappus of Besa is the following Latin inscription: C(aius) Julius C(aii) F(ilius) Fab . Antiochus . Philopappus . Cos. Frater . Arvalis . Electus . Inter . Prætorios . ab . Imp . Cæsare . Nerva . Trajano . Optumo . Germanico . Dacico. And on the left one, in the time of Ciriaco,[1] the following one in Greek: Βασιλεὺς Ἀντίοχος Φιλόπαππος, Βασιλέως Ἐπιφάνους, τοῦ Ἀντιόχου.

We take from Leake's work on the 'Topography of Athens' the following explanation of the monument (App. viii.): "We learn from Josephus that in the fourth year of Vespasian (A.D. 72) Samosata, the capital of Commagene, was taken by Pætus, whom Vespasian had left in the government of Syria. Antiochus, the King of Commagene, retired to Cilicia with his wife and daughter, but his two sons, Epiphanes and Callinicus, held out for a short time in arms, and even engaged successfully in action with the Romans, but at length, having been deserted by their soldiers, they crossed the Euphrates into the territory of Vologeses, King of Parthia. Vespasian showed no resentment against them, but permitted both the father and sons to proceed to Rome,

[1] ap. Leake, vol. i. p. 191.

where he treated them with distinction. We may infer from the inscriptions that Philopappus of Besa and King Antiochus Philopappus were sons of Epiphanes, and had assumed the name of Philopappus from respect to the grandfather, the last *de facto* king of their family. The name was similar to many adjuncts of those days, such as Philometor and Philoromæus. While one of the brothers affected the republican simplicity of an Attic citizen, the other still adhered to the empty title of king, which of course he bestowed also on his father Epiphanes. As to the Latin inscription, I am inclined to believe with Stuart that it was intended for a son of Callinicus; he could not have been a brother of the titular King Antiochus Philopappus, their two Greek names having been the same; but for that very reason he was likely to have been a first cousin. The Caii Filius show that his father was a citizen of Rome as well as himself, and it appears that they were enrolled in the Fabian tribe and Julian family."

From the Latin inscription we learn nearly the date of the monument. Trajan is styled Dacicus, but not Parthicus, which title, if the Senate had then bestowed it upon him, would not have been omitted, especially as there was sufficient space for it on the pilaster. The monument, therefore, was erected between the years 101 and 108 of the Christian era.[1] As Epiphanes is stated by Josephus to have been young in the year 72, his son Philopappus must have died at a middle age; and the monument was probably erected by his surviving brother and cousin, who may have intended to explain this fact by their own statues having been erect while the two others were seated. The treatise of Plutarch on 'How to distinguish a Flatterer from a Friend' is addressed to Antiochus Philopappus, and in another place he mentions a Βασιλεὺς Φιλόπαππος as having executed with great munificence the office of agonothetes, and that of choregus for all the tribes on some particular occasion (Quæst. Symp. i. 10). The title and the two names are suited

[1] If we refer the titles Dacicus and Parthicus to the two triumphs of Trajan, the years will be 105 and 115, instead of 101 and 108. The title of Optimus was bestowed upon Trajan as early as the year 99, though seldom found on monuments till near the end of his reign. But Philopappus would probably be early in doing honour to his patron.

to the person whose statue stood on the left hand of Philopappus of Besa. But it is possible that Plutarch may have referred to two persons, and that one of them may have been Philopappus of Besa, who, residing among the Athenians, may have been known as King Philopappus, although an Attic citizen; for it was probably in the latter capacity that he filled the offices mentioned by Plutarch. The magnificence of the monument, and its position within the city in one of the most honourable and conspicuous situations, show it to have been that of some person who had obtained the special favour of the Athenians.

With regard to the Latin inscription, we feel rather inclined to agree with M. Breton,[1] that no inference can be drawn from it with regard to the date of the mausoleum. It must surely have been erected in honour of the person represented by the central and most conspicuous statue, viz. Philopappus of Besa, and not of a person who had no statue, but only an inscription, and that relegated to the top of the pilaster. For we also agree with M. Breton, that there could have been no statues on the top of these pilasters, as Stuart supposed, there being no place to hold them; and even if there had been, statues in such a position must have been subordinate in dignity to the middle one. M. Breton is of opinion that the bas-relief relates not to any triumph of Trajan, but that of Titus after the capture of Jerusalem, in which Antiochus IV. assisted. Hence he thinks that the building might have been erected towards the close of the first century, perhaps in the reign of Domitian or Nerva; and that the Latin inscription was added afterwards, on the burial there of another member of the family.

The next hill to the Musæum on the north-west, commonly called the Pnyx Hill, contains one of the most extensive and remarkable ruins in Athens; yet, as Pausanias has left it unnoticed, its destination appears to be still capable of question. The greater part of this ruin, if such it can be called, is formed out of the solid rock, and the remainder was completed by a huge wall of Cyclopean character. The whole consists of an upper and a lower terrace. The former, near the summit of the hill, is about 60 mètres, or 65 yds. 1 ft. 6 in. in length,

[1] Athènes, p. 331 sq.

and 40 mètres, or 43 yds. 2 ft. 3 in. in breadth, at its broadest part. It is bounded on the south side by a sort of cliff or wall, cut out of the rock, 8 ft. or 9 ft. high at its highest point. A few steps in this wall lead to the summit of the hill, which has a rapid descent towards the south. The floor of this terrace is levelled out of the solid rock, and smoothed with the chisel. In the wall or cliff is an arched niche, and in the floor before it three round holes of no great size at equal distances from one another, in which apparently poles may have been inserted, to form a temporary partition. There are also vestiges of the foundations of small quadrangular buildings in the eastern part of this area. On the opposite side stands, quite detached, a cubic mass resembling a large altar, the top of which has evidently been mutilated with violence. It is not built of masonry, but is part of the rock, left standing when the floor of the terrace was hewn out. It is partly surrounded by a low step, and a gutter runs round it, having at its north-west angle a round hole. This seems intended to receive the blood of victims, and marks the object as an altar. That it could have been a bema, as Dr. Wordsworth and some other writers have imagined, appears to us quite untenable, and, besides its resemblance to an altar, for these reasons: first, it is not so situated that an orator could have addressed from it an audience in the lower terrace; secondly, the upper terrace is not large enough to have contained an assembly of the people; thirdly, there are no steps by which to ascend this object.

Such is the upper terrace; the lower one is considerably larger. It is separated from the upper one by a wall cut out of the solid rock, like that just described, but longer and higher; being in length about 115 mètres, or nearly 126 yards, and in height where highest, namely, on the eastern side of the bema, from 12 ft. to 15 ft. above the present level. This wall is not perfectly straight, but inclines slightly inwards towards the centre, so as to form there a very obtuse angle. Here there is a large projecting cubic object cut out of the rock, like the altar before mentioned, from which however it differs materially. It is much larger, being 11 ft. both in length and breadth, and 5 ft. in height; and instead of standing isolated, it projects from the cliff or wall. It is

mutilated on the top, like the altar. The above are the dimensions of
the cube alone; but it stands upon a base, also cut in the rock, which
adds greatly to its dimensions. This base, or platform, consists of
three steps, together nearly 5 ft. in height. The lowest of them is
more than 30 ft. in length, and 20 ft. in breadth. The third step leads
to a broad landing place, or platform, from which rise steps on each
side of the cubic block, for the purpose of ascending it; and these,
which would be useless for an altar, indubitably mark it for the bema,
or the λίθος ἐν τῇ πυκνί,[1] the command of which gave the favourite
orator as much power as the prime minister of England. The whole
arrangement of the terraces and bema will be better understood by
referring to the plan in the Appendix.

The wall of the lower terrace just described formed the chord of a
vast semicircular space, stretching before it northwards, the enclosure
of its arc being a huge Cyclopean sort of wall of masonry. The radius
of the semicircle measures about 70 mètres (between 76 and 77 yards)
from the bema just described to the centre of this wall. At the part
opposite the bema, the Cyclopean wall is still well preserved for a
length of about 20 ft., and a height of from 12 ft. to 15 ft. In the
middle of it, at the lower part, is a large square hole, apparently an
emissary for drainage. The wall consists of huge blocks of stone,
pretty accurately squared and fitted together, and lying at one part in ·
two courses, at another in three. The semicircular line it described
may still be traced, especially on the western side, till it joined each
end of the cliff wall. That it was originally much loftier is allowed on
all hands, the upper courses having been removed, probably for building
purposes; and there can be little doubt that when perfect it equalled
in height the cliff wall. Göttling allows that the upper part of the
wall has fallen.[2] And Pittakys holds that anciently it rose not merely
to the level of the cliff wall, but 8 ft. above it, as one of the huge stones
still remains on the cliff where the wall joined it on the west.[3] Wheler,

---

[1] ὅστις κρατεῖ νῦν τοῦ λίθου τοῦ 'ν τῇ
πυκνί.—Aristoph. Pax, 680.

[2] Das Pelasgikon in Athen (Gesamm.
Abhandl. p. 80).

[3] L'anc. Athènes, p. 457.

in a cut of the Pnyx,[1] which, however, he misnames the Odeium, represents the circular wall as complete, but unfortunately does not say
whether it then existed in that state, or whether the sketch is a fanciful
restoration. At all events, enough of it must have then remained to
indicate its line with certainty. The whole place, therefore, must have
had, and indeed still preserves, somewhat of the appearance of a theatre;
so that Wheler suspected it might have been the Odeium of Pericles,
while Stuart took it for that of Regilla.[2] Of the number of spectators
that such an area could accommodate, different writers have given
surprisingly various estimates. Leake says that the area of the platform
was capable of containing between 7000 and 8000 persons, allowing a
square yard to each.[3] Dr. Wordsworth says that the area of the Pnyx
covers more than 12,000 square yards,[4] in which estimate he probably
included both terraces; but even then it seems a good deal too high.
Curtius makes the contents only 2586 square mètres,[5] which is not a
very great deal less than the same number of square yards (about 2828);
but this measure is absurdly below the mark, and one can hardly help
suspecting that it was adopted to favour the author's theory that this
structure could not have been the Pnyx, because these dimensions would
not have sufficed to hold the citizens assembled in ecclesia. The true
area seems to be 6230 square yards, and we have the authority of an
eminent architect for saying that such an area would accommodate
about 11,000 persons seated. A square yard, therefore (Leake's allowance), is a great deal too liberal for one person. We do not find in
ancient authors[6] notices of more than from 5000 or 6000 persons having

[1] Journey, &c. p. 382.
[2] Athens, vol. iii. ch. 8.
[3] Topography of Athens, p. 518.
[4] Athens and Attica, p. 58.
[5] Attische Studien, No. i. p. 32.
[6] Thucydides (viii. 72) says that, through
absence in war, &c., so many as 5000 had
never met; yet a public debtor could not
be discharged, nor a stranger admitted to
Athenian citizenship, by fewer votes than
6000 (Demosth. c. Timocr. p. 715, Reiske;

c. Neær. p. 1375). But the occasions on
which either of these things was done
were probably rare; and it is possible that
there might have been some alteration
respecting the numbers after the time of
Eucleides (Andoc. de Myst. p. 42, Reiske).
If 6000 actually voted on any such occasion
we may suppose that there must have been
more than that number actually present;
but probably not a great many more; as
such motions would not be brought for-

been assembled in ecclesia at one time ; and therefore, on the score of
its capacity, all objections vanish as to this place having been the
Pnyx. Dr. Chandler first identified it as such, and everything con-
spires to show that his view was correct. For, first, it answers to the
description of Pollux, who says that it was a *place* (not a *building*) near
the Acropolis arranged in the simple, ancient fashion, and not with the
elaborateness of a theatre.[1] From the last words it is plain that it
suggested the idea of a rude theatre, as we have shown above, and the
allusion to its ancient simplicity evidently means the construction of
it out of the living rock.

Secondly, the Pnyx, like the place in question, was on a hill, as is
directly testified by the scholiast on Æschines.[2] Hence the people
were said to "go up to it;"[3] when they were assembled in it to "sit
up above;"[4] and when leaving it, to "descend."[5] And hence in the
'Knights' of Aristophanes, Cleon is represented as looking out from it
after the tributes like a fisherman on a height after the tunnies :

$$\kappa\dot{a}\pi\dot{o} \ \tau\hat{\omega}\nu \ \pi\epsilon\tau\rho\hat{\omega}\nu \ \ddot{a}\nu\omega\theta\epsilon\nu \ \tauο\dot{\upsilon}\varsigma \ \phi\dot{o}\rho o\upsilon\varsigma \ \theta\upsilon\nu\nuο\sigma\kappaο\pi\hat{\omega}\nu.—\text{v. 313.}$$

> "—— and from the rocks above
> Spying for tributes, just as they were tunnies."

Where we see that the 'rocks,' or in the singular, 'the rock,'[6] was a
name for it, no doubt from the nature of the place, as having been hewn
out of the rock. So Euripides calls the Acropolis the Cecropian rock

---

wards except there was a tolerable certainty
of their being carried.

[1] ἐνεκκλησίαζον δὲ πάλαι μὲν ἐν τῇ πυκνί ·
πνὺξ δὲ ἦν χωρίον πρὸς τῇ ἀκροπόλει, κατε-
σκευασμένον κατὰ τὴν παλαιὰν ἁπλότητα, οὐκ
εἰς θεάτρου πολυπραγμοσύνην.—viii. 132.

[2] ἦν δὲ πάγος ὑψηλός, λόφος καλούμενος
πνύξ.—Æsch. c. Timarch. p. 24, Dind.
(Oxon. 1852). See the authorities collected by Ross, Die Pnyx u. das Pelasgikon,
p. 1.

[3] εἰς τὰς ἐκκλησίας ἀναβαίνουσιν.—Dem.

c. Aristog. p. 772, cf. 775, Reiske.

[4] πᾶς ὁ δῆμος ἄνω καθῆτο.—Id. de Cor.
p. 285, cf. Plut. Nic. 7.

[5] καταβάς.—Dem. c. Aristog. p. 782.

[6] Thus in the same play : ὅταν δ' ἐπὶ ταυ-
τησὶ καθῆται τῆς πέτρας (v. 754); and, ἐπὶ
ταῖσι πέτραις οὐ φροντίζει σκληρῶς σε
καθήμενον οὕτως (v. 783). Where some
commentators have thought that the allusion is to stone benches; but this can
hardly be the case with the example in
the singular (τῆς πέτρας).

(Κεκρόπια πέτρα.—Ion, 936). And the Pnyx was notoriously a stony place.[1] There were no doubt stone seats hewn out of the terrace wall, for they may still be traced on each side of the bema ; but in the pit, or amphitheatre, before the bema, the benches were more probably of wood. At all events they are so called in the following passage of the ' Acharnenses :'

εἶτα δ' ὠστιοῦνται πῶς δοκεῖς
ἐλθόντες ἀλλήλοισι περὶ πρώτου ξύλου.—v. 24.

" And then just fancy how they shove about,
Each man contending for a foremost seat."

though it must be allowed that ξύλον is sometimes used of any bench.

Thirdly, it was in a deserted place, surrounded with λάκκοι, or underground cellars, and the ruined foundations of buildings (οἰκόπεδα),[2] which description remains true to the present day. Hence it was occupied by the persons who retired, or absconded, under the rule of the Thirty :

ἐν ταῖς φυγαῖς μετὰ τἀνδρὸς ᾤκησ' ἐν πυκνί.[3]

" —— During the flight we dwelt,
I and my husband, i' the Pnyx."

And, as may be inferred from the contents of Æschines' speech against Timarchus just alluded to, it seems also, from its solitariness, to have been used for purposes of low and cheap debauchery.

Fourthly, we know that the Pnyx was in the quarter called Melitë,[4] which, as we have shown when speaking of the regions of the city, may have comprehended the Pnyx Hill, but could hardly have included the Museum also, where some would place the ecclesia. To the proof of site may be added some inscriptions found in the neighbourhood. Göttling affirms[5] that he saw and pointed out to Preller and Pittakys, on a rock on the side of the Pnyx Hill, between the Cyclopean wall and the road leading under the Nymphs' Hill, and about forty-five paces from the latter, the inscription ΓΥϘΝΙ, which, from the use of the

[1] πνὺξ δὲ πετρώδης ἐστι τόπος.—Schol. ad Æsch. l. c.

[2] Æsch. c. Timarch. p. 106, Reiske.

[3] Aristoph. Eccl. 243 et ibi schol.

[4] Schol. ad Aristoph. Av. 998.

[5] Das Pelasgikon u. die Pnyx, p. 20.

koppa, for kappa, must have been one of the oldest at Athens. That letter is found on old coins of Croton and Syracuse, but some have questioned whether it was ever used at Athens.[1] Such boundary inscriptions are not unfrequently found on the Athenian hills. The site of this one very satisfactorily defines the place of the Pnyx. Curtius indeed asserts[2] that only the first two letters are certain; but even if this be so, considering the place where the inscription was found, it is a good deal. Another inscription in ancient characters, ὅρος Πυκνός, on a piece of marble, was found in the hole which we have already described at the north-west corner of the rock-altar on the upper terrace; but its original position was ten mètres south of this altar, where another hole contained a little tufa pedestal, part of which still adhered to the inscribed marble.[3] The latter is now preserved in the Acropolis. But here also Curtius contests the spot at which it was discovered.[4] Another inscription found, according to M. Pittakys, on a block of marble in a hole on the horizontal rock of the Pnyx, had the words Λακκιαδῶν τριττύος. For administrative purposes, the people were divided into trittyes, and this boundary-stone seems to have marked out the place in the assembly of the trittys of the Lacciadæ.[5]

Fifthly, that this was the site of the Pnyx may also be established from descriptions of the objects which might be seen from it. That it had a view into the agora may be inferred from the 'Acharnenses' of Aristophanes (v. 20–40), where Dicæopolis sees the people in it; and this would have been possible from no other height than the Pnyx Hill, over the lower part of the Areiopagus Hill, and the valley which lies between it and the Nymphs' Hill.[6] The Propylæa could be seen from it, as we learn from several allusions in the orators, where they bid the people look at them;[7] and this will not so well suit any other locality that can be named for the Pnyx. Harpocration observes, that

---

[1] Ross, Pnyx u. Pelasgikon, p. 28.

[2] Att. Studien, i. 56, note.

[3] Rangabé, Ant. Hell. t. ii. p. 579; Philologus, ix. 642.

[4] Ibid. p. 55.

[5] Rangabé, ibid. p. 586.

[6] See Ross, Das Theseion, p. 60.

[7] ἀνιστάμενοι οἱ ῥήτορες ἀποβλέπειν εἰς τὰ προπύλαια τῆς ἀκροπόλεως ἐκέλευον ἡμᾶς.—Æsch. de f. Leg. p. 253, Reiske; Demosth. c. Androt. p. 617, προπύλαια ταῦτα.

such allusions may be made because the Propylæa were visible from the
Pnyx, which is enough for our purpose, though he goes on to say that
the demonstrative pronoun in the passages (προπύλαια ταῦτα) may be
also used concerning well-known things, though not actually present.[1]
Nor will this last explanation suit the passage we have quoted from
Æschines, where the word ἀποβλέπειν proves actual view. Another
proof of the locality may be found in Lucian's 'Bis Accusatus' (c. 9),
where Mercury bids Justice sit down on the Areiopagus and look at
the Pnyx which lies over against it.   M. Rangabé, a resident of Athens,
declares that he has searched all round the Acropolis to discover
whether there is any other place capable of holding a numerous
assembly, from which can be seen the Areiopagus, the Propylæa, and
the sea (Plut. Them. 19)—to which he might have added a view into
the agora—and he positively declares that there is none;[2] an affirma-
tion which we can confirm from local observation.   The only place
that might afford the smallest chance is the Musæum Hill; but this
M. Rangabé particularly examined, and he gives the following account
of it: "I have traversed, step by step, all the western side of the hill.
Before arriving at the double tomb of Zosimus, on the north, there is
not the slightest space at all level, and the sea is completely masked.[3]
Above the tomb there are some points from which may be seen at the
same time the Areiopagus, the Propylæa, and the sea; but at these the
orator would have his audience either a great deal above his head or
below his feet, and the ground is so broken that it could not accommodate more than a few hundred persons.   On the other side, and to
the south of the tomb, neither the Propylæa nor the Areiopagus are
visible."

So striking is the identity of the place we have described with all
that we know about the Pnyx, that we should not have thought it
worth while to enter into even this brief discussion of its site had not

---

[1] Harpocr. (in προπ. ταῦτα) δύναται μὲν
δεικτικῶς λέγεσθαι ἅτε ὁρωμένων τῶν προπυλαίων ἀπὸ τῆς πυκνός, κ.τ.λ.

[2] Antiquités Helléniques, t. ii. p. 580
sq.

[3] The view of the sea is, we think, un-
necessarily imported into the argument,
from the fanciful reason given by Plutarch
(Them. 19) for altering the direction of the
bema. See Appendix iii.

a section of German scholars recently attempted to controvert it. The idea that the bema, which we have described, was an altar of Zeus, seems to have first occurred to Ulrichs about the year 1842, but he never developed it to any extent, and he died in the following year. Welcker, however, to whom he had communicated it, brought it forward about ten years afterwards in a paper read at the Berlin Academy of Sciences.[1] It will be seen from the title-page that he also identified the place with the Pelasgicum, that is, the Pelasgic fortification ($\tau\grave{o}$ Πελασγικὸν τεῖχος), which he took to be a separate and distinct thing from the Pelasgicum at the Acropolis; but as this extravagant view has not, so far as we know, been adopted even by any of his countrymen, except Göttling, we may be excused from discussing it. We may say the same of Göttling's theory,[2] which differs, however, considerably from Welcker's, inasmuch as, though he thought that the place in question was the Pelasgic fortification in which the Peisistratidæ were besieged, yet he allows that it was subsequently converted into the Pnyx. But this theory does not appear to have found much favour even in Germany. Thus, according to Welcker's view, the place was at once the Pelasgic fortification, and a temenos of Zeus; and according to Göttling, the fortress first and the Pnyx afterwards. The substance of Welcker's paper is: that the building with the bema, taken since Chandler's time for the Pnyx, was a temenos and rockaltar of Zeus Hypsistos, also called Pelasgicum; that the site of the Pnyx cannot be determined from ancient testimony, and that its construction was incompatible with the present remains. It must be sought in some other part of the town, and probably at the Museium. The view of the bema having been an altar of Zeus is derived from some votive tablets found near it, which are evidently of a late Roman period;[3] and that it is to be referred to the time of the Pelasgi is

[1] Der Felsaltar des höchsten Zeus und das Pelasgikon zu Athen, bisher genannt die Pnyx. Eine in der kgl. Akademie der Wissenschaften zu Berlin gelesene Abhandlung von F. G. Welcker. Berlin, 1852 (75 pp. in 4to).

[2] See his 'Pelasgikon in Athen,' in Rhein. Mus. 1846, iv. 321; and his pamphlet, 'Das Pelasgikon und die Pnyx,' Jena, 1853.

[3] Some of these are in the British Museum, and have been described in the

inferred from the sort of Cyclopean wall before alluded to, which, however, is evidently not Pelasgic, but of a much later date. The stones
are in general not polygonal, but carefully squared and fixed. If, as we
contend, it belongs to the Pnyx, it could hardly have been anterior to
the time of Solon, who is commonly regarded as the founder of the
ecclesia.[1] Curtius himself admits that it has not so very antique a
character. Thus he says in his 'Attische Studien' (No. i. p. 43 sq.):
"The wall itself is not of such a kind that it need be ascribed to the
oldest period of Attic constructions. For, notwithstanding the huge-
ness of the stones, it bears evident marks of a certain elegance, as
shown by the parallel lines which the ancient masons have drawn round
the edges of the separate pieces. Sir Wm. Gell has very clearly
shown this refinement in his specimens of town walls of ancient
Greece."

There can be no doubt that the Pnyx, from the time of its establishment, was dedicated to Zeus Agoræus, just as the senate house was
to Zeus Boulæus, and that the ecclesia was opened with sacrifice to
that deity. Cleon, in the 'Knights' of Aristophanes, by way of
imprecation on himself if he should be outdone in impudence, wishes
that he may never again be present, in that case, at the sacrifice to
Zeus Agoræus, where, as became a demagogue, and one of the "masters
of the stone," he swears by the presiding deity of the popular assembly.[2]
The scholiast on that passage remarks that there was an image of Zeus
Agoræus both in the agora and in the ecclesia.[3] This sacrifice is also
alluded to by the orators, and Æschines quotes the law by which it was
ordained that nobody should be allowed to speak before the lustration
(τὸ καθάρσιον) had been carried round and the herald had pronounced
the customary prayers.[4] The lustration consisted of the blood of suck-

---

little work on the Elgin marbles, published
in the 'Library of Entertaining Knowledge,' vol. ii. p. 103 sqq.

[1] Ross (Die Pnyx, &c. p. 6) assigns it
to a period long before Solon; whereby,
as Göttling observes (Pelasgikon, &c. p. 7)

he strangles his own argument.

[2] ἢ μή ποτ' ἀγοραίου Διὸς σπλάγχνοισι
παραγενοίμην.—v. 410.

[3] Ἀγοραῖος Ζεὺς ἵδρυται ἐν τῇ ἀγορᾷ καὶ
ἐν τῇ ἐκκλησίᾳ.

[4] ἐπειδὰν τὸ καθάρσιον περιενεχθῇ, καὶ

ing pigs, which were called *peristia* (περίστια) ; and the priest who performed the sacrifice (περιστίαρχος) sprinkled the blood over the seats.[1]
A passage in the 'Thesmophoriazusae' (v. 295 sqq.) is doubtless,
mutatis mutandis, a close parody of the preliminary ceremonies in the
ecclesia.

The fashion of the place of which we are speaking answers admirably for all the requirements of the ecclesia. The altar which we have
described on the upper terrace was doubtless that at which the purify-
ing sacrifice was performed. It would have been in the sight of the
people assembled in the lower terrace, whilst round about it on this
higher platform we may suppose that the chief magistrates were
grouped. At the western extremity of the higher terrace a broad flight
of steps leads down to the lower one, by which the peristiarchus may
have descended for the purpose of sprinkling the seats with the lustral
blood. By the same steps, likewise, the people may have ascended to
give their votes by ballot, when the question was not one to be decided
by a show of hands. The voting pebbles were not distributed to
the people as they sat in their places, but were given to them by
the Prytanes as they advanced to vote (προσιόντι τῷ δήμῳ), no doubt
at the top of these stairs.[2] The Prytanes had previously arranged the
ballot boxes, which were probably placed in some of those buildings on
the eastern side of the higher terrace, to whose foundations, as being
still visible, we have already adverted. Thus, having entered the
upper terrace on the western side, they would have left it on the
eastern ; where there are still numerous traces in the rock of steps
leading down the hill in the direction of that road which we have before
mentioned as leading from the agora to the Pnyx, between the
Acropolis and the Areiopagus.[3]

ὁ κῆρυξ τὰς πατρίους εὐχὰς εὔξηται . . .
μετὰ ταῦτα ἐπερωτᾷ ὁ κῆρυξ, τίς ἀγορεύειν
βούλεται, κ.τ.λ.—Æsch. c. Timarch. p. 48 ;
cf. Demosth. De fals. Leg. p. 363; c.
Timocr. p. 706.

[1] Suid. voc. περιστίαρχος; schol. ad
Aristoph. Ach. 44 ; Poll. viii. s. 104.

[2] τοὺς δὲ πρυτάνεις κελεύει τιθέναι τοὺς
καδίσκους ὁ νόμος, καὶ τὴν ψῆφον διδόναι
προσιόντι τῷ δήμῳ, κ.τ.λ. — Demosth. c.
Neær. p. 1375, Reiske.

[3] These steps were remarked also by
Burnouf: "Le Pnyx est également remar-
quable par ses escaliers presque effacés ;

The Pnyx having been consecrated to Zeus Agoræus, it is easy to see how, after it had become deserted by the course of political events, it may still have been regarded with a sort of religious awe; and as its cliff walls offered opportunities for making niches and depositing anathemata, a favourite superstition among the Athenians, and practised also, as we have seen, along the northern cliff of the Acropolis, as well as at the rock on which stands the chapel of Agios Athanasios, it is not at all surprising that they should have been appropriated to such a use. Only the name of the deity would of course have been changed. That of Agoræus would have been no longer applicable, and it would have been natural to substitute for it that of Hypsistus, as one not defined by any particular locality, or any minor and peculiar attribute, but a general one denoting his highest and universal power. That the little arched niche near the bema could have held a statue of the god with which the ancient Athenians would have been satisfied, or which could have held its place through the classic times of Athens, is too ridiculous a supposition to merit a serious thought. Such a statue must evidently have been the work of the declining days of the city, as well as the votive offerings found on this spot, to which we have already referred. If the place which we are discussing, and which we have no doubt was the Pnyx, had really been a huge temenos dedicated to Zeus, as Welcker, and after him, Curtius, have supposed, it is utterly impossible but that some allusion must have been made to it by the classic writers; but Curtius admits that there is none.[1] This fact alone, to any mind not preoccupied by an hypothesis, is quite decisive. But as Curtius has devoted the greater part of a number of his 'Attische Studien' to the proof of such a view, we have thought it due to a writer of eminence to examine his arguments in an Appendix (No. iii.), where also will be found an account of his excavations at the place in question.

---

vers son angle sud-est le rocher en est tout convert, et ceux-là doivent être fort anciens, car ils paraissent avoir été destinés à la foule qui s'écoulait du vieux Pynx."—Archives des missions littéraires, &c., t. v. p. 82.

[1] "Die erstere Stätte [that in question] hat sich in alterthümlicher Einfachheit erhalten, ist aber von den alten Schriftstellern nirgends erwähnt."—Erläuternder Text to his maps of Athens, p. 16.

The hill lying to the west of the Areiopagus, and north-west of the
Pnyx, on which is the modern Observatory, was called by the earlier
topographers Lycabettus; but that appellation has now been rightly
transferred to the lofty Hill of St. George, on the north-east side of
Athens, and that in question has obtained the name of the Nymphs'
Hill. It rests, however, only on the authority of an inscription on the
rock, and so far as we are aware it is not mentioned by any classical
author, nor by Pausanias. For this reason it is of small importance,
and we need only remark upon it, that it has, like the Pnyx Hill,
vestiges of the foundations of very ancient dwellings.

As Pausanias, for some reason or another, passes over all this
quarter of Melitë, so we look in vain for an account of two temples of
some renown which stood in it. One of these was a temple of Heracles
Alexicacus, or the averter of evil. We have already adverted to the
story of Heracles having been initiated in Melitë; a temple appears to
have been erected to him in this quarter in the time of the great plague
of Athens, the cessation of which was attributed to him. The statue in
it was the work of Geladas, or Ageladas, the master of Pheidias.[1] In
Melitë also was the house of Themistocles, and near it the temple
which he erected to Artemis Aristoboulë.[2]

Before quitting the city, we must note a few particulars respecting
its more ordinary and domestic life. Athens was of course provided
with baths (βαλανεῖα). In ancient times warm baths were not allowed
within the walls, as they were considered to be injurious; but with the
progress of luxury they came to be introduced even into private houses.[3]
Isæus alludes to one outside the Thracian Gate, or Dipylum, near the
statue of Anthemocritus;[4] which must, therefore, have been one of the
more ancient ones, if indeed they were already admitted within the city
in his time. An institution peculiar to the Greeks was the *lesche*
(λέσχη), a sort of public place in which fires were lighted in the winter,

---

[1] Γελάδου τοῦ Ἀργείου μὲν ἦν μαθητὴς Φειδίας τοῦ ἐν Μελίτῃ Ἀττικῆς πλάσαντος Ἡρακλέα. — Tzetz. Chil. viii. 192
(325); cf. schol. ad Aristoph. Ran. v. 504.
[2] Plut. Them. 22.
[3] Athen. i. 32.
[4] Apud Harpocr. voc. Ἀνθεμόκριτος.

and were therefore frequented by the poor and those out of work. It is said that there were at Athens no fewer than 360 of these places, which suggests the idea of a vast proletarian population. They were under certain laws and regulations intended to make them something better than merely places of idle resort; but in what these regulations consisted we are not informed.[1] In the cold weather the poor resorted in the night to the smiths' forges, and other workshops where fires were lighted.[2]

Having now described all the principal objects within the walls of Athens, we are in a position to give some account of the processions which on certain solemn festivals paraded the streets. Of these, the principal were the Panathenaïc processions, the Greater and the Less; both of which appear to have been celebrated in the month Hecatombæon; but the Greater recurred only once in every Olympiad, and were celebrated during several days, while the latter took place every year, and lasted only two days. It is only of the route of the Great Panathenaïc procession that we have any particular account; but the authorities are somewhat divergent and contradictory, so that we are not able to distinguish very clearly between the usages at the two festivals, chiefly, as Leake suggests,[3] from the ambiguous meaning of the word *peplus* (πέπλος).

The adorning of the image of Athena with a robe, or shawl, called *peplus*, was a very ancient custom, and is described in the Iliad (v. 286 sqq.), where Hecuba, accompanied by the Trojan matrons, is represented as taking from her chamber her best and newest Sidonian shawl, and laying it on the knees of the goddess in the Trojan Acropolis; whence we may infer that the statue was in a sitting posture (cf. v. 92). The same ceremony was, no doubt, practised at Athens in very early times, when the festival in which it was done seems to have been called *Athenæa* (τὰ 'Αθήναια);[4] but after the synoicismos effected by Theseus,

---

[1] Schol. ap. Hesiod. Oper. et Dies, v. 491.

[2] Ibid.

[3] Topography of Athens, app. xvi.

[4] The only express testimony for a yearly peplus, and therefore in the Lesser Panathenæa, appears to be the scholiast on

Aristoph. Eq. v. 563. Meursius (Panath. cap. 17) condemns it as erroneous, quoting against it Plato, Euthyphron, Plaut. Merc. act i. sc. 1; and a fragment of the same author, quoted by Servius, ad Æn. i. v. 480; Virgil's Ciris; Harpocr. in voc. and a pas-it obtained the name of Panathenæa, as being participated by all the people of Attica. At a still later period, about which we have no precise accounts, but probably in the time of Peisistratus, another and more splendid festival of the same kind appears to have been instituted, which was celebrated every four years, and obtained, from its more elaborate magnificence, the name of the Great Panathenæa. It was afterwards made still more splendid by Lycurgus the orator, who, besides other vessels for the procession, presented some golden Victories and ornaments for a hundred maidens, or canephoroi.[1] For this festival a larger and richer peplus was woven under the superintendence of the two young maidens, called Errephoroi, as before described (supra, p. 427). This, no doubt, was the peplus alluded to by one of the scholiasts on the 'Knights' of Aristophanes, who says that it formed the sail of the Panathenaïc ship, which the Athenians rigged out for Athena every four years.[2] Another scholiast on the same passage, however, refers the word to a garment prepared *every year*, and also carried in procession in the Panathenæa; that is, of course, the lesser Panathenæa.[3] Now, the question is, which peplus did Aristophanes mean? The line which is the subject of these comments, runs as follows:

ἄνδρες ἦσαν τῆσδε τῆς γῆς ἄξιοι καὶ τοῦ πέπλου.

"For they were worthy of the land and also of the peplus."

where Aristophanes doubtless alludes to a custom noticed by a third scholiast of weaving into the peplus portraits of distinguished warriors.[4]

---

sage of Moschopulus. But in these passages the more splendid peplus only is alluded to seemingly *par excellence*, and without necessarily excluding another. Nor can it be supposed that a custom dating at least from the Homeric times should only have been adopted at Athens when the Greater Panathenæa were instituted. It is more probable that only a more splendid one was used on that occasion.

[1] Pausan. c. 29, 16.

[2] πέπλος, τὸ ἅρμενον τῆς Παναθηναϊκῆς νεώς, ἣν οἱ Ἀθηναῖοι κατασκευάζουσι τῇ

θεῷ διὰ τετραετηρίδος.—v. 563. Cf. τῇ δὲ Ἀθηνᾷ ἤγοντο (τὰ μέγαλα Παναθήναια) διὰ πέντε ἐτῶν, ὅτε καὶ ἡ ναῦς ἐπὶ γῆς πλέει παρ' αὐτοῖς.—Schol. ad Pac. 417.

[3] ἐπεσκευάζετο οὖν ὁ πέπλος καθ' ἕκαστον ἐνιαυτόν, καὶ ἐπομπεύετο ἐν τοῖς Παναθηναίοις.—Ibid.

[4] νικήσαντες πέπλον ἐποίησαν τῇ Ἀθηνᾷ καὶ ἐνέθεντο τοὺς ἀρίστους ἐν αὐτῷ.—Ibid. Suidas, voc. πέπλος, has the same, except that he writes ἐνέγραψαν for ἐνέθεντο, which might mean that their names were inscribed.

Plato, in his 'Euthyphro,'[1] mentions a peplus adorned with representations of the wars of the gods, being carried in procession to the Acropolis in the Great Panathenæa; but though he does not advert here to portraits of men, this does not necessarily exclude the idea that there may have been such, or at least occasionally. Both the more ancient and the more modern peplus appear to have contained the wars of the gods, as described by Euripides,[2] and particularly the figure of Enceladus; but the insertion of portraits was doubtless peculiar to the later one. Of those who had obtained this honour, a biographical account appears to have been written, with the title of 'Peplos,' by one of the numerous authors named Aristoteles.[3] Leake (vol. i. p. 568) thinks that the later peplus was used as a curtain before the statue of Athena in the Parthenon, referring to Pausanias' description of a similar curtain in the temple of Zeus, at Olympia; but, had such been the case, it would have been easy for Pausanias to say so when describing the Parthenon. We can only certainly conclude that there were two distinct pepli; but the destination of the larger one cannot be determined by any positive evidence. Arguing from the account given by Pollux,[4] we might conclude that the smaller was merely an embroidered chiton, or ordinary article of dress; whilst the larger one, which he characterizes as an $\epsilon\pi\iota\beta\lambda\eta\mu\alpha$, or covering, may have been intended to throw over and conceal the statue when it was stripped in order to be cleaned during the Plynteria. For we know from Xenophon and Plutarch that it was covered up on that occasion; and it was considered a bad omen for Alcibiades that he should have returned to Athens while the goddess was in that condition.[5] At all events, as the whole

---

[1] p. i. t. i. p. 363, Bekker. Cf. schol. in Remp. init.

[2] Hecuba, v. 466 sqq. We have already seen from Homer that the peplus of Athena was in use in the time of the Trojan queen.

[3] Eustath. ad Il. ii. 557. The author of the poem called 'Ciris,' attributed to Virgil, alludes to the custom of carrying the peplus in the Great Panathenæa, v. 21 sqq.

[4] καὶ ὅτι μὲν ἐπίβλημά ἐστι (ὁ πέπλος) τεκμήραιτ' ἄν τις ἐκ τῶν τῆς Ἀθηνᾶς πέπλων. ὅτι δὲ καὶ χιτών, κ.τ.λ.—Poll. vii. 50.

[5] ἡμέρᾳ, ᾗ Πλυντήρια ἦγεν ἡ πόλις, τοῦ ἕδους κατακεκαλυμμένου τῆς Ἀθηνᾶς.— Xenoph. Hellen. i. 4, 12. Where ἕδος is of course the ancient image. Cf. Plut. Alcib. 34.

festival was in honour of Athena Polias, we do not think that this splendid peplus could have been appropriately used except in the Erechtheium.

We are of opinion that Aristophanes, in the passage cited from the 'Knights,' was really alluding to the Great Panathenaea, and the larger and more splendid peplus. If the first scholiast is right, then this was displayed as the sail of a ship as early at least as the date of that play. And evidence is not altogether wanting that this was the case. Strattis, who was contemporary with Aristophanes, though younger, says in a fragment of his 'Macedones,' preserved by Harpocration : [1]

τὸν πέπλον δὲ τοῦτον
ἕλκουσ' ὀνεύοντες τοπείοις ἄνδρες ἀναρίθμητοι
εἰς ἄκρον, ὥσπερ ἱστίον, τὸν ἱστόν.

"Innumerable men
With ropes and pullies to the top o' the mast
Haul up this peplus, as it were a sail."

We have another confirmation of that custom though at a period of nearly a century later. From an inscription discovered in the Dionysiac theatre at Athens, in May, 1862, it appears that the comic poet Philippides obtained from the Thracian king Lysimachus, in the archonship of Euctemon (B.C. 299), a mast and yard-arm for hoisting the peplus. [2] There can be little doubt that the peplus rent by a storm while passing through the Ceramcicus seven or eight years before this—an accident attributed to the anger of the gods, because the likenesses of Demetrius and Antigonus had been woven into it together with those of Zeus and Athena [3]—was also carried on a mast, though Plutarch does not say so. Hence Photius remarks, that the apparatus of a mast and yard-arm to which the peplus was often attached resembled the letter Tau (T). [4]

---

[1] voc. τοπεῖον. We have printed the passage as given by Meineke, Frag. Com. Graec. p. 432. ὀνεύοντες, *hauling up*. Why countless numbers should aid in hauling, was, perhaps, because the doing so was thought to procure the goodwill of the goddess.

[2] διελέχθη δὲ (ὁ Φιλλιππίδης) καὶ ὑπὲρ κεραίας καὶ ἱστοῦ, ὅπως ἂν δοθῇ τῇ θεῷ εἰς τὰ Παναθήναια τῷ πέπλῳ, ἃ ἐκομίσθη ἐπ' Εὐκτήμονος ἄρχοντος. Ἀρχαιολ. Ἐφημερίς, June, 1862, p. 116. The article describing it is by M. Rousopoulcs.

[3] Plut. Demetr. 12.

[4] Lex. voc. ἱα.ὸς καὶ κεραία.

The ship was, no doubt, an emblem of the maritime supremacy of the Athenians, achieved under the protection of Athena, and therefore may have figured in the procession any time after Themistocles, but before that it was probably carried as a banner. An anathema, consisting of a bronze model of such a vessel, about a foot in length, was found in the Erechtheium, in February, 1862.[1] Sailing or rowing matches formed part of the contests with which the Great Panathenæa were celebrated. An inscription relating to these games and contests found near the Parthenon in 1839, and published by Rangabé, adverts to these matches,[2] which are also mentioned in a passage of the comic poet Plato,[3] from which we also see that they took place at Peiræeus, as they might be viewed from the tomb of Themistocles there (supra, p. 121). Another proof that the naval glory of Athens was connected at an early period with the Great Panathenaïc festival. The custom of carrying the peplus as a sail was continued many centuries later, and the fullest description of the procession which we possess will be found in Philostratus' 'Lives of the Sophists.' It is there said in the life of Herodes Atticus, that in the same Panathenæa in which the stadium he had so magnificently adorned was opened to the public, he exhibited the sail of a ship, swelling with the wind, beautifully adorned with pictures; and that the vessel to which it belonged was not drawn by cattle, but gently impelled by machinery beneath it. It seemed to have a thousand oars, and starting from the Cerameicus it proceeded to the Eleusinium, made the tour of that temple, and then coasting along the Pelasgicum, arrived at the Pythium.[4]

Those who have followed our description of the Athenian agora and its neighbourhood will have little difficulty in tracing the route here laid down. Two things only might occasion some difficulty, the starting point and the goal, the Cerameicus and the Pythium. We have already

[1] Ephem. May, 1862, p. 91 sq.; with a cut.

[2] Ant. Hell. t. ii. No. 960, l. 28: νικη-τήρια νεῶν ἁμίλλης. The editor, however, misunderstood it, and wrote νέων. Sauppe

corrected his reading. De Inscr. Panath. p. 10 sq.

[3] Preserved in Plut. Them. 32.

[4] Philostr. Vit. Soph. i. 2, s. 5.

seen that, in the practice of later writers, the Cerameicus means the agora; and we are inclined to think that in such writers it always does so, unless qualified by the addition of *inner* or *outer*. In the earliest account which we have of the Panathenæa, namely, that of Thucydides (vi. 56), respecting the procession in the time of Hippias and Hipparchus, it appears to have been mustered in the Cerameicus; not in the *outer* Cerameicus, as A. Mommsen[1] and other writers say, forgetting that at that time there could have been only one Cerameicus, and that the distinction between an inner and an outer one must have arisen when the district was intersected by the wall of Themistocles. A passage in the sophist Himerius,[2] which shows that the Panathenaïc ship still figured in the procession in the fourth century of our æra, makes it start from one of the gates, but does not specify which. From the context, however, it may be gathered that it was not from the Dipylum, and therefore not from the outer Cerameicus, but rather from the Peiraïc gate. For it is described as passing through a straight road *descending* from the gate, and lined with porticoes on each side; a description which answers to the street or road which we have before described as leading from the Peiraïc gate to the agora, but which would not at all suit the Dipylum, the road from which, whether lined with porticoes or not, must have *ascended* towards the agora, as the Dipylum lies many feet below its level. This passage, to be sure, would afford no criterion for the earlier times, as in the course of several centuries the practice may have altered. All that we can be sure about is, that the ship must have traversed the Cerameicus or agora. We have already adverted to a passage in Athenæus (iv. 64) where the grandson of Demetrius Phalereus is described as erecting for his mistress Aristagora a scaffolding higher than the Hermæ, in order that she might

---

[1] Heortologie, p. 189.

[2] ἐν τῇδε τῇ πανηγύρει τὴν ἱερὰν ᾽Αθηναῖοι τριήρη τῇ θεῷ πέμπουσιν. ἄρχεται μὲν εὐθὺς ἐκ πυλῶν, οἷον ἔκ τινος εὐδίου λιμένος τῆς ἀναγωγῆς ἡ ναῦς· κινηθεῖσα δὲ ἐκεῖθεν ἤδη καθάπερ κατά τινος ἀκυμάντου θαλάσσης, διὰ μέσου τοῦ δρόμου κομίζεται, ὃς εὐθυτενής τε καὶ λεῖος καταβαίνων ἄνωθεν σχίζει τὰς ἑκατέρωθεν αὐτῷ παρατεταμένας στοάς, ἐφ᾽ ὧν ἀγοράζουσιν οἱ ᾽Αθηναῖοί τε καὶ οἱ λοιποί, κ.τ.λ. Cf. Wachsmuth, Rh. Mus. 1868, p. 53.

obtain a good view of the Panathenaïc procession as it passed through the market place. Mommsen (p. 191) adverts to a passage in Xenophon's Hipparchicus (iii. 2), which we have already cited on another occasion, where the cavalry is described as starting from the Hermæ and galloping to the Eleusinium, and thinks that Philostratus' account of the course of the ship is thereby confirmed; but the argument, though affording a strong presumption, is not conclusive. The procession of the Lesser Panathenæa also went through the agora, as appears from a passage of Menander's 'Hypobolimæus,' preserved by Photius and Suidas.[1]

With regard to the goal, we think, with Leake and Dr. Wordsworth, that by the 'Pythium' Philostratus means the temenos of Apollo Patroüs near the Areiopagus. It has been shown that the Pythium, properly so called, was near the Olympium. This could not have been the place meant by Philostratus, since he says that the ship, after going round the Eleusinium, which was at the eastern extremity of the agora (above, p. 222 sq.), proceeded along the Pelasgicum, which lay westward of it. Its resting-place, therefore, must have been the temenos of Apollo Patroüs; where, indeed, Pausanias seems to have seen it when he was leaving the Acropolis (above, p. 457).

M. Beulé disputes,[2] and with considerable show of reason, the commonly received opinion that the chariots and horsemen of the procession actually ascended to the Acropolis. This view, for which there is no ancient authority, seems to have been suggested, he remarks, by the frieze of the Parthenon. It was inferred from it that what was represented on the temple must really have existed around it, just as a shadow projected on a wall necessarily implies the presence of the body which it figures. Horses and chariots are shown on the frieze, therefore horses and chariots made the circuit of the Parthenon. In confirmation of this opinion, some travellers have imagined that they could discover the ruts of wheels on the pavement of the Acropolis. M. Beulé

---

[1] Μικρὰ Παναθήναι᾽ ἐπειδὴ δι᾽ ἀγορᾶς πέμποντά σε,
Μοσχίων, μήτηρ ἑώρα τῆς κόρης ἐφ᾽ ἅρματος.—Suidas, voc. πέμπειν.

[2] L'Acropole, &c., t. i. p. 147 sqq.

declares that there are none, and asks how deep holes could have been worked in the stone by carriages which passed over it once in four years? He further observes that the construction of the steps, and the steepness of the ascent, would have made it impossible for chariots to go up, and still more so to go down. To these remarks we may perhaps add, that the surface of the Acropolis, crowded as it was with temples, statues, and other monuments, would hardly have afforded sufficient space for the evolutions of chariots and horsemen.

We must suppose, then, that the procession halted at the foot of the ascent, where the chariots, horsemen, and also the Panathenaïc ship, quitted it; whilst another procession, consisting of the priests, the magistrates, the old men (or θαλλοφόροι), the canephoroi, and other privileged persons ascended on foot. This privilege of bearing a branch of olive (θαλλός) was confined to citizens, and the handsomest old men appear to have been selected for it: they were permitted to accompany the procession to the temple. On the other hand, freedmen and other barbarians were allowed to carry a branch of oak in the procession, but not to proceed beyond the agora.[1] The oxen, also, must have been dragged up to the sacrifice, for we know that sacrifice was offered on this occasion. An inscription found at the Propylæa in 1846, which, from the characters, M. Rangabé takes to belong to Olympiad 110 (B.C. 340), shows that when the procession ascended, two sacrifices were made by the hieropoioi; one to Athena Hygieia, and the other on the Areiopagus.[2] This inscription, therefore, could not refer to the Great Panathenæa, because we are expressly told, on the authority of Aristotle, that the hieropoioi—who were ten in number, consequently one for each tribe—superintended all the sacrifices, including the Pentaëterides, or those recurring every five years, *except* those at the Panathenæa.[3]

---

[1] δρῦν φέρειν διὰ τῆς ἀγορᾶς.—Bekk. Ancc. Gr. p. 242.

[2] θ]ύειν δὲ τοὺς ἱεροποιοὺς τὰς μὲν δύο [θυσίας τήν τε τῇ] Ἀθηνᾷ τῇ Ὑγιείᾳ καὶ τὴν ἐν τῷ Ἀρε[ίῳ πάγῳ τελου]μένην καθάπερ πρότερον.—Rangabé, Ant. Hell. No. 814 (t. ii. p. 439).

[3] Ἱεροποιοί, κληρωτοὶ ἄρχοντές εἰσι δέκα τὸν ἀριθμόν, οἱ . . . καὶ θυσίας τὰς νομιζομένας ἐπιτελοῦσι, καὶ τὰς πενταετηρίδας ἁπάσας διοικοῦσι, πλὴν παναθηναίων. ταῦτα δὲ Ἀριστοτέλης ἱστορεῖ ἐν τῇ Ἀθηναίων πολιτείᾳ.—Etym. M. in voc. p. 468, 56. This passage is not to be found in

The inscription, therefore, must refer to the Lesser Panathenæa ; but it is probable that there were sacrifices of the same sort, if under different superintendence, at both festivals. The other pentaëterid sacrifices were those at Delos, at Brauron, that of the Heracleia, and that at Eleusis ; and these were all superintended by the hieropoioi.[1] The sacrifice on the Areiopagus was no doubt to the Semnæ. For such sacrifices there appear also to have been ten special hieropoioi.[2] Photius, indeed (in voc.), says that the number was indefinite ; and from a passage in Demosthenes[3] it has been inferred that there were only three ; an inference which also acquires plausibility from the number of the Semnæ. But the passage is very probably corrupt ; whilst, not only are the words of Deinarchus plain and positive, but it is also more consonant with probability that each of the ten tribes should have been represented by a hieropoios.

After the two preliminary sacrifices to Athena Hygieia and the Semnæ, the inscription published by Rangabé proceeds to give directions about the sacrifice of the hecatomb. The hecatomb did not always mean a hundred victims ; but in this case, at all events, they must have amounted to more than half that number, taking the price of an ox or cow at 75 drachms, or an average between 50 and 100, as laid down by

_ _ _ _ _

the 'Politics' as we possess them. The sacrifices were actually performed by the μάντεις, or soothsayers : ἱεροποιὸν δὲ καλοῦσι τὸν ἐποπτεύοντα τοὺς μάντεις ὅτε θύουσι, μήπου τι κακουργῶσιν ἐν ταῖς θυσίαις.—Schol. ad Demosth. c. Mid. Rangabé (ibid. p. 441).

[1] Pollux, viii. 107. The text has Ἡρακλειδῶν. Ἡρακλείων is an emendation of Meursius.

[2] Etym. M. voc. ἱεροποιοί from Deinarchus : καὶ τὰς σεμνὰς θεὰς αἷς ἐκείνος ἱεροποιὸς καταστὰς δέκατος αὐτός.

[3] περιεῖδε δὲ ταῖς σεμναῖς θεαῖς ἱεροποιὸν αἱρεθέντα ἐξ Ἀθηναίων ἁπάντων τρίτον αὐτόν, καὶ καταρξάμενον τῶν ἱερῶν.—c. Mid.

p. 552, Reiske. It is remarkable, however, that the Etymologicus, who quotes this passage, instead of τρίτον αὐτὸν καί, reads καὶ περὶ τὸν αὐτὸν καιρόν. Kühn, however (ad Poll. viii. 107, note 90), would not amend Demosthenes, and thinks that by τρίτον αὐτὸν he merely means that he was the third elected among the ten. But we doubt very much whether αὐτὸς after an ordinal number can ever mean anything but the whole number designated by the ordinal. Mommsen, however (Heortologie, p. 171, note), adopts the number of three from this doubtful passage, without adverting to other authorities.

Boeckh;[1] for the price set apart for the purchase of them is 41 minæ, or 4100 drachms.[2] The hecatomb was to be sacrificed "at the great altar of Athena" (ἐπὶ τῷ βωμῷ τῆς Ἀθηνᾶς τῷ μεγάλῳ l. 19); by which we can hardly understand, with Rangabé (p. 443), the altar of the θυηχόος before described, at the entrance of the Erechtheium. It seems more likely to have been the great altar before the eastern front of the Parthenon, which was not very far from the temple of Polias. Previously to the sacrifice of the hecatomb, one of the heifers, selected for its beauty, was offered up at the temple of Athena Nikë.[3] The inscription also gives directions about the division of the flesh of the victims, and especially enjoins that the *pannychis* (παννυχίς), or vigil, which preceded every Panathenaïc procession, and in which the Lampadephoria and other sports were exhibited, should be celebrated with all possible splendour; after which the procession was to begin with the rising sun.

We are unable to connect any other of the Athenian pomps to any great extent with the topography of the city. The most important of them were the Eleusinian and Dionysiac processions. In the former, when the image of Iacchus was carried from Athens to Eleusis—called ἐξελαύνειν τὸν Ἴακχον—it seems to have been taken, myrtle-crowned, like the mystæ themselves, and bearing a torch, from the Iaccheium near the Peiraïc Gate by the Iacchagogus. Hence the route would have lain through the agora and Inner Cerameicus, entering on the Holy Way at the Dipylum. Of the route thence to Eleusis we shall have occasion to speak further on. The return of the image from Eleusis to Athens seems to have been accomplished in a more disorderly manner, if the passage in Herodotus describing the dust raised by three myriads of men, at the time of the battle of Salamis, is to be referred to that occasion.[4] There appears also to have been a procession on the fourth day of the festival, when the *calathus* was paraded in a car drawn by oxen, and apparently in the city, since

---

[1] Pub. Œc. of Athens, Lewis' trans. p. 75.
[2] Inscr. l. 16.
[3] μίαν δὲ ἐπὶ τῷ (βωμῷ) τῆς Νίκης, προ-

κρίναντες ἐκ τῶν καλλιστευουσῶν βοῶν.—
Rangabé, Ant. Hell. No. 184 (t. ii. p. 440).
[4] lib. viii. 65; cf. Plut. Them. 15.

the people were forbidden to view it from the housetops, or from any
height :

> τὸν κάλαθον κατιόντα χαμαὶ θάσησθε, βέβαλοι,
> μηδ' ἀπὸ τοῦ τέγεος, μηδ' ὑψόθεν αὐγάσσησθε.[1]

> " From housetop, or from any height, refrain
> The holy calathus to view, profane!"

But we cannot tell its route. This was the slowly-rolling waggon
alluded to by Virgil :

> " Tardaque Eleusinæ matris volventia plaustra."
>
> Georg. i. 163.

The procession on the occasion of the Great Dionysia, in the month
of Elaphebolion, does not seem to have been an extensive one. The
day appears to have been inaugurated with sacrifice and pæans in the
temple of Asclepius, followed by the Dionysiac proagon, seemingly a
sort of rehearsal, in the theatre.[2] In the night of that day the statue
of Dionysus, probably that of Alcamenes (see above, p. 305), which was
the more splendid one, was carried from the temple to the theatre by
torch light,[3] and erected in the orchestra.[4] That there was a procession
on the following day we know from the law quoted by Demosthenes,[5]
and because canephoroi, with their golden baskets, took part in it.[6] A
decree in honour of one Zopyrus, who had sent his daughter as a
canephoros in the Great Dionysia, was found in the theatre in June,
1862. He was to be rewarded with an ivy crown, while all the epi-
meletæ or stewards of the pomp were to have crowns of gold.[7] Plutarch

---

[1] Callimachus, Hymn in Cer.

[2] τῇ ὀγδόῃ ἱσταμένου τοῦ Ἐλαφηβολιῶνος
μηνός, ὅτε ἦν τῷ Ἀσκληπίῳ ἡ θυσία, καὶ ὅτ'
ἦν προαγὼν ἐν τῇ ἱερᾷ ἡμέρᾳ.—Æsch. c.
Ctesiph. p. 455, Reiske ; cf. A. Mommsen,
Heortol. p. 391.

[3] εἰσήγαγον δὲ καὶ τὸν Διόνυσον ἀπὸ τῆς
ἐσχάρας εἰς τὸ θέατρον μετὰ φωτός.—Inscr.
in Arch. Ephem. 1861, No. 4098, ap.
Mommsen, p. 392.

[4] τὸν Διόνυσον ἐπὶ τὴν ὀρχήστραν τιθέασιν.— Dion Chrys. Orat. xxxi. p. 386,

Teubner.

[5] καὶ τοῖς ἐν ἄστει Διονυσίοις ἡ πομπή.—
Demosth. c. Meid. p. 517, Reiske.

[6] κατὰ τὴν τῶν Διονυσίων ἑορτὴν παρὰ
τοῖς Ἀθηναίοις αἱ εὐγενεῖς παρθένοι ἐκανη-
φόρουν. ἦν δὲ ἐκ χρυσοῦ πεποιημένα τὰ
κανᾶ, ἐφ' ὧν τὰς ἀπαρχὰς ἁπάντων ἐτίθεσαν.
—Schol. ad Aristoph. Acharn. v. 241.

[7] Ἐλαφηβολιῶνος δεκάτῃ ὑστέρᾳ . . .
δεδόχθαι τῷ δήμῳ ἐπαινέσαι τὸν πατέρα τῆς
κανηφόρου Ζώπυρον Δικαίου Μελιτέα καὶ
στεφανῶσαι αὐτὸν κιττοῦ στεφάνῳ . .

notes the superfluous splendour of the procession in his day, as compared with the simplicity of ancient times. Formerly, he says, the feast was celebrated in a plebeian and merry fashion; there was a cask of wine and a branch of clematis; then came a fellow dragging along a goat; another followed bearing a basket of figs; and last of all came the phallus. But now all this is neglected and has disappeared, and gold cups and splendid robes are carried about instead, and there are chariots and maskers.[1] The chorus danced and sung round the altar of the Twelve Gods in the agora, besides paying the same devotions to other deities.[2] The ἕδος, or antique statue, of Dionysus (τοῦ Διονύσου τοῦ Ἐλευθερέως) was carried in one of the Dionysiac festivals to a small temple in the Academy, as we shall learn presently from Pausanias; but whether this took place in the Great Dionysia, or in the Anthesteria, does not seem clear.[3]

ἐπαινέσαι τοὺς ἐπιμελητὰς τῆς πομπῆς καὶ στεφανῶσαι ἕκαστον αὐτῶν χρυσῷ στεφάνῳ, κ.τ.λ.—Arch. Ephem. July 6, 1862, No. 180, p. 174. The archon was also named Zopyrus.

[1] De cupid. divit. p. 527 (t. viii. p. 91, Reiske).

[2] Xenoph. Hipparch. iii. 2. Among the Twelve, however, Dionysus was not to be found. Ennius thus sums them up (ap. Appul. De Deo Socr. p. 123):

" Juno, Vesta, Minerva, Ceres, Diana,
    Venus, Mars,
    Mercurius, Jovi', Neptunus, Vulcanus,
    Apollo."

[3] Pausanias, i. 29, 2, only says, ἀνὰ πᾶν ἔτος ἐν τεταγμέναις ἡμέραις. A passage in Philostratus : ὁπότε δὲ ἥκοι Διονύσια καὶ κατίοι ἐς Ἀκαδημίαν τὸ τοῦ Διονύσου ἕδος (Vit. Soph. ii. 1, 3), does not specify which Dionysia.

CHAPTER XIII.

PAUSANIAS has now finished his description of the interior of the city, but we will accompany him on his way through some of the suburbs (c. 29, 2 sqq.). There were, he says, in the boroughs, or demes, outside the city and along the roads, temples of the gods, and tombs of men and heroes. Not far from the walls is the ACADEMY, once the property of a private individual, but now a gymnasium. On the way thither is an enclosure, sacred to Artemis, containing rude images of her (ξόανα) as the "best" and "most beautiful." That these were surnames of Artemis is confirmed by the poems of Sappho. There is to be sure another account of them, he observes, which however I will pass over. There is also a small temple to which the image of the Eleutherean Dionysus—viz. that in his temple at the Limnæ—is carried every year. These were all the temples on the road.

In the next chapter he proceeds to describe the objects at the Academy. Before the entrance was an altar of Eros, and the inscription on it purported that Charmus was the first Athenian who dedicated one to that deity. The altar of Anteros in the city was said to have been dedicated by the metics, or denizens. In the Academy was an altar of Prometheus, where the competitors in the Lampadephoria lighted their torches and ran with them into the city. The skill of it was, to keep the

torch alight while running. First one runs, then another, and whoever
brings in his torch alight is proclaimed victor ; but if none succeeds,
there is no prize. There are also altars of Hermes and of the Muses,
and in the interior one of Athena and one of Heracles. Here, too, is an
olive tree, said to have been the second created. Near the Academy is
a monument of Plato. Pausanias then goes on to relate the dream of
Socrates, how on the eve when Plato was to become his disciple, a white
swan flew into his bosom. The story is also told by Apuleius, who
adds that the swan rose from the altar of Eros, and afterwards flew up
to heaven, delighting with its song both gods and men.[1]

The account of Pausanias must be corrected and supplemented from
other authorities. Besides an altar, there was also a statue of Eros. It
was usual to place this deity in gymnasia along with Hermes and
Heracles.[2] The epigram on the altar was :

$$\pi o \iota \kappa \iota \lambda o \mu \acute{\eta} \chi a \nu\text{'} \text{ }\text{"}E \rho \omega s, \sigma o \grave{\iota} \tau \acute{o} \nu \delta\text{'} \text{ } \dot{\iota} \delta \rho \acute{\nu} \sigma a \tau o \beta \omega \mu \grave{o} \nu$$
$$X \acute{a} \rho \mu o s \dot{\epsilon} \pi \grave{\iota} \sigma \kappa \iota \epsilon \rho o \hat{\iota} s \tau \acute{\epsilon} \rho \mu a \sigma \iota \gamma \nu \mu \nu a \sigma \acute{\iota} o \nu.[3]$$

"For thee, in this gymnasium's circling shade,
  Charmus, O trickster Love, this altar made."

Charmus lived in the reign of Peisistratus, so that the Academy
must have been a gymnasium even then ; and indeed we have seen that
Hipparchus built a wall round it.[4] According to Plutarch,[5] the statue
was dedicated by Peisistratus, who was an admirer of Charmus. In the
same passage it is said that the torches for the Lampadephoria were lit
here ; so that the altar and statue must have been near that of Prometheus, at the entrance. The Lampadephoria was celebrated in the
Panathenæa and in the festivals of Hephæstus and Prometheus ; and
the torch is said to have been first used in sacrifices to the former.
There was also a torch game in honour of Pan and Prometheus.[6]
Torches were lit and carried on the fourth day of the Eleusinia, sym-
bolizing the search of Demeter for Corë, which was called $\lambda a \mu \pi a \delta \epsilon \acute{\nu} \epsilon \sigma \theta a \iota$;
but this was a different thing from the Lampadephoria ; for though

---

[1] De Dogm. Plat. lib. i. init.
[2] Athen. xiii. 12.   [3] Ibid. c. 89.
[4] Suidas in τὸ Ἱππάρχου τεῖχος.

[5] In Solon. 1.
[6] Phot. Lex. voce. λαμπάδος and λαμπάς :
Bekk. An. Gr. vo ·. λαμπάς, p. 277.

the mystæ appear to have run with them in the temple of Demeter, there was no contest, and the torches were handed from one to another.[1] According to Istros, the torches were lighted and hymns sung in honour of Hephæstus in the festival of the Apaturia.[2] Of the conjunction of the worship of Hephæstus with that of Athena we have already had occasion to speak (supra, p. 227). In the Academy Prometheus was added to the group, and there was an ancient statue of him ($\mathring{\iota}\delta\rho\upsilon\mu\alpha$) with an altar, in the temenos of Athena here. On an ancient base or pediment, at the entrance, was a bas-relief of Prometheus and Hephæstus, the former being represented as the elder and first in rank, with a sceptre in his right hand. There was also sculptured in the bas-relief an altar common to both.[3]

By the second created olive Pausanias appears to mean the sacred plants called *moriæ* ($\mu o\rho\acute{\iota}\alpha\iota$ or $\mu o\rho\acute{\iota}\alpha\iota$ $\grave{\epsilon}\lambda\alpha\hat{\iota}\alpha\iota$), reputed to be offshoots from the primitive olive on the Acropolis, and from which was made the oil given as a prize in the Panathenaïc contests.[4] They grew near the temple of Athena in the Academy, where also was an altar of Zeus Catæbates ($\kappa\alpha\tau\alpha\iota\beta\acute{\alpha}\tau\eta s$, *descending in the thunderbolt*—Jupiter Elicius) called also Morios ($\mu\acute{o}\rho\iota os$) here as guardian of these trees.[5]

All that we learn from Pausanias about the site of the Academy is, that it was not far from the city; but he does not even tell us on which side it lay. We know, however, from Cicero and Livy, that the road to

[1] "Tuque, Actæa Ceres, cursu cui semper anhelo
Votivam taciti quassamus lampada mystæ."—Stat. Silv. iv. 8, 50.
Schol. ad Juv. xv. 141: "in templo Cereris sibi invicem facem cursores tradunt." So Lucretius:
"Et quasi cursores vitai lampada tradunt."—ii. 77.
See Meurs. Eleus. c. 26.

[2] Harpocr. voc. λαμπάς; cf. Hesych. and Phavorinus.

[3] Schol. ad Soph. Œd. Col. v. 56; from Apollodorus and Lysimachides. Leake (vol. i. p. 600) strangely misinterprets this

scholium, confounding the altar of Prometheus with that represented on the base, and omitting the statue of Prometheus. Whether he had a temple, as Leake says, or merely an altar, depends on whether we read βωμὸς or ναός. The former is the reading of the Laurentian MS., edited by Elmsley (schol. in Soph. Oxon. 1825, p. 45).

[4] Aristot. ap. schol. Soph. Œd. Col. v. 701.

[5] περὶ 'Ακαδημίαν ἐστὶν ὅ τε τοῦ Καταιβάτου Διὸς βωμός, ὃν καὶ Μόριον καλοῦσι, (ἀπὸ?) τῶν ἐκεῖ μορίων παρὰ τὸ τῆς 'Αθηνᾶς ἱερὸν ἱδρυμένων.—Ibid. v. 705; cf. Aristoph. Nub. 1001, and Schol.

it was through the Dipylum, and that it must consequently have been
on the north side of Athens. The former of these authorities calls the
distance of it from the gate six stadia,[1] and the latter *about* a mile;
whence we may conclude that it was somewhat under the latter measure.[2]
We find it sometimes identified with the Ceramicus,[3] whence we may
infer that it was included within the bounds of that suburb. About a
century ago it appears to have been identified with a low hill to the
north of the city, called Acathymia;[4] but it is not very easy at present
to discover its exact site, and all that Gell tells of it is, that it is supposed to have been in the direction of Sepolia.[5] It is said to have
derived its name from a hero called Academus, or Hecademus; in consideration of whom the Lacedæmonians abstained from ravaging the
Academy when they invaded Attica; though according to another
account they did so for fear of the curses attaching to such an act.[6]

The site of the Academy was not reckoned very healthy,[7] probably
from the dampness arising from the waters of the Cephisus. The
same cause, however, rendered the spot favourable to vegetation, and
even at this day, all this side of Athens, along the course of the river,
is marked by a belt of olive and other trees. Most of these trees,
M. Le Normant is of opinion,[8] were planted in ancient times. Some of
them are twenty feet in circumference; the oldest are entirely hollow,
and live only in their bark, so that it is impossible to calculate their age.
Two amongst the youngest, which had been cut down, showed by the
successive layers that they had existed 652 and 530 years respectively.
Hence the Academy is called by Diogenes Laërtius a well wooded
suburb.[9] Its natural qualities in this way were improved by art.

[1] "Inde vario sermone sex illa a Dipylo
stadia confecimus; cum autem venissemus
in Academiæ non sine causa nobilitata
spatia," &c.—Cic. de Fin. v. 1.

[2] "Limes mille ferme passus in Academiæ gymnasium (ab Dipylo)."—Liv.
xxxi. 24.

[3] Hesych. Steph. in voc.

[4] Walpole's 'Turkey,' p. 146.

[5] Itinerary, p. 48.

[6] Plut. Thes. 32; schol. ad Soph. Œd.
Col. 701.

[7] νοσεροῦ χωρίου λεγομένου εἶναι τῆς
'Ακαδημίας.—Æl. Var. Hist. ix. 10.

[8] Voie Sacrée, t. i. p. 197 sq.

[9] γυμνάσιον προάστειον ἀλσῶδες.—iii. 7;
cf. Plut. Sull. 12: δενδροφορωτάτην προ-
αστείων οὖσαν.

Cimon introduced into it streams of water, made shady walks and broad and open drives.[1] It was along the last probably that the cavalry exercised, for we know from Xenophon that this was one of the places where they displayed their evolutions.[2] These drives, or rides, are alluded to by Eupolis as being also shady :

$$\text{ἐν εὐσκίοις δρύμοισιν Ἀκαδήμου θεοῦ.}^{3}$$

" In god-like Academus' shady drives."

The same characteristic is alluded to by Horace :

" Atque inter silvas Academi quærere verum."[4]

In later times it was still further improved by Attalus, who laid out some gardens here, which afterwards obtained the name of the Lacydeium, because the philosopher Lacydes, the founder of the third or new Academy, was accustomed to teach in them.[5] The king alluded to seems to have been Attalus Philometor, who lived in the second century before our era. He seems to have been a good gardener, though a bad man ; the many poisonous herbs which he cultivated, and his skill in preparing them, may perhaps have helped him to make away with some of his friends and relations.[6] Much of the beauty of the Academy must have been destroyed by Sulla when he invested Athens, and cut down the trees of the Academy and the Lyceium for the purpose of making implements of war.[7] But this damage was doubtless made good afterwards.

The Academy owes its celebrity chiefly to its having been the residence and the school of Plato, and thus giving birth to what has been called after it the Academic sect. Plato's house, to which a garden seems to have been attached, must have been modest enough, since it is said to have cost only 3000 drachmas, and the yearly value of

[1] Plut. Cim. 13.

[2] Hipparch. iii. 1.

[3] In his Ἀστράτευτοι, ap. Diog. Laërt. iii. 7. The enormous plane trees, or rather tree, mentioned by Leake as being in the Academy (vol. i. p. 197 sq.), appears rather to have been in the Lyceum ; but the mis-take is Pliny's. See Sillig ad xii. 1, 5 (t. ii. p. 331).

[4] Ep. ii. 2, 45.

[5] Diog. Laërt. iv. 60.

[6] Plut. Demetr. 20.

[7] Plut. loc. cit. ; App. B. M. p. 191.

it was estimated at only three pieces of gold ; but afterwards, through the gifts and bequests of the patrons of learning, it became worth 3000.[1] The little garden seems to have been extant in the time of Cicero, who adverts to it as bringing back not only the memory but even the very form itself of the great philosopher.[2] Nevertheless, in spite of his poverty, Plato adorned the Academy by erecting a temple to the Muses,[3] which must have been that mentioned by Pausanias. It was in this temple probably that Mithridates placed the statue of Plato, made by Silanion and dedicated to the Muses.[4] Speusippus erected in it statues of the Graces.[5] Plato was buried near the Academy—Diogenes Laërtius says in it,[6] and that his body was accompanied to the tomb by all the population of the neighbourhood, whence we may infer that this suburb was then pretty thickly inhabited. The memory of such a man and of the philosophers by whom he was succeeded, and the lofty nature of their teaching, seem to have invested the place with a certain awful solemnity. Aristophanes alludes in the ' Clouds' to the sober character of the youths who frequented it :

> ἀλλ' εἰς 'Ακαδήμειαν κατιὼν ὑπὸ ταῖς μορίαις ἀποθρέξει
> στεφανωσάμενος καλάμῳ λευκῷ μετὰ σώφρονος ἡλικιώτου.—v. 1005.

" In the Academy, under the shade
By the boughs of the olives conveniently made
With a steady companion like thyself thou wilt scamper,
Having first bound thy brow with white reeds for a damper."[7]

There was an Attic saying that in ancient times no laughter was allowed there;[8] but this was probably an exaggeration. The solemnity of the place must have been augmented by the pit at which, according to immemorial custom, the polemarchs offered sacrifice to the souls of

---

[1] Plut. de Exil. p. 603 (t. viii. 379, Reiske); Suidas, in Πλάτων.

[2] "Cujus etiam illi hortuli propinqui non memoriam solum mihi afferunt, sed ipsum videntur in conspectu meo ponere."—De Fin. v. 2.

[3] Diog. Laërt. Vit. Speus. (iv. 1, 1). Leake (i. 601) erroneously attributes the

temple to Xenophon

[4] Idem, Vit. Plat. iii. 25.

[5] Diog. Laërt. iv. 1.

[6] Ibid. 40.

[7] λιτὸς γὰρ καὶ ἀπερίεργος ὁ τοιοῦτος στέφανος.—Schol. ad loc.

[8] Æl. V. H. iii. 35.

heroes (Parentalia).[1] Banquets, however, seem to have been sometimes celebrated at the Academy, and also at the Lyceium, as we have before remarked (supra, p. 290).

Pausanias also describes in his 29th chapter the tombs of celebrated men which lay on the road from the Dipylum to the Academy. The first met with was that of Thrasybulus, who overthrew the Thirty Tyrants. Next occurred those of Pericles, Chabrias and Phormio. That of Pericles must have stood a little out of the road, on the right, as Cicero mentions having quitted the main road a little in order to view it.[2] We may suppose that the tomb of Chabrias must have been a rather magnificent structure, as the Athenians had expended a thousand drachmas upon it; and his spendthrift son was not ashamed to sell the stones of it, to eke out his profligate luxury;[3] for which he was branded by several of the comic poets. Indeed, it was found necessary to restrain by a law the splendour sometimes displayed in these monuments; and it was enacted—Cicero does not say at what date—that nobody should have a finer sepulchre than what ten men could execute in three days. It was not to be architecturally adorned, nor to have a Hermes placed upon it; nor was the deceased to be eulogised, except when the funeral was a public one, and then only by a person publicly appointed for that purpose.[4] Another tomb in the Cerameicus mentioned by Pausanias (c. 29, 5) was that of Cleisthenes, the author of the new arrangement of the tribes. There also lay Harmodius and Aristogeiton, the philosophers Zeno and Chrysippus, Nicias, the animal painter, the rhetoricians Ephialtes, the reformer of the Areiopagus, and Lycurgus, who adorned Athens with so many beautiful buildings (ib. s. 15, 16).

---

[1] ἐπειδὴ κατὰ τὸν βόθρον ἐγένετο τὸν ἐν Ἀκαδημίᾳ (πάντως γινώσκεις ἔνθα τοῖς ἥρωσι οἱ πολέμαρχοι τὸ πάτριον ἐναγίζουσιν), κ.τ.λ. —Heliodor. Æthiop. i. 17 (ap. Meurs. Cer. c. 26).

[2] De Fin. v. 2, 5.

[3] Athen. iv. 60.

[4] " Sed post (Solonem) aliquanto, propter has amplitudines sepulcrorum, quas in Ceramico videmus, lege sancitum est, NE QUIS SEPULCRUM FACERET OPEROSIUS QUAM QUOD DECEM HOMINES EFFECERINT TRIDUO. Neque id opere tectorio exornari, nec Hermas hos, quos vocant, licebat imponi; nec de mortui laude, nisi in publicis sepulturis; nec ab alio, nisi si qui publice ad eam rem constitutus esset, dici licebat."—Cic. De Rep. ii. 26.

The honour was conferred upon Zeno at the request of King Antigonus.[1] Servius Sulpicius appears to have procured for his friend M. Marcellus a marble tomb in the Academy itself, where also his body was burnt.[2]

Along the road leading to the Academy were also the tombs of all who had fallen in battle, with the exception of those slain at Marathon; for these were all buried in the field on which they fell, in memory of their valour (Paus. 29, 4 sqq.). Thucydides has a classical passage on the method of interring those who had fallen in war, which we will here insert. "Three days before the funeral takes place the bones of the dead are placed in a tent erected for the purpose, and their relatives bring any offerings they may think proper. On the day of the funeral each tribe sends in a waggon a chest, or coffin, made of cypress wood, in which are placed the remains of those belonging to the respective tribes. One empty bier, with coverlets, is brought for those whose bodies were not found. Whoever please to do so, citizens or strangers, follow the procession, and the female relatives of the defunct are present at the sepulchre, where they indulge their lamentations. The remains are placed in a public monument in the most beautiful suburb of the city (viz. the Cerameicus), where those who fall in battle are always interred, except those slain at Marathon; for as the valour of these was deemed unparalleled, so they were buried where they fell. After they are interred, a man chosen by the city, and considered pre-eminent in wisdom and dignity, pronounces over them a suitable panegyric, after which the assembly disperses."[3] The custom is alluded to by Aristophanes in the 'Birds':

> ὁ Κεραμεικὸς δέξεται νώ.
> δημόσια γὰρ ἵνα ταφῶμεν,
> φήσομεν πρὸς τοὺς στρατηγοὺς
> μαχομένω τοῖς πολεμίοισιν
> ἀποθανεῖν ἐν Ὀρνεαῖς.—v. 394 sqq.

> "'T were strange indeed if two fellows like us
> Couldn't get interred in the Cerameicus,

---

[1] Diog. Laërt. vii. 15. Of Lycurgus cf. Ps. Plut. in Vita.

[2] Servius Ciceroni (Epist. ad Fam. iv. 12).

[3] Thucyd. ii. 34.

> For to the general we'll swear,
> Though sure enough we were not there,
> That fighting with the enemy
> We got killed at Ornea,
> And so the public will inter us."

Demosthenes, in a fine passage of his oration 'De Corona,' invokes those buried in the public sepulchres, as well as those who had fallen at Marathon.[1] Over the sepulchres were stelæ, or marble pillars, with inscriptions recording where the inmates of them fell.[2] The polemarchs appear to have celebrated yearly in the Academy funeral games in their honour;[3] probably at the spot where, as we have already mentioned, they performed the Parentalia to heroes. Unless indeed Academy be there used as synonymous with Cerameicus, as seems to be sometimes the case. Nor was the honour of public sepulture confined to Athenian citizens. Thus there were tombs of the Thessalian knights, who came to the aid of Athens in the Peloponnesian war, and near them of some Cretan bowmen. Some of the Lacedemonians who fell when Thrasybulus was engaged against the Thirty Tyrants were also buried here.[4] Even slaves who had faithfully and valiantly stood by their masters in war were by a public decree admitted to this honour, and their names engraved on the column (c. 29, 5 and 6).

Among the earlier monuments of this kind were those of the Athenians slain by the Edoni in Thrace, and those who invaded the Æginetans before the Persian war. Also, among others, of those who had fought under Alcibiades, of those who had conquered the Syracusans before the arrival of Demosthenes, of those who had shared in the naval battle at the Hellespont, of those who had fought with Cimon at the Eurymedon, and of those who had opposed the Macedonians at Chæroneia. There also were tombs of Conon and Timotheus.

The tomb of Cimon himself is supposed to have been quite on the opposite side of the city, under the north-west side of the Museium Hill. His grandfather of the same name, who flourished in the time of Peisis-

[1] p. 297, Reiske.
[2] Schol. ad Aristoph. loc. cit. Pausan.
[3] Philostr. Vit. Soph. ii. 30 fin. p. 623; et Poll. viii. ix. 4.
[4] Xenoph. Hell. ii. 4, 33.

tratus, appears from the testimony of Herodotus to have been interred at this spot, "beyond the road called Cœlë," and opposite to him the horse with which he had thrice carried off the Olympic prize.[1] This was no doubt the sepulchre called Cimoneia (Κιμώνεια), where his grandson, the son of Miltiades, was also buried,[2] and to which we have before had occasion to advert when speaking of the city regions (supra, p. 100). The probability is strengthened by the circumstance that Cimon cohabited with his sister, Elpinicë, on the neighbouring Pnyx Hill.[3] Thucydides was also interred near the same spot.[4]

Some tombs in the Cerameicus, to which we have before alluded (ch. 4), just outside the Dipylum, near the little church of Agia Triada, were accidentally discovered in 1863 by a peasant employed in digging for sand. They seem to have owed their preservation to the circumstance of their having been buried in ancient times to a depth of about thirty feet. As there could have been no houses just outside the wall by whose ruins they could have been covered, and as indeed the soil itself, from its nature, could not have been formed of such materials, it is most probable, as we have said, that they were buried under a mound formed by Philip V. The Athenians themselves could hardly have committed so sacrilegious an act; it was doubtless done by military violence, and as there was no siege of Athens from the time of Sulla to that of the Goths, it is most natural to refer the heaping-up of this sand either to him or Philip. For as the tombs found on its surface were of the first and second century of our era, it was evidently long prior to the time of the Gothic siege.[5] Near the same spot was found in 1860 an enormous mass of human bones, the results, it has been conjectured, of the massacre committed by Sulla.[6] But we have before had occasion to observe that this spot seems to have been used as a common place of sepulture. Owing to what must now be considered the fortunate

---

[1] Herod. vi. 103.

[2] Plut. Cim. 19.

[3] Δίδυμος δέ φησιν οὐχ ὅτι (ὁ Κίμων) ἐλακώνιζεν, ἀλλ' ὅτι ἐν Πυκνὶ τῇ ἀδελφῇ συνῆν.—Arg. in Orat. Arist. in Cimonem (Meurs. Ath. Att. ii. 9).

[4] Marcell. V. Thucyd.

[5] See Lenormant, La voie Sacrée, p. 168 sq.; cf. Arch. Ephemeris for June and September, 1863, pp. 279 sqq.; 295 sqq.

[6] Lenormant, Voie Sacrée, i. 22.

circumstance of the mound just mentioned, some fine and curious relics
of the best times of Athens have been preserved to us.

The tombs are arranged on the left hand side of a road, which in
the more ancient times may have been that leading to the Academy and
Eleusis, but which could not have been that trodden by Pausanias, as of
course in his time it was still covered by the mound. Some of the
tombs, as appears from the characters of the inscriptions, are of the
Macedonian times. Among the largest and best preserved is one of
Pentelic marble, in the form of a temple, with an inscription in six
elegiac lines to one Dionysius, from which it would appear that he was
a foreigner naturalized at Athens.[1] Close to this tomb was found a
finely executed image of a bull, which had adorned its summit. As the
bull was the symbol of Dionysus, the image was no doubt allusive to
the name of the inmate of the tomb.[2] One of these tombs, inscribed to
Agathon, presented one of the most perfect examples yet discovered of
painting on marble. Such painted tombs are alluded to several times in
Greek epigrams, and two or three of them—but not at Athens—are
described by Pausanias.[3] But by far the most beautiful and interesting
of these monuments is that inscribed to Dexileos, one of five knights
who fell at Corinth, and born in the archonship of Peisander—or rather
Teisander—B.C. 414. The name of this archon rests only on the authority
of Diodorus Siculus; the epitaph reads distinctly *Teisander;* and therefore several distinguished critics are inclined to correct by it the text of
Diodorus. The battle of Corinth, in the archonship of Eubulides, is
related at great length by Xenophon (Hell. iv. 2, 9 sqq.). It was a
bloody day for the Athenian hoplites; but though they appear to have
had 600 cavalry in the field, it would seem from this epitaph that only
five were slain; unless, indeed, the meaning be that Dexileos was one of

---

[1] σῶμα μὲν ἐνθάδε σόν, Διονύσιε, γαῖα
καλύπτει,
ψυχὴν δ' ἀθάνατον κοινὸς ἔχει ταμίας·
σοῖς δὲ φίλοις καὶ μητρὶ κασιγνήταις τε
λέλοιπας
πένθος ἀείμνηστον σῆς φιλίας φθί-
μενος·

δισσαὶ δ' αὖ πατρίδες σ', ἡ μὲν φύσει
ἡ δὲ νόμοισιν
ἔστερξαν πολλῆς εἵνεκα σωφροσύνης.
Ephem. p. 298.

[2] Ibid. p. 67.

[3] Paus. ii. 7, 4; vii. 22, 4; 25, 7; Brunck,
Analecta, t. ii. p. 4; t. iii. p. 68, 294.

five who had most distinguished themselves. The figure of a cavalier, of the size of life, sculptured on it in high relief in a style not unworthy of the time of Pheidias, shows a youth about the age of twenty, in the act of transfixing with his lance a prostrate enemy. On the marble are observed a number of small holes, which no doubt served to fix upon the figure, by means of pins or nails, certain objects in metal, as the

TOMB OF DEXILEOS.

lance, &c.; and especially traces of bronze cramps round the head show that originally it had, in all probability, a Thessalian hat, or petasus, similar in form to that worn by the horsemen on the frieze of the Parthenon. The design of this sculpture seems not to have been peculiar to this tomb, as three repetitions of it are known, with slight variations; one in the Museum at Berlin, sent by Ludvig Ross; another at Rome, in the gallery of the Villa Albani; and a third in the Museum

2 K

of the Vatican.[1] A cast from that at Athens would be a valuable addition to the Elgin room of the British Museum. The characters of the inscription confirm the age of the monument, and show it to have been a little later than the archonship of Eucleides. Thus the omega is used, but the ancient orthography is preserved, as in the use of the omicron for the diphthong ου, and of γ for ν before κ. The inscription will be seen in the foregoing cut of the monument, engraved from a photograph; but it may be convenient to repeat it here:

ΔΕΞΙΛΕΩΣ ΛΥΣΑΝΙΟ ΘΟΡΙΚΙΟΣ
ΕΓΕΝΕΤΟ ΕΓΙ ΤΕΙΣΑΝΔΡΟ ΑΡΧΟΝΤΟΣ
ΑΓΕΘΑΝΕ ΕΓ ΕΥΒΟΛΙΔΟ
ΕΓ ΚΟΡΙΝΘΩΙ ΤΩΝ ΓΕΝΤΕ ΙΓΓΕΩΝ.

i.e. Dexileos, son of Lysanias, of Thoricus, was born in the archonship of Teisander, died in that of Eubulides, one of the five knights killed at Corinth.[2]

The oldest kind of tombs known in Attica appear to have been *tumuli*, or little hills of earth, in which was the sepulchral chamber.[3] These appear to have been as old as the Homeric age. Next may be mentioned the quadrangular towers, mostly *polyandria*, or places where many were buried together. A very ancient kind were those hewn out of the rock, like the Cimoneia already mentioned, and the many smaller graves (θῆκαι) found in great numbers on the western hills of Athens. Although there is a difference in these two kinds: the larger and more sumptuous ones, like the Cimoneia, being hewn horizontally out of the cliffs and above the surface of the earth; while the smaller are below it and sunk vertically in the rock. Bodies deposited in the earth were enclosed in sarcophagi of marble, stone, or earthenware; those of the poorer classes in wooden coffins. When the bodies were burnt, the ashes

---

[1] Lenormant, Voie Sacrée, i. 72.

[2] Arch. Ephem. June, 1863, p. 283; Lenormant, ibid. A full description of these tombs has been published by M. Antonio Salinas, Turin, 1863, 4to, entitled, "I monumenti sepolcrali scoperti presso la chiesa della Sta. Trinità in Atene;" with five plates of the tombs and surrounding topography. Cf. Lenormant, Voie Sacrée, i. p. 38 sqq.

[3] On this subject see Pervanoglu, Grabsteine der alten Griechen, p. 6 sq.

were deposited in urns, or vessels of marble, terra-cotta, bronze, or other metal. The graves were often adorned with tomb-stones, of which perhaps the oldest and most common form was the simple *stelï*, or column, adorned at the top with sculptures of flowers, or sometimes an *ἀέτωμα*, or pediment. Underneath was inscribed the name of the deceased; and if there were several, the names were often separated by rosettes.[1] Sometimes there were longer inscriptions, sculptures of figures, &c.; and many of these stelæ appear to have been painted. But it would be endless to enumerate all the different forms which these monuments assumed, and we shall therefore content ourselves with describing a very ancient one, now preserved under a glass cover in the so-called Theseium at Athens. This records not only the name of the warrior to whom it was dedicated, but also presents us with a portrait of him, in bas-relief, of the size of life. This interesting relic was found at Velanidhéza,[2] a desert place near the eastern coast of Attica, opposite Carysto, in Eubœa, where there are numerous tumuli. It is a square marble column about 7 feet in height, 1 ft. 6 in. in breadth, but tapering towards the top, and 4 or 5 inches thick. It stands on a pedestal about 2 ft. 3 in. broad, and 1 ft. high. The figure, which fills the whole column, is that of a warrior in complete armour with a lance in his hand. The traces of colour on it are still very plain. The pedestal bears the name of Aristion ('Αριστίωνος), no doubt that of the person represented; whilst under the column is inscribed ἔργον 'Αριστοκλέος, " the work of Aristocles." This artist lived at the beginning of the fifth century B.C., and was the father of Cleætas, who flourished in the time of Pericles. The characters of the inscriptions, as well as the style of the work, bear out this early date. Thus the Γ is written Λ, the Λ, V, the Σ, ϟ, the E, Ɛ, &c. The rigidity of the contours of the figure belongs to the Dædalian school, and from these marks Rangabé would assign the work to the period between the seventieth and eightieth Olympiad (500—460 B.C.).[3] Pausanias adverts to a similar monument of Androclus, son

[1] See Ross, Aufsätze, i. p. 40 sqq.
[2] Leake, vol. ii. p. 75.
[3] See Rangabé, Ant. Hell. t. i. No. 21,

p. 18 sq., and the coloured plate at the end of the volume.

of Codrus, which he saw at Ephesus,[1] and a stelé very similar to that of Aristion, though apparently still more ancient, was found a few years ago by Dr. Conze, on the banks of the Cephisus, but in a very damaged state.[2]

In order to keep this subject of the tombs together, we will here insert what Pausanias says a few chapters further on (36, 3 sqq.) respecting the tombs on the ἱερὰ ὁδός, or Holy Way leading to Eleusis ; and we will advert at the same time to other objects on that road. The first which presented itself was that of Anthemocritus, an Athenian herald, slain by the Megarians in violation of the law of nations, when sent to forbid them cultivating the holy land. Plutarch also alludes to this tomb as being outside the Thriasian Gate ; which seems to have been the name for it in the time of Pericles, when the decree for the burial of Anthemocritus there was made ; but which in the time of Plutarch had come to be called Dipylum.[3] The tomb appears to have been surmounted by a statue.[4] The deed of the Megarenses was regarded as inexpiable, even down to the time of Hadrian, who refused to show them any favour. The next tomb was that of Molottus or Molossus, whom the Athenians made their general when they crossed over to Eubœa to support Plutarch, in the time of Philip of Macedon.[5] Here also, near a torrent, was the place called Sciron, from the following cause. When the Eleusinians were making war upon Erechtheus, a soothsayer named Sciros, who erected the ancient temple of Athena Scira at Phalerum, came to their aid, and having fallen in battle, the Eleusinians buried him near a torrent ; and both the place and the torrent took their name from the hero.

Sciron appears to have been a favourite resort of gamblers and courtezans.[6] This was one of the places from which Athena took her surname of Sciras, the other being at Phalerum. The former was the place to which, on the festival called Skirophoria, a procession was made

---

[1] ἐπίθημα δὲ τῷ μνήματι ἀνήρ ἐστιν ὡπλισμένος.—vii. 2, 6.

[2] Pervanoglu, Grabsteine, &c., p. 11.

[3] Vit. Pericl. c. 30.

[4] Isæus, ap. Harpocr. voc. Ἀνθεμόκριτος.

[5] Plut. Vit. Phoc. 12 sq.

[6] Alciphr. Epp. iii. 8 ; Stephan. in Σκίρος ; Phot. Lex. σκιράφια.

by the priest of Athena Polias, of Poseidon Erechtheus, and of Helios, under a white canopy held by the Eteobutadae.[1]

Near this was the tomb of Cephisodorus, who opposed Philip V. of Macedon, the son of Demetrius, and crossing over into Italy obtained the help of the Romans; an event which ended not long after in the overthrow by them of the Macedonian kingdom and the captivity of King Perseus. Next to this was the monument of Heliodorus, whose portrait might be seen in the great temple of Athena. He must, therefore, have been a distinguished man, but we are unable to say whether he was the tragic poet of that name or the author of a Periegesis of Athens, or, indeed, either of them. Here also was buried Themistocles, the son of Poliarchus, and great-grandson of that Themistocles who defeated Xerxes. A little further on was the temenos of the hero Lacius and the deme of the Laciadae named after him; to which the family of Miltiades belonged.[2] Also the monument of the Tarentine Nicocles, the most celebrated of all citharists, and an altar of Zephyrus and temple of Demeter and Corë, with whom also Athena and Poseidon were worshipped. The little church of St. Demetrius appears to mark the site of this temple;[3] for it was customary with the early Christians to be attracted by the analogy of a name in dedicating their churches. It is in this place that Phytalus is said to have received Demeter in his house, for which the goddess rewarded him with a fig-tree. Here was the suburb, hence called ἱερὰ συκῆ, or 'the holy fig-tree,' where, according to Philostratus, a halt was made when bringing the sacred utensils from Eleusis to Athens.[4] From a recently discovered inscription we further learn that these sacred utensils (ἱερὰ) were met at the shrine of Echo

---

[1] Phot. Lex. voc. σκιρόν; cf. Harpocr.

[2] Plut. Cim. 4.

[3] Gell, Itinerary, p. 30; Dodwell, 'Tour in Greece,' ii. p. 169.

[4] ἐτάφη δὲ (ὁ 'Απολλώνιος) ἐν τῷ προαστείῳ τῆς ἐν 'Ελευσῖνι λεωφόρου· ὄνομα τῷ προαστείῳ ἱερὰ συκῆ· τὰ δὲ 'Ελευσινόθεν ἱερά, ἐπειδὴ ἐς ἄστυ ἄγωσιν, ἐκεῖ ἀναπαύουσιν. — Philostr. Vit. Soph. ii. 20, 3. From the words ἐν 'Ελευσῖνι, it

might be supposed that Hiera Syce was a suburb of Eleusis, not Athens. But it is evident from the description of the route that it could not be so; and M. Lenormant has pointed out a passage in which the words are used in precisely the same manner by Hesychius of the Attic Cephisus: Γεφυρισταί, οἱ σκῶπται, ἐπεὶ ἐν 'Ελευσῖνι ἐπὶ τῆς γεφύρας, κ.τ.λ.—Voie Sacrée. i. p. 231.

by armed ephebi, who escorted them on their further journey along the
Holy Way;[1] and it seems therefore to have been this procession which
rested at the Holy Fig Tree. Now, on what occasion did it take place?
A. Mommsen is of opinion that on the day before the great procession to
Eleusis, certain sacred utensils necessary for it were brought from
Eleusis; were met at the shrine of Echo, the position of which is not
exactly known, by the ephebi, and escorted by them to Athens; where
they were deposited in the Iaccheium, near the Peiraïc Gate, till the
following day,[2] when the image of Iacchus was carried in solemn procession to Eleusis. Sainte-Croix[3] and Guigniaut[4] are of opinion that
this took place on the return of the grand procession; whilst Preller[5]
thought that it was on the return from the seashore on the day of the
festival, called Ἅλαδε μύσται, on the 16th Boüdromion,[6] and in this last
view M. F. Lenormant concurs.[7] But we must confess that we are
rather inclined to agree with Mommsen. It is true that we do not hear
of this procession of the ephebi in any other authorities than Philostratus and the inscriptions cited; but it is equally true that we do not
hear of it at all on the day called Ἅλαδε μύσται, nor of any sacred
objects being carried on that day. Again, the mystæ on that occasion
do not appear to have gone any further than the streams called Rheiti;
while, according to Philostratus, the ἱερά, or sacred objects in question,
were brought from Eleusis. Gell places the house of Phytalus and the
Holy Fig Tree at the church of Agia Sabas, about a mile and a half
from Athens.[8] The fruit of the fig-tree was called ἡγητηρία, either as
being the produce of the first fruit-tree, or as conducting to a civilized
life,[9] the acorn being then abandoned; and hence a mass of dried figs
was carried in procession in the Plynteria. An Attic family called the
Phytalidæ claimed to be descended from this Phytalus. To the tombs here

<hr />

[1] ὑπαπάντησαν δὲ καὶ τοῖς ἱεροῖς ἐν ὅπλοις
μέχρι τῆς Ἠχοῦς καὶ προέπεμψαν αὐτά.—
Inscr. in Arch. Ephem. 1860, No. 4097.

[2] Heortologie, p. 252.

[3] Recherches sur les Mystères, t. i. p. 382.

[4] Religions de l'Antiquité, t. iii. p. 1185.

[5] De Via Sacra, disp. i. p. 14.

[6] Polyæn. Strateg. iii. 11, 2.

[7] Voie Sacrée, p. 282 sqq.

[8] Itinerary of Greece, p. 30.

[9] ἡγεμὼν τοῦ καθαρίου βίου.—Athen. iii. 6
et ibi Casaubon.

mentioned by Pausanias, may be added that of the sophist Apollonius.[1]
A little before crossing the Cephisus was the monument of Theodorus, an
infamous character, but the best tragic actor of his time, who is said to
have drawn tears from Alexander, the cruel tyrant of Pheræ.[2]   On the
bank of the stream were statues of Mnesimachē and of her son, cutting
off his hair as an anathema to the river Cephisus ;[3] an ancient Greek
custom, as is evident from Homer.

Pausanias does not say how the river was crossed ; whether by a ford,
a ferry, or a bridge.   A. Mommsen[4] positively denies that there was
any bridge here in the olden times, though he admits that there was
one in the time of Strabo.   But it is hardly probable that so considerable a stream as the Cephisus should have been left unbridged.
The epigram attributed to Simonides proves, we think, the existence of
a bridge :

ὦ ἴτε Δήμητρος πρὸς ἀνάκτορον, ὦ ἴτε μύσται,
  μήδ' ὕδατος προχοὰς δείδετε χειμερίους·
τοῖον Ξεινοκλῆς γὰρ ὁ Λίνδιος ἀσφαλὲς ὕμμιν
  ζεῦγμα διὰ πλατέος τοῦδ' ἔβαλεν ποταμοῦ.[5]

"O mystics, to Demeter's shrine proceed,
    Ye need no more the storm-swoln torrent dread ;
  But o'er it on the bridge, just newly raised
      By Lindian Xenocles securely tread."

The epigram, though wrongly ascribed to Simonides, is doubtless an
ancient one.   An architect named Xenocles was, we know, employed in
erecting the temple at Eleusis,[6] and it is therefore highly probable that
he should have built a bridge over the Cephisus.   We attach no
importance to the circumstance that while the epigram calls him a
native of Lindus, Plutarch designates him as of the deme Cholargos.

---

[1] See the passage of Philostratus quoted above, p. 501.
[2] Æl. V. H. xiv. 40 et ibi not. He seems to have been a tragic poet as well as actor ; cf. Plut. Sympos. ix. 2 ; Demosth. de fals. Leg. p. 418, Reiske ; Aristot. Polit. vii. 17.
[3] Siebelis (ad loc.) observes that Mnesi-

machē and her son, whoever they were, must have been of the heroic age, as Pausanias calls their statues ἀγάλματα.
[4] Heortologie, p. 255, note 2.
[5] Ap. Casaub. ad Strab. ix. p. 400 ; cf. Brunck, Anal. i. p. 138.
[6] Plut. Pericl. 13.

One of the authors may have been mistaken on that point, or Xenocles may have been a Lindian naturalised at Athens, and residing in that deme. That the river, bridge, and mysteries referred to in the epigram should have been in Rhodes, as suggested by Jacobs,[1] is highly improbable.

At this bridge were enacted, on the return of the procession with Iacchus from Eleusis, those scenes of ribaldry and abuse called *gephyrisms* (γεφυρισμοί). Whether they were so named from the bridge, or from the race of Gephyræans settled here, of whom we have spoken before, we shall not stop to inquire; but it is probable enough that the term γέφυρα for a bridge may have originated from them, who, from their location at Tanagra, on the banks and among the marshes of the Asopus, were compelled to construct bridges.[2] In these gephyrisms either a woman or man masked (συγκαλυπτόμενος, Hesych. voc. γεφυρίς) uttered the grossest abuse against the most distinguished citizens by name; a tradition doubtless from Baubo or Iambë. The whole, however, seems to have been taken in good part; for the gods themselves, according to Plato, love a joke,[3] and the most successful wit was rewarded with a fillet.[4] Similar scenes took place on one of the days of the Thesmophoria, called Stenia (στήνια), but the abuse on that occasion was among the women only.[5] As the women were carried in carts in the Eleusinian and other festivals, this scurrility came to be called ἐξ ἁμάξης λέγειν, and, as is well known, became the origin of comedy.[6]

On the other side of the river was an ancient altar of Zeus Meilichios, or 'the Placid,' at which Theseus was said to have been purified by the descendants of Phytalus after slaying, among others, the robber Sinis, who was connected with Theseus on the maternal side. Here was a tomb of Theodectes of Phaselis, a pupil of Aristotle's, a rhetorician and also apparently a tragic poet. Alexander the Great had had some acquaintance with him, and when staying at Phaselis, having got rather

---

[1] Anim. in Anth. Græc. i. p. 240.

[2] Etym. M. voc. γέφυρα.

[3] φιλοπαίσμονες γὰρ καὶ οἱ θεοί.—Cratyl. p. 406.

[4] Aristoph. Ran. 392.

[5] Aristoph. Thesm. 841, and schol. Hesych. and Phot. in voc.

[6] Bentley, Phalaris, p. 288, &c.

drunk, crowned with wreaths a statue which had been erected to
Theodectes in his native town. The author of the life of Isocrates
describes the monument on the Sacred Way as being in a ruinous condition. Theodectes seems to have erected a statue to himself there,
and also statues of several poets, of which, however, only that of Homer
was extant in the time of the author.[1] Here also was a monument to
Mnesitheus, a good physician, who dedicated many statues of gods, and
amongst them one of Iacchus. Beside the road was a small temple
of Cyamites,[2] but Pausanias did not know whether he was the first who
sowed beans, or some hero of that name. Pausanias here observes his
usual reticence respecting things connected with the mysteries.
Cyamites seems to be identical with Bacchus or Iacchus.[3] The bean
was considered an obscene object, and abstinence from it was enjoined
in the mysteries.[4] But two monuments surpassed the rest in size and
beauty; one of a Rhodian, who settled in Athens; the other was
erected by a Macedonian named Harpalus, who absconded from Alexander when in Asia. It was in memory of Pythionicë, whom he had
married and passionately loved, though she had been a prostitute both
at Corinth and Athens. Pausanias, who had seen so many things of
this sort, describes it as one of the finest in Greece. Plutarch, however, tells how Harpalus was cheated by Charicles, to whom he had
intrusted the work, and declares that the monument was not worth the
thirty talents said to have been expended on it.[5] The same author
adds that the monument was in the demus Hermus.[6] Here also was a
temple in which were statues of Demeter and Corë, Athena and Apollo.
It was near Mount Pœcilum, and was at first dedicated only to Apollo.
This part of the chain is usually called Corydallus. The temple having
originally been dedicated only to Apollo, was probably erected by the

---

[1] Plut. Op. t. ix. p. 330, Reiske; Val.
Max. viii. 14, 3; Plut. V. Alex. M. c. 17.
Athenæus has preserved some lines of
Theodectes, lib. x. 80.

[2] This temple is also mentioned in the
life of Isocrates (loc. cit.) under the name
of Cyamitis.

[3] Hesych. in voc. and the emendation
of Meursius (Att. Lect. iv. 20).

[4] Pausan. viii. 15, 1; Plut. Sympos.
ii. 3; Aul. Gell. N. A. iv. 11.

[5] Vit. Cim. c. 22.

[6] On this see Leake, vol. ii. p. 142.

Ionians; and the addition of the images of Demeter, Corë, and Athena, points to the union of the worship of Eleusis with that of Athens.[1] After this came a temple of Aphroditë, and before it a wall of unhewn stones, worthy of notice.

This part of the road, traces of which may still be seen, is at the pass over Mount Ægaleos, now called the pass of Daphni. Near the entrance of the pass, to the right, on an isolated hill, stands the church of Agios Elias, supposed to have occupied the site of a temple in the deme of the Hermeii. As the pass was important in a military point of view, it appears from some remains to have been strongly fortified. At the highest point of the pass stands the monastery of Daphni, in the church of which were three fluted Ionic columns, parts of which were brought to England by Lord Elgin, in 1801, and are now in the British Museum.[2] From the size of them they must have belonged to a considerable temple, which it is conjectured was that of Apollo mentioned by Pausanias. Less than a mile further on are the foundations of another temple, thought to be that of Aphroditë. It stood on the northern side of the valley, under rocks, the sides of which, rendered artificially perpendicular, contain niches for votive offerings. Under these, doves of white marble have been found, which appear to have fallen from them; and these anathemata, as well as inscriptions under the niches, in which the words Φίλη 'Αφροδίτη are legible, are sufficient proof that the temple was dedicated to that goddess. It appears to have been built in honour of Phila (Φίλα), mother of Demetrius Poliorcetes; hence it was dedicated to Φίλα 'Αφροδίτη, and the whole enclosure called Philæum.[3] From some remains, it appears to have been of the Doric order. Probably, however, an older temple had stood here, as the peribolus was enclosed by huge irregular masses of stone, like the walls of Tiryns; the ἀργοὶ λίθοι spoken of by Pausanias, remains of which are still extant.[4] Dionysius, son of Tryphon, quoted in the above passage of Athenæus, says that the temple was at Thria; whence we may infer

---

[1] Lenormant, Recherches à Eleusis, p. 257.

[2] See 'Elgin Marbles,' vol. ii. p. 112.

[3] Athen. vi. 56.

[4] Leake, ib. p. 147.

Cf. Leake, vol. ii. p. 145, &c.

that the demus Thria, which gave name to the Eleusinian plain, was situated here.

After passing the temple of Aphroditö, and getting into the plain, Pausanias arrives at the streams called Rheiti ('Ρεῖτοι) (c. 28, 1), which, he says, by their flowing, resembled a river, but were quite salt. They were two brooks running apparently in a ravine;[1] and from their saltness they were thought to flow under ground from the Euripus. They were sacred to Demeter and Corë; and according to Phavorinus (in voc.), the more eastern one, or that nearest Athens, was sacred to Corë, and the further one to her mother. The circumstance of these border rivers being sacred to these deities, seems to indicate how peculiarly their worship belonged to the Eleusinians; who indeed, when they subjected themselves to the Athenians, reserved the right of performing the mysteries. Hence, too, the temple of Demeter and Persephonë, in the very heart of Athens, bore the name of Eleusinium. Nobody but the priests was allowed to fish in the Rheiti. They are insignificant streams,[2] but they formed the boundary between the Eleusinian and Attic territory in ancient times. The modern road to Eleusis leaves them to the right, keeping along the shore, but in ancient times it appears to have run on the other side of them. Above half a mile further is a tomb with an inscription recording it to be that of Strato, a Cydathenæan,[3] not mentioned by Pausanias; who indeed appears to have selected only a few tombs out of the vast number that lined the road. Beyond this tomb, the Sacred Way assumes the form of a raised causeway over the low and marshy ground, which extends as far as Eleusis. The plain through which it runs was called the Thriasian plain.

The district westward of the Rheiti was said once to have belonged to King Crocon, who married Sæsara, a daughter of Celeus. Pausanias could find no tomb of his, but there was one of Eumolpus, whose history he here gives, to which we have before alluded. His youngest son, Ceryx (Κήρυξ), was the founder of the race of heralds; who however

---

[1] Etym. M. voc. 'Ρείτης.

[2] Walpole, Turkey, p. 333.

[3] Leake, vol. ii. p. 147 sq.

affirmed that he was not a son of Eumolpus, but of Hermes and Aglauros the daughter of Cecrops. Here also was an heroum of Hippothoon, the eponymous hero of one of the Attic tribes, and near it one of Zarex, whom Apollo is said to have taught music. Pausanias thought that the latter was no Athenian, but a Lacedæmonian by birth, and founder of Zarex, a town on the coast of Laconia.

Pausanias now arrives at the Eleusinian Cephisus, which he says had a much more impetuous stream than the Attic river of the same name. Near it was a place called Erineos, where it was said Pluto descended when he carried off Corë. It was on the banks of this Cephisus that Theseus slew the robber Polyphemon, surnamed Procrustes.

Pausanias now arrives at Eleusis. He says (c. 38, 6) that there was there a temple of Triptolemus and another of Artemis Propylæa and Father Poseidon. Also a well called Callichorus, where the Eleusinian women first formed a chorus and sung in honour of the goddess. The Rharian plain, it is said, was the first that was sown, and produced crops; whence it was customary to make barley cakes from the grain produced there to be used in the sacrifices. There was also a threshing floor, said to be that of Triptolemus, and an altar dedicated to him. Of what was within the sacred precincts the dream before mentioned (c. 14, 2) forbade Pausanias to speak; and what the uninitiated were prevented from seeing, it was plainly improper for them to hear. The town was named after the hero Eleusis, who some said was the son of Hermes and Daeira, a daughter of Oceanus, whilst others fabled that Ogyges was her father. For the ancient Eleusinians having no genealogies, had given occasion to much fiction, and especially concerning the races of heroes. According to other authorities, however, the place derived its name from the advent (ἔλευσις) of Demeter.

Of Eleusis, once the most famed and holiest place, not merely of Attica, but of the whole pagan world,[1] scarcely anything remains but the slightly altered name (*Lepsina*). It is now a miserable village with

---

[1] "Omitto Eleusina sanctam illam et augustam, ‘ *Ubi initiantur gentes orarum ultima.*’"—Cic. N. Deor. i. 42, 119.

a few ruins of walls and buildings. The temple and its appurtenances lay on a rocky height of moderate elevation which runs along the Bay of Eleusis, opposite to the island of Salamis and at a little distance from the sea, while the town occupied part of the level underneath it. The wall of the upper town, which on the eastern side was probably identical with the outer peribolus of the great temple, ran along the northern and southern side of the height, and at the western extremity of the town, its highest point, formed a small Acropolis, now occupied by a Frankish tower. Thus the sacred buildings, standing on the eastern extremity of the height, would first strike the eyes of the mystæ on their approach from Athens. The first object arrived at, as we see from the description of Pausanias, was the temple of Triptolemus, the site of which is now occupied by the church of Agios Zacharias, which is entirely built out of ancient materials, and contains many inscriptions and fragments of statues. The temple of Artemis Propylæa and Poseidon, which followed next, stood before the entrance to the peribolus of the great temple. M. Breton thinks that its site is now marked by the little church of St. George.[1] It was entirely built of Pentelic marble, and consisted of one cell with a double entrance, each supported by two Doric columns between antæ. This temple was 40 feet long and 20 feet broad, and was raised upon five steps. It is now, with the Propylæum beyond it, a vast heap of ruins. The mission of the Dilettanti in 1764 was not able to discover any remains of the temples of Triptolemus or of Artemis and Poseidon.[2] But the site of the former at the church of St. Zachary has been since shown by the discovery there of a piece of sculpture called " the Eleusinian relief," now preserved in the so-called Thescium at Athens.[3] There are also still in the church apparently two ancient columns of Egyptian form, which were thought to testify the Eastern origin of the worship of Demeter. But Bötticher, who examined them closely, says that they are

[1] Athènes, p. 370.

[2] Leake, vol. ii. p. 164.

[3] Found in 1859, No. 67 in Kekulé's ' Description of the Sculptures in the Theseium.' It represents Triptolemus, as a boy, standing between Demeter and Persephatta, who hold lighted torches. Figured in Breton's Athènes, p. 371. Kekulé thinks it belongs to a period soon after Pheidias.

of Greek workmanship, and form colossal representations of the torches
which are often seen in the hands of Demeter enthroned, and especially
in a wall painting at Pompeii.[1]   But the columns have been reversed
in the Christian times, and the cup-formed upper end, where the flames
were, converted into the basis.   The shaft is an imitation of a bundle
of pine rods, of which the ancient torches were made.   The height of
these columns is between seven and eight feet.   But they have been
mutilated ; pieces of them were found inside the church, and Bötticher
is of opinion that originally they were fourteen feet high.   They would
have formed an appropriate symbolical entrance to the temple of Triptolemus, and serve to confirm its site.[2]

The Propylæum which gave admission into the peribolus was almost
an exact imitation of the Propylæum of the Acropolis.   We take from
Leake the following description of the remains at Eleusis.   "At a distance
of fifty feet from the Propylæum was the north-eastern angle of the
inner inclosure, which was in shape an irregular pentagon. Its entrance
was at the angle just mentioned, where the rock was cut away both
horizontally and vertically, to receive another Propylæum, much
smaller than the former, which consisted of an opening thirty-two feet
wide, between two parallel walls of fifty feet in length.   Towards the
inner extremity this opening was narrowed by transverse walls to
a gateway of twelve feet in width, which was decorated with antæ,
opposed to two Ionic columns.   Between the inner front of this Propylæum and the site of the great temple lay, until the year 1801, the
colossal bust of Pentelic marble, crowned with a basket, which is now
deposited in the public library at Cambridge.   It has been supposed to
be a fragment of the statue of Ceres which was adored in the temple ;
but to judge from the position in which it was found, and from the unfinished appearance of the surface in those few parts where any original
surface remains, the statue appears rather to have been that of a cisto-

---

[1] Bötticher appears to mean the Ceres
in the house of the Quæstor ; but she is
not there enthroned but standing erect.
See cut in Overbeck's Pompeii, t. ii. p. 201.

She holds an enormous torch in her right
hand, and the calathus in her left.
[2] See Bötticher, Bericht, p. 226 sqq.

phorus, serving for some architectural decoration, like the caryatides
of the Erechtheium. . . . . The north-west side of the pentagonal
enclosure of the hierum of Eleusis was formed by a perpendicular excavation in the rock of the Acropolis, which left a platform thirty-six feet
wide between the perpendicular rock and the back of the temple.

" The μυστικὸς σηκὸς or τελεστήριον, or temple itself, the largest
ever erected by the Greeks in honour of the idols of their superstition, is
described by Strabo[1] as capable of containing as many persons as
a theatre. It was one of the edifices designed in the administration of
Pericles by the architect of the Parthenon; but it was probably
executed in part only before the Peloponnesian war, as three successive
artists were employed in building it, and its portico was not constructed
until the time of Demetrius Phalereus, when Philo was the fourth or
fifth architect of this temple.[2] When complete, it ranked as one of the
four finest examples of Greek architecture in marble. It faced the
south-east, and consisted (if the mission of the Dilettanti is correct in
its conclusion) of a cella 166 feet square within.[3] Unfortunately, the
centre of the modern village occupies the exact site of this building,
and some of the cottages are built upon a slope formed by its ruins, in
consequence of which the mission could not succeed in obtaining all the
details which a more complete excavation of the ruins would probably
give. Comparing, however, the fragments which they found with the

[1] p. 395. According, however, to
Plutarch (Pericl. 13), the building was
begun by Corœbus, continued by Metagenes the Xypetian, and finished by
Xenocles the Cholargean. Leake (ii. p.
163, note) would reconcile these authorities by supposing that Ictinus only designed the temple. But Strabo's words,
ὃν κατεσκεύασεν Ἴκτινος hardly admit
this. Vitruvius also attributes the building to Ictinus : " Eleusine Cereris et Proser-
pinæ cellam immani magnitudine Ictinus
Dorico more sine exterioribus columnis ad
laxamentum usus sacrificiorum pertexuit."
—lib. vii. præf. 16. It therefore had at

first no portico, and Vitruvius goes on to
say that Philo added one, and made it
prostylon. The ancient temple had been
burnt by the Persians. Herod. ix. 65.

[2] It may be added that Appius Claudius,
a contemporary of Cicero's, either built or
thought of building a propylæum here.
Epp. ad Att. vi. 1, 26. Cf. vi. 6.

[3] If these were its dimensions, it is
evident that we must not take Strabo's
words of its being able to contain as many
spectators as a theatre (ὄχλον θεάτρου) of
such a theatre as the Dionysiac. Unless
Strabo meant the whole peribolus.

description of Plutarch, they thought themselves warranted in concluding that the roof of the cella was covered with tiles of marble, like the temples of Athens; that it was supported by twenty-eight Doric columns of a diameter (measured under the capital) of 3 ft. 2 in., that the columns were disposed in two double rows across the cella, one near the front, the other near the back; and that they were surmounted by ranges of smaller columns, as in the Parthenon, and as we still see exemplified in one of the existing temples at Præstum. The cella was fronted with a magnificent portico of twelve Doric columns, measuring 6 ft. 6 in. at the lower diameter of the shaft, but fluted only in a narrow ring at the top and bottom.[1] The platform at the back of the temple was twenty feet above the level of the pavement of the portico. An ascent of steps led up to this platform on the outside of the northwestern angle of the temple, not far from where another flight of steps ascended from the platform to a portal adorned with two columns, which perhaps formed a small propylæum[2] communicating from the Hierum to the Acropolis."[3]

Eleusis was so intimately connected with the history and antiquities of Athens that some account of it was indispensable. It forms no part of our plan to describe the other Attic boroughs; but there are one or two places which we have passed over, that, for the same reason as Eleusis, demand notice. After describing the Academy, Pausanias proceeds to mention in its neighbourhood the tower of Timon the misanthrope (c. 30, 4), whose only road to happiness was by avoiding his fellow men. He belonged, by birth, to the deme of Collytus, which lay on the opposite side of the city.[4]

Between the Academy and the modern village of Sepolia which lies to the north of it, two low and small hills were supposed to mark the site of Colonus Hippius, renowned as the scene of the 'Œdipus

---

[1] This must have been the portico erected by Philo in the time of Demetrius Phalereus.

[2] May not this have been the propylæum added by Appius Claudius? If, indeed, it was ever built.

[3] See Leake's Topography of Athens, vol. ii. p. 159 sqq.; Bursian, Geogr. von Griechenland, B. i. S. 328 f.

[4] Lucian, Timon, § 7. Leake, therefore, is incorrect in saying that Collytus was Timon's residence.—vol. i. p. 443, note 3.

Colonus' of Sophocles. Thucydides says that it was a hierum dedicated to Poseidon,[1] by which we must understand a considerable peribolus or enclosure. We have before adverted to Colonus as an Attic demo when speaking of the city regions (supra, p. 96). According to the same passage of Thucydides, it appears to have been at a distance of about ten stades from the city. The correctness of this has, however, been questioned by Meursius on the following grounds: Cicero, in a passage of his 'De Finibus,' before quoted (supra, p. 489), says that the Academy was only six stades from the Dipylum; and a few lines further on, his brother Quintus, who accompanied him thither, remarks that on the road his eyes had been attracted by Colonus.[2] Hence Meursius was led to think that in the text of Thucydides for δέκα we should read δ΄, that is, four; and that the corruption has arisen from the numeral letter being followed by καί:[3] an emendation approved of by Hudson in his note on the passage. There appears, however, to be no necessity for it. Cicero seems rather to have understated the distance of the Academy from the walls, for while he calls it only six stadia, Livy, as we have seen, makes it about a mile, or eight stadia (supra, p. 489); and if, as it appears to have been, Colonus was on a height, it might easily have been descried at a distance of a quarter of a mile; which, according to the statements of Thucydides and Livy, would have been the interval between it and the Academy. That it was a place of considerable size may be inferred from the fact that Pisander and his colleagues summoned an ecclesia in it, as we learn from the same chapter of Thucydides; and this circumstance also confirms the view that it was an enclosed place, though it was doubtless surrounded by a village.[4] No indication of its site can be derived from the chorus of the 'Œdipus Coloneus' (v. 668 sqq.) except that it was distinguished by the whiteness of its soil (τὸν ἀργῆτα

---

[1] ἔστι δὲ (ὁ Κολωνὸς) ἱερὸν Ποσειδῶνος ἔξω τῆς πόλεως, ἀπέχον σταδίους μάλιστα δέκα.—viii. 67.

[2] "Nam me ipsum huc modo venientem convertebat ad sese Colonus ille locus, cujus incola Sophocles ob oculos versabatur."—

[3] De Fin. v. 1, 3.   [3] De Pop. Att. in voc.

[4]
οἱ δὲ πλησίοι γύαι
τὸν ἱππότην Κολωνὸν εὔχονται σφίσιν
ἀρχηγὸν εἶναι, καὶ φέρουσι τοὔνομα
τὸ τοῦδε κοινὸν πάντες ὠνομασμένοι.
Œd. Col. 58 sq

Κολωνόν); for the allusion to the waters of the Cephisus seems to apply to the rivulets which had been deduced from it, and, as we have seen, served to water the Academy,[1] so that it cannot be inferred hence that it was actually near the river.

Pausanias goes on to observe that Œdipus was said to have gone to Colonus Hippios on arriving in Attica, but that this differed from the account of Homer. Here, he continues, was an altar of Poseidon Hippios and of Athena Hippia; and heroa of Peirithoüs and Theseus, and of Œdipus and Adrastus. Antigonus, he adds, burnt down the grove and temple of Poseidon when he invaded Attica, from which it follows that the altar of that deity and Athena was not merely one in the open air. As Poseidon was the creator, so Athena was the tamer of the horse, though, according to some views, Poseidon derived his name of Hippios from the same cause as Athena.[2]

Homer says that Œdipus was buried at Thebes, and seems not to have known the story of his blindness and flight to Attica.[3] The latter therefore was probably an Attic legend; and we have here a proof that in this case at least the Pisistratidæ did not alter the text of Homer in order to suit Athenian traditions. Besides the objects mentioned by Pausanias, there was also at Colonus a *temenos* of the Semnæ, or Furies,[4] alluded to by Sophocles:

OI. τίς δ' ἔσθ' ὁ χῶρος; τοῦ θεῶν νομίζεται;
ΞΕΝ. ἄθικτος οὐδ' οἰκητός· αἱ γὰρ ἔμφοβοι
θεαί σφ' ἔχουσι, Γῆς τε καὶ Σκότου κόραι.

Œd. Col. 38 sq.

"Œd.   What place is this? to what god dedicate?
Host.   'Tis uninhabitable; for 'tis held
         By the dread Semnae, born of Earth and Night."

---

[1]   οὐδ' ἄϋπνοι
κρῆναι μινύθουσιν
Κηφισοῦ νομάδες ῥεέθρων.—v. 386 sq. The scholiast observes: ὡς ὁ Κηφισὸς ἐπινέμεται· λέγοι δ' ἂν ἐν τῇ Καδμείᾳ. Where we should read, perhaps, ἐν τῇ Ἀκαδημείᾳ.

[2] Pausan. vii. 21, 3; cf. viii. 47, 1.

[3] Iliad, xxiii. 679 sq.; cf. Odyss. xi. 270 sqq.; and schol. on v. 271, 275. There were various traditions about the end of Œdipus. One was that he was finally buried at Eteonos. Schol. ad Soph. Œd. Col. v. 91.

[4] Apollod. iii. 6, 9; 2nd hypothesis to Œd. Col.

According to a scholiast on the 'Œdipus Coloneus' (v. 57) there were
also some copper mines,[1] the entrance to which is alluded to more
than once in the same drama, under the names of χαλκόπους ὁδός
(v. 57) and καταρράκτης ὁδός (v. 1590), and was considered to be a
descent into Hades. In its neighbourhood was a garden, where Plato
in his later years philosophised, instead of at the Academy.[2] But the
greatest glory of Colonus was that it was the birthplace of Sophocles,[3]
who from that circumstance, perhaps, may have been led to illustrate
and render it for ever memorable by his last and perhaps finest
tragedy. On the hill supposed to be Colonus have been erected
monuments to two learned archæologists, Karl Ottfried Müller and
Charles Lenormant. It is a small low hill with a flat summit, having
no trees and little vegetation in its immediate vicinity. The view
from it, however, is very charming, the Acropolis standing out well
on the horizon, with the sea in the distance.

Such was the state of Athens in the time of the Antonines; and
here, for the student of its topography and antiquities, all interest
ceases. From this period decadence and decay set in; no new monuments were added, and the ancient ones began to experience the
dilapidations resulting from the effects of time, or from violent destruction. Art and taste declined after the extinction of paganism;
and the Byzantine Christians, though they preserved some of the
temples by converting them into churches, disfigured or destroyed the
statuary and other ornaments with which they were adorned. Paganism
however appears to have survived at Athens longer than elsewhere.
We have seen that towards the end of the fifth century, and long after
the reign of Theodosius, the Athena of the Parthenon continued to
be worshipped. There may, however, have been a small section of
Christians at Athens from the earliest times, as St. Paul had converted

---

[1] But there seems to be no other evidence of this fact. Brunck wrote ὁδός for
οὐδός on the authority of the scholiast on
v. 1590; but the MSS. appear to have ὁδός.

[2] Diog. Laërt. iii. 5, 5.
[3] Scholiast in Vit.; Suidas; Cic. Fin.
loc. cit.

Dionysius the Areiopagite, and a few others.[1] The reputation and ancient glory of Athens had attracted the favour of some of the early Christian emperors. Constantine accepted the office of strategus, was honoured with a statue, and made the Athenians an annual donation of corn.[2] The apostasy of Julian naturally led him to regard with favour the stronghold of paganism, more especially as he had there imbibed the principles of his philosophy and religion.

In the reign of Gallienus (A.D. 262), the Goths penetrated to and captured Athens; but they were ultimately driven out by Dexippus, the orator, who appears to have taken a signal vengeance upon them.[3] The reparation of the walls by Valerian, said to have been effected a few years previously, proved therefore no protection. In the second year of Arcadius and Honorius (A.D. 396), the terrible Alaric appeared before Athens; but by offering a ransom, the citizens saved it from assault, which indeed Alaric was hardly in a condition to deliver. According to Zosimus,[4] he was deterred from the attack by the apparition of Achilles and Athena Promachus. But he entered the city in a friendly manner, and departed with the presents which had purchased his goodwill. More than a century later Justinian repaired the walls.[5] It was by an edict of the same emperor that the schools of Athens were shut up (A.D. 529),[6] and an end put to that philosophical or sophistical teaching which had flourished a thousand years.

[1] Acts xvii. 34.

[2] Julian, Orat. i.

[3] See the fragments of Dexippus in the Bonn ed. of Scriptores Hist. Byz. t. i.; Aur. Victor, De Cæsar. xxxiii. 3; Trebellius Pollio, Gallienus, 5.

[4] lib. v. 5.

[5] Procop. De Æd. iv.

[6] Malala, t. ii. p. 451; cf. Procop. t. iii. p. 459.

APPENDIX.

I.

On the Fountain Enneacrunus.

The irregularity with which Pausanias is charged in his first walk arises from the confusion by his expounders of two fountains, Enneacrunus and Callirrhoë; and the source of this confusion lies in the circumstance of Thucydides incidentally mentioning (ii. 15) that the Enneacrunus, before it obtained that name from its being fitted with pipes by the Peisistratidæ, had been called Callirrhoë. The lexicographers repeat this, and tell us that Enneacrunus was a fountain which was *previously* called Callirrhoë;[1] thus implying that it had subsequently lost the latter name. Yet commentators assume that it continued occasionally to bear it, and that it might be called indifferently either Callirrhoë or Enneacrunus. This mistaken view appears to have arisen from the fact that there was really another fountain, or perhaps more accurately speaking a cascade, at the Ilissus, called Callirrhoë. But that this was distinct from Enneacrunus appears from Pliny,[2] who enumerates the Attic springs as being Cephisia, Larinë, Calliroë, Enneacrunos. Harduin and Sillig, indeed, thinking that the last two were identical, print Calliroe Enneacrunos, without a comma between them; supposing, like Meursius, that the names are here placed in apposition, and stand for the same fountain. It is incredible that Pliny should have so written when professing to give an accurate enumeration of the Attic springs; and that he did not is plain from his follower and expounder Solinus, who mentions them in a way which indisputably shows that he considered them to be distinct.[3] And Harduin allows that earlier editions of Pliny have the comma.

[1] Ἐννεάκρουνος · κρήνη τις ἐν Ἀθήναις · πρότερον δ' ἐκαλεῖτο Καλλιρόη.—Harpocr. Cf. Hesych.

[2] H. N. iv. 24.

[3] "Callirhoën stupent fontem, nec ideo Cruneson fontem alterum nullæ rei numerant."—p. 64 sq. (Mommsen's ed.). The various readings in the MSS. consulted by Mommsen are only *croneson*, *crunescon*; but that Solinus meant Enneacrunos will be evident to any one who compares the whole paragraph with that of Pliny; of which it is a sort of paraphrase.

The Enneacrunus, as a fountain in Athens, is mentioned by Thucydides in the passage before cited, by Herodotus (vi. 137), by several lexicographers, and by Pausanias (i. 14, 1): which shows that it had borne that name several centuries, and renders it still more improbable that it should have had a double name. But that there existed at the same time another fountain called Callirrhoë appears from the Platonic dialogue entitled 'Axiochus.' In this piece Socrates is represented as having gone out of the city and arrived on the banks of the Ilissus; when hearing himself called, he turns, and sees Kleinias *running towards Callirrhoë*.[1] This fountain, therefore, was *outside the walls*, and was no doubt the pool which still bears the same name. But the Enneacrunus of Pausanias was within the city, for he mentions it as the only spring in it, though there were many wells.[2]

The compiler of the 'Etymologicum Magnum,' who lived in the tenth or eleventh century, is the only authority who says, in plain terms, that Enneacrunus was *at the Ilissus*.[3] If this were a fact, it is singular that it should not have been mentioned by Harpocration, Hesychius, and the earlier lexicographers. But the two fountains had now become confounded, as is plain from a passage in the Lexicon of Photius, who lived a century or two earlier. Photius had written, that in wedding ceremonies water was brought from the fountain of Enneacrunus, once called Callirrhoë; to which, as Porson annotates, a later scribe has added: " but it is called Callirrhoë *now*."[4] It seems probable therefore that, about the ninth century, the Enneacrunus had disappeared, perhaps through an earthquake or some other natural cause; and, as the Callirrhoë at the Ilissus still continued to exist, ill-informed writers began to identify it with the former Enneacrunus. This confusion is well exemplified by a passage in Suidas, also a late and injudicious compiler, who, reversing the account of Thucydides and the earlier lexicographers, says that Callirrhoë was a fountain in Athens, previously called Enneacrunus![5] It is perfectly incredible that the artificial fountain should ever have regained the name it bore when in its natural state.

Thucydides says (ii. 15) that the fountain Enneacrunus was near the

---

[1] Εξιόντι μοι ἐς Κυνόσαργες καὶ γενομένῳ μοι κατὰ τὸν Ἰλισσόν, διῆξε φωνὴ βοῶντός του, Σώκρατες, Σώκρατες· ὡς δὲ ἐπιστραφεὶς περι εσκόπουν ὁπόθεν εἴη, Κλεινίαν ὁρῶ τὸν Ἀξιόχου θέοντα ἐπὶ Καλλιρόην.—Axioch. init.

[2] φρέατα μὲν γὰρ καὶ διὰ πάσης τῆς πόλεώς ἐστι, πηγὴ δὲ αὕτη μόνη.—i. 14. 1. So also Harpocration mentions it as in Athens (ἐν Ἀθήναις), not at Athens (Ἀθήνησιν).

[3] Ἐννεάκρουνος, κρήνη Ἀθήνησι παρὰ τὸν Ἰλισσόν. ἡ πρότερον Καλλιρόη ἔσκεν.

[4] τὰ δὲ λουτρὰ ἐκόμιζον ἐκ τῆς νῦν μὲν Ἐννεακρούνου καλουμένης κρήνης, πρότερον δὲ Καλλιρόης.—Phot. 231. " Addit m. recens, ἀλλὰ καὶ νῦν αὕτη Καλλιρόη καλεῖται."— Porson's note.

[5] Καλλιρόη· κρήνη ἡ ἐν Ἀθήναις ἥτις πρό τερον Ἐννεάκρουνος ἐκαλεῖτο. Ed. Küster. Gaisford, however, in his edition of Suidas, omits all the words after κρήνη. And under Ἐννεάκρουνος. Suidas has the usual account, taken apparently from Harpocration.

Acropolis; whereas had it been at the Ilissus, it would have been about a
mile distant. That this is the meaning of the passage appears, we think, from
the whole context; and this view is confirmed by the scholiast, who to the
words ἐγγὺς οὔσῃ appends the note: ὡς ἀκροπόλει δηλονότι. As we have
observed in another place,[1] Leake seems to misapprehend this passage ('Topography of Athens,' p. 173) and makes Thucydides say that the fountain was
near the sanctuaries, i.e. the Olympium, Pythium, and others recited by the historian, instead of near the Acropolis. He also mistranslates a passage in the
Hippiatrics of Hierocles,[2] and makes Tarantinus say that when the Athenians
were building the temple of Zeus (i.e. the Olympium) *near Enneacrunus*, they
ordered all the beasts of burden to be driven into the city, instead of to be
driven into the city *near Enneacrunus*, as Meursius correctly renders. For it
would hardly have been necessary to identify the site of so magnificent a
temple as the Olympium by saying that it was near a fountain. The other
passages cited by Leake in favour of his view utterly fail to substantiate it.
That from Herodotus (vi. 137), or rather Hecataeus, whom he quotes, proves
nothing about the situation of Enneacrunus, which he must have named by
a *prolepsis;* for it was not so called till the time of the Peisistratidæ, and he
is speaking of the Pelasgi. A prolepsis which he may have used in order
that the reader should not confound the Callirrhoë at the Ilissus with the
fountain anciently so called at the Acropolis. The fragment of Cratinus
proves nothing at all, for a fountain with *twelve* pipes is surely not Enneacrunus; and the lines of Statius (Theb. xii. 629)—

> " Et quos Callirrhoë novies errantibus undis
> Implicat, et raptæ qui conscius Orythyiæ
> Celavit Geticos ripis Ilissus amores"—

only show that he was talking at random, and took Callirrhoë for a stream
with nine channels, instead of a fountain with nine pipes.

Ancient texts, then, do not bear out the view that Enneacrunos was at the
Ilissus; and if we weigh the probabilities of the matter, we shall find still less
reason to place it there. It is highly improbable, as we have already observed,
that Pausanias should have made so purposeless a deviation from his route.
And it is perhaps a still greater improbability that Peisistratus, or whoever was
the founder of the original Odeium, should have built it in such an out-of-the-
way place, far outside the ancient, or Thesean, walls of the city. For the
Odeium, as well as the temple of Demeter and Corë, and the little temple of

---

[1] In an article in the 'Cambridge Journal
of Philology,' 1870, vol. iii. p. 81 sqq.; where
the reader will find the subject treated at
greater length.

[2] Ταραντῖνος δὲ ἱστορεῖ τὸν τοῦ Διὸς ἐῶν
κατασκευάζοντας Ἀθηναίους Ἐννεακρούνου
πλησίον εἰσελαθῆναι ψηφίσασθαι τὰ ἐκ τῆς
Ἀττικῆς εἰς τὸ ἄστυ ζεύγη ἅπαντα.

Eucleia, were close to the Enneacrunus, wherever it may have been. And this group, which cannot be separated, adds greatly to the improbability. For Pausanias says that the temple of Demeter was *above* Enneacrunus—ὑπὲρ τὴν κρήνην (c. 14, 1), and Forchhammer, who follows the received view about Enneacrunus, is consequently obliged to place the temple on the further, or left, bank of the Ilissus, because there is no high ground on the right. Siebelis indeed asserts that ὑπὲρ here and in other places means *beyond*, not *over*.[1] But we are rather disposed to agree with Forchhammer[2] who translates *oberhalb, above.* The preposition ὑπὲρ with an accusative may be construed in both ways, and the meaning of *above* is very usual with Pausanias.[3] But Forchhammer is very naturally surprised that Pausanias does not mention having crossed the stream, and labours very hard to explain away this omission. Another inconvenience is that the temple would then have been in close proximity to the other temple of Demeter at Agræ. Further, the temple of Demeter, Corë, and Triptolemus was evidently the Eleusinium, as we have shown (supra, p. 222); but the Eleusinium could not have been in this part of the town; whereas if it was under the north side of the Acropolis, as we take Pausanias to mean, this would save us the trouble of searching for a second Eleusinium at some imaginary spot, a question which has sorely puzzled the topographers.

We shall only further urge on this subject the improbability that the temple of Eucleia, of which the Athenians were very proud, as having been built out of the Marathonian spoil,[4] should have been erected in an obscure corner, outside the Themistoclean walls, where comparatively few would see it. That it was near the agora, where all the monuments of Athenian glory were collected as in a focus, is much more probable; and this forms an additional reason that the Enneacrunus was there also.

We shall only add here that Wheler appears to have also come to the conclusion that the Enneacrunus and temple of Demeter were on the north-west side of the Acropolis; and he identified the fountain with a spring of water which he observed near the top of the hill (Journey, p. 384). To this spring, which seems to be sometimes confounded with the Clepsydra, we have adverted at the beginning of our 12th chapter (p. 444).

---

[1] See his note here, and at § 5.

[2] Topographie, p. 47.

[3] We will cite one or two instances about which there cannot possibly be any doubt: ἀνιοῦσι δὲ εἰς τὸν Ἀκροκόρινθον (ἡ δέ ἐστιν ὄρους ὑπὲρ τὴν πόλιν κορυφή).—ii. 4, 7. And again in the same section, ὑπὲρ τοῦτο, *above* this temple; for he continues ascending.

[4] φρονῆσαι δὲ Ἀθηναίους ἐπὶ τῇ νίκῃ ταύτῃ μάλιστα εἰκάζω.—Pausan. i. 14, 4.

II.

ON THE THYMELË AND THE ARRANGEMENT OF THE CHORUS IN THE ORCHESTRA.

THERE is no reason to suppose that, in the classic days of the Attic drama, the thymelë formed a part of the theatre on which either the actors or the chorus performed. Phrynichus, who flourished in the time of the Antonines, in his 'Εκλογή, written to warn Cornelianus against words not of the true Attic type, excludes the name altogether from the theatre, and allows only of the logeium for the actors and the orchestra for the chorus. We transcribe the article: Θυμέλην· τοῦτο οἱ μὲν ἀρχαῖοι ἀντὶ τοῦ θυσίαν ἐτίθουν· οἱ δὲ νῦν ἐπὶ τοῦ τύπου ἐν τῷ θεάτρῳ, ἐν ᾧ αὐληταὶ καὶ κιθαρῳδοὶ καὶ ἄλλοι τινὲς ἀγωνίζονται. σὺ μέντοι ἔνθα μὲν κωμῳδοὶ καὶ τραγῳδοὶ ἀγωνίζονται, λογεῖον ἐρεῖς. ἔνθα δὲ οἱ αὐληταὶ καὶ οἱ χοροί, ὀρχήστραν· μὴ λέγε δὲ θυμέλην (p. 163, Lobeck). Where we also see indicated a different use of the orchestra by the ancient and of the thymelë by the more modern Athenians: the orchestra having been used by the flute players and chorus; the thymelë by flute players, citharœdists, *and others;* by which, as we shall see presently, Phrynichus probably meant mimes and dancers; for in connection with the thymelë a regular dramatic chorus is not mentioned. Timæus, who lived perhaps a century later than Phrynichus, says much the same thing in his Lexicon Platonicum: Ὀκρίβας· πῆγμα τὸ ἐν τῷ θεάτρῳ τιθέμενον, ἐφ' οὗ ἵστανται οἱ τὰ δημόσια λέγοντες. θυμέλη γὰρ οὐδέπω ἦν. λέγει γοῦν τις, Λογεῖόν ἐστι πῆξις ἐστορεσμένη ξύλων, εἶτα ἐξῆς, Ὀκρίβας δὲ ὀνομάζεται. Where we see that ὀκρίβας was another name for λογεῖον, as also appears from the passage of Plato which this article is intended to explain: εἰ ἰδὼν τὴν σὴν ἀνδρίαν καὶ μεγαλοφροσύνην ἀναβαίνοντος ἐπὶ τὸν ὀκρίβαντα μετὰ τῶν ὑποκριτῶν (Sympos. p. 124 ᴅ); where the scholiast observes: Ὀκρίβαντα· τὸ λογεῖον, ἐφ' οὗ οἱ τραγῳδοὶ ἠγωνίζοντο. By δημόσια Timæus probably means speeches delivered in the theatre when it was used for political purposes. He then affirms that, in the time of Plato, there was no such thing as a thymelë. It appears, indeed, to have been a kind of enlarged logeium, constructed when the mimes, buffoons, and dancers were introduced, so as to afford room for their evolutions; therefore probably in the Roman times. Lobeck observes (ad Phrynich. loco cit.): "Θυμέλη pro orchestra apud veteres non memini me legere (sic), præter quod Pratinas (Ath. xiv. 8, 236) Διονυσιάδα πολυπάταγα θυμέλην in hunc sensum dixisse videtur; sæpius apud recentiores pro scena et re scenica atque musica occurrit." And he then goes on to quote passages from Plutarch, Lucian, Procopius, scholiasts, &c., where it is used in that sense; but not a single authority from the classic times of Greek literature; from which, indeed, as we have seen, Phrynichus excludes the word. The same also is the case with the word θυμελικός, derived from it, to denote an actor, which is to be found only in the later writers. With regard to the verses of Pratinas alluded to by Lobeck :

τίς ὁ θόρυβος ὅδε ;
τί τάδε τὰ χορεύματα ;
τίς ὕβρις ἔμολεν
ἐπὶ Διονυσιάδα
πολυπάταγα θυμέλαν ; κ.τ.λ.

we may observe, first, that when they were written the theatre most probably was not in existence; secondly, that they belong to a hyporcheme, and not a drama. Hence they can be of no authority with regard to the theatre. The classical meaning of θυμέλη was, any altar, or place for sacrifice ; and the altar of Dionysus in the middle of the orchestra, like any other one, always bore this name. But besides this, in the early times and before the drama was perfected, θυμέλη appears also to have signified a large table near the altar of Dionysus, on which the victims sacrificed were cut up. Thus Phavorinus : Θυμέλη· ὁ βωμός. Θυμέλη· ἡ τοῦ θεάτρου, μέχρι νῦν ἀπὸ τῆς τραπέζης ὠνόμασται, διὰ τὸ ἐπ' αὐτῆς τὰ θύη μερίζεσθαι, τουτέστι, τὰ θυόμενα ἱερεῖα· τράπεζα ἦν, ἐφ' ἧς ἑστῶτες ἐν τοῖς ἀγροῖς ᾖδον, μήπω τάξιν λαβούσης τραγῳδίας. The Etymologicum M. (in voc.) has the same. These authors, in calling it a part of the theatre, are speaking according to the usage of their own times. In the lines of Pratinas it may mean the sacrificial table, which was the cradle of the drama. from an actor getting upon it and holding a dialogue with the chorus ; but it seems probable that this had really been enlarged so as to form a platform or orchestra near the altar. This τράπεζα, or table, was also called ἐλεός, or ἐλεόν ; and before the time of Thespis, says Pollux, somebody would get upon it and hold a dialogue with the chorus. (Ἐλεὸς δ' ἦν τράπεζα ἀρχαία, ἐφ' ἦν πρὸ Θεσπίδος εἴς τις ἀναβάς, τοῖς χορευταῖς ἀπεκρίνατο, iv. 123.) But when the drama had been perfected, and a regular theatre constructed, this table disappeared. Previously, the spectators must have stood around the performers, and hence it was necessary to raise these last a few feet, in order that they might be seen by all. But in the theatre, where the audience sat tier above tier, such a contrivance became useless ; and hence we hear nothing about it from the classical authors.

In the palmy days of the Attic drama, the scene with the narrow wooden stage called logeium (or ὀκρίβας) before it, and the semicircular orchestra extending under it, served for the performers: the scene and logeium being appropriated to the actors, and the orchestra to the chorus. But in process of time, as we have before observed, after the introduction of mimes and buffoons, and the consequent increase in the number of performers, the logeium no longer sufficed to contain them, and it was therefore enlarged by being extended over half the orchestra, and as far as the thymelë, or altar of Dionysus, in the middle of it. The action was now carried on in dumb show, gesticulation and pantomime, and the performer was said *to dance* a character (ὀρχεῖσθαι) instead of *to act* it (ὑποκρίνεσθαι). Thus Lucian: μικροῦ ὀρχηστοῦ εἰσελθόντος καὶ τὸν Ἕκτορα ὀρχουμένου (De Salt. 76). So also in Latin, saltare pastorem, and even tragœdiam saltare ("et pantomimus Mnester tragœdiam *saltavit*, quam olim Neoptolemus tragœdus . . . *egerat.*" Suet. Cal. 57). This was not, however, altogether a novel art. Even in the time of Æschylus there were among the choreutæ— not the actors—some who could represent by dancing the whole action of a play, as that of the 'Seven against Thebes' (Athen. i. 39); but it does not seem to have been an art that was exhibited in the theatre, or for which prizes were given. This exhibition seems to have been first introduced in provincial theatres, and their construction altered accordingly, so that even the name of logeium became obsolete. But this alteration was probably never adopted in the Dionysiac theatre at Athens. O. Müller, in his edition of Festus (p. 180), says : "*Orchestra* a Festo eo sensu intelligitur, quo id v. neque in antiquo Græco neque in Romano theatro instructum erat, sed in scenicis ludis senescentis Græciæ, apud Alexandrinos, puto, et Antiochenos. In his proscenio additum erat pulpitum inferius, ab aliis thymelë, ab aliis orchestra dictum, in quo musici artifices, saltatores, mimi committerentur." This new stage seems to have obtained the name of *thymelë* either from a reminiscence of the table or platform in use in early times, or from its extending as far as the altar of Dionysus, or thymelë, in the orchestra. However this may be, it is certain that the innovation revolutionised the theatrical nomenclature. The descriptions of the late lexicographers are quite wild. Thus Suidas confines the name of *scene* to *the middle door* of the theatre; the parascenia, or side scenes, are on each side of the middle door; immediately after the scene and side scenes came the orchestra, a place floored with boards, on which the mimes acted. Next to the orchestra was an altar of Dionysus, called θυμέλη from θύειν, to sacrifice. Beyond the thymelë was the *conistra*, or lowest floor of the theatre: Σκηνή ἐστιν ἡ μέση θύρα τοῦ θεάτρου. παρασκήνια δὲ τὰ ἔνθεν καὶ ἔνθεν τῆς μέσης θύρας, ἵνα δὲ σαφέστερον εἴπω· μετὰ τὴν σκήνην εὐθὺς καὶ τὰ παρασκήνια, ἡ ὀρχήστρα· αὕτη δὲ ἐστιν ὁ τόπος ὁ ἐκ σανίδων ἔχων τὸ ἔδαφος, ἀφ' (ἐφ') οὗ θεατρίζουσιν οἱ μῖμοι· ἔστι μετὰ τὴν ὀρχήστραν βῶμος τοῦ Διονύσου, ὃς καλεῖται θυμέλη, παρὰ τὸ θύειν· μετὰ δὲ τὴν θυμέλην ἡ κονίστρα, τουτέστι, τὸ κάτω ἔδαφος τοῦ θεάτρου. What a confusion is here ! The scene, instead of being the whole wall with its three doors, is confined to the middle one, which is called the door " of the theatre," a name properly applicable to the audience part; the logeium is altogether ignored, and immediately next to the scene comes a scaffolding, which is called the orchestra, extending as far as the altar of Dionysus in the middle of the orchestra, properly so called. Upon this scaffolding it is no longer the actors (ὑποκριταί) who contend (ἀγωνίζονται), but the mimes who, to coin an equivalent word, theatralize (θεατρίζουσιν); a word not found in any classical author. The thymelë, as an altar, is the only correct part of the account, agreeably to classic notions, though the description no doubt answered well enough to a theatre of the lower ages. Beyond the thymelë, he continues, is the conistra (κονίστρα), literally, an arena covered with dust. Suidas, we believe, is the only author who applies this name to any part of a theatre; it was in his view the furthest part of the orchestra from the scene, left bare and open, and may probably in the later ages have been converted into a place for gymnastic exercises. The Etymologicum Magnum (voc. σκηνή) has an almost similar article, except that for κονίστρα it reads ὀρχήστρα; an evident mistake of the copyists, as ὀρχήστρα had occurred before for the scaffolding. The description here given of the orchestra by Suidas and the Etymologist may be refuted from older and better lexicographers. Thus Timæus calls the orchestra the middle space of the theatre ('Ορχήστρα· τὸ τοῦ θεάτρου μέσον χωρίον, Lex. Plat. in voc.); and Photius defines it as the lowest hemicycle of the theatre (therefore not a scaffolding) on which the chorus sung and danced ('Ορχήστρα· τοῦ θεάτρου τὸ κάτω ἡμίκυκλον· οὗ καὶ οἱ χοροὶ ᾖδον καὶ ὠρχοῦντο; and again: 'Ορχήστρα· τὸ νῦν τοῦ θεάτρου λεγόμενον σίγμα· ἐκεῖ γὰρ ὠρχοῦντο οἱ χοροί). In later times the orchestra had come to be called sigma; no doubt from its semicircular form, resembling that letter, C. Thus in the Λέξεις 'Ρητορικαί: 'Ορχήστρα· τοῦ θεάτρου τὸ νῦν λεγόμενον σίγμα· ὠνομάσθη δὲ οὕτως ἐπεὶ ὠρχοῦντο οἱ χοροί (Bekk. An. Gr. p. 286). The new moon also obtained the name of sigma from its shape (Boeckh, Corp. Inscr. Gr. i. p. 85).

As in these passages of Suidas and the Etymologicum the thymelë is confounded with the orchestra, so also we sometimes find it confounded with the scene. Thus we read in the Σοφιστικὴ Παρασκευή· νῦν μὲν θυμέλην καλοῖμεν τὴν τοῦ θεάτρου σκηνήν (Bekk. An. Gr. p. 42). And in the Etymologicum M.: σκηνὴ δέ ἐστιν ἡ νῦν θυμέλη λεγομένη (voc. Παρασκήνια, p. 592, ed. Lips. 1816). The reason is obvious. The logeium, which was an appendage of the ancient scene, was now in abeyance; the thymelë for the mimes had usurped its place. What had anciently been called the scene, was now only regarded as an entrance to the theatre.

That the scaffolding, which Suidas and the Etymologist call the orchestra, was by others called the thymelë, Müller has observed in the passage above quoted. We have indeed already seen that Phrynichus, in the article cited at the beginning of this Appendix, adverts to its having this name, which he condemns. When the mimes came in, the name of logeium was superseded by that of thymelë, which signified a more extensive platform than the logeium, and one adapted for dancing. Thus Lucian represents the Antiochians crying out to a very fat dancer, who was attempting to cut extraordinary capers, to have mercy on the thymelë (καὶ ἐπὶ τοῦ παχέος δὲ καὶ πιμελοῖς ὀρχηστοῦ, πηδᾶν μεγάλα πειρωμένου, Δεόμεθα, ἔφασαν, φεῖσαι τῆς θυμέλης.— De saltatione, 76). Hence the new thymelë having superseded the ancient logeium, and extinguished its name, it is no wonder that late writers, when describing a performance of the classic times, should, according to their lights, call the logeium, thymelë. We will give an example from the scholia on the 'Knights' of Aristophanes. Demosthenes and Nicias are on the stage, when the sausage-maker appears, and Demosthenes says to him :

> ὦ μακάριε
> ἀλλαντοπῶλα, δεῦρο δεῦρ', ὦ φίλτατε,
> ἀνάβαινε, σωτὴρ τῇ πόλει καὶ νῷν φανείς.—147 sqq.

The scholia on which run as follows : ἵνα, φησὶν, ἐκ τῆς παρόδου ἐπὶ τὸ λογεῖον ἀναβῇ.—διὰ τί οὖν ἐκ τῆς παρόδου; τοῦτο γὰρ οὐκ ἀναγκαῖον. λεκτέον οὖν ὅτι ἀναβαίνειν ἐλέγετο τὸ ἐπὶ τὸ λογεῖον εἰσιέναι.—ὃ καὶ πρόσκειται · λέγεται γὰρ καταβαίνειν, τὸ ἀπαλλάττεσθαι ἐντεῦθεν ἀπὸ τοῦ παλαιοῦ ἔθους . . . ὡς ἐν θυμέλῃ δὲ τὸ ἀνάβαινε.

We clearly recognise here the hands of three commentators of different ages, or at all events of different degrees of information. The first and second correctly use the word λογεῖον of the stage on which the actors were standing; but the first mistakes the meaning of the word ἀνάβαινε, and thinks it signifies *to come up*—that is, from the πάροδος in the orchestra, which of course lay below.[1] But the second scholiast corrects him, and says that ἀναβαίνειν was used of any entrance upon the stage, and καταβαίνειν of an exit,

---

[1] We do not know whether the meaning of "a passage in the orchestra" is to be found in the lexicons, but that it had that meaning appears very plainly from Pollux (iv. 126), where after stating that of the two side doors of the scene, the right led from abroad and the left from the city, he adds, τῶν μέντοι παρόδων, ἡ μὲν δεξιὰ ἀγρόθεν, ἡ ἐκ λιμένος, ἡ ἐκ πόλεως ἄγει · οἱ δὲ ἀλλαχόθεν πεζοὶ ἀφικνούμενοι, κατὰ τὴν ἑτέραν εἰσίασιν. εἰσελθόντες δὲ κατὰ τὴν ὀρχήστραν, ἐπὶ τὴν σκηνὴν διὰ κλιμάκων ἀναβαίνουσι. It appears very plainly from this that πάροδος did not mean the side doors of the scene as it is sometimes taken to do, with a reference to Athenæus (xiv. 16,

see Liddell and Scott's Lexicon), where it has not necessarily that signification. It rather means the side entrances to the orchestra. For Pollux had already described the use of the side doors, and then goes on to describe the use of the πάροδοι, which were therefore different; and that these must have been in the orchestra appears from the circumstance that persons who had entered by them had to get upon the stage by steps. This it was that misled the first scholiast as to the meaning of the word. The only entrance to the stage from the scene appears to have been through one of the three doors.

according to the ancient and traditionary manner of speaking (ἀπὸ τοῦ παλαίου ἔθους), derived, no doubt, from the table which served the first actors as a stage and on which they had to mount. Then a third scholiast, making the same mistake as the first about ἀναβαίνειν, adds the further one of substituting *thymelë* for *logeium*, the latter name having in his time become obsolete.

Having thus determined the meaning of the word 'thymelë,' when applied to a place in the theatre used by the performers, and shown that in that view it was unknown in the Attic theatre in the days of Sophocles and Aristophanes, and was first introduced when the stage was enlarged for the use of the mimes and musicians, we are now in a condition to examine some modern hypotheses respecting the arrangement of the chorus. And first we will turn to Donaldson's 'Theatre of the Greeks,' being a book much in the hands of students. Here we read (p. 151, 6th ed. 1849): "The orchestra was a levelled space twelve feet lower than the front seats of the κοῖλον, by which it was bounded. Six feet above this was a boarded stage, which did not cover the whole area of the orchestra, but terminated where the line of view from the central *cunei* was intercepted by the boundary line. It ran, however, to the right and left of the spectators' benches, till it reached the sides of the scene. The main part of this platform, as well as an altar of Bacchus in the centre of the orchestral circle, was called the θυμέλη. The segment of the orchestra not covered by this platform was termed the κονίστρα, arena, or 'place of sand.' In front of the elevated scene, and six feet higher than the platform in the orchestra (i.e. on the same level with the lowest range of seats), was the προσκήνιον mentioned above, and called also the λογεῖον, or 'speaking stage.' There was a double row of steps (κλιμακτῆρες) from the *arena* (κονίστρα) to the platform in the orchestra, and another of a similar description from this orchestral platform to the προσκήνιον, or real stage. There were also two other flights of steps leading to the orchestral platform from the chambers below the stage." Dr. Donaldson further says, in a note: "We believe that in the time of Euripides, at all events, the thymelë signified the platform for the chorus, and not merely the altar which stood upon it. See Eurip. *Electr.* 712 sqq."

The lines of the 'Electra' here referred to are the following:

> χοροὶ δ' Ἀτρειδᾶν ἐγέραιρον οἴκους·
> θυμέλαι δ' ἐπίπλαντο χρυ-
> σήλατοι, πελαγεῖτο δ' ἀν' ἄστυ
> πῦρ ἐπιβώμιον Ἀργείων.

Here Dr. Donaldson seems to think that θυμέλαι has reference to the preceding χοροί, thus making them stages for choral dances. But they rather appear to relate to the following πῦρ ἐπιβώμιον. For dancing floors would scarcely be adorned with beaten gold, though movable altars might; and such altars might without impropriety be said to be *filled*, i.e. with sacrifices, so that the whole city shone with the fires upon them. For they have at all events nothing to do with the theatre, as they were erected in the streets (ἀπ' ἄστυ). This passage, therefore, can hardly form an exception to Lobeck's remark that he did not remember to have found Θυμέλη in the sense of *orchestra* in the ancient writers ; and no other is adduced by Dr. Donaldson in support of the very precise description which he has given of the arrangement of the orchestra, but only a reference to a German periodical (Jahrb. f. Phil. u. Pädag. li. i. pp. 22–32), which we have not at hand. The reader who has perused the preceding pages will see that his account is taken from Suidas, and that he has thus applied to the classic period the orchestral arrangements that prevailed in the decline of the drama.

Schlegel, also, in his third lecture on the ancient drama, adopts the thymelë as the station of the chorus, and affirms that it rose "as high as the stage," without indicating its length or breadth.[1] But he gives no authorities.

Müller, in his 'Dissertation on the Eumenides,' has devoted a section to the thymelë. He correctly points out from Suidas the change which the thymelë of the theatre underwent ;[2] though perhaps it would be more correct to say that it was the logeium, not the thymelë, that was altered. He seems to think, however—for he does not express himself very clearly—that in the classical times part of the chorus stood upon the thymelë, that is, on the steps of the altar ; and that at least the hegemon of the chorus took his station on it, he being in the middle of the left file of choreutæ ; and that from this station he spoke with the persons on the stage over the heads of the two other files, posted in straight lines between the thymelë and the stage.

Hermann, in his review of Müller's work, ridicules this arrangement. But as his own hypothesis is founded on the account of Suidas, which he applies to the theatre of the classical times, it becomes still more absurd.[3] He adopts Suidas' name of κονίστρα for the orchestra ; the thymelë, he thinks, was a large altar, with steps in the middle of the conistra ; that the flute players stood on the steps ; that the altar was, perhaps, movable, which indeed was probably the case ; that in the performance of dithyrambs the altar was surrounded with a low planking for the use of the chorus, which gave occasion to the name of *orchestra* for the whole *conistra*. But such a planking, he observes, would not have served for the regular drama. Vitruvius says (v. 8 (7)) that the stage was not less than ten nor more than twelve feet above the orchestra— that is, the conistra. Hence, according to Hermann, it necessarily follows that the tragic and comic chorus, which had often not only to speak with the actors,

[1] See Donaldson's Gr. Theatre, p. 171.   [2] p. 250. Eng. trans.
[3] Opuscula, t. ii. p. ii. p. 152 sqq.

but also to take part in what was going forward on the stage, could not have stood at such a depth below it, but must have been stationed on a scaffold not more than two feet lower than the stage. This scaffold, as Suidas and the Etymologist say, reached from the stage to the thymelë or altar; and as the space between the middle of the thymelë to the wall of the scene was at least 150 feet, it must have been 120 feet broad, allowing 20 feet for the proscenium, and 10 feet for half the thymelë;[1] which would have been more than sufficient room for the choral dances of fifteen or twenty-four persons. This platform being higher than the altar, or thymelë, properly so called, nearly concealed the flute players and police, who stood on its steps. Where we may remark that it must have concealed the altar also; and then, what became of the preliminary sacrifice to Dionysus, with which, no doubt, the performance began? There must have been steps, Hermann proceeds, for the chorus to ascend the platform. As the chorus entered on the right of the spectators, the hegemon would be the middle man in the file nearest to them, when the songs were addressed to them; but when he had to speak with the actors, an evolution was made by which this line became nearest to the stage, and therefore he had not to speak over the heads of the other two lines.

All these views, except Müller's, are more or less founded on the anachronous and ill-understood article of Suidas, and on the passage in Vitruvius quoted by Hermann in the preceding extract; from which it is inferred that the stage rose ten or twelve feet above the orchestra, and that the seats of the first row of spectators were of the same height.[2] Of the article in Suidas we have already spoken. Respecting the passage of Vitruvius, let us observe that he is not there describing an ancient Greek theatre, but directing how one should be built. ("In Græcorum theatris non omnia iisdem rationibus *sunt facienda.*") As gladiators had come to be exhibited on the orchestras of Greek theatres, a lofty podium might have become necessary to prevent accidents like that recorded by Dion Chrysostom (see above, p. 177). However this may be, in a theatre constructed on Vitruvius' plan it must be allowed that a scaffold for the choreutæ would be absolutely necessary. A chorus standing on the floor of the orchestra would have been almost hidden from the sight of the spectators; whilst an actor addressing the choreutæ *de haut en bas* would have had a most ridiculous effect. A theatre so constructed, if intended for the representation of the classic drama, is repugnant to the most obvious dictates of common sense. Why should the level of the orchestra have been

---

[1] We know not from what theatre Hermann took these dimensions, which, with regard to the Dionysiac theatre, are very much exaggerated.

[2] "Ejus logei altitudo non minus debet esse pedum decem, non plus duodecim."—Vitr. v. 7 (8). Vitruvius says nothing about the height of the first row of seats, which seems to be a modern inference, though perhaps a necessary one.

so low as to require to be remedied by an artificial platform? Surely it would have been both an easier and more sightly plan to have placed the stage, the orchestra, and the spectators on such levels as would have required no further alteration. We say a more sightly plan; for to see the chorus scrambling up steps eight or ten feet in height would have been a most absurd spectacle. And when they had got to the top of the platform they would have deprived themselves of the use of the greater part of the orchestra. We may further observe that the stage of a classic Greek theatre could not, as a rule, have had the height assigned to it by Vitruvius; since the *hyposcenium* or wall under it, which separated it from the orchestra, is described by Pollux, in a passage before quoted (p. 312), as ornamented with small figures (ἀγαλματίοις), as we have seen that the Dionysiac theatre at Athens really was, and must therefore have been a low one. Such small figures on a wall ten or twelve feet high would have been quite inappropriate and absurd.

We will now turn to survey the theatre at Athens, as revealed to us by the excavations, and consider whether its arrangement at all agrees with the different hypotheses concerning it which we have just adduced. The first things that strike us are, that the stage is only four or five feet in height, instead of twelve; and that the first row of spectators' seats, instead of being level with the stage, is level with the orchestra. Under these circumstances a platform for the chorus, so far from being required, would absolutely have intercepted the view of the stage from the chief priests and magistrates, who sat in the first circle; while, on the other hand, as the stage was raised four or five feet above the orchestra, they would have had a very good view of the actors over the heads of the choreutæ who stood at some distance. Nor would such a difference of level between the actors and the chorus have produced any bad effect.

We will now consider the rhomboidal figure in the middle of the orchestra, which the reader will have observed in the plan. That this was meant to indicate the station of the chorus, will hardly admit of a question. We know from Hesychius that their position in the orchestra was marked out by lines.[1] There would have been no use for such lines if the choreutæ stood on a quadrangular scaffold; and this, again, would have hidden the lines. It will be observed that this rhomboidal figure was much better adapted for the station of the chorus than a square or oblong one, which, we believe, all the commentators assume. Müller makes his chorus stand in three ranks of five each, thus forming an oblong figure between the thymelë, or altar, and the stage. No tetragonal figure so completely fills the area of a semicircle as the lozenge; besides which, it has the additional advantage of bringing the hegemon of the chorus, supposing that he stood at the angle nearest the stage, into immediate

---

[1] γραμμαὶ ἐν τῇ ὀρχήστρᾳ ἦσαν, ὡς τὸν χορὸν ἐν στοίχῳ ἵστασθαι.—Hesych. voc. Γραμμαί.

proximity with the actors; at the same time placing him there *alone*, and in a conspicuous station aloof from the rest; whereas, as a square figure would have presented an extended front to the stage, he would not have been distinguished from the neighbouring choreutæ. We will only further observe that if this figure really marks the station of the chorus, commonly but improperly called the thymelë, it is the only trace of one discovered in any theatre yet excavated.

We know little about the evolutions of the chorus, except their mode of entry, which has been described by Pollux.[1] The tragic chorus in general came in either three abreast and five in file, or five abreast and three in file. It was on very rare occasions that they entered singly. Those in line, or abreast, formed a ζυγόν; those in file, or following one another, a στοῖχος. The left file was towards the spectators; and they must consequently have entered from the left side of the theatre. This left file was more honourable than the others, and in the middle of it was the coryphæus, or hegemon of the chorus. A scholium on Aristeides[2] may help to explain their mode of entry. It is there said that when they came in singing their hymns, they walked obliquely (πλαγίως βαδίζοντες). The rhomboidal figure is well adapted to such an oblique march. Entering from the left or western side of the theatre, they would have proceeded along and outside the north-west side of the lozenge. On arriving at its northernmost angle, in the central line of the orchestra, they would then, wheeling to their right, have continued their march along its north-east side, thus literally marching obliquely. Thus they would have made the whole circuit of the orchestra, and shown themselves to all the spectators. How they entered the space marked out by the lozenge and arranged themselves upon it, we will not, in the absence of all authority, pretend to determine; though it is probable, as we have before remarked, that the hegemon stood at the southern-most angle, the nearest to the stage. The thymelë, or altar of Dionysus, would have stood in the centre of the figure, where there is a hole for the reception of its base. Around it the flute players would have been stationed.

This, we submit, is a more convenient and graceful arrangement of the chorus than any of those proposed by the authorities whom we have quoted; and we will add that it is not only more conformable to what we can gather from ancient authorities, but also to the present appearances in the orchestra of the Dionysiac theatre.

---

[1] lib. iv. s. 109.   [2] In the oration Ὑπὲρ τεσσάρων, t. ii. p. 161, Jebb.

III.

ON THE PNYX.

As Dr. CURTIUS, though not the originator of the hypothesis that the place commonly regarded as the Pnyx was in fact a temenos of Zeus, is the most prominent advocate of that view, we propose in this Appendix to examine the arguments which he has adduced in support of it. He recapitulates them as follows:[1] "If we assemble in one view the separate points that have been adverted to—(1) the very antique construction of the two terraces; (2) the situation of them, which was so well adapted to unite the town and country districts; (3) their unmistakeable connexion with the ancient rock-city of the Cranai; (4) their adaptation for worship and for religious assemblies, deducible from their arrangement; (5) the testimony to the worship of Zeus Hypsistos there afforded by memorials (urkundlich bezeugt); (6) the traces of several altars symmetrically placed; (7) the analogy which the spot has with the Argive κοινοβωμία, as a most ancient place of worship of the θεοὶ ἀγώνιοι or ἀγοραῖοι; lastly, (8) the tradition of an ἀγορὰ θεῶν in Cyzicus, Eleusis, and Athens—an examination of these points will lead us to understand with certainty these very ancient Athenian foundations, and to recognize in them a primitive Agora of the Gods, in the midst of which Zeus Hypsistos had his throne as highest of the gods."

To this it may be answered:

1. There is nothing in the construction of these terraces that compels us to refer them to a very high antiquity. If such a view is derived from their being hewn out of the rock, it might be proved by the same argument that the Dionysiac theatre, which is partly constructed in the same manner, must also be very ancient; whereas we know that it was not begun till five centuries B.C. The polygonal wall surrounding the lower terrace, which has sometimes been adduced in support of the same view, proves just the reverse. The best judges have determined that it is not Cyclopean or Pelasgic. But we need not go into this point, because Curtius himself admits that it is not of very high antiquity, and that it was a comparatively modern addition to the original design of the terraces.[2]

[1] Attische Studien, No. 1, S. 42.
[2] "Die Mauer selbst ist durchaus nicht der Art, dass sie der allerältester Zeit attischer Bauthätigkeit zugeschrieben zu werden

2. The fanciful argument from situation requires no serious answer. Any situation near any town may with equal justice be called adapted to unite town and country; and the maintainers of the Pnyx hypothesis may assert with a great deal more appropriateness that the spot was admirably adapted for the meeting of the public assembly.

3. With regard to the third argument, we may observe that the vestiges of dwellings on the southern hills are very far from having been proved to have belonged to the ancient Cranaan city. On the contrary, we have endeavoured to show in our first chapter that they were more probably additions to it, and that the Cranaan city was only another name for Cecropia, or the subsequent Athenian Acropolis, which, according to Thucydides, was the original city.

4. What are the grounds on which Curtius deduces from the arrangement of the terraces that they are more suitable for a place of worship than for a public assembly? Before we can examine these we must give an account of the excavations which he made here, by translating his own description of them.[1] We also insert his plan.

"I had," he says, "three objects in view: first, to lay open the outer boundary of the (lower) terrace and its approaches; second, to excavate at the back wall down to the surface of the rock; lastly, to get a knowledge of the floor of the terrace itself in its original condition.

"As regards the first point, the whole extent of the polygonal wall, of which only the lower part was visible, was laid bare; it goes up in a regular curve of the same masonry on both sides of the hill, and terminates at the rock cliff, or wall. It forms a kind of girdle round the lower slope, and corresponds, as a lower boundary, to the opposite cliff, which bounds the terrace above.[2]

"Secondly, as regards the cliff wall at the back of the terrace, trenches were made here on both sides of the (so-called) bema, which showed that the perpendicularly hewn rock goes a great deal below the present surface. Thus, on the east, the rock floor lies 4·302 mètres (about 14 feet) below the lowest step of the bema, and on the west 3·50 mètres (10 feet 6 inches). It further appeared that at both ends of the back wall margins, or edges, sharply cut in the rock, and 18 mètres (59 feet) long, project in the direction of the upper part of the polygonal wall, as if to meet it, and to complete in conjunction with

brauchte. Denn bei aller Mächtigkeit der Werkstücke trägt sie schon die deutlichen Spuren einer gewissen Zierlichkeit, wie dies besonders die Parallellinien bezeugen, mit denen die alten Steinmetzen die Ränder der einzelnen Werkstücke umzogen haben. Der treffliche Sir W. Gell hat in seiner Ansicht der Mauer (Probestücke von Städtemauern des alten Griechenlands, T. 30) diese gesuchte Zierlichkeit sehr deutlich wiedergegeben."—Att. Studien, No. 1, S. 43 f.

[1] Attische Studien, No. 1, p. 24 sqq.

[2] It may be observed that this is no new discovery. Wheler, as we have seen (above, p. 464), describes the wall as semicircular, and has even given a view of it.

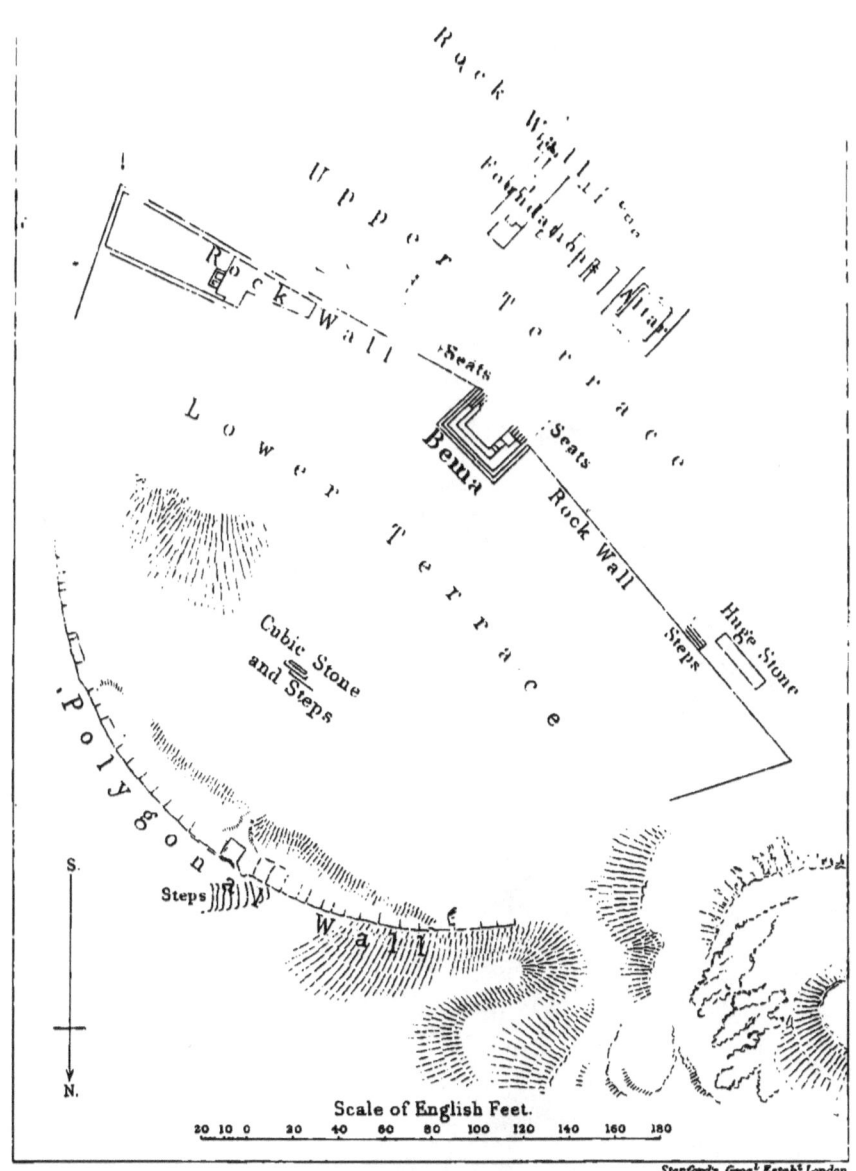

Rock Wall Chi...

Polygon...? [Wall]

Upper Terrace

Rock Wall

Seats

Bema

Seats

Rock Wall

Lower Terrace

Steps

Huge Stone

Cubic Stone and Steps

Polygon Wall

Steps

S.

N.

Scale of English Feet.

20 10 0   20   40 60 80 100 120 140 160 180

Stanford's Geog.l Estab.t London.

London: Bell & Daldy.

it the boundary of the whole terrace. There is, however, on both sides an interval of about 28 mètres (nearly 92 feet), a space in which apparently the entrances were.

"On uncovering the eastern margin, a singular construction was discovered in the angle which it forms with the perpendicular back wall. Immediately at the foot of this wall is a piece of rock about 30 mètres (98 feet 6 inches) long, cut out almost at right angles by deep and neatly executed canals, or gutters, from about 1 foot 6 inches to 2 feet broad. The breadth of this piece of rock diminishes towards the west, or in the direction of the bema, and projects towards it like a sort of beak. The extremity of this beak is about midway between the bema and the east angle of the cliff wall. This isolated piece of rock is cut through in the middle by a depression; but the whole upper surface is so rough and broken that no conclusion can be drawn respecting the meaning and use of this enigmatical piece of rock-work. Only this much is certain, that the whole construction is the result of art and of considerable labour. The view that these are incomplete works, and that the intention was by means of the canals, or gutters, to work off the mass of rock which they surround, and thus make a level, is opposed not only by their depth and their careful execution, but also by their narrowness, for labourers could scarce move in them, and would be quite unable to use their arms.

"We must, therefore, assume that this isolated mass of rock was an essential part of the whole terrace, and that at one time its surface was made level with gravel and rubbish, so as to form a place on which people could assemble. The two margins or edges, before mentioned, running towards the polygonal wall, in conjunction with the lofty back wall, form the boundary of an upper part of the terrace, in contrast to the lower one, which is not enclosed by cuttings in the rock.

"With regard to ancient vestiges behind the bema on the border of the back wall, there are, first, the incisions in the rock resembling steps on each side of the bema, and similar incisions to the west of them, 18 mètres (59 ft.) from the N.W. corner, where the back wall and side rock-boundary meet together in an acute angle. These steps must have served for stairs, (or a 'kind of stairs,' as Welcker cautiously says, 'Felsaltar,' S. 285, 21) which led from the upper to the lower terrace. Meanwhile, an excavation that was made here showed that the distance between the lowest step and the level of the terrace was so great that it was impossible there could have been an ascent here. These steps, therefore, could only have served to exhibit objects on. Above them[1] lies an immense block of stone, hewn into a rectangular shape, and visible from a great distance; it looks like a remnant of

---

[1] Not exactly, but just to the west of them.

a cyclopean wall, but, on turning up the ground, no continuation of it could be discovered.

"After the boundaries of the terrace and the construction of the back wall had been examined, my third care was to investigate the floor of the terrace. For this purpose a trench more than 4 ft. broad was dug in a straight line from the middle of the bema to the lower, or polygonal, wall. This immediately showed that the ancient floor was covered with rubbish, whilst hitherto we had believed that we stood upon it: nay, it further showed that the old level was higher than the present one, and that the sinking of the stones of the lower wall, which supported it, had occasioned a sinking of the whole terrace. At first (near the back wall) it was only thin layers of earth and dust that covered the original rock-floor. This floor begins to sink immediately from the bema, and is neatly finished, so that there can be no doubt that it was meant to lie open and exposed. (Curtius here refers to a drawing showing the profile of the present soil, and that of the floor of the trench which he opened, being that of the original floor.) On continuing the trench, the surface of the ancient rock-floor appeared to have been forcibly injured, and the labourers came upon some walling of a later time. I caused it to be broken through, when I discovered under it, at a depth of 6 mètres (19 ft. 6 in.), and 36 mètres (118 ft.) from the bema, three steps hewn in the rock, and, where that did not suffice, completed with masonry. The trench was now enlarged so as to discover the angles of this object; when it appeared that it was no stairs, but a construction resembling the bema in the middle of the back wall, with which it is in a line, so that the steps of both are parallel. Hence it is probable that here, as above, the steps were surmounted by a cubic block of rock. The junction of it (or foundation) is plainly seen, but it has been destroyed down to the level of the floor, with the view, apparently, of erecting a later building over it. The rubbish turned up in these excavations showed an upper layer of coarse potsherds, mixed with rubble, and underneath a thicker layer of finer potsherds belonging to smaller vessels, as drinking-cups, lamps, &c., including, also, fragments of ancient sculptures and monuments. Then there was a fragment of an inscribed stone on which might clearly be read ΙΙΠΟΘΟΩΝΤΙΣ; further, two fragments of small marble bas-reliefs with human limbs on them. On one of these were the letters ΕΜΟ ; where the second and third lines are evidently to be read: Δὰ ΙΣΤΣ ἰψ[ίστ]ῳ εὐ]χή. Hence they belong to the same group of anathemata ΧΗ as those which Lord Aberdeen found in the niches in the rock, and to which also belong the 'tablettes votives d'Athènes,' published by Ross in the 'Annali dell' Instituto,' 1843, p. 322.

"Beyond the newly discovered steps, the soil is covered with rubbish and large pieces of rock, in such a manner that it was impossible to clear it ; so that the original nature of the floor between these lower steps and the polygonal wall remains unknown. The immense stones which lie here impressed me with the notion that they were placed here at a remote period, and that they were intended to form the foundation of a level surface extending from the lower (newly discovered) steps to the polygonal wall. Nor were any antique potsherds found in this part, so far as it was opened.

" With regard to the polygonal wall itself, it is probable that it was at least one course of stones higher than it is at present, as the topmost ones show traces of having had another layer upon them. The square opening in the front of the wall has not the least appearance of being accidental ; I caused it to be examined, in order to ascertain if it was the mouth of any subterraneous gutter ; but the labourers found only firmly-packed stones.

" I caused the soil beneath and outside the wall to be laid open, and discovered on the western side a considerable flight of low steps cut in the rock, extending close to the wall, and about 15 ft. wide. They, however, do not follow the ascent of the wall, but disappear at its foot.

" Lastly, I sought to discover, by means of excavations, how the two terraces were connected with the surrounding town districts. In accordance with the facts discovered about the locality, it was to be expected that the side entrances lay in the intervals between the rock margins above and the polygonal wall below. I caused the rock-surface to be laid bare in the direction of the Nymphs' Hill, where steps in the rock seemed to give a clue to the line, but no levelled paths could be discovered. On the other hand, a broad approach to the upper rock terrace was plainly to be seen ; a carriage road about 8 ft. wide, levelled in the rock, which led in a straight line from the ravine which ascends to the Nymphs' Hill to the level of the upper terrace. Close to it, on the town side, is a considerable level space, or plateau, on the rock, which seems to have been prepared for the reception of some building. On the opposite, or eastern, side of the (Pnyx) hill, traces are seen of paths and steps cut in the rock ; though it is impossible to lay down any defined lines, and to point out a regular approach to the terrace." (See above, p. 471, and note [3].)

Such were the results of Curtius' excavations ; and from these, in connection with the entire arrangement of the terraces, he comes to the conclusion that the whole formed what he calls an ἀγορὰ θεῶν, or Forum of the Gods ; that the stone commonly called the bema was an altar of Zeus Hypsistos ; that the cubic stone on the upper terrace, and the steps discovered by his excavation in the lower terrace, from which the cube had been broken off, were also altars, but he does not say to what gods dedicated ; that there may be other altars hidden under the made soil of the lower terrace ; that the altar of Zeus at first stood alone, and that the others were subsequent additions when the whole place was enlarged; that the original rock floor of the lower terrace, which sinks away from the back wall, and so-called bema, was admirably adapted for a λαῶν χῶρος, or place for the people to assemble to behold the sacrifices to Zeus; that the mutilated state in which the three altars are is to be attributed to the Byzantine Christians; that the area of the lower terrace was at the same period covered up with rubbish; that, besides the defacement of the third altar, discovered by him in the lower terrace, a chapel was also built over it; and that this shows that, in the Byzantine times, the original rock floor of this terrace must have lain exposed, consequently that the superincumbent rubbish must have been heaped upon it at a later period.

In examining this hypothesis, we will at present confine ourselves to local appearances. First, then, we must remember that the lowest step of the object which Curtius calls the altar of Zeus, lay 12 or 13 ft. above the original floor of the terrace, and therefore the spectators would have to survey the sacrifices made there at a distance above their heads. Now, as the victims were always slaughtered before the altars, it occurs to inquire how they could have been got up to this height? The difficulty had suggested itself to Curtius himself, who offers two solutions of it: first, the victims might have been brought up alive to the terrace or platform before the altar by means of planking, or by the heaping up of earth; or, secondly, they might have been slaughtered below, and only the pieces destined for the gods carried up to the altar.[1] Of these clumsy contrivances the reader must be left to form his own judgment; and we will only observe, with regard to the latter, that some examples should have been given of victims sacrificed at a distance from the altar.

We leave out of our consideration here that the object in the middle of the back wall was evidently not an altar. It has steps at the sides to enable a person to mount upon its surface; very necessary appendages to a bema, but useless for an altar, and, so far as we know, unheard of. The stone cube on the upper terrace was evidently an altar; but it stands free, and has no steps at its sides.

Secondly, with regard to the mutilation of these objects. That they were all mutilated at the same time, or that the original rock floor of the lower terrace could have been exposed in the Byzantine times, is highly improbable. The improbability of the latter hypothesis will appear from a consideration of the nature of the lower terrace, as described by Curtius himself. First, it is impossible to regard the solid polygonal wall at the bottom of it as a

---

[1] Att. Studien, i. 36.

mere boundary. An infinitely slighter wall would have answered that purpose. From the solidity of its construction, it was evidently intended for a buttress, or supporting-wall of some superincumbent weight; and this weight could have been no other than the rubbish with which the area of the lower terrace is filled. If this be so, the building of the wall and the filling in of the rubbish must have been contemporaneous; they were parts of the same plan, and that they were so, is plain from Curtius' description of the nature of the rubbish. He tells us that from the steps which he discovered down to the polygonal wall the filling matter consisted of huge stones, through which his workmen could not penetrate. Now no people would have taken the trouble to bring in these large blocks merely to desecrate a place. The intention of them is evident. As the original floor of the terrace was on a slope, which was to be filled up to a level, these huge stones were placed at the lowest part of the semicircle, to help in supporting, in conjunction with the polygonal wall, the higher superincumbent rubbish, which from the slope would have a natural tendency to press downwards. The wall and the adjustment of the rubbish were therefore, as we have said, parts of one and the same plan, consequently contemporary; and nobody, we suppose, will maintain that the polygonal wall was built in the Byzantine times. The artificial manner in which the rubbish was placed is further shown by Curtius' description. It was not shovelled in promiscuously and pêle-mêle, as it would have been had the intention only been to desecrate and deform; but it was placed in regular layers.

All this shows Curtius' hypothesis that the original floor lay open in the Byzantine times to be quite untenable. The steps and mutilated cube which he discovered could not, therefore, have been built over by the Byzantines for the purpose of founding a chapel. It was not their custom to build chapels, but to convert pagan temples, already existing, into Christian churches. Nor does Curtius' description of the wall which he found here at all answer to the foundations of a building. The mutilated object which he discovered was most probably walled over when this lower terrace was reconstructed; and it must be a very discriminating person indeed who can fix precisely the date of a wall which has been buried many centuries under rubbish.

But when was the object under it mutilated, whatever it may have been? If there is any justice in what we have remarked, it could not have been in the Byzantine times. The only other epoch that we can suggest is that of the capture of Athens by Lysander, and the reign of the Thirty Tyrants, when the Long Walls were demolished. But in that case the mutilated object discovered by Curtius could hardly have been an altar, but might very well have been a bema, the mouthpiece of popular liberty, the throne of a people-king. And that a new bema was constructed at this time we know on the authority of Plutarch, which we will now examine.

We will preface our remarks by admitting that the reason which Plutarch assigns for the altering of the bema is absurd, namely, that the original bema looked towards the sea, and that the Thirty, holding that the maritime power of the Athenians was the origin of their democracy, turned it away from the sea and made it look towards the country, because the agricultural population was less disinclined to an oligarchy.[1] Nevertheless we have two traditions here which are not to be entirely discarded ; namely, that the direction of the bema was completely reversed in the time of the Thirty, and that whereas it before looked towards the sea, or southwards, it was now made to look towards the land, or northwards. Indeed Curtius himself accepts the tradition so far as regards the turning of the bema, and makes it the subject of a singular piece of archæology. Assuming the turning, he remarks that the bema at all events must consequently have been a moveable object that could be turned round, and therefore not hewn out of the rock, like the so-called bema, respecting which no such tradition could have been current.[2] But Plutarch's words by no means imply a turning round of the bema itself ; on the contrary, they show that it was a fixed object. For he says that it was *constructed* to look towards the sea ; whereas, had it been moveable, it would not have been made to look any way in particular. And the following word ἀπέστρεψαν does not mean that it was turned round, but that its direction, or view, was averted from seawards to landwards ; consequently a new bema was made, but in the same Pnyx ; for there is no hint that the place of assembly was changed. In fact, the bema must have been so placed that the orator should have the whole assembly, or the great bulk of them, before him ; consequently a moveable bema would have been an absurdity ; for if it was turned round, being kept in the same place, the orator would have turned his back on his audience.

We assume, therefore, that the alteration mentioned by Plutarch was the making of a new bema in the ancient Pnyx, facing in a contrary direction to the older one. Now this new bema was no other than the object still existing in the centre of the back wall of the lower terrace. First, it answers to Plut-

---

[1] διὸ καὶ τὸ βῆμα τὸ ἐν Πνυκί, πεποιημένον ὥστ' ἀποβλέπειν πρὸς τὴν θάλασσαν, ὕστερον οἱ τριάκοντα πρὸς τὴν χώραν ἀπέστρεψαν, οἰόμενοι, τὴν μὲν κατὰ θάλατταν ἀρχὴν γένεσιν εἶναι δημοκρατίας, ὀλιγαρχίᾳ δ' ἧττον δυσχεραίνειν τοὺς γεωργοῦντας.—Plut. Them. 19.

[2] " Endlich noch die Erzählung von der Umkehrung der Rednerbühne unter den Dreissig. Mag man darüber urtheilen, wie man will, sie war in Athen verbreitet ; es muss also doch auf jeden Fall die Bühne ein Gegenstand gewesen sein, welcher beweglich war und umgedreht werden konnte ; es kann also kein aus dem Gestein gehauener sein, wie das gemeinhin sogenannte Bema, von welchem eine solche Erzählung gar nicht in Umlauf kommen konnte."—Att. St. i. 33.

arch's account by facing towards the country, or north, as he says that the new one did. Secondly, it is evidently an addition to, or alteration in, a former plan or structure. The back wall of the lower terrace was no doubt originally straight, without any bema, or projection, in the middle. Had this projection formed part of the first plan, the designer of it would scarcely have obtained it by means of such singular-looking obtuse angles as the wall now presents. He would have made it project from a straight line. But when it was determined out of a straight line to obtain a projection in the centre to serve for a new bema, it is evident that these obtuse angles would have saved an immense deal of labour in hollowing out the rock. (See Plan.) Another proof that this bema was not in the original plan is, that there would have been, as we have seen, a depth of twelve or thirteen feet from its first step to the original floor below, thus making it perfectly useless, whether for an altar or a bema. It would have remained altogether inaccessible until the filling up of the area below with rubbish brought its surface to a level with the step. The same would have been the case with the stairs at the western extremity of the rock wall. All this shows that both these stairs and the bema were parts of a new plan, which could only be completed by raising the former level with rubbish, so as to make them accessible; and this rubbish required the polygonal wall to bound and support it.

The reader now begins perhaps to anticipate our view of the whole place. The rock floor sinking with a gradual descent towards the object discovered by Curtius, bounded on the south by the straight and perpendicular rock wall twelve to fourteen feet high, which formed the chord of the arc, and by cuttings in the rock to describe its semicircle, was the original Pnyx, and the steps discovered by Curtius were the steps of the original bema. As the semicircle formed by the cuttings was smaller than that subsequently made by the polygonal wall, this bema would have lain very near the boundary. The orator consequently would have had the greater part of the assembly before him, rising gradually upwards towards the southern boundary wall; thus, in fact, resembling an inverted theatre, the audience part rising up to, instead of from, the chord of the semicircle, and the orator, instead of being in the middle of the chord, like an actor, taking his place in the middle of the arc.

And this agrees with Plutarch's account, that at first the orator looked towards the sea, that is, towards the south. That he could have seen it is of course out of the question. Plutarch does not say that he did, but only that he looked in that direction. We have already observed that the reason he gives is a vain and frivolous one, and his record is only valuable as showing *the direction* of the two bemas, with which the remains correspond.

But it is not only the back wall that shows signs of reconstruction; there is evidence that the whole lower terrace also has been enlarged. This has been shown by Curtius from the steps he discovered under the polygonal wall, which have been cut off by it, so as to be at present perfectly useless, but which must originally have served for an approach to the lower terrace.[1] But even these were not the only alterations. It is quite evident that the upper terrace was no part of the original plan, but a subsequent addition, made when the polygonal wall was built[2] and the level of the lower terrace raised. The steps in the back wall of the lower terrace near its western termination suffice to show this. Curtius observes (supra, p. 533) that from the depth between them and the original rock floor there could have been no ascent here, and that they could only have served for the exhibition of objects. What sort of objects? There is not the slightest probability in this view, which is only a desperate guess to account for a construction which does not accord with his hypothesis. It is evident that these steps were not made till the floor of the lower terrace had been raised, and that they then served as an approach from it to the upper one. The use of them, as well as of the upper terrace itself, as an appendage to the Pnyx, we have explained in the text (supra, p. 471).

According to our view, then, as founded on the appearance of the place, it was in the lower terrace that the great bulk of the ecclesia assembled. We hold that its surface, when altered, did not slope down from the bema, as it does now, but that it was at least level with it at the most distant part; consequently, that the polygonal wall was two or three times as high as it is at present. Curtius says that, from appearances, there must have been at least another course of stones above the actual topmost ones; and this being so, there is no saying how many more courses there might have been. Their disappearance is easily accounted for. These fine square blocks were admirably adapted for building purposes, and were no doubt so applied in the middle ages. The wonder, perhaps, is that so many should remain, rather than that so many should have disappeared, when we consider that nearly all the enormous columns of the Olympium have vanished. When the made soil was deprived of the support of the upper courses of the wall, the rains would naturally have washed it down and produced the present slanting profile.

It remains to consider the reasons for these alterations, and the time when

[1] "Von einer solchen Erweiterung der Terrasse scheint die alter Steintreppe zu zeugen, welche jetzt gerade auf den Fuss der Polygonmauer hinführt und unter den Steinen derselben aufhört, so dass die Fortsetzung derselben verbaut zu sein scheint; denn wie sie jetzt auf die Mauer stösst, ist sie vollkommen zwecklos. Sie scheint also einen älteren Zugang gebildet zu haben und die Polygonenmauer erst bei Gelegenheit eines späteren Erweiterung aufgeführt worden zu sein."— Att. St. i. 43.

[2] We have already seen that Curtius allows the lower wall not to have been so very ancient (supra, p. 531).

they were effected. With regard to the latter, the reign of the Thirty may be a sufficiently probable epoch; perhaps they were earlier, they could hardly have been later. The sculptured and other fragments found among the rubbish with which the lower area was raised would answer to that period well enough, and could not possibly have belonged to a very remote era. The later anathemata to Zeus Hypsistos from the niches in the rock wall may have got mingled with this rubbish in the course of ages. Plutarch's reason for changing the bema cannot, of course, be accepted. It is not unlikely, however, that the Lacedæmonians, on the taking of Athens, or the Thirty Tyrants whom they established, in their common hatred of democracy, may have injured and defaced the original Pnyx in a way to render it almost useless. The same Tyrants, however, were not likely to construct a new one; nor, indeed, would the short span of less than a year during which their reign lasted, have sufficed for such a purpose. It is more probable that the new Pnyx was made after their overthrow by Thrasybulus. Its reconstruction on a larger and more convenient scale may have been preferred to repairing the old one; and the reversal of the bema may have been suggested by the convenience offered by the rock wall for making one. The whole arrangement would thus have been rendered more theatre-like; the orator, like the actor, being placed in the middle of the chord of the arc, and thus having a greater number of his audience within convenient reach of his voice.

5. Curtius' fifth argument is drawn from the proofs of Zeus-worship on the Pnyx Hill afforded by the votive tablets found there; but as we have already said, these are of a late Roman period, and therefore are no proofs of a primitive Zeus-worship at this place (supra, p. 469). We shall only add here, that if this was the most ancient, or one of the most ancient, sanctuaries of Zeus at Athens, how comes it that we have no traditions about it? All traditions relating to Zeus-worship at Athens point for their locality either to the Acropolis or to the Olympium. How the Pnyx became sacred to Zeus we have already explained (supra, p. 472).

6. The proof from several (three) altars symmetrically placed vanishes if one of them at least, if not two, are shown to have been rostra, and not altars.

7 and 8 we may take together. The analogy of the Argive κοινοβωμία also vanishes in the same manner. Moreover, Curtius' attempt to make out the existence of an ancient κοινοβωμία, or ἀγορὰ θεῶν, at Athens from classical writers is abortive. He is obliged to go to foreign cities for it. His only attempt (p. 39–41) from classic Athenian writers is from the 'Supplices' of Æschylus, in which Danaüs mentions a κοινοβωμία (v. 222), and where his allusions to the scenery might bear some resemblance to the Pnyx Hill. But then, unfortunately, the scene of the 'Supplices' is not at Athens, but Argos. He next goes (p. 41)

to Cyzicus for a Forum of the Gods, mentioned in the Panegyric of Aristeides on that city (t. i. p. 239, Jebb). He then affirms (p. 42), from Zenobius (iv. 30), that there were also θεῶν ἀγοραὶ at Eleusis and Athens, though Pausanias does not mention them. But we have before suggested that the ἀγορὰ θεῶν at Athens, which is mentioned only by late writers, may have been the Pantheon of Hadrian (supra, p. 254, note). Surely so striking an object, had it existed earlier, could hardly have escaped all allusion to it by Pausanias and by the classical writers. Curtius seems to have felt this defect himself, and in order to remedy it, falls back (p. 44) on the following line of Cratinus:

ἔνθα Διὸς μεγάλου θᾶκοι πεσσοί τε καλοῦνται.

Θᾶκος, he says, means (Atticè) a place where many meet together, which corresponds with the θεῶν ἀγορὰ of Zenobius. Then again, πεσσοὶ may refer to the dice-like form of the rock altars! Some, too, read ψῆφοι for πεσσοί; and, according to Suidas, there was a sacred place at Athens called Διὸς ψῆφος, where the gods pronounced judgment in the suit of Poseidon *v.* Athena. "Bergk," continues Curtius (p. 45), "has explained in his Aphorisms ('Philologus,' xii. S. 579), that the so-called Pnyx Hill was the height named Διὸς ψῆφος, without, indeed, producing any reasons for it, but, as I think, with perfect justice." For our parts, we must confess that we should like to see the reasons. The legend about Athena and Poseidon can hardly be separated from the Acropolis. We have already adverted to this point in Chapter XI. (p. 388), where we have endeavoured to show that the spot called Διὸς ψῆφος was before the western front of the Parthenon, where the sculptures in the pediment above represented the judgment.

It will, we think, be allowed that these attempts to find classical authority for an ἀγορὰ θεῶν at the Pnyx Hill are not very successful. And, indeed, Curtius himself seems tacitly to have abandoned them in the explanatory text to his maps of Athens, where he says that the Pnyx, as a sanctuary of Zeus, is nowhere mentioned by the ancient writers (p. 16). That denomination, therefore, rests merely on conjecture, and, as appears to us, not a very happy one.

For a very sensible refutation of Welcker's theory respecting the Pnyx, too long to be inserted here, the reader is referred to M. Rangabé's 'Antiquités Helléniques,' t. ii. pp. 579–586.

INDEX.

www.ingramcontent.com/pod-product-compliance
Lightning Source LLC
Chambersburg PA
CBHW021935110726
47901CB00003B/851